D1540941

AMERICAN PUBLIC OPINION AND HEALTH CARE

AMERICAN PUBLIC
OPINION AND
HEALTH CARE

OBERT J. BLENDON, MOLLYANN BRODIE,

OHN M. BENSON, AND DREW E. ALTMAN

CQ PRESS

A Division of SAGE
Washington, D.C.

CQ Press
2300 N Street, NW, Suite 800
Washington, DC 20037

Phone: 202-729-1900; toll-free, 1-866-4CQ-PRESS (1-866-427-7737)

Web: www.cqpress.com

The Kaiser Family Foundation is a non-profit private operating foundation, based in Menlo Park, California, dedicated to producing and communicating the best possible information and analysis on health issues. For fifteen years the Foundation has operated a large scale public opinion and survey research program conducting polls itself and with major news organization partners. The Kaiser Family Foundation is not associated with Kaiser Permanente or Kaiser Industries.

Portions of text from Chapter 13 (pp. 328–329) were previously published and adapted from "The American Public and the Terri Schiavo Case," by Robert J. Blendon, John M. Benson, and Melissa J. Herrmann in the *Archives of Internal Medicine*, vol. 165 (Dec. 2005), pp. 2580–2584. Copyright © 2005 American Medical Association. All Rights Reserved. Used with permission.

CQ Press gratefully acknowledges Harvard University, the Kaiser Family Foundation, and the Roper Center for Public Opinion Research for generously allowing us to reprint public opinion poll data in this volume.

Cover design: Matthew Simmons, www.myselfincluded.com
Composition: C&M Digitals (P) Ltd.

⊗ The paper used in this publication exceeds the requirements of the American National Standard for Information Sciences—Permanence of Paper for Printed Library Materials, ANSI Z39.48-1992.

Printed and bound in the United States of America

14   13   12   11   10   1   2   3   4   5

Library of Congress Cataloging-in-Publication Data

American public opinion and health care / Robert J. Blendon . . . [et al.].
    p. cm.
  Includes index.
  ISBN 978-0-87289-384-9 (case : alk. paper) 1. Health surveys—United States. 2. Medical care—United States—Public opinion. I. Blendon, Robert II. Title.

  RA407.3.A44 2011
  362.10973—dc22

2010030509

CONTENTS

Chapter 3: Attitudes about the U.S. Health System and Priorities for Government Action

Chapter 4: Attitudes about Health Care Costs

Chapter 5:   The Uninsured and Efforts to Expand Coverage

Chapter 6:   The Massachusetts Health Reform Law: A Case Study

Chapter 7: Medicare and Medicaid

Chapter 8: Public Opinion on Prescription Drugs

Chapter 9: Quality of Care and Medical Errors

Chapter 10: Attitudes about HIV/AIDS

Chapter 11: Attitudes about Abortion

Chapter 12: Attitudes about Stem Cell Research

Chapter 13: End-of-Life Care

Chapter 14: Public Opinion and Obesity

Chapter 15: Emerging Infectious Diseases

Chapter 16: Pandemic Influenza

Chapter 17: Americans' Views about Racial and Ethnic Health Care Disparities

Chapter 18: The Views of African Americans and Hispanics on Health Policy

Chapter 19: Women's Perspectives on Health Care Policy

Chapter 20: Elections, Partisan Views, and Health Policy

Chapter 21: Public Opinion on Health Care Reform through the Prism of Obama's 2009–2010 Reform Effort

About the Authors

Robert J. Blendon, M.B.A., Sc.D., is professor of health policy and political analysis at the Harvard School of Public Health and Harvard's Kennedy School of Government. He directs the Harvard Opinion Research Program. Dr. Blendon is also a past president of the Association of Health Services Research and winner of their Distinguished Investigator Award. He is a recipient of the Baxter Award for lifetime achievement in the health services research field and the Warren J. Mitofsky Award for Excellence in Public Opinion Research. He teaches a course called "Public Opinion, Polling and Public Policy" at Harvard's Kennedy School of Government.

Mollyann Brodie, Ph.D., is a senior vice president and the director of public opinion and survey research at the Kaiser Family Foundation. For the last fifteen years she has directed the foundation's public opinion survey efforts, including a variety of public knowledge and survey-related projects and ongoing survey partnerships with the *Washington Post,* National Public Radio, and *USA Today.* Her research efforts focus on understanding the public's opinion, experiences, and knowledge on health care policy issues, and the role of opinion in health policy debates. She received her Ph.D. in health policy from Harvard University.

John M. Benson, M.A., is managing director of the Harvard Opinion Research Program at the Harvard School of Public Health. He has directed numerous national and international polling projects leading to more than one hundred publications in policy and polling journals. He has played a major role in the design and analysis of surveys with the *Washington Post,* National Public Radio, the Kaiser Family Foundation, and the Robert Wood Johnson Foundation. Previously he was associate editor of *Public Perspective* and senior opinion analyst at the Roper Center for Public Opinion Research.

Drew E. Altman, Ph.D., is president and chief executive officer of the Kaiser Family Foundation based in Menlo Park, California, with major facilities in Washington, D.C. In late 1990 Dr. Altman joined the foundation and directed a complete overhaul of its mission and operating style, leading to its standing today as a leader in health policy and communications. He is a former commissioner of the Department of Human Services for the state of New Jersey under Governor Tom Kean (1986–1989). Dr. Altman earned his Ph.D. in political science from the Massachusetts Institute of Technology, served in the Carter administration, and was a vice president of the Robert Wood Johnson Foundation and director of the Health and Human Services Program at the Pew Charitable Trusts.

About the Contributors

Sara Bleich, Ph.D., is an assistant professor in the Department of Health Policy and Management at the Johns Hopkins Bloomberg School of Public Health with expertise in obesity policy.

Tami Buhr, A.M., is senior project manager at Opinion Dynamics Corporation.

John M. Connolly, Ph.D., is a senior policy analyst at the Kaiser Family Foundation.

Claudia Deane, M.A., is associate director of public opinion and survey research at the Kaiser Family Foundation.

Carolina S. Gutiérrez, M.A., is a survey analyst with the public opinion and survey research group at the Kaiser Family Foundation.

Elizabeth C. Hamel is associate director of public opinion and survey research at the Kaiser Family Foundation.

Melissa J. Herrmann, M.A., is president of Social Science Research Solutions.

Gillian K. SteelFisher, Ph.D., is a research scientist and assistant director of the Harvard Opinion Research Program at the Harvard School of Public Health.

Tara Sussman Oakman, Ph.D., is a research fellow at the Harvard School of Public Health.

Kalahn Taylor-Clark, Ph.D., is research director at the Brookings Institution in the Engelberg Center for Health Care Reform, where she leads activities related to policy solutions to reduce health disparities.

Kathleen J. Weldon is project coordinator at the Harvard Opinion Research Program at the Harvard School of Public Health.

Chapter 1

INTRODUCTION: PUBLIC OPINION ON HEALTH POLICY

Robert J. Blendon, Mollyann Brodie, John M. Benson, Drew E. Altman, Claudia Deane, and Tami Buhr

This book examines Americans' views about the country's health system and the policies that shape its future direction. What people think about health policy is relevant because this area of decision making directly affects their day-to-day lives and it involves decisions about ways to reduce deaths, pain, suffering, disabilities, and financial hardships for the population as a whole. Unlike many other areas of public policy, such as foreign affairs, transportation, agriculture, or space exploration, where most attitudes are not based on experience, opinions on health policy draw on the life experiences of people in general.

In the course of a year, the average American sees a physician about four times.[1] One in fourteen Americans is hospitalized.[2] Nearly half of the population takes at least one prescription drug per month.[3] Personal health expenditures, from various sources, are more than $6,000 per person.[4] Health is also a visible area of government policymaking. Because of concerns about the health, safety, and financial security of the public, the health sector is highly regulated, and government currently pays for 46 percent of all personal health care expenditures.[5] The health sector is also an important part of the economic fabric of communities. It represents one-sixth of the American economy and employs 10 percent of the nation's workforce.[6]

Taken together these factors make health care an issue that Americans think, talk, and have opinions about, and public opinion polls seek to capture these views. Polls not only provide a scientific measure of Americans' views on the state of health care both nationally and personally, but also report on people's experiences with the health system. Poll results suggest areas of support or opposition, as well as opportunities for future action by the government, the professions, and health institutions to improve the health of the public. In particular, opinion polls give the public a voice in deliberations about their future health system. Hundreds of interest groups crowd Washington and state capitals to try to shape government policymaking in ways that reflect their own views.[7] Opinion polls give the public an independent voice in this process and provide a counterweight to those who are represented by powerful and influential interest groups.

Polls also serve as an educational medium for elected officials in the area of health policy. With more than 300 million people, the United States is diverse in experiences and views. Polls present a picture of this diversity in a single set of findings and track how attitudes may change.

Over the years, increased attention has been paid to measuring public opinion on health policy issues. This rise in interest is reflected in the volume of polling questions on the subject. The number of health-related polling questions grew from 338 in the 1960s to 22,963 in the decade 2000–2009 (**Table 1–1**).[8]

Several factors have been suggested as to why public opinion polling on health care has increased so sharply. Some of these factors are broad societal changes; others are unique to the health field.

One major societal change relates to the public belief that governments should be more responsive to concerns of their citizens.[9] Opinion surveys show that the vast majority of Americans believe that the views of the public should have a great deal (68 percent) or a fair amount (26 percent) of influence on the decisions made by elected and government officials in Washington. Public opinion polling is seen by a large majority as a very good (28 percent) or somewhat good (56 percent) way of communicating public views to government decision-makers. In addition, three-fourths believe that polls are very useful (22 percent) or somewhat useful (54 percent) for elected and government officials to know how the public feels about important issues (**Table 1–2**).[10] Surveys also show that the overwhelming majority of Americans (76 percent) believe the public can make sound judgments about the general direction government officials should take on health care (**Table 1–3**).[11]

Another factor is the decline in public trust in government decision-makers, experts, and authority figures. This includes a decline in public trust specifically in regard to the leaders of medicine, a term often taken to refer to people who head major institutions in health care, such as the American Medical Association, medical schools and centers, and the nation's hospitals. Americans have traditionally relied on these leaders to help shape health policy decision making in the United States.[12]

In addition, the electorate in the United States has broadened during the past century, making the views of diverse populations more important to those involved in electoral politics. The voting population is more heterogenous now than in the early twentieth century, when women and younger adults (ages 18 to 20) were constitutionally prohibited from voting and African Americans and many immigrant groups faced major barriers in gaining access to the ballot box.

Other factors have created interest in public opinion on health care. They include: (1) the significance of health care as a voting issue in recent elections, making responsiveness to public views more important to the electoral success of politicians;[13] (2) the increasing number of health-related ballot initiatives in state elections, creating a mechanism for public opinion directly affecting state health policy;[14] and (3) the growing impact of consumer movements in health where the public and their organized representative groups have sought more influence on how health services are organized, provided, and financed.[15]

What Public Opinion Polls Can Tell Us: Cancer as a Case Study

Polls can provide a picture of how the public as a whole looks at a particular health problem—how worried they are about being affected by it, how important they think the problem is, what priority for government action it should receive. But polls can also give voice to people who are grappling with a specific health challenge, revealing their experiences and attitudes, how the health care system is working for them and how it is not, and then feeding this information into the ongoing evolution of national and state health policy.

Polling about cancer is an example. Polls of the general public find that cancer is the disease that Americans most worry about getting, the one they believe poses the greatest health threat to the public, and the disease that should be the highest priority for federally funded medical research.

When asked to think about health problems that might affect them in the future, the public chose some form of cancer—lung, breast, or prostate (depending on the respondent's gender), or other forms of cancer—as the health problem they worried about most.[16] When people were asked in 2009 to say in their own words what two diseases or health conditions they thought posed the greatest threat to the American public, cancer topped the list, named by 57 percent, well ahead of heart disease (28 percent) and HIV/AIDS (25 percent) (**Table 1–4**).[17] In a similarly open-ended question, this one not restricted to diseases or health conditions, the public was asked what they thought was the most urgent health problem facing the country today. Cancer again topped the list (named by 28 percent), followed by health insurance and the uninsured (18 percent), and health care costs (17 percent).[18]

This concern is reflected in the public's list of priorities for federal government spending on medical research. More than twice as many people named cancer (37 percent) as Alzheimer's (15 percent), heart disease (14 percent), and HIV/AIDS (14 percent) as the highest priority from a list of seven health problems.[19]

In 2006 *USA Today*, the Kaiser Family Foundation, and the Harvard School of Public Health conducted a poll of people from households affected by cancer—the 10 percent of Americans who say that they or another family member in their household has been diagnosed or treated for cancer in the past five years—to better understand their attitudes and specific experiences.[20] In particular, the poll was able to catalog the massive financial impact of cancer on these families, and in doing so highlight hot-button policy issues such as the personal impact of rapidly rising health care costs and the extent to which even those with insurance are not always well-protected against catastrophic illness.

The survey found that nearly half (46 percent) of people whose families were affected by the disease said the costs of cancer care were a burden on the family, including one in six (17 percent) who said costs were a major burden (**Table 1–5**). In addition, significant minorities reported some serious consequences of the financial costs: one in four said they had used up all or most of their savings, and about one in ten (11 percent) reported being unable to pay for basic necessities such as food, heat, and housing. One in eight (13 percent) had been contacted by a collection agency, and 3 percent had declared bankruptcy. For some, cost had affected treatment decisions. Eight percent said they had delayed or had not gotten care for cancer because of the cost. Each of these findings has policy implications in the sense that they point out ways the current system can fail families—often even those families with solid health insurance coverage—at a time of great need.

The poll also provided another channel to examine some of the duplication and confusion that currently plagues the American health care system, duplication that current reformers hope to weed out with new reforms. Significant minorities reported problems with coordination of care, including receiving conflicting information from different health care providers (25 percent), being sent for duplicate tests (21 percent), and being confused about medication they were prescribed (20 percent). About one-fourth (26 percent) rated the American health care system when it came to treating cancer as fair or poor (**Table 1–6**).

Polling can also show the public's reaction to a controversial policy decision. For many years, medical guidelines have called for most women to have their first mammogram at age forty and to have follow-up mammograms every year. In November 2009, in the midst of a contentious and partisan debate over health care reform, the U.S. Preventive Services Task Force (USPSTF), a panel of medical experts commissioned by the federal government to review the scientific evidence regarding preventive medical services and develop practice guidelines, announced a new recommendation: the age for a first mammogram should be increased to fifty and that follow-up mammograms be conducted every two years instead of every year.[21] The recommendation was immediately controversial, taken up as a weapon in the contentious health reform debate.

A poll conducted shortly after the announcement found that roughly three-fourths (76 percent) of women aged thirty-five to seventy-five disagreed with the recommendations, 47 percent of them strongly. This group was suspicious of the motives behind the panel's recommendations. Only 16 percent believed that the new recommendations were based mainly on a fair assessment of the medical risks and benefits of mammograms for women in their forties. More than three-fourths (76 percent) believed that the new recommendations were based on the potential for cost savings in the health care system. Eighty-four percent of women aged thirty-five to forty-nine said that they personally intended to have a mammogram before they turned fifty, and only 13 percent said they would wait until age fifty (**Table 1–7**).[22]

Although it is difficult to link public opinion directly to public policy, cancer is the disease that receives the largest amount of funding from the federal government, corresponding to the public's preferences. Similarly, following the immediate negative response from women to the new mammography recommendations, Kathleen Sebelius, secretary of Health and Human Services, issued a statement encouraging women and clinicians to continue current practices despite the findings and suggesting that public and private insurance practices regarding mammograms would not and should not change. In the health reform debate, Sen. Barbara Mikulski, D-Md., proposed an amendment that would require that all women be guaranteed preventive health screenings (including mammograms). To this amendment, Sen. David Vitter, R-La., added a directive that the government ignore the USPSTF's most recent guideline change. The Senate passed the amendment by a vote of 61 to 39.[23]

There are countless other examples of polls that have become part of the policymaking process at every level.

- At the local level, a series of 2006 and 2008 surveys of post-Katrina New Orleans helped inform local and state leaders of the scope of the hurricane's human impact, as well as laying out residents' priorities for the official recovery process. The 2006 survey found that 77 percent of those then living in the greater New Orleans area had experienced a deterioration in their economic situation, physical/mental health, or family relations after the hurricane, making clear the extent of the challenge facing city and state leaders. The survey discovered that fully half of those living in the area were facing problems with health care coverage and access, including 27 percent who had no regular source of care outside the emergency room. Not surprisingly, the project found that getting medical facilities up and running in the damaged city ranked third only behind levee repair and crime control on the public's priority list.[24] These and other findings were presented to the official recovery czar as well as the head of Louisiana's Department of Health and Hospitals and in testimony before Congress.[25]

- At the national level, surveys that measured the impact of direct-to-consumer (DTC) advertising of prescription drugs may have affected the crafting of legislation to regulate such advertising. A 2008 survey was presented to the House Energy and Commerce Subcommittee on Oversight and Investigations as evidence that indeed DTC ads were prompting Americans to speak to their physicians about drugs they had seen advertised. Specifically, 32 percent of Americans reported having spoken to a doctor about a particular medication after seeing an ad, and 82 percent of this group said the doctor recommended a prescription drug as a result, findings that were echoed in a corresponding survey of physicians. The survey found that although majorities were satisfied with the job DTC ads do in explaining the potential benefits of a drug, more than half felt ads did only a fair or poor job explaining potential side effects. The survey revealed that there was some appetite for increased government regulation when it came to ensuring that advertising claims are not misleading.[26]

- Finally, ongoing surveys that measure the extent to which Americans defer needed care due to cost, and the problems they have paying the medical bills they do incur, became an important part of the public record in 2009 and 2010 as Congress made a historic effort to reform the health care system.[27]

How Polls Are Conducted

The vast majority of polls cited in this book were conducted by telephone with a randomly selected sample of a population. Using a technique called random digit dialing, telephone numbers are selected randomly from a sample frame of all possible telephone numbers, including, in recent years, cell phone numbers.[28] Referring back to the cancer-related polls discussed above, the first four of those were surveys of the general public, the most common sort of poll.

Most polls of the sort used in this book are conducted over relatively short periods of time in order to reflect the most current views of the respondents.[29] As a result, some proportion of the sample cannot be reached during the poll's field period and does not get interviewed. Some groups in the population, such as young adults, are especially hard to reach, while others, such as people age sixty-five and over, are easier to reach. Some other people simply do not want to be interviewed, either in general or because it is inconvenient when they are contacted. To compensate for this "nonresponse bias" and help ensure that the results are more representative, the data are weighted to reflect the actual composition of the population, calculated on the basis of data from the U.S. Census Bureau, according to age, sex, education, region, race or ethnic background, and the number of adults in the household.[30]

Typically polls interview between 1,000 and 1,500 respondents, although some have samples as small as 500 or as large as 4,000 or more. All surveys are subject to sampling error. Results may differ from what would have been obtained if the whole adult population had been interviewed, which is clearly impossible to do. The size of the sampling error varies with the number surveyed and the magnitude of difference in the responses to each question. For example, an analysis of a sample of 500 persons will, with a 95 percent degree of confidence (i.e., in 19 out of 20 cases), have a statistical precision (often called "margin of error") of approximately plus or minus 5 percentage points; for a sample of 1,500 persons, plus or minus 3 percentage points.

Also included in the discussion of the cancer-related polls was a more specialized survey of adults from households affected by cancer. Because the incidence of this group is relatively low—10 percent of the national adult population—the sample for that survey was screened first from a general public sample by asking a short series of questions. Those who did not meet the criteria were excluded from the sample. (A proportion of those who were excluded were asked demographic questions for the purposes of weighting the data.)

In a somewhat simpler screening process, only adult women were included in the sample for the mammogram poll described above. Some of the questions were asked only of subgroups of women who would be affected by the new guidelines.

At times, instead of screening for a subpopulation that is of special interest to the topic being examined, that subpopulation is oversampled, meaning that a higher proportion of that group is interviewed than would occur in the actual overall population. This technique is commonly used to look in more detail at the responses of a particular subgroup, but also to learn the opinions of the rest of the population. One might oversample women to ask their views about the new mammogram guidelines and when they expect to get a mammogram, which would allow for a more detailed examination of the views of particular age groups of women. But one might also be interested in learning what men think about the guidelines. Oversampling is often used when looking at the views of racial/ethnic minorities or other groups that do not make up a large proportion of the population. Even though one group is oversampled, an overall result for the total population can be obtained by weighting the responses of the oversampled group back to its proportion in the actual population, as measured by the U.S. Census.

Because polling questions most often ask respondents for opinions, there is no external validation for most of the findings. Surveys' claims to validity are based on the statistical theory of sampling. The underlying assumption is that if one chooses a sample using probability techniques, one can generalize from that sample back to the population.[31] Practically speaking, however, the reputation of public opinion polls in general rests upon the success of preelection polls to predict election results, where the outcome is known. In presidential elections since 1956, preelection polls of short duration that were analyzed with the use of reweighted data have accurately predicted the voting distribution, with an average error of ±1.9 percentage points.[32] Also, a 2009 study comparing responses to polls using probability sampling to actual measures that could be validated from official records (e.g., the proportion of adults who have passports and driver's licenses) found that probability samples yield quite accurate results.[33]

Polls have proliferated, but not all polls are of equal quality. Professional organizations and individual researchers involved in the field have published guidelines to help survey practitioners design better polls and to teach poll users how to tell good polls from bad polls.[34]

Overview of the Book

Archival research shows that over the years hundreds of polls involving thousands of survey questions have been conducted on health and health care issues. The goal of *American Public Opinion and Health Care* is to help interested readers sort out what public opinion really is on the critical health policy issues facing the nation today. The book is not a simple compendium of data. Instead, it attempts, in a readable and accessible way that is free of jargon, to provide expert analysis of and insight into American public opinion on health care policy.

After this introduction, the book is divided into 20 chapters, each of which deals with an important health policy issue in depth and draws on current and historical polling data. Chapter 2 discusses public trust in government and health care institutions. Chapters 3 through 9 deal with public opinion about major issues having to do with the health care system: views of the health care system as a whole, health care costs, the uninsured, and efforts to expand health insurance coverage, including a case study of the Massachusetts health reform law, Medicare and Medicaid, prescription drugs, and quality of care and medical errors.

Chapters 10 through 16 discuss Americans' views about crucial public health issues: HIV/AIDS, abortion, stem cell research, end-of-life care, obesity, and emerging infectious diseases, including a case study of pandemic flu and H1N1 (swine) flu. Chapter 17 examines Americans' views about disparities in health care.

Chapters 18 and 19 look at the health care attitudes and experiences of African Americans, Hispanics, and women. Chapter 20 examines how views about health care issues differ by political party identification. The book concludes with a discussion of public opinion on health care policy through the prism of President Barack Obama's 2009–2010 reform effort, revisiting several major themes of the book.

Each chapter begins with a review of the main policy debates on the subject being discussed, often in historical context. Then, using a wealth of recent polling results, as well as substantial trend data when appropriate, each chapter examines public opinion on the major policy questions being debated.

Extensive and detailed endnotes follow the text of each chapter. Tables found at the end of each chapter present the key public opinion findings, often with trends over time or the responses of certain subgroups of the population.

Each of the public opinion tables shows the public response (in percent), the wording of the questions, and the sources of the data presented. Generally, the percentage is shown for each substantive response offered in the question, although sometimes similar responses are combined; "strongly agree" and "somewhat agree" may be combined into "agree." For ease of comparison among multiple questions, sometimes the percentage for only one response category, such as the percentage who approve of various proposals, is shown.

Volunteered responses of "Don't know," "no answer," "not sure," and "uncertain" are left in the base of people responding when calculating percentages, even when those categories are not shown. Often, when the total of these volunteered responses is less than 10 percent, they are not shown, but their absence from the table is noted. For simplicity and convenience, these responses are often short-handed as "Don't know" because the meanings of the various labels are similar.

Data Selection

In general, the data selected for discussion and display are from the latest well-written question(s) on a given subject, except when talking about certain historical events or trends. Whenever possible, trends consist of responses to substantially identical questions. When exceptions are made to this rule, the question wordings shown on the trend tables inform the reader of the variation.

The data are derived from general public samples except where noted. Responses are sometimes shown for closely related groups, such as registered or likely voters, particularly when discussing elections, or groups whose views are particularly relevant to the issue being discussed, such as the views of adults age sixty-five or over in the case of Medicare.

Data from partisan or advocacy group polls are excluded except when explicitly making a point about that group's position or where the question adds a particular insight on one of a range of policy options. Again, these exceptions are clearly noted. Except in rare cases, which are also noted, Internet polls are not included.

Sources of Data

The data presented in this book come from more than 300 public opinion polls from a wide variety of sources. The largest proportion of the polls represented here were conducted by major polling organizations, such as Gallup, Harris Interactive, and the Pew Research Center for the People and the Press, and by polling groups at major media organizations: ABC News/*Washington Post*, CBS News/*New York Times*, NBC News/*Wall Street Journal*, FOX News, the *Los Angeles Times, USA Today, Time, Newsweek*, and the Associated Press. In addition, a large amount of data comes from polls conducted by the Kaiser Family Foundation and by the Harvard School of Public Health.

Major resources for finding these data include the Kaiser Family Foundation Web site, kff
.org; the Gallup, Harris Interactive, and Pew Research Center Web sites; and the iPOLL database
of the Roper Center for Public Opinion Research. Because most of the nonproprietary data of
the major polling firms are archived at the Roper Center, many of the references in this book cite
the Roper Center as the place of publication. Most of the health-related questions and responses
can be found online at the Kaiser Family Foundation's Health Poll Search, http://www.kff.org/
kaiserpolls/healthpoll.cfm.

Notes

[1] National Center for Health Statistics, "Americans Make Nearly Four Medical Visits a Year on
Average," August 6, 2008, http://www.cdc.gov/nchs/pressroom/08newsreleases/visitstodoctor
.htm. This number includes visits to doctors' offices, hospital outpatient departments, and
hospital emergency departments.

[2] National Center for Health Statistics, *Health, United States, 2008* (Hyattsville, Md.: National
Center for Health Statistics, 2009), Table 101.

[3] Ibid., Table 98.

[4] Micah Hartman, Anne Martin, Patricia McConnell, Aaron Catlin, and the National Health
Expenditure Accounts Team, "National Health Spending in 2007: Slower Drug Spending
Contributes to Lowest Rate of Overall Growth Since 1998," *Health Affairs* 28 (January/
February 2009): 246–261.

[5] Ibid.

[6] Ibid.; National Center for Health Statistics, *Health, United States, 2008*, Table 108.

[7] Katherine A. Hinckley and Bette S. Hill, "On Treacherous Ground: The Strategic Choices of
Health Interest Groups," in Theodor J. Litman and Leonard S. Robins, eds., *Health Politics
and Policy,* 3rd ed. (Albany, N.Y.: Delmar, 1997), 231–262; Kay Lehman Schlozman and
John T. Tierney, *Organized Interests and American Democracy* (New York: Harper and
Row, 1986).

[8] Based on a count of questions on health-related topics in the iPOLL database at the Roper
Center for Public Opinion Research, the nation's largest archive of public opinion polls. The
holdings of the Roper Center archive are more complete for recent decades, so the growth of
health care polling may be slightly overestimated.

[9] Thomas Lamatsch, "Ideological Measurement," in Samuel J. Best and Benjamin Radcliff, eds.,
Polling America: An Encyclopedia of Public Opinion (Westport, Conn.: Greenwood Press,
2005), 313–318.

[10] Kaiser Family Foundation/*Public Perspective,* "National Survey of the Role of Polls in
Policymaking," June 2001, http://www.kff.org/kaiserpolls/loader.cfm?url=/commonspot/
security/getfile.cfm&PageID=13842.

[11] Ibid.

[12] See Chapter 2.

[13] Robert J. Blendon, Drew E. Altman, John M. Benson, Mollyann Brodie, Tami Buhr, Claudia
Deane, and Sasha Buscho, "Voters and Health Reform in the 2008 Presidential Election," *New
England Journal of Medicine* 359 (November 6, 2008): 2050–61. See also Chapter 20.

[14] National Conference of State Legislatures, "Ballot Measures Database," http://www.ncsl.org/programs/legismgt/elect/dbintro.htm.

[15] Nancy Tomes, "Patients or Health Care Consumers? Why the History of Contested Terms Matters," in Rosemary A. Stevens, Charles E. Rosenberg, and Lawton R. Burns, eds., *History and Health Policy in the United States* (New Brunswick, N.J.: Rutgers University Press, 2006), 83–110.

[16] Stony Brook University Poll (Storrs, Conn.: Roper Center for Public Opinion Research, May 12–July 2, 2006).

[17] Harvard School of Public Health/Robert Wood Johnson Foundation Poll (Storrs, Conn.: Roper Center for Public Opinion Research, June 24–28, 2009).

[18] Kaiser Family Foundation Poll (Storrs, Conn.: Roper Center for Public Opinion Research, January 26–March 8, 2009).

[19] AP/Ipsos Poll (Storrs, Conn.: Roper Center for Public Opinion Research, July 19–21, 2004).

[20] *USA Today*/Kaiser Family Foundation/Harvard School of Public Health, "National Survey of Households Affected by Cancer," August 1–September 14, 2006, http://www.kff.org/kaiserpolls/pomr112006pkg.cfm.

[21] Gina Kolata, "Panel Urges Mammograms at 50, Not 40," *New York Times,* November 17, 2009, http://www.nytimes.com/2009/11/17/health/17cancer.html; U.S. Preventive Services Task Force, "Screening for Breast Cancer: U.S. Preventive Services Task Force Recommended Statements," *Annals of Internal Medicine* 151 (November 17, 2009): 716–726, http://www.annals.org/content/151/10/716.full.pdf+html.

[22] Gallup Poll, "Women Disagree with New Mammogram Advice," November 24, 2009, http://www.gallup.com/poll/124463/Women-Disagree-New-Mammogram-Advice.aspx.

[23] "Senate Health Care Follies," *New York Times,* December 6, 2009, http://www.nytimes.com/2009/12/06/opinion/06sun1.html?scp=1&sq=senate%20health%20care%20follies&st=cse.

[24] Kaiser Family Foundation, "Giving Voice to the People of New Orleans: The Kaiser Post-Katrina Baseline Survey," 2006, http://www.kff.org/kaiserpolls/pomr051007pkg.cfm; Kaiser Family Foundation, "New Orleans Three Years After the Storm: The Second Kaiser Post-Katrina Survey: 2008," http://www.kff.org/kaiserpolls/posr081008pkg.cfm.

[25] Diane Rowland, "Health Care in New Orleans: Progress and Remaining Challenges," Testimony before the U.S. House of Representatives Committee on Oversight and Government Reform," December 3, 2009, http://www.kff.org/uninsured/upload/8026.pdf; Diane Rowland, "Health Care in New Orleans from the People's Perspective," Testimony before the U.S. House of Representatives Committee on Energy and Commerce Subcommittee on Oversight and Investigation, August 1, 2007, http://www.kff.org/uninsured/upload/7678.pdf.

[26] Mollyann Brodie, "Public Views of Direct-to-Consumer Prescription Drug Advertising," Testimony before the U.S. House of Representatives Committee on Energy and Commerce Subcommittee on Oversight and Investigation, May 8, 2008, http://www.kff.org/kaiserpolls/upload/7774.pdf.

[27] Diane Rowland, "The Adequacy of Health Insurance," Testimony before the U.S. Senate Committee on Health, Education, Labor, and Pensions, http://www.kff.org/uninsured/upload/7870.pdf.

[28] Whitney Murphy and Colm O'Muircheartaigh, "Random Digit Dialing (RDD)," in *Polling America: An Encyclopedia of Public Opinion,* ed. Samuel J. Best and Benjamin Radcliff (Westport, Conn.: Greenwood Press, 2005), 652–657.

[29] Henry E. Grady and Gary R. Orren, "Polling Pitfalls: Sources of Error in Public Opinion Surveys," in *Media Polls in American Politics,* ed. Thomas E. Mann and Gary R. Orren (Washington D.C.: Brookings Institution, 1992), 55–94.

[30] D. Stephen Voss, Andrew Gelman, and Gary King, "Pre-election Survey Methodology: Details from Eight Polling Organizations, 1988 and 1992" *Public Opinion Quarterly* 59 (Spring 1995): 98–132.

[31] Norman M. Bradburn and Seymour Sudman, *Polls and Surveys: Understanding What They Tell Us* (San Francisco: Jossey-Bass, 1988), Chapter 1.

[32] Michael W. Traugott, "The Accuracy of the National Preelection Polls in the 2004 Presidential Election," *Public Opinion Quarterly* 69 (Special Issue 2005): 642–654.

[33] David S. Yeager, Jon A. Krosnick, LinChiat Chang, Harold S. Javitz, Matthew S. Levindusky, Alberto Simpser, and Rui Wang, "Comparing the Accuracy of RDD Telephone Surveys and Internet Surveys Conducted with Probability and Non-Probability Samples," August 2009, http://www.knowledgenetworks.com/insights/docs/Mode-04_2.pdf.

[34] American Association for Public Opinion Research, "Best Practices," http://www.aapor.org/Best_Practices/1480.htm; Michael W. Link and Robert W. Oldendick, " 'Good' Polls/'Bad' Polls—How Can You Tell? Ten Tips for Consumers of Survey Research," http://www.ipspr.sc.edu/publication/Link.htm.

Table 1-1 Number of Polling Questions about Health and Health Care, by Decade

Before 1940*	70
1940–1949	362
1950–1959	326
1960–1969	338
1970–1979	2352
1980–1989	8404
1990–1999	20358
2000–2009	22963
Total	55173

Note: *Polling was first developed during the 1930s, so the number of health questions shown for the period before the 1940s is low. The holdings of the Roper Center are more complete for recent decades, so that growth of health care polling may be slightly overestimated in this table.

Source: iPoll database, Roper Center for Public Opinion Research.

Table 1-2 Americans' Attitudes about the Role of Public Opinion (in percent)

	Great deal	A fair amount	Not too much	None at all
Influence the views of majority of Americans should have on federal government officials	68	26	4	1

	A very good way	Somewhat good	Not too good	Not good at all
As a way for elected and government officials to learn what the majority of Americans think, conducting a public opinion poll is . . .	28	56	10	3

	Very useful	Somewhat useful	Not too useful	Not useful at all
Usefulness of polls for elected and government officials to know how the public feels about important issues	22	54	13	8

Note: Don't know responses not shown.

Question: How much influence do you think the views of the majority of Americans should have on the decisions of elected and government officials in Washington? A great deal, a fair amount, not too much, or none at all?

Question: There are different ways elected and government officials could try to learn what the majority of people in our country think about important issues. Is conducting a public opinion poll a very good, somewhat good, not too good, or not at all good way to learn what the majority of people in our country think?

Question: To what extent do you think opinion polls are useful for elected and government officials in Washington to understand how the public feels about important issues? Very useful, somewhat useful, not too useful, or not useful at all?

Source: Kaiser Family Foundation/*Public Perspective,* "National Survey of the Role of Polls in Policymaking," June 2001.

Table 1-3 Americans' Views about the Ability of the Public to Make Sound Judgments (in percent)

The public can make sound judgments about the general direction elected officials should take regarding . . .	Yes	No	Don't know
Education issues	76	19	5
Health care issues	76	21	3
Economic issues	66	30	4
Foreign policy issues	50	44	6

Question: For each of the following issues, please tell me if you think the public can make sound judgments about the general direction elected officials should take. Do you think the public can make sound judgments about the general direction officials should take regarding (education issues, such as how much money should be spent or testing for teachers;health care issues, such as whether to expand health insurance coverage to the uninsured;economic issues, such as what taxes should be or how the budget surplus ought to be spent;foreign policy issues, such as whether to send our troops to another country or expand our military), or don't you feel this way?

Source: Kaiser Family Foundation/*Public Perspective,* "National Survey of the Role of Polls in Policymaking," June 2001.

Table 1-4 Americans' Views of Cancer as a Health Threat and Priority for Federally Funded Medical Research (in percent)

Diseases or health conditions that pose the greatest threats to the American public *[1]	
Cancer	57
Heart disease	28
HIV/AIDS	25
Influenza	17
Diabetes	13
Obesity	9
Health problem that should be the federal government's highest priority for medical research spending **[2]	
Cancer	37
Alzheimer's disease	15
Heart disease	14
AIDS	14
Obesity	10
Smoking	4
Stroke	3

Note: *Open-ended question. Top six responses shown add to more than 100 percent because multiple responses were allowed. **Volunteered responses "something else" and "Don't know" not shown.

Question: What two diseases or health conditions do you think pose the greatest threats to the American public? (open-ended)

Question: I'm going to read you a list of health problems facing the United States today. Please tell me which of these health problems you think should be the federal government's highest priority for spending on medical research: cancer, Alzheimer's disease, heart disease, AIDS, obesity, smoking, stroke.

Sources: [1]Harvard School of Public Health/Robert Wood Johnson Foundation Poll (Storrs, Conn.: Roper Center for Public Opinion Research, June 24–28, 2009). [2]AP/Ipsos Poll (Storrs, Conn.: Roper Center for Public Opinion Research, July 19–21, 2004).

Table 1-5 Financial Effects of Cancer, among Adults in Households Affected by Cancer* (in percent)

Burden of costs of cancer care in family	
Major burden	17
Minor burden	29
Not a burden	52
Results of financial costs of dealing with cancer	
Used up all or most savings	25
Contacted by collection angency	13
Unable to pay for food, heat, or housing	11
Delayed or decided not to get cancer care because of costs	8
Declared bankruptcy	3

Note: *Adults who said that they or another family member in their household had been diagnosed or treated for cancer in the past five years.

Question: How much of a burden on (your/your [family member with cancer]'s) family (were/are) the costs of (your/his/her) overall medical care, including any services ((you needed/need)/(he/she needed/needs)) to cope with (your/his/her) cancer—a major burden, a minor burden, or not a burden at all?

Question: (Did/Have) any of the following things ever (happen/happened) to (you/your [family member with cancer]) as a result of the financial cost of dealing with (your/his/her) cancer, or not? (You/He/She) (was/were) unable to pay for basic necessities like food, heat, or housing/(You/He/She) (was/were) contacted by a collection agency/(You/He/She) declared bankruptcy.

Question: (Did you/Have you)/(Did/Has your [family member with cancer]) ever delay(ed) or decide(d) not to get care for (your/his/her) cancer because of the cost?

Source: USA Today/Kaiser Family Foundation/Harvard School of Public Health, "National Survey of Households Affected by Cancer," August 1–September 14, 2006.

Table 1-6 Experiences of Cancer Treatments, among Adults in Households Affected by Cancer* (in percent)

Problems with coordination of care	
Received conflicting information from different health care professionals	25
Sent for duplicate tests or diagnostic procedures	21
Confused about the medicine the doctor prescribed	20
Rating of health care system when it comes to providing cancer care	
Excellent	22
Very good	21
Good	26
Fair	14
Poor	12
Don't know	4

Note: *Adults who said that they or another family member in their household had been diagnosed or treated for cancer in the past five years.

Question: During the course of (your/his/her) cancer treatment, ((Did you receive/Have you received)/(Did your [family member with cancer] receive/Has your [family member with cancer] received)) conflicting information about (your/his/her) cancer from different doctors or health care professionals, or not?

Question: When getting care for (your/his/her) cancer, (was there ever/has there ever been) a time when ((You were/Your [family member with cancer] was) sent for duplicate test or diagnostic procedures by different doctors, nurses, or healthcare workers/(You were/[family member with cancer] was) confused about the medication the doctor prescribed), or not?

Question: How would you rate the health care system in America today when it comes to providing cancer care? Would you say it is excellent, very good, good, fair, or poor?

Source: USA Today/Kaiser Family Foundation/Harvard School of Public Health, "National Survey of Households Affected by Cancer," August 1–September 14, 2006.

Table 1-7 Attitudes about New Mammogram Guidelines, among Women (in percent)

Opinion of new recommendations that women get first mammogram at age 50 and follow-ups every two years (among women aged 35–75)	
Strongly agree	5
Agree	17
Disagree	29
Strongly disagree	47
Views about the reason behind new recoomendations (among women aged 35–75)	
Fair assessment of medical risks and benefits of mammograms	16
Potential for cost savings in health care system	76
Plans for timing of next mammogram (among women aged 35–49)	
Will have next mammogram before age 50	84
Will wait until age 50	13

Note: "Don't know" responses not shown.

Question: (Asked of women aged 35 to 75) As you may know, medical guidelines have called for most women to have their first mammograms at age 40 and then to have follow-up mammograms every year. The [U.S. Preventive Services Task Force] advisory panel now recommends increasing the age for a first mammogram to age 50, and changing the frequency to every two years. What is your opinion of the new recommendations, do you strongly agree, agree, disagree, or strongly disagree with them?

Question: (Asked of women aged 35 to 75) Just your best guess, do you think the panel's recommendations were mainly based on a fair assessment of the true medical risks and benefits of mammograms for women in their 40s, or mainly based on the potential for cost savings in the healthcare system?

Question: How would you rate the health care system in America today when it comes to providing cancer care? Would you say it is excellent, very good, good, fair, or poor?

Question: (Asked of women aged 35 to 49) Do you think you will, personally, wait until age 50 to get your next mammogram, or will you get one sooner than that?

Source: Gallup Poll, "Women Disagree with New Mammogram Advice," November 24, 2009.

Chapter 2

TRUST IN GOVERNMENT AND HEALTH CARE INSTITUTIONS

Tami Buhr and Robert J. Blendon

One factor that has affected health policy in the United States is the decline in public confidence in a variety of institutions over the past fifty years. Confidence has fallen in government in general, specific government institutions such as Congress and the executive branch, private institutions such as major companies and law firms, and oppositional institutions such as the news media. Americans' confidence in the medical establishment also has declined during this time. There is a great deal of research examining the forces associated with the decline of trust in government, but considerably less on those affecting the decline in confidence in other institutions, including medicine. As the rise and fall in confidence of many of these institutions roughly mirrors the pattern for trust in government and government institutions, an underlying element may be common to them all.

The decline in trust has consequences for public policy broadly. Faced with a skeptical public, elected officials have less room for error. Public support is an important source of political power.[1] A decline in support hampers a politician's ability to lead in many areas, including health care reform. With a public less likely to give elected officials the benefit of the doubt, after a few missteps, the officials may find themselves lacking influence over others.

The decline in political trust has particular consequences for health policy. Reforming or changing the health care system almost always involves large-scale changes in government policy. These changes are often complex and involve shifting resources from one group to another. A skeptical public is least inclined to trust the government to manage redistributive programs that may take resources from the many to benefit the few.[2] As a result, large-scale health reform that would provide health care coverage for Americans without health insurance has been hampered by the overall mood of distrust toward the government.

Given the ties between trust in government and efforts to reform the health system, we begin this chapter by documenting changes in political trust since 1958. We present public opinion on confidence in government and a variety of institutions and attempt to provide some understanding of these changes by summarizing the theories and evidence explaining changes in trust over time.

In the second section of this chapter, we turn our attention to public trust in the leaders of the health professions and institutions. As we discover, trust in personal physicians remains high, but confidence in the leaders of medicine has declined.

Trust in Government

Over the years, public opinion scholars have developed a number of measures to track public trust in government. The American National Election Study (ANES) has asked questions about confidence in government for nearly a half century, from 1958 through 2006.[3] The 1958 survey asked three questions:

1. How much of the time do you think you can trust the government in Washington to do what is right—just about always, most of the time, or only some of the time?
2. Do you think that quite a few of the people running the government are crooked, not very many are, or do you think hardly any of them are crooked?
3. Do you think that people in government waste a lot of the money we pay in taxes, waste some of it, or don't waste very much of it?

In 1958 the answers revealed a largely trusting public. A large majority of respondents expressed faith in their government, with 16 percent saying they could trust the government to do what is right "just about always" and 57 percent "most of the time" (**Table 2–1**). Few felt that government officials were corrupt: one-quarter (24 percent) felt that quite a few officials were crooked, 44 percent felt not many, and 26 percent believed that hardly any or not many were crooked. Americans were more skeptical about tax money, with 43 percent saying that a lot was wasted, 42 percent some, and 10 percent not very much. The questions were not asked again until 1964, when a fourth was added to the series:

4. Would you say the government is pretty much run by a few big interests looking out for themselves or that it is run for the benefit of all people?

Confidence in government remained high in 1964. On this new question, nearly two-thirds (64 percent) felt that government was run for the benefit of all people (**Table 2–1**). Responding to the other three questions, a majority of Americans also continued to express faith in their government.

Four years later, however, the next time all four questions were asked, fewer Americans gave a trusting response. In 1968 a majority (61 percent) still said they could trust the government to do what is right all or most of the time, but this percentage was a significant decline from the 73 percent who gave these responses in 1958. About half (51 percent) of Americans in 1968 believed that government was run for the benefit of all, also a sharp decline from four years earlier.

By 1968 a majority (59 percent) of the public also believed that the government wasted a lot of tax money. The late 1960s marked the beginning of a long decline in confidence in government. By 1980 trust in government was nearly opposite what it was twenty years earlier, with 73 percent saying they could trust the government "some" or "none" of the time, and only 25 percent saying "most of the time" or "just about always." Seven in ten thought government was "run pretty much by a few big interests looking out for themselves," and 78 percent believed that government wasted a lot of tax money.

Since 1980 public confidence in government has risen and fallen several times. Trust rebounded slightly during the 1980s before declining once more and reaching a series low in 1994. From this low point, trust in government increased throughout the rest of 1990s. Following the terrorist attacks of September 11, trust shot up to levels unseen since the late 1960s, but the increase was short-lived. In the 2002 ANES, 56 percent of Americans said they trusted the government to do the right thing all or most of the time. Two years later, the percentage had dropped to 47 percent. By 2006 trust had returned nearly to its all-time low, and it remains low in 2010, with only 26 percent giving a trusting response.[4] A trust index, which is created by averaging the ANES questions after they have been scaled to range from 0 to 100, highlights the changes in trust over time (**Table 2–1**).[5]

Confidence in National versus State or Local Government

Americans have more confidence in governments that are closer to home. When asked in the same survey how much they trust federal, state, and local governments to do what is right, Americans consistently give higher ratings to state and local government (**Table 2–2**).[6]

A similar pattern is seen when looking at congressional job approval. The public is more approving of the job performance of their member of Congress than they are of Congress as a whole. Shortly before the 2008 election, 50 percent of Americans approved of the job their member of Congress was doing, compared to 15 percent who approved of the job being done by the institution of Congress (**Table 2–2**).[7]

Causes of Decline in Trust in Government

By the early 1970s, scholars had noted the drop in people's trust in government as measured by the ANES. The first studies proposed two different theories on the causes and consequences of decline in trust. According to the first theory, the decline in public trust represented a loss of support for the American system of government.[8] Ultimately, the legitimacy of the political system would be at risk if the situation continued. The other side contended that the drop in trust was specific to the current government officials and policy decisions.[9] A change in leadership and policy direction could reverse the decline. So the question is: Have Americans become less trusting of the institutions of government or of the incumbents in charge of running those institutions? The passage of time and additional evidence has provided more support for the latter theory than the former.

Surveys have asked people about their feelings toward the American system of government and generally have found a satisfied American public. Although the proportion of Americans who say they are satisfied with the U.S. system of government has declined since 2001, a majority

(53 percent) still express satisfaction (**Table 2–3**).[10] Americans overwhelmingly feel that, "whatever its faults," the United States has the best system of government in the world (81 percent in 2007, only a slight decline from 89 percent in 2000).[11]

Nevertheless, people also sense that things are not operating as well as they should. Many feel that fundamental changes are needed (62 percent), but far fewer feel the system needs to be completely rebuilt (17 percent).[12] Likewise, although a large majority (86 percent) feels that the system is broken, most believe it can be fixed (81 percent) compared to those who feel it is broken and cannot be fixed (5 percent).[13] The dissatisfaction appears to be more with the leaders than the institutions. Two-thirds (66 percent) agreed that the U.S. system of government is good, but the people running it are incompetent.[14]

Fluctuations in trust levels over time also suggest that incumbent performance matters more than government institutional structures. Changes in public perceptions of the economy, presidential job performance, and presidential image are tied to changes in trust in government.[15] Presidential performance on major issues, such as the economy and foreign policy crises, are particularly important.

The initial decline in trust in government that began in the late 1960s and continued through the 1970s occurred during a time of great political and social unrest. Protests surrounding the Vietnam War and race relations marked the end of Lyndon Johnson's presidency. Trust continued its downward slide during Richard Nixon's presidency with the continuation of the Vietnam War, increasing economic uncertainty, and the Watergate scandal. By the time Jimmy Carter took office, trust in government and other institutions had fallen so low he described the public mood as a "crisis in confidence."[16]

Since the Carter presidency, the nation has experienced two periods of renewed trust followed by decline. The first renewal came during Ronald Reagan's administration and coincided with an improvement in the economy and an increase in public approval of the president's job performance. Trust fell again during George H. W. Bush's administration as the economy softened. Trust continued to drop and hit a new low in 1994 during Bill Clinton's first term with the failure of his health care reform plan and other administration priorities. But with a growing economy and higher approval levels for Clinton, despite personal scandal, trust rebounded and by 2000 equaled the high during the Reagan administration.

George W. Bush's presidency saw both high and low levels of trust in government. Both trust and presidential approval spiked with a "rally around the flag" effect following the September 11, 2001, terrorist attacks, but as Bush's approval declined with the lengthening of the Iraq War, so did trust.

Additional evidence that trust is tied to incumbent leaders rather than political institutions is found by examining differences in trust by party identification. Partisans are more trusting of government when the party with which they identify controls the institutions of government.[17] Looking once again at the Trust Index from the ANES, we see that during Republican presidential administrations, Republicans are significantly more trusting of government and that Democrats are more trusting during Democratic presidencies (**Table 2–4**).[18] This variation is indicative of the skeptical view Americans have of their political system: they have confidence that it works only when their own party is in charge. Political independents, who lack a party affiliation, display trust levels similar to members of the out party.

Impact of Decline in Trust in Government

Although political trust is tied more to incumbent performance and less to institutions, trust has remained consistently lower than it was fifty years ago. Replacing elected officials has not caused trust to rebound to its late 1950s and early 1960s levels. Marc Hetherington argues that researchers have focused too much on the causes of the decline and have not paid enough attention to the consequences.[19] He finds that evaluations of incumbent leaders not only impact levels of trust, but also that trust itself impacts evaluations of leaders. Causality runs in both directions, so we cannot understand the causes of the decline of trust without considering the consequences of the decline. Studies using ANES data show that higher levels of trust are associated with more positive evaluations of elected officials and political institutions. In turn, positive evaluations of officials, government effectiveness, and the country's economic situation are associated with higher political trust. Elected officials find themselves in a vicious cycle. Americans are skeptical of elected officials and therefore evaluate them less positively. Officials with low levels of public support find themselves lacking the political capital needed to govern.[20] Lacking political capital, officials have difficulty successfully pursuing their initiatives, providing further evidence of government ineffectiveness, which causes citizens to trust government even less.

The overall decline in political trust has impacted some policy areas more than others. Redistributive programs that provide benefits to select groups are particularly at risk. The public at large is still supportive of government spending programs, but less so for those that are not seen as benefiting middle-income Americans. With these programs, the American public is being asked to pay for a benefit or services that most do not receive. Research shows that those who are less trusting of government are less likely to support redistributive programs that would benefit lower-income Americans.[21] People who do not trust the government to manage effectively a program that provides no benefits to them are not willing to make sacrifices or trade-offs to support that program. For those on the receiving end of program benefits (low-income Americans), however, trust levels do not impact program support. The implication of these results is that there is less public support for redistributive policies—reducing poverty, narrowing the gap in income, helping poor citizens meet basic needs—due to the decline in public trust the country has experienced since the 1960s.

Confidence in Institutions

Leaders of nongovernmental institutions trying to bring about change face the same dilemma as government leaders. Public confidence in a variety of institutions also has declined substantially since the mid-1960s. In 1966 the Harris Poll asked Americans how much confidence they had in the people in charge of running ten different institutions. The institutions were "governmental" (Congress, Supreme Court, etc.), "private" (organized religion, major companies, medicine, etc.), and "oppositional" (organized labor, the press, etc.). Confidence has varied across institutions. In

1966 the proportion expressing confidence ranged from 73 percent for the people running medicine to only 22 percent for the leaders of organized labor (**Table 2–5**).[22] In general, people had the most confidence in private and government institutions and the least in oppositional.

Similar to the decline in trust in government documented by the ANES series, confidence in a variety of American institutions dropped in the five years between 1966 and 1971, the next time the Harris series was asked. The percentage of people expressing a great deal of confidence in the executive branch, Congress, the Supreme Court, and the military fell by approximately one-half.

The Harris data show that confidence in "government" institutions also rose and fell over time in a fashion similar to the ANES "trust in government" questions. After the initial decline in the 1970s, confidence rose during the early 1980s before dropping in the early 1990s, and then rising in the mid- to late 1990s. A sharp increase in response to 9/11 is evident and then a decline to pre-9/11 levels.

Among the government institutions, people generally have more confidence in the military than in other entities. Although confidence in the military, like all other institutions, declined, it appears to have recovered better than the rest. In 1966, 61 percent expressed a great deal of confidence in the military compared to 27 percent in 1971, during the later stages of the Vietnam War. By 2010, 59 percent had a great deal of confidence in the military. Confidence in the U.S. Congress, on the other hand, dropped from 42 percent in 1966 to 19 percent in 1971. Despite some short-lived increases over the years, only 8 percent expressed a great deal of confidence in Congress in 2010.[23]

The decline in confidence was not limited to government institutions. Confidence fell in medicine, colleges, major corporations, organized religion, and the press. The movement of confidence in medicine and major educational institutions mirrors that of government institutions, although with smaller year-to-year changes. Educational institutions and medicine remained the most respected among private institutions in 2010, with 35 percent and 34 percent, respectively, expressing a great deal of confidence. Still, these numbers represent a considerable decline from 61 percent and 73 percent in 1966.[24]

The General Social Survey (GSS) also has asked people about their confidence in a variety of institutions beginning in 1973 (**Table 2–6**). The relative confidence across institutions in the GSS is similar to the Harris surveys. Like those reported by Harris, the GSS confidence numbers show people having the most confidence in private institutions on average, followed by government institutions, and then oppositional institutions. Among government entities, the military and the Supreme Court fare better than the executive branch and Congress. The military received a large boost in confidence in 1991 at the time of the first Gulf War and then another following the 9/11 attacks and subsequent Iraq War.

The GSS data show a large difference in the level of confidence in different private institutions. Medicine and the scientific community inspire the most confidence. Major companies, banks, and financial institutions generally have fared less well in the public's view. Although confidence fell for five of the private institutions in the GSS over time, Americans express about as much confidence in the scientific community in 2008 (39 percent) as they did in 1973

(41 percent) when the series started. Confidence in all the other private institutions declined, including medicine. In 1973, 55 percent had a great deal of confidence in medicine, compared to 39 percent in 2008.[25]

Trust in the Medical Community

Periodically through the decades, the leaders of medicine have been urged to take the initiative in fixing the health care system. But they too confront the same phenomenon as do other institutions: trust in the medical community and its leaders has declined since the early 1970s. This section examines trust in medicine more closely, focusing first on trust in the leaders of medicine. This term is often taken to refer to people who head the major health care institutions, such as the American Medical Association, medical schools, and the nation's hospitals. Next, this section considers trust in doctors and other medical professionals more generally and in individual physicians.

Trust in the Leaders of Medicine

Trust in the leaders of medicine, like most other institutions, has declined since the mid-1960s. Both the Harris and the GSS series show a decline in confidence in medical leaders. In 1966, when the Harris series began, 73 percent said they had a "great deal of confidence in the people in charge of running medicine." In 2010 only 34 percent expressed that level of confidence. The GSS series started in 1973 with 55 percent expressing a great deal of confidence in the people running medicine. (The Harris number was similar that year at 57 percent.) By 2008 that proportion had dropped to 39 percent (**Tables 2–5 and 2–6**).[26]

A number of theories have been proposed to explain the decline in confidence in medicine.[27] At the center of many of these theories are rising health care costs. Medical technology has grown tremendously during the past half century, which in turn has led to higher medical costs. Between 1960 and 2007, the cost of medical goods and services rose by 1,474 percent, compared to 600 percent for all goods and services on which the Bureau of Labor Statistics calculates the inflation rate. Rising costs have caused insurers, employers, and public officials to look more closely at the decisions doctors make in treating patients. Those paying the bills began to question the efficacy of treatments and weigh that against costs. Doctors have been painted as being profit-driven by prescribing needless treatments in an attempt to grow rich. At the same time, they have been accused of putting the interests of insurance companies above those of their patients by not recommending expensive treatments. Patients are caught in the middle. Added to the tensions created by increased medical costs, the growth of investigative journalism has led to highly publicized stories of medical errors and the corrupt billing practices. The average American is left to wonder if these cases are the exception or the norm. Finally, as we documented above, the public has become skeptical of all professions. In this environment, confidence in the medical profession has been damaged.

Even though confidence in the leaders of medicine (the group that helped shape the current health system[28]) has declined, most Americans are not in favor of replacing the current health care system with something entirely different. In 2009 about one-third (31 percent) said that there was so much wrong with the U.S. health care system that it needed to be completely rebuilt.[29] Earlier in this chapter we saw that only 17 percent of Americans said the U.S. system of government had so much wrong it that it needed to be rebuilt (**Table 2–3**).[30] Both polls show that although Americans are often dissatisfied with the performance of the leaders of government and medicine, they are not so unhappy that they are willing to scrap the current way of doing things and start over.

Trust in Doctors and Other Medical Professionals

Corresponding to the fall of trust in leaders of medicine has been a decline in many measures of trust in the medical community as a whole. Two surveys, the first conducted in 1976 and the second in 1998, asked the same series of questions addressing some of the theories suggested for the decline in confidence in medicine (**Table 2–7**). The questions asked about doctors in general and the respondent's personal doctor, which we detail in the next section. In general, the responses show a decline in positive assessments of doctors between 1976 and 1998. Fewer people in 1998 than in 1976 felt that doctors treat patients with respect (51 percent vs. 67 percent) and do their best to keep patients from worrying (51 percent vs. 60 percent).[31]

Americans also had more negative views in 1998 than in 1976 about treatment decisions. More than half (55 percent) in 1998 disagreed with the statement, "Doctors always avoid unnecessary patient expenses," an increase from 42 percent in 1976. The proportion who thought doctors sometimes take unnecessary risks in treating patients rose from 24 percent to 34 percent. In addition, more people in 1998 than in 1976 disagreed with the statement, "Doctors never recommend surgery (an operation) unless there is no other way to solve the problem" (34 percent to 22 percent).[32]

Despite the decline in confidence in the medical profession more generally, the proportion of Americans feeling that doctors have high ethical standards has increased. Since 1976 the Gallup Poll has asked people to rate the honesty and ethical standards of different professions. In 1976, 56 percent said doctors had very high or high ethical standards. By 2008 this number had increased to 64 percent. The public's view of the ethical standards of two other medical professions, nurses and pharmacists, also has improved (**Table 2–8**).[33] Of the twenty-one professions included in the 2008 survey, doctors were the fourth highest rated, behind nurses, pharmacists, and high-school teachers.[34]

Trust in Their Own Physician

Despite dissatisfaction with the U.S. health care system, leaders of medicine, and some medical professionals, people's confidence in their own physician remains high. In 2002 most Americans trusted their doctor to do the right thing for their care. Nearly half (48 percent) trusted their doctor to do the right thing "just about always," and one-third (33 percent), "most of the time" (**Table 2–9**).[35] Although there is no directly comparable figure for doctors generally, the responses to other questions suggest that trust would be lower: many fewer Americans in 2002 reported having "a great deal" of confidence in the people running medicine (Harris, 29 percent; GSS, 37 percent).[36]

The GSS of 1998 that asked about various attitudes toward doctors and their work also asked questions about the respondent's own doctor. Overall, more people gave positive responses to questions about their own doctor than doctors in general (**Table 2–7**). A large majority felt their doctor would refer them to a specialist when needed (84 percent). Most do not worry that their doctor is putting cost considerations above their care (59 percent), that they are being denied needed treatment (62 percent), or that their doctor is being prevented from telling about the full range of treatment options (58 percent). But just over 20 percent voiced each of these concerns, which indicates that a sizable minority is concerned that their doctor cares more about the costs of their care than its quality.[37]

The GSS asked five additional questions about people's attitudes toward their own doctor on three separate occasions: 1998, 2002, and 2006. In each of the surveys, a large majority expressed a high degree of confidence in their doctors (**Table 2–10**). Across all three years, most Americans trusted their doctor's judgments about their medical care and trusted their doctor to put their medical needs above all. Fewer people, but still sizable majorities, felt that their doctor cared about them as a person, trusted their doctor to admit a mistake made in treatment, and believed their doctor was a real expert in their medical problems. Although the percentage of positive responses is high across all years, confidence appeared to increase in 2002 with more respondents giving the most positive response about their doctor. It is not clear what caused this increase in confidence, but it is consistent with other surveys conducted in the period following the 9/11 terrorist attacks that showed an increase in trust of institutions and individuals.[38] By the 2006 survey, the numbers were lower and closer to their 1998 level.

Although most Americans express confidence in their own physicians, for the people who do not trust their physician, earlier work has shown that this personal distrust is associated with distrust of the broader medical profession. For this group, lack of trust in one's doctor can have a negative impact on care. People who do not trust their doctor are less likely to seek care, comply with treatment recommendations, or reveal sensitive information.[39]

Trust in Nongovernmental Groups to Recommend the Right Thing for the Country on Health Care

In 2009, while the debate on health care reform was ongoing, the public was asked how much confidence they had in each of eleven nongovernmental groups to recommend the right thing for the country when it came to health care. Once again, the most trusted were nurses' groups (79 percent of the public expressed a great deal or a fair amount of confidence). About two-thirds said they had confidence in groups representing patients (70 percent), doctors' groups (65 percent), and groups representing seniors (64 percent). A majority also had confidence in hospitals (61 percent), small business groups (60 percent), and consumer groups (54 percent).

At the other end of the spectrum, only about one-third expressed confidence in health insurance companies (35 percent), groups representing major corporations (32 percent), and drug companies (31 percent). Forty-three percent had confidence in labor unions (**Table 2–11**).[40]

Conclusion

Over the past fifty years, public confidence in government and other major institutions, including medicine, has fallen. The loss of public confidence in leaders has significant implications for the future of health policy, but less impact on future doctor-patient relationships.

A major health care reform law was narrowly passed by Congress and signed into law by President Obama in 2010. This legislation differs from what is found in Canada and much of Europe in that the role of government, both in providing health insurance and in regulating health care, is substantially less. This reflects in part the American public's distrust of a more centralized, government-directed program. With a public that is increasingly skeptical of government leaders, dealing with future problems in the health care system may continue to be difficult.

Notes

[1] Richard E. Neustadt, *Presidential Power: The Politics of Leadership* (New York: Wiley, 1960).

[2] Marc J. Hetherington, *Why Trust Matters: Declining Political Trust and the Demise of American Liberalism* (Princeton, N.J.: Princeton University Press, 2005).

[3] American National Election Studies, *The 1948–2004 ANES Cumulative Data File* [dataset] (Palo Alto, Calif.: Stanford University; Ann Arbor, Mich.: University of Michigan, 2005); American National Election Studies, *The 2006 ANES Pilot Study* [dataset] (Palo Alto, Calif.: Stanford University; Ann Arbor, Mich.: University of Michigan, 2007).

[4] Ibid.; CNN/Opinion Research Corporation Poll (Storrs, Conn.: Roper Center for Public Opinion Research, February 12–15, 2010).

[5] Because all four questions were not asked on every survey, some of the trust index values are based on fewer than four questions, making it difficult to compare all years. In particular, the index in 1966 is based on two questions, and those in 1986 and 2006 were drawn from only one question. The values in those years should be treated with caution as they are higher than the surrounding years despite a decline in trust in the overall trust in government question.

[6] NPR/Kaiser Family Foundation/Kennedy School of Government Poll (Storrs, Conn.: Roper Center for Public Opinion Research, May 26–June 25, 2000); American National Election Studies, *The 2006 ANES Pilot Study* [dataset], 2007; CNN/Opinion Research Corporation Poll, February 12–15, 2010.

[7] CBS News/*New York Times* Poll (Storrs, Conn.: Roper Center for Public Opinion Research, October 25–29, 2008).

[8] Arthur H. Miller, "Political Issues and Trust in Government: 1964–1970," *American Political Science Review* 68 (September 1974): 951–972.

[9] Jack Citrin, "Comment: The Political Relevance of Trust in Government," *American Political Science Review* 68 (September 1974): 973–988; Jack Citrin and Donald Philip Green, "Presidential Leadership and the Resurgence of Trust in Government," *British Journal of Political Science* 16 (October 1986): 431–453.

[10] Gallup Polls (Storrs, Conn: Roper Center for Public Opinion Research, January 10–14, 2001; January 7–9, 2002; January 13–16, 2003; January 12–15, 2004; January 3–5, 2005; January 9–12, 2006; January 15–18, 2007; January 4–6, 2008).

[11] ABC News/*Washington Post* Poll (Storrs, Conn: Roper Center for Public Opinion Research, December 12–15, 2000); ABC News/Facebook Poll (Storrs, Conn: Roper Center for Public Opinion Research, December 16–19, 2007).

[12] CBS News/*New York Times* Poll (Storrs, Conn: Roper Center for Public Opinion Research, July 21–25, 2006).

[13] CNN/Opinion Research Corporation Poll, February 12–15, 2010.

[14] Post-Modernity Project, University of Virginia Poll (Storrs, Conn.: Roper Center for Public Opinion Research, January 27–April 14, 1996).

[15] Citrin and Green, "Presidential Leadership and the Resurgence of Trust in Government"; Jack Citrin and Samantha Luks, "Political Trust Revisited: Déjà Vu All Over Again," in *What Is It About Government that Americans Dislike?* ed. John R Hibbing and Elizabeth Theiss-Morse (Cambridge: Cambridge University Press, 2001), 9–27.

[16] Seymour Martin Lipset and William Schneider, *The Confidence Gap: Business, Labor and Government in the Public Mind* (New York: Free Press, 1983).

[17] Luke Keele, "The Authorities Really Do Matter: Party Control and Trust in Government," *Journal of Politics* 67 (August 2005): 873–886.

[18] American National Election Studies, *The 1948–2004 ANES Cumulative Data File* [dataset], 2005.

[19] Marc J. Hetherington, "The Political Relevance of Political Trust," *American Political Science Review* 92 (December 1998): 791–808; Hetherington, *Why Trust Matters.*

[20] Ibid.; Richard E. Neustadt, *Presidential Power.*

[21] Hetherington, *Why Trust Matters.*

[22] Harris Interactive, "Virtually No Change in Annual Harris Poll Confidence Index from Last Year," March 9, 2010,. http://news.harrisinteractive.com/profiles/investor/ResLibraryView.asp?ResLibraryID=36697&GoTopage=4&Category=1777&BzID=1963&t=30.

[23] Ibid. The question about confidence in the people running Congress yields a different response from the job approval question about Congress, cited earlier, partly because the questions measure slightly different things and partly because the questions use different response scales.

[24] Ibid.

[25] James Allan Davis and Tom W. Smith, *General Social Surveys, 1972–2008* [dataset] (Chicago: National Opinion Research Center, producer; Storrs, Conn.: Roper Center for Public Opinion Research, distributor, 2008).

[26] Harris Interactive, "Virtually No Change in Annual Harris Poll Confidence Index from Last Year,"; Davis and Smith, *General Social Surveys, 1972–2008.*

[27] Mark Schlesinger, "A Loss of Faith: The Sources of Reduced Political Legitimacy for the American Medical Profession," *Milbank Quarterly* 80 (June 2002): 185–235.

[28] Paul Starr, *The Social Transformation of American Medicine* (New York: Basic Books, 1982).

[29] CBS News Poll (Storrs, Conn.: Roper Center for Public Opinion Research, October 5–8, 2009).

[30] CBS News/*New York Times* Poll, July 21–25, 2006.

[31] Ronald Andersen and Lu Ann Aday, *National Survey of Access to Medical Care, 1975–1976* [dataset] (Chicago: University of Chicago, Center for Health Administration Studies; Ann Arbor, Mich.: Inter-university Consortium for Political and Social Research, 1998); Davis and Smith, *General Social Surveys, 1972–2008*.

[32] Ibid.

[33] Gallup Polls (Storrs, Conn.: Roper Center for Public Opinion Research, June 11–14, 1976; August 19–22, 1977; July 24–27, 1981; May 20–23, 1983; July 12–15, 1985; September 23–26, 1988; February 8–11, 1990; May 16–19, 1991; June 26–July 1, 1992; July 19–21, 1993; September 23–25, 1994; October 19–22, 1995; November 9–11, 1996; November 6–9, 1997; October 23–25, 1998; November 4–7, 1999; November 13–15, 2000; November 26–27, 2001; November 22–24, 2002; November 14–16, 2003); for 2004–2008, Gallup Poll, "Honesty/Ethics in Professions," 2008, http://www.gallup.com/poll/1654/Honesty-Ethics-Professions.aspx.

[34] Gallup Poll, "Honesty/Ethics in Professions," 2008.

[35] Kaiser Family Foundation/Harvard School of Public Health Poll (Storrs, Conn.: Roper Center for Public Opinion Research, August 22–September 23, 1997); NPR/Kaiser Family Foundation/ Kennedy School of Government Poll (Storrs, Conn.: Roper Center for Public Opinion Research, March 28–May 1, 2002).

[36] Harris Interactive, "Virtually No Change in Annual Harris Poll Confidence Index from Last Year"; Davis and Smith, *General Social Surveys, 1972–2008*.

[37] Davis and Smith, *General Social Surveys, 1972–2008*.

[38] Ibid.

[39] Mark A. Hall, Fabian Camacho, Elizabeth Dugan, and Rajesh Balkrishnan, "Trust in the Medical Profession: Conceptual and Measurement Issues," *Health Services Research* 37 (October 2002): 1419–39.

[40] NPR/Kaiser Family Foundation/Harvard School of Public Health, "Survey on the Role of Health Care Interest Groups," September 2009, http://www.kff.org/kaiserpolls/upload/7991.pdf.

Table 2-1 Confidence in Government, 1958–2010 (in percent)

	1958[1]	1964	1966	1968	1970	1972	1974	1976	1978	1980	1982	1984	1986	1988	1990	1992	1994	1996	1998	2000	2002	2004	2006[2]	2010[3]
Trust in Government																								
Just about always	16	14	17	7	6	5	2	3	2	2	2	4	3	4	3	3	2	3	4	4	5	4	1	2
Most of the time	57	62	48	54	47	48	34	30	27	23	31	40	35	36	25	26	19	30	36	40	51	43	24	24
Some of the time	23	22	28	36	44	44	61	62	64	69	62	53	57	56	69	68	74	66	58	55	44	52	74	69
None of the time (volunteered)	0	0	2	0	0	1	1	1	4	4	3	1	2	2	2	2	3	1	1	1	0	1	1	5
Government Officials Are Crooked																								
Hardly any	26	18	—	19	16	14	10	13	13	9	—	14	—	11	9	9	8	9	12	13	14	10	—	—
Not many	44	49	—	52	49	45	42	40	42	42	—	50	—	45	40	44	39	47	46	49	56	53	—	—
Quite a few	24	29	—	25	32	36	45	42	39	47	—	32	—	40	48	46	52	44	41	36	30	35	—	—
Government Wastes Tax Money																								
Not very much	10	7	—	4	4	2	1	3	2	2	2	4	—	2	2	2	2	1	3	3	3	2	—	—
Some	42	44	—	34	26	30	22	20	19	18	29	29	—	33	30	30	27	39	34	38	49	37	—	—
A lot	43	47	—	59	69	66	74	74	77	78	66	65	—	63	67	67	70	59	61	59	48	61	—	—
Government Run for:																								
Benefit of all	—	64	53	51	41	38	25	24	24	21	29	39	—	31	24	20	19	27	32	35	51	40	—	—
Few big interests	—	29	33	40	50	53	66	66	67	70	61	55	—	64	71	75	76	69	64	61	48	56	—	—
Trust Index	49	52	61*	45	39	38	29	30	29	27	31	38	47*	34	29	29	26	32	34	36	43	37	41*	—

Note: "Don't know" responses not shown. The trust index is created by recoding the question categories so they range from 0 to 100. The values are summed and divided by the number of questions asked in a given year. Except where noted, the index is only created for years in which at least three of the questions were asked. No trust index was calculated for 2010. * Index is based on only 1 or 2 of the questions making it difficult to compare to other years.

Question: How much of the time do you think you can trust the government in Washington to do what is right: just about always, most of the time, or only some of the time?

Question: Do you think that quite a few of the people running the government are crooked, not very many are, or do you think hardly any of them are crooked?

Question: Do you think that people in government waste a lot of money we pay in taxes, waste some of it, or don't waste very much of it?

Question: Would you say the government is pretty much run by a few big interests looking out for themselves or that it is run for the benefit of all people?

Sources: [1]American National Election Studies, *The 1948–2004 ANES Cumulative Data File* [dataset] (Palo Alto, Calif.: Stanford University; Ann Arbor, Mich.: University of Michigan, 2005). [2]American National Election Studies, *The 2006 ANES Pilot Study* [dataset] (Palo Alto, Calif.: Stanford University; Ann Arbor, Mich.: University of Michigan, 2007). [3]CNN/Opinion Research Corporation Poll (Storrs, Conn: Roper Center for Public Opinion Research, February 12–15, 2010).

Table 2-2 Confidence in Federal, State, and Local Government (in percent)

	2000[1]	2006[2]	2010[3]
Federal			
Just about always	5	1	2
Most of the time	24	24	24
Some of the time	59	74	69
None of the time*	11	1	5
State			
Just about always	5	4	3
Most of the time	33	35	30
Some of the time	52	59	62
None of the time*	8	2	5
Local			
Just about always	7	—	—
Most of the time	33	—	—
Some of the time	49	—	—
None of the time*	10	—	—

Views about Congress and their own representative[4]	Approve	Disapprove	Don't know
Congress (2008)	15	75	10
Own Member of Congress (2008)	50	31	19

Note: *"None of the time" was an explicitly offered response in 2000, but could only be volunteered by respondents in 2006. This accounts for the larger percentage giving this response in 2000. "Don't know" responses not shown.

Question: How much of the time do you trust the federal government to do what is right: just about always, most of the time, some of the time, or none of the time? (2000)

Question: How much of the time do you trust (the state/your state's) government to do what is right: just about always, most of the time, some of the time, or none of the time? (2000)

Question: How much of the time do you trust the local government to do what is right: just about always, most of the time, some of the time, or none of the time? (2000)

Question: How much of the time do you think you can trust the government in Washington to do what is right: just about always, most of the time, or only some of the time? (2006, 2010)

Question: How much of the time do you think you can trust the government in [insert R's state] to do what is right: just about always, most of the time, or only some of the time? (2006)

Question: Do you approve or disapprove of the way Congress is handling its job? (2008)

Question: How about the representative in Congress from your district? Do you approve or disapprove of the way your representative is handling his or her job? (2008)

Sources: [1]NPR/Kaiser Family Foundation/Kennedy School of Government Poll (Storrs, Conn.: Roper Center for Public Opinion Research, May 26–June 25, 2000). [2]American National Election Studies, *The 2006 ANES Pilot Study* [dataset] (Palo Alto, Calif.: Stanford University; Ann Arbor, Mich.: University of Michigan, 2007). [3]CNN/Opinion Research Corporation Poll (Storrs, Conn.: Roper Centers for Public Opinion Research, February 12-15, 2010). [4]CBS News/*New York Times* Poll (Storrs, Conn.: Roper Centers for Public Opinion Research, October 25–29, 2008).

Table 2-3 Opinion of the American System of Government (in percent)

Satisfaction with system[1]	Very satisfied	Somewhat satisfied	Somewhat dissatisfied	Very dissatisfied
2001	16	52	21	9
2002	25	51	16	7
2003	19	45	25	10
2004	17	44	26	13
2005	18	42	24	15
2007	17	39	25	18
2008	14	39	27	20

U.S. has best system of government in the world[2]	Agree	Disagree
1994	84	13
1996	83	15
2000	89	11
2007	81	17

Does system need fixing[3]	System is NOT broken	System is broken but CAN be fixed	System is broken and CANNOT be fixed
2006	22	71	7
2010	14	81	5

Does system need to be rebuilt[4]	Minor changes needed	Fundamental changes needed	Need to completely rebuild
1992	12	62	23
1999	20	61	18
2006	21	62	17

	Completely agree	Mostly agree	Mostly disagree	Completely disagree
U.S. system is good, but people running it are incompetent (1996)[5]	16	50	30	4

Note: "Don't know" responses not shown.

Question: I'm going to read some aspects of life in America today. For each one, please say whether you are—very satisfied, somewhat satisfied, somewhat dissatisfied, or very dissatisfied. How about . . . our system of government and how well it works?

Question: I'm going to read you some statements that may or may not describe your own feelings about politics and government. Please tell me whether you agree or disagree with each one. Whatever its faults, the United States still has the best system of government in the world.

Question: Which of the following statements comes closest to your view? . . . Our system of government is broken and cannot be fixed, our system of government is broken but can be fixed, our system of government is not broken.

Question: Which of the following three statements comes closest to expressing your overall view of the system of government and politics in the United States? . . . On the whole, the political system works pretty well and only minor changes are necessary to make it work better. There are some good things in our political system, but fundamental changes are needed. Our political system has so much wrong with it that we need to completely rebuild it.

Question: I want you to consider a series of objections that some have expressed regarding politics and the government. For each one, please tell me whether you completely agree, mostly agree, mostly disagree, or completely disagree with the complaint. . . . Our system of government is good, but the people running it are incompetent.

Sources: [1]Gallup Polls (Storrs, Conn: Roper Center for Public Opinion Research, January 10–14, 2001; January 7–9, 2002; January 13–16, 2003; January 12–15, 2004; January 3–5, 2005; January 9–12, 2006; January 15–18, 2007; January 4–6, 2008). [2]ABC News Polls (Storrs, Conn: Roper Center for Public Opinion Research, September 8–11, 1994; April 30–May 6, 1996); ABC News/*Washington Post* Poll (Storrs, Conn: Roper Center for Public Opinion Research, December 12–15, 2000); ABC News/Facebook Poll (Storrs, Conn: Roper Center for Public Opinion Research, December 16–19, 2007). [3]CNN/Opinion Research Corporation Poll (Storrs, Conn: Roper Center for Public Opinion Research, October 13–15, 2006; February 12–15, 2010). [4]CBS News/*New York Times* Polls (Storrs, Conn: Roper Center for Public Opinion Research, June 17–20, 1992; July 21–25, 2006); CBS News Poll (Storrs, Conn: Roper Center for Public Opinion Research, September 14–18, 1999). [5]Post-Modernity Project, University of Virginia Poll (Storrs, Conn: Roper Center for Public Opinion Research, January 27–April 14, 1996).

Table 2-4 Trust in Government Index, by President and Party Identification, 1958–2004

	All	Democrats	Republicans	Independents	Difference (Dem. – Repub.)
Eisenhower*	49.5	48.1	52.5	49.0	−4.4
Johnson	52.3	56.5	48.0	48.8	8.5
Nixon/Ford	33.6	32.1	38.3	32.2	−6.2
Carter	28.3	31.0	26.5	26.3	4.5
Reagan	36.7	34.5	41.8	35.3	−7.3
George H. W. Bush	28.7	28.4	31.0	27.4	−2.6
Clinton	32.0	34.5	31.4	29.8	3.1
George W. Bush**	40.8	37.2	46.7	38.9	−9.5

Note: The trust index is created by recoding the question categories so they range from 0 to 100. The values are summed and divided by the number of questions asked in a given year. *Based only on 1958. **Based only on 2002 and 2004.

Question: How much of the time do you think you can trust the government in Washington to do what is right: just about always, most of the time, or only some of the time?

Question: Do you think that quite a few of the people running the government are crooked, not very many are, or do you think hardly any of them are crooked?

Question: Do you think that people in government waste a lot of money we pay in taxes, waste some of it, or don't waste very much of it?

Question: Would you say the government is pretty much run by a few big interests looking out for themselves or that it is run for the benefit of all people?

Source: American National Election Studies, *The 1948–2004 ANES Cumulative Data File* [dataset] (Palo Alto, Calif.: Stanford University; Ann Arbor, Mich.: University of Michigan, 2005).

Table 2-5 Harris Confidence in Institutions, 1966–2010 (percent expressing "great deal" of confidence)

	Government Institutions					Private Institutions						Oppositional Institutions		
	Executive Branch	Congress	Supreme Court	White House	Military	Major Educ. Insts.	Medicine	Organized Religion	Major Companies	Law Firms	Wall Street	Press	TV News	Org. Labor
1966	41	42	50	—	61	61	73	41	55	—	—	29	—	22
1971	23	19	23	—	27	37	61	27	27	—	—	18	—	14
1972	27	21	28	—	35	33	48	30	27	—	—	18	—	15
1973	19	—	33	18	40	44	57	36	29	24	—	30	41	20
1974	28	18	40	28	33	40	50	32	21	18	—	25	31	18
1975	13	13	28	—	24	36	43	32	19	16	—	26	35	14
1976	11	9	22	11	23	31	42	24	16	12	—	20	28	10
1977	23	17	29	31	27	37	43	29	20	14	—	18	28	14
1978	14	10	29	14	29	41	42	24	22	18	—	23	35	15
1979	17	18	28	15	29	33	30	20	18	16	—	28	37	10
1980	17	18	27	18	28	36	34	22	16	13	12	19	29	14
1981	24	16	29	28	28	34	37	22	16	24	—	16	—	12
1982	—	13	25	20	31	30	32	20	18	—	—	14	24	8
1983	—	20	33	23	35	36	35	22	18	12	—	19	24	10
1984	—	28	35	42	45	40	43	24	19	17	—	18	28	12
1985	19	16	28	30	32	35	39	21	17	12	—	16	23	13
1986	18	21	32	19	36	34	33	22	16	14	—	19	27	11
1987	19	20	30	23	35	36	36	16	21	15	—	19	29	11
1988	16	15	32	17	33	34	40	17	19	13	—	18	28	13
1989	17	16	28	20	32	32	30	16	16	—	8	18	25	10
1990	14	14	32	14	43	35	35	20	9	—	21	12	27	18
1991	—	9	15	—	—	—	23	21	20	—	14	—	9	21
1992	—	16	30	25	50	29	22	11	10	13	13	—	12	11

(Table continues)

Table 2-5 *Continued*

1993	15	12	26	23	57	23	22	—	16	11	13	15	23	—
1994	12	8	31	18	39	25	23	—	19	8	15	13	20	—
1995	9	10	32	13	43	27	26	24	21	9	13	11	16	8
1996	12	10	31	15	47	30	29	—	21	11	17	14	21	—
1997	12	11	28	15	37	27	29	20	18	7	17	11	18	9
1998	17	12	37	20	44	37	38	25	21	11	18	14	26	13
1999	17	12	42	22	54	37	39	27	23	10	30	15	23	15
2000	18	15	34	21	48	36	44	26	28	12	30	13	20	15
2001	20	18	35	21	44	35	32	25	20	10	23	13	24	15
2002	33	22	41	50	71	33	29	23	16	13	19	16	24	11
2003	26	20	34	40	62	31	31	19	13	12	12	15	21	14
2004	23	13	29	31	62	37	32	27	12	10	17	15	17	15
2005	—	16	29	31	47	39	29	27	17	11	15	12	16	17
2006	—	10	33	25	47	38	31	30	13	10	15	14	19	12
2007	—	10	27	22	46	37	37	27	16	13	17	12	20	15
2008	—	8	25	15	51	32	28	25	14	10	11	10	16	11
2009	—	9	28	36	58	40	34	30	11	11	4	12	22	16
2010	—	8	31	27	59	35	34	26	15	13	8	13	17	14
Δ 1966–2010	−18*	−34	−19	9**	−2	−26	−39	−15	−40	−11**	−4***	−16	−24**	−8

Note: *Difference between 1966 and 2004. **Difference between 1973 and 2010. ***Difference between 1980 and 2010.

Question: As far as people in charge of running [insert institution] are concerned, would you say you have a great deal of confidence, only some confidence, or hardly any confidence at all in them?

Source: Harris Interactive, "Virtually No Change in Annual Harris Poll Confidence Index from Last Year," March 9, 2010.

Table 2-6 General Social Survey Confidence in Institutions, 1973–2008 (percent expressing "great deal" of confidence)

	Government Institutions				Private Institutions						Oppositional Institutions		
	Executive Branch	Congress	Supreme Court	Military	Education	Medicine	Organized Religion	Major Companies	Banks/Fin. Institutions	Scientific Community	The Press	Television	Org. Labor
1973	30	24	33	33	38	55	36	31	—	41	23	19	16
1974	14	18	35	41	50	61	45	33	—	50	26	24	19
1975	14	14	32	37	32	51	26	20	33	42	25	18	11
1976	14	14	38	42	38	55	33	23	41	49	29	19	13
1977	29	20	37	38	41	52	41	28	43	45	26	18	15
1978	13	13	29	31	29	46	32	23	33	40	21	14	12
1980	13	10	26	29	31	53	37	29	33	46	23	16	16
1982	18	13	31	30	36	45	34	22	26	39	18	16	14
1983	13	10	28	30	29	52	29	25	24	44	14	13	8
1984	19	13	35	37	29	52	32	32	33	47	17	13	9
1986	21	17	31	32	28	47	26	25	21	41	19	15	8
1987	18	16	36	35	37	52	30	29	28	45	19	13	12
1988	17	16	36	35	30	52	21	26	27	42	19	14	11
1989	21	17	36	34	31	47	22	25	19	44	17	14	10
1990	24	16	37	34	27	46	24	26	18	41	15	14	11
1991	27	18	39	61	31	48	26	21	13	44	17	15	12
1993	12	7	32	43	23	40	24	22	15	41	11	12	9
1994	12	8	31	38	25	42	25	26	18	41	10	10	11
1996	11	8	30	39	23	45	26	24	25	43	11	10	12
1998	14	11	33	37	27	45	28	28	26	43	10	10	12
2000	14	13	34	40	27	44	29	29	30	45	10	10	14
2002	27	13	37	55	25	37	19	18	22	39	10	10	12
2004	22	15	32	58	28	38	24	19	29	43	9	11	13
2006	16	12	34	48	28	40	25	18	30	44	10	9	12
2008	11	10	31	51	29	39	20	16	19	39	9	9	12
Δ 1973–2008	−19	−14	−2	18	−9	−16	−16	−15	−14*	−2	−14	−10	−4

Note: *Difference between 1975 and 2008.

Question: I am going to name some institutions in this country. As far as the people running these institutions are concerned, would you say you have a great deal of confidence, only some confidence, or hardly any confidence at all in them?

Source: James Allan Davis and Tom W. Smith, *General Social Surveys, 1972–2008* [dataset] (Chicago: National Opinion Research Center, producer; Storrs, Conn.: The Roper Center for Public Opinion Research, distributor, 2008).

Table 2-7 Attitudes toward Doctors and How They Do Their Work, 1976 and 1998 (in percent)

	1976[1]			1998[2]		
	Strongly agree/ Agree	Uncertain	Strongly disagree/ Disagree	Strongly agree/ Agree	Uncertain	Strongly disagree/ Disagree
Doctors Generally						
Doctors always treat their patients with respect.	67	16	17	51	14	34
Doctors always do their best to keep the patient from worrying.	60	23	17	51	20	38
Doctors never recommend surgery (an operation) unless there is no other way to solve the problem.	43	34	22	43	19	34
Doctors cause people to worry a lot because they don't explain medical problems to patients.	42	20	38	41	16	43
Doctors aren't as thorough as they should be.	41	22	38	50	14	35
Doctors are very careful to everything when examining their patients.	38	25	38	34	20	44
Sometimes doctors take unnecessary risks in treating their patients.	24	42	34	34	24	38
Doctors always avoid unnecessary patient expenses.	22	36	42	22	20	55
Own Doctor or Care						
The medical problems I've had in the past are ignored when I seek care for anew medical problem.	15	20	46	18	14	64
My doctor is willing to refer me to a specialist when needed.	—	—	—	84	8	5
I worry that my doctor will put cost considerations above the care I need.	—	—	—	24	15	59
I worry that I will be denied the treatment or services I need.	—	—	—	23	13	62
I worry that my doctor is being prevented from telling me the full range of options for my treatment.	—	—	—	21	17	58

Note: "Don't know" responses not shown.

Question: As you read each of the following statements, please think about the medical care you are now receiving. If you have not received any medical care recently, circle the answer based on what you would expect if you had to seek care today. Even if you are not entirely certain about your answers, we want to remind you that your best guess is important for each statement.

Sources: [1]Ronald Andersen and Lu Ann Aday, *National Survey of Access to Medical Care, 1975–1976* [dataset] (Chicago: University of Chicago, Center for Health Administration Studies; Ann Arbor, Mich.: Inter-university Consortium for Political and Social Research, 1998). [2]James Allan Davis and Tom W. Smith, *General Social Surveys, 1972–2008* [dataset] (Chicago: National Opinion Research Center, producer; Storrs, Conn.: The Roper Center for Public Opinion Research, distributor, 2008).

Table 2-8 Ethical Standards of Professions, 1976–2008 (percent saying "very high" or "high")

	Nurses	Druggists, pharmacists	Medical doctors
1976	—	—	56
1977	—	—	51
1981	—	60	50
1983	—	61	53
1985	—	65	58
1988	—	66	53
1990	—	62	52
1991	—	60	54
1992	—	66	52
1993	—	65	51
1994	—	62	47
1995	—	66	54
1996	—	64	55
1997	—	69	56
1998	—	64	57
1999	73	69	58
2000	79	67	63
2001	84	68	66
2002	79	67	63
2003	83	67	68
2004	79	72	67
2005	82	67	65
2006	84	73	69
2007	83	71	64
2008	84	70	64

Question: Please tell me how you would rate the honesty and ethical standards of people in these different fields: very high, high, average, low, or very low?

Sources: Gallup Polls (Storrs, Conn.: Roper Center for Public Opinion Research, June 11–14, 1976; August 19–22, 1977; July 24–27, 1981; May 20–23, 1983; July 12–15, 1985; September 23–26, 1988; February 8–11, 1990; May 16–19, 1991; June 26–July 1, 1992; July 19–21, 1993; September 23–25, 1994; October 19–22, 1995; November 9–11, 1996; November 6–9, 1997; October 23–25, 1998; November 4–7, 1999; November 13–15, 2000; November 26–27, 2001; November 22–24, 2002; November 14–16, 2003); for 2004–2008, Gallup Poll, "Honesty/Ethics in Professions," 2008.

Table 2-9 Trust in Own Doctor (in percent)

	1997[1]	2002[2]
Just about always	52	48
Most of the time	31	33
Some of the time	12	16
None of the time (volunteered)	1	0
Do not have regular doctor (volunteered)	2	2
Don't Know	2	0

Question: How often do you trust the doctor you usually see to do the right thing for your care? Would you say just about always, most of the time, or only some of the time? [1997 poll]

Question: How often do you trust your primary care or family doctor to do the right thing for your care? Would you say . . . just about always, most of the time, or only some of the time? [2002 poll]

Sources: [1]Kaiser Family Foundation/Harvard School of Public Health Poll (Storrs, Conn.: Roper Center for Public Opinion Research, August 22–September 23, 1997). [2]NPR/Kaiser Family Foundation/Kennedy School of Government Poll (Storrs, Conn.: Roper Center for Public Opinion Research, March 28–May 1, 2002).

Table 2-10 Confidence in Own Doctor, 1998–2006 (percent)

	I doubt that my doctor really cares about me as a person.			I trust my doctor's judgments about my medical care.			I trust my doctor to put my medical needs above all other considerations when treating my medical problems.			My doctor is a real expert in taking care of medical problems like mine.			I trust my doctor to tell me if a mistake was made about my treatment.		
	1998	2002	2006	1998	2002	2006	1998	2002	2006	1998	2002	2006	1998	2002	2006
Strongly agree	2	7	5	12	43	26	10	43	22	9	36	19	7	37	18
Agree	14	14	13	69	47	56	63	41	55	50	42	52	53	34	50
Neither agree nor disagree	15	10	19	11	4	11	15	6	14	26	11	21	16	8	16
Disagree	55	27	41	6	4	4	10	7	6	10	7	4	16	11	10
Strongly disagree	12	41	21	1	1	2	1	2	2	1	1	1	5	8	4
Don't know	2	2	2	1	1	2	2	2	2	4	3	2	3	2	2

Question: As I read each of the following statements, please think about the medical care you are now receiving. If you have not received any medical care recently, circle the answer based on what you would expect if you had to seek care today. Even if you are not entirely certain about your answers, we want to remind you that your best guess is important for each statement. How much do you agree with the following statement? (Read statement) Strongly agree, agree, neither agree nor disagree, disagree, strongly disagree.

Source: James Allan Davis and Tom W. Smith, *General Social Surveys, 1972–2006* [dataset] (Chicago: National Opinion Research Center, producer; Storrs, Conn.: Roper Center for Public Opinion Research, distributor, 2006).

Table 2-11 Confidence in Nongovernmental Groups to Recommend the Right Thing for the Country on Health Care (in percent)

	A Great deal	A Fair number	Only a Little	None
Nurses groups	33	46	14	3
Groups representing patients	27	43	18	5
Doctors groups	24	41	25	7
Groups representing senior citizens	26	38	26	7
Hospitals	20	41	26	10
Small business groups	24	36	30	8
Consumer groups	15	39	32	9
Labor unions	17	26	30	23
Health insurance companies	9	26	39	25
Groups representing the country's major corporations	9	23	39	24
Pharmaceutical or drug companies	10	21	38	30

Note: "Don't know" responses not shown. Ranked by percentage responding "A great deal" + "A fair amount."

Question: As I read the names of some people and groups, please tell me how much confidence you have in each of them to recommend the right thing for the country when it comes to health care. How much confidence do you have in (READ ITEM) to recommend the right thing for the country on health care: a great deal, a fair amount, only a little or none?

Source: NPR/Kaiser Family Foundation/Harvard School of Public Health, "Survey on the Role of Health Care Interest Groups," September 2009.

Chapter 3

ATTITUDES ABOUT THE U.S. HEALTH SYSTEM AND PRIORITIES FOR GOVERNMENT ACTION

Robert J. Blendon and John M. Benson

For more than sixty years the nature and functioning of the U.S. health system have been issues of great public controversy and debate. The U.S. health system differs substantially from those of other industrialized countries, where health care is financed and directed primarily by government. Instead, the United States has a mixed private insurance/public system with relatively little government planning and direction and a strong reliance on market forces and private sector decision making.

Table 3–1 presents a comparison of health indictors for the United States, United Kingdom, Canada, and the average for all countries belonging to the Organisation for Economic Cooperation and Development (OECD).[1] The United States spends more on health care than any other OECD country, both in terms of percentage of gross domestic product (GDP) and per capita expenditure.[2] Despite the greater spending, comparative international health statistics show that Americans' health care and level of health lag behind those of many other countries. Indicators in a comparison with thirteen other developed nations placed the United States at the bottom in rankings for low birth-weight percentages, infant mortality, and years of potential life lost, and near the bottom for post–neonatal mortality; life expectancy at one year, fifteen years, and forty years; and age-adjusted mortality.[3] Moreover, the American health system has been criticized for its lack of emphasis on preventive care and public health.[4]

The United States is also the only industrialized country without universal health insurance coverage of its entire population. In 2008 the number of non-elderly uninsured people in the United States was 45.7 million.[5] Critics of the U.S. health system have used these indicators as a basis for advocating major reform of the existing system or the possible adoption of a Canadian- or European-style health system.

On the other side of this contentious debate are those who see the U.S. health system as the best in the world. They point to the lack of long waiting lines and the absence of rationing, particularly for advanced treatments, problems that are more common in many other nations. They emphasize the extraordinary achievements by the United States in medical sciences, the unique opportunities for medical innovation, and the number of people who come to the United States from all over the world to receive specialized treatment. They also value the protection from government interference in the provision of health care. In addition, they argue that citizens with national health systems are less satisfied with the systems than critics of the American system suggest.[6]

Public opinion polling has been in the thick of the debate from the outset. In this chapter we examine public views along five dimensions: (1) public satisfaction with the current U.S. health care system—both as a whole and as it impacts individuals' health care experiences; (2) the satisfaction of Americans, in comparison with the citizens of other industrialized countries, with their health care system; (3) Americans' views of other countries' health care systems and "socialized medicine" in comparison with the current U.S. system; (4) public satisfaction with the nation's public health system, which focuses on broad preventive services and protecting the public from health threats; and (5) Americans' priorities for improvements and changes in the health care and public health systems in the future.

Public Satisfaction with the Health Care System

Against the background of more than a half century of debate about the merits and shortcomings of the U.S. system, how satisfied or dissatisfied are Americans with their system and health care, and how much change do they think is needed? As we show, the answers to these questions are complex.

Views of the Health Care System as a Whole

Most polling about the nation's health system concerns the system for delivering medical care. A well-functioning health system from the public's perspective involves what doctors, hospitals, emergency rooms, ambulances, health centers, insurance agencies, and government officials do to provide and finance health care. This is often called the health care or medical care system.

In a number of recent opinion surveys, a majority of Americans have expressed dissatisfaction with the nation's health care system, although their dissatisfaction has not reached the point at which they believe the system to be in crisis and that a completely new health care system is needed.

In 2009 most Americans said they were dissatisfied with the U.S. health care system. About two-thirds (69 percent) rated the nation's system for providing medical care as fair or poor, and 28 percent rated it as excellent or good.[7] When asked in 2005 about five major systems in the United States, the public rated the health care system as the lowest, behind the tax, Social Security, legal, and education systems.[8] Furthermore, in 2008 only 36 percent of Americans expressed a great deal or quite a lot of confidence in the nation's medical system (**Table 3–2**).[9]

Each year since 1982 Americans have been asked whether they think their health care system works pretty well and needs only minor changes, has some good things but needs fundamental changes, or has so much wrong with it that it needs to be rebuilt completely (**Table 3–3**).[10] By this measure, a majority of Americans have never been completely satisfied with the U.S. health care system and wanted some degree of change. They were the most positive in 1987, when 29 percent said that they saw the system working pretty well. In 1991, often seen as the starting point of the great health care reform debate of the early 1990s, only 6 percent held this favorable view. In that year Democrat Harris Wofford won a special Senate election in Pennsylvania on a platform calling for national health insurance. Also in 1991, 42 percent of Americans expressed the view that the health care system should be completely rebuilt, the highest level ever recorded. In 2009, 15 percent saw the system as working pretty well, and 31 percent thought it should be completely rebuilt.[11]

The forces behind these shifts in opinion have been difficult to isolate. They likely relate to reports of rising costs, increasing numbers of uninsured, cutbacks in employee health benefits by businesses, and media accounts of serious problems experienced by Americans when faced with illness and the high cost of care.

Similarly, and very likely related to these other trends, only about one in three Americans (34 percent) reported in 2010 that they had a great deal of confidence in the leaders of medicine. This term is often taken to refer to people who head the major institutions in health care, such as the American Medical Association, medical schools, and the nation's hospitals. The proportion of Americans currently expressing confidence in these leaders is significantly lower than it was during the early 1970s, but higher than the low point of 22 percent in 1992 and 1993, just before and during the early stages of the debate over President Bill Clinton's health reform plan (**Table 3–4**).[12]

Added to their overall negative views of the health care system, a significant proportion of Americans in 2009 believed that private health insurers and pharmaceutical companies in the United States were not doing a good job for those they served. Nearly six in ten (58 percent) thought health insurance companies were doing a bad job serving their consumers. In addition, more than four in ten (45 percent) believed pharmaceutical companies were doing a bad job (**Table 3–5**).[13]

Despite this continued and widespread public criticism of the health care system, the level of concern has never reached the point of being considered a crisis by the American public as a whole. In 2009 only 18 percent described the health care system as being in a state of crisis. A slight majority (52 percent) said it had serious problems but was not in crisis, a view that has remained relatively constant since 1994. Also in 2009 about one in four (28 percent) believed the health care system had either minor problems or no problems at all (**Table 3–6**).[14]

Personal Views of Health Care Experiences and Health Professionals

A majority of Americans have negative feelings about the health care system, but they have far more positive views of their own health care and health professionals. Most are satisfied with the health care they receive. In 2008 more than eight in ten Americans who had received medical care from a doctor or other health professional during the past year rated the overall care they used as excellent (44 percent) or good (38 percent).[15] Eighty-three percent rated the quality of care they received as excellent (36 percent) or good (47 percent), and 16 percent said it was only fair or poor (**Table 3–7**).[16]

In 2003 about nine in ten Americans reported being very (62 percent) or fairly (30 percent) satisfied with the medical care they received the last time they saw a doctor, and 8 percent were dissatisfied.[17] In 2006 about eight in ten said they were satisfied with their ability to get a doctor's appointment when they wanted one (82 percent), see top-quality medical specialists if necessary (79 percent), and get the latest, most sophisticated medical treatments (78 percent). Among those who had health insurance, nearly nine in ten rated their insurance coverage as excellent (33 percent) or good (55 percent).[18]

Despite not having much confidence in the leaders of U.S. medicine in general, a majority of Americans trust the health care professionals with whom they have contact and who provide their care. In 2009 more than three-fourths (78 percent) of Americans believed that hospitals were doing a good job for their patients. In contrast, only about four in ten Americans think health insurance companies (39 percent) and HMOs and managed care companies (35 percent) are doing a good job (**Table 3–5**).[19] In 2002 about nine in ten said they trusted nurses (90 percent) and doctors (88 percent) to make the right decisions about their health care.[20]

In addition, Americans have a high level of respect for the honesty of health professionals. Large majorities in 2008 rated the honesty and ethical standards of nurses (84 percent), pharmacists (70 percent), and doctors (64 percent) as very high or high, making these professions among the highest ranked.[21]

The low level of confidence in the leaders of medicine seems to be related to their perceived inability to deal with national problems affecting health care, such as rising costs, the growing number of uninsured people, and the problem of medical errors. In contrast, most Americans trust their own doctors, whom they do not hold responsible for these broad national problems in health care.

At the same time that most Americans are relatively satisfied with their own health care and health care professionals, many are worried that in the future they might not be able to afford health care or might lose their own health insurance. In early 2007, four in ten (40 percent) said they were very worried about having to pay more for their health care or health insurance. Nearly three in ten (29 percent) of insured Americans were very worried about losing health insurance coverage.

These worries were even more widespread among low-income Americans. More than half (54 percent) of people from households with an annual income of less than $20,000 said they were very worried about having to pay more for their health care or health insurance. Forty-four percent of low-income Americans who had health insurance were very worried about losing their coverage (**Table 3–8**).[22]

Comparative Satisfaction with the Health Care System

For decades a national debate has gone on about whether Americans are more or less satisfied with their health system than citizens of other industrialized countries are with theirs. What do public opinion data show?

Comparative surveys show a high level of public dissatisfaction with the health care systems in many industrialized countries. In 2003 the majority of the public in the United States (68 percent), Canada (64 percent), and Great Britain (67 percent) believed that their health care system was either in a state of crisis or had major problems.[23]

Recognizing this dissatisfaction across countries, it is also true that surveys have shown repeatedly that Americans are more dissatisfied with their health care system than are citizens of other industrialized countries. Between 2004 and 2006 international public opinion surveys showed that only a minority of residents of Spain (28 percent), United Kingdom (26 percent), Canada (21 percent), and the United States (13 percent) were completely satisfied with their health care system. Of the four countries, Americans expressed the highest level of dissatisfaction. More than one-third (37 percent) believed the U.S. health care system needed to be rebuilt completely. This percentage is nearly three times that of Canadian (14 percent), Spanish (13 percent), and U.K. residents' (13 percent) views of their own country's health care system (**Table 3–3**).[24]

This pattern, which has continued for many years, is apparent when the opinions of Americans are compared with those of people from a larger number of countries. When asked how satisfied they were with their country's health care system, the proportion who expressed satisfaction was lower in the United States (40 percent) than in most of the countries of the European Union and in Canada (46 percent). In eleven European countries, a majority (from 57 percent in the United Kingdom to 91 percent in Denmark) said they were satisfied with their own country's health care system. In only three countries (Italy, Portugal, and Greece) was the proportion satisfied lower than it was in the United States (**Table 3–9**).[25]

Americans are far less satisfied with the availability of affordable health care in their country than the Canadians and British are with theirs. Nearly three-fourths (72 percent) of Americans in 2003 expressed dissatisfaction with the availability of affordable health care. Only one in four was satisfied, a proportion significantly smaller than that in the United Kingdom (43 percent) and Canada (57 percent).[26] In 2008 nearly three-fourths (72 percent) of Americans remained dissatisfied with the availability of affordable health care, including 47 percent who were very dissatisfied (**Table 3–10**).[27]

This comparative picture is different when it comes to quality of care. Residents of all three countries were about evenly divided in their opinions about the quality of medical care available in their country. In 2005 about half of U.S. (53 percent), U.K. (55 percent), and Canadian (52 percent) residents rated the quality of health care in their country as excellent or good.[28] In 2008, 57 percent of Americans rated the quality of health care in the United States as excellent or good.[29]

Where residents of the three countries differ is in their responses about the quality of care they receive as individuals. Significantly more Britons (25 percent) and Canadians (24 percent) than Americans (16 percent) rated the quality of their own health care as only fair or poor.[30]

Therefore, it is in cost and availability of care that the United States lags behind Canada and the United Kingdom in the ratings given by each country's residents. But for quality of care, U.S. residents rate their country about the same as Canadians and Britons rate theirs, and they rate the quality of their own care more highly than those respondents in other countries.

Americans' Views of Other Countries' Health Care Systems and "Socialized Medicine"

Given the comparatively high level of public dissatisfaction on many dimensions, we might expect that Americans would want to replace their current health system with that of another country. For such a change to occur, Americans would not only have to be dissatisfied, but also believe that another country's health care system is better than the U.S. system. A 2008 survey found that Americans were generally split on the issue of whether the United States has the best health care system in the world: 45 percent believed it is the best; 39 percent believed that other countries had better systems; 16 percent said they did not know (**Table 3–11**).[31]

In addition, although many Americans view the health care systems of other countries as better than the U.S. system in general, the survey showed that they did not identify as better those specific countries that have been most frequently compared with the United States.[32] In head-to-head comparisons with the health care systems of Canada, France, and Great Britain, a large proportion of Americans were not sure how the United States compared overall. Fifty-three percent of Americans said they did not know how the United States compares with France, and 40 percent said they did not know if the U.S. system was better or worse than Great Britain's. About a quarter (26 percent) was not sure how the U.S. health care system compared with the Canadian system. Only three in ten Americans thought the U.S. system was worse than Canada's. Fewer than one in five thought the U.S. system was worse than those of Great Britain (17 percent) and France (14 percent).[33]

The view that the U.S. health care system lags other countries' seems largely driven by the view that the United States is behind in controlling health care costs and providing affordable access to everyone. In comparing how the United States stacked up against other countries in specific areas, a slim majority of Americans believed that the U.S. health care system is better in terms of the quality of care patients receive (55 percent) and shorter waiting times to see specialists or be admitted to a hospital (53 percent). Very few, however, believed that the United States has the edge in providing affordable access to everyone (26 percent) and controlling health care costs (21 percent).[34]

Part of the resistance to adopting the type of health care system found in other industrialized countries may relate to the stigma that Americans have long associated with government involvement in a national health care system. In the 1940s these types of national, government-directed programs were often called "socialized medicine," implying similarity to the policies either of the old Soviet Union or of left-leaning governments in parts of Europe. Historically, this phrase has been used to attack health reform proposals in the United States if they in any way resembled those of other countries.[35]

What does this phrase mean to Americans today and how does it influence opinions about current debates? A 2008 survey found that Americans were divided on whether a socialized medical system would be better or worse than the current health care system. Among those who said they had at least some understanding of the phrase (82 percent), a plurality (45 percent) said such a system would be better, and 39 percent thought it would be worse (**Table 3–12**).[36]

Although a majority of Americans said they understood the term *socialized medicine* very well (34 percent) or somewhat well (33 percent), about one in three were uncertain what it meant (15 percent not very well; 15 percent not at all). When offered descriptions of what such a system could mean, one-third (32 percent) felt that socialized medicine was a system where "the government tells doctors what to do." Strong majorities believed that it meant that "the government makes sure everyone has health insurance" (79 percent) and "the government pays most of the cost of health care" (73 percent).

A majority of those surveyed felt that the American health care system already had elements that could be described as socialized medicine. Sixty percent believed that Medicare was socialized medicine, and about half (47 percent) felt that the veterans' health care system was socialized medicine.

Compared with seniors (ages 65 and older), young adults (ages 18 to 34) were more likely to view socialized medicine positively (55 percent to 30 percent). Young adults were also more likely than seniors to view Medicare as socialized medicine (67 percent to 47 percent). The uninsured do not view socialized medicine as negatively as those who have health insurance. Only 19 percent of the uninsured thought that a socialized medicine system would be worse than the current system, while 57 percent thought it would be better. Those with health insurance were divided on whether socialized medicine would be better (44 percent) or worse (41 percent).[37]

The divided views Americans hold about the comparison with other countries' health care systems and about whether a socialized medicine type of system would be better or worse leads to a split over whether changing to another nation's health care system would lead to a better outcome. The result of this division can be seen when Americans were asked if they wished to replace their health care system with an alternative. In a three-country survey, Canadians and Britons were asked a similar question about their own systems.

In the United States the public was asked which of the following two approaches they would prefer: replacing the current system with a new government-run health care system or maintaining the current system based mostly on private health insurance. In Canada and Great Britain, residents were asked the reverse, whether they would prefer replacing their current system with a new system based mostly on private insurance or maintaining the government-run system.[38] Majorities in all three countries favored staying with their existing health care system. But Americans were much more likely to favor replacing the U.S. system (38 percent) based on private insurance than the British (21 percent) and Canadians (13 percent) were to favor replacing their current government systems with private insurance plans.

These survey results reinforce the earlier findings, that Americans are highly dissatisfied with their current health care system in general and on many aspects. But this level of dissatisfaction has not reached a point where most would replace the current health system with one like Canada's or Great Britain's.

Satisfaction with the Public Health System

The second part of the U.S. health system is the *public health* system. The job of the public health system is to improve the nation's overall health by protecting the population from health threats; preventing disease; encouraging better diets; reducing environmental risks, violence, injuries, and tobacco use; and improving water supplies and living conditions. Although this system is not as widely discussed as the health care delivery system is, Americans do have views about it.

Since 2000 the country has faced a number of public health threats: SARS, anthrax, smallpox, avian or pandemic flu, obesity, and H1N1 or swine flu. These threats and how they were handled have raised concerns about the adequacy of the U.S. public health system.

In 2010 the majority (56 percent) of Americans rated the nation's system overall for protecting the public from health threats and preventing illness as fair or poor, while 42 percent rated it as excellent or good.[39] Asked in 2009 about some more specific aspects, 54 percent rated the nation's system for preventive care and preventing illnesses such as cancer, heart disease, and seasonal flu as fair or poor. A majority (52 percent) gave a positive (excellent or good) rating to the nation's system protecting the public from health threats such as SARS and H1N1 or swine flu, and 45 percent gave a negative rating. A plurality (49 percent) gave a positive rating to the nation's system protecting against terrorism using biological means such as smallpox and anthrax, while 43 percent gave a negative rating.[40]

Although Americans say they are dissatisfied with the nation's public health system in the aggregate, they voice a high level of satisfaction with the leading federal government public health agency, the Centers for Disease Control and Prevention (CDC). In 2010, 62 percent rated the job being done by the CDC as excellent or good. This rating compares favorably to the public's rating of the Department of Homeland Security (43 percent positive) and the Food and Drug Administration (43 percent) (**Table 3–13**).[41]

One of the reasons for the contrast between the low rating of the public health system overall and the high rating of the CDC may relate to the public's perception that the overall system is poorly planned and coordinated, even if the leading federal agency is performing well. In the United States public health functions and responsibilities are widely dispersed. They are performed by nonprofit groups, such as the American Cancer Society and American Red Cross, as well as by a wide range of government agencies at the federal, state, and local level. In this type of mixed, decentralized system, it is not clear who is responsible for the provision of preventive services or who the lead group is during a public health crisis.

Although the public remains critical of the overall public health system, Americans' support for more spending on these activities has been high for almost forty years. Since 1973 a majority of Americans have said that the United States is spending too little on improving and protecting the nation's health. In 2008, three-fourths (75 percent) thought the country was spending too little, while only 5 percent thought the nation was spending too much (**Table 3–14**).[42]

Americans' Priorities for Improving the Health Care and Public Health Systems

Given Americans' high level of dissatisfaction with the current health system and their general interest in reforming it, one would expect the public to rank health care as a top priority for national government action. Elected officials can work on only a limited number of major issues at one time. Has health care change been a top public priority?

Health Care as a National Priority

Since the 1988 presidential election, health care and/or Medicare have been among the top five issues that voters have said are important in their voting choices. Moreover, health care has consistently ranked higher as a priority for Democratic voters than for Republican voters. This means that when the Democratic Party holds the presidency and majorities in both houses of Congress, major health care legislation is likely to be debated. At the time of the 2008 election, health care was the second-ranked issue for Democratic voters, behind only the economy.[43]

Health Care Priorities for Government Action

Understanding the public's priorities for action by government in the health care area is important because they suggest what might be the best opportunities for change. Surveys show that no single problem area in health care is identified by the majority as the most important priority for government to address. In December 2008, when asked which of three goals they thought should be the most important for any health care reform plan—the most important health care problems for the government to address—Americans cited making health care and health insurance more affordable as the most important goal (39 percent), followed by finding a way to provide health insurance coverage to most Americans (30 percent), and reforming the existing health care system to provide higher-quality, more cost-effective care (18 percent).[44] Their responses suggest that the public's agenda for health reform is diverse, involving multiple issues. (See Chapters 4, 5, and 9 for extensive discussion of Americans' attitudes about health care costs, the problems of the uninsured and access to health care, and quality of care.)

Most Urgent Health Problems Facing the Nation

Another way to look at Americans' priorities is to ask what they think is the most urgent health problem facing the country. Some Americans name major diseases as the most urgent concerns, and others name health care system issues. The distribution of answers to this question has changed substantially since the early 1990s. In 1991, 69 percent of Americans selected as the single most urgent health problem a particular disease such as HIV/AIDS, cancer, or heart disease. That year, only 12 percent named a systemic problem such as health care costs or the number of uninsured. In 2009, 50 percent of the public named a health care system problem as most urgent, and only 37 percent cited a particular disease. Over time, health system problems have become more salient to Americans in comparison to the disease threats facing our society. The trend is occasionally disrupted when a new disease threat emerges, such as avian or pandemic flu in 2005, when about the same proportion named diseases and health system problems as the most urgent health problem. The overall dominance of health system issues resumed in the following year (**Table 3–15**).[45]

Although health system issues have grown in importance to the general public, the overall priorities for specific diseases and health conditions continue to impact the health system and are worth understanding. Health problems and diseases that the public sees as the most important often receive more federal funding and voluntary private giving, which has a significant impact on the nature and shape of the U.S. health system.

In 2001 the public was given comprehensive lists of eighty-five diseases and conditions and asked to rate their relative seriousness. Three conditions—cancer (87 percent), heart disease (80 percent), and HIV/AIDS (80 percent)—ranked at the top of the public's list of diseases the public considered "very serious problems." [46]

Poverty, infant mortality, substandard housing, and racial discrimination, issues often named by health policy and public health researchers as major health problems, were not seen as very serious health problems by a majority of the public. It is possible that the public ranks some of these problems lower because they do not see them mainly as health problems.

In addition, although cancer was the top-rated item, there was a variation among types of cancer. Breast cancer (named by 84 percent) was at the top of the "very serious problem" list, while prostate cancer (named by 61 percent) did not rank as highly, even among men.

A wide range of chronic diseases appeared on the lists presented in the study. The public's ratings varied for specific diseases. Cancer, heart disease, and HIV/AIDS were seen as very serious problems, while allergies and chronic fatigue syndrome were rated as much less serious. Chronic disease generically ranked in the middle of these extremes (named by 55 percent as very serious).

Of historical note, these health priorities change over long periods of time. In 1940 syphilis was the public's top national health concern (46 percent), followed by cancer (29 percent), tuberculosis (16 percent), and polio (9 percent).[47] Asked in 2009 what they believed were the diseases or health conditions that posed the greatest threats to Americans, the public rated cancer first (named by 57 percent), followed by heart disease (28 percent) and HIV/AIDS (25 percent).[48] Of the original health threats, only cancer has remained as a top concern for sixty-six years.

Conclusions

American public opinion on the U.S. health system is more complex and nuanced than might be thought at first. Americans are critical of their overall health care system, but they do not see other countries' health care systems as being better. They remain worried about their economic security as it relates to their health insurance coverage. But on a day-to-day basis, most Americans are satisfied with the health care they receive from health professionals and institutions.

Americans are more dissatisfied with their health system than citizens of most other industrialized countries, particularly when it comes to the cost and availability of care. The overall general dissatisfaction level has not, however, reached a point where Americans would consider switching to an alternative system like Canada's.

Two issues tend to dominate Americans' concerns about the health care system—high costs and insecure access to insurance and care. Three diseases dominate Americans' thinking—cancer, heart disease, and HIV/AIDS.

A major health care reform law was passed by Congress and signed by President Barack Obama in 2010. But many issues, such as containing high health care costs, have not yet been fully addressed. What is clear from this review is that public pressure for substantial change in both the health care and public health system will remain an important part of political life even after the 2010 law has been implemented.

Notes

[1] Organisation for Economic Co-operation and Development, "OECD Health Data 2009: How Does the United States Compare," http://www.oecd.org/dataoecd/46/2/38980580.pdf; "OECD Health Data 2009: How Does the United Kingdom Compare," http://www.oecd.org/dataoecd/46/4/38980557.pdf; "OECD Health Data 2009: How Does the Canada Compare," http://www.oecd.org/dataoecd/46/33/38979719.pdf.

[2] Gerard F. Anderson, Peter S. Hussey, Bianca K. Frogner, and Hugh R. Waters, "Health Spending in the United States and the Rest of the Industrialized World," *Health Affairs* 24 (July/August 2005): 903–914; Gerard F. Anderson, Bianca K. Frogner, and Uwe E. Reinhardt, "Health Spending in OECD Countries in 2004: An Update," *Health Affairs* 26 (September/October 2007): 1481–89; Stephen F. Jencks and George J. Schieber, "Containing U.S. Health Care Costs: What Bullet to Bite?" *Health Care Financing Review* (Annual Supplement, 1991): 1–12; Gerard F. Anderson, Uwe E. Reinhardt, Peter S. Hussey, and Varduhi Petrosyan, "It's the Prices, Stupid: Why the United States Is So Different from Other Countries," *Health Affairs* 22 (May/June 2003): 89–105.

[3] Barbara Starfield, "Is US Health Really the Best in the World?" *JAMA: Journal of the American Medical Association* 282 (July 26, 2000): 483–485.

[4] James F. Fries, C. Everett Koop, Carson E. Beadle, Paul F. Cooper, Mary Jane England, Roger F. Greaves, Jacque J. Sokolov, and Daniel Wright, "Reducing Health Care Costs by Reducing the Need and Demand for Medical Services," *New England Journal of Medicine* 329 (July 29, 1993): 321–325.

[5] Kaiser Family Foundation, "The Uninsured: A Primer," October 2009, http://www.kff.org/uninsured/upload/7451-05.pdf.

[6] Tyler Cowen, "Poor U.S. Scores in Health Care Don't Measure Nobels and Innovation," *New York Times,* October 5, 2006; Thomas Boehm, "How Can We Explain the American Dominance in Biomedical Research and Development?" *Journal of Medical Marketing* 5 (April 2005): 158–166; Michael Tanner, "In Praise of U.S. Health Care," *Washington Times,* October 1, 2005, A13.

[7] Harvard School of Public Health/Robert Wood Johnson Foundation Poll (Storrs, Conn.: Roper Center for Public Opinion Research, June 17–21, 2009).

[8] Pew Research Center for the People and the Press Poll (Storrs, Conn.: Roper Center for Public Opinion Research, January 5–9, 2005).

[9] Gallup Poll, "Confidence in Institutions," 2009, http://www.gallup.com/poll/1597/Confidence-Institutions.aspx.

[10] For 1982–2002, Harris Interactive, "Attitudes toward the United States' Health Care System: Long-Term Trends," *Health Care News,* August 21, 2002, http://www.harrisinteractive.com/news/newsletters/healthnews/HI_HealthCareNews2002Vol2_Iss17.pdf. For 2004–2006, Robert J. Blendon, Mollyann Brodie, John M. Benson, Drew E. Altman, and Tami Buhr, "Americans' Views about Health Care Costs, Access, and Quality," *Milbank Quarterly* 84 (December 2006):

623–657. For 2007–2008, CBS News/*New York Times* Polls (Storrs, Conn.: Roper Center for Public Opinion Research, July 9–17, 2007; September 12–16, 2008). For 2009, CBS News Poll (Storrs, Conn.: Roper Center for Public Opinion Research, October 5–8, 2009).

[11] CBS News Poll, October 5–8, 2009.

[12] Harris Interactive, "Virtually No Change in Annual Harris Poll Confidence Index from Last Year," March 9, 2010, http://news.harrisinteractive.com/profiles/investor/ResLibraryView.asp?ResLibraryID=36697&GoTopage=4&Category=1777&BzID=1963&t=30.

[13] Harris Interactive, "Big Drop since Last Year in Reputation of Car Manufacturers, Investment and Brokerage Firms, and Banks," August 18, 2009, http://www.harrisinteractive.com/harris_poll/pubs/Harris_Poll_2009_08_18.pdf.

[14] For 1994–2005, Gallup Poll trend data, published in Robert J. Blendon, Kelly Hunt, John M. Benson, Channtal Fleischfresser, and Tami Buhr, "Understanding the American Public's Health Priorities: A 2006 Perspective," *Health Affairs* 25 (Web exclusive, October 17, 2006): w508–w515. For 2006–2008, Gallup Poll, November 9–12, 2006; Gallup Poll (Storrs, Conn.: Roper Center for Public Opinion Research, November 11–14, 2007); Harvard School of Public Health/Robert Wood Johnson Foundation Polls (Storrs, Conn.: Roper Center for Public Opinion Research, March 26–30, 2008; June 17–21, 2009).

[15] Harvard School of Public Health/Robert Wood Johnson Foundation Poll, March 26–30, 2008.

[16] Gallup Poll (Storrs, Conn.: Roper Center for Public Opinion Research, November 13–16, 2009).

[17] Harvard School of Public Health/Robert Wood Johnson Foundation Poll (Storrs, Conn.: Roper Center for Public Opinion Research, February 18–23, 2003).

[18] ABC News/Kaiser Family Foundation/*USA Today* Poll, October 2006, http://www.kff.org/kaiserpolls/upload/7573.pdf.

[19] Harris Interactive Poll, "Big Drop since Last Year in Reputation of Car Manufacturers, Investment and Brokerage Firms, and Banks," August 18, 2009.

[20] Harris Interactive Poll (New York: Harris Interactive, March 2002).

[21] Gallup Poll, "Honesty/Ethics in Professions," 2008, http://www.gallup.com/poll/1654/Honesty-Ethics-Professions.aspx.

[22] Kaiser Family Foundation Poll (Storrs, Conn.: Roper Center for Public Opinion Research, March 8–13, 2007).

[23] Gallup Poll, "Greener on the Other Side? Universal vs. Private Healthcare," January 20, 2004, http://www.gallup.com/poll/10339/Greener-Other-Side-Universal-vs-Private-Healthcare.aspx.

[24] For U.S., Blendon et al., "Americans' Views about Health Care Costs, Access, and Quality." For Canada and U.K., Cathy Schoen, Robin Osborn, Phuong Trang Huynh, Michelle Doty, Karen Davis, Kinga Zapert, and Jordan Peugh, "Primary Care and Health System Performance: Adults' Experiences in Five Countries," *Health Affairs* Web exclusive , October 28, 2004, http://content.healthaffairs.org/cgi/reprint/hlthaff.w4.487v1?maxtoshow=&hits=10&RESULTFORMAT=&fulltext=schoen+osborn+primary&searchid=1&FIRSTINDEX=0&resourcetype=HWCIT. For Spain, Albert Jovell, Robert J. Blendon, Maria Dolors Navarro, Channtal Fleischfresser, John M. Benson, Catherine M. DesRoches, and Kathleen J. Weldon, "Public Trust in the Spanish Health Care System," *Health Expectations* 10 (December 2007): 350–357.

[25] Robert J. Blendon, Minah Kim, and John M. Benson, "The Public Versus the World Health Organization on Health System Performance," *Health Affairs* 20 (May/June 2001): 10–20.

[26] Gallup Poll data, published in Blendon et al., "Americans' Views about Health Care Costs, Access, and Quality."

[27] Gallup Poll (Storrs, Conn.: Roper Center for Public Opinion Research, January 4–6, 2008).

[28] Gallup Poll data, published in Blendon et al., "Americans' Views about Health Care Costs, Access, and Quality."

[29] Gallup Poll, November 13–16, 2008.

[30] Gallup Poll, "Healthcare System Ratings: U.S., Great Britain, Canada," March 25, 2003, http://www.gallup.com/poll/8056/Healthcare-System-Ratings-US-Great-Britain-Canada.aspx.

[31] Harvard School of Public Health/Harris Interactive Poll, "Debating Health: Election 2008; Americans' Views on the U.S. Health Care System Compared to Other Countries," March 2008, http://www.hsph.harvard.edu/news/press-releases/files/Topline__Best_HC_Havard_Harris.doc.

[32] In 2000 the World Health Organization ranked the U.S. health care system as thirty-seventh best in the world in overall performance. France was rated first, Great Britain eighteenth, and Canada thirtieth. World Health Organization, *The World Health Report 2000: Health Systems: Improving Performance,* http://www.who.int/whr/2000/en/whr00_en.pdf. This report's findings were criticized by Glen Whitman, "WHO's Fooling Who? The World Health Organization's Problematic Ranking of Health Care Systems," Cato Institute Briefing Paper, no. 101, February 28, 2008, http://www.cato.org/pubs/bp/bp101.pdf. In a 2007 Commonwealth Fund study comparing health care in Australia, Canada, Germany, New Zealand, the United Kingdom, and the United States, the U.S. finished last. Karen Davis, Cathy Schoen, Stephen C. Schoenbaum, Michelle M. Doty, Alyssa L. Holmgren, Jennifer L. Kriss, and Katherine K. Shea, "Mirror, Mirror on the Wall: An International Update on the Comparative Performance of American Health Care," May 2007, http://www.commonwealthfund.org/usr_doc/1027_Davis_mirror_mirror_international_update_final.pdf?section=4039.

[33] Harvard School of Public Health/Harris Interactive Poll, "Debating Health: Election 2008; Americans' Views on the U.S. Health Care System Compared to Other Countries," March 2008.

[34] Ibid.

[35] Paul Starr, *The Social Transformation of American Medicine* (New York: Basic Books, 1982), 280–289.

[36] Harvard School of Public Health/Harris Interactive Poll, "Debating Health: Election 2008; Americans' Views on Socialized Medicine," February 2008, http://www.hsph.harvard.edu/news/press-releases/files/Topline__Socialized_Med_Havard_Harris.pdf.

[37] Ibid.

[38] Gallup Poll, "Healthcare System Ratings: U.S., Great Britain, Canada," March 25, 2003.

[39] Harvard School of Public Health Poll (Storrs, Conn.: Roper Center for Public Opinion Research, January 13–17, 2010).

[40] Harvard School of Public Health/Robert Wood Johnson Foundation Poll (Storrs, Conn.: Roper Center for Public Opinion Research, June 24–28, 2009).

[41] Pew Research Center for the People and the Press, "March 2010 Trust in Government Survey: Final Topline," March 11–21, 2010, http://people-press.org/reports/questionnaires/606.pdf.

[42] James A. Davis, Tom W. Smith, and Peter V. Marsden, *General Social Surveys, 1972–2008* (Chicago: National Opinion Research Center, 2008).

[43] Robert J. Blendon and Karen Donelan, "The 1988 Election: How Important Was Health?" *Health Affairs* 8 (Fall 1989): 6–15; Robert J. Blendon, Drew E. Altman, John M. Benson,

Humphrey Taylor, Matt James, and Mark Smith, "The Implications of the 1992 Presidential Election for Health Care Reform," *JAMA: Journal of the American Medical Association* 268 (December 16, 1992): 3371–5; Robert J. Blendon, John M. Benson, Mollyann Brodie, Drew E. Altman, Diane Rowland, Patricia Neuman, and Matt James, "Voters and Health Care in the 1996 Election," *JAMA: Journal of the American Medical Association* 277 (April 16, 1997): 1253–8; Robert J. Blendon, Drew E. Altman, John M. Benson, and Mollyann Brodie, "The Implications of the 2000 Election." *New England Journal of Medicine* 344 (March 1, 2001): 679–684; Robert J. Blendon, Mollyann Brodie, Drew E. Altman, John M. Benson, and Elizabeth C. Hamel, "Voters and Health Care in the 2004 Election," *Health Affairs* 24 (January-June 2005 supplement): w86–w96; Robert J. Blendon, Drew E. Altman, John M. Benson, Mollyann Brodie, Tami Buhr, Claudia Deane, and Sasha Buscho, "Voters and Health Care Reform in the 2008 Presidential Election," *New England Journal of Medicine* 359 (November 6, 2008): 2050–61.

[44] Kaiser Family Foundation/Harvard School of Public Health Poll (Storrs, Conn.: Roper Center for Public Opinion Research, December 4–14, 2008).

[45] For 1991–2007, Gallup Poll, "'Access' Gains as Top Perceived U.S. Health Problem," December 3, 2007, http://www.gallup.com/poll/102964/Access-Gains-Top-Perceived-US-Health-Problem.aspx. For 2008–2009, Gallup Polls (Storrs, Conn.: Roper Center for Public Opinion Research, November 13–16, 2008; November 5–8, 2009).

[46] Robert J. Blendon, Kimberly Scoles, Catherine DesRoches, John T. Young, Melissa J. Herrmann, Jennifer L. Schmidt, and Minah Kim, "Americans' Health Priorities: Curing Cancer and Controlling Costs," *Health Affairs* 20 (November/December 2001): 222–232.

[47] Gallup Poll (Storrs, Conn.: Roper Center for Public Opinion Research, March 8–13, 1940).

[48] Harvard School of Public Health/Robert Wood Johnson Foundation Poll, June 24–28, 2009. Responses add to more than 100 percent because each respondent could give up to two different responses.

Table 3-1 Health Indicators 2006–2007

	United States	United Kingdom	Canada	OECD average
Life expectancy at birth (in years) (2005–2006)	78.1	79.1	80.7	79.0
Infant mortality (per 1,000 live births) (2006–2007)	6.7	4.8	5.0	4.9
Total expenditure on health per capita (in PPPs) (2007)	7290.0	2992.0	3895.0	2964.0
Practicing physicians per 1,000 population (2007)	2.4	2.5	2.2	3.1
Acute care beds per 1,000 population (2007)	2.7	2.6	2.7	3.8
Percentage of GDP spent on health care (2007)	16.0	8.4	10.1	8.9
Public expenditure as percentage of total health expenditure (2007)	45.0	82.0	70.0	73.0

Sources: Organisation for Economic Co-operation and Development, "OECD Health Data 2009: How Does the United States Compare," "OECD Health Data 2009: How Does the United Kingdom Compare," "OECD Health Data 2009: How Does Canada Compare."

Table 3-2 Public Confidence in American Institutions (in percent)

	Great deal/ Quite a lot	Some	Very little/ none (vol)
The military	82	12	5
Small business	67	26	7
The police	59	29	11
The Church or organized religion	52	29	17
The presidency	51	24	23
The U.S. Supreme Court	39	41	18
The public schools	38	39	22
The medical system	36	41	23
The criminal justice system	28	44	27
Newspapers	25	43	31
Television news	23	41	35
Banks	22	49	29
Organized labor	19	40	39
Health maintenance organizations, or HMOs	18	44	35
Congress	17	45	38
Big business	16	42	41

Note: "Don't know" reponses not shown. "(Vol)" = Volunteered response

Question: I am going to read you a list of institutions in American society. Please tell me how much confidence you, yourself, have in each one: a great deal, quite a lot, some or very little.

Source: Gallup Poll, "Confidence in Institutions," 2009.

Table 3-3 Public Attitudes about the Health Care System in Four Countries, 1982–2009 (in percent)

		Works pretty well, only minor changes are necessary	Some good things, but fundamental changes are needed	So much wrong need to completely rebuild it
1982	U.S.	19	47	28
1987	U.S.	29	47	19
1991	U.S.	6	50	42
1994	U.S.	14	54	31
1998	U.S.	15	49	30
2000	U.S.	15	52	30
2002	U.S.	17	49	31
2004	U.S.	13	50	36
2004	Canada	21	63	14
2004	U.K.	26	59	13
2006	Spain	28	58	13
2006	U.S.	13	49	37
2007	U.S.	11	50	38
2008	U.S.	14	50	35
2009	U.S.	15	53	31

Note: "Don't know" responses not shown

Question: Which of the following statements comes closest to expressing your overall view of the country's health care system? On the whole, the health care system works pretty well and only minor changes are necessary to make it work better; there are some good things in our health care system, but fundamental changes are needed to make it work better; or our health care system has so much wrong with it that we need to completely rebuild it?

Sources: For U.S. 1982–2002, Harris Interactive, "Attitudes toward the United States' Health Care System: Long-Term Trends," *Health Care News*, 21 August 2002. For U.S. 2004–2006, Robert J. Blendon, Mollyann Brodie, John M. Benson, Drew E. Altman, and Tami Buhr, "Americans' Views about Health Care Costs, Access, and Quality," *Milbank Quarterly* 84, no. 4 (2006): 623–657. For U.S. 2007–2008, CBS News/*New York Times* (Storrs, Conn.: Roper Center for Public Opinion Research, July 9–17, 2007; September 12–16, 2008). For U.S. 2009, CBS News (Storrs, Conn.: Roper Center for Public Opinion Research, October 5–8, 2009). For Canada and U.K., Cathy Schoen, Robin Osborn, Phuong Trang Huynh, Michelle Doty, Karen Davis, Kinga Zapert, and Jordan Peugh, "Primary Care and Health System Performance: Adults' Experiences in Five Countries," *Health Affairs* 23 (Supplement 2):W4-487-503. For Spain, Albert Jovell, Robert J. Blendon, Maria Dolors Navarro, Channtal Fleischfresser, John M. Benson, Catherine M. DesRoches, and Kathleen J. Weldon, "Public Trust in the Spanish Health Care System," *Health Expectations* 10 (December 2007): 350–357.

Table 3-4 Public Confidence in Leaders of Medicine, 1971–2010 (percent saying great deal)

1971	61
1974	50
1977	43
1980	34
1983	35
1986	33
1989	30
1992	22
1995	26
1998	38
2001	32
2004	32
2007	37
2008	28
2009	34
2010	34

Question: As far as people in charge of running medicine are concerned, would you say you have a great deal of confidence, only some confidence, or hardly any confidence at all in them?

Source: Harris Interactive, "Virtually No Change in Annual Harris Poll Confidence Index from Last Year," March 9, 2010.

Table 3-5 Public Rating of the Job Health Care Industries Do for Their Customers (in percent)

	Good job	Bad job	Not sure
Hospitals	78	19	3
Pharmaceutical companies	54	45	1
Health insurance companies	39	58	3
Managed care companies, such as HMOs	35	54	10

Question: Do you think (hospitals/pharmaceutical and drug companies/health insurance companies/managed care companies, such as HMOs) generally do a good job or bad job serving their customers?

Source: Harris Interactive, "Big Drop since Last Year in Reputation of Car Manufacture, Investment and Brokerage Firms, and Banks," August 18, 2009.

Table 3-6 Americans' Views of the U.S. Health Care System, 1994–2009 (in percent)

	1994	2000	2002	2003	2005	2006	2007	2008	2009
State of crisis	17	12	11	14	18	16	17	18	18
Major problems	52	58	54	54	52	55	56	51	52
Minor problems	29	28	32	30	28	25	24	26	24
No problems	1	1	2	1	1	3	3	4	4

Note: "Don't know" responses are not shown.

Question: Which of these statements do you think best describes the U.S. health care system today: it is in a state of crisis, it has major problems, it has minor problems, or it does not have any problems?

Sources: For 1994–2005, Gallup Poll trend data, published in Robert J. Blendon, Kelly Hunt, John M. Benson, Channtal Fleischfresser, and Tami Buhr, "Understanding the American Public's Health Priorities: A 2006 Perspective," *Health Affairs* 25 (web exclusive, October 17, 2006): w508–w515. For 2006, Gallup Poll (Storrs, Conn.: Roper Center for Public Opinion Research, November 9–12, 2006). For 2007, Gallup Poll (Storrs, Conn: Roper Center for Public Opinion Research, November 11–14, 2007). For 2008–2009, Harvard School of Public Health/Robert Wood Johnson Foundation Polls (Storrs, Conn.: Ropert Center for Public Opinion Research, March 26–30, 2008; June 17–21, 2009).

Table 3-7 Americans' Views about Their Own Health Care Arrangements (in percent)

	Excellent	Good	Fair/Poor
Rating of the overall medical care you receive (among those who received medical care from a doctor or other health professional during the past 12 months)[1]	44	38	18
Rating of the quality of care you receive[2]	36	47	16
Rating of your health insurance coverage (among insured)[3]	33	55	12

Satisfaction with:	Satisfied	Dissatisfied
Medical care you received the last time you saw a doctor[4]	92	8
Your ability to get a doctor's appointment when you want one[3]	82	17
Your ability to see top-quality medical specialist if you need one[3]	79	16
Your ability to get latest, most sophisticated medical treatments[3]	78	18

Note: "Don't know" responses not shown

Question: (Asked of those who had received medical care from a doctor or some other health professional in the past 12 months) Overall, how would you rate that medical care, excellent, good, fair or poor?

Question: Overall, how would you rate the quality of health care you receive, as excellent, good, only fair, or poor?

Question: (Asked of those who have health insurance) How would you rate your overall health insurance coverage: excellent, good, not so good or poor?

Question: Thinking about the last time you saw a medical doctor about yourself, would you say you were very, fairly, not too, or not at all satisfied with the medical care you received?

Question: For each specific item I name, please tell me whether you are very satisfied with it, somewhat satisfied, somewhat dissatisfied or very dissatisfied: your ability to (get a doctor's appointment when you want one/get to see top-quality medical specialists, if you ever need one/get the latest, most sophisticated medical treatments).

Sources: [1]Harvard School of Public Health/Robert Wood Johnson Foundation Poll (Storrs, Conn.: Roper Center for Public Opinion Research, March 26–30, 2008). [2]Gallup Poll (Storrs, Conn.: Roper Center for Public Opinion Research, November 13–16, 2008). [3]ABC News/Kaiser Family Foundation/ *USA Today* Poll, October 2006. [4]Harvard School of Public Health/Robert Wood Johnson Foundation Poll (Storrs, Conn.: Roper Center for Public Opinion Research, February 18–23, 2003).

Table 3-8 Americans' Health Care Worries about the Future, by Household Income (percent very worried)

	Having to pay more for health care of health insurance	Losing your health insurance (insured respondents)
Total	40	29
By household income		
<$20,000	54	44
$20,000–49,999	39	34
$50,000+	32	19

Question: How worried are you about having to pay more for your health care or health insurance? Are you very worried, somewhat worried, not too worried, or not at all worried?

Question: (Asked of those who have health insurance) How worried are you about losing your health insurance coverage? Are you very worried, somewhat worried, not too worried, or not at all worried?

Source: Kaiser Family Foundation Poll (Storrs, Conn.: Roper Center for Public Opinion Research, March 8-13, 2007).

Table 3-9 The Public's Satisfaction with Their Own Health Care System in Seventeen Countries (percent saying very or fairly satisfied)

Denmark	91
Finland	81
Austria	73
Netherlands	70
Luxembourg	67
France	65
Belgium	63
Ireland	58
Germany	58
Sweden	58
United Kingdom	57
Canada	46
Spain	43
United States	40
Italy	20
Portugal	16
Greece	16

Question: In general, would you say you are very satisfied, fairly satisfied, neither satisfied nor dissatisfied, fairly dissatisfied, or very dissatisfied with the way health care runs in [name of respondent's country]?

Source: Robert J. Blendon, Minah Kim, and John M. Benson, "The Public Versus the World Health Organization on Health System Performance," *Health Affairs* 20 (May/June 2001): 10–20.

Table 3-10 Ratings of Health Care Availability and Quality in Three Countries (in percent)

Availability of affordable health care in your country	Very Satisfied	Somewhat Satisfied	Somewhat Dissatisfied	Very Dissatisfied
2003 Canada[1]	16	41	24	17
2003 U.K.[1]	7	36	27	25
2003 U.S.[1]	6	19	28	44
2007 U.S.[2]	8	17	27	46
2008 U.S.[3]	7	18	25	47

Quality of health care	Excellent	Good	Only fair	Poor
2005 Canada[1]	8	44	34	14
2005 U.K.[1]	11	44	30	15
2005 U.S.[1]	16	37	33	14
2006 U.S.[4]	16	37	32	14
2008 U.S.[3]	17	40	30	12

Note: "Don't know" responses not shown

Question: We'd like to know how you feel about the state of the nation in each of the following areas. For each one, please say whether you are very satisfied, somewhat satisfied, somewhat dissatisfied, or very dissatisfied. If you don't have enough information about a particular subject to rate it, just say so. How about the availability of affordable health care?

Question: Overall, how would you rate the quality of health care in this country . . . as excellent, good, only fair, or poor?

Sources: [1]Gallup Poll data, published in Robert J. Blendon, Mollyann Brodie, John M. Benson, Drew E. Altman, and Tami Buhr, "Americans' Views about Health Care Costs, Access, and Quality," *Milbank Quarterly* 84 (December 2006): 623–657. [2]Gallup Poll (Storrs, Conn.: Roper Center for Public Opinion Research, January 15–18, 2007). [3]Gallup Poll (Storrs, Conn.: Roper Center for Public Opinion Research, January 4–6, 2008). [4]Gallup Poll (Storrs, Conn.: Roper Center for Public Opinion Research, November 9–12, 2006).

Table 3-11 Americans' Views about U.S. Healthcare System vs. Those of Other Countries (in percent)

	U.S. has the best	Other countries have better	Don't know
U.S. health care system vs. other countries (in general)	45	39	15

U.S. health care system compared with:	U.S. system is better	U.S. system is worse	Same (vol)	Don't know
Canada	40	30	4	26
Great Britain	37	17	6	40
France	31	14	3	53

U.S. health care system compared with these countries when it comes to . . .	U.S. system is better	U.S. system is worse	Same (vol)	Don't know
Quality of care patients receive	55	16	8	21
Waiting times to see specialists or be admitted to the hospital	53	16	6	25
Making sure everyone can get affordable health care	26	52	4	18
Controlling health care costs	21	56	4	19

Note: "(vol)" = volunteered response

Question: Some people say that the United States has the best health care system in the world. Others say that the health care systems of some other countries are better than the United States. How about you? Do you think that in general the United States has the best health care system or are there other countries with better health care systems?

Question: Specifically thinking about (Canada/France/Great Britain), would you say that overall the United States has a better health care system than (Canada/France/Great Britain) or a worse health care system than (Canada/France/Great Britain)?

Question: Thinking about the countries I have just mentioned, would you say that in general the United States has a better health care system or a worse health care system than these countries when it comes to (the quality of care that patients receive/waiting times to see specialists or be admitted to the hospital/making sure everyone can get affordable health care/controlling health care costs)?

Source: Harvard School of Public Health/Harris Interactive Poll, "Debating Health: Election 2008; Americans' Views on the U.S. Health Care System Compared to Other Countries," March 2008.

Table 3-12 Americans' Views about Socialized Medicine (in percent)

Among those who say they have at least some understanding of what "socialized medicine" means:

If U.S. had socialized medicine, the health care system would be . . .	Better	Worse	About the same (vol)	Don't know
Total	45	39	4	12
By age				
18–34	55	30	4	11
35–64	45	38	4	13
65+	30	57	2	11
By health insurance status				
Insured	44	41	3	11
Uninsured	57	19	8	17
Percent who think "socialized medicine" means . . .				
The government makes sure everyone has health insurance	79			
The government pays most of the cost of health care	73			
The government tells doctors what to do	32			
Percent who think of the following as being systems of socialized medicine				
Medicare	60			
The veterans' health care system	47			

Question: So far as you understand the phrase, do you think that if we had socialized medicine in this country that the health care system would be better or worse than what we have now?

Question: Which of the following do you understand by the words "socialized medicine"? Do you think it means a system where (the government makes sure everyone has health insurance/the government pays most of the cost of health care/the government tells doctors what to do)? (Yes/No to each)

Question: Do you think of the following as being systems of socialized medicine or not? (Medicare, the system for seniors and people with disabilities/the veterans' health care system)

Source: Harvard School of Public Health/Harris Interactive Poll, "Debating Health: Election 2008; Americans' Views on Socialized Medicine," January-February 2008.

Table 3-13 Public Ratings of Federal Government Agencies (in percent)

	Excellent	Good	Only fair	Poor	Don't know
Centers for Disease Control and Prevention (CDC)	14	48	24	7	7
Federal Bureau of Investigation (FBI)	10	48	24	7	11
Central Intelligence Agency (CIA)	8	38	29	11	15
Department of Homeland Security	9	34	37	16	4
Environmental Protection Agency (EPA)	7	36	36	16	5
Food and Drug Administration (FDA)	7	36	35	17	5
Internal Revenue Service (IRS)	5	35	38	16	6
Department of Education	5	28	35	29	2

Question: As I name some federal government agencies and institutions, please tell me if it is your impression that each one is doing an excellent, good, only fair, or a poor job. Would you say (the Centers for Disease Control and Prevention, the CDC/the Federal Bureau of Investigation, the FBI/the Central Intelligence Agency, the CIA/the Department of Homeland Security/the Environmental Protection Agency, the EPA/the Food and Drug Administration, the FDA/the Internal Revenue Service, the IRS/the Department of Education) is doing an excellent, good, only fair, or a poor job?

Source: Pew Research Center for the People and the Press, "March 2010 Trust in Government Survey: Final Topline."

Table 3-14 Americans' Attitudes About Spending to Improve and Protect the Nation's Health, 1973–2008 (in percent)

	Too little	About right	Too much
1973	61	31	5
1974	64	28	5
1975	63	28	5
1976	60	31	5
1977	56	33	7
1978	55	34	7
1980	55	34	8
1982	56	32	6
1983	57	34	5
1984	58	32	7
1985	58	33	6
1986	59	34	4
1987	68	26	4
1988	66	28	3
1989	68	25	3
1990	72	22	3
1991	69	26	3
1993	72	17	8
1994	64	23	9
1996	66	23	8
1998	67	25	6
2000	72	23	4
2002	74	21	4
2004	78	17	4
2006	73	21	5
2008	75	18	5

Note: "Don't know" responses not shown

Question: (We are faced with many problems in this country, none of which can be solved easily or inexpensively. I'm going to name some of these problems, and for each one I'd like you to tell me whether you think we're spending too much money on it, too little money, or about the right amount.) Are we spending too much, too little, or about the right amount on improving and protecting the nation's health?

Source: James A. Davis, Tom W. Smith, and Peter V. Marsden, *General Social Surveys*, 1972–2008 (Chicago: National Opinion Research Center, 2008).

Table 3-15 Americans' Views of the Most Urgent Health Problem Facing the Country, 1991–2009 (in percent)

	Healthcare system issues	Health and disease problems	Bioterrorism	Other
1991	12	69	—	15
1992	30	48	—	18
1997	22	55	—	18
1999	14	67	—	13
2000	38	47	—	8
2001	22	39	22	9
2002	39	44	1	7
2003	52	33	1	8
2004	58	25	*	9
2005	42	46	*	5
2006	51	33	*	8
2007	56	32	—	4
2008	55	31	—	4
2009	50	37	—	3

Note: "Don't know" responses not shown. *= less than .5 percent.

Question: What would you say is the most urgent health problem facing this country at the present time? (open-ended)

Sources: For 1991–2007, Gallup Poll, "'Access' Gains as Top Perceived U.S. Health Problem," December 3, 2007. For 2008, Gallup Polls (Storrs, Conn.: Roper Center for Public Opinion Research, November 13–16, 2008; November 5–8, 2009).

Chapter 4

ATTITUDES ABOUT HEALTH CARE COSTS

Mollyann Brodie, Claudia Deane, Elizabeth C. Hamel, John M. Connolly

Health care is a bedeviling combination for consumers: both completely necessary and increasingly costly. And because these services are so indispensable, their price is impossible to ignore.

For the majority of Americans with health insurance coverage, costs show up as premiums that every year take up a greater share of their paychecks, as rising deductibles or co-payments when they visit a doctor's office or pharmacy, and as direct payments to practitioners for visits or treatments that may not be covered under their particular plan. All these aspects of coverage have become more expensive in recent years.

In 1999 the average worker paid $1,543 per year in premiums for family coverage. By 2009 that average worker was paying more than double that amount—$3,515 per year—and the total annual premium cost of an employer-sponsored family health insurance policy (including the share the employer paid) had topped $13,000 (**Table 4–1**).[1] Looked at in slightly different terms to provide a broader comparison, from 1999 to 2009 the cost of health insurance premiums increased by 131 percent, while workers' earnings increased by only 38 percent and overall inflation was 28 percent.[2]

Deductibles and co-payments are also trending upward. In 2006 the average deductible for a person with single coverage in a PPO (preferred provider organization) was $473. Three years later, it was $634.

The numbers mean that a large share of the public is spending more on health care than ever before. In 1996 about 16 percent of Americans were spending more than 10 percent of their family income on health care. By 2003 the share experiencing this level of burden was more than 19 percent, representing an additional 11.7 million people.[3]

These costs impact a wide range of important life decisions. Determining what level of coverage to sign up for requires a constant balance between Americans' estimates of what health care services they and their family may need and what insurance plan they can afford. The availability of health care benefits, or lack thereof, impacts individuals' choices about which jobs to take, which to keep, and which to leave. And paying for coverage and care often involves decisions about what other important goods and services individuals will have to live without.

These problems are magnified tremendously for the more than 46 million Americans who face the health care marketplace with no insurance whatsoever. And the number of uninsured Americans—those most vulnerable to the explosive rise in health care costs—is also on the rise, increasing steadily each year since 2000. Between 2007 and 2008, the number of uninsured grew from 45.7 to 46.3 million.[4]

As much as the rising cost of health care is a challenge for individuals and employers, it is an equally overwhelming challenge for the federal and state governments that provide public insurance for large groups of Americans including the elderly, the disabled, low-income mothers and children, and veterans. In 2007 the government paid for 40 percent of all health services and supplies, running up a bill of $845.8 billion.[5] Total national health spending increased from about 6 percent of GDP (gross domestic product) in 1965 to more than 16 percent in 2007, and it is projected to reach 20 percent of GDP by 2018. Faced with these projections, many have raised concerns about the long-term impact of rising health care costs on the federal budget deficit.[6]

Aware of the budgetary implications of rising health care costs and the growing public frustration surrounding the topic, policymakers have repeatedly, and unsuccessfully, attempted to find ways to rein in prices. Over the last several decades, each attempt at controlling the rise of health care costs has failed.[7]

In the 1960s the creation of Medicare and Medicaid, government health care programs for elderly and poor Americans, helped to reduce the burden of medical expenses on the private sector, but only temporarily, and health care costs began to rise rapidly once again in the late 1960s. In the early 1970s wage and price controls slowed the rise of costs, but within a few years prices rose swiftly once again. In the 1990s managed care—incorporating greater use of health maintenance organizations (HMOs)—was touted as a potential solution to the cost problem. This approach not only failed to control costs, which reached a double-digit rate of growth by 2001, but also proved unpopular with consumers. Neither government regulation nor private competition in the marketplace has effectively controlled the rate of growth in health care costs for more than a few years at a time. Health care costs were once again at the forefront of the 2009–2010 national debate over health care reform, and it remains to be seen what impact, if any, the recently passed Patient Protection and Affordability Act will have on the trajectory of these costs.

While policymakers search for ways to address the health care cost challenge, Americans continue to face the problem of high prices on a day-to-day basis, often with profound effects on their lives. As the price of health care continues to rise, some Americans have gone without health insurance, risked their health by not seeking medical attention when they needed it, or endured financial hardships as a result of the enormous expense of some procedures. More generally, rising health care costs have increased the levels of stress and concern that many Americans feel about paying for health care and the way health problems might impact their general financial well-being. In this chapter we examine Americans' attitudes about this ongoing problem, their experiences with rising health care costs, and their opinions about possible policy solutions.

Attitudes about Health Care Costs

Even though a large majority of the public—more than eight in ten—have some sort of health insurance, many worry about being able to pay for the health care that they and their families need. These worries have driven the cost issue to the forefront of the public's agenda for government.

Personal Worries about Affording Health Care

No matter what their actual experiences are, most Americans report experiencing at least some worry about the way rising prices may affect their ability to get care. When asked to compare their health care concerns with their worries about other possible problems, Americans consistently put health care at or near the top of their list. Worries about having to pay more for health care or insurance were most common (a range of 31 percent to 49 percent said they were "very worried"), and they were almost tied with more general concerns about their income not keeping up with rising prices (36 percent to 47 percent were "very worried"). The share saying they were very worried about not being able to afford the health care services they think they need (28 percent to 42 percent) has consistently ranked third. In fact, since early 2004 the proportion of the public saying they were very worried about medical or health care issues (including paying for prescription drugs) outranked worries about paying a mortgage or rent, being a victim of violent crime or terrorist attacks, or losing a job (**Table 4–2**).[8]

A considerable share of Americans have doubts about their ability to pay for the usual health care costs that a family requires. In 2010 about three in ten (31 percent) said they were either "not too confident" or "not at all confident" that they had enough money or health insurance to pay for these costs. In addition, nearly four in ten (38 percent) said they were either "not too confident" or "not at all confident" they had enough money or insurance to pay for a major illness. Both of these proportions have remained fairly steady since the late 1970s, indicating that this fear has been an enduring problem for a sizable minority across the nation (**Table 4–3**).[9]

A notable proportion of adults also have concerns about paying for health care in the future. In 2005, four in ten said they were "very worried" about not being able to pay medical costs when they are elderly, and nearly as many (36 percent) said they were "very worried" about not being able to afford nursing home or home care services. Three in ten insured adults (32 percent) were "very worried" about health insurance becoming too expensive, and two in ten of the insured were "very worried" about losing their health insurance. Three in ten adults (31 percent) were "very worried" about not being able to afford prescription drugs.[10]

Given this widespread worry, it follows that the health care cost problem is one that Americans most often view through a personal lens. When asked what concerns them most about rising health care costs, the plurality (35 percent) said increases in the amount people pay for their health insurance premiums and other out-of-pocket costs. Fewer people mentioned big picture concerns, such as increases in what the nation as a whole spends on health (mentioned by 20 percent), increased spending on government health insurance programs (15 percent), or increases in insurance premiums paid by employers (14 percent).[11]

In a 2009 survey, 47 percent of Americans said they were dissatisfied with their health care costs, and a similar share (48 percent) said they were at least "somewhat satisfied" with their own costs. People were much more likely to report dissatisfaction with the cost of their health care than with the quality of care they received (78 percent said they were at least somewhat satisfied with their quality of care, while 18 percent were dissatisfied).[12]

Most Important Health Care Problem for Government to Address

Perhaps as a result of their worries, concerns, and dissatisfaction, Americans have consistently put health care costs at the top of their list when it comes to the health care issue they would most like to see government address. Asked in an open-ended format to name the one or two most important problems in health care, since 2000 Americans have consistently put costs above other major worries, including access to care and seniors' health concerns, such as the Medicare program. The proportion naming the issue has also been on the rise over the time period, from roughly one-quarter to closer to four in ten (37 percent in August 2006) (**Table 4–4**).[13]

When people were given a closed-ended list of options, meaning they were provided a set number of responses from which to choose rather than answering the question in their own words, they still chose affordable health care and health insurance (38 percent) as their top concern, and they placed expanding coverage to most Americans just behind (34 percent) (**Table 4–5**).[14] When controlling costs versus increasing coverage were pitted directly without other options offered, a larger share chose costs (59 percent) over coverage (39 percent) in a September 2009 survey.[15]

Health Care Seen as Overpriced

Finally, the public overwhelmingly believes health care services are unreasonably priced. In 2006 more than eight in ten Americans said hospital charges and prescription drug prices were unreasonably high compared to other goods and services they purchase. Significant majorities said the same about health insurance premiums (70 percent), nursing home charges (63 percent), and physician fees (59 percent). The one exception was generic drugs, which three in four thought *were* reasonably priced.[16] As is true in many cases when it comes to public opinion, views are more positive when people are asked about their own doctors; in 2009 roughly two-thirds thought their own doctors' charges were reasonable, while about a quarter said they were unreasonable.[17]

Experiences Paying for Health Care

As overall national spending on health care continues to rise, individual Americans report experiencing the effects of this trend. The public reports not only paying more for health care, but also experiencing many other financial consequences that affect their daily lives as a result of this obligation. In 2009, half the public said that their health care costs had increased in the previous year, including 21 percent who said they went up "a lot."[18] When asked about the cost of health care relative to other expenses, another 2009 survey found nearly six in ten (59 percent) said that the cost of their health care had gone up compared to other household expenses.[19] Taking a longer-term view, in 2005, two in three insured adults said that their health insurance premiums, which they pay directly, had gone up in the past five years, with 38 percent saying they went up a lot. Fifty-two percent said their co-payments for medical visits and services went up, with two in ten saying they went up a lot. And nearly half (49 percent) said their insurance deductibles had gone up, with 25 percent saying they went up a lot.[20]

Difficulty Paying for Health Care

A relatively large group of Americans report having difficulty paying for the medical care they need. In 2005 about one in five (21 percent) said they currently had medical bills that were overdue.[21] In surveys from 2006 through 2009, between one in five and one-third reported that during the past year they or another family member in their household had had problems paying medical bills.[22] Among those who had problems paying bills, six in ten (61 percent) said the amount owed was more than $1,000. These burdensome bills were for a variety of services: 29 percent of those who claimed they had problems paying said the bills were mainly for doctor visits; 25 percent said they were mainly emergency room visits; 15 percent cited prescription drugs; and 14 percent said their problem bills were mainly for hospital stays.[23]

Some Americans also reported that medical bills have caused a number of negative financial consequences in their lives. Twelve percent said they have had difficulty paying other bills in the past year because of medical bills; 11 percent said they had been contacted by a collection agency; 11 percent said they had used up all or most of their savings; 7 percent said they had been unable to pay for basic necessities, such as food, heat, or housing; 6 percent said they had borrowed money or gotten a loan; and 2 percent said they had declared bankruptcy. Nearly two in ten (19 percent) Americans said they had at least one of these problems in the past year (**Table 4–6**).[24]

Prescription Drugs

Obtaining prescription drugs is a common way that Americans use the health care system and a major component of medical treatment. A majority of Americans (54 percent) report that they currently take prescriptions drugs, and nearly two in ten (19 percent) say they regularly take four or more such medications. In 2008, four in ten adults said it was at least somewhat of a problem for their family to pay for the prescription medicines they needed, including 16 percent who said it was a serious problem. On the other hand, 58 percent said it was not much of a problem.[25]

Consequences of Rising Health Care Costs

In 2008 nearly half of adults (47 percent) said that during the past year they or a family member had done one of the following because of the cost: postponed getting needed health care, not filled a prescription, skipped a recommended treatment or test, cut pills in half or skipped doses of medicine, or had problems getting mental health care. Many of those who reported these types of problems said their medical conditions worsened as a result (**Table 4–7**).[26]

Fifteen percent of adults in 2005 said there was a time in the past year when either they or a family member living in their household needed medical care but did not get it. When these people were asked why they did not get the needed care, nearly six in ten (59 percent) said it was because it would have cost too much. Many in this heavily impacted group reported that they had experienced a number of other, secondary effects of not receiving needed medical care. Majorities of them said they lost a significant amount of time at work, school, or other important life activities (53 percent) or experienced a serious increase in their stress level (79 percent). Half said that not getting the medical care they needed resulted in a temporary disability that included a significant amount of pain and suffering, and a smaller share said that they developed a long-term disability (15 percent).[27]

Vulnerable Populations

Vulnerable populations, such as those who are chronically ill or uninsured, have particular difficulty paying for health care and are more likely to report going without the care they need due to cost. They are also more likely to experience additional consequences in their financial situations and lifestyles as a result of their health care expenses.

The Chronically Ill

Chronic illnesses are a pervasive challenge, currently impacting a significant number of U.S. families. In 2008 nearly three in ten Americans (28 percent) said either they or a household member had a chronic health condition or a disability that kept them from participating fully in work, housework, school, or other activities, including 18 percent who said they personally had such a condition. Faced with more persistent, ongoing medical needs, those grappling with chronic illnesses are significantly more likely to be affected by the high cost of health care.

Across a range of financial impacts, adults in households where someone has a chronic condition or disability that limits daily activity were more likely to say they had problems paying for their medical or health care. In 2008 this group was more likely than those in households without a chronic condition (55 percent to 41 percent) to say that they or a family member postponed getting needed care, skipped a recommended test or treatment, did not fill a prescription, cut pills or skipped doses of a medicine, or had problems getting mental health care in the past year because of cost. They were also more likely to say that they or a family member had problems paying medical bills in the past year (39 percent to 26 percent) and that these problems had a major impact on their family (26 percent to 14 percent) (**Table 4–8**).[28]

A 2006 survey of households dealing with a current or recent occurrence of cancer highlighted the ways Americans facing a life-threatening illness are particularly vulnerable to financial problems. Nearly half (46 percent) of those whose families had been affected by the disease said the costs of cancer care were a burden on their family, including 17 percent who said such costs were a "major burden." One-quarter said they used up all or most of their savings, and one in ten reported being unable to pay for basic necessities, including food, heat, and housing. Thirteen percent said they borrowed money from relatives; 11 percent sought the aid of a charity or public assistance; and 7 percent borrowed money or took out another mortgage on their home. In some cases, cost can be a factor that affects the treatment decisions of people with cancer: one in twelve (8 percent) said they delayed or did not get care for cancer because of the cost.[29]

The Uninsured

Health care costs have an especially heavy impact on the uninsured in the United States. First, the price of insurance stands as a barrier to gaining coverage. Among the 16 percent of adults who said they were uninsured in 2008, cost was at the top of the list of reasons for their plight, with 37 percent of this group saying that they did not have insurance due to excessive cost, followed by 22 percent who mentioned unemployment or job loss as the main reason they were uninsured.[30]

Facing the system with no additional resources outside their own personal finances, the uninsured are significantly more likely to report problems paying for the medical and health care they need. Among insured Americans, 27 percent said they or a family member had problems paying medical bills in the past year, but more than twice as many uninsured Americans (62 percent) reported the same problem. Those without insurance were two to three times as likely as their insured counterparts to say that they or a family member had taken various steps in the past year because of cost, including relying on home remedies or over-the-counter drugs instead of seeing a doctor, skipping dental care or checkups, putting off needed care, skipping a recommended test or treatment, not filling a prescription, and cutting pills in half or skipping doses of medication (**Table 4–9**).[31]

Returning to the study of families impacted by cancer, nearly half (46 percent) of those facing cancer without health insurance said they used up all or most of their savings to pay for treatments, and more than four in ten (41 percent) said they were unable to pay for basic necessities. More than a third (34 percent) had been contacted by a collection agency.[32]

Health Insurance No Guarantee of Protection against Costs

Having health insurance is a major hedge against facing the full costs of the increasingly expensive health care system, but it does not provide Americans with ironclad protection. The large majority (69 percent) of those who reported having problems paying their medical bills during the last year were in fact insured.[33]

This situation is particularly common when insured Americans face an illness that is both serious and chronic, as in the case of cancer. The study of households dealing with cancer found that although most people (95 percent) reported being covered by insurance during their treatment, cost and billing issues remained a difficult problem. Among those with insurance, nearly one in four said their plan paid less than expected for a bill; one in eight said they were surprised to find out their plan would not pay anything for a bill they thought was covered; one in ten reached the limit of what their insurance would pay for cancer treatment; and one in twelve were turned away or unable to get a specific type of treatment because of insurance issues.[34]

Exposure to cost-related problems also varies *across* the insured population itself. Non-elderly Americans with moderate and lower incomes (less than $75,000 a year) were significantly more likely to report problems than their wealthier counterparts or the senior population that relies on public insurance programs such as Medicare (**Table 4–10**).[35]

Lowering Health Care Costs

As costs continue to rise and public concern over the issue continues to grow, policymakers attempting to address the problem must worry not only about the content of their policy proposals, but also about how Americans might react to them. Unfortunately, public opinion on cost containment does not offer clear directives or easy choices.

But one thing is clear: a substantial appetite exists for action on the problem of high health care costs. A November 2006 survey found that three in four Americans thought that Congress should do something about the perceived "unreasonably high" prices of everything from hospital stays to prescription drugs. At least some of this desire to have the government address health care costs may stem from the public's concern about the impact of rising health care costs on the overall economy. In 2009 about three-quarters (76 percent) said the rising cost of health care was a serious threat to the nation's economy, including nearly half (49 percent) who perceived the threat as "very serious."[36]

Furthermore, the public has high expectations when it comes to the potential impact that policymakers can have on the problem: in 2008 nearly six in ten registered voters (58 percent) said the president and Congress can do "a lot" when it comes to addressing the high cost of health care, and a quarter said they could do "a little." Only 15 percent thought health care costs were "mostly beyond [the president's and Congress's] control."[37]

Perceived Reasons for Rising Health Care Costs

To understand what solutions Americans are willing to embrace to solve the problem of rising costs, it helps to begin by looking at their views on what is *causing* higher prices. As is true in other domains of public opinion, the most popular reasons have to do with corporate bad actors and general feelings about fraud and waste, rather than those that concern systemic changes in both the population and the treatments developed to serve them.

Asked to rate the importance of a series of possible reasons for rising costs, half the public named drug and insurance company profit margins as "one of the single biggest factors" in 2006. More than a third pointed to the number of malpractice lawsuits (37 percent), the amount of fraud and waste in the health care system (37 percent), and "doctors and hospitals making too much money" (36 percent) as the biggest factors. About three in ten identified insurance administrative costs (30 percent); "people getting medical treatments they don't really need" (30 percent); unhealthy lifestyles (29 percent); and the use of expensive new drugs, treatments, and technology (28 percent) as the biggest factors. A somewhat smaller share cited the aging of the population (23 percent). Just 12 percent said that "more people are getting better medical care than ever before" was one of the single biggest reasons for rising health care costs.[38] Similar results have been found in surveys dating back to 2002 (**Table 4–11**).[39]

Although pharmaceutical companies do stand out as particularly profitable (ranking as the country's third most profitable industry in 2008), experts are more likely to point to the expanding use of expensive high-tech medical equipment, surgical procedures, and drugs as the strongest reason for the cost boom.[40] As noted, fewer than a third of the public pointed to medical technology as one of the most important factors causing higher health costs, ranking eighth on a list of ten possible factors.

Government versus Marketplace Strategies for Reducing Health Costs

Decades of study and policy experimentation have made one thing clear: there is no one easy solution to the nation's health cost problem. In general, proposals can be divided into two broad categories, those that primarily involve government regulation and those that rely on market competition in the private sector. Asking about these potentially complex solutions in simple, straightforward questions is a challenge for survey researchers, and results in this area are often frustratingly vague.

A 2006 survey found that most Americans seem to think that *both* government regulation and market forces would be at least somewhat effective at controlling costs, with 80 percent choosing market forces, and 62 percent choosing government regulation. In evaluating this sentiment, however, it is worth noting that in the same survey, 67 percent said that the current system is at least somewhat effective in controlling costs (**Table 4–12**).[41]

Although Americans have a healthy distrust of the federal government's ability to execute critical tasks, surveys suggest that government regulation is not anathema in the area of health costs. In 2008 about half the public (51 percent) said that there was not enough government regulation of health care costs, while a quarter said there was too much regulation, and 21 percent said there was about the right amount.[42] Similarly, about half said there was not enough government regulation when it came to the cost of health insurance (51 percent) and prescription drugs (48 percent).[43]

Historically, Americans have favored price controls for medical expenses, with support rising during the 1980s and remaining stable through the mid-1990s. Surveys in more recent years, however, show that support varies among different types of health care services and products, with larger shares favoring price controls for prescription drugs than for doctor bills, where opinion is more evenly divided (**Table 4–13**).[44]

To take one specific policy example: Congress has debated whether the Medicare prescription drug program should be amended so that the government could use its buying power to directly negotiate with pharmaceutical companies to reduce prices for beneficiaries. Even though six in ten believe such negotiations would lead to government price controls on prescription drugs, fully 85 percent would back such a proposal, suggesting that price controls are acceptable in some situations.[45]

But at the same time that government regulation appears somewhat popular, Americans also have expressed a fondness for marketplace solutions to health care problems, with large majorities supporting tax credits for people to purchase private insurance as a way to expand coverage. In a more specific example of backing for a market-based solution to the cost problem, roughly seven in ten supported legalizing the importation of prescription drugs from Canada as a means of potentially lowering prices.[46]

Given that both types of solutions meet with initial approval from the public, survey researchers have attempted to push the issue by pitting primarily government-based solutions head-to-head against market-based solutions, asking the public to choose which would be more effective. Results here are somewhat mixed. A 2006 survey found that the majority (59 percent) said that Congress should involve the government in limiting what doctors, hospitals, and insurance companies can charge, while 34 percent would prefer to see the legislative branch use tax incentives to change consumer behavior.[47] The government also came out somewhat ahead in a 2009 poll that asked whether it would "do a better or worse job than private insurance companies in holding down health care costs"; 47 percent said better, and 38 percent said worse.[48] But a 2008 survey that asked more generically about whether federal regulation or the marketplace would be more effective at controlling costs found the public evenly divided between the two (**Table 4–14**).[49]

Reducing Overtreatment as a Way to Lower Health Care Costs

During the 2009–2010 debate over health reform, a number of additional strategies were discussed as ways to lower health care costs. Some experts suggested that as much as 30 percent of medical care is unnecessary, producing no clinical benefit, and that reducing such unnecessary care provides an opportunity for lowering costs.[50] But surveys suggest that the public may be at odds with experts on this issue. As noted above, only three in ten see overtreatment as one of the biggest reasons for rising health care costs; overtreatment ranks fifth on a list of ten possible causes. Further, although about half the public (49 percent) believes the American health care system has a "major problem" with "too many patients getting medical tests and treatments that they don't really need," only 16 percent believe that they themselves have received unnecessary care. Americans are even more likely to feel the country's health care system has a problem with undertreatment than with overtreatment; 67 percent say that "too many patients not getting the medical tests and treatments they need" is a major problem with the U.S. system.[51]

Comparative Effectiveness Research

Many health policy experts have touted "comparative effectiveness research," which involves comparing different ways of treating particular conditions on the basis of factors such as benefits, risks, or costs, as a means of controlling rising health care costs. Legislation passed in early 2009 provided federal funding for such research, specifying that the funding be used to compare the clinical outcomes, effectiveness, risk, and benefits (but not the costs) of various technologies and treatments, and that such research could not be used to mandate coverage, reimbursement, or other policies for public or private payers.[52]

Surveys suggest the public is at least somewhat open to the idea of using such comparisons to make decisions about which treatments should be covered by insurance, but they are less comfortable with the idea of having the government get involved in those decisions. A 2008 survey found that more than half the public (56 percent) thought that insurance companies should not have to cover expensive new treatments that have not been proven more effective than other, less expensive options, while four in ten thought such treatments should be covered. Opinion was more narrowly divided when the public was asked about an expensive new treatment "recommended by a doctor," with 51 percent saying the insurance company should not have to pay for the treatment if there are other less expensive options, and 45 percent saying they should have to pay.[53]

The public is more skeptical when it comes to the government weighing in on such matters. Although 55 percent said they would trust "a panel of experts from an independent scientific organization" to make recommendations about which tests and treatments should be covered by insurance, support dropped to 41 percent when the words "appointed by the federal government" were added. Support was at a similar level for having the National Institutes of Health or "another government health agency" make such recommendations; 42 percent said they would trust such an agency, and 57 percent would not.[54]

Health Information Technology

Another strategy that has gained attention as a potential long-term cost-saver is greater use of electronic medical records (EMRs) and other health information technology. The public sees benefits to nationwide adoption of this technology, with about two-thirds saying that it would lead to improvements in quality of care for both the country as a whole (67 percent) and for their own families (62 percent). More than half also say that if the United States adopted an EMR system, fewer people would get unnecessary medical care (58 percent), and fewer would get sick or die as a result of medical errors (53 percent).[55]

When it comes to lowering costs, however, the public takes a distinctly different view from the proponents of EMRs. In 2009 a larger proportion thought the adoption of EMRs would increase the cost of health care in America than said it would decrease the cost (34 percent vs. 22 percent), and more than a third (36 percent) thought it would not have much impact either way. Views were even more pessimistic about the impact on personal costs, with 39 percent saying nationwide adoption of EMRs would increase their own family's health care costs, compared with 12 percent who thought it would bring their costs down, and 43 percent who thought they would stay about the same.[56]

Managed Care

One of the most widespread attempts in the past fifteen years to tackle rising health care costs has been the use of managed care plans. Under managed care, organizations such as health maintenance organizations (HMOs) attempt to improve efficiency and quality by coordinating care, and to cut costs by controlling consumers' choice of health care providers and the types of procedures an insurer will cover. The move toward increasing participation in this sort of insurance arrangement was instigated in earnest by the private marketplace in the 1990s, and adopted as a national policy proposal by President Bill Clinton in his failed legislative bid to reform the health care system.

But managed care has failed to fulfill its initial promise. Although higher enrollment and the possibility of a Clinton-backed overhaul had a dramatic effect in slowing the rate of increase in health spending in the mid-1990s, by the late 1990s spending was on the rise again, and with a vengeance.[57] Consumers took note of the trend, with a majority saying that they thought the increased use of HMOs had made no difference in controlling costs (**Table 4–15**).[58] At the same time, American consumers turned against the system, demanding more flexibility and voting with their feet. The share of covered workers enrolled in HMOs has declined since 2000, as more people chose PPO plans that provide more choice.[59]

Personal Strategies to Lower Health Care Costs

With little visible impact on rising health care costs being made on the policy front, Americans are left with little recourse in the battle against rising costs other than attempting to tackle the problem on an individual basis. These personal cost containment efforts are not currently widespread.

In 2005 about one in ten adults (11 percent) said they had negotiated with a physician or other health care provider to try to get a lower price for health care services in the past year; 24 percent of the uninsured population said they had negotiated with a provider. Those who negotiated for health care services did so for many different types of services, and the largest share reported negotiating for the price of a doctor or other provider visit. Fifty-eight percent of those who negotiated said they were successful in securing a lower price for services.[60]

Smaller shares of the public also said they attempted a variety of other strategies to reduce costs. A small proportion used the Internet to try to find a lower price for prescription drugs (9 percent), switched doctors to reduce the amount they pay directly out of their own pocket (7 percent), or surfed the Web to find a lower price for other types of health care services (6 percent) (**Table 4–16**).[61]

Despite the worries and concerns Americans have about their health care costs, most say that they do not often talk to their doctors about the cost of procedures and medications. When asked how often they ask about cheaper treatment options or medications when visiting a doctor, a third say they rarely or never discuss this with their doctor, while about a quarter (23 percent) say they do this "sometimes." Sixteen percent say they "often" discuss less costly treatments with their doctor, and 27 percent say they "always" do.[62] Similarly, more than half the public (55 percent) said in 2008 that when their doctor writes them a prescription for a drug they have not taken before, they do not usually talk to the doctor about its cost.[63] In 2009 fewer than a quarter of Americans (22 percent) said that in the past two years, they had asked their doctor what would be charged for a medical or lab test, and just about half (51 percent) said they think their doctor knows how much is charged for a medical test when he or she orders it.[64]

Conclusion

Health care costs are on the rise. These rising costs affect both the national economy and Americans' personal finances. Surveys suggest that Americans are well aware of the rising cost curve, that a significant proportion of them experience difficulty paying for the care they need, and that a majority, although not currently facing such extreme problems, are worried about being able to afford coverage and treatment. The cost of health care bears most heavily on the nation's vulnerable populations, particularly those with chronic illnesses and the uninsured. These personal concerns have driven the cost issue to the top of the public's list of pressing health care issues for the government to address.

Although the recently passed Patient Protection and Affordability Act contains many provisions designed to rein in health care costs over the long term, most of them will not be implemented until several years in the future, and it may take many more years before their effect, if any, is felt. In the short term, it is likely that people's premiums and out-of-pocket costs will continue to rise at a rate faster than their wages.

Currently, the public appears to adopt a welcoming attitude to a variety of possible solutions, including those based on greater government regulation and those based on marketplace competition. At the same time, there is no real consensus as to which of these would be the better approach. And more important, this apparent welcome is likely based more on frustration with the current situation than on an awareness of the ways that actual, concrete proposals might affect them personally.

Surveys suggest there are several general principles of public opinion to keep in mind as we try to understand how the public might react to the implementation of cost-related measures in the new law, and to any further attempts to contain health care costs. First, the public is not totally averse to government regulation—even price controls in certain circumstances—when the goal is reducing costs. The public is also generally interested in market-based solutions, such as consumer-directed arrangements where individuals shop around for the best prices or tax credits to influence consumer or employer behavior. And, given that advances in medical technology rank as experts' number one culprit in rising costs, the public's willingness to consider the idea that insurance companies should have to cover only those new technologies that are proven to be more effective than less expensive existing treatments may provide an opening for policymakers.

At the same time, only a small minority now practice the kinds of "smart shopper" behaviors necessary for market-based solutions to succeed. Limiting policymakers in future efforts at cost containment, the managed care experiment and survey research done on topics such as universal coverage suggest that any proposal that threatens individuals' flexibility to choose providers and treatments will not be warmly received by a significant portion of the public.

All these factors put together mean that despite the desire for action, there will be significant room to move public opinion away from any given policy solution once the specific details are laid out and implementation begins, and suggest that serious challenges lie ahead for policymakers trying to garner significant public support for measures to contain costs.

Notes

[1] Kaiser Family Foundation and the Health Research and Educational Trust, "Employer Health Benefits: 2009 Annual Survey," http://ehbs.kff.org/pdf/2009/7936.pdf.

[2] Ibid.; Bureau of Labor Statistics, "Seasonally Adjusted Data from the Current Employment Statistics Survey" (April to April), http://data.bls.gov/PDQ/outside.jsp?survey=ce; Bureau of Labor Statistics, "Consumer Price Index, U.S. City Average of Annual Inflation" (April to April), http://data.bls.gov/PDQ/outside.jsp?survey=cu.

[3] Jessica S. Banthin and Didem M. Bernard, "Changes in Financial Burdens for Health Care: National Estimates for the Population Younger than 65 Years, 1996 to 2003," *JAMA: Journal of the American Medical Association* 296 (December 13, 2006): 2712–9.

[4] U.S. Census Bureau, "Income, Poverty, and Health Insurance Coverage in the United States: 2008," http://www.census.gov/prod/2009pubs/p60–236.pdf.

[5] Micah Hartman, Anne Martin, Patricia McDonnell, Aaron Catlin, and the National Health Expenditure Accounts Team, "National Health Spending in 2007: Slower Drug Spending Contributes to Lowest Rate of Overall Growth Since 1998," *Health Affairs* 28 (January-February 2009): 246–261.

[6] Peter R. Orszag, "Testimony of Peter R. Orszag, Director of the Office of Management and Budget, before the Committee on Finance, U.S. Senate, March 10, 2009," http://www .whitehouse.gov/omb/assets/testimony/031009_healthcare.pdf.

[7] Drew E. Altman and Larry Levitt, "The Sad Story of Health Care Cost Containment as Told in One Chart," *Health Affairs,* Web Exclusive, January 23, 2002, http://content.healthaffairs .org/cgi/reprint/hlthaff.w2.83v1.

[8] Kaiser Family Foundation polls (Storrs, Conn.: Roper Center for Public Opinion Research, February 4–8, 2004; April 1–5, 2004; June 4–8, 2004; August 5–8, 2004; October 14–17, 2004; December 2–5, 2004; March 31–April 3, 2005; October 4–9, 2005; February 2–7, 2006; August 3–8, 2006; October 5–10, 2006; March 8–13, 2007; May 31–June 5, 2007; November 28–December 9, 2007; April 3–13, 2008; September 8–13, 2008; October 8–13, 2008; July 7–14, 2009).

[9] American Medical Association polls (Storrs, Conn.: Roper Center for Public Opinion Research, January 1977, September 1978, September 1979, July 1981, August 1982, January 1990, January 1991, January-February 1992, January-February 1993, January-February 1994); Harvard School of Public Health/Robert Wood Johnson Foundation Poll (Storrs, Conn.: Roper Center for Public Opinion Research, August 16–20, 2000); *USA Today*/Kaiser Family Foundation/Harvard School of Public Health, "Health Care Costs Survey: Summary and Chartpack," August 2005, http://www.kff.org/newsmedia/upload/7371.pdf; Kaiser Family Foundation, "Kaiser Health Tracking Poll: May 2010," http://www.kff.org/kaiserpolls/ upload/8075-T.pdf.

[10] *USA Today*/Kaiser Family Foundation/Harvard School of Public Health, "Health Care Costs Survey: Summary and Chartpack," August 2005.

[11] Kaiser Family Foundation, "Kaiser Health Tracking Poll: July 2009," http://www.kff.org/ kaiserpolls/upload/7943.pdf.

[12] CBS News/*New York Times* Poll (Storrs, Conn.: Roper Center for Public Opinion Research, September 19–23, 2009).

[13] Kaiser Family Foundation poll trend date, 2000–2006.

[14] Kaiser Family Foundation, "Kaiser Health Tracking Poll: February 2009, Toplines," http:// www.kff.org/kaiserpolls/upload/7867.pdf.

[15] Gallup/*USA Today* Poll (Storrs, Conn.: Roper Center for Public Opinion Research, September 11–13, 2009).

[16] Kaiser Family Foundation/Harvard School of Public Health, "The Public's Health Care Agenda for the New Congress and Presidential Campaign," December 2006, http://www.kff .org/kaiserpolls/upload/7598.pdf.

[17] NPR/Kaiser Family Foundation/Harvard School of Public Health, "The Public and the Health Care Delivery System," April 2009, http://www.kff.org/kaiserpolls/upload/7888.pdf.

[18] Ibid.

[19] CBS News/*New York Times* Poll (Storrs, Conn.: Roper Center for Public Opinion Research, April 1–5, 2009).

[20] *USA Today*/Kaiser Family Foundation/Harvard School of Public Health, "Health Care Costs Survey: Summary and Chartpack," August 2005.

[21] Ibid.

[22] Kaiser Family Foundation, "Kaiser Health Tracking Poll: September 2009, Topline," http://www.kff.org/kaiserpolls/upload/7988.pdf.

[23] Kaiser Family Foundation, "Kaiser Health Tracking Poll: February 2009, Toplines."

[24] Kaiser Family Foundation, "Kaiser Health Tracking Poll: August 2009, Topline," http://www.kff.org/kaiserpolls/upload/7964.pdf.

[25] See Chapter 8 for more on prescription drug spending. *USA Today*/Kaiser Family Foundation/Harvard School of Public Health, "The Public on Prescription Drugs and Pharmaceutical Companies," March 2008, http://www.kff.org/kaiserpolls/upload/7747.pdf.

[26] Kaiser Family Foundation, "Kaiser Health Tracking Poll: Election 2008," Issue 11, October 2008, http://www.kff.org/kaiserpolls/upload/7832.pdf.

[27] *USA Today*/Kaiser Family Foundation/Harvard School of Public Health, "Health Care Costs Survey: Toplines," August 2005, http://www.kff.org/newsmedia/upload/7372.pdf.

[28] Kaiser Family Foundation Poll (Storrs, Conn.: Roper Center for Public Opinion Research, October 8–13, 2008).

[29] *USA Today*/Kaiser Family Foundation/Harvard School of Public Health, "National Survey of Households Affected by Cancer," November 2006, http://www.kff.org/kaiserpolls/upload/7590.pdf.

[30] NPR/Kaiser Family Foundation/Harvard School of Public Health, "The Public and the Health Care Delivery System."

[31] Kaiser Family Foundation Poll (Storrs, Conn.: Roper Center for Public Opinion Research, September 11–18, 2009).

[32] *USA Today*/Kaiser Family Foundation/Harvard School of Public Health, "National Survey of Households Affected by Cancer."

[33] ABC News/Kaiser Family Foundation/*USA Today*, "Health Care in America 2006 Survey," October 2006, http://www.kff.org/kaiserpolls/upload/7573.pdf.

[34] *USA Today*/Kaiser Family Foundation/Harvard School of Public Health, "National Survey of Households Affected by Cancer."

[35] Kaiser Family Foundation Poll, September 11–18, 2009.

[36] CBS News/*New York Times* Poll (Storrs, Conn.: Roper Center for Public Opinion Research, July 24–28, 2009).

[37] Kaiser Family Foundation/Harvard School of Public Health, "Pre-Election Poll: Voters, Health Care and the 2008 Election: Toplines," October 2008, http://www.kff.org/kaiserpolls/upload/7829.pdf.

[38] ABC News/Kaiser Family Foundation/*USA Today*, "Health Care in America 2006 Survey," October 2006.

[39] Kaiser Family Foundation polls (Storrs, Conn.: Roper Center for Public Opinion Research, March 28–May 1, 2002; February 6–10, 2003; October 14–17, 2004); Kaiser Family Foundation/Harvard School of Public Health Poll (Storrs, Conn.: Roper Center for Public Opinion Research, November 4–28, 2004); *USA Today*/Kaiser Family Foundation/Harvard School of Public Health, "Health Care Costs Survey: Summary and Chartpack," August 2005.

[40] *Fortune* magazine, "Fortune 500: Top Industries: Most Profitable," 2009, http://money.cnn.com/magazines/fortune/fortune500/2009/performers/industries/profits/; Congressional Budget

Office, "Technological Change and the Growth of Health Care Spending," January 2008, http://www.cbo.gov/ftpdocs/89xx/doc8947/01–31-TechHealth.pdf.

[41] ABC News/Kaiser Family Foundation/*USA Today*, "Health Care in America 2006 Survey."

[42] Kaiser Family Foundation/Harvard School of Public Health, "The Public's Health Care Agenda for the New President and Congress," January 2009, http://www.kff.org/kaiserpolls/upload/7853.pdf.

[43] Kaiser Family Foundation, "Kaiser Health Tracking Poll: Election 2008."

[44] Cambridge Reports Polls (Storrs, Conn.: Roper Center for Public Opinion Research, January 1979, July 1981, October 1982, October 1984); ABC News Poll (Storrs, Conn.: Roper Center for Public Opinion Research, January 14–17, 1994); Harris Interactive polls (Storrs, Conn.: Roper Center for Public Opinion Research, April 10–15, 2003; August 10–15, 2004).

[45] Kaiser Family Foundation/Harvard School of Public Health, "The Public's Health Care Agenda for the New Congress and Presidential Campaign," December 2006.

[46] Kaiser Family Foundation/Harvard School of Public Health, "The Public's Health Care Agenda for the New President and Congress," January 2009.

[47] Ibid.

[48] CBS News Poll (Storrs, Conn.: Roper Center for Public Opinion Research, August 27–31, 2009).

[49] Kaiser Family Foundation, "Kaiser Health Tracking Poll: Election 2008," Issue 11.

[50] Peter R. Orszag, "Increasing the Value of Federal Spending on Health Care," Testimony before the Committee on the Budget, U.S. House of Representatives, July 16, 2008, Congressional Budget Office, http://www.cbo.gov/ftpdocs/95xx/doc9563/07–16-HealthReform.pdf.

[51] NPR/Kaiser Family Foundation/Harvard School of Public Health, "The Public and the Health Care Delivery System."

[52] Kaiser Family Foundation, "Health Care Costs: A Primer," March 2009, http://www.kff.org/insurance/upload/7670_02.pdf.

[53] Kaiser Family Foundation/Harvard School of Public Health, "The Public's Health Care Agenda for the New President and Congress," January 2009.

[54] NPR/Kaiser Family Foundation/Harvard School of Public Health, "The Public and the Health Care Delivery System."

[55] Ibid.

[56] Ibid.

[57] Altman and Levitt, "The Sad Story of Health Care Cost Containment as Told in One Chart," *Health Affairs*.

[58] Kaiser Family Foundation/Harvard School of Public Health Polls (Storrs, Conn.: Roper Center for Public Opinion Research, August 22–September 23, 1997; August 6–20, 1998; April 10–22, 1999; July 2–August 8, 2001); Kaiser Family Foundation Poll (Storrs, Conn.: Roper Center for Public Opinion Research, August 5–8, 2004).

[59] Kaiser Family Foundation and the Health Research and Educational Trust, "Survey of Employer Health Benefits 2006," http://www.kff.org/insurance/7527/upload/7561.pdf.

60 *USA Today*/Kaiser Family Foundation/Harvard School of Public Health, "Health Care Costs Survey: Summary and Chartpack," August 2005.

61 Ibid.

62 Employee Benefit Research Institute Poll (Storrs, Conn.: Roper Center for Public Opinion Research, May 8–June 2, 2009).

63 *USA Today*/Kaiser Family Foundation/Harvard School of Public Health, "The Public on Prescription Drugs and Pharmaceutical Companies," March 2008.

64 NPR/Kaiser Family Foundation/Harvard School of Public Health, "The Public and the Health Care Delivery System."

Table 4-1 The Cost of Health Insurance Premiums, 1999–2009

		Worker Contribution	Employer Contribution	Total Premium
1999	Single	$318	$1,878	$2,196
	Family	$1,543	$4,247	$5,791
2000	Single	$334	$2,137	$2,471
	Family	$1,619	$4,819	$6,438
2001	Single	$355	$2,334	$2,689
	Family	$1,787	$5,269	$7,061
2002	Single	$466	$2,617	$3,083
	Family	$2,137	$5,866	$8,003
2003	Single	$508	$2,875	$3,383
	Family	$2,412	$6,657	$9,068
2004	Single	$558	$3,136	$3,695
	Family	$2,661	$7,289	$9,950
2005	Single	$610	$3,413	$4,024
	Family	$2,713	$8,167	$10,880
2006	Single	$627	$3,615	$4,242
	Family	$2,973	$8,508	$11,480
2007	Single	$694	$3,785	$4,479
	Family	$3,281	$8,824	$12,106
2008	Single	$721	$3,983	$4,704
	Family	$3,354	$9,325	$12,680
2009	Single	$779	$4,045	$4,824
	Family	$3,515	$9,860	$13,375

Source: Kaiser Family Foundation and the Health Research and Educational Trust, "Employer Health Benefits: 2009 Annual Survey."

Table 4-2 Americans' Worries about the Future, 2004–2009

Percent very worried	2/04	4/04	6/04	8/04	10/04	12/04	4/05	10/05	2/06	8/06	10/06	3/07	5/07	11/07	4/08	9/08	10/08	7/09
*Having to pay more for your health care or insurance	47	47	46	45	47	47	49	40	38	46	47	40	41	41	37	34	38	31
Your income not keeping up with rising prices	40	44	45	42	46	41	46	40	36	46	45	42	45	46	43	41	47	37
*Not being able to afford the health care services you think you need	38	39	36	40	38	37	42	34	32	34	39	35	36	35	29	28	31	34
*Not being able to afford the prescription drugs you need	36	37	34	38	35	35	35	32	28	31	37	33	33	31	27	27	25	27
*The quality of health care services you receive getting worse	29	31	29	30	30	34	32	28	27	25	33	30	32	33	26	24	26	28
Not being able to pay your rent/mortgage	27	28	24	31	27	26	29	22	23	22	30	27	25	27	21	21	25	29
Being the victim of a terrorist attack	20	20	23	20	23	22	19	18	21	21	23	23	25	22	18	18	19	20
Being the victim of violent crime	19	17	18	17	19	21	18	16	17	16	23	23	21	21	18	17	18	***
**Losing your job	21	23	20	25	18	21	23	16	20	17	24	18	19	23	21	21	27	28

Notes: *Indicates a health care issue; **Based on those who were employed; ***Question was not asked in 2009.

Question: I'm going to read you a list of things that some people worry about and others do not. I'd like you to tell me how worried you are about each of the following things. How worried are you about (READ ITEM)? Are you very worried, somewhat worried, not too worried, or not at all worried?

Sources: Kaiser Family Foundation polls (Storrs, Conn.: Roper Center for Public Opinion Research, February 4–8, 2004; April 1–5, 2004; June 4–8, 2004; October 14–17, 2004; December 2–5, 2004; March 31–April 3, 2005; October 4–9, 2005; February 2–7, 2006; August 3–8, 2006; October 5–10, 2006; November 28–December 9, 2007; April 3–13, 2008; October 8–13, 2008; July 7–14, 2009).

Table 4-3 Americans' Confidence in Their Ability to Pay Health Care Costs, 1977–2010 (in percent)

Have enough money or health insurance to pay for . . .		
	Confident	Not confident
The usual medical costs a family requires		
1977	69	29
1978	71	29
1979	62	38
1981	66	34
1982	72	27
2005	66	33
2010	67	31
A major illness		
1978	50	50
1979	47	53
1981	49	51
1982	59	41
1990	66	31
1991	64	35
1992	55	45
1993	54	46
1994	58	41
2000	67	33
2005	59	40
2010	60	38

Note: "Don't know" responses not shown.

Question: Generally, how confident are you that you have enough money or health insurance to pay for the usual medical costs that (a family requires/that you and your family require)? Would you say you are very confident, somewhat confident, not too confident, or not at all confident? (1977–1982, 2005, 2010)

Question: Generally, how confident are you that you have enough money or health insurance to pay for a major illness? Are you very confident, somewhat confident, not very confident, or not at all confident? (1978–1990)

Question: How confident are you that you have enough money or health insurance to pay for each of the following? Are you very confident, somewhat confident, not very confident, or not at all confident that you have enough money or insurance to pay for a major illness? (1991–1994)

Question: How confident are you that you would have enough money or health insurance to pay for a major illness? Are you very confident, somewhat confident, not too confident, or not at all confident? (2000, 2005)

Question: How confident are you that you would have enough money or health insurance to pay for a major illness, such as a heart attack, cancer, or a serious injury that required hospitalization? Would you say you are very confident, somewhat confident, not too confident, or not at all confident? (2010)

Sources: American Medical Association polls (Storrs, Conn.: Roper Center for Public Opinion Research, January 1977, September 1978, September 1979, July 1981, August 1982, January 1990, January 1991, January-February 1992, January-February 1993, January-February 1994); Harvard School of Public Health/Robert Wood Johnson Foundation (Storrs, Conn.: Roper Center for Public Opinion Research, August 16–20, 2000); *USA Today*/Kaiser Family Foundation/Harvard School of Public Health Poll, "Health Care Costs Survey: Summary and Chartpack," August 2005; Kaiser Family Foundation, Kaiser Health Tracking Poll: May 2010.

Table 4-4 Americans' Views on the Most Important Health or Health Care Problems for Government to Address, 2000–2006

Percent saying each is one of the top two for government to address

	Costs	Access to care	Seniors' issues	Medical conditions	Insurance company concerns	Other policy concerns
2000						
October	27	14	20	6	10	12
December	22	13	20	7	11	8
2001						
February	22	16	18	9	8	6
April	24	12	21	12	9	5
June	32	24	23	19	9	15
August	34	15	22	14	10	11
October	27	19	20	13	11	13
December	27	19	20	18	11	10
2002						
February	26	19	22	14	9	12
April	24	18	17	17	9	8
June	31	16	16	7	7	4
October	35	20	21	14	10	8
December	36	22	19	12	8	9
2003						
February	35	17	32	19	8	10
April	35	23	23	16	8	9
June	38	23	19	16	6	8
August	42	19	22	11	8	9
October	39	22	23	13	5	11
December	35	14	25	9	8	7
2004						
February	44	23	24	17	6	9
April	43	19	21	20	9	9
August	46	26	15	10	4	8
December	46	25	16	12	6	7
2005						
February	42	21	16	18	8	8
April	43	26	17	11	6	10
August	39	23	13	12	3	10
December	32	18	15	11	6	9
2006						
April	39	25	14	11	4	9
August	37	25	13	11	8	15

Question: What do you think is the most important problem in health or health care for the government to address? Is there another health problem you think is almost as important?

Source: Kaiser Family Foundation poll trend data, 2000–2006.

Table 4-5 The Goals Americans Think Should Be Most Important in Health Reform (in percent)

Making health care and health insurance more affordable	38
Finding a way to provide health insurance coverage to most Americans	34
Reforming the existing health care system to provide higher quality, more cost-effective care	14
Combination/All of these are most important	4
None of these is very/most important	10

Note: Percentage shown includes those who named only one item as very important, as well as those who chose the item in the forced-choice follow-up.

Question: If the new president and Congress decide to take on health care reform, how important is each of the following as a goal of any health care reform plan? Making health care and health insurance more affordable/Finding a way to provide health insurance coverage to most Americans/Reforming the existing health care system to provide higher quality, more cost-effective care. Is this very important, somewhat important, not too important, or not at all important as a goal of health care reform? Those who said more than one item was "very important" were asked: Of the things you said are very important, which of these do you think should be the most important goal of any health care reform plan?

Source: Kaiser Family Foundation, "Kaiser Health Tracking Poll," February 2009.

Table 4-6 Americans' Problems Paying Medical Bills

Percent who say they had problems paying medical bills, and have had each of the following problems in the past twelve months because of medical bills:

Had difficulty paying other bills	12
Been contacted by a collection agency	11
Used up all or most of savings	11
Been unable to pay for basic necessities	7
Borrowed money/gotten loan/second mortgage on home	6
Declared bankruptcy	2
Had any of the above problems	19

Question: In the past twelve months, did you or another family member in your household have any problems paying medical bills, or not? (Asked if had problems paying medical bills:) In the past twelve months, have you (had difficulty paying other bills/been contacted by a collection agency/used up all or most of your savings/been unable to pay for basic necessities like food, heat, or housing/borrowed money or gotten a loan or another mortgage on your home/declared bankruptcy) because of medical bills?

Source: Kaiser Family Foundation, "Kaiser Health Tracking Poll: August 2009."

Table 4-7 Consequences of Health Care Costs

	Percent who say they or a family member have done each of the following in the past year because of cost	Percent who say their condition got worse as a result
Put off or postponed getting needed health care	36	22
Skipped a recommended treatment or test	31	19
Didn't fill a prescription	27	17
Cut pills or skipped doses of medicine	22	14
Had problems getting mental health care	12	9
Did any of the above	47	

Question: In the past year, have you or another family member living in your household (put off or postponed getting health care you needed/skipped a recommended medical test or treatment/not filled a prescription for a medicine/cut pills in half or skipped doses of medicine/had problems getting mental health care) because of the cost, or not?

Question: Did the condition get worse as a result of (putting off or postponing getting health care you needed/skipping a recommended medical test or treatment/not filling a prescription/cutting pills in half or skipping doses of medicine/having problems getting mental health care)?

Source: Kaiser Family Foundation, "Kaiser Health Tracking Poll: Election 2008," Issue 11, October 2008.

Table 4-8 Financial Impact on American Households in Which Someone Has a Chronic Condition or Disability

Percent who say in the past year, they or a family member . . .	Chronic condition or disability in household	No chronic condition or disability in household
Put off or postponed getting needed care because of cost	40	33
Skipped a recommended test or treatment because of cost	38	27
Didn't fill a prescription because of cost	37	20
Cut pills in half or skipped doses of a medicine because of cost	32	15
Had problems getting mental health care because of cost	15	9
Did any of the above	55	41
Have had problems paying medical bills	39	26
Problems paying medical bills have had a major impact on family	26	14

Question: In the past year, have you or another family member living in your household (put off or postponed getting health care you needed/skipped a recommended medical test or treatment/not filled a prescription for a medicine/cut pills in half or skipped doses of medicine/had problems getting mental health care) because of the cost, or not?

Question: In the past twelve months, did you or another family member living in your household have any problems paying medical bills, or not?

Question: (If had problems paying medical bills:) How much of an impact have these bills had on you and your family—a major impact, a minor impact, or no real impact on you and your family?

Source: Kaiser Family Foundation Poll (Storrs, Conn.: Roper Center for Public Opinion Research, October 8–13, 2008).

Table 4-9 Financial Impact on Americans without Health Insurance

Percent who say in the past twelve months, they or another family member living in their household . . .	Insured (all ages)	Uninsured (under 65)
Had problems paying medical bills	27	62
Relied on home remedies or over the counter drugs instead of going to see a doctor because of cost	37	77
Skipped dental care or checkups because of cost	27	70
Put off or postponed getting needed health care because of cost	25	67
Skipped a recommended test or treatment because of cost	21	61
Didn't fill a prescription because of cost	19	57
Cut pills in half or skipped doses of medicine because of cost	16	45
Had problems getting mental health care because of cost	7	17

Question: In the past 12 months, did you or another family member in your household have any problems paying medical bills, or not?

Question: In the past twelve months, have you or another family member living in your household (relied on home remedies or over the counter drugs instead of going to see a doctor/skipped dental care or checkups/put off or postponed getting health care you needed/skipped a recommended medical test or treatment/not filled a prescription/cut pills in half or skipped doses of medicine/had problems getting mental health care) because of the cost, or not?

Source: Kaiser Family Foundation Poll (Storrs, Conn.: Roper Center for Public Opinion Research, September 11–18, 2009).

Table 4-10   Consequences of Health Care Costs, by Age and Income

Percent who say in the past twelve months, they or another family member living in their household . . .	Insured non-elderly earning less than $75,000	Insured non-elderly earning $75,000 or more	Insured seniors (age 65+)
Had problems paying medical bills	33	18	24
Relied on home remedies or over the drugs instead of going to see a doctor because of cost	47	29	27
Skipped dental care or checkups because of cost	35	15	26
Put off or postponed getting needed health care because of cost	34	15	18
Skipped a recommended test or treatment because of cost	30	9	18
Didn't fill a prescription because of cost	28	6	17
Cut pills in half or skipped doses of medicine because of cost	21	9	14
Had problems getting mental health care because of cost	10	2	7

Question: In the past 12 months, did you or another family member in your household have any problems paying medical bills, or not?

Question: In the past twelve months, have you or another family member living in your household (relied on home remedies or over the counter drugs instead of going to see a doctor/skipped dental care or checkups/put off or postponed getting health care you needed/skipped a recommended medical test or treatment/not filled a prescription/cut pills in half or skipped doses of medicine/had problems getting mental health care) because of the cost, or not?

Source: Kaiser Family Foundation Poll (Storrs, Conn.: Roper Center for Public Opinion Research, September 11–18, 2009).

Table 4-11   Americans' Views of the Causes of Rising Health Care Costs, 2006 (in percent)

	One of the single biggest factors	Major factor but not one of the biggest	Less of a factor
Drug and insurance companies making too much money	50	36	13
Too many malpractice lawsuits	37	41	19
Fraud and waste in the system	37	40	20
Doctors and hospitals making too much money	36	33	29
Administrative costs in handling insurance claims	30	46	21
People getting treatments they don't really need	30	36	31
People needing more care because of unhealthy lifestyles	29	49	19
The use of expensive new drugs, treatments, and medical technology	28	52	16
The population is aging	23	51	25
More people are getting better medical care than ever before	12	40	44

Note: "Don't know" responses not shown.

Question: For each item I name, please tell me if you think it's one of the single biggest factors in rising health care costs, a major factor but not one of the single biggest ones, or less of a factor than that: Drug and insurance companies making too much money/Too many medical malpractice lawsuits/Fraud and waste in the health care system/Doctors and hospitals making too much money/Administrative costs in handling medical insurance claims/People getting medical treatments they don't really need/People needing more medical care because of unhealthy lifestyles/The use of expensive new drugs, treatments, and medical technology/The population is aging/More people are getting better medical care than ever before.

Source: ABC News/Kaiser Family Foundation/*USA Today,* "Health Care in America 2006 Survey," October 2006.

Table 4-12 Americans' Views about the Effectiveness of Various Ways to Control Health Care Costs (in percent)

	Very effective	Somewhat effective	Not too effective	Not at all effective	Don't know
Current system: most people have employer purchase insurance from private insurance companies on behalf of workers	11	56	17	13	3
Letting individuals shop around for the best prices they can get for health care and health insurance	37	43	10	8	2
Having the government regulate health care costs	21	41	18	18	2

Question: The current system for most people has employers purchase insurance on behalf of workers from private insurance companies. Do you think this system is very effective, somewhat effective, not too effective, or not at all effective at controlling health care costs?

Question: How about letting individuals shop around for the best prices they can get for health care and health insurance? Do you think that would be very effective, somewhat effective, not too effective, or not at all effective at controlling health care costs?

Question: How about having the government regulate health care costs? Do you think that would be very effective, somewhat effective, not too effective, or not at all effective at controlling health care costs?

Source: ABC News/Kaiser Family Foundation/*USA Today,* "Health Care in America 2006 Survey," October 2006.

Table 4-13 Americans' Views about Price Controls on Medical Costs, 1979–2004 (in percent)

	Strongly support	Somewhat support	Somewhat oppose	Strongly oppose
Price controls for medical expenses				
1979	38	30	12	15
1981	36	25	19	14
1982	41	26	16	13
1984	50	27	10	9
1994	52	20	10	17

Federal government price controls on:	Favor	Oppose
Prescription drugs		
2003	56	39
2004	60	35
Hospital charges		
2003	48	52
2004	55	39
Doctor bills		
2003	43	57
2004	48	46

Note: "Don't know" responses not shown.

Question: I'm going to read you some particular measures that have been proposed to help control health care costs. I'd like you to tell me whether you strongly favor, somewhat favor, somewhat oppose, or strongly oppose each one: Government price controls and regulations on what doctors and hospitals can charge. (1979–1984)

Question: I'm going to name some suggestions for changes in the health care system. Please tell me if you support or oppose each item I name: Federal price controls on medical expenses such as doctors' fees, hospital charges, and drug prices. (If support/oppose) Do you support/oppose that strongly or only somewhat? (1994)

Question: Would you favor or oppose federal government price controls of the following products and services? Prescription drugs/hospital charges/doctor bills. (2003–2004)

Sources: Cambridge Reports Polls (Storrs, Conn.: Roper Center for Public Opinion Research, January 1979, July 1981, October 1982, October 1984); ABC News Poll (Storrs, Conn.: Roper Center for Public Opinion Research, January 14–17, 1994); Harris Interactive polls (Storrs, Conn.: Roper Center for Public Opinion Research, April 10–15, 2003; August 10–15, 2004).

Table 4-14 Americans' Views of the Effectiveness of Government versus the Marketplace at Holding Down Health Care Costs (in percent)

Which approach should Congress take[1]	
Government dealing directly with doctors, hospitals, and insurance companies and establishing limits on what they can charge	59
Government giving consumers tax incentives to buy high-deductible health plans to encourage them to shop for lower-priced health care	34
Both (vol.)	2
Neither (vol.)	3
Don't know	3
Government vs. private insurance companies[2]	
Government would do a better job than private insurance companies in holding down health care costs	47
Government would do a worse job than private insurance companies in holding down health care costs	38
Same (vol.)	4
Don't know	11
Which would do a better job at keeping health care costs down[3]	
Regulation by the federal government	46
Competition in the marketplace	43
Both (vol.)	2
Neither (vol.)	3
Don't know	5

Note: (vol.) = volunteered response.

Question: A number of health experts think that there are two different approaches Congress could take to help lower the cost of health care. The first involves the government trying to solve the problem by dealing directly with doctors, hospitals, and insurance companies and establishing limits on what they can charge. The second involves the government giving consumers tax incentives to buy high-deductible health plans to encourage them to shop for lower-priced health care based on cost and quality information. Which approach do you prefer Congress to follow? (options were rotated)

Question: Do you think the government would do a better or worse job than private insurance companies in holding down health care costs?

Question: Which of the following do you think would do a better job at keeping health care costs down? Regulation by the federal government or competition in the marketplace?

Sources: [1]Kaiser Family Foundation/Harvard School of Public Health, "The Public's Health Care Agenda for the New Congress and Presidential Campaign," December 2006. [2]CBS News Poll (Storrs, Conn.: Roper Center for Public Opinion Research, August 27–31, 2009). [3]Kaiser Family Foundation, "Kaiser Health Tracking Poll: Election 2008," Issue 11, October 2008.

Table 4-15 Americans' Views of the Role of HMOs/Managed Care Plans in Keeping Health Care Costs Down, 1997–2004 (in percent)

	Helped	Haven't made much difference	Made costs go up (vol.)	Don't know/Refused
1997	28	55	5	12
1998	21	59	8	12
1999	21	55	8	16
2001	21	59	8	12
2004	13	63	7	17

Note: "(vol.)" = volunteered response.

Question: During the past few years, do you think HMOs and other managed care plans have helped keep health care costs down, or haven't they made much difference?

Sources: Kaiser Family Foundation/Harvard School of Public Health Poll (Storrs, Conn.: Roper Center for Public Opinion Research, August 22–September 23, 1997; August 6–20, 1998; April 10–22, 1999; July 2–August 8, 2001); Kaiser Family Foundation Poll (Storrs, Conn.: Roper Center for Public Opinion Research, August 5–8, 2004).

Table 4-16 Actions That Americans Say They Have Taken to Lower Health Care Costs (in percent)

Negotiated with a physician or other health care provider to try and get a lower price for health care services in the last year	11
Gone on the Internet to try to find a lower price for prescription drugs	9
Switched doctors to lower the amount you pay directly out of your own pocket	7
Gone on the Internet to try to find a lower price for any other type of health care services	6

Question: In the past year, have you (negotiated with a physician, a hospital, or any other health care provider to try and get a lower price for health care services/gone on the Internet to try and find a lower price for prescription drugs/switched doctors to lower the amount you pay directly out of your own pocket/gone on the Internet to try and find a lower price for any other type of health care services), or not?

Source: USA Today/Kaiser Family Foundation/Harvard School of Public Health, "Health Care Costs Survey: Summary and Chartpack," August 2005.

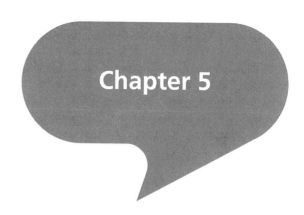

Chapter 5

THE UNINSURED AND EFFORTS TO EXPAND COVERAGE

Claudia Deane, Mollyann Brodie, Elizabeth C. Hamel, and Carolina S. Gutiérrez

In 2008 more than 45 million Americans under age sixty-five lacked health insurance, representing 17 percent of the country's non-elderly population.[1] To think of the size of that group in another way, the number is nearly as large as the entire West Coast population of the United States or everyone living in California, Oregon, and Washington combined.

To understand how this lack of coverage came about, it is helpful first to understand how insured Americans get their coverage. Currently, the United States relies primarily on an employer-based system, with most people getting health insurance through their jobs. Among adults under age sixty-five, six in ten were covered by employer-sponsored insurance in 2008.[2] One reason that the number of uninsured has gone up is the rising cost of health care premiums, forcing some employers to stop offering health coverage to their employees.[3] The rising cost of coverage also affects employees—not only those who can no longer afford their share of insurance costs, but also those buying insurance in the individual market.

Existing alongside the employer-based system are federal and state programs. Seniors who are sixty-five and older and people with permanent disabilities who qualify for Social Security are eligible to participate in the federal Medicare program, and virtually all do.[4] The federal and state governments also jointly finance the Medicaid program, which serves certain groups of poor and near poor Americans, including children and their parents, pregnant women, people with severe disabilities, and the elderly.[5] Coverage of lower-income children was further enhanced in the late 1990s with the passage of the State Children's Health Insurance Program, or SCHIP (now simply referred to as the Children's Health Insurance Program, or CHIP), a federal block grant to states. Despite these large swaths of coverage, millions of Americans—and particularly working-age adults without dependent children—are left without an easy path to affordable health insurance.

Not having health insurance is a problem only if it is associated with lessened access to care and poorer health outcomes, and numerous studies have shown that this is precisely the case. More than half of uninsured adults have no regular source of health care, and they are much less likely than insured adults to receive preventive care or screening services.[6] The title of the Institute of Medicine's 2002 report on the topic succinctly summed up the results of this kind of access disparity: *Care without Coverage: Too Little, Too Late.*[7] Researchers found that working-age Americans with no health insurance coverage did not receive enough care, and the care they did get usually came too late. Once inside the hospital system, they received poorer care. Overall, they were sicker and died sooner.

Aside from paying the ultimate cost—with their health and in some cases their lives—individuals without health insurance also carry a financial burden. Most obviously, they must pay the high cost of health care and coverage without the help of a subsidy from an employer or the government. And the cost of their care is not marked down because of their lack of insurance; in fact, hospitals often charge them at least twice what health insurers and public programs are paying for the same services.[8] Research also has found that the uninsured have lower annual earnings because of their generally poorer health.[9]

The problem of the uninsured also has society-wide financial implications. Many of those without insurance, and without the ability to pay the full cost of care, still receive some health care services, particularly in emergency circumstances. This care, provided to individuals without regard for their ability to pay, must still somehow be paid for. Americans who spent any part of 2008 uninsured will receive roughly $56 billion in uncompensated care, about 75 percent of which will be financed by government programs.[10] Society also pays the much larger and less-tangible cost of what experts term "health capital foregone," the additional productivity Americans would have if they spent less time being sick.

So who are the uninsured Americans? The large majority of them—roughly eight in ten—are employed or are part of a family where at least one person is employed.[11] Here, it is often the case that either their employer does not offer health care coverage, that they cannot afford the coverage offered, or that they do not qualify for that coverage because they work part-time or are relatively new to the job. The first of these phenomena is more common among low-wage workers, those who work in small businesses, service industries, or in blue collar jobs.[12] The uninsured are more likely to be low income, with two-thirds of this population coming from families with incomes below twice the poverty level.[13] Surveys show that the main reason the uninsured give for not having coverage is their inability to afford it.[14]

Research also shows racial and other demographic disparities in access to health insurance. African Americans, Native Americans, and Hispanics are more likely than whites to be uninsured, in large part because they are more likely to work in the kind of low-wage jobs that do not come with insurance benefits.[15] The rate for Hispanics is particularly high: 34 percent are uninsured, compared to 12 percent of whites.[16] There is some truth to the stereotype of younger people being more likely to be uninsured. But it is also true that most uninsured adults (six in ten) are over age thirty. And although noncitizens are less likely to have health insurance, nearly eight in ten of the uninsured are U.S. citizens.[17]

In the modern political era, U.S. presidents have attempted to expand coverage to a greater number of Americans, or even to all, but until recently none met with substantial success. Harry Truman unsuccessfully proposed a national health insurance plan that would have been financed through Social Security.[18] Richard Nixon tried to expand coverage in 1974, only to see his legislative agenda stopped in its tracks by the Watergate scandal. Jimmy Carter had his turn in 1977, also unsuccessful. And in 1993–1994 Bill Clinton created a task force, headed by his wife, Hillary Rodham Clinton, that proposed a plan intended to cover all American citizens. The Clintons and their allies could not persuade either the American public or Congress to back the plan. Proponents of coverage expansion were more successful, however, when they moved from efforts to make comprehensive change to those involving particular groups of Americans. During Lyndon Johnson's tenure in office, the executive branch worked with Congress to pass Medicare and Medicaid. And in 1997 Congress and the Clinton administration created CHIP, which allowed states to provide coverage to an additional number of low-income children.

It was not until 2010 that the combination of a Congress controlled by Democrats and a newly elected Democratic president—Barack Obama, who as a candidate had made health reform one of his top priorities—managed to pass legislation that is expected to make a major dent in the number of uninsured in America. After a year of contentious debate that reached from the corridors of Capitol Hill to the boardrooms of corporate America to public town hall meetings nationwide, Congress passed and President Obama signed into law the Patient Protection and Affordable Care Act. The legislation is expected to reduce the number of uninsured by 32 million by 2019 using a wide variety of policy mechanisms.[19] The new law's provisions, however, are scheduled to be put into practice over a number of years, years during which other political and policy developments could impact the speed and specifics of its implementation.

In all these debates, public opinion—either support, opposition, or just plain lack of interest—was a major factor. In this chapter, we consider the current state of public opinion on the topic of the uninsured, beginning with an assessment of Americans' perceptions of this population. We look at the extent of concern over the issue, where it falls in the public's priority list, and who Americans think should bear the responsibility for resolving it. We also consider how people view various means of expanding coverage and the challenges and opportunities these views posed in the recent health care reform effort. Although expanding coverage is occasionally spoken of as synonymous with health care reform, the latter topic is much broader, encompassing, among other things, delivery system reform and cost controls. In this chapter, we focus only on the comparatively narrower, but still challenging, issue of expanding coverage.

Americans' Views of the Uninsured

Americans' perceptions of the uninsured—who they are and what experiences they face—is somewhat mixed, more accurate in some aspects than in others. The public does seem to be aware that the number of uninsured has been growing. In 2000 more than six in ten adults believed correctly that the number of Americans without health insurance had increased over the previous decade.[20] A majority also believes this trend will continue, at least in the short term: in the summer of 2007, 63 percent said they thought that the number of uninsured Americans would increase over the next six to twelve months.[21]

Asked in an open-ended question to name the "one or two types of people [who] would come to your mind first . . . if you were going to describe uninsured Americans," the public's top two answers were "poor people" (named by 33 percent) followed by mentions of working families or employed individuals (18 percent). Nearly one in ten (8 percent) mentioned members of racial and ethnic minority groups (**Table 5–1**). Research backs up each of these characterizations. The other two responses that reached double-digit percentages suggest a somewhat less accurate perception of who makes up the bulk of the uninsured population, with 16 percent naming "unemployed people" and 13 percent citing the elderly.[22] Although it is certainly true that the unemployed are uninsured at a high rate, the large majority of uninsured Americans are members of working families, and the elderly have access to coverage through Medicare.

Asked more directly whether more uninsured Americans come from working families or families where no one is employed, roughly six in ten Americans choose the latter option or say they do not know. This misperception has been remarkably persistent over more than ten years of repeated askings.[23]

The majority of the public does seem to grasp some of the main problems faced by people who do not have health insurance. Seven in ten recognize that the uninsured are more likely to postpone seeking needed care, and 58 percent are aware that this population is less likely to have a regular source of care (**Table 5–2**).[24] At least six in ten also said that the uninsured were less likely to have seen a doctor recently, to have gotten care they needed, or to have received preventive health services.[25]

Despite the list of challenges to getting care, a majority (58 percent) believes that most uninsured people in their own community are able to get the care they need from doctors and hospitals.[26] Although it may be true that many uninsured individuals can get *some* care, research suggests that large numbers of those without coverage do not, in fact, get the care they need.[27] That most Americans believe the uninsured in their community are getting the care they need is particularly worth noting in the context of attempts to expand coverage, as this perception undermines the arguments for providing health insurance to more people.

Lack of Coverage a Serious National Issue

Surveys suggest that Americans' feelings about the provision of health care often cross into the realm of values and morality, a powerful force in the national psyche. A large majority agrees that "health care should be provided equally to everyone," as in the case of public education.[28] About two-thirds say they think of health care mostly as a right, while just over a third think of it more as a privilege (**Table 5–3**).[29]

Given that many view access to health care as something every American deserves and that many also recognize that being uninsured hampers a person's ability to remain healthy, it is not surprising that a large majority of people say that the current number of Americans without insurance is a real problem. Roughly three in four call the situation "very serious."[30] Roughly half go even further and call the problem "critical" (**Table 5–4**).[31]

Another point of general agreement is that the federal government should do more to help more Americans obtain coverage. Overall, 75 percent of Americans said they would favor the federal government taking additional action.[32] As will become clear in upcoming sections, however, little agreement is found on what "doing more" should look like.

The interest in doing more to cover the uninsured echoed through the 2008 presidential election. In the months preceding the November vote, just under half of registered voters (47 percent) said they would like to see the candidates propose "a new health plan that would make a major effort to provide health insurance for all or nearly all of the uninsured," even if it "would involve a substantial increase in spending." In comparison, 30 percent said they would like to see a more limited plan that cost less and covered somewhat fewer people, and 17 percent hoped the candidates would propose leaving things as they are.[33]

There are real distinctions in the intensity with which partisans of different stripes characterize the issue of the uninsured and in their appetite for action, differences that were reflected in their support for and opposition to particular proposals. Roughly nine in ten Democrats believe the uninsured problem is "very serious," compared to seven in ten political independents and five in ten Republicans.[34] Shortly before the 2008 presidential election, two-thirds (67 percent) of registered voters who said they intended to vote for Senator Obama hoped the next president would propose a major expansion of coverage, while less than half as many (26 percent) who intended to vote for Senator John McCain had the same interest.[35]

In addition to the values aspect of Americans' widespread support for attention to the issue of the uninsured is the economic aspect. Just over half of registered voters (53 percent) believe that universal coverage would improve the overall economic situation in the United States. Democrats are nearly twice as likely as Republicans (69 percent to 36 percent) to see expanded coverage as having an economic benefit.[36]

The Uninsured, the Policy Agenda, and Competing Priorities

Although most Americans see the continued growth in the nation's uninsured population as a serious problem, and one that government should do something about, it would be wrong to think that this is the only item on the national agenda. Instead, the overarching issue of health care competes with a variety of other pressing topics for the public's attention. And once health care does get the spotlight, the issue splinters into many issues that compete with the expansion of coverage.

The nation's public policy agenda varies as the country's needs and challenges change. Health care's ranking on this agenda rises and falls. One way to look at this is in the context of elections, when the public's priority list becomes important to those in power or seeking power. Early in the 2008 presidential race, health care was for a while at the top of the domestic priority list, trailing only the war in Iraq as the country's top issue overall. With the onset of a crisis in the home mortgage market, the failure of several large financial institutions, and talk of recession, however, the economy displaced both health care and Iraq as the country's most pressing issue. Health was pushed down, but still remained in the top three issues, driven by its top three ranking among Democrats and independents; Republicans were less interested in action on this front.[37] The emphasis on health care distinguishes the 2008 election from the 2006 midterm or the 2004 presidential contest, when health ranked significantly farther down the list.

Even in a year when health care is a top-tier issue, however, the issue of the uninsured may not be guaranteed to be a top priority. Rising health care costs also rank high in the public's mind. Surveys have measured the rankings of health care priorities in many different ways and found that cost has generally edged out coverage as a public priority. One measure places cost and coverage concerns within a long list of public concerns related to health care and other issues. Here, just over two-thirds (69 percent) say that reducing health care costs is a "top priority" for the president and Congress, compared to just over half (54 percent) who say the same about providing health insurance to the uninsured. In terms of ranking, reducing costs was third only to the economy and terrorism. Expanding coverage ranked eleventh out of twenty-one options.[38]

When the public is asked to rank a list consisting just of possible health care priorities, cost and coverage again come out on top, with cost named by 38 percent and coverage by 34 percent.[39] Putting the two priorities head-to-head similarly divides the public, with a larger proportion choosing cost (59 percent) than coverage (39 percent) (**Table 5–5**).[40] As noted above, there is also a partisan aspect to this prioritization. In August 2009, perhaps the most publicly controversial month of the Obama health reform debate, twice as many Democrats as Republicans (43 percent compared to 19 percent) ranked increasing coverage as the most important of four possible major goals for health reform; the other three were insurance reform, reining in health costs, and strengthening prevention.[41]

It is worth keeping in mind that in the real world of policymaking, multiple priorities can be addressed at the same time (in fact, many argue that is the *only* way to make health reform happen), and that controlling costs and expanding coverage can theoretically be addressed simultaneously. This was, in the end, the combination that managed to pass the House and the Senate in 2010. Still, all these findings combined serve to temper the conclusions of the last section: although most Americans see the number of uninsured as a serious problem and one deserving of action, they have other priorities for the political system as well. Expanding coverage must continually compete with these for attention.

Expanding Coverage: Whose Responsibility?

Surveys suggest at least two noteworthy themes concerning the public's views about who should bear primary responsibility for making sure that Americans have access to health care and health insurance. First, the public believes the federal government has a role here. Second, the public has a strong preference for solutions that spread the responsibility beyond the federal government to state government, employers, insurance companies, and consumers themselves.

One question, asked over several years, measures whether Americans think the federal government should "guarantee" health care coverage for all Americans, or whether this is not a federal responsibility. Consistently, majorities have said that the government does have this responsibility, varying in a relatively narrow range between 51 percent and 69 percent.[42] An earlier series that asked whether it was the responsibility of the federal government to guarantee medical care for the uninsured found support in the range of 59 percent to 77 percent. These questions are general and do not mention any specific means, but they do indicate that the majority of the public sees some sort of federal involvement here (**Table 5–6**).[43]

Additional questions ask about other groups that could be seen as responsible for ensuring health insurance coverage, specifically employers and individuals. Asked which of the three— government, employers, or individuals—should bear the primary responsibility for ensuring that people have health insurance, the public was split, with roughly a third (36 percent) choosing government, three in ten (31 percent) choosing individuals, and a somewhat smaller share (24 percent) choosing employers.[44] The Democratic-leaning Democracy Corps asked likely voters about paying for "health care costs" and also found responses split, but with employers holding an edge; 41 percent said employers should pay most of the cost, 31 percent said government, and 20 percent said individuals.[45] This hint that the public might be interested in solutions that shared responsibility across the three is borne out in the answers to a question that specifically offers this option. Asked whether "insurance costs" should be mostly paid for by individuals, employers, or the government, or whether they should be "shared by" the three, 66 percent chose the shared costs option.[46]

Some evidence suggests that the government might be seen by more people as having a role when the question focuses not on the population at large but on those currently without health care coverage. A survey sponsored by the conservative Galen Institute found that six in ten likely voters thought the government should be most responsible for providing health coverage to the uninsured (43 percent specified the federal government, and 20 percent the state government), while only 11 percent named employers and business.[47]

Approaches to Expanding Coverage

Advocates for the uninsured, both inside government and outside, have proposed any number of ways of bringing health care coverage to more people, many of which became part of the significant coverage expansion built into the 2010 Patient Protection and Affordable Care Act. This section considers the public's views on many of these ideas. The challenges to measuring public opinion on this type of health reform plan are many, however, and should be kept in mind. First, although the plans themselves tend to be complex, questions about them must, by necessity, be boiled down to fairly simplified outlines. Second, although many plans take a smorgasbord approach—combining various elements of different plans as did the 2010 legislation—it is more difficult to do this in a survey question, and much of the historical work on specific policy options tends to examine opinion on one approach at a time. Third, because the goal of bringing health insurance to more people is popular, nearly any proposed plan to meet this goal is met with initial warmth. As we show later in the chapter, however, spelling out the costs of such a plan, as well as the possible personal impact, erodes support rather quickly. After laying out opinion on some of the broad-brush approaches to expanding coverage, we further complicate things by showing what happens when the public is asked to choose among them, and we examine whether the kinds of smorgasbord plans discussed above are more or less popular with the public.

Most of these themes are shown in **Table 5–7**, which lays out some broad ways to expand coverage, all of which—with one major exception—are at first glance popular with the American public. The rest of this section examines these one by one, with full recognition that they are used in combination.[48] In the conclusion of the chapter, we consider the ways that the coverage expansion of 2010 did and did not reflect these trends in public opinion.

Single-Payer Plan

In the recent past, the comparatively least popular approach to expanding health care coverage is also one of only a few proposals that would require major system change.[49] This proposal is the so-called single-payer plan, which would shift from the employer-based system to a taxpayer-financed national health system. Under such a plan, all citizens would get their insurance from a single government plan or from multiple government-sponsored plans that offer common benefits.

The main public opinion finding here is that the single-payer plan is one of the few methods of coverage expansion that in most cases does not meet with initial majority approval among Americans, even as the minority who favor it seem to be particularly strong in their support. In September 2009, 40 percent said they favored a single-payer plan, but the percentage in favor varies depending on the question wording, usually hovering in the 40 percent to 50 percent range compared to other expansion proposals, which score substantially higher.[50] Asked a similarly worded question in 2007, on its own rather than embedded in a longer list of possible plans, 47 percent backed the plan.[51] Another item described a "government-run, government-financed health insurance program" that "would be administered like the current Medicare for citizens sixty-five and over." This plan received slightly more support, garnering the backing of 54 percent of the public.[52] Perhaps the highest level of support measured in a recent survey was the response to a 2006 question that asked whether people would prefer to keep the current employer-backed system or to move to a "universal health insurance program in which everyone is covered under a program like Medicare that is run by the government and financed by taxpayers." Fifty-six percent chose the universal coverage option, but as will be shown below, this broader level of support tends to be somewhat shallow (**Table 5–8**).[53]

Possibly fueling the lack of support for a single-payer government plan is much public opinion research pointing to Americans' distrust of government, particularly when it comes to competence.[54] Roughly one in four say they are "extremely" or "very" confident that the federal government could provide "quality health care coverage" to all its citizens, but a significantly larger percentage (42 percent) say they are "not too confident" or "not at all confident," with a large chunk in the middle expressing just some faith (31 percent).[55] Asked whether the government would do a better or worse job than the private sector in providing coverage, more chose worse (44 percent) than chose better (30 percent).[56]

Values also influence acceptance of a national health care plan. Overall, nearly half the public (48 percent) says that it would be "unfair" for the government to require participation in such a plan, compared to 43 percent who see it as fair.[57] A 2008 survey found at least some resistance—although perhaps less than in the past—to the idea of so-called "socialized" medicine. About four in ten say that if the United States had "socialized medicine," the health care system would be worse than it is now, with a slightly larger percentage (45 percent) saying it would be better. Again, a concept that divides the public.[58]

The Public Option

Another option for expanding coverage that would involve greater government participation, the so-called public option, was the subject of a particularly contentious debate during the most recent national health reform effort. As Congress ironed out the specifics of various health overhaul bills, many paid close attention to whether the final bill would include some version of a public option, a government-created health insurance plan that would compete with private insurance. A public option can take on many different forms, depending on a range of factors such as whether prices under the public plan would be linked to Medicare reimbursement rates, who is and is not allowed to buy into the plan, and whether individual states would have the ability to "opt out" of the plan. Given the intense public focus on this issue throughout the 2009–2010 debate, it is perhaps not surprising that no fewer than twenty-two publicly released polls sought to measure support for the public option in the spring and summer of 2009.

Levels of support varied depending on the specific question wording, but most polls found at least a slim majority in favor of such a plan. In each pollster's asking of the question in the summer and fall of 2009, support ranged from a high of 62 percent to a low of 44 percent.[59] Support was highest (62 percent in favor, 31 percent opposed) when the plan was described as "the government offering everyone a government administered health insurance plan—something like the Medicare coverage that people 65 and older get—that would compete with private health insurance plans."[60] The lowest level of support was found in a Fox News Poll of registered voters that asked about "the creation of a government-run health insurance plan that would compete in the marketplace against private insurance plans," with 44 percent in favor and 48 percent opposed.[61]

In the case of the public option, public support varied not only with question wording, but also when different aspects or potential consequences of the plan were mentioned. Support increased from 55 percent to 76 percent in a September 2009 poll when those initially opposed were asked to consider the caveat that the plan would be available only to people who were unable to get insurance from a private plan.[62] In a July poll, support started out at 59 percent, but was pushed as high as 72 percent when opponents were asked to consider that the plan would "give people more choice among health insurance plans," and as low as 35 percent when supporters were told that the plan could "give the government plan an unfair advantage over private insurance companies."[63]

The public was also split on the effect a public plan might have on the private insurance market. Forty-five percent said the creation of a government-administered public plan would be more likely to cause private companies to become more efficient and provide better products at a lower price, and nearly as many (43 percent) said it would be more likely to drive private companies out of the health insurance business.[64]

Expanding Existing Public Programs

A less-dramatic, more incremental approach to expanding government's role in providing health care insurance calls for existing public programs to be extended to additional groups of individuals rather than to the whole population. One proposal would be to expand Medicare by allowing people to enroll at age fifty-five. Another would expand existing state government programs aimed at lower-income residents—such as Medicaid and CHIP—to include more people.

Both of these approaches are broadly popular as general proposals, supported by roughly seven in ten. Building on the current structure—in this case three relatively popular programs, Medicare, Medicaid, and CHIP—seems to be an appealing solution to many Americans (**Table 5–7**).[65]

Strengthening the Employer-Based System

Given that most Americans currently receive their health care coverage through their employer or their spouse's or a parent's employer, many proposals begin by focusing on ways to increase the number of employers who offer such coverage. Some suggest offering employers financial sweeteners in the form of additional tax subsidies, while others favor an employer mandate. Some create "pay or play" plans, in which employers must either provide coverage or contribute to a general fund.

Using the tax code to increase employer activity is a popular idea, according to surveys. About eight in ten Americans are in favor of offering businesses tax deductions, tax credits, or other financial assistance to help them provide health insurance to their employees (**Table 5–9**).[66] The idea of an employer mandate—or a requirement that businesses offer private health insurance to their employees—is also popular, at least as a general concept. In addition to the multiple-item question at the start of this chapter, which found that 67 percent of Americans would back an employer mandate (see Table 5–7), other questions have also found large majorities in support. One question gave people the option of saying that "employers should either provide health insurance to their employees or contribute to a fund that would help cover workers without health insurance," or that employers should not have to provide or contribute, and found that eight in ten chose the former. A survey by the Employee Benefit Research Institute (EBRI) put the number in favor of an employer mandate even higher, at nine in ten.[67]

This support, however, comes with exceptions. In a follow-up question, EBRI researchers found that a narrow majority thought that small businesses—those with fewer than thirty employees—should not be included in such a mandate, and that many people would like to see that definition of small business be even broader. In addition, Americans do not yet have strong views about this (or likely any) proposal for coverage expansion. When given the option, nearly half the public volunteered that they were not yet sure whether the employer mandate was a good idea or a bad idea.[68]

Tax Incentives for Individuals

Rather than approaching coverage expansion from the employer perspective, other proposals would use the tax code to encourage *individuals*—either the uninsured or everyone in the United

States—to purchase coverage on their own. Because the tax code as currently written promotes employer-based coverage, most proposals of this variety entail a substantial shift in emphasis. One of the more straightforward proposals would offer tax deductions or tax credits to the uninsured to help them buy private health insurance. The tax code already provides advantages to saving for health costs in an HRA (health reimbursement arrangement) or an HSA (health savings account), both of which, if and when paired with a high deductible health plan (HDHP), are intended to make coverage more affordable and therefore more widespread, an approach that was central to President George W. Bush's health care proposals. Surveys suggest that proposals involving tax credits for individuals tend to be quite popular. As will be shown below, however, the popularity of these types of changes depends on the details.

In general, roughly two in three Americans (67 percent) say they are in favor of expanding coverage by offering tax deductions or credits to those without insurance.[69] In a survey by a Democratic-leaning organization, two in three likely voters said they would be at least somewhat more likely to support a candidate for Congress if he or she advocated tax deductions for families and individuals more generally.[70] Support for this concept drops if the question makes clear that the plan would not place "restrictions on health insurance companies' ability to decide who to cover and at what price." In this case, 44 percent back the approach, 46 percent oppose it, and 11 percent are not sure.[71] Many people are also not sure that they would be able to purchase appropriate health coverage at certain levels of tax credit. In 2003 about half the public said they thought they would be able to get a plan that met their needs if the tax credit was $3,000 for a family and $1,000 for an individual. Another one in four said they did not think this amount would be enough to get the right plan, and just as many were not sure.[72] It is difficult to find a reliable estimate of the average price of health plans available in the individual market, but as a rough comparison, it is worth noting that in 2003 the average annual premium for employer-sponsored family coverage was about $9,000.[73]

The tax code also has been used to promote the availability of lower premium policies—such as high deductible health plans—that would give consumers more of a stake in their spending by creating tax-preferred savings accounts such as HSAs and HRAs that can be paired with certain plans.[74] In general, public awareness of the existence of these plans remains somewhat limited. In a February 2006 survey, about three in ten Americans said they knew what the term "health savings account" meant, unchanged from a survey fielded in November 2004.[75] At least at first, public resistance to such plans was about two to one. Asked in the spring of 2005 whether they preferred to "pay for health care through an insurance plan that your employer provides, or pay for health care through a tax-free savings account that you set up and contribute money to," 64 percent of Americans chose the employer option, and 30 percent chose the savings account. According to experts, use of the accounts is growing, albeit slowly. In 2008 an estimated 8 percent of covered workers were enrolled in some sort of high deductible health plan with a tax-preferred savings option, up from 4 percent in 2006.[76] Such plans obviously do not address the issue of those without access to employer coverage. The bottom line: survey data, along with information about the public's real life choices, suggest that making such plans more available is likely not the fastest way to a big boost in coverage.

Imposing an Individual Mandate

Another option that many experts insisted would need to be a part of any serious coverage expansion strategy is the individual mandate, which would move toward universal coverage by requiring that every person obtain health insurance. Most individual mandate proposals include, at a minimum, some subsidy for low-income residents who cannot afford to purchase a policy on their own. These proposals have the public opinion advantage of not changing most people's health care arrangements: the bulk of the population would still get insurance through their employers. This type of mandate was also one aspect of a broad and high-profile overhaul of the health care system in Massachusetts in 2006 (see Chapter 6).

To the extent that the average American understands the concept of these often complex plans, opinion seems to be mixed. When the individual mandate idea was presented as one of a number of possible options for expanding coverage, two-thirds said they favored the approach (**Table 5–7**).[77] A 2008 survey fielded in the midst of intense debate on the topic in the Democratic presidential primaries, and presenting the option as a stand-alone question, found that 47 percent supported an individual mandate, and nearly as many (44 percent) opposed it.[78] But other polls taken later in the reform debate found support for an individual mandate ranging from 49 percent to 72 percent.[79] A June 2009 survey found the public was almost evenly split on the question of a law requiring "all Americans to have health insurance, either getting it from work or buying it on their own" (49 percent support, 47 percent opposed). Support increased, however, when different potential provisions of such a law were mentioned: 62 percent would support such a law if it included an employer mandate; 68 percent would support it if it included a rule that insurance companies must accept people regardless of preexisting conditions; and 70 percent would back a law if it included tax credits or other aid to help low-income people afford insurance. Conversely, support fell to 44 percent if the law included a financial penalty for those who do not get insurance (**Table 5–10**).[80]

Two reasons that resonate most with those who back the individual mandate plan: "making sure everyone has health insurance is the right thing to do" (87 percent named this as a major reason for their support) and "people with health insurance would get preventive and more continuous health care" (73 percent major reason). Somewhat less unanimity was found as to the top reasons for opposing the plan. Among the most popular: "people shouldn't be required to buy insurance if they can't afford it" (61 percent said "major reason"); "this approach will lead to higher taxes" (52 percent); and "this approach will lead to government run health care" (51 percent).[81]

Shifting from Employer-Sponsored Insurance to an Individual Market

A particularly dramatic shift toward making coverage an individual responsibility would be to move from an employer-based system to a system where all Americans are responsible for purchasing their own insurance in the individual market. As with the major change at the other end of the spectrum—a publicly financed single-payer plan—surveys suggest that the majority of Americans are not interested in this kind of change.

Asked about moving toward a more individually based system in a generic way, Americans are divided. About four in ten (42 percent) would support switching to a system where they bought their own health insurance, and a marginally higher proportion (45 percent) would prefer to build on the current employer-based system (**Table 5–11**).[82]

But responses look somewhat different when people are asked to think about the change in terms of their own personal situation. Asked whether, assuming the cost was the same, they would prefer to get health insurance through their employer or prefer to buy insurance on their own, nearly half of those with work-based insurance said they prefer to leave the responsibility to their employers; a third said they did not care either way; and 14 percent said they would prefer to do the purchasing themselves.[83]

A follow-up question suggests an attachment to the employer-based system that might be somewhat stronger: at least six in ten believe that if they had to buy health insurance on their own it would be harder to find a plan that matched their needs, particularly if they are in poor health, harder to get a good price, and harder to handle the associated administrative issues.[84] Overcoming these negative perceptions would be a difficult hurdle for proponents of converting to an individual market.

Public Opinion and the Real World: Lack of Consensus, Partisan Differences, and the Allure of Combined Approaches

As complicated as the above tour of public views on coverage expansion is, it falls far short of the complexity of public opinion in the real world of policy and politics. Three strands of public opinion on this issue apply to any proposal that might be introduced, and so are worth discussing. First is the time-honored finding that rather than coalescing around one of these many plans, public support tends to splinter among them. Second is the fairly dramatic partisan differences in opinion as to the right way forward. And third is the finding that combining aspects of various plans often attracts more supporters than one plan on its own.

Asked about different ways of guaranteeing health insurance for more Americans, significant majorities said they would favor each one, with the exception of a single-payer plan. When forced to decide which *one* of these plans that they *most* prefer, however, respondents reveal no consensus. Each plan receives double-digit support, but no plan is most preferred by more than 15 percent of the public (**Table 5–12**).[85]

This phenomenon is not new: as far back as the Truman administration a large majority (82 percent) of the public expressed a desire to "make it easier for people to pay for doctor and hospital care," but did not agree about the best way to achieve expanded coverage. The public was divided in their support between plans advanced by the insurance industry, the federal government, and a doctors' organization.[86] During the debate over the Nixon health reform plan, most Americans agreed that a new national health insurance plan was needed, but they were split between a large group who wanted it to come from the government and a similarly large group who preferred to see it come from private companies.[87] At the start of the 1993–1994 attempt to overhaul the health care system, the public split three ways: some preferred a version of the Clinton plan, some preferred a Republican-inspired tax credit plan, and others wanted a single-payer system.[88]

Moreover, the uninsured themselves do not coalesce around one particular approach to expanding coverage. Asked which would be the best way for their family to have greater access to health care, 40 percent said they would prefer publicly sponsored health insurance along the lines of Medicaid; 33 percent said they would prefer a tax credit that they could use to buy their own coverage; and 19 percent would prefer to see a free or reduced-cost public clinic made available in their area.[89]

Forcing the public to choose among the different plans does, however, provide some interesting insights. Although the idea of a single government health plan received dramatically less support than the other options as a stand-alone plan, it still attracted roughly the same amount of support as the other plans when people were asked to choose just one plan from the list. This result suggests that the group of hard-core supporters for a single-payer plan (about 15 percent) rivals the size of hard-core supporters of other proposals.[90]

Another way to show the lack of consensus is to look at questions that pit competing proposals head-to-head and ask the public to choose between them. When asked whether they preferred an individual mandate or a system of health savings accounts and tax credits, 40 percent picked individual mandate; 49 percent picked savings accounts and tax credits; and 11 percent were unsure: no clear majority there.[91] Again in the case of tax credits versus expanding state government programs, the public is split, with 43 percent choosing the former and 47 percent the latter.[92]

In addition to the general divisions between proponents of various plans, consistent partisan differences become apparent, with rank-and-file Democratic voters and rank-and-file Republican voters being interested in somewhat different plans. These divisions have significance in a political system where candidates of both parties survive mainly by appealing to their own constituencies. Broadly speaking, Democrats are more likely than Republicans to prioritize action on the problem of the uninsured and are therefore more likely to back any number of plans. Within the spectrum of proposed plans, and consistent with their overarching tendencies in areas other than health care, Democrats are more likely to support solutions that involve government participation, and Republicans are more likely to support market-based solutions. Independents tend to be somewhere in the middle (see Chapter 19).

Democrats and Republicans are often, in fact, mirror images of each other in terms of support and opposition. Sixty-five percent of Democrats say they would back a government-run, government-financed health insurance program, and 62 percent of Republicans say they would oppose it. About half of political independents favor such a plan.[93] When it comes to the basic concept of an individual mandate to reach universal coverage, 55 percent of Democrats support it, 56 percent of Republicans oppose it, and independents are in the middle, divided between support and opposition (46 percent to 47 percent).[94] Asked to choose between expanding coverage through an extension of existing public programs or through additional tax credits, a majority (56 percent) of Republicans chose the tax credit option, and a majority of Democrats (61 percent) chose the expansion of Medicaid and CHIP.[95]

As support is splintered across a variety of proposals and partisans differ in their interests, it follows that any plan seeking to win broad public support will incorporate a variety of different strategies for expanding coverage. Survey questions are not able to replicate the complexity of this type of plan, but a simple experiment shows the appeal of combining various approaches that are separately popular. Half the respondents on a national survey were asked whether they supported or opposed a fairly straightforward individual mandate (**Table 5–10**). The other half of the sample was asked about an individual mandate combined with responsibilities for businesses (an employer mandate), government (expanded public programs), and insurance companies (regulations to prevent discrimination based on preexisting conditions). The version that asked only about an individual mandate found the public roughly split in half (47 percent in favor to 44 percent opposed). The version that put the mandate in the context of what many term "shared responsibility" found a clear majority (59 percent to 35 percent) in favor.[96]

Children as a Special Case

One population of uninsured individuals serves as an exception to many of the patterns discussed above, and that group is children. A fair degree of consensus exists among the public that children deserve to be at the top of the list when it comes to expanding coverage, and policies that target this population tend to be popular across partisan lines. Because it is less expensive to insure children than adults, it is also true that plans to expand coverage for kids likely do not seem as big, bold, or financially overwhelming to the public as universal health care does. This trend in public thinking helps explain why in the wake of the failure of the more broadly targeted Clinton health reform plan in 1993 and 1994, Congress was still able to pass CHIP in 1997. (President Bush vetoed an expansion of CHIP in late 2007, but President Obama signed a similar bill into law in early 2009.)

Surveys fielded in 1997 found that among those who had heard of the new program, support was overwhelming, roughly nine in ten.[97] Ten years later, two-thirds of the public believed that the government was doing "too little" to provide health insurance to children who lacked it.[98] And among the 85 percent who thought the government should do more to expand coverage in general, the majority thought children should be covered ahead of the poor and the working poor.[99] It follows that when Congress considered a CHIP expansion bill in 2007, a majority of Americans—about seven in ten—backed the proposal (**Table 5–13**).[100]

Expanding Coverage: Challenges

For those who have been interested in successfully planning, passing, and implementing significant expansions in health care coverage, the public's complex and sometimes conflicting views on the topic offered both challenges and opportunities. This was as true for those seeking change in 2010 as it was in earlier debates. But it is important to recognize that public support is only one of many ingredients needed to create change, which also requires not only the involvement and support of stakeholders and policymakers, but also a funding plan to pay for it.[101] The following discussion stays within the confines of public opinion, running through some of the highlights of public opinion on plans to expand coverage, beginning with the obstacles that confronted reform advocates in the most recent debate as well as in earlier efforts.

To put it simply, in most years, health care is not the top issue on Americans' priority lists. In the new millennium, a foreign war, terrorism, and the economy also have preoccupied the public and the nation's leaders. And even when the public does turn its gaze to health care issues, expanding coverage must compete with other problems, particularly those associated with rising costs.

Limited Willingness to Foot the Bill

No matter the plan, providing health coverage to a greater number of Americans will cost money. And thus far, a substantial proportion of the public has been unwilling to pay.

To some extent, public opinion data on the question of financial sacrifice reflects Americans' internal conflict between their desire to see more of their fellow citizens have coverage and their questions about whether they, and the country in general, can afford such a change. When people are asked which is more important, universal coverage or holding down taxes, two-thirds (66 percent) choose universal coverage.[102] And over the past five years more than six in ten say that they favor the "government guaranteeing health insurance for all citizens, even if it means raising taxes."[103] When the focus is on the goal and the personal cost is implicit, then, many Americans are willing to say that generic "taxes" could be raised (**Table 5–14**).

When the question is phrased so that the personal cost is explicit, however, people provide a different response. In response to a question asked several times since 1996—"would you be willing to pay more, either in higher health insurance premiums or higher taxes" to cover more Americans, at least four in ten, and sometimes up to 58 percent, as in a 2007 survey, say they would not.[104] This sentiment reaches back even further. In a 1944 survey roughly two-thirds of the public said they would be in favor of having Social Security cover medical care. But that support dropped nearly thirty percentage points when those who opposed a payroll tax increase and those who preferred the private sector provide care were removed from the tally.[105]

Although the public is reluctant to pay more themselves to expand coverage, surveys suggest they are willing to ask others to pay more to fund such an expansion. In an October 2009 survey, more than six in ten (62 percent) said they would favor increasing taxes on upper-income individuals and families as a way to cover more of the uninsured, and more than half (55 percent) said they would favor taxing health insurance companies that offer expensive policies.[106]

Fear about Changing a Largely Satisfactory Status Quo

Although many Americans express dissatisfaction with the state of health care in the United States generally, large majorities of those with coverage—in the neighborhood of nine in ten—express satisfaction with their own insurance coverage and the quality of their own health care.[107] This satisfaction with their own arrangements can translate into risk aversion, a fear that change from the status quo will bring about a worsening of personal conditions. The effect is exacerbated by the common misperception that the uninsured are primarily unemployed Americans, leading employed people to a perhaps misplaced feeling of safety.

Surveys that ask Americans how they imagine a generic universal health insurance system would affect them personally find real division as to whether their lot would get better, worse, or stay the same, with the public breaking roughly into thirds on the question (**Table 5–15**).[108] A similar pattern of perception, with the negatives even more pronounced, was seen during President Clinton's 1994 attempt at health care reform, an attempt that was unsuccessful in large part because opponents were able to frighten the public about the personal effects of change.[109]

Messages Matter

For all the reasons laid out above, it is relatively easy to dampen public enthusiasm for comprehensive health care reform plans. And the way a policy debate plays out in the public arena has an important impact on the public's support or opposition to any plan. Despite the relative stability of public views, messages that tap into values, concerns, and Americans' general risk aversion are powerful. As political scientist Lawrence Jacobs describes it, "political conflict and its coverage by the press also can heighten the public awareness of the uncertainty and risks of altering the status quo, which in turn invites cynicism and distrust about the uses of government and erodes support for policy reform."[110]

An example from survey research: an October 2008 survey found that 49 percent of the American public was in favor of a universal health insurance program run by the government. But when those who backed the change to a universal system were asked whether they would continue supporting the plan even if it meant they would have to pay more, wait longer for some treatments or not have them covered, or have fewer choices of physicians, support dropped dramatically, ranging from 12 percent to 25 percent.[111] Whether a universal single-payer plan would indeed cause any of these results is debatable, but the survey shows that such messages can change the complexion of public opinion rapidly.

Another example concerns opinion on an individual mandate. As was mentioned above, a September 2009 survey found 68 percent in favor of requiring all Americans to have health insurance, with financial help for those unable to afford it. But when supporters were asked how they would feel if people would be required to buy insurance that they thought too expensive or did not want, support dropped to 29 percent. Conversely, when opponents were asked whether their opinion would change if they heard that without a mandate, insurance companies would be able to deny coverage to people who are sick, support rose to 76 percent.[112]

When President Clinton initially proposed his reform plan, 59 percent of the public approved of the proposal. But a mere six months later, after an intensive public campaign between advocates and opponents had played out in the media, support had dropped to four in ten.[113] The attacks on the proposal, launched by "some Democrats, many Republicans, and a coalition of interest groups, such as the HIAA [Health Insurance Association of America] were transmitted and amplified by the press in a way that activated the public's well-established philosophical conservatism toward government interference and its uncertainty and sense of personal risk."[114]

Similarly, during Truman's attempted overhaul, opposition to the president's health reform plan went from 38 percent in March 1949 to 61 percent in November 1950.[115] The public is wary when it comes to changes that affect something as vital to their families' day-to-day lives as health care, and the messages they get from the media, policymakers, and friends matter.

Expanding Coverage: Opportunities

Just as there are challenges to any comprehensive coverage expansion, there are also opportunities for those who see it as a pressing issue. Public opinion data point to some of these opportunities in regard to the public's worries, the importance of leadership, concerns about cost, and the efficacy of combining approaches and beginning with the familiar.

First and foremost, underneath the public's broad-based satisfaction with their health care are ongoing worries about the stability of these arrangements. In the summer of 2009, more than half of insured Americans were at least somewhat worried about losing their coverage. Nearly seven in ten overall were worried about having to pay more for their health care or insurance, and more than six in ten worried that they might not be able to afford needed services (**Table 5–16**).[116]

And these worries have persisted over time. Surveys fielded at the beginning and end of the 1990s found that roughly two-thirds worried that their future health care costs would not be covered.[117] In a January 2006 survey roughly six in ten said they had a lot of concern about their current and future health care costs, a proportion that remained roughly the same in fall 2008.[118] This widespread worry is a possible motivation for embracing proposals that would expand insurance coverage.

Surveys also suggest that just as message campaigns can dampen support for proposed coverage expansions, they can also whet the appetite for such plans. Although the conventional wisdom is that public clamoring for health care reform led to the introduction of the Clinton plan, survey data shows that the situation was more complex than that. Instead, a receptive public with personal concerns about the future of health care and an interest in domestic issues combined with a group of policymakers interested in reform. As **Figure 5–1** shows, leadership by the executive and legislative branches, and the ensuing media coverage, preceded the movement of health care up the public's priority list.[119] This pattern suggests that leadership matters, and when it comes to leadership, the president may have an advantage over Congress, which inevitably speaks with multiple voices.

At least as many Americans are concerned about health care costs as are concerned about expanding coverage. And the issue of costs impacts each person in the country in a way that the lack of health care coverage for all does not. Even those with comprehensive coverage through their employers are seeing their premiums rise at rates significantly faster than their paychecks.[120] Costs, therefore, are an entry point for health care reform plans. In addition, the public believes that the president and Congress can have an impact in this arena: nearly six in ten registered voters say that the executive and legislative branches "can do a lot" about the cost of health care.[121] This is not to say, however, that the public will accept any reform if it addresses only cost. Just as is true with plans to expand coverage, plans to rein in costs will be more or less popular depending on how they affect people's individual arrangements. Still, by linking coverage expansions with the country's other major health care preoccupation—rising costs—a reform plan has a larger base of support on which to draw.

As the analysis in this chapter demonstrates, multiple paths to increased coverage are popular, each with different groups of Americans. Simple math would suggest that combining approaches would build a larger group of supporters. The data also suggest that rather than beginning with major system change, plans that are less disruptive to people's existing arrangements would be more popular. The employer-based system is familiar, and employers are often viewed as having their employees' best interests at heart. Among those insured through an employer, eight in ten say they believe their employer "is doing the best they can" to provide "affordable health insurance coverage."[122] Building a coverage expansion plan on existing employer-based arrangements, then, would seem to be another way to court public approval.

Conclusion

Between the time we began working on this chapter and the time this book went to press, Congress passed and the president signed into law the biggest expansion in health care coverage since the creation of the Medicare program. The Patient Protection and Affordable Care Act of 2010 was a comprehensive reform package, including not only coverage expansion but also other major changes, from insurance reform to cost containment efforts. In this final section, however, we focus on how the content of the law reflects the public's policy preferences as summarized above. We also assess how public opinion challenges and opportunities played out in the deeply political process of passing a major piece of policy legislation. Chapter 21 provides a more extended discussion of public opinion and the health reform efforts of 2010.

Taking Advantage of Public Opinion Opportunities

The health reform law as passed reflected the realities of public opinion in many ways, but perhaps most in how it combined approaches to coverage expansion and built on the familiar employer-based health system. Although expansion via either a single-payer plan or a conversion to a purely individual market were popular on the left and right ends of the elite's ideological spectrum, they have not been embraced by the general public and were never seriously discussed by legislative leaders during the debate. Instead, the Patient Protection and Affordable Care Act exploited the opportunity to have people hold on to what they know, with advocates continually reassuring the public that if they had employer-sponsored coverage and liked it, the law would not require them to make substantial changes in their arrangements.[123] Much of the coverage expansion will take place by expanding existing public programs, particularly Medicaid, an approach that the public has embraced. The act also attempts to maximize employer-based coverage by assessing fees on employers with more than fifty workers if they do not provide health insurance. And an individual mandate was included in combination with insurance reforms and subsidies, some of the elements that surveys found made it more palatable, even though the mandate included a yearly financial penalty for those who fail to obtain coverage, an element that surveys suggest depressed support.

The passage of health reform in 2010 also demonstrates how President Obama took advantage of another public opinion opportunity: the power of presidential leadership in pushing a policy topic to the top of the nation's agenda. Perhaps in part because of his focus, most Americans were receptive to the idea of health reform throughout the economic hardships of 2009. The continued advocacy of the Obama administration and its effort to partner with Democratic leadership in both houses of Congress led to the legislation's passage, even though the final bill did not enjoy majority support from the public.

Finally, policymakers harnessed the public's concerns about the cost of health care and health insurance—issues that impact everyone rather than just a segment of the nation—as part of the comprehensive legislation that was also tackling lack of coverage more directly. Even part of the title of the bill, the "Affordable Care Act," references this goal. Surveys show that a portion of those who support the bill do so because they believe it will make health care more affordable and bring down costs generally.[124]

Overcoming Public Opinion Challenges

Advocates of this particular health reform bill faced some very steep public opinion challenges. In one important way, they overcame the challenges: the bill is now law. In another way, however, advocates were less successful. The public remains quite divided on the final legislation, even as they look favorably on many of its component parts.[125] Chief among the public opinion concerns were paying for the expansion (raising the issue of national and personal costs), the threat people felt to their personal health care status quo, and the extreme partisan divisions within the general public, focusing primarily on the role of government in implementing reform.

Many Americans were loath to incur any personal cost for expanding coverage to others, which proved challenging for policymakers looking to add coverage subsidies while trying to trim costs nationally. In the end, the revenue mechanisms relied on avoided focusing directly on large swaths of the general public, instead operating in a more indirect way through excise taxes on high-cost insurance and savings derived through the Medicare program, among others. Still, the overall cost of the bill and the fear that it will raise prices for Americans generally remain major reasons for public opposition to the law. In fact, in the end, advocates were not able to convince more than a third of the public that they would benefit from health reform.[126] The silver lining here was that they kept the proportion who thought they might be harmed to a similar percentage. Adding in those who did not expect a change either way neutralized the issue enough to ensure passage.

Last, but far from least, the increasingly partisan divide among the public on health reform mirrored the stark divisions at the elite level and posed a continuing public opinion challenge to passage. At the start of the debate, rank-and-file Republicans were opposed to tackling coverage expansion during an economic crisis (if ever), and at the end, most of them opposed the bill as passed. Democrats, in contrast, were in favor of both the effort in general and of the specific legislation. Independents were divided, tilting negative. Much of the opposition followed familiar ideological divides, such as the role of government in mandating individual coverage and setting up national standards, and the extent to which each group is comfortable with government spending. These challenges promise to continue as the legislation is implemented.

Coverage Expansion: What Next?

It is tempting to think that public opinion on the uninsured and the expansion of coverage is less relevant now that a major expansion has become law. But at the time of writing, the law is a mere infant, months old, and implementation stretches ahead over a period of years. Many decisions about how to implement the law have yet to be made, and the country's leadership will undoubtedly shift and change before the decisions are final, guaranteeing points where policy too can shift and change. The public's views on the uninsured, then, remain relevant. It will be important to understand whether Americans become more knowledgeable about who the uninsured are even as their ranks diminish and to see whether the strain of opposition to the law based in the view that some people who now will get insurance are somehow undeserving continues. Americans' views about this particular coverage expansion law also bear watching over time, as what was an abstract discussion becomes concrete changes in people's own lives and the lives of their friends and acquaintances. As this happens, opinion will also no doubt react.

Notes

[1] Kaiser Commission on Medicaid and the Uninsured, "The Uninsured: A Primer," October 2009, http://www.kff.org/uninsured/upload/7451–05.pdf. The data are from a KCMU/Urban Institute analysis of 2008 Annual Social and Economic Supplement to the Current Population Survey.

[2] Ibid.

[3] Kaiser Family Foundation and the Health Research and Educational Trust, "Employer Health Benefits: 2009 Annual Survey," http://ehbs.kff.org/pdf/2009/7936.pdf.

[4] Kaiser Family Foundation, "Medicare: A Primer," March 2007, http://www.kff.org/medicare/upload/7615.pdf.

[5] Kaiser Commission on Medicaid and the Uninsured, "Medicaid Facts: The Medicaid Program at a Glance," November 2008, http://www.kff.org/medicaid/upload/7235_03–2.pdf.

[6] Kaiser Commission on Medicaid and the Uninsured, "The Uninsured: A Primer," October 2009.

[7] Institute of Medicine, *Care without Coverage: Too Little, Too Late*, May 2002, http://www.iom.edu/~/media/Files/Report%20Files/2003/Care-Without-Coverage-Too-Little-Too-Late/Uninsured2FINAL.ashx.

[8] Gerard F. Anderson, "From 'Soak the Rich' to 'Soak the Poor': Recent Trends in Hospital Pricing," *Health Affairs* 26 (May-June 2007): 780–789.

[9] Jack Hadley, "Sicker and Poorer—The Consequences of Being Uninsured: A Review of the Research on the Relationship between Health Insurance, Medical Care Use, Health, Work, and Income," *Medical Care Research and Review* 60 (Supplement June 2003): 76S–112S.

[10] Jack Hadley, John Holahan, Teresa Coughlin, and Dawn Miller, "Covering the Uninsured in 2008: Current Costs, Sources of Payment, and Incremental Costs," *Health Affairs* 27 (September/October 2008): w399–w415.

[11] Kaiser Commission on Medicaid and the Uninsured, "Five Basic Facts on the Uninsured," September 2008, http://www.kff.org/uninsured/7806.cfm. The data are from a KCMU/Urban Institute analysis of March 2008 Current Population Survey.

[12] Kaiser Family Foundation Poll (Storrs, Conn.: Roper Center for Public Opinion Research, April 30–July 20, 2003); Diane Rowland, "Health Care Affordability and the Uninsured," April 15, 2008.

[13] Kaiser Commission on Medicaid and the Uninsured, "Five Basic Facts on the Uninsured."

[14] ABC News/Kaiser Family Foundation/*USA Today*, "Health Care in America 2006 Survey," October 2006, http://www.kff.org/kaiserpolls/upload/7573.pdf; *The Newshour with Jim Lehrer*/ Kaiser Family Foundation, "National Survey on the Uninsured," April 2000, http://www.kff .org/uninsured/upload/3013toplines.pdf; Kaiser Family Foundation Poll, April 30–July 20, 2003; *USA Today*/Kaiser Family Foundation/Harvard School of Public Health, "Health Care Costs Survey," August 2005, http://www.kff.org/newsmedia/upload/7372.pdf.

[15] Sara R. Collins, Cathy Schoen, Diane Colasanto, and Deirdre A. Downey, "On the Edge: Low-Wage Workers and Their Health Insurance Coverage," Commonwealth Fund, April 2003, http://www.commonwealthfund.org/usr_doc/collins_ontheedge_ib_626.pdf?section=4039.

[16] Kaiser Commission on Medicaid and the Uninsured, "The Uninsured: A Primer," October 2008.

[17] Ibid.

[18] Robert J. Blendon and Mollyann Brodie, "Public Opinion and Health Policy," in *Health Politics and Policy*, 4th ed., ed. Theodor J. Litman and Leonard S. Robins (Albany, N.Y.: Delmar, 2008), 249–270.

[19] Kaiser Family Foundation, "Summary of Coverage Provisions In the Patient Protection and Affordable Care Act," April 2010, http://www.kff.org/healthreform/upload/8023-R.pdf.

[20] *The Newshour with Jim Lehrer*/Kaiser Family Foundation, "National Survey on the Uninsured."

[21] Robert Wood Johnson Foundation/Public Opinion Strategies Poll (Storrs, Conn.: Roper Center for Public Opinion Research, August 4–7, 2007).

[22] *The Newshour with Jim Lehrer*/Kaiser Family Foundation, "National Survey on the Uninsured."

[23] Kaiser Family Foundation/Harvard School of Public Health polls (Storrs, Conn.: Roper Center for Public Opinion Research, February 17–24, 1994; June 20–July 9, 1996; November 4–December 6, 1998; October 8–12, 1999); Kaiser Family Foundation polls (Storrs, Conn.: Roper Center for Public Opinion Research, May 2–30, 1998; February 6–10, 2003; April 1–5, 2004; May 31–June 5, 2007); *The Newshour with Jim Lehrer*/Kaiser Family Foundation, "National Survey on the Uninsured"; *Washington Post*/Kaiser Family Foundation/Harvard University Poll (Storrs, Conn.: Roper Center for Public Opinion Research, July 5–18, 2000).

[24] Kaiser Family Foundation Poll, April 1–5, 2004.

[25] *The Newshour with Jim Lehrer*/Kaiser Family Foundation, "National Survey on the Uninsured."

[26] Harvard School of Public Health/Robert Wood Johnson Foundation Poll (Storrs, Conn.: Roper Center for Public Opinion Research, June 17–21, 2009).

[27] J. Z. Ayanian, J. S. Weissman, E. C. Schneider, J. A. Ginsburg, and A. M. Zaslavsky, "Unmet Health Needs of Uninsured Adults in the United States," *JAMA: Journal of the American Medical Association* 284 (October 25, 2000): 2061–9.

[28] *The Newshour with Jim Lehrer*/Kaiser Family Foundation, "National Survey on the Uninsured."

[29] World Public Opinion/Brookings Institution, "American Public Opinion on Health Care Reform," October 2009, http://www.worldpublicopinion.org/pipa/pdf/oct09/USHealthCare_ Oct09_quaire.pdf.

[30] NPR/Kaiser Family Foundation/Harvard School of Public Health, "The Public on Requiring Individuals to Have Health Insurance: Summary and Chartpack," February 2008, http://www .kff.org/kaiserpolls/upload/7753.pdf.

[31] ABC News/Kaiser Family Foundation/*USA Today,* "Health Care in America 2006 Survey."

[32] Kaiser Family Foundation, "Kaiser Health Tracking Poll: Election 2008," October 2008, http://www.kff.org/kaiserpolls/upload/78161.pdf.

[33] Robert J. Blendon, Drew E. Altman, John M. Benson, Mollyann Brodie, Tami Buhr, Claudia Deane, and Sasha Buscho, "Voters and Health Reform in the 2008 Presidential Election," *New England Journal of Medicine* 359 (November 6, 2008): 2050–61.

[34] NPR/Kaiser Family Foundation/Harvard School of Public Health, "The Public on Requiring Individuals to Have Health Insurance."

[35] Blendon et al., "Voters and Health Reform in the 2008 Presidential Election."

[36] Kaiser Family Foundation, "Kaiser Health Tracking Poll: Election 2008," March 2008, http://www.kff.org/kaiserpolls/upload/7751.pdf.

[37] Kaiser Family Foundation, "Kaiser Health Tracking Poll," October 2008.

[38] Pew Research Center for the People and the Press, "January Political Survey," January 9–13, 2008, http://people-press.org/reports/questionnaires/388.pdf.

[39] Kaiser Family Foundation, "Kaiser Health Tracking Poll," February 2009, http://www.kff.org/kaiserpolls/upload/7867.pdf.

[40] Gallup/*USA Today* Poll (Storrs, Conn.: Roper Center for Public Opinion Research, September 11–13, 2009).

[41] Kaiser Family Foundation, "Kaiser Health Tracking Poll," August 2009, http://www.kff.org/kaiserpolls/upload/7964.pdf.

[42] CBS News/*New York Times* polls (Storrs, Conn.: Roper Center for Public Opinion Research, July 13–16, 2000; January 20–25, 2006; February 23–27, 2007); Gallup polls (Storrs, Conn.: Roper Center for Public Opinion Research, November 11–14, 2002; November 3–5, 2003; November 7–10, 2005; November 9–12, 2006; November 11–14, 2007).

[43] CBS News/*New York Times* polls (Storrs, Conn.: Roper Center for Public Opinion Research, June 17–20, 1992; September 16–19, 1993; July 14–17, 1994; February 22–24, 1996).

[44] NBC News/*Wall Street Journal* Poll (Storrs, Conn.: Roper Center for Public Opinion Research, February 26–March 1, 2009).

[45] Democracy Corps/Greenberg Quinlan Rosner Research Poll (Storrs, Conn.: Roper Center for Public Opinion Research, May 29–31, 2007).

[46] Commonwealth Fund, "2007 Commonwealth Fund Biennial Health Insurance Survey," http://www.commonwealthfund.org/surveys/surveys_show.htm?doc_id=701249.

[47] Galen Institute/Zogby International Poll (Storrs, Conn.: Roper Center for Public Opinion Research, June 18–21, 2003).

[48] Kaiser Family Foundation, "Kaiser Health Tracking Poll," October 2008.

[49] Robert J. Blendon, John M. Benson, and Catherine M. DesRoches, "Americans' Views of the Uninsured: An Era for Hybrid Proposals," *Health Affairs* W3 (Web exclusive, August 27, 2003): 405–414.

[50] Kaiser Family Foundation, "Kaiser Health Tracking Poll," September 2009, http://www.kff.org/kaiserpolls/upload/7988.pdf.

[51] Kaiser Family Foundation, "Kaiser Health Tracking Poll: Election 2008," August 2007, http://www.kff.org/kaiserpolls/upload/7690.pdf. For a similar finding, see Gallup Poll (Storrs, Conn.:

Roper Center for Public Opinion Research, November 11–14, 2007), where 41 percent would favor "replacing the current health care system with a new government-run health care system."

[52] *Los Angeles Times*/Bloomberg Poll, October 19–22, 2007.

[53] ABC News/Kaiser Family Foundation/*USA Today*, "Health Care in America 2006 Survey."

[54] Blendon and Brodie, "Public Opinion and Health Policy."

[55] Ruth Helman and Paul Fronstin, "2007 Health Confidence Survey: Rising Health Care Costs Are Changing the Ways Americans Use the Health Care System," *EBRI Notes* 28 (November 2007): 2–11, http://www.ebri.org/pdf/notespdf/EBRI_Notes_11a-20071.pdf.

[56] CBS News/*New York Times* Poll (Storrs, Conn.: Roper Center for Public Opinion Research, February 23–27, 2007).

[57] Ibid.

[58] Harvard School of Public Health/Harris Interactive Poll, "Debating Health: Election 2008; Americans' Views on Socialized Medicine," February 2008, http://www.hsph.harvard.edu/news/press-releases/files/Topline__Socialized_Med_Havard_Harris.pdf.

[59] ABC News/*Washington Post* Poll (Storrs, Conn.: Roper Center for Public Opinion Research, September 10–12, 2009); NBC News/*Wall Street Journal* Poll (Storrs, Conn.: Roper Center for Public Opinion Research, September 17–20, 2009); Kaiser Family Foundation Poll (Storrs, Conn.: Roper Center for Public Opinion Research, September 11–18, 2009); Quinnipiac University Poll (Storrs, Conn.: Roper Center for Public Opinion Research, July 27–August 3, 2009); CBS News Poll (Storrs, Conn.: Roper Center for Public Opinion Research, October 5–8, 2009); *Time*/Abt SRBI Poll (Storrs, Conn.: Roper Center for Public Opinion Research, July 27–28, 2009); Pew Research Center for the People and the Press Poll (Storrs, Conn.: Roper Center for Public Opinion Research, September 30–October 4, 2009); Fox News/Opinion Dynamics Poll (Storrs, Conn.: Roper Center for Public Opinion Research, July 21–22, 2009).

[60] CBS News Poll (Storrs, Conn.: Roper Center for Public Opinion Research, October 5–8, 2009).

[61] Fox News/Opinion Dynamics Poll (Storrs, Conn.: Roper Center for Public Opinion Research, July 21–22, 2009).

[62] ABC News/*Washington Post* Poll (Storrs, Conn.: Roper Center for Public Opinion Research, September 10–12, 2009).

[63] Kaiser Family Foundation, "Kaiser Health Tracking Poll," July 2009, http://www.kff.org/kaiserpolls/upload/7943.pdf.

[64] Ibid.

[65] Kaiser Family Foundation, "Kaiser Health Tracking Poll," September 2009.

[66] Commonwealth Fund, "2007 Commonwealth Fund Biennial Health Insurance Survey."

[67] Helman and Fronstin, "2007 Health Confidence Survey."

[68] CBS News/*New York Times* Poll, February 23–27, 2007.

[69] Kaiser Family Foundation, "Kaiser Health Tracking Poll," September 2009.

[70] Democracy Corps/Greenberg Quinlan Rosner Research Poll, May 29–31, 2007.

[71] *Los Angeles Times*/Bloomberg Poll, October 19–22, 2007.

[72] Kaiser Family Foundation Poll, April 30–July 20, 2003.

[73] Kaiser Family Foundation and the Health Research and Educational Trust, "Employer Health Benefits: 2003 Summary of Findings," http://www.kff.org/insurance/upload/Kaiser-Family-Foundation-Summary-of-Findings.pdf.

[74] Alliance of Community Health Plans, "Health Savings Accounts," February 2006, http://www.achp.org/library/download.asp?id=7361.

[75] Kaiser Family Foundation Poll (Storrs, Conn.: Roper Center for Public Opinion Research, February 2–7, 2006); Kaiser Family Foundation/Harvard School of Public Health, "Health Care Agenda for the New Congress," January 2005.

[76] Kaiser Family Foundation and the Health Research and Educational Trust, "Employer Health Benefits: 2008 Annual Report."

[77] Kaiser Family Foundation, "Kaiser Health Tracking Poll," September 2009.

[78] NPR/Kaiser Family Foundation/Harvard School of Public Health, "The Public on Requiring Individuals to Have Health Insurance."

[79] Kaiser Family Foundation, "Kaiser Health Tracking Poll," November 2009, http://www.kff.org/kaiserpolls/upload/8018.pdf; Pew Research Center for the People and the Press Poll (Storrs, Conn.: Roper Center for Public Opinion Research, September 30–October 4, 2009); CBS News/*New York Times* Polls (Storrs, Conn.: Roper Center for Public Opinion Research, September 19–23, 2009; April 5–12, 2010); ABC News/*Washington Post* Polls (Storrs, Conn.: Roper Center for Public Opinion Research, September 10–12, 2009; October 15–18, 2009; February 4–8, 2010); Gallup/*USA Today* Poll (Storrs, Conn.: Roper Center for Public Opinion Research, July 10–12, 2009); *Newsweek*/Princeton Survey Research Associates International Poll (Storrs, Conn.: Roper Center for Public Opinion Research, February 17–18, 2010).

[80] ABC News/*Washington Post* Poll (Storrs, Conn.: Roper Center for Public Opinion Research, June 18–21, 2009).

[81] NPR/Kaiser Family Foundation/Harvard School of Public Health, "The Public on Requiring Individuals to Have Health Insurance."

[82] Kaiser Family Foundation, "Kaiser Health Tracking Poll: Election 2008," April 2008, http://www.kff.org/kaiserpolls/upload/7771.pdf.

[83] Kaiser Family Foundation, "Kaiser Health Tracking Poll: Election 2008," August 2008, http://www.kff.org/kaiserpolls/upload/7807.pdf.

[84] Ibid.

[85] Kaiser Family Foundation Poll, February 2–7, 2006.

[86] Stanley L. Payne, "Some Opinion Research Principles Developed through Studies of Social Medicine," *Public Opinion Quarterly* 10 (Spring 1946): 93–98; Robert J. Blendon, John M. Benson, Mollyann Brodie, Drew E. Altman, Matt James, and Larry Hugick, "Voters and Health Care in the 1998 Election," *JAMA: Journal of the American Medical Association* 28 (July 14, 1999): 189–194.

[87] Opinion Research Corporation Poll, 1972, cited in Blendon and Brodie, "Public Opinion and Health Policy."

[88] Kaiser Family Foundation/Commonwealth Fund Poll (Storrs, Conn.: Roper Center for Public Opinion Research, August 6–20, 1993).

[89] Kaiser Family Foundation Poll, April 30–July 20, 2003.

[90] Kaiser Family Foundation Poll, February 2–7, 2006.

[91] NBC News/*Wall Street Journal* Poll (Storrs, Conn.: Roper Center for Public Opinion Research, November 1–5, 2007).

[92] Kaiser Family Foundation/Harvard School of Public Health, "Post-Election Survey: The Public and the Health Care Agenda for the New Administration and Congress," January 25, 2001, http://www.kff.org/kaiserpolls/loader.cfm?url=/commonspot/security/getfile.cfm&PageID=13785.

[93] *Los Angeles Times*/Bloomberg Poll, October 19–22, 2007.

[94] NPR/Kaiser Family Foundation/Harvard School of Public Health, "The Public on Requiring Individuals to Have Health Insurance."

[95] Kaiser Family Foundation/Harvard School of Public Health, "Post-Election Survey: The Public and the Health Care Agenda for the New Administration and Congress," January 25, 2001.

[96] NPR/Kaiser Family Foundation/Harvard School of Public Health, "The Public on Requiring Individuals to Have Health Insurance."

[97] Pew Research Center for the People and the Press Poll (Storrs, Conn.: Roper Center for Public Opinion Research, August 7–10, 1997).

[98] NPR/Kaiser Family Foundation/Harvard School of Public Health, "Public Views on SCHIP Reauthorization: Chartpack," October 2007, http://www.kff.org/kaiserpolls/upload/7703.pdf.

[99] Kaiser Family Foundation/Harvard School of Public Health, "The Public's Health Care Agenda for the New Congress and Presidential Campaign," December 2006, http://www.kff.org/kaiserpolls/upload/7598.pdf.

[100] ABC News/*Washington Post* Poll (Storrs, Conn.: Roper Center for Public Opinion Research, September 27–30, 2007); NPR/Kaiser Family Foundation/Harvard School of Public Health, "Public Views on SCHIP Reauthorization."

[101] Lawrence R. Jacobs and Michael Illuzzi, "In the Shadow of 9/11: Health Care Reform in the 2004 Presidential Election," *Journal of Law, Medicine and Ethics* 32 (Fall 2004): 454–460.

[102] ABC News/*Washington Post* Poll (Storrs, Conn.: Roper Center for Public Opinion Research, June 12–15, 2008).

[103] Data from 2003–2007 presented in Pew Research Center for the People and the Press, "August 2007 Religion and Public Life Survey," http://people-press.org/reports/questionnaires/353.pdf; Pew Research Center for the People and the Press/Pew Forum on Religion and Public Life Poll (Storrs, Conn.: Roper Center for Public Opinion Research, July 31–August 10, 2008).

[104] Kaiser Family Foundation/Harvard School of Public Health polls (Storrs, Conn.: Roper Center for Public Opinion Research, November 6–10, 1996; November 4–December 6, 1998; October 8–12, 1999; November 13–December 13, 2000; February 6–10, 2003; November 4–28, 2004; December 4–14, 2008); *Washington Post*/Kaiser Family Foundation/Harvard School of Public Health polls (Storrs, Conn.: Roper Center for Public Opinion Research, May 3–June 3, 2007); Kaiser Family Foundation polls (Storrs, Conn.: Roper Center for Public Opinion Research, June 1–5, 2009; July 7–14, 2009; August 4–11, 2009; September 11–18, 2009).

[105] Payne, "Some Opinion Research Principles."

[106] Kaiser Family Foundation, "Kaiser Health Tracking Poll," October 2009, http://www.kff.org/kaiserpolls/upload/7998.pdf.

[107] ABC News/Kaiser Family Foundation/*USA Today*, "Health Care in America 2006 Survey"; Kaiser Family Foundation, "Kaiser Health Tracking Poll," August 2009.

[108] Kaiser Family Foundation, "Kaiser Health Tracking Poll," October 2008.

[109] Gallup/CNN/*USA Today* Poll (Storrs, Conn.: Roper Center for Public Opinion Research, April 16–18, 1994).

[110] Lawrence R. Jacobs, "Manipulators and Manipulation: Public Opinion in a Representative Democracy," *Journal of Health Politics, Policy and Law* 26 (December 2001): 1361–74.

[111] Kaiser Family Foundation, "Kaiser Health Tracking Poll," October 2008.

[112] Kaiser Family Foundation, "Kaiser Health Tracking Poll," September 2009.

[113] Robert J. Blendon, Mollyann Brodie, John M. Benson, Drew E. Altman, and Tami Buhr, "Americans' Views about Health Care Costs, Access, and Quality," *Milbank Quarterly* 84 (December 2006): 623–657.

[114] Jacobs, "Manipulators and Manipulation."

[115] Blendon et al., "Americans' Views about Health Care Costs, Access, and Quality."

[116] Kaiser Family Foundation, "Kaiser Health Tracking Poll," July 2009.

[117] ABC News/*Washington Post* Poll (Storrs, Conn.: Roper Center for Public Opinion Research, December 11–15, 1991); ABC News/*Money* Poll (Storrs, Conn.: Roper Center for Public Opinion Research, September 14–26, 1999).

[118] CBS News/*New York Times* polls (Storrs, Conn.: Roper Center for Public Opinion Research, January 20–25, 2006; March 28–April 2, 2008).

[119] NBC News/*Wall Street Journal* (1990–1992) and Harris Interactive polls (1993–2006), cited in Mollyann Brodie, "Insights into the Public's Views about Health Insurance: Challenges and Opportunities for Would-Be Reformers," Presentation at the Annual Conference of the National Academy of Social Insurance, February 2, 2007, http://www.nasi.org/usr_doc/Mollyann_Brodie_NASI_Presentation_02_02_07.pdf; Harris Interactive polls (Storrs, Conn.: Roper Center for Public Opinion Research, February 2–5, 2007; April 20–23, 2007; July 6–9, 2007; September 7–10, 2007; October 5–8, 2007; November 30–December 3, 2007: February 6–10, 2008; April 2–6, 2008; June 4–8, 2008; August 6–10, 2008; September 17–21, 2008; October 16–19, 2008; January 7–11, 2009).

[120] Kaiser Family Foundation and the Health Research and Educational Trust, "Employer Health Benefits: 2009 Annual Survey."

[121] Kaiser Family Foundation/Harvard School of Public Health, "Pre-Election Poll: Voters, Health Care and the 2008 Election: Toplines," October 2008, http://www.kff.org/kaiserpolls/upload/7829.pdf.

[122] Kaiser Family Foundation Poll, April 30–July 20, 2003.

[123] Kaiser Family Foundation, "Kaiser Health Tracking Poll," March 2010, http://www.kff.org/kaiserpolls/upload/8058-T.pdf.

[124] Kaiser Family Foundation, "Kaiser Health Tracking Poll," May 2010, http://www.kff.org/kaiserpolls/upload/8075-T.pdf.

[125] Kaiser Family Foundation, "Kaiser Health Tracking Poll," April 2010, http://www.kff.org/kaiserpolls/upload/8067-T.pdf.

[126] Kaiser Family Foundation, "Kaiser Health Tracking Poll," March 2010.

Table 5-1 Americans' Beliefs about Who the Uninsured Are (in percent)

Which types of people come to mind if you were to describe the uninsured[1]

Poor people	33
Working families/Employed	18
Unemployed people	16
The elderly	13
Children	8
Members of minority groups	8
Homeless	6
Younger people/30 and under	6
Immigrants	4
People like yourself	2
Single parents	2
Other	6
Don't know	13

Employed or not employed[2]	Employed	Unemployed	Don't Know
1994	34	56	10
1996	42	50	8
1998 (mid)	36	52	12
1998 (late)	47	43	10
1999	49	41	9
2000 (early)	39	57	4
2000 (mid)	45	49	6
2003	39	51	11
2004	40	49	11
2007	44	45	11

Question: If you were going to describe uninsured Americans—those with no health insurance at all—which one or two types of people would come to your mind first? (open-ended)

Question: Would you say that more uninsured Americans are employed or from families where someone is employed, or that more of these uninsured Americans are unemployed or from families where no one is employed?

Sources: [1]*The Newshour with Jim Lehrer*/Kaiser Family Foundation, "National Survey on the Uninsured," April 2000. [2]Kaiser Family Foundation/ Harvard School of Public Health polls (Storrs, Conn.: Roper Center for Public Opinion Research, February 17–24, 1994; June 20–July 9, 1996; November 4–December 6, 1998; October 8–12, 1999); Kaiser Family Foundation polls (Storrs, Conn.: Roper Center for Public Opinion Research, May 2–30, 1998; February 6–10, 2003; April 1–5, 2004; May 31–June 5, 2007); *The Newshour with Jim Lehrer*/Kaiser Family Foundation, "National Survey on the Uninsured," April 2000; *Washington Post*/Kaiser Family Foundation/Harvard University Poll (Storrs, Conn.: Roper Center for Public Opinion Research, July 5–18, 2000).

Table 5-2 Views of the Effects of Being Uninsured (in percent)

Uninsured compared to insured[1]	More likely	Less likely	Same	Don't know
Put off or postpone seeking care	73	10	13	4
Have a regular source where they get medical care	20	58	14	8
Have hospital or ER visits that could have been avoided	50	22	21	7

Uninsured in community able to get medical care[2]

Able to get treatment	58
Not able	34
Don't know	7

Question: Do you think Americans with no health insurance are more likely, less likely, or about the same as those with health insurance to (put off or postpone seeking care/have a regular source where they get medical care/have hospital or ER visits that could have been avoided)?

Question: Do you think that most people in your community without health insurance are unable to get medical treatment, or that these uninsured people are still able to get medical care they need from doctors and hospitals?

Sources: [1]Kaiser Family Foundation Poll (Storrs, Conn: Roper Center for Public Opinion Research, April 1–5, 2004). [2]Harvard School of Public Health/Robert Wood Johnson Foundation Poll (Storrs, Conn.: Roper Center for Public Opinion Research, June 17–21, 2009).

Table 5-3 Attitudes about Health Insurance as a Right (in percent)

Health care should be provided equally to everyone, just as public education is[1]

Strongly agree	62
Somewhat agree	22
Somewhat disagree	8
Strongly disagree	7

Think of health care mostly as . . .

A right	63
A privilege	36

Note: "Don't know" responses not shown.

Question: Do you strongly agree, somewhat agree, somewhat disagree or strongly disagree that health care should be provided equally to everyone, just as public education is?

Question: Do you mostly think of health care as a right or as a privilege?

Sources: [1]*The Newshour with Jim Lehrer*/Kaiser Family Foundation, "National Survey on the Uninsured," April 2000. [2]World Public Opinion/Brookings Institution, "American Public Opinion on Health Care Reform," October 2009.

Table 5-4 Attitudes about the Seriousness of the Uninsured Problem (in percent)

	Very serious	Somewhat serious	Not too serious	Not at all serious
Seriousness of number of Americans who do not have health insurance[1]	74	19	4	2

	Critical problem	Serious but not critical	Problem but not serious	Not much of a problem
How critical is the uninsured problem[2]	52	36	7	4

Note: "Don't know" responses not shown.

Question: An issue that has received attention in the news lately is the number of Americans who do not have health insurance. How serious do you think this problem is?

Question: Thinking now about the number of Americans who have no health insurance—do you think that's a critical problem for the country, a serious problem but not a critical one, a problem but not serious, or not much of a problem at all?

Sources: [1]NPR/Kaiser Family Foundation/Harvard School of Public Health, "The Public on Requiring Individuals to Have Health Insurance," February 2008. [2]ABC News/Kaiser Family Foundation/*USA Today*, "Health Care in America 2006 Survey," October 2006.

Table 5-5 The Uninsured as a Health Care Priority (in percent)

Most important goal of any health care reform plan*[1]

Making health care and health insurance more affordable	38
Finding a way to provide health insurance coverage to most Americans	34
Reforming the existing health care system to provide higher quality, more cost-effective care	14
Combination/All of these are most important	4
None of these is very/most important	10

More important goal in terms of health care[2]

Controlling rising health care costs	59
Expanding health care coverage to include nearly all Americans	39
Neither (vol.)	1

Notes: "Don't know" responses not shown; (vol.) = volunteered response. *Percentage shown includes those who named only one item as very important, as well as those who chose the item in the forced-choice follow-up.

Question: If the new president and Congress decide to take on health care reform, how important is each of the following as a goal of any health care reform plan? Making health care and health insurance more affordable/Finding a way to provide health insurance coverage to most Americans/Reforming the existing health care system to provide higher quality, more cost-effective care. Is this very important, somewhat important, not too important, or not at all important as a goal of health care reform? Those who said more than one item was "very important" were asked: Of the things you said are very important, which of these do you think should be the most important goal of any health care reform plan?

Question: If you had to choose, which goal would you say is more important in terms of health care—expanding health care coverage to include nearly all Americans or controlling rising health care costs in the U.S. today?

Sources: [1]Kaiser Family Foundation, "Kaiser Health Tracking Poll," February 2009. [2]Gallup/*USA Today* Poll (Storrs, Conn.: Roper Center for Public Opinion Research, September 11–13, 2009).

Table 5-6 Attitudes about the Federal Government's Responsibility to Guarantee Medical Care (in percent)

Responsibility of federal government to guarantee medical care for people who don't have health insurance[1]	Yes, should guarantee	No, not its responsibility	Don't know
1992	77	17	6
1993	65	27	8
1994	59	32	10
1996	64	29	7

Responsibility of federal government to guarantee health insurance/health care coverage for all Americans	Yes, should guarantee	No, not its responsibility	Don't know
2000[2]	62	29	9
2002[3]	62	35	3
2003[3]	59	39	2
2005[3]	58	38	4
January 2006[2]	62	31	7
November 2006[3]	69	28	2
February 2007[2]	64	27	9
November 2007[3]	64	33	3
November 2008[3]	54	41	5
March 2009[2]	62	30	8
June 2009[2]	64	30	6
July 2009[2]	55	38	7
September 2009[2]	51	40	9

Whose responsibility is it to ensure people have health insurance[4]

Federal government	36
Employers and businesses	24
Individuals themselves	31
All (vol.)	6
None/Other (vol.)	3

Who should pay for most of the cost of health care (of likely voters)[5]

Employers	41
Government	31
Individuals	20
Mix/all (vol.)	3
Don't know/Refused	4

Who should pay for most of the cost of health insurance[6]

Mostly individuals	6
Mostly employers	8
Mostly government	15
Shared by all three	66
Don't know/Refused	5

(Table continues)

Table 5-6 *Continued*

Who should have most responsibility for providing health coverage to uninsured (of likely voters)[7]

Federal government	43
State government	20
Employers and business	11
Other (vol.)	10
None of these (vol.)	8
Not sure	8

Note: (vol.) = volunteered response.

Question: Do you think the government in Washington should guarantee medical care for all people who don't have health insurance, or isn't this the responsibility of the government in Washington?

Question: Do you think the federal government should guarantee health insurance for all Americans, or isn't this the responsibility of the federal government? (2000, January 2006, February 2007, March 2009, June 2009, July 2009, September 2009)

Question: Do you think it is the responsibility of the federal government to make sure all Americans have health care coverage, or is that not the responsibility of the federal government? (2002, 2003, 2005, November 2006, November 2007, November 2008)

Question: Which one of the following do you think should have the most responsibility for helping ensure that Americans receive health insurance coverage: the federal government, employers and businesses, or individuals themselves?

Question: As you may know, health care costs can be paid by three different sources: the government, employers, and individuals. Of these three sources, which do you think should pay for most of the cost of health care?

Question: Who do you think should pay for health insurance for all Americans? Should insurance costs be mostly paid for by individuals, mostly by employers, mostly by the government, or should insurance costs be shared by individuals, employers, and the government?

Question: Which one of the following should be most responsible for providing health coverage to uninsured adults and children: the federal government, the state government, or business and employers?

Sources: [1]CBS News/*New York Times* polls (Storrs, Conn.: Roper Center for Public Opinion Research, June 17–20, 1992; September 16–19, 1993; July 14–17, 1994; February 22–24, 1996). [2]CBS News/*New York Times* polls (Storrs, Conn.: Roper Center for Public Opinion Research, July 13–16, 2000; January 20–25, 2006; February 23–27, 2007; March 12–16, 2009; June 12–16, 2009; July 24–28, 2009; September 19–23, 2009). [3]Gallup polls (Storrs, Conn.: Roper Center for Public Opinion Research, November 11–14, 2002; November 3–5, 2003; November 7–10, 2005; November 9–12, 2006; November 11–14, 2007; November 13–16, 2008). [4]NBC News/*Wall Street Journal* Poll (Storrs, Conn.: Roper Center for Public Opinion Research, February 26–March 1, 2009). [5]Democracy Corps/Greenberg Quinlan Rosner Research Poll (Storrs, Conn.: Roper Center for Public Opinion Research, May 29–31, 2007). [6]Commonwealth Fund, "2007 Commonwealth Fund Biennial Health Insurance Survey." [7]Galen Institute/Zogby International Poll (Storrs, Conn.: Roper Center for Public Opinion Research, June 18–21, 2003).

Table 5-7 Attitudes about Ways to Increase the Number of Americans Covered by Health Insurance (in percent)

	Favor	Oppose	Don't know
Expanding state government programs for low-income people, such as Medicaid and the Children's Health Insurance Program	82	16	2
Expanding Medicare to cover people between the ages of 55 and 64 who do not have health insurance	74	20	6
Requiring all Americans to have health insurance, either from their employer or from another source, with financial help for those who can't afford it	68	29	3
Requiring employers to offer health insurance to their workers or pay money into a government fund that will pay to cover those without insurance	67	28	5
Offering tax credits to help people buy private health insurance	67	26	7
Creating a government-administered public health insurance option to compete with private health insurance plans*	59	36	5
Creating a government-administered public health insurance option similar to Medicare to compete with private health insurance plans*	57	37	6
Having a national health plan, or single-payer plan, in which all Americans would get their insurance from a single government plan	40	56	5

Note: *These two items were asked of separate groups of respondents as a wording experiment.

Question: I'm going to read you some different ways to increase the number of Americans covered by health insurance. As I read each one, please tell me whether you would favor it or oppose it. (Expanding state government programs for low-income people, such as Medicaid and the Children's Health Insurance Program/Expanding Medicare to cover people between the ages of 55 and 64 who do not have health insurance/Requiring all Americans to have health insurance, either from their employer or from another source, with financial help for those who can't afford it/Requiring employers to offer health insurance to their workers or pay money into a government fund that will pay to cover those without insurance/Offering tax credits to help people buy private health insurance/Creating a government-administered public health insurance option to compete with private health insurance plans/Creating a government-administered public health insurance option similar to Medicare to compete with private health insurance plans/Having a national health plan, or single-payer plan, in which all Americans would get their insurance from a single government plan.)

Source: Kaiser Family Foundation, "Kaiser Health Tracking Poll," September 2009.

Table 5-8 Atttitudes about Government Health Insurance (in percent)

Preference for health insurance[1]

Current system, in which most people get their health insurance from private employers, but some people have no insurance	40
Universal program, in which everyone is covered under a program like Medicare that is run by the government and financed by taxpayers	56

Confidence that federal government could provide quality health care coverage to all citizens who need it[2]

Extremely confident	12
Very confident	14
Somewhat confident	31
Not too confident	19
Not at all confident	23

Government would do a better or worse job than private insurance companies in providing medical coverage[3]

Better	36
Worse	47
Same (vol.)	5
Don't know	12

Fairness of federal government requiring all Americans to participate in a national health care plan, funded by taxpayers[4]

Fair	43
Unfair	48

Socialized medicine compared to system we have now (among those who said they were at least somewhat familiar with the phrase "socialized medicine" = 83%)[5]

Better	45
Worse	39
About the same (vol.)	4
Don't know	12

Notes: "Don't know" responses not shown if less than 10%; (vol.) = volunteered response.

Question: Which would you prefer—the current health insurance system in the United States, in which most people get their health insurance from private employers, but some people have no insurance; or a universal health insurance program, in which everyone is covered under a program like Medicare that's run by the government and financed by taxpayers?

Question: How confident are you that . . . The federal government could provide quality health care coverage to all citizens who need it?

Question: Do you think the government would do a better or worse job than private insurance companies in providing medical coverage?

Question: Do you think it would be fair or unfair for the government in Washington to require all Americans to participate in a national health care plan, funded by taxpayers?

Question: (Asked of those who said they were at least somewhat familiar with the phrase "socialized medicine") So far as you understand the phrase, do you think that if we had socialized medicine in this country that the health care system would be better or worse than what we have now?

Sources: [1]*ABC News/Kaiser Family Foundation/USA Today,* "Health Care in America 2006 Survey," October 2006. [2]Ruth Helman and Paul Fronstin, "2007 Health Confidence Survey: Rising Health Care Costs Are Changing the Ways Americans Use the Health Care System," *EBRI Notes* 28 (November 2007). [3]CBS News Poll (Storrs, Conn.: Roper Center for Public Opinion Research, August 27–31, 2009). [4]CBS News/*New York Times* Poll (Storrs, Conn.: Roper Center for Public Opinion Research, February 23–27, 2007). [5]Harvard School of Public Health/Harris Interactive Poll, "Debating Health: Election 2008; Americans' Views on Socialized Medicine," February 2008.

Table 5-9 Attitudes about Employment-Based Health Insurance (in percent)

Believe employers should either provide health insurance to their employees or contribute to a fund that would help cover workers without health insurance[1]	81

Requiring all Americans to have health insurance: employers would be required to provide insurance for all their workers or pay into a fund that would be used to buy insurance for people who do not have insurance[2]

Good idea	36
Bad idea	17
Unsure	46

Note: "Don't know" responses not shown.

Question: Some people say that to help pay for the cost of health insurance for all Americans, employers should either provide health insurance to their employees or contribute to a fund that would help cover workers without health insurance. Others say that employers should not have to provide or contribute. Which comes closer to your opinion?

Question: Some people have suggested requiring all Americans to have health insurance. Under this plan, employers would be required to provide insurance for all their workers or pay into a fund that would be used to buy insurance for people who do not have insurance. Does this sound like a good idea to you, a bad idea or are you unsure?

Sources: [1]Commonwealth Fund, "2007 Commonwealth Fund Biennial Health Insurance Survey." [2]CBS News/*New York Times* Poll, February 23–27, 2007.

Table 5-10 Attitudes about Requiring People to Have Health Insurance Coverage (in percent)

Require all Americans to have health insurance: Most people would still get insurance through their work. People who don't get insurance from work would have to buy it themselves, or pay a fine if they don't. People with lower incomes would get help from the government paying the cost of health insurance.[1]

Support	47
Oppose	44
Don't know	8

A law that requires all Americans to have health insurance, either getting it from work or buying it on their own[2]

Support	49
Oppose	47
No opinion	4

A law requiring all Americans to have health insurance if it included:

A rule that working Americans who don't get insurance through work or on their own would have to pay money into a government health insurance fund[2]

Support	44
Oppose	52
No opinion	4

A rule that all employers either offer health insurance to their employees or pay money into a government health insurance fund[2]

Support	62
Oppose	34
No opinion	4

A rule that insurance companies sell coverage to people regardless of preexisting conditions[2]

Support	68
Oppose	27
No opinion	5

A tax credit or other aid to help low-income Americans pay for health insurance[2]

Support	70
Oppose	28
No opinion	2

Question: I'm going to read you a description of a plan to make sure everyone has health insurance, and then I'm going to ask you if you support or oppose this plan. This proposal would require all Americans to have insurance. Most people would still get insurance through their work. People who don't get insurance from work would have to buy it themselves, or pay a fine if they don't. People with lower incomes would get help from the government paying the cost of health insurance. Would you support or oppose this kind of plan?

Question: Would you support or oppose a law that requires all Americans to have health insurance, either getting it from work or buying it on their own?

Question: Would you support or oppose a law that requires all Americans to have health insurance if it included: (a rule that working Americans who don't get insurance through work or on their own would have to pay money into a government health insurance fund/a rule that all employers either offer health insurance to their employees or pay money into a government health insurance fund/a rule that insurance companies sell coverage to people regardless of preexisting conditions/a tax credit or other aid to help low-income Americans pay for health insurance)

Sources: [1]NPR/Kaiser Family Foundation/Harvard School of Public Health, "The Public on Requiring Individuals to Have Health Insurance," February 2008. [2]ABC News/*Washington Post* Poll (Storrs, Conn., Roper Center for Public Opinion Research, June 18–21, 2009).

Table 5-11 Attitudes about the Individual Health Insurance Market (in percent)

Preferred direction on health care[1]

Building on the current system, where most people get insurance through their employers and many of those with low incomes have their health care paid for by the government through public programs	45
Moving toward a system in which most individuals would buy their own insurance but people with more modest incomes would receive a government tax credit to help them with the cost of the plan	42
Don't know	12

Preferred way to get health insurance, if cost to you were the same (among those covered by health insurance from their/their spouse's employer)[2]

Get health insurance through your/your spouse's employer	47
Buy health insurance yourself	14
Doesn't make much difference	36
Don't know	4

If you were to buy health insurance on your own, would each of the following be easier/harder/wouldn't make much difference (among those covered by health insurance from their/their spouse's employer)[2]	Easier	Harder	No difference
Get a good price for health insurance	5	82	8
Find or keep health insurance if you are sick	5	78	12
Handle administrative issues, such as filing a claim or signing up for a policy	8	65	22
Find a plan that matches your needs well	16	62	17

Question: Which of the following best describes the direction you would like to see the country take when it comes to health care? Building on the current system, where most people get insurance through their employers and many of those with low incomes have their health care paid for by the government through public programs or moving toward a system in which most individuals would buy their own insurance but people with more modest incomes would receive a government tax credit to help them with the cost of the plan?

Question: (Asked of those covered by health insurance/a health plan through their/their spouse's employer) Assuming the cost to you was about the same, would you prefer to get health insurance through your/your spouse's employer at work, or would you prefer to buy health insurance on your own, or doesn't it make much difference to you?

Question: (Asked of those covered by health insurance/a health plan through their/their spouse's employer) If you were to buy health insurance on your own, do you think it would be easier or harder to (do each), or wouldn't it make much difference compared to your current situation?

Sources: [1]Kaiser Family Foundation, "Kaiser Health Tracking Poll: Election 2008," April 2008. [2]Kaiser Family Foundation, "Kaiser Health Tracking Poll: Election 2008," August 2008.

Table 5-12 Lack of Public Consensus about Ways to Cover the Uninsured (in percent)

Which option preferred most among ways to increase the number of Americans covered by health insurance (2006)[1]	
Requiring employers to either offer health insurance or pay money into a government pool	15
Having all Americans get their insurance from a single government plan	15
Expanding Medicare to those uninsured who are aged 55 to 64	14
Offering tax breaks to businesses that do offer health insurance	14
Requiring all Americans to have health insurance, with tax credits or other aid to help those who can't afford it	14
Offering tax credits to help people buy private health insurance	12
Expanding state government programs for low-income people	11
Health reform plan you prefer for yourself (1945)[2]	
Insurance company plan	39
Federal government plan	34
Doctor organization plan	12
No preference	15
Preference as way to help cover those without health insurance (2007)[3]	
Requiring all Americans to have health insurance, with the federal government helping pay for health insurance for low-income families	40
Providing health savings accounts and tax credits to help individuals and employers purchase health insurance	49
Neither/other (vol.)	6
Preferred way to provide health insurance coverage to more people (2001)[4]	
Offering uninsured Americans income tax deductions, tax credits, or other financial assistance to help them purchase private health insurance on their own	43
Expanding state government programs, such as Medicaid and the Children's Health Insurance Program, to provide coverage for low-income people without health insurance	47
Don't prefer either (vol.)	7

Notes: "Don't know" responses not shown if less than 10%; (vol.) = volunteered response.

Question: Of those options you just said you favored, which one do you most prefer: requiring employers to either offer health insurance or pay money into a government pool/having all Americans get their insurance from a single government plan/expanding Medicare to those uninsured who are aged 55 to 64/offering tax breaks to businesses that do offer health insurance/requiring all Americans to have health insurance, with tax credits or other aid to help those who can't afford it/offering tax credits to help people buy private health insurance/expanding state government programs for low-income people?

Question: Which of these three [health] plans would you prefer for yourself—group insurance through an insurance company, a federal government plan as part of the Social Security program, or a doctor-organization plan?

Question: When it comes to the issue of health care, which of the following two options would you prefer to help cover those without health insurance? Requiring all Americans to have health insurance, with the federal government helping pay for health insurance for low-income families or providing health savings accounts and tax credits to help individuals and employers purchase health insurance.

Question: If you had to choose between the following two ways to provide health insurance coverage to more uninsured people, which one would you prefer: offering uninsured Americans income tax deductions, tax credits, or other financial assistance to help them purchase private health insurance on their own or expanding state government programs, such as Medicaid and the Children's Health Insurance Program, to provide coverage for low-income people without health insurance?

Sources: [1]Kaiser Family Foundation Poll (Storrs, Conn.: Roper Center for Public Opinion Research, February 2–7, 2006). [2]Stanley L. Payne, "Some Opinion Research Principles Developed through Studies of Social Medicine," *Public Opinion Quarterly* 10 (Spring 1946): 93–98. [3]NBC News/*Wall Street Journal* Poll (Storrs, Conn.: Roper Center for Public Opinion Research, November 1–5, 2007). [4]Kaiser Family Foundation/Harvard School of Public Health, "Post-Election Survey: The Public and the Health Care Agenda for the New Administration and Congress," January 25, 2001.

Table 5-13 Attitudes about Providing Health Insurance Coverage for Children (in percent)

How much government is doing to provide health insurance to children who don't have it[1]	
Too much	6
Too little	67
About the right amount	20
Which group should we try to provide health insurance coverage for first (among those who favor the federal government doing more to help provide health insurance = 85%)[2]	
Children	57
Working people who are currently uninsured	19
Low-income people	21
Increase federal spending on children's health insurance by $35 billion over the next five years[3]	
Support strongly	49
Support somewhat	23
Oppose somewhat	8
Oppose strongly	17
Spending an additional $35 billion over the next 5 years in order to maintain coverage for those already in the program and expand coverage to an additional 3.8 million uninsured children. The expansion would be financed by an increase in cigarette taxes. In general, would you say you support or oppose the increased funding for this program?[1]	
Support	70
Oppose	26

Note: "Don't know" responses not shown.

Question: In general, do you think the government is doing too much, too little, or about the right amount in providing health insurance to children who don't have it?

Question: (Asked of those who favor the federal government doing more to help provide health insurance for more Americans) If Congress doesn't think we can afford to guarantee health insurance for everyone, which one of the following groups do you think we should try to provide with health insurance coverage first? Is it children, working people who are currently uninsured, or low-income people?

Question: There's a proposal to increase federal spending on children's health insurance by $35 billion over the next five years. It would be funded by an increase in cigarette taxes. Supporters say this would provide insurance for millions of low-income children who are currently uninsured. Opponents say this goes too far in covering children in families that can afford health insurance on their own. Do you support or oppose this increased funding for this program? Do you feel this way strongly or somewhat?

Question: The State Children's Health Insurance Program, or SCHIP, is a program in which the federal government joins with states to fund health insurance for children whose parents make too much to qualify for Medicaid. Currently, approximately 6 million children get health insurance through this program at a cost to the federal government of $25 billion over 5 years. Congress is proposing to spend an additional $35 billion over the next 5 years in order to maintain coverage for those already in the program and expand coverage to an additional 3.8 million uninsured children. The expansion would be financed by an increase in cigarette taxes. In general, would you say you support or oppose the increased funding for this program?

Sources: [1]NPR/Kaiser Family Foundation/Harvard School of Public Health, "Public Views on SCHIP Reauthorization," October 2007. [2]Kaiser Family Foundation/Harvard School of Public Health, "The Public's Health Care Agenda for the New Congress and Presidential Campaign," December 2006. [3]ABC News/*Washington Post* Poll (Storrs, Conn.: Roper Center for Public Opinion Research, September 27–30, 2007).

Table 5-14 Willingness to Pay in Order to Increase the Number of Americans with Health Insurance (in percent)

Which is more important[1]

Providing health care for all Americans	66
Holding down taxes	31

The U.S. government guaranteeing health insurance for all citizens, even if it means raising taxes[2]

Strongly favor	30
Favor	33
Oppose	21
Strongly oppose	13

Willingness to pay more in order to increase the number of Americans who have health insurance[3]	Yes, willing	No, not willing
1996	47	47
1998	46	49
1999	39	52
2000	46	49
2003	52	42
2004	45	51
2007	39	58
2008	47	49
June 2009	41	54
July 2009	51	44
August 2009	42	55
September 2009	49	46

Note: "Don't know" responses not shown.

Question: Which of these do you think is more important: providing health care coverage for all Americans, even if it means raising taxes or holding down taxes, even if it means some Americans do not have health care coverage?

Question: All in all, do you strongly favor, favor, oppose, or strongly oppose . . . the U.S. government guaranteeing health insurance for all citizens, even if it means raising taxes?

Question: Would you be willing to pay more—either in higher health insurance premiums or higher taxes—in order to increase the number of Americans who have health insurance or not? (1996–2004, 2008, 2009)

Question: In order to increase the number of Americans who have health insurance, would you be willing to pay more—either in higher health insurance premiums or higher taxes—or would you not be willing to pay more? (2007)

Sources: [1]ABC News/*Washington Post* Poll (Storrs, Conn.: Roper Center for Public Opinion Research, June 12–15, 2008). [2]Pew Research Center for the People and the Press/Pew Forum on Religion and Public Life Poll (Storrs, Conn.: Roper Center for Public Opinion Research, July 31–August 10, 2008). [3]Kaiser Family Foundation/Harvard School of Public Health polls (Storrs, Conn.: Roper Center for Public Opinion Research, November 6–10, 1996; November 4–December 6, 1998; October 8–12, 1999; November 13–December 13, 2000; February 6–10, 2003; November 4–28, 2004; December 4–14, 2008); *Washington Post*/Kaiser Family Foundation/Harvard School of Public Health Poll (Storrs, Conn.: Roper Center for Public Opinion Research, May 3–June 3, 2007); Kaiser Family Foundation polls (Storrs, Conn.: Roper Center for Public Opinion Research, June 1–5, 2009; July 7–14, 2009; August 4–11, 2009; September 11–18, 2009).

Table 5-15 Attitudes about Changing the Status Quo in the Health Care System (in percent)

Expected effect of universal health insurance[1]	Worse	Same	Better
The quality of your own health care	31	38	25
The availability of health care treatments to you and your family	31	35	29
The cost of health care for you and your family	25	33	33
Your choice of doctors and hospitals	34	39	21
	Increase	Stay the same	Decrease
Expected effect of Clinton plan on total amount you pay for medical care[2]	54	26	17
	Fewer choices	About the same	More choices
Expected effect of Clinton plan on number of choices when it comes to doctors and medicine you can receive[2]	48	33	16
	Decline	Stay about the same	Improve
Expected effect of Clinton plan on quality of medical care available to you[2]	39	40	20
	Worse off	Won't make much difference	Better off
Overall, if Congress passes a health care plan, effect on you personally[2]	40	37	19

Note: "Don't know" responses not shown.

Question: Do you think a universal health insurance system would make (each) better, worse, or would it stay about the same?

Question: Under [President Bill] Clinton's [health care reform] plan, would you expect the total amount of money you pay for medical care—including health insurance—to increase, decrease, or stay about the same?

Question: Under Clinton's [health care reform] plan, would you expect to have more choices, fewer choices, or about the same number of choices as you now have when it comes to doctors and the medical care you receive?

Question: Under Clinton's [health care reform] plan, would you expect the quality of medical care available to you to improve, decline, or stay about the same?

Question: Overall, if Congress passes a health care plan, do you think you personally will be better off, worse off, or won't the health care plan make much of a difference to you?

Sources: [1]Kaiser Family Foundation, "Kaiser Health Tracking Poll," October 2008. [2]Gallup/CNN/*USA Today* Poll (Storrs, Conn.: Roper Center for Public Opinion Research, April 16–18, 1994).

Table 5-16 Americans' Worries about Health Insurance (in percent)

	Very worried	Somewhat worried	Not too worried	Not at all worried
Having to pay more for your health care or health insurance	31	38	17	13
Not being able to afford the health care services you think you need	34	28	21	17
Losing your health insurance coverage (among those insured)	29	23	24	22

Note: "Don't know" responses not shown.

Question: I'm going to read you a list of things that some people worry about and others do not. I'd like you to tell me how worried you are about each of the following things. How worried are you about having to pay more for your health care or health insurance/not being able to afford the health care services you think you need/losing your health insurance coverage (among those insured)?

Source: Kaiser Family Foundation, "Kaiser Health Tracking Poll," July 2009.

Figure 5-1 **Priority of Health Care, 1990–2008**

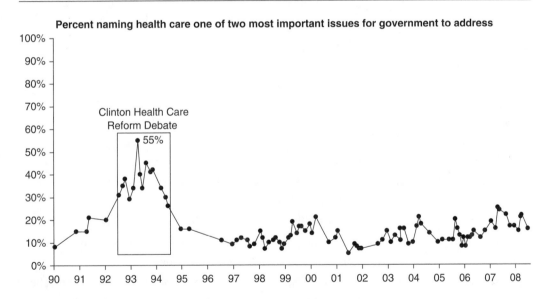

Note: "Don't know" responses were included in the base when percentages were calculated.

Question: What would you say are the two or three most important issues or problems facing the nation today that you personally would like to see the federal government in Washington do something about? (1990–1992)

Question: What do you think are the two most important issues for the government to address? (1993–2008)

Sources: NBC News/*Wall Street Journal* (1990–92) and Harris Interactive polls (1993–2006), cited in Mollyann Brodie, "Insights into the Public's Views about Health Insurance: Challenges and Opportunities for Would-Be Reformers," Presentation at the Annual Conference of the National Academy of Social Insurance, February 2, 2007; Harris Interactive polls (Storrs, Conn.: Roper Center for Public Opinion Research, February 2–5, 2007; April 20–23, 2007; July 6–9, 2007; September 7–10, 2007; October 5–8, 2007; November 30–December 3, 2007; February 6–10, 2008; April 2–6, 2008; June 4–8, 2008; August 6–10, 2008; September 17–21, 2008).

Chapter 6

THE MASSACHUSETTS HEALTH REFORM LAW: A CASE STUDY

Tara Sussman Oakman, Robert J. Blendon, and Tami Buhr

On April 12, 2006, Governor Mitt Romney of Massachusetts signed into law sweeping changes to the state's health insurance system. The legislation, "An Act Providing Access to Affordable, Quality, Accountable Health Care," aimed to provide nearly universal health coverage to Bay State residents within three years. Massachusetts is the only state that has enacted a law that covers more than 97 percent of its population.

This chapter provides a case study of the role of public opinion in a debate over health care reform. It addresses three main issues: background information on the political culture in Massachusetts, what influenced the shape of the 2006 reform law from public opinion to leadership, and public support for the law and its main features at three points of its implementation. These three points are: September 2006, when Massachusetts had passed the legislation, before any substantive changes to the health care system were implemented, and after the local media had reported some concerns; June 2007, one year after implementation when the individual mandate had taken effect and several groups were expressing concerns about affordability for some Massachusetts residents; and June 2008, after the penalties for not having insurance had been executed in the state income tax forms and the statehouse was addressing a $150 million budget shortfall. The chapter also looks at overall support of the law in 2009, three years after implementation and during a severe recession. The discussion of public opinion data in this chapter draws extensively from an article published by the authors in *Health Affairs* in 2008.[1]

Massachusetts Political Culture

The political culture in Massachusetts fostered an environment supportive of the 2006 legislation. First, universal coverage was appealing to the core political values of the majority of Massachusetts residents: in 2007, 92 percent of them thought health care was a right.[2] The political party distribution in Massachusetts, highly skewed toward Democrats and independents, was also relevant to health reform, as people who identify with each political party tend to have different views on what should be done about the health care system.[3] Democrats and independents are much more supportive of universal coverage proposals than are Republicans. In a February 2008 nationwide survey, 65 percent of Democrats said that they wanted a new health plan that would make a major effort to provide health insurance for all uninsured. Forty-seven percent of independents shared this view, but only 26 percent of Republicans did. At the same time, 28 percent of Republicans—compared to 6 percent of Democrats and 12 percent of independents—thought things should be kept as they were.[4]

Second, Massachusetts has a unique history when it comes to health reform. The state has produced several leaders, namely, Senators Ted Kennedy and John Kerry and Governor Michael Dukakis, who rose to national prominence as presidential candidates and campaigned on providing universal health insurance coverage. Among the reasons for the predominance of Massachusetts politicians on the national stage are that the state is considered to have a "hyperpolitical" culture and its leaders often believe they are equipped to handle national roles.[5]

In addition, Massachusetts has wrestled with the idea of universal coverage on several occasions. In April 1988, in the midst of his campaign for president, Dukakis signed the Health Security Act to provide universal health coverage in his state.[6] Its universal coverage feature, a mandate requiring all employers to offer insurance to their employees or pay a fine, however, was never implemented. In 1995 Governor William Weld, a Republican, proposed a health reform plan advertised as "universal coverage without an employer mandate." Among its other features, the plan expanded Medicaid eligibility (necessitating that the U.S. government grant the state a waiver to surpass basic federal requirements), provided tax credits to businesses that gave health benefits to their workers, and created a program (now called Insurance Partnership) to assist small employers and low-wage workers in buying health insurance.[7]

The legislature made significant modifications to Weld's proposal and passed it in July 1996. Three major features of this legislation were to provide health coverage to most of the 160,000 children (through age 19) who lacked health insurance, to help the elderly with their prescription drug costs, and to impose a new cigarette tax of 25 cents per pack, as well as a 15 percent tax on cigars and smoking tobacco to help fund these benefits.[8]

With this law, Massachusetts moved into the vanguard of health reform legislation in the country.[9] Over the next several years, Massachusetts made additional incremental changes to its system to address the issue of the uninsured. In 1998, during the tenure of Governor Paul Cellucci, the state got a federal waiver to make it possible to give financial assistance to families earning up to 200 percent of the federal poverty level who were participating in employer-provided health insurance. Massachusetts thus became the first state in the country to subsidize private health insurance for employees who could not afford the premiums in plans offered by their employers.[10]

By the time the next health reform debate began several years later, Massachusetts residents were comfortably familiar with the issue of universal coverage. Public opinion data from 2003 showed that the public supported a major initiative to cover the uninsured. When asked what they thought the government should do for people in Massachusetts who do not have health insurance, only 11 percent said that things should be kept as they are now. Forty-seven percent believed that the government should "make a major effort to provide health insurance for most uninsured Massachusetts residents, which might require a tax increase to pay for it." Thirty-four percent said they preferred a "limited effort," which might "mean more government spending" (**Table 6–1**). About six in ten (59 percent) thought that the situation for the uninsured in Massachusetts had gotten worse during the past two years; only 5 percent thought it had gotten better.[11]

Although the environment was favorable to moving health reform forward, the Massachusetts public was divided on the best way to proceed. When asked about various alternatives for expanding coverage, a majority supported each one, from a single-payer government plan, to tax credits, to an expansion of existing state programs. But when respondents were presented with arguments against these coverage expansion approaches, overall support for each alternative, other than expanding state programs, fell below a majority (**Table 6–2**).[12]

Survey results also showed that Massachusetts residents did not agree about who should pay for the uninsured. Fifteen percent said the uninsured themselves were responsible, and 16 percent gave the responsibility to businesses. Although a majority (57 percent) thought that government should be responsible, the public did not agree on which level of government: 35 percent said the federal government, 18 percent said the state, and 1 percent local governments (**Table 6–3**).[13]

Actors in the Health Reform Debate

The opinion environment in Massachusetts provided an opportunity for leadership, from the grassroots level to the governor, to craft legislation that would take advantage of the support for reform and maintain that support despite the complexity of views among the public. We now look at the major actors in the process.

Grassroots and Interest Groups

In May 2005 a coalition called MassACT launched an initiative to put health care coverage on the November 2006 ballot.[14] Political leaders took the ballot initiative seriously, presumably because they expected it to pass. In a March 2005 poll, 66 percent of Massachusetts voters said they would be inclined to vote yes on an amendment to the state constitution that would "require the governor and legislature to enact a plan, subject to the approval of the voters, that provides comprehensive, affordable health insurance coverage for every Massachusetts resident."[15] In reflecting on the 2006 health reform debate, Massachusetts House Speaker Salvatore DiMasi said, "I used the threat of the ballot measure to pressure the business community. . . . I told them you'd better do something or you're going to lose the ballot question."[16]

The Health Care Sector

In 2005 Partners HealthCare and Blue Cross Blue Shield of Massachusetts (BCBSMA) joined together as part of an initiative advocating health care reform.[17] Together, Partners and BCBSMA framed the uninsured issue as an economic crisis.

BCBSMA also influenced the health reform debate through its charitable foundation. The BCBSMA Foundation, founded in 2001 to improve access to health care in Massachusetts, began the *Roadmap to Coverage* initiative in 2003. On November 16, 2004, the foundation released a report, "Caring for the Uninsured in Massachusetts," prepared by the Urban Institute in Washington, D.C. It concluded that providing coverage for the uninsured would increase health care spending in the state, but it would also result in social benefits and economic benefits of up to $1.7 billion because people would be healthier.[18] The report drew an immediate response from Massachusetts leadership, which promised to make health reform a priority for the upcoming legislative session.[19]

The Federal Government

In November 2004 the federal government began to apply its own pressure on Massachusetts to reform its health care system. The U.S. Department of Health and Human Services (HHS) threatened to cut a substantial amount of funds it had been providing to Massachusetts as part of the Section 1115 Medicaid waiver the state received in 1997 and renewed in 2002. The funds were directed to safety net systems at Boston Medical Center and Cambridge Health Alliance. As part of an overall effort to limit federal spending, the Bush administration was cracking down on state Medicaid funds. Governor Romney and Senator Kennedy joined together to try to convince federal officials that Massachusetts was using the money wisely to help the uninsured and was not taking advantage of federal generosity.[20] In January 2005 HHS officials agreed that Massachusetts could keep the funds if, by July 2006, the state had provided a plan to help people to get insurance rather than reimburse institutions that provided care for the uninsured.[21] This federal threat put enormous pressure on the governor and state legislature to move forward on health reform.

The Governor

After his election as governor, Romney made reforming the health care system one of his highest priorities. In June 2005 he released his full health care proposal, which included an individual mandate.[22] An individual mandate requires all state residents to have health insurance that they either get through their employers or buy themselves. People with low incomes would get help from the government to pay their health insurance premiums. Romney marketed the individual mandate as a conservative idea, that people should be responsible for their own care and not look to government to take care of them if they can afford to take care of themselves. The Heritage Foundation gave Romney many of his ideas for health reform. The conservative think tank also gave Romney political cover from Republican critics who accused him of being too liberal in developing a plan for expanding the state's health coverage.[23] As *The Almanac of American Politics* observed, "In heavily Democratic Massachusetts, Romney has not hesitated to be a strong Republican partisan."[24]

As Romney announced his plans for health reform, many people continued to wonder about his ambition for higher office. This speculation was bolstered in early 2006 when Romney declared that he would not run for a second term as governor. Commentators suggested that he wanted to use health reform as a political trophy.[25] Recognizing that he needed the legislature's help to move concrete accomplishments forward, Romney began running ads in spring 2005 talking about his efforts to reach across the aisle to have another "year of action in the Legislature."[26]

The Massachusetts Legislature

Senate president Robert Travaglini announced a health reform plan on April 6, 2005. Before becoming Senate president, Travaglini had proposed a single-payer plan for Massachusetts, but now he offered a more moderate plan.[27] On November 9 the state senate passed a version similar to Travaglini's.[28]

On November 3 Speaker DiMasi presented his plan to the House floor. This plan aimed to cover 95 percent of the state's uninsured through a combination of an individual mandate, Medicaid expansion, and an employer mandate in the form of a payroll tax on employers who did not offer health insurance within a three-year period. DiMasi called upon Massachusetts lawmakers to live up to the state's reputation for leadership: "Massachusetts has been known, throughout its history, throughout the country's history, for being the first in many things. What we are proposing today is a bold proposal. It takes bold and courageous leadership to pass this for our citizens, to control the health care costs in our commonwealth, provide health care for everyone."[29]

DiMasi's plan passed the House on November 4, 2005.

At an Impasse

The plans passed by the House and Senate were very different versions of health reform. Travaglini said he thought the House plan would strain Massachusetts resources. Some leaders of the House, including Democrat Patricia Walrath, chair of the Health Care Financing Committee, thought the Senate plan would not meet standards set forth by the federal government to hold on to the Medicaid funding that had been at risk.[30]

Reactions outside the legislature were divided as well. The MassACT coalition supported the House plan. The business community was divided, especially because of the payroll tax. Retailers and the National Federation of Independent Business opposed any sort of charge to employers. A group of construction industry associations and some individual executives supported it. A loose coalition of business groups that included Greater Boston Chamber of Commerce, Associated Industries of Massachusetts, Massachusetts Business Roundtable, and Massachusetts Taxpayers Foundation supported overall efforts to achieve health care reform but opposed the payroll tax specifically.[31]

By February 2006 talks between the Massachusetts House and Senate in conference committee had bogged down, and DiMasi and Travaglini began one-on-one negotiating. DiMasi seemed optimistic at that point that an agreement would be reached, but Travaglini began to show signs of skepticism. DiMasi insisted on the payroll tax and the more generous coverage goal, and Travaglini was in favor of a more gradual approach without the mandates.[32]

Governor Romney pressured the House and Senate to compromise. In February he personally delivered letters to DiMasi and Travaglini urging them to come to an agreement. Romney continued to oppose the payroll tax, however, and told DiMasi that if the compromise bill included a payroll tax, he would not use his influence with Michael Leavitt, secretary of the U.S. Department of Health and Human Services, to get federal approval of the Massachusetts plan and save their Medicaid funds.[33]

Ted Kennedy also got involved in the health reform process. When the state House and Senate passed their plans in November, Kennedy did not endorse either one but praised both the individual and employer mandate features of the House plan. When the conference committee appeared at a standstill, he called legislative leaders at home. DiMasi said of Kennedy's interest in the issue, "I think he really wants to see us do something dramatic and bold so we can insure as many people as possible in the next three years and comply with the waiver. He thinks Massachusetts can be a leader in this area, and he's very excited about it."[34]

By the end of February, Travaglini announced that hopes for a Massachusetts reform plan were all but dead and that they should work on a scaled-back plan that both sides could agree on to meet the federal deadline and not lose the Medicaid funding.[35] The Senate passed just such a scaled-back plan on February 28. That bill aimed to make available basic, more affordable private insurance plans for which poorer residents could receive subsidies on a sliding scale. Upon Governor Romney's request, the plan also included an individual mandate; Romney suggested that the federal government would not accept the plan without a mandate.[36] Speaker DiMasi, however, continued to say that he would not support a bill without any sort of employer assessment and wanted to hold out for a more ambitious plan. In the meantime the MassACT Coalition continued to push ahead for a universal coverage initiative on the November 2006 ballot.[37]

The Compromise

On March 1 Jack Connors, chairman of Partners Healthcare, convened a secret meeting of Boston business executives to help broker a deal and break the health reform impasse. Together, they devised a plan to impose a $295 charge per employee for businesses with eleven or more workers and did not offer health coverage. This proposal was intended to appease both the business community and the legislature. DiMasi and Travaglini met with this group and agreed with their suggestions. Within forty-eight hours, the two leaders stood together at the State House announcing that they had reached a compromise.

The legislature passed the compromise bill on April 4, 2006, with the House voting 154 to 2 and the Senate voting 37 to 0. The revised bill intended to provide coverage to 95 percent of the state's uninsured over three years at a price of $1.2 billion. It assessed companies with more than ten employees that did not offer insurance $295 per year for each worker.

The compromise legislation not only brought together a coalition of supporters among state leadership and interest groups, but also reflected the complexity of public opinion. Research has suggested that one way to attain majority support of universal coverage legislation is for leaders to craft a solution that includes multiple approaches so nearly everyone gets some part of their preferences.[38] Reflecting the lack of public consensus on a particular solution, policymakers had pieced together multiple approaches to covering the uninsured. They also included government, employers, and individuals as part of a "shared responsibility" plan that mirrored the lack of agreement among the public as to who should pay for the uninsured.

When the legislature officially sent the bill to the governor for his signature, Romney said, "Today, Massachusetts has set itself apart from every other state in the country. An achievement like this comes along once in a generation."[39] In a separate interview, he also remarked, "This is a Democratic ideal, which is getting health care for everybody, but achieved in a Republican way, which is reforming the private marketplace and insisting on personal responsibility."[40] Supporters of health reform celebrated the passage of this landmark legislation, and the MassACT Coalition decided to drop their ballot initiative.

Public Opinion on the Reform, 2006 to 2009

From the early days of the Massachusetts health care reform law, observers noted the importance of paying attention to public support for the law over time, and many implementation decisions were made with an eye toward bolstering it.[41] Public support for the new health law in Massachusetts would be critical to its success and survival. As health care costs grew and state budgets tightened, a loss of support among the public could result in pressure on the government to repeal or cut the legislation, as had happened in other states.[42]

Awareness of and Support for the Law

From the time the health reform law was passed in 2006, more than three-fourths of Massachusetts residents said that they had heard or read at least a little about the law: 80 percent in 2006, 86 percent in 2007, 93 percent in 2008, and 89 percent in 2009. The proportion who said they had heard or read a great deal or quite a lot about the law increased from less than one-fourth (22 percent) in 2006 to about half in 2008 (54 percent) and 2009 (49 percent) (**Table 6–4**).[43]

Despite some negative press coverage after the law's passage,[44] public support for it increased between 2006 and 2008. Among those who had heard or read at least a little about the law, the proportion who supported it increased from 61 percent in September 2006 to 69 percent in June 2008 (**Table 6–5**).[45]

In 2009, when Massachusetts was facing the impact of a severe recession, state budget and fiscal problems, and continued high health care costs, public support for the law declined, but 59 percent were still behind it. Support varied by party affiliation: only 35 percent of Republicans favored the law, compared to 76 percent of Democrats, and 56 percent of independents.[46]

In June 2007 Massachusetts residents were asked about their reasons for supporting or opposing the reform law. An overwhelming majority (90 percent) of proponents said that a major reason for their support was that "making sure everyone has health insurance is the right thing to do." Another popular reason (79 percent) was that "people with health insurance get preventive and more continuous health care, which can keep everyone's future health care premiums down." Most supporters (59 percent) also said that a major reason was that "people won't face higher health care costs to cover the unpaid bills of those who don't have health insurance."

The individual mandate provided the basis for the two most popular reasons to oppose the reform. Seventy-two percent of opponents cited as their major objection that "people shouldn't be required to buy insurance if they can't afford it," and 61 percent said "people shouldn't be required to buy insurance if they don't want it or don't think they need it" (**Table 6–6**).[47]

The Individual Mandate

From the beginning, the individual mandate was one of the most politically controversial features of the new Massachusetts law.[48] As discussed above, it was one of the primary differences between the various legislative proposals before the legislators reached a compromise. Once the mandate became law, administrators were still unclear how the public would react. Many of the administrative decisions about who would be eligible for subsidized plans and who would be exempt from the mandate because insurance was deemed unaffordable were made with an eye toward public opinion, knowing that these decisions could make or break public support.[49]

Throughout the first two years of implementation, a modest majority of Massachusetts residents approved of the mandate: 52 percent in 2006, 57 percent in 2007, and 58 percent in 2008. Support among groups who might be feeling the brunt of the mandate because they were less likely to have insurance, such as the young, the least educated, and the $25,000–$49,999 income group hovered around 50 percent. Democrats' support strengthened over time. In choosing to back the individual mandate, Romney had suggested that this approach would appeal to conservatives because of its focus on individual responsibility. Republicans, however, remained evenly divided on the mandate issue (**Table 6–7**).[50]

One of the primary implementation decisions related to the mandate concerned eligibility for subsidized plans. As of June 2008 about one-half of the previously uninsured population in Massachusetts qualified for subsidized plans. The remainder of the uninsured population was required to purchase insurance without assistance, unless they were eligible for Medicaid.[51] Survey data from June 2007 suggested that whether the uninsured were required to enroll in a subsidized or unsubsidized plan made a real difference in terms of popular perceptions of the fairness of this requirement. After hearing a description of a subsidized and an unsubsidized plan, the Massachusetts public was more inclined to think that mandatory purchase of subsidized insurance plans was fair, as compared to unsubsidized plans. Overall, 44 percent thought it was unfair to require a typical uninsured person to purchase a subsidized insurance plan, and 62 percent thought the same about an unsubsidized plan. A substantial majority of the youngest (77 percent), poorest (79 percent), and least well educated groups (74 percent) thought that it would be unfair to mandate purchase of unsubsidized plans (**Table 6–8**).[52]

When asked generally about subsidized insurance plans in June 2008, support was high. Seventy-seven percent said they agreed with providing subsidized insurance to people earning less than 300 percent of federal poverty level.[53]

Employer Responsibility

The business-related requirement in the health reform law was one of the most divisive features among the leadership. Their hesitation to include employer responsibility in the law may have been based on the knowledge that an employer mandate had not fared well under the Dukakis plan years earlier. The public, however, has been consistently supportive of the requirement that all companies that employ more than ten people either offer health insurance to their employees or pay a penalty of up to $295 per employee per year (**Table 6–9**).

One of the main reasons for this positive reaction may be that the public has come to expect employers to provide insurance for their employees. Since the post–World War II era, the U.S. health insurance system has been rooted in the private sector.[54] In September 2006, 70 percent of Massachusetts residents supported the employer responsibility included in the new law, and 75 percent did so in 2008. A substantial majority of all groups, including Republicans, approved it.[55] Public opinion nationally about an employer mandate generally favors employer participation in health care.[56]

Moreover, research conducted on Massachusetts employer perceptions of the health reform showed that employers agree that they should have some responsibility for health insurance. This is true even among smaller businesses—employers with fewer than fifty workers—which many perceived to be hurt by this legislation.[57]

Perceptions of Who Is Helped and Hurt

One might expect that a law that aims to provide universal coverage would be perceived as helping the uninsured and those groups most likely to be uninsured—the poor and young adults. In 2006 and 2007 Massachusetts residents were asked to predict the impact of the law on various groups. In June 2008 they were asked their perceptions about the actual impact the law was having. In the two earlier years, the majority expected the law to help the uninsured, the poor, and young adults, but in 2008 respondents were more divided, with the majority thinking that the law had either hurt these groups or had no impact.

On the other hand, in this same period, a majority of the public felt that the law was either helping or having no impact on the middle class, large corporations, and the insured. Across all three survey periods, a majority thought the law had or would have no impact on them personally. This finding is important because earlier research had shown that a plan that a majority of individuals believe may hurt their care and/or the care of the middle class can threaten overall support for the plan as a whole.[58] These results suggest that one reason the Massachusetts plan is popular is that most people do not feel threatened by it. One group that the public does think has been hurt by the law is small business (**Table 6–10**).[59]

Two-thirds of Massachusetts residents initially expected the uninsured to be helped by the reform law, but by 2008 that proportion had dropped to about half (**Table 6–10**). The 2008 survey showed that those who were uninsured at some point during the last twelve months or those who had gotten insurance or changed their insurance because of the law were significantly less supportive of the law and more likely to say that the law was hurting them, as compared to other Massachusetts residents. The directly affected group was also less likely than other Massachusetts residents to support the mandate and more likely to think that the law had caused their health care costs to go up (**Table 6–11**).[60]

Public Views on Costs Associated with Reform

Since passage of the law in 2006, observers have noted that rising health care costs could provide the biggest threat to its success, because of its impact on individuals as well as on the state budget and economy.[61]

In 2008 a slight majority (54 percent) of Massachusetts residents thought the law had not had much impact on what they paid for health care and insurance. One-third, however, thought the law had caused their health care costs to go up. Thirty-nine percent thought the law had raised the cost of health care in Massachusetts. The same percentage thought the law was hurting the state budget, and 35 percent thought it was hurting the state's economy (**Table 6–12**).[62]

In 2008 the state government was dealing with costs of subsidized insurance plans that were higher than projected, leading to an estimated $150 million budget shortfall. When asked in June 2008 about options that might be used to deal with this deficit, a majority favored several different solutions. The most popular were increasing the cigarette tax and penalizing businesses with many part-time employees receiving subsidized insurance. Requiring insurers to contribute was also a popular option. The least popular alternatives were limiting the number of people receiving subsidized insurance and creating a waiting list and increasing the state sales tax (**Table 6–13**).[63] In June 2008, before these survey results were released, the state passed a $1 increase in the cigarette tax to help to address the budget shortfall.[64]

Public Views on the Future of Health Reform

Three years into the reform, the public showed some reservations about the law but little support for abolishing it. Only 11 percent of Massachusetts residents thought it should be repealed. Fifty-seven percent thought it should be continued with some changes, although it was unclear from the survey what those changes would mean, and 22 percent thought the law should continue as it was. Sixty-four percent of people thought the new law had been successful at reducing the number of uninsured in the state.[65]

Conclusion

Governor Mitt Romney, House Speaker Salvatore DiMasi, and Senate president Robert Travaglini, in conjunction with major stakeholders, were all crucial to the creation of a compromise health reform plan that addressed the substantive goals of expanding coverage in Massachusetts in a politically viable way. The law was not only passed, but also enjoyed high levels of support three years into implementation.

The political culture in Massachusetts, including its partisan leanings and its prior exposure to health care reform, provided a favorable environment for the new health law. Popular interest in addressing the uninsured issue put pressure on legislators to act, especially when some groups initiated the ballot referendum. Moreover, the design of the law took into account the complexity of public opinion. First, it included multiple approaches to expanding coverage. In a public divided as to the best way to cover the uninsured, this strategy has the potential to bolster support, as nearly everyone sees that their preferred alternative has been included. Second, the law mirrored the lack of agreement among the public as to who should pay for the uninsured by including government, employers, and individuals as part of a "shared responsibility" approach.

Surveys of Massachusetts residents in the three years after the state's health reform law was passed suggest that it is likely to survive. A majority supported the law overall, as well as its main features, including the mandate, employer responsibility, and subsidized plans. When asked specifically about whether the law should be repealed, an overwhelming number did not think so. In addition, a majority of people did not feel threatened by the law, a perception that had hurt universal coverage efforts in the past.

Some potential threats to the law, especially rising health care costs, do exist. If more people perceive that their already high cost of living is rising because of the law, or if attention is drawn to increasingly expensive unsubsidized plans that people are forced to purchase, it is possible that support for the law could change. A shift in employer attitudes or withdrawal of federal support could also provide a serious threat. At this point, however, it seems that the innovative Massachusetts health law, rooted in compromise, will last into the future. Although the new federal health care reform law passed in 2010 will require some changes in Massachusetts, it is structured to allow the state to continue with its general policy direction.

Notes

[1] Robert J. Blendon, Tami Buhr, Tara Sussman, and John M. Benson, "Massachusetts Health Reform: A Public Perspective from Debate through Implementation," *Health Affairs* 27 (Web exclusive, October 28, 2008): w556–w565. doi: 10-1377/hlthaff.27.6. w556. Published and copyrighted by Project HOPE/Health Affairs. Archived and available online at http://healthaffairs.org. Used with permission.

[2] Suffolk University, "Poll Reveals Disconnect on Mass. Health Care Law," June 17, 2007, http://www.suffolk.edu/20588.html.

[3] Robert J. Blendon, Drew E. Altman, Claudia Deane, John M. Benson, Mollyann Brodie, and Tami Buhr, "Health Care in the 2008 Presidential Primaries," *New England Journal of Medicine* 358 (January 24, 2008): 414–422; Robert J. Blendon, Mollyann Brodie, Drew E. Altman, John M. Benson, and Elizabeth C. Hamel, "Voters and Health Care in the 2004 Election," *Health Affairs* 24 (Web exclusive, March 1, 2005): 86–96.

[4] Kaiser Family Foundation, "Kaiser Health Tracking Poll Election 2008," March 2008 (conducted February 7–16, 2008), http://www.kff.org/kaiserpolls/upload/7751.pdf.

[5] Michael Barone and Richard E. Cohen, *The Almanac of American Politics 2006* (Washington, D.C.: National Journal, 2005), 806.

[6] Susan A. Goldberger, "The Politics of Universal Access: The Massachusetts Health Security Act of 1988," *Journal of Health Politics, Policy and Law* 15 (Winter 1990): 857–885.

[7] John E. McDonough, "The Road to Universal Health Coverage in Massachusetts," *New England Journal of Public Policy* 20 (Fall/Winter 2004/2005): 57–64; Dolores Kong, "Beacon Hill Reopens Health Care Debate: Coverage for Uninsured Still at Issue," *Boston Globe*, May 1, 1995, 17.

[8] Alex Pham, "Variety of Health Care Measures Awaiting Action by Legislature," *Boston Globe*, July 23, 1996, C2.

[9] Richard A. Knox, "State Widens Health Plan for Children, Teen-agers," *Boston Globe,* November 3, 1996, A1.

[10] Chris Black, "U.S. OK's Mass. Medical Plan; Uninsured to Get Medicaid Coverage," *Boston Globe,* May 30, 1998, B1.

[11] Robert J. Blendon, Catherine M. DesRoches, Elizabeth Raleigh, and John M. Benson, *The Uninsured in Massachusetts: An Opportunity for Leadership* (Boston: Blue Cross Blue Shield of Massachusetts Foundation, 2003).

[12] Ibid.; Blendon et al., "Massachusetts Health Reform."

[13] Blendon et al., *The Uninsured in Massachusetts.*

[14] Notably, the ACT initiative did not provide the only chance for universal health care to appear on the November 2006 ballot. In July 2004 lawmakers had approved a potential constitutional amendment requiring the legislature to come up with a plan for universal coverage. Legislators would need to approve the measure in another constitutional convention either in 2005 or in 2006 for that measure to appear on the ballot. The ACT ballot initiative did not seek to amend the constitution and was more specific. See Scott S. Greenberger, "Mass. Group Set to Push for Universal Health Care," *Boston Globe,* May 26, 2005, A1.

[15] Kiley and Company Opinion Research Consultants, *A Study of Attitudes among Voters in Massachusetts* (Boston: Kiley and Company Opinion Research Consultants, 2005).

[16] Pam Belluck, "The Nurturing of Health Care," *New York Times,* April 6, 2006.

[17] Massachusetts Health Care Reform Coalition, http://www.massachusettshealthreform .org. Partners HealthCare was founded in 1994 by Brigham and Women's Hospital and Massachusetts General Hospital and developed an integrated health care system throughout the Boston area.

[18] John Holahan, Randall Bovbjerg, and Jack Hadley, *Caring for the Uninsured in Massachusetts: What Does It Cost, Who Pays and What Would Full Coverage Add to Medical Spending?* November 2004, http://bluecrossfoundation.org/foundationroot/en_US/documents/ roadmapReport.pdf; John Holahan, Linda J. Blumberg, Alan Weil, Lisa Clemens-Cope, Matthew Buettgens, Fredric Blavin, and Stephen Zuckerman, *Roadmap to Coverage: Synthesis of Findings,* October 2005, http://www.urban.org/UploadedPDF/411327_roadmap_synthesis .pdf.

[19] Scott S. Greenberger, "State Leaders Aim at Healthcare Gap; Look to Cut Ranks of the Uninsured," *Boston Globe,* November 17, 2004, A1.

[20] Alice Dembner, "U.S. Threatens to Cut $600M in Medicaid," *Boston Globe,* November 11, 2004, A24.

[21] John E. McDonough, Brian Rosman, Fawn Phelps, and Melissa Shannon, "The Third Wave of Massachusetts Health Care Access Reform," *Health Affairs* 25 (Web exclusive, September 14, 2006): w420–w431.

[22] Scott S. Greenberger, "Governor Romney Eyes Penalties for Those Lacking Insurance; Costs are Key in Health Plan," *Boston Globe,* June 22, 2005, A1.

[23] Alan Wirzbicki, "Romney Defends Health Plan to Skeptical Conservatives," *Boston Globe,* April 26, 2006, B5.

[24] Barone and Cohen, *The Almanac of American Politics 2006,* 809.

25 Scott S. Greenberger, "Governor Romney Lobbies in Person on Health," *Boston Globe,* February 2, 2006, B8.

26 Scott S. Greenberger, "Romney, In Tone Shift, Reaches Out to Democrats," *Boston Globe,* April 13, 2005, B1.

27 Scott S. Greenberger, "State Leaders Aim at Healthcare Gap; Look to Cut Ranks of the Uninsured," *Boston Globe,* November 17, 2004, A1.

28 McDonough et al., "The Third Wave of Massachusetts Health Care Reform"; Scott S. Greenberger, "State Senate OK's Healthcare Plan," *Boston Globe,* November 10, 2005, A1.

29 Scott S. Greenberger, "House Approves Healthcare Overhaul," *Boston Globe,* November 4, 2005, A1.

30 Jim O'Sullivan, "House Health Plan Consultant Questions Its Estimates of the Uninsured," *State House News Service,* November 9, 2005.

31 McDonough et al., "The Third Wave of Massachusetts Health Care Reform"; Massachusetts Taxpayers Foundation, "Health Care Reform: Expanding Access without Sacrificing Jobs," December 2005, http://www.masstaxpayers.org/files/Health%20Care%20Reform_0.PDF.

32 Greenberger, "Governor Romney Lobbies."

33 Ibid.

34 Scott S. Greenberger, "Kennedy Joins Mass. Healthcare Push," *Boston Globe,* December 5, 2005, B1.

35 Scott Helman and Frank Phillips, "Hopes Fade on Reforms in Healthcare; Travaglini Shifts to Lesser Mass. Plan," *Boston Globe,* February 26, 2006, A1.

36 Scott Helman, "Senate OK's Scaled-Down Health Bill; The Uninsured Could Pay Costs or Penalties," *Boston Globe,* March 1, 2006, A1.

37 Scott Helman, "Leaders Look to Bridge Gap on Health Bill; Meeting Today; DiMasi Balks at Senate Plan," *Boston Globe,* March 3, 2006, A1.

38 Robert J. Blendon, Mollyann Brodie, John M. Benson, Drew E. Altman, and Tami Buhr, "Americans' Views of Health Care Costs, Access, and Quality," *Milbank Quarterly* 84 (December 2006): 623–657; Robert J. Blendon, John Benson, and Catherine M. DesRoches, "Americans' Views of the Uninsured: An Era for Hybrid Proposals," *Health Affairs* 22 (Web exclusive, August 27, 2003): 7–23.

39 Scott Helman, "Mass. Bill Requires Health Insurance," *Boston Globe,* April 4, 2006, A1.

40 Ron Fournier, "Clinton Praises Romney Health Care Plan," *Forbes,* April 5, 2006.

41 Nancy C. Turnbull, "The Massachusetts Model: An Artful Balance," *Health Affairs* 25 (Web exclusive, September 14, 2006): w453–w456; Alice Dembner, "Health Plan May Exempt 20 Percent of the Uninsured," *Boston Globe,* April 12, 2007; Alice Dembner, "Universal Plan Can Cost $300, Insurers Say; Monthly Price Is Closer to Goal," *Boston Globe,* February 5, 2007.

42 Robert Jablon, "Officials Look for Fixes after Health Care Measure Fails," *Associated Press,* November 6, 2004; Jonathan Oberlander, "Health Reform Interrupted: The Unraveling of the Oregon Health Plan," *Health Affairs* 26 (Web exclusive, December 16, 2006): w96–w105.

43 Robert J. Blendon, Tami Buhr, Channtal Fleischfresser, and John M. Benson, *The Massachusetts Health Reform Law: Public Opinion and Perception* (Boston: Harvard School of Public Health/ Blue Cross Blue Shield of Massachusetts Foundation, 2006); Kaiser Family Foundation/Harvard

School of Public Health/Blue Cross Blue Shield of Massachusetts Foundation, "Massachusetts Health Reform Tracking Survey," June 2007, http://www.kff.org/kaiserpolls/upload/7658 .pdf; Harvard School of Public Health/Blue Cross Blue Shield of Massachusetts Foundation, "Massachusetts Health Reform Survey," June 2008, http://www.bcbsmafoundation.org/ foundationroot/en_US/documents/MassHealthReform_Topline_071008.pdf; Harvard School of Public Health/*Boston Globe,* "Fifty-nine Percent Support Massachusetts Landmark 2006 Health Reform Law," September 28, 2009, http://www.hsph.harvard.edu/news/press–releases/2009-releases/fifty-nine-percent-support-massachusetts-2006-health-reform-law.html.

[44] Cheri Andes, "Real People Behind Real Life Pressures," *Boston Globe,* September 1, 2006; "Health Law Uncertainties," *Boston Globe,* June 10, 2006; Alice Dembner, "200,000 May Need to Get More Insurance; State Healthcare Law Sets Higher Minimums," *Boston Globe,* January 30, 2007; Liz Kowalczyk, "Thousands Face Delay in Healthcare Enrollment," *Boston Globe,* August 3, 2006; "Busy Signal on Health," *Boston Globe,* August 18, 2006.

[45] Blendon et al., "Massachusetts Health Reform."

[46] Harvard School of Public Health/*Boston Globe,* "Fifty-nine Percent Support Massachusetts Landmark 2006 Health Reform Law."

[47] Blendon et al., "Massachusetts Health Reform."

[48] Stephanie Ebbert, "Conservatives Split on Mandate and Business Fees," *Boston Globe,* April 13, 2006; Christopher Rowland, "Mass. Health Plan Seems Unlikely to Be US Model; Demographics in State's Favor," *Boston Globe,* April 14, 2006.

[49] Jerry Geisel, "Massachusetts Proposal Exempts Some from Health Insurance Mandate; Compromise May Defuse Opposition to Coverage Law," *Business Insurance,* April 16, 2007; Alice Dembner, "Health Plan May Exempt 20 Percent of the Uninsured," *Boston Globe,* April 12, 2007.

[50] Blendon et al., "Massachusetts Health Reform."

[51] Robert Steinbrook, "Health Care Reform in Massachusetts: A Work in Progress," *New England Journal of Medicine* 354 (May 18, 2006): 2095–8.

[52] Blendon et al., "Massachusetts Health Reform"; Kaiser Family Foundation/Harvard School of Public Health/Blue Cross Blue Shield of Massachusetts Foundation, "Massachusetts Health Reform Tracking Survey," June 2007.

[53] Ibid.

[54] Jacob S. Hacker, *The Divided Welfare State: The Battle over Public and Private Social Benefits in the United States* (Cambridge: Cambridge University Press, 2002).

[55] Blendon et al., "Massachusetts Health Reform"; Blendon et al., *The Massachusetts Health Reform Law;* Harvard School of Public Health/Blue Cross Blue Shield of Massachusetts Foundation, "Massachusetts Health Reform Survey," June 2008.

[56] Blendon, Benson, and DesRoches, "Americans' Views of the Uninsured: An Era for Hybrid Proposals."

[57] Jon R. Gabel, Heidi Whitmore, and Jeremy Pickreign, "Report from Massachusetts: Employers Largely Support Health Care Reform, and Few Signs of Crowd-Out Appear," *Health Affairs* 27 (Web exclusive, November 14, 2007): w13–w23.

[58] Robert J. Blendon, Mollyann Brodie, and John Benson, "What Happened to Americans' Support for the Clinton Health Plan?" *Health Affairs* 14 (Summer 1995): 7–23.

[59] Blendon et al., "Massachusetts Health Reform."

[60] Ibid. It is possible that the responses of the directly affected group can be better understood by looking at differences in income or in eligibility for subsidized insurance. Because of the small sample sizes of these groups in our study, we are unable to analyze these particular populations.

[61] Turnbull, "The Massachusetts Model"; J. Holahan and L. Blumberg, "Massachusetts Health Care Reform: A Look At the Issues," *Health Affairs* 25 (Web exclusive, September 14, 2006): w432–w443.

[62] Harvard School of Public Health/Blue Cross Blue Shield of Massachusetts Foundation, "Massachusetts Health Reform Survey," June 2008.

[63] Blendon et al., "Massachusetts Health Reform."

[64] "MA Cigarette Tax Jumps $1 per Pack," *Associated Press*, June 30, 2008.

[65] Harvard School of Public Health/*Boston Globe*, "Fifty-nine Percent Support Massachusetts Landmark 2006 Health Reform Law."

Table 6-1 Overall Views among Massachusetts Residents about What Their State Government Should Do for the Uninsured, 2003 (in percent)

Make a major effort to provide health insurance for most uninsured Massachusetts residents, which might require a tax increase to pay for it	47
Make a limited effort to provide health insurance for some of the uninsured, which would mean more government spending	34
Keep things as they are now	11
Don't know	8

Question: Which one of the following three statements comes closest to what you think the government should do for people in Massachusetts who don't have health insurance?

Source: Robert J. Blendon, Catherine M. DesRoches, Elizabeth Raleigh, and John M. Benson, *The Uninsured in Massachusetts: An Opportunity for Leadership* (Boston: Blue Cross Blue Shield of Massachusetts Foundation, 2003).

Table 6-2 How Negative Arguments Affect Public Support for Proposals to Cover the Uninsured in Massachusetts, 2003 (in percent)

	Initial support	Support after argument
Expanding existing state programs argument: *What if you heard that expanding these programs would require raising taxes to pay for the cost?*	82	55
Employer mandate argument: *What if you heard that it would be so expensive that employers would be forced to lay off workers?*	76	35
Tax credits and deductions for the uninsured argument: *What if you heard that the amount of tax relief would not be enough to cover the cost of a private plan?*	70	36
Legally requiring all residents to have health insurance argument: *What if you heard that even with the government's help, people won't be able to afford insurance and the law will cause financial hardship?*	56	22
Single-payer government plan argument: *What if you heard that you would have to wait longer for some hospital and specialty care?*	50	30

Question: I'm going to read you one way to guarantee health insurance for more people who live in Massachusetts. After I read it, please tell me whether you would favor or oppose it:

Question: Expanding state government programs for low-income state residents such as MassHealth, to provide coverage for state residents without health insurance? (If favors) What if you heard the following argument: expanding state government programs would require raising taxes to pay for the expansion. Would you still favor this plan or would you now oppose it?

Question: Requiring businesses to offer private health insurance for their employees. Under this type of plan, your employer would be required by law to pay a fixed amount of your health insurance premium while you pay the rest. (If favors) What if you heard the following argument: requiring employers to provide insurance would be so expensive that they would be forced to lay off workers. Would you still favor requiring employers to provide insurance or would you now oppose it?

Question: Offering uninsured state residents income tax deductions, tax credits, or other financial assistance to help them purchase private health insurance on their own. (If favors) What if you heard the following argument: the amount of the tax credit would not be enough to cover the cost of an individual health insurance plan. Would you still favor this plan or would you now oppose it?

Question: Having a law that requires all state residents to have health insurance that they buy themselves or get through an employer. This would be similar to the law that requires people who drive cars to have auto insurance. People with low incomes would get help from the government to pay their health insurance premiums. (If favor) What if you heard the following argument: many uninsured people will not be able to afford to buy their own insurance even with government help and this would cause financial hardship. Would you still favor this plan or would you now oppose it?

Question: A state health plan, financed by taxpayers, in which all Massachusetts residents would get their insurance from a single government plan? (If favors) What if you heard the following argument: under this type of plan, you would wait longer for some hospital and specialty care. Would you still favor this type of plan or would you now oppose it?

Source: Robert J. Blendon, Tami Buhr, Tara Sussman, and John M. Benson, "Massachusetts Health Reform: A Public Perspective from Debate through Implementation," *Health Affairs* 27 (Web exclusive, October 28, 2008): w556–w565; Robert J. Blendon, Catherine M. DesRoches, Elizabeth Raleigh, and John M. Benson, *The Uninsured in Massachusetts: An Opportunity for Leadership* (Boston: Blue Cross Blue Shield of Massachusetts Foundation, 2003).

Table 6-3 Massachusetts Residents' Opinions on Who Should Pay Most of the Cost of Helping the Uninsured Get Health Insurance in Massachusetts, 2003 (in percent)

Government	57
Federal	35
State	18
Local	1
Don't know which level	2
Businesses	16
The uninsured themselves	15
Charities	4
Don't know	9

Question: In your opinion, who should pay most of the cost of helping the uninsured in Massachusetts get health insurance? Businesses, charities, the uninsured themselves, or government? (If government) You said that the government should pay most of the cost of helping the uninsured in Massachusetts get health insurance. Should it be local government, the state government, or the federal government?

Source: Robert J. Blendon, Catherine M. DesRoches, Elizabeth Raleigh, and John M. Benson, *The Uninsured in Massachusetts: An Opportunity for Leadership* (Boston: Blue Cross Blue Shield of Massachusetts Foundation, 2003).

Table 6-4 Familiarity with the Massachusetts Health Reform Law among Massachusetts Residents, 2006–2009 (in percent)

Heard or read . . .	2006	2007	2008	2009
A great deal	7	12	27	26
Quite a bit	15	22	27	23
Just some	28	27	22	27
Only a little	29	25	16	13
Nothing at all	20	13	6	10

Note: "Don't know" responses not shown.

Question: As you may know, Governor Mitt Romney and the Massachusetts Legislature recently approved a new law that is aimed at providing health insurance for all Massachusetts residents. How much have you heard or read about the recently enacted Massachusetts Universal Health Insurance Law? Would you say a great deal, quite a bit, just some, only a little, or nothing at all? (2006)

Question: As you may know, Massachusetts has a law that is aimed at assuring that virtually all Massachusetts residents have health insurance. How much have you heard or read about the Massachusetts law? Would you say a great deal, quite a bit, just some, only a little, or nothing at all? (2007–2009)

Sources: Robert J. Blendon, Tami Buhr, Channtal Fleischfresser, and John M. Benson, *The Massachusetts Health Reform Law: Public Opinion and Perception* (Boston: Harvard School of Public Health/Blue Cross Blue Shield of Massachusetts Foundation, 2006); Kaiser Family Foundation/Harvard School of Public Health/Blue Cross Blue Shield of Massachusetts Foundation, "Massachusetts Health Reform Tracking Survey," June 2007; Harvard School of Public Health/Blue Cross Blue Shield of Massachusetts Foundation, "Massachusetts Health Reform Survey," June 2008; Harvard School of Public Health/*Boston Globe*, "Fifty-nine Percent Support Massachusetts Landmark 2006 Health Reform Law," 2009.

Table 6-5 Massachusetts Residents' Support for the Health Reform Law, 2006–2009 (in percent)

	2006	2007	2008	2009
Total	61	67	69	59
By party identification				
Democrat	68	76	76	76
Independent	60	64	70	56
Republican	56	57	44	35

Note: The question was asked of respondents who had heard at least a little about the law: 80 percent in 2006; 86 percent in 2007; 93 percent in 2008; 89 percent in 2009.

Question: Given what you know about it, in general, do you support or oppose this new Massachusetts Universal Health Insurance Law?

Sources: Robert J. Blendon, Tami Buhr, Tara Sussman, and John M. Benson, "Massachusetts Health Reform: A Public Perspective from Debate through Implementation," *Health Affairs* 27 (Web exclusive, October 28, 2008): w556–w565; Harvard School of Public Health/*Boston Globe*, "Fifty-nine Percent Support Massachusetts Landmark 2006 Health Reform Law," 2009.

Table 6-6 Massachusetts Residents' Reasons for Supporting or Opposing the Health Reform Law, 2007 (in percent)

Percent saying each is a major reason for supporting the law (among those who support the law)	
Making sure everyone has health insurance is the right thing to do	90
People with health insurance get preventive and more continuous health care, which can keep everyone's future health care premiums down	79
People won't face higher health care costs to cover the unpaid medical bills of those who don't have insurance	59
I like that business will have to contribute to the costs of their employees' health insurance	54
As a result of the new law, my health care costs won't rise as much	45

Percent saying each is a major reason for opposing the law (among those who oppose the law)	
People shouldn't be required to buy insurance if they can't afford it	72
People shouldn't be required to buy insurance if they don't want it or don't think they need it	61
The new law will hurt me or my family, by increasing my taxes or health care costs	58
The new law will lead to government-run health care	47
The new law will hurt small businesses	46
The new law is the wrong approach. We need a single government health program for everyone	44

Question: I'm going to read you some reasons people give for (supporting/opposing) the new health care law. After I read each one, please tell me if it is a major reason, minor reason, or not a reason why you (support/oppose) the law.

Source: Robert J. Blendon, Tami Buhr, Tara Sussman, and John M. Benson, "Massachusetts Health Reform: A Public Perspective from Debate through Implementation," *Health Affairs* 27 (Web exclusive, October 28, 2008): w556–w565.

Table 6-7 Massachusetts Residents' Support for the Individual Mandate, 2006–2008 (in percent)

	2006	2007	2008
Total	52	57	58
By sex			
Male	53	59	52
Female	51	55	62
By age			
18–29	44	57	48
30–49	53	56	56
50–64	56	62	65
65 plus	51	54	62
By household income			
Less than $25,000	43	50	53
$25,000–$49,999	47	55	49
$50,000–$74,999	58	61	57
$75,000 plus	60	63	69
By education			
HS degree or less	50	48	45
Some college	44	61	58
College graduate	60	64	69
By party identification			
Democrat	56	66	65
Independent	53	53	58
Republican	51	52	48

Question: The new law requires that all uninsured Massachusetts residents either purchase health insurance or pay a fine of up to 50 percent of what health insurance would cost. If a state agency determines that a person can't afford a policy, they would not be required to buy one. People whose incomes fall below a certain level would receive help paying part or all of their insurance premiums. Do you support or oppose state government requiring uninsured residents to purchase health insurance?

Sources: Robert J. Blendon, Tami Buhr, Tara Sussman, and John M. Benson, "Massachusetts Health Reform: A Public Perspective from Debate through Implementation," *Health Affairs* 27 (Web exclusive, October 28, 2008): w556–w565.

Table 6-8 Massachusetts Residents' Opinions on Whether Requiring Uninsured Person to Sign Up and Pay for Unsubsidized and Subsidized Plans Is Unfair, 2007

	% Saying unfair	
	Unsubsidized	Subsidized
Total	62	44
By sex		
Male	60	41
Female	65	47
By age		
18–29	77	62
30–49	63	42
50–64	53	35
65 plus	58	39
By household income		
Less than $25,000	79	61
$25,000–$49,999	72	50
$50,000–$74,999	60	38
$75,000 plus	47	33
By education		
HS degree or less	74	61
Some college	63	39
College graduate	49	28
By party identification		
Democrat	59	43
Independent	62	46
Republican	68	39

Question: The new health insurance law requires all uninsured Massachusetts adults to buy health insurance or pay a fine, unless coverage is determined to be unaffordable. Private insurers have put together many different health plans that have been approved by the Commonwealth as being affordable and providing reasonable health benefits. I'd like to get your opinion about the costs and benefits of some of these health insurance plans for different individuals.

Question: Unsubsidized individual plan for an uninsured 37-year-old single adult whose income is $42,000 a year. This plan includes three doctor visits a year that cost the patient $25 a piece. The individual must pay $1,500 in other medical expenses before he or she starts receiving benefits. After this deductible is met, this person will pay for 20 percent of the cost of doctor visits, hospital stays, and tests. The maximum amount this person will have to pay for medical services in a year is $5,000. Prescription drugs will cost $15 for generic brands and 50 percent of the cost of other brands. The plan would cost $259 a month. Do you think it is fair or unfair to require an uninsured person like this to sign up and pay for a plan like this?

Question: Subsidized individual plan for an uninsured 37-year-old single adult whose income is $30,000 a year. Under this plan, the cost of a visit to a regular doctor is $10 and a specialist is $20. Hospital stays cost $250. Prescription drugs are covered for a co-payment of $10 to $45 depending on the drug. The maximum amount this person would have to pay in a year is $750 for medical expenses and $500 for prescription drugs. The plan would cost this person $105 a month. Do you think it is fair or unfair to require an uninsured person like this to sign up and pay for a plan like this?

Source: Robert J. Blendon, Tami Buhr, Tara Sussman, and John M. Benson, "Massachusetts Health Reform: A Public Perspective from Debate through Implementation," *Health Affairs* 27 (Web exclusive, October 28, 2008): w556–w565; Kaiser Family Foundation/Harvard School of Public Health/Blue Cross Blue Shield of Massachusetts Foundation, "Massachusetts Health Reform Tracking Survey," June 2007.

Table 6-9 Massachusetts Residents' Support for the Employer Responsibility, 2006–2008 (in percent)

	2006	2008
Total	70	75
By sex		
Male	66	74
Female	73	77
By age		
18–29	70	84
30–49	77	74
50–64	64	75
65 plus	63	70
By household income		
Less than $25,000	67	75
$25,000–$49,999	68	77
$50,000–$74,999	79	76
$75,000 plus	73	78
By education		
HS degree or less	71	74
Some college	67	74
College graduate	70	76
By party identification		
Democrat	77	81
Independent	70	76
Republican	62	60

Question: The law requires that businesses that employ more than ten people either provide health insurance for their employees, or pay a penalty of $295 per employee per year. Do you support or oppose requiring businesses to provide health insurance or pay a penalty?

Sources: Robert J. Blendon, Tami Buhr, Channtal Fleischfresser, and John M. Benson, *The Massachusetts Health Reform Law: Public Opinion and Perception* (Boston: Harvard School of Public Health/Blue Cross Blue Shield of Massachusetts Foundation, 2006); Harvard School of Public Health/Blue Cross Blue Shield of Massachusetts Foundation, "Massachusetts Health Reform Survey," June 2008.

Table 6-10 Massachusetts Residents' Perceptions of Whom the Health Reform Law Is Helping and Hurting, 2006–2008 (in percent)

	% Helped			% Hurt			% Not impacted		
	2006	2007	2008	2006	2007	2008	2006	2007	2008
People who are uninsured	67	72	45	15	17	33	13	6	14
Poor people	66	66	44	17	21	31	2	10	14
Young adults	50	60	32	19	18	29	24	16	28
The middle class	27	40	27	28	22	26	39	34	40
Large corporations	15	30	19	18	15	11	64	49	56
People who are insured	17	27	26	19	12	18	58	57	48
Small businesses	14	25	13	63	52	56	19	15	19
You personally	20	24	14	18	12	18	60	62	67

Note: "Don't know" response not shown.

Question: Generally speaking, do you think the new Massachusetts Health Insurance Law will help or hurt (people who do not have health insurance/poor people/young adults/the middle class/large corporations/people who do have health insurance/small businesses/you personally) or don't you think it will have much of an impact one way or another? (2006, 2007)

Question: Generally speaking, do you think the Massachusetts Health Insurance Reform Law is helping, hurting, or not having much of an impact on (people who do not have health insurance/poor people/young adults/the middle class/large corporations/people who do have health insurance/small businesses/you personally)? (2008)

Sources: Robert J. Blendon, Tami Buhr, Tara Sussman, and John M. Benson, "Massachusetts Health Reform: A Public Perspective from Debate through Implementation," *Health Affairs* 27 (Web exclusive, October 28, 2008): w556–w565.

Table 6-11 Perceptions of Massachusetts Health Reform Law among a Directly Affected Group, 2008 (in percent)

	Total	Directly affected	Other Mass. residents
Overall support for law	61	52	72
Support for the mandate	52	37	62
Impact of law on uninsured			
Helping	45	35	47
Hurting	33	44	31
Not much impact	14	18	13
Impact of law on you personally			
Helping	14	22	13
Hurting	18	50	11
Not much impact	67	26	75
Impact on health care costs			
Go up	33	51	30
Go down	6	14	4
Not much impact	54	30	59

Note: Directly affected respondents are those who were uninsured at some point during the last 12 months or those who had gotten insurance or changed their insurance due to the law. "Don't know" responses not shown.

Question: Given what you know about it, in general, do you support or oppose this new Massachusetts Universal Health Insurance Law? (Asked of those who had heard at least a little about the law)

Question: The new law requires that all uninsured Massachusetts residents either purchase health insurance or pay a fine of up to 50 percent of what health insurance would cost. If a state agency determines that a person can't afford a policy, they would not be required to buy one. People whose incomes fall below a certain level would receive help paying part or all of their insurance premiums. Do you support or oppose state government requiring uninsured residents to purchase health insurance?

Question: Generally speaking, do you think the Massachusetts Health Insurance Reform Law is helping, hurting, or not having much of an impact on (people who do not have insurance/you personally)?

Question: Do you think the health insurance law has caused what you pay for health care and insurance to go up, go down, or don't you think it has had much impact on how much you pay for insurance?

Source: Robert J. Blendon, Tami Buhr, Tara Sussman, and John M. Benson, "Massachusetts Health Reform: A Public Perspective from Debate through Implementation," *Health Affairs* 27 (Web exclusive, October 28, 2008): w556–w565.

Table 6-12 Massachusetts Residents' Views on the Economic Impact of the Health Reform Law (in percent)

	Caused it to go up	Not much impact	Caused it to go down	Don't know
What you pay for health care and insurance	33	54	6	6

	Hurting	Not much impact	Helping	Don't know
State budget	39	26	14	20
Cost of health care in Massachusetts	39	30	20	12
Massachusetts economy	35	31	22	11

Questions: Do you think this health insurance law has caused what you pay for health care and insurance to go up, go down, or don't you think it has had much impact on how much you pay for health care and insurance?

Question: Generally speaking, do you think this health insurance law is helping, hurting, or not having much of an impact on (the state budget/the cost of health care in Massachusetts/the Massachusetts economy)?

Source: Harvard School of Public Health/Blue Cross Blue Shield of Massachusetts Foundation, "Massachusetts Health Reform Survey," June 2008.

Table 6-13 Massachusetts Residents' Support for Various Options to Cover Health Care Reform Budget Shortfall, 2008 (in percent)

	Strongly favor	Somewhat favor	Somewhat oppose	Strongly oppose
Increase cigarette tax	57	13	8	21
Penalize businesses with many part-time employees receiving subsidized insurance	47	27	11	11
Require insurers to contribute to fund for the uninsured	36	25	11	24
Increase business penalty	30	23	18	27
Reduce payments to doctors and hospitals for patients receiving subsidized care	22	29	20	23
Increase premiums, co-pays, and deductibles for those receiving subsidized insurance	16	24	22	33
Cut other government programs	14	19	23	33
Limit number of people receiving subsidized insurance and create a waiting list	10	17	21	45
Increase state sales tax	7	16	16	59

Note: "Don't know" responses not shown.

Question: Since the law went into effect, approximately 175,000 people have gotten health insurance through this subsidized program. The number is more than was expected so the program is projected to be roughly $150 million dollars over budget this year. I'm going to read some ways that might be used to deal with these additional costs and would like you to tell me whether you favor or oppose each method of dealing with this budget shortfall.

Question: To deal with this budget shortfall, do you favor or oppose (increasing the cigarette tax/requiring insurers to make a contribution to a fund that provides subsidized coverage for the uninsured/reducing payments to hospitals and physicians for people who have subsidized insurance/increasing the premiums, co-pays, and deductibles of those who receive subsidized insurance/cutting other government programs/limiting the number of uninsured people who would receive subsidized insurance and creating a waiting list for them/increasing the state sales tax)? Would this be strongly (favor/oppose) or somewhat (favor/oppose)?

Question: Under the current law, businesses that employ more than ten people must either provide health insurance for their employees or pay a penalty of $295. To deal with this budget shortfall, do you favor or oppose increasing the penalty for businesses that don't provide health insurance? Would this be strongly (favor/oppose) or somewhat (favor/oppose)?

Question: Under the current law, businesses that employ more than ten people must either provide health insurance for their employees or pay a penalty of $295. Some large companies don't pay this penalty because they provide coverage for their full-time workers, but some companies also have a lot of part-time workers who aren't provided insurance. Many of these workers are getting subsidized insurance from the new state program. To deal with the budget shortfall, do you favor or oppose charging these large companies for some of the costs that the state must pay to provide health care to their workers? Would this be strongly (favor/oppose) or somewhat (favor/oppose)?

Source: Robert J. Blendon, Tami Buhr, Tara Sussman, and John M. Benson, "Massachusetts Health Reform: A Public Perspective from Debate through Implementation," *Health Affairs* 27 (Web exclusive, October 28, 2008): w556–w565.

Chapter 7

MEDICARE AND MEDICAID

Elizabeth C. Hamel, Claudia Deane, and Mollyann Brodie

Medicare and Medicaid were established by an act of Congress in 1965 to provide health insurance coverage for low-income, disabled, and elderly Americans. Together they make up the bulk of the publicly funded safety net intended to protect the health of those who are perceived as most vulnerable, covering roughly 96 million Americans. Together they also represent one of the government's most significant financial commitments, and with recent rises in health care costs, they represent a growing share of the federal budget and pose serious challenges to the country's fiscal health. Given their scope, both in terms of the number of people covered and dollars spent, the size and structure of these programs is a topic of ongoing public policy debate.

Medicare is a federal government program that provides health insurance coverage for Americans ages sixty-five and older, as well as younger adults with permanent disabilities. Medicaid, a joint federal and state government program, covers health and long-term care for certain groups of low-income Americans, including working families, the elderly poor, and people with physical and mental disabilities. Although the two programs are distinct and differ in many ways, they are the nation's two largest health care programs and are often discussed together. This chapter begins with a brief introduction to each program and then examines public attitudes and knowledge about both programs. Because Medicare's coverage of prescription drugs was the subject of a high-profile policy debate, a significant portion of this chapter is devoted to a case study of public opinion on that topic.

The authors would like to thank Tricia Neuman, vice president and director of the Medicare Policy Project at the Kaiser Family Foundation, for her contributions to this chapter.

Medicare: The Basics

When the Medicare program was established, nearly 40 percent of America's seniors were living at or below the poverty line, and roughly half of them lacked health insurance. Today, Medicare provides health insurance coverage for virtually all Americans ages sixty-five and older, regardless of income, as well as people under age sixty-five with permanent disabilities who receive Social Security Disability Income payments. In 2010 Medicare covered 47 million people, including 39 million seniors and more than 8 million younger adults with disabilities. Nearly half of Medicare beneficiaries live at or below 200 percent of the federal poverty line ($21,660 for an individual or $29,140 for a couple in 2010), and more than four in ten (44 percent) have three or more chronic conditions.[1]

Medicare spending accounts for 12 percent of the federal budget and 23 percent of total national expenditures on health. The Congressional Budget Office (CBO) projects Medicare spending will nearly double from $528 billion in 2010 to $1,038 billion in 2020. Medicare is financed by a combination of general revenues (40 percent), payroll taxes (38 percent), premiums collected from beneficiaries (12 percent), and interest on the Medicare Trust Fund and other sources (9 percent).

Medicare provides coverage of basic health services, including hospital care, physician visits, diagnostic tests, and preventive services. Medicare Part A pays for inpatient hospital, skilled nursing facility, home health, and hospice care, and Part B pays for physician, outpatient, preventive services, and home health visits. As of 2006 Medicare also covers outpatient prescription drugs through coverage provided by private plans (Medicare Part D). Medicare does not cover routine dental or vision care, and it does not cover long-term care services for its beneficiaries, either at home or in a nursing home.

Medicare is less generous than the typical private health plan that workers get from their employers. Compared with most employer-sponsored insurance, Medicare has relatively high cost-sharing requirements (including a $1,100 deductible in 2010 and a coverage gap in the prescription drug benefit, often referred to as the "doughnut hole"), and no cap on out-of-pocket spending. As a result, most Medicare beneficiaries have some sort of "wraparound" coverage to compensate for these deficiencies. In 2007 about a third had supplemental coverage from a former employer, and about one in six (17 percent) purchased supplemental private insurance, known as Medigap, on their own. About 15 percent of Medicare beneficiaries with low incomes and modest assets also qualified for Medicaid in 2007; for these individuals (known as "dual eligibles"), Medicaid helps with the cost of Medicare's premiums and cost-sharing and pays for long-term care.

Since the 1970s Medicare beneficiaries have had the option of receiving their benefits through private health plans. Currently, about a quarter of beneficiaries are enrolled in private plans under Medicare, now known as "Medicare Advantage" (MA) plans (also known as Medicare Part C). Enrollment in such plans has increased rapidly in recent years, more than doubling from 5.3 million in 2003 to 11.4 million in early 2010. During this time, Congress increased payments to private plans under Medicare in an effort to encourage beneficiaries to enroll in these plans. As a result, in 2009 the average Medicare payment to MA plans was 114 percent of the cost of similar benefits under traditional fee-for-service Medicare.[2] The recently passed Patient Protection and Affordable Care Act, however, freezes payments to MA plans in 2011 and phases in reductions in MA payments relative to fee-for-service costs beginning in 2012, so over time this "overpayment" to private plans should be reduced or eliminated.[3]

The public and political debate continues about private plans in Medicare. Public attitudes on this topic are also explored in this chapter, particularly with regard to prescription drug coverage.

Medicaid: The Basics

Medicaid is the nation's principal safety-net health insurance program, covering health and long-term care services for low-income Americans. Medicaid was initially created to provide help with medical costs to individuals and families who were already receiving cash assistance (or welfare), but it has been incrementally expanded by Congress over the years to cover more people living at or below the poverty level. Today, Medicaid covers 59 million of the poorest and sickest Americans, including children and parents (mostly in working families), seniors, and people with disabilities.[4]

Medicaid accounts for 16 percent of total national spending on personal health care, and it is the principal source of financing for long-term care in the country, paying 40 percent of the total national bill for nursing home and long-term care services overall. Medicaid is jointly financed by the federal government and the states, and each state administers its own Medicaid program within broad federal guidelines.

Currently, to qualify for Medicaid, a person must have a family income below a certain level and belong to one of several "categorically eligible" groups: children; parents with dependent children; pregnant women; people with disabilities; and seniors. Federal law requires that all states offer coverage to people in these categories, but states also may expand Medicaid coverage beyond the federal minimum standards. States have wide discretion regarding other aspects of Medicaid, such as which benefits are covered and how providers are paid. As a result, Medicaid operates as more than fifty distinct programs in the states, the District of Columbia, and each U.S. territory. The 2010 health reform law included a significant expansion of Medicaid eligibility, so that beginning in 2014, all individuals under age sixty-five with incomes up to 133 percent of the federal poverty level will be covered.

In 2005 Medicaid provided coverage to 29.4 million children,[5] 15.2 million adults (primarily poor working parents), 6.1 million seniors, and 8.3 million individuals with disabilities. Seniors and adults with disabilities make up just one-quarter of Medicaid enrollees, but they account for more than 70 percent of Medicaid spending because of their greater use of acute and long-term care than other groups.

Historical Support for Medicare and Medicaid

Before examining public opinion on today's Medicare and Medicaid, we need to look at the historical context of opinion before the programs were enacted. Surveys conducted as early as the

1930s showed strong support for the idea of the government helping people who could not afford to pay for health care. In several questions asked between 1937 and 1943, roughly eight in ten Americans supported the idea of the government providing free medical care for those unable to pay.[6] In 1944, two in three said it would be a good idea "if the Social Security law also provided paying the doctor and hospital care that people might need in the future."[7] This sentiment existed even when tax increases were mentioned. In 1945 more than half (52 percent) favored "increasing the present tax rates to include payment of benefits for sickness, disability, doctor and hospital bills" under Social Security (**Table 7–1**).[8]

In the 1960s, as discussion and debate about a national health insurance plan once more began in earnest, pollsters again started to ask about the idea of a government health insurance plan for the elderly. The idea remained popular. In 1961, two-thirds of the public favored "having the Social Security tax increased in order to pay for old age medical insurance."[9] In late 1964, when asked specifically about Congress's plans regarding Medicare, six in ten Americans said they approved.[10] And just after Medicare was passed, in December 1965, more than eight in ten Americans said they approved of the bill passed by Congress.[11]

Public Opinion on Medicare and Medicaid

Since their enactment, Medicare and Medicaid have been popular programs among the public, although Americans are more familiar with Medicare than with Medicaid (see the section on public knowledge). Large majorities of the public describe both programs as "very important."[12] And since the 1970s the public has shown strong support for maintaining or increasing federal government spending on Medicare and Medicaid. In addition, the public has been reluctant to cut these programs as a way to balance the federal budget or reduce the federal budget deficit (**Table 7–2**).

In thirteen public opinion surveys from 1971 through 2009, large majorities (between 88 percent and 96 percent) said that government spending on Medicare should either be kept the same or increased. In eleven of the thirteen surveys, more than half chose the "increased" option, and in none of the surveys did as many as one in ten say Medicare spending should be decreased (**Table 7–3**).[13]

Support for Medicaid spending was similarly high, with between eight and nine in ten saying that funding should be kept the same or increased in nine surveys dating back to 1972. Notably, given the dire economic situation facing the country at the end of 2008, support for additional funding for both programs was lowest in a poll taken in December of that year (43 percent for Medicare, and 34 percent for Medicaid). Still, at that time only 6 percent said spending on Medicare should be *decreased,* and just 11 percent said the same about Medicaid (**Table 7–3**).[14]

Support for maintaining Medicare and Medicaid spending is strong across party identification, ideology, and age. Although Republicans and conservatives are somewhat less likely to say funding for these programs should be *increased,* fewer than two in ten in any group say such funding should be *decreased* (**Table 7–4**).[15]

In another measure of public support for the programs, cutting back spending on Medicare and Medicaid is unpopular as a way to balance the federal budget or reduce the federal deficit.

In ten surveys between 1987 and 2006, majorities of the public were opposed to cutting back spending on one or both of these programs to reduce the deficit. Support for cutting Medicaid spending was highest in a 1995 survey that asked about such cuts "to balance the federal budget and avoid raising taxes" (42 percent were in favor). When it comes to Medicare, a 2006 survey found somewhat greater support (35 percent) for "slowing the rate of growth in Medicare spending" as a way to reduce the deficit, but a majority remained opposed even when the question was phrased this way.[16]

Similarly, a 2005 survey found that the public is generally opposed to cutting Medicaid to deal with state budget problems. When asked whether they would support or oppose "making some cuts to the Medicaid program in your state" to help balance the state budget, nearly-three quarters were opposed, including 52 percent who were "strongly" opposed. When asked which of three ways they thought was best for their state to reduce its budget problems, about one in five (21 percent) chose cuts in Medicaid funding. Roughly equal shares chose cutting other programs (24 percent) or raising taxes (21 percent), and 23 percent said the state should do none of these or volunteered another way the state should deal with its budget problems (**Table 7–5**).[17]

Moreover, expanding Medicare and Medicaid is one of the most popular options when the public is asked about different ways to cover more of the uninsured in the United States. In surveys between 1999 and 2009, majorities ranging from 57 percent to 79 percent said they would favor expanding Medicare to cover people between the ages of fifty-five and sixty-four, and between 70 percent and 84 percent said they would favor expanding state government programs like Medicaid to provide coverage for people without insurance (**Table 7–6**).[18] In fact, expanding Medicaid to cover more people is one of the major provisions of the 2010 Patient Protection and Affordable Care Act.

Perceptions and Knowledge about Medicare and Medicaid

Perceptions of Medicare and Medicaid are generally positive. Most people (between six and seven in ten) say they have a favorable opinion of Medicare, and just about half have a favorable opinion of Medicaid. Fewer than a third say they have an unfavorable view of either program (**Table 7–7**).[19]

Surveys also show that seniors who are enrolled in Medicare give their insurance higher ratings and report fewer problems accessing care than younger people enrolled in private insurance. A 2002 study by the Commonwealth Fund found that nearly a third of elderly Medicare enrollees rated their health insurance as excellent, compared with one in five non-elderly adults in private plans. The same study also found that seniors on Medicare were less likely to report negative experiences with their health plan, less likely to say they went without needed care due to the cost, and more likely to report being very satisfied with their health care compared to younger adults in private plans.[20] A 2009 survey found that seniors were much more likely than younger adults with insurance coverage to give their health plan a rating of "excellent."[21]

Despite their overall favorable views of both programs, many in the general public lack knowledge about certain aspects of Medicare and Medicaid. When it comes to understanding who is covered by each program, public knowledge is somewhat greater for Medicare than for Medicaid. In a 2005 survey, six in ten knew that Medicare is the main source of coverage for people over sixty-five regardless of income, while just under half (47 percent) knew that Medicaid is the main source of coverage for many low-income families regardless of age. Fewer than four in ten (38 percent) knew that Medicaid is the main source of coverage for low-income people who need nursing home care or long-term home care.[22]

Prior to the enactment of the Medicare prescription drug benefit in 2003, nearly half (49 percent) of the public incorrectly thought that Medicare *already* covered prescription drugs. Nearly four in ten (39 percent) incorrectly thought it covered long-term care.[23]

The public is somewhat more knowledgeable about Medicare and Medicaid funding, but less knowledgeable about the size of Medicare spending relative to the federal budget. About three-quarters know Medicare is a federal government program, and about half know that Medicaid is jointly funded by federal and state governments.[24] In 2009, however, just a third identified Medicare as one of the two largest areas of spending by the federal government, compared to more than half who correctly identified defense as one of the largest areas of spending (**Table 7–8**).[25]

Perceptions of Medicare's Long-term Financial Solvency

Medicare is expected to face significant financing challenges in the future because of overall increases in health care costs, the aging of the population, and the declining ratio of workers to beneficiaries. Medicare spending is growing at a faster rate than the overall economy, and if current trends continue, Medicare expenditures as a percentage of GDP are expected to increase from 3.5 percent in 2010 to 6.4 percent by 2030. The solvency of the Medicare Part A Trust Fund (from which Medicare pays for hospital stays and other benefits covered under Part A) is the measure of the program's financial health that typically receives the most public attention. According to the Medicare trustees, spending from the Part A Trust Fund has exceeded income since 2008. In May 2009, the trustees projected that the fund would be depleted in 2017, with insufficient funds to pay benefits.

The 2010 health care reform law includes a number of changes that are expected to reduce the growth in Medicare spending over time, including delivery system reforms, reductions in payments to providers and MA plans, and the establishment of a new Independent Payment Advisory Board to recommend additional strategies to reduce spending. Combined, these changes are expected to improve Medicare's financial outlook in the future. The CBO estimates the new law will lead to a net reduction in Medicare spending of $428 billion between 2010 and 2019, and the Centers for Medicare and Medicaid Services project the solvency of the Part A Trust Fund will be extended from 2017 to 2029.[26]

Most people in the general public seem to be aware of Medicare's financial problems, and many are concerned about how they may be affected. In survey questions from 1995 through 2005, about one in five Americans said that Medicare is in crisis, and about half said it has major problems. In 2009, when the question was framed specifically in terms of Medicare's *financial* problems, three in ten said the program is in crisis, and another 44 percent said it has major problems (**Table 7–9**).[27] In 2009 more than half said Medicare will not be able to cover its share of seniors' hospital bills in the near future; 16 percent saw this happening in the next five years, and another 39 percent said it will happen in the next five to ten years.[28]

Many people also worry that Medicare will not be there for them when they retire. In a 2009 survey by the Employee Benefits Research Institute (EBRI), most workers (61 percent) said they are not too confident or not at all confident that Medicare will continue to provide benefits of at least equal value to the benefits received by retirees today, while just 5 percent said they are very confident. This level of concern has remained fairly steady in EBRI surveys dating back to 1992 (**Table 7–10**).[29]

Retirees, most of whom are already receiving Medicare, are more likely than workers to express confidence, with nearly six in ten (59 percent) saying they are at least somewhat confident in the value of future benefits paid by Medicare. Although overall confidence has remained fairly steady for retirees over time, the 2008 and 2009 surveys had the smallest share saying they were "very confident" (8 percent and 9 percent, respectively) since EBRI began tracking in 1992.[30]

A 2009 survey found that nearly six in ten (58 percent) of those under age sixty-five were "very concerned" that the current level of Medicare benefits would not be available for them when they retire. A 2003 survey found that half of those on Medicare were very concerned that they would not continue to receive their current level of Medicare benefits in the future (**Table 7–11**).[31]

How to Deal with Medicare's Financial Problems

Despite the public's awareness of Medicare's financial challenges and people's concerns about the future, little public consensus exists on how to deal with the program's financial problems. During flush financial times, the public was in favor of using the federal budget surplus to help shore up Medicare, but in leaner times there has been little public support for most proposals to keep Medicare financially sound, particularly proposals that involve cuts to the program.

In the late 1990s, when the federal budget ran a surplus, the public expressed a preference for using a large part of that surplus to shore up both Medicare and the Social Security program. When asked in a series of questions from 1998 to 2001 whether the budget surplus should mostly be used to cut taxes, pay down the national debt, increase spending on domestic programs, or help make Medicare and Social Security financially sound, Americans usually picked Medicare and Social Security as the top priority, by pluralities of between 37 percent and 50 percent (**Table 7–12**).[32]

Since that time, instead of a surplus, the U.S. budget is running a considerable deficit, and surveys have found little public support for most of the proposals put forward to make Medicare financially sound. (**Table 7–13** shows public support for a range of options).[33] There are exceptions, however, and chief among them is to allow the federal government to negotiate lower prices with drug companies as part of the Medicare drug benefit, which was backed by nine in ten Americans in 2008 and 2009.[34] Experts do not, however, believe this option would save the federal government much money.[35] Three-quarters in 2009 also said they would support "having

Medicare pay for new treatments and technologies only if they provide better results than current treatments" as a way to help ensure Medicare's financial security.

Aside from these two proposals, the most popular historically have been rolling back tax cuts (with about three-quarters support in 2003 and 2006).[36] Support for rolling back tax cuts for upper-income Americans was, however, somewhat lower (46 percent) in December 2008, possibly due to the economic recession and because the tax cuts had been in place for several years by then. The only other proposals that garner majority support are reducing Medicare payments to HMOs and other private insurers (66 percent in 2009), reducing payments to doctors and hospitals (65 percent), and requiring higher-income seniors to pay higher premiums (53 percent).[37]

As another indicator of the popularity of the program, the *least* popular proposals for keeping Medicare financially sound are those that involve program cutbacks, in terms either of benefits or of who is covered. Proposals opposed by large majorities include increasing out-of-pocket costs for all seniors (79 percent opposed in 2009), cutting back the Medicare drug benefit (74 percent opposed in 2008), turning Medicare into a program that only serves low-income seniors (73 percent opposed in 2008), and gradually raising the age of eligibility to sixty-seven (57 percent opposed in 2009). Half (50 percent in 2009) also opposed increasing Medicare payroll taxes.[38] Seniors' opinions on these questions have usually been similar to those of the general public.[39]

Medicare/Medicaid Payments and Health Reform

During the health reform debate in 2009 and 2010, several surveys asked about limiting or changing payments under Medicare and/or Medicaid as a way to pay for health reform. In polling conducted between June and August 2009, these proposals received a lukewarm reception from the public. About half (47 percent to 53 percent) said they would favor limiting future increases in Medicare payments to doctors and hospitals.[40] About half (47 percent) said that it was "acceptable" to reduce payments to doctors and hospitals for services they provide to patients covered by Medicare and Medicaid (47 percent) and to reduce payments to hospitals and drug makers for the services or products they provide to patients in these two programs (48 percent).[41] About four in ten (38 percent) said they would favor "saving money by cutting back on Medicare costs," and 58 percent were opposed.[42] One-third (33 percent) said they would favor "tighter restrictions on what medical procedures Medicare and Medicaid will cover," and 58 percent were opposed.[43] The legislation passed in March 2010 included a provision to limit future increases in Medicare payments to health care providers, and an April 2010 survey found that 57 percent of the public had a favorable impression of this provision. Although this represents majority support, it was the least popular of eleven of the early implementation provisions tested in the survey.[44]

Medicaid's Funding Challenges

Medicaid has its own unique set of financing challenges. Because it is funded in part by state income taxes, available funding for Medicaid decreases during tough economic times when income tax revenues go down. It is also during tough times that Medicaid enrollment spikes, as people lose their jobs and their employer-sponsored health insurance. The joint federal-state funding structure is particularly important during such times, as the federal government may need to step in to fill the gaps caused by state budget problems. The public is generally supportive of the federal government helping out the states in this way. The economic stimulus bill passed by Congress and signed by President Obama in 2009 included money to help states meet the growing Medicaid enrollment due to the recession and to avoid deep cuts to the program. A January 2009 survey found that three-quarters (76 percent) of the public thought that providing aid to states to avoid cuts in Medicaid and education was a "good idea."[45]

As was true for Medicare, however, most people see major financial problems in the Medicaid program, but they do not support a variety of proposals to deal with those problems, particularly the proposals that would make cuts to the program. A 2005 survey found that 22 percent of Americans thought the Medicaid program was in a financial crisis, and an additional 39 percent thought it had major problems. But none of the six proposals to deal with Medicaid's financial problems garnered majority support. Most proposals were favored by about four in ten adults. The least popular proposal was limiting which prescription drugs Medicaid will pay for (32 percent favor, 65 percent oppose) (Table 7–14).[46]

Medicaid: State Flexibility and What Should Be Covered

Another Medicaid restructuring proposal that policymakers have discussed is increasing states' flexibility in determining which benefits are offered. Surveys suggest, however, that the public's long-standing interest in "leaving things to the states" may be outweighed in this instance by a desire to see each Medicaid recipient receive similar benefits. In a 2005 survey, nearly six in ten Americans (58 percent) said that all states should be required to offer the same set of core health care benefits to receive federal funding, and about four in ten (39 percent) said states should be able to decide their own benefits (Table 7–15).[47]

More than eight in ten in the same survey said that various benefits—some of which are optional under current law—should be essential in Medicaid coverage, including: hospital stays (87 percent), prescription drugs (87 percent), medical equipment such as wheelchairs and artificial limbs (85 percent), mental health services (83 percent), emergency room visits (82 percent), nursing home care (82 percent), physical therapy (81 percent), and doctor visits (81 percent).[48]

Medicare and Private Plans

As mentioned in the introduction to this chapter, there has been much public debate over the years about what role, if any, private health insurance plans should play in Medicare. This debate played out in a high-profile way when it came to discussion and development of the Medicare Part D prescription drug benefit, addressed in the case study below.

In general, when asked who is more trusted to provide health insurance to seniors, the general public splits about evenly between Medicare and private plans. Seniors themselves, however, are more likely to prefer Medicare. And when asked about their preferences for the future, most seniors say they would prefer to continue getting their benefits through Medicare, while most younger adults would prefer to get insurance through a private plan when they retire (**Table 7–16**).[49] This finding is not surprising, given that surveys often find people "like what they know."

There is also a generational divide when it comes to perceptions of the generosity of benefits and the choice of doctors and hospitals available through Medicare compared with employer-sponsored private plans. Younger adults are nearly three times as likely as seniors to say that employer-sponsored private plans offer more generous benefits than Medicare (46 percent versus 16 percent), and they are twice as likely to say private plans offer more choice than Medicare (41 percent versus 20 percent). Pluralities of seniors think that Medicare and employer-sponsored private plans are about equal when it comes to benefits (45 percent) and choice of doctors and hospitals (38 percent).[50]

Comparisons to private plans are somewhat less favorable on perceptions of fraud and abuse. A 1998 survey found that about half of seniors *and* younger adults think there is the same amount of fraud and abuse in Medicare as in private plans, and a third of both groups think there is *more* fraud and abuse in Medicare.[51]

Despite being somewhat split on these questions of Medicare versus private plans, when asked about changes to the Medicare system, the public has consistently expressed a preference for continuing with the current system rather than moving toward a system of enrolling most seniors in private plans. In the mid-1990s, there was discussion in Washington about doing away with the traditional Medicare program and instead providing seniors with a voucher for a fixed amount of money that they could use to purchase their own private insurance plan. This proposal was not popular among the public, with about a third (32 percent to 35 percent) in favor of the proposal, and about six in ten (55 percent to 64 percent) opposed.[52]

Questions about the role of private insurance arose again during the debate over whether and how to expand Medicare to include prescription drug coverage. Surveys during this time showed that the public consistently favored expanding Medicare to cover drug costs, as opposed to the government helping people buy private insurance. To provide context to this debate, the case study below gives some background on prescription drug coverage under Medicare and then examines public opinion on private plans, as well as other aspects of Medicare prescription drug coverage.

Public Opinion Case Study: Medicare and Prescription Drugs

In December 2003 President George W. Bush signed into law the largest expansion of Medicare since its inception: the Medicare Prescription Drug, Improvement, and Modernization Act (MMA), otherwise known as Medicare Part D. Until the passage of the MMA, Medicare did not generally cover outpatient prescription drugs. But in the forty-five years since Medicare was enacted, patterns of prescription drug use in the United States had changed dramatically. In the past, prescription drugs were commonly used to treat diagnosed diseases or conditions, often in a time-limited course of treatment. Today, more medications are used to control and prevent chronic conditions such as heart disease, high blood pressure, and diabetes, meaning more people are dependent on prescription drugs for longer periods of time. At the same time, prescription drug costs have been rising rapidly. These factors combined made a strong case for a major revision to the Medicare program.

The 1988 Medicare Catastrophic Act

The 2003 Part D legislation was not the first attempt to add prescription drug coverage to Medicare. Perhaps the most interesting attempt, and the one that set the stage for the ultimately successful legislation, was the ill-fated Medicare Catastrophic Coverage Act signed into law by President Ronald Reagan in 1988. This law was aimed at providing beneficiaries better protection against catastrophic medical expenses. It altered program benefits and financing, and for the first time included prescription drug coverage that would have been phased in beginning in 1991.

The Medicare Catastrophic legislation also included a progressive financing system that raised premiums on wealthier beneficiaries to subsidize poorer beneficiaries. Although the legislation started out with strong bipartisan and public support, it soon came to symbolize how strong initial support for a potential policy does not guarantee success once that policy is actually enacted. After passage, Medicare Catastrophic suffered a strong backlash from middle- and upper-income beneficiaries who balked at the higher premiums and from drug companies who feared it would set federal price controls on prescription drugs. The law was repealed one year later in 1989, but not before at least one well-known politician was threatened in the street by angry seniors:

> Congressman Dan Rostenkowski, one of the most powerful politicians in the United States, was booed and chased down a Chicago street Thursday morning by a group of senior citizens after he refused to talk with them about federal health insurance. . . . Eventually, the six-foot four-inch Rostenkowski cut through a gas station, broke into a sprint and escaped into his car, which minutes earlier had one of the elderly protesters, Leona Kozien, draped over the hood.[53]

Two features of Medicare Catastrophic were particularly important in its downfall, and they heavily influenced the authors of the next prescription drug coverage law. The first was the unpopularity of the "pay now, benefit later" structure in which higher-income seniors were to begin paying supplemental premiums for the benefit in 1990, a full year before drug coverage was scheduled to take effect. The second important feature was that the program was mandatory, not voluntary.

Historical Support for a Prescription Drug Benefit

Despite the failure of the Medicare Catastrophic Coverage Act, the growing reliance on prescription drugs to treat chronic diseases and the increasing cost of these drugs translated into strong public support for another attempt at legislation to add prescription drug coverage to Medicare. Between 1994 and 2003, more than eight in ten Americans said they would favor a proposal to guarantee prescription drug coverage to everyone on Medicare (**Table 7–17**).[54]

This support remained high even when the question included mention of potential cost increases. Over the same time period, around seven in ten favored a proposal "to guarantee prescription drug coverage to everyone on Medicare even if it means an increase in premiums or taxes to cover the costs."[55]

Furthermore, surveys from 2000 through 2003 also showed a consistent and clear preference for expanding Medicare to cover drug costs, as opposed to the government helping people buy private insurance (**Table 7–18**).[56] This support for traditional Medicare over private plans is not surprising: surveys often find that the public is somewhat conservative when it comes to reform measures, preferring proposals that make smaller changes within a known system over plans that convert to an entirely new system.

Medicare Part D Takes Shape

Shortly after taking office in 2001, President Bush proposed legislation to Congress that would help Medicare beneficiaries with the cost of prescription drugs. The House and Senate debated different versions of the legislation throughout 2002 and 2003, and in December 2003, the president signed Medicare Part D into law.

The Medicare Part D policy provides coverage through *private* companies, representing a fundamental change in how seniors get health benefits through Medicare. Private companies were encouraged to develop individual plans, and the result is that seniors who decide to enroll in the benefit have forty or more drug plans to choose from—each offering a different selection of covered medications, premium costs, co-pays, and so forth. The decision to use this approach was largely based on ideology and was considered necessary by many to get Republican lawmakers to support the legislation. Although it seems to run counter to public opinion, this approach may not have been entirely unacceptable to the public, given that pluralities of seniors see private plans as equal to Medicare in terms of generosity of benefits and choice of providers, and most seniors and younger adults think there is at least as much fraud and abuse in Medicare as in private plans.

Two features of the legislation showed that lawmakers learned some lessons from the experience of Medicare Catastrophic and responded accordingly. First, unlike the "pay now, benefit later" structure of the earlier legislation, the new law included a provision for a drug discount card that was immediately available and provided some financial help to seniors paying for prescription drugs. The discount card program ended when the full benefit took effect: beginning in November 2005 seniors could start enrolling in the new Medicare prescription drug plans, with benefits to begin in January 2006.

The second important feature is that Medicare Part D was marketed to seniors as a voluntary program (unlike Medicare Catastrophic, which was mandatory). In truth, the Part D program is voluntary only to a certain extent. Seniors were given until May 15, 2006, to enroll in a drug plan; after that, anyone without drug coverage that is at least as good as the standard Medicare drug benefit ("creditable coverage") is subject to a 1 percent premium penalty for each month they delay enrollment.

Furthermore, to fit the law into the prescribed budget constraints, the structure of the standard drug benefit under Medicare Part D is complicated and includes a variety of cost-sharing arrangements. One such arrangement, coined the "doughnut hole," describes a gap in coverage (between $2,510 and $5,726 in drug costs in 2008), where beneficiaries pay 100 percent of drug costs in addition to the plan's premium costs (see below for more detail).

Overall Impressions of the Benefit

Public opinion surveys starting in February 2004—three months after legislation passed and nearly a year before enrollment began—showed that, at least initially, many seniors were suspicious of the new law. In ten of eleven tracking surveys between February 2004 and April 2006, more seniors said they had an unfavorable than a favorable impression of the Medicare drug benefit.

Once enrollment began and seniors began to have experience with the program, however, larger numbers of them reported a favorable impression. In November 2006 (the last time this question was asked), roughly four in ten seniors (42 percent) said they had a favorable impression of the drug benefit, and about a third (34 percent) reported an unfavorable impression (**Table 7–19**).[57] Furthermore, those seniors who said they were enrolled in a Medicare drug plan were significantly more likely to report a favorable impression than those who were not enrolled (56 percent compared with 32 percent).[58]

Enrolled Seniors' Opinions about Medicare Part D

As of February 2009, the Centers for Medicare and Medicaid Services reported that 26.7 million Medicare beneficiaries, or 59 percent of all beneficiaries, were enrolled in Medicare Part D plans (an additional 32 percent had prescription drug coverage through a former employer or some other source, and 10 percent lacked drug coverage).[59] Overall, seniors' reported experiences in the Medicare Part D program have been mostly positive. Early on, in November 2006, three-quarters of seniors enrolled in Part D said their experiences using their plan were positive, including nearly half (46 percent) who said they were "very positive."[60] Two and three years into the program, surveys in 2007 and 2008 found that about six in ten seniors in Part D were "extremely" or "very" satisfied with their prescription drug plan (59 percent in 2007 and 56 percent in 2008), and just about one in ten were "not very" or "not at all" satisfied. Satisfaction was somewhat lower when enrollees were asked about the amount of the monthly premium they paid for coverage, but still about half were extremely or very satisfied (**Table 7–20**).[61]

Surveys also found that most people enrolled in Medicare Part D felt they were saving money on their prescriptions. In a 2006 survey, just over half (52 percent) of seniors who were enrolled and had filled at least one prescription under Part D said they were saving money on prescriptions compared to the previous year, about three in ten (31 percent) said they were paying about the same, and 14 percent said they were paying more.[62] In 2007, 44 percent of seniors with Part D coverage said that prescriptions under the program were more affordable (including two in ten who said "much" more affordable), and more than half said they had saved money compared to the previous year (including 19 percent who said they saved "a great deal" of money) (**Table 7–21**).[63]

Criticisms of Part D: Complicated, Too Many Plans

Despite the overall popularity of the prescription drug program, Medicare Part D is not immune to criticism. One criticism voiced from the beginning was that the benefit is too complicated for seniors to navigate. Surveys as early as 2004—just after the law was passed but before implementation began—and continuing through 2006 found that large majorities (between 69 percent and 81 percent) of seniors agreed with this sentiment (**Table 7–22**).[64] A 2006 survey also found that among the 45 percent of seniors with an unfavorable impression of the drug benefit, nearly eight in ten (78 percent) said a major reason for their unfavorable impression was that "it is too complicated for people on Medicare to understand."[65] Two surveys in 2006 also found that overwhelming majorities of physicians (92 percent) and pharmacists (91 percent) agreed that the benefit was too complicated, including about six in ten in both groups who "strongly" agreed.[66]

With time, understanding about Medicare Part D improved, but in the early period confusion was a serious problem. As enrollment began in late 2005, nearly six in ten seniors said they did not have enough information about the benefit to understand how it would impact them personally. In April 2006, with just one month to go before the end of enrollment, this situation had improved somewhat, and seniors were split on whether they understood the personal impact of the benefit—47 percent said they did understand, 46 percent said they did not (**Table 7–23**).[67]

At the root of much of this confusion was the large number of private plans, each with different specific coverage limitations and cost-sharing arrangements, that seniors had to consider. In 2005 polling just before the benefit was implemented, seniors were roughly split as to whether people on Medicare would have too many (22 percent) or too few (20 percent) drug plans to choose from, with three in ten each saying they would have the right amount of plans or they did not know.[68] In November 2006, about a year into the benefit, seniors' opinions about the number of plans were more negative, with nearly four in ten (39 percent) saying there were too many.[69]

When told that most people on Medicare would have at least forty different plans to choose from, large majorities of both seniors (73 percent in 2005) and the general public (61 percent in 2006) believed that "having many plans to choose from makes it confusing and difficult to pick the best plan," and much smaller shares (22 percent and 31 percent) instead thought that "having many plans to choose from is helpful and provides an opportunity to find the best plan."[70]

In 2006, six in ten seniors thought that Medicare should select a handful of plans meeting certain standards so it would be easier for seniors to choose one, but about half as many thought Medicare should offer dozens of plans so people can find one that meets their needs. The same survey found that 60 percent of the general public, and 68 percent of seniors, were in favor of "simplifying the new drug benefit by reducing the number of available plans seniors have to choose from."[71]

Seniors themselves reported at least some difficulty choosing between the different Part D plan options, but surveys show that most of those who chose a Part D plan were satisfied with the one they chose. In April 2006, about half (51 percent) of Part D enrollees said it was easy to choose a Medicare drug plan, and about half (48 percent) said it was difficult (including 25 percent who said it was "very difficult").[72] In surveys in 2006, 2007, and 2008, about three-quarters of those enrolled in Part D said that they thought they had made a "good choice," and fewer than one in ten said they would have been better off with a different plan (**Table 7–24**).[73] Beneficiaries enrolled in Part D plans may switch plans once a year, between November 15 and December 31.

Continuing Challenges with Part D

Despite overall positive experiences, a small but important proportion of those with Part D coverage have reported problems getting all of the medications they need. More than one in ten say that since joining their new drug plan, they decided not to fill a prescription (12 percent in 2007 and 2008), skipped a dose (17 percent in 2007 and 19 percent in 2008), or took less than the prescribed dose of a medicine (13 percent in 2007 and 17 percent in 2008). Six percent of enrollees in 2007 and 16 percent in 2008 said they have inquired about a drug manufacturer's prescription assistance program.[74]

One of the biggest ongoing criticisms voiced about the Medicare Part D benefit is the coverage gap, or "doughnut hole." The standard benefit in 2010 had a $310 deductible and 25 percent co-insurance up to an initial coverage limit of $2,830 in total drug costs, followed by a coverage gap in which enrollees pay 100 percent of their drug costs until they have spent $4,550 out of pocket, excluding the Part D premium.[75] In 2007, an estimated 3.4 million Medicare beneficiaries had spending in the coverage gap. There is evidence that among those with chronic conditions who reached the coverage gap, some stopped taking their medications or took less than the prescribed dose.[76]

Seniors, and the public at large, are supportive of federal outlays to "fill in" the doughnut hole. In surveys in both 2006 and 2008, large majorities said they favored (and about half "strongly" favored) spending federal money to eliminate the coverage gap (**Table 7–25**).[77] The newly passed health reform law includes provisions that gradually reduce the amount enrollees are required to pay in the coverage gap. In 2010 Part D enrollees with spending in the gap received a $250 rebate. Beginning in 2011 Medicare will phase in additional coverage of generic drugs in the coverage gap, and pharmaceutical companies will be required to provide a 50 percent discount on brand-name drugs in the gap. In 2013 Medicare will begin to provide subsidies on brand-name drugs in the gap so that by 2020 enrollees will be responsible for paying 25 percent of drug costs in the coverage gap, compared with 100 percent in 2009.[78] A survey taken just before the law's passage found that 71 percent of the public thought closing the coverage gap was an "extremely" or "very" important element of health reform, and another survey taken soon after passage found that just over half (56 percent) knew that this provision was included in the final bill.[79]

Finally, it is worth mentioning one potential reform to the drug benefit under Medicare that is very popular with the public: having the government negotiate with drug companies to get lower prices on prescription drugs. Currently, the Medicare prescription drug law actually prohibits the government from such direct negotiations with drug companies. As mentioned above, nine in ten supported such negotiation as a way to deal with Medicare's financial problems in a 2008 survey (but again, experts question how much money this would actually save). More detail on public opinion about this issue can be found in Chapter 8.

Conclusion and Future Challenges

As the two largest government health care programs, Medicare and Medicaid are critical components of the U.S. health care system. Surveys consistently show that these programs are popular among the public and that people are resistant to making major changes in them. Moreover, despite experts' concerns about financing challenges, people do not want to see cutbacks made in Medicare and Medicaid, either in the benefits offered or in the number of people covered. These findings demonstrate a common theme in public opinion: that even when problems exist, the public is often comfortable with what is familiar, and is resistant to change and to making hard choices that could require some people to receive less or pay more.

Policymakers are likely to face many difficult challenges relating to Medicare and Medicaid in the future, the most daunting of which is how to continue financing care for an aging population, particularly at a time when health care costs are rising much faster than the rate of inflation. This challenge becomes even more complicated when considering the public opinion environment in which people do not want cuts made to these programs.

Ideological differences in attitudes toward the role of private plans in these public programs present another challenge. Again, we have seen that most people "like what they know" and prefer that coverage be provided directly through Medicare, as opposed to through private plans. Medicare Part D provides an interesting case study in this area, as policymakers were able to pass a law that ran counter to the public's desire to stick with the familiar and provided drug coverage to seniors through private plans, rather than through a direct expansion of Medicare. As younger generations who are more comfortable with private insurance near the age of Medicare eligibility, it is also possible that this preference for public over private plans will be mediated somewhat.

Notes

[1] Unless otherwise noted, all information in this section comes from Kaiser Family Foundation, "Medicare: A Primer, 2010," http://www.kff.org/medicare/upload/7615–03.pdf.

[2] Scott Harrison and Carlos Zarabozo, "The Medicare Advantage Program," paper presented at the Medicare Payment Advisory Commission (MedPAC) Public Meeting, December 5, 2008, http://www.medpac.gov/transcripts/MA1208presentation%20final%20NO%20NOTES.pdf.

[3] Kaiser Family Foundation, "Summary of Key Changes to Medicare in 2010 Health Reform Law," May 2010, http://www.kff.org/healthreform/upload/7948–02.pdf.

[4] Unless otherwise noted, all information in this section comes from Kaiser Family Foundation, "Medicaid: A Primer, 2009," http://www.kff.org/medicaid/upload/7334–03.pdf.

[5] An additional 7 million children in 2007 received coverage through the State Children's Health Insurance Program (SCHIP). For more details on SCHIP and children's health insurance coverage, see Chapter 5, on the uninsured.

[6] Gallup Poll (Storrs, Conn.: Roper Center for Public Opinion Research, June 16–21, 1937); Gallup Poll (Storrs, Conn.: Roper Center for Public Opinion Research, May 22–27, 1938); Office of Opinion Research Poll (Storrs, Conn.: Roper Center for Public Opinion Research, March 1943).

[7] National Opinion Research Center Poll (Storrs, Conn.: Roper Center for Public Opinion Research, August 1944).

[8] Gallup Poll (Storrs, Conn.: Roper Center for Public Opinion Research, June 1–5, 1945).

[9] Gallup Poll (Storrs, Conn.: Roper Center for Public Opinion Research, May 17–22, 1961).

[10] Institute for International Social Research Poll (Storrs, Conn.: Roper Center for Public Opinion Research, October 1964).

[11] Harris Poll (Storrs, Conn.: Roper Center for Public Opinion Research, December 1965).

[12] NPR/Kaiser Family Foundation/Kennedy School of Government, "National Survey of Americans on Social Security," May 20, 1999 (conducted March 4–24, 1999), http://www.kff .org/kaiserpolls/loader.cfm?url=/commonspot/security/getfile.cfm&PageID=14902; Kaiser Family Foundation, "National Survey of the Public's Views about Medicaid," June 2005 (conducted April 1–May 1, 2005), http://www.kff.org/medicaid/upload/National-Survey-of-the-Public-s-Views-About-Medicaid-Toplines.pdf; Kaiser Family Foundation, "Kaiser Health Tracking Poll," April 2009 (conducted April 2–8, 2009), http://www.kff.org/kaiserpolls/upload/7892.pdf.

[13] Opinion Research Corporation Poll (Storrs, Conn.: Roper Center for Public Opinion Research, May 7–25, 1971); ABC News/*Washington Post* polls (Storrs, Conn.: Roper Center for Public Opinion Research, February 19–20, 1981; February 6–12, 1986; January 13–19, 1987; August 17–21, 1989. Marist College Institute for Public Opinion Poll (Storrs, Conn.: Roper Center for Public Opinion Research, January 29–31, 1990); Pew Research Center for the People and the Press polls (Storrs, Conn.: Roper Center for Public Opinion Research, May 15–18, 1997; April 18–22, 2001; February 12–18, 2002; May 1–June 14, 2009); Kaiser Family Foundation, "National Survey of the Public's Views about Medicaid," June 2005; AARP Poll (Storrs, Conn.: Roper Center for Public Opinion Research, January 4–9, 2006); Kaiser Family Foundation/Harvard School of Public Health, "The Public's Health Care Agenda for the New President and Congress," January 2009 (conducted December 4–14, 2008), http://www.kff.org/kaiserpolls/upload/7853.pdf.

[14] Gallup/Potomac Associates Poll (Storrs, Conn.: Roper Center for Public Opinion Research, May 1972); ABC News/*Washington Post* polls, February 19–20, 1981; February 6–12, 1986; January 13–19, 1987; August 17–21, 1989); Harris Poll (Storrs, Conn.: Roper Center for Public Opinion Research, April 22–27, 1998); Kaiser Family Foundation, "National Survey of the Public's Views about Medicaid," June 2005; AARP Poll, January 4–9, 2006; Kaiser Family Foundation/Harvard School of Public Health, "The Public's Health Care Agenda for the New President and Congress," January 2009.

[15] Kaiser Family Foundation/Harvard School of Public Health, "The Public's Health Care Agenda for the New President and Congress," January 2009.

[16] Harris Poll (Storrs, Conn.: Roper Center for Public Opinion Research, October 29–November 4, 1987); *Time*/CNN/Yankelovich Partners Poll (Storrs, Conn.: Roper Center for Public Opinion Research, August 4–5, 1993); *Los Angeles Times* Poll (Storrs, Conn.: Roper Center for Public Opinion Research, January 19–22, 1995); ABC News/*Washington Post* Poll (Storrs, Conn.: Roper Center for Public Opinion Research, January 26–29, 1995): *Reader's Digest* Poll (Storrs, Conn.: Roper Center for Public Opinion Research, February 26–March 5, 1995); Kaiser Family Foundation/Harvard School of Public Health Poll (Storrs, Conn.: Roper Center for Public Opinion Research, May 31–June 5, 1995); Harris Poll (Storrs, Conn.: Roper Center for Public Opinion Research, June 8–11, 1995); *Washington Post*/Kaiser Family Foundation/Harvard University Poll (Storrs, Conn.: Roper Center for Public Opinion Research, July 20–September 18, 1995); AARP Poll, January 4–9, 2006; Kaiser Family Foundation/Harvard School of Public Health, "The Public's Health Care Agenda for the New President and Congress," January 2009.

[17] Kaiser Family Foundation, "National Survey of the Public's Views about Medicaid," June 2005.

[18] Kaiser Family Foundation/Harvard School of Public Health Poll (Storrs, Conn.: Roper Center for Public Opinion Research, December 3–13, 1999); *NewsHour with Jim Lehrer*/Kaiser Family

Foundation, "National Survey on the Uninsured," April 2000 (conducted January 10–February 9, 2000), http://www.kff.org/uninsured/upload/3013toplines.pdf; Kaiser Family Foundation/Harvard School of Public Health, "Post-Election Survey: The Public and the Health Care Agenda for the New Administration and Congress," January 2001 (conducted November 13–December 13, 2000), http://www.kff.org/kaiserpolls/loader.cfm?url=/commonspot/security/getfile.cfm&PageID=13785; NPR/Kaiser Family Foundation/Kennedy School of Government Poll (Storrs, Conn.: Roper Center for Public Opinion Research, March 28–May 1, 2002); Kaiser Family Foundation/Harvard School of Public Health, "Health Agenda for the New Congress," January 2005 (conducted November 4–28, 2004), http://www.kff.org/kaiserpolls/upload/Health-Care-Agenda-for-the-New-Congress-Survey-Toplines.pdf; Kaiser Family Foundation, "Kaiser Health Tracking Poll: Election 2008," October 2008 (conducted September 8–13, 2008), http://www.kff.org/kaiserpolls/upload/78161.pdf; Kaiser Family Foundation/Harvard School of Public Health, "The Public's Health Care Agenda for the New President and Congress," January 2009; Kaiser Family Foundation polls (Storrs, Conn.: Roper Center for Public Opinion Research, April 2–8, 2009; June 1–5, 2009; July 7–14, 2009; August 4–11, 2009).

[19] Cato Institute/Public Opinion Strategies Poll (Storrs, Conn.: Roper Center for Public Opinion Research, March 27–31, 1996); Cato Institute/Public Opinion Strategies Poll (Storrs, Conn.: Roper Center for Public Opinion Research, June 12–16, 1996); NPR/Kaiser Family Foundation/Kennedy School of Government, "Attitudes toward Government," May 26–June 25, 2000, http://www.kff.org/kaiserpolls/upload/NPR-Kaiser-Kennedy-School-Poll-Attitudes-Toward-Government.pdf; Robert Wood Johnson Foundation/Public Opinion Strategies Poll (Storrs, Conn.: Roper Center for Public Opinion Research, August 4–7, 2007).

[20] Karen Davis, Cathy Schoen, Michelle Doty, and Katie Tenney, "Medicare Versus Private Insurance: Rhetoric and Reality," *Health Affairs* 21 (Web exclusive, October 9, 2002): w311–w324, http://content.healthaffairs.org/cgi/reprint/hlthaff.w2.311v1.

[21] Kaiser Family Foundation, "Data Note: Americans' Satisfaction with Insurance Coverage," September 2009, http://www.kff.org/kaiserpolls/upload/7979.pdf.

[22] Kaiser Family Foundation, "National Survey of the Public's Views about Medicaid," June 2005.

[23] Kaiser Family Foundation/Harvard School of Public Health, "National Survey of the Public's Views on Medicare," April 25–June 1, 2003, http://www.kff.org/medicare/loader.cfm?url=/commonspot/security/getfile.cfm&PageID=14304.

[24] Kaiser Family Foundation/Harvard School of Public Health Poll (Storrs, Conn.: Roper Center for Public Opinion Research, May 31–June 5, 1995); *Washington Post*/Kaiser Family Foundation/Harvard University, "Survey of Americans' Knowledge and Attitudes about Entitlements," March 1997, http://www.kff.org/medicare/loader.cfm?url=/commonspot/security/getfile.cfm&PageID=14513; *Washington Post*/Kaiser Family Foundation/Harvard University, "Issues in the 2000 Election: Health Care," July 2000, http://www.kff.org/kaiserpolls/upload/3038.pdf; Kaiser Family Foundation/Harvard School of Public Health, "National Survey of the Public's Views on Medicare," April 25–June 1, 2003; Kaiser Family Foundation, "National Survey of the Public's Views about Medicaid," June 2005.

[25] Kaiser Family Foundation "Survey of Americans on the U.S. Role in Global Health," May 2009, http://www.kff.org/kaiserpolls/upload/7894.pdf.

[26] Kaiser Family Foundation, "Medicare, A Primer, 2010."

[27] Gallup/CNN/*USA Today* Poll (Storrs, Conn.: Roper Center for Public Opinion Research, September 22–24, 1995); *Washington Post*/Kaiser Family Foundation/Harvard University,

"Survey of Americans' Knowledge and Attitudes about Entitlements," March 1997; Kaiser Family Foundation/Harvard School of Public Health, "National Survey on Medicare Policy Options," August 14–September 20, 1998, http://www.kff.org/medicare/loader.cfm?url=/commonspot/security/getfile.cfm&PageID=14658; *Washington Post*/Kaiser Family Foundation/Harvard University Poll (Storrs, Conn.: Roper Center for Public Opinion Research, August 2–September 1, 2002); ABC News/*Washington Post* Poll (Storrs, Conn.: Roper Center for Public Opinion Research, January 30–February 1, 2003); Quinnipiac University Poll (Storrs, Conn.: Roper Center for Public Opinion Research, January 25–31, 2005); Kaiser Family Foundation, "Kaiser Health Tracking Poll," April 2009.

[28] Kaiser Family Foundation, "Kaiser Health Tracking Poll," April 2009.

[29] Employee Benefit Research Institute, "The 2009 Retirement Confidence Survey: Economy Drives Confidence to Record Lows; Many Looking to Work Longer," Issue Brief no. 328, April 2009, http://www.ebri.org/pdf/briefspdf/EBRI_IB_4–2009_RCS2.pdf.

[30] Ibid.

[31] Kaiser Family Foundation/Harvard School of Public Health, "National Survey of the Public's Views on Medicare," April 25–June 1, 2003; Kaiser Family Foundation, "Kaiser Health Tracking Poll," April 2009.

[32] Pew Research Center for the People and the Press, "February 2001 News Interest Index: Final Topline," http://people–press.org/reports/questionnaires/17.pdf.

[33] Kaiser Family Foundation/Harvard School of Public Health, "The Public's Health Care Agenda for the New President and Congress," January 2009; Kaiser Family Foundation, "Kaiser Health Tracking Poll," April 2009.

[34] See the case study at the end of this chapter and Chapter 8 on prescription drugs for more detail on this topic.

[35] In a letter to senators dated March 3, 2004, the Congressional Budget Office stated that striking the "noninterference" provision of the Medicare drug law would have a "negligible" effect on federal spending. See http://cbo.gov/doc.cfm?index=5145&type=0.

[36] Kaiser Family Foundation/Harvard School of Public Health, "National Survey of the Public's Views on Medicare," April 25–June 1, 2003; Kaiser Family Foundation/Harvard School of Public Health, "The Public's Health Care Agenda for the New Congress and Presidential Campaign," December 2006 (conducted November 9–19, 2006), http://www.kff.org/kaiserpolls/upload/7598.pdf.

[37] Kaiser Family Foundation, "Kaiser Health Tracking Poll," April 2009.

[38] Kaiser Family Foundation/Harvard School of Public Health, "The Public's Health Care Agenda for the New President and Congress," January 2009.

[39] Ibid.

[40] Kaiser Family Foundation polls (Storrs, Conn.: Roper Center for Public Opinion Research, June 1–5, 2009; August 4–11, 2009).

[41] NBC News/*Wall Street Journal* polls (Storrs, Conn.: Roper Center for Public Opinion Research, June 12–15, 2009; July 24–27, 2009).

[42] Gallup/*USA Today* Poll (Storrs, Conn.: Roper Center for Public Opinion Research, July 10–12, 2009).

[43] Pew Research Center for the People and the Press Poll (Storrs, Conn.: Roper Center for Public Opinion Research, July 22–26, 2009).

[44] Kaiser Family Foundation, "Kaiser Health Tracking Poll," April 2010, http://www.kff.org/kaiserpolls/upload/8067-T.pdf.

[45] NBC News/*Wall Street Journal* Poll (Storrs, Conn.: Roper Center for Public Opinion Research, January 9–12, 2009).

[46] Kaiser Family Foundation, "National Survey of the Public's Views about Medicaid," June 2005.

[47] Ibid.

[48] Ibid.

[49] Kaiser Family Foundation/Harvard School of Public Health, "National Survey on Medicare Policy Options," August 14–September 20, 1998; *Time*/CNN/Yankelovich Partners Poll (Storrs, Conn.: Roper Center for Public Opinion Research, September 6–7, 2000); Kaiser Family Foundation/Harvard School of Public Health, "National Survey of the Public's Views on Medicare," April 25–June 1, 2003.

[50] Kaiser Family Foundation/Harvard School of Public Health, "National Survey of the Public's Views on Medicare," April 25–June 1, 2003.

[51] Kaiser Family Foundation/Harvard School of Public Health, "National Survey on Medicare Policy Options," August 14–September 20, 1998.

[52] Kaiser Family Foundation/Harvard School of Public Health Poll (Storrs, Conn.: Roper Center for Public Opinion Research, May 31–June 5, 1995); NBC News/*Wall Street Journal* Poll (Storrs, Conn.: Roper Center for Public Opinion Research, July 29–August 1, 1995); Kaiser Family Foundation/Harvard School of Public Health, "Survey of Americans on Health Policy," July 1996 (conducted June 20–July 9, 1996), http://www.kff.org/kaiserpolls/loader.cfm?url=/commonspot/security/getfile.cfm&PageID=14464.

[53] William Recktenwald, "Insurance Forum Turns Catastrophic for Rostenkowski," *Chicago Tribune*, August 18, 1989, 1. For a more extensive discussion of this incident, see Ken Kollman, *Outside Lobbying: Public Opinion and Interest Group Strategies* (Princeton, N.J.: Princeton University Press, 1998), 28–31.

[54] *New York Times* Poll (Storrs, Conn.: Roper Center for Public Opinion Research, March 8–11, 1994); Harris Poll (Storrs, Conn.: Roper Center for Public Opinion Research, September 17–21, 1999); *NewsHour with Jim Lehrer*/Kaiser Family Foundation, "National Survey on the Uninsured," April 2000; Pew Research Center for the People and the Press Poll (Storrs, Conn.: Roper Center for Public Opinion Research, June 13–17, 2001); *Time*/CNN/Harris Interactive Poll (Storrs, Conn.: Roper Center for Public Opinion Research, July 16–17, 2003).

[55] Kaiser Family Foundation, "The Public on Medicare Part D—The Medicare Prescription Drug Benefit," Kaiser Public Opinion Spotlight, April 2006, http://www.kff.org/spotlight/medicarerx/upload/Spotlight_Apr06_MedicareRX-3.pdf.

[56] Kaiser Family Foundation/Harvard School of Public Health, "Post-Election Survey: The Public and the Health Care Agenda for the New Administration and Congress," January 2001; NPR/Kaiser Family Foundation/Kennedy School of Government Poll (Storrs, Conn.: Roper Center for Public Opinion Research, March 28–May 1, 2002); *Washington Post*/Kaiser Family Foundation/Harvard University Poll (Storrs, Conn.: Roper Center for Public Opinion Research, August 2–September 1, 2002); Kaiser Family Foundation/Harvard School of Public Health Poll (Storrs, Conn.: Roper Center for Public Opinion Research, February 6–10, 2003).

[57] Kaiser Family Foundation, "The Public on Medicare Part D—The Medicare Prescription Drug Benefit," Kaiser Public Opinion Spotlight, April 2006.

58 Kaiser Family Foundation/Harvard School of Public Health, "The Public's Health Care Agenda for the New Congress and Presidential Campaign," December 2006.

59 Kaiser Family Foundation, "The Medicare Prescription Drug Benefit," Medicare Fact Sheet, March 2009, http://www.kff.org/medicare/upload/7044-09.pdf.

60 Ibid.

61 AARP Poll (Storrs, Conn.: Roper Center for Public Opinion Research, October 5–26, 2007); AARP Poll (Storrs, Conn.: Roper Center for Public Opinion Research, November 8–20, 2008).

62 Kaiser Family Foundation/Harvard School of Public Health, "The Public's Health Care Agenda for the New Congress and Presidential Campaign;" December 2006.

63 AARP Poll, October 5–26, 2007.

64 Kaiser Family Foundation/Harvard School of Public Health, "Health Agenda for the New Congress," January 2005; NBC News/*Wall Street Journal* Poll (Storrs, Conn.: Roper Center for Public Opinion Research, December 9–12, 2005); NBC News/*Wall Street Journal* Poll (Storrs, Conn.: Roper Center for Public Opinion Research, January 26–29, 2006); NBC News/*Wall Street Journal* Poll (Storrs, Conn.: Roper Center for Public Opinion Research, April 21–24, 2006); Kaiser Family Foundation/Harvard School of Public Health, "The Public's Health Care Agenda for the New Congress and Presidential Campaign," December 2006.

65 Kaiser Family Foundation, "Selected Findings on Seniors' Views of the Medicare Prescription Drug Benefit," February 2006, http://www.kff.org/kaiserpolls/upload/7462.pdf.

66 Kaiser Family Foundation, "National Survey of Physicians: Findings on Medicare Part D," September 2006 (conducted April 25–July 8, 2006), http://www.kff.org/kaiserpolls/upload/7554.pdf; Kaiser Family Foundation, "National Survey of Pharmacists: Findings on Medicare Part D," September 2006 (conducted April 21–June 27, 2006), http://www.kff.org/kaiserpolls/upload/7555.pdf.

67 Kaiser Family Foundation, "The Public on Medicare Part D—The Medicare Prescription Drug Benefit," Kaiser Public Opinion Spotlight, April 2006.

68 Kaiser Family Foundation/Harvard School of Public Health, "The Medicare Drug Benefit: Beneficiary Perspectives Just before Implementation," November 2005 (conducted October 13–31, 2005), http://www.kff.org/kaiserpolls/upload/-The-Medicare-Drug-Benefit-Beneficiary-Perspectives-Just-Before-Implementation-Toplines.pdf; Kaiser Family Foundation, "Selected Findings on Seniors' Views of the Medicare Prescription Drug Benefit," February 2006.

69 Kaiser Family Foundation/Harvard School of Public Health, "The Public's Health Care Agenda for the New Congress and Presidential Campaign," December 2006.

70 Kaiser Family Foundation/Harvard School of Public Health, "The Medicare Drug Benefit: Beneficiary Perspectives Just before Implementation," November 2005; Kaiser Family Foundation, "Selected Findings on Seniors' Views of the Medicare Prescription Drug Benefit," February 2006.

71 Kaiser Family Foundation/Harvard School of Public Health, "The Public's Health Care Agenda for the New Congress and Presidential Campaign," December 2006.

72 Kaiser Family Foundation, "Seniors' Early Experiences with the Medicare Prescription Drug Benefit," April 2006, http://www.kff.org/kaiserpolls/upload/7501.pdf.

73 Kaiser Family Foundation, "May/June 2006 Kaiser Family Health Poll Report Survey: Selected Findings on Health Care," July 2006 (conducted June 12–19, 2006), http://www.kff.org/kaiserpolls/upload/7545.pdf; AARP Poll, October 5–26, 2007; AARP Poll, November 8–20, 2008.

74 AARP Poll, October 5–26, 2007; AARP Poll, November 8–20, 2008.

75 Kaiser Family Foundation, "Medicare: A Primer, 2010."

[76] Jack Hoadley, Elizabeth Hargrave, Juliette Cubanski, and Tricia Neuman, "The Medicare Part D Coverage Gap: Costs and Consequences in 2007," Kaiser Family Foundation, August 2008, http://www.kff.org/medicare/upload/7811.pdf.

[77] Kaiser Family Foundation/Harvard School of Public Health, "The Public's Health Care Agenda for the New Congress and Presidential Campaign," December 2006; Kaiser Family Foundation/Harvard School of Public Health, "The Public's Health Care Agenda for the New President and Congress," January 2009.

[78] Kaiser Family Foundation, "Medicare: A Primer, 2010."

[79] Kaiser Family Foundation, "Kaiser Health Tracking Poll," February 2010, http://www.kff.org/kaiserpolls/upload/8051-T.pdf; Kaiser Family Foundation, "Kaiser Health Tracking Poll," April 2010.

Table 7-1 Public Support for Government Helping People Who Cannot Afford to Pay for Health Care, 1937–1965 (percent)

	Favor/Yes	Oppose/No	No opinion
Federal government providing free medical care for those unable to pay (1937)[1]	76	19	5
Government should be responsible for providing medical care for those unable to pay (1938)[2]	78	18	3
After the war, government should provide free medical care for all who need it and can't afford it (1943)[3]	83	15	2
Good/bad idea if Social Security law also provided paying doctor and hospital care that people might need (1944)[4]	68	19	13
Increase tax rates to include payment of benefits under Social Security for sickness, disability, doctor and hospital bills (1945)[5]	52	37	11
Social Security tax increase to pay for old age medical insurance (1961)[6]	68	26	7
Compulsory medical insurance program covering hospital and nursing home care for elderly/financed from increased Social Security taxes (1964)[7]	61	31	8
(After Medicare passed) approve/disapprove of bill passed to provide medical care for the aged (1965)[8]	82	18	0

Question: Should the federal government provide free medical care for those unable to pay?

Question: Do you think the government should be responsible for providing medical care for people who are unable to pay for it?

Question: After the war do you think the government should provide free medical care for all who need it and can't afford it?

Question: Do you think it would be a good idea or a bad idea if the Social Security law also provided paying the doctor and hospital care that people might need in the future?

Question: At present the Social Security program provides benefits for old age, death, and unemployment. Would you favor increasing the present tax rates to include payment of benefits for sickness, disability, doctor and hospital bills?

Question: Would you favor or oppose having the Social Security tax increased in order to pay for old age medical insurance?

Question: Congress has been considering a compulsory medical insurance program covering hospital and nursing home care for the elderly. This Medicare program would be financed out of increased Social Security taxes. In general, do you approve or disapprove of this program?

Question: Now I want to hand you a list of bills passed by this last Congress. For each, tell me if you approve or disapprove of that bill from what you know or have heard of it. . . . Medical care for the aged.

Sources: [1]Gallup Poll (Storrs, Conn.: Roper Center for Public Opinion Research, June 16–21, 1937). [2]Gallup Poll (Storrs, Conn.: Roper Center for Public Opinion Research, May 22–27, 1938). [3]Office of Opinion Research Poll (Storrs, Conn.: Roper Center for Public Opinion Research, March 1943). [4]National Opinion Research Center Poll (Storrs, Conn.: Roper Center for Public Opinion Research, August 1944). [5]Gallup Poll (Storrs, Conn.: Roper Center for Public Opinion Research, June 1–5, 1945). [6]Gallup Poll (Storrs, Conn.: Roper Center for Public Opinion Research, May 17–22, 1961). [7]Institute for International Social Research Poll (Storrs, Conn.: Roper Center for Public Opinion Research, October 1964). [8]Harris Poll (Storrs, Conn.: Roper Center for Public Opinion Research, December 1965).

Table 7-2 Americans' Views about the Importance of Medicare and Medicaid, 1999–2009 (percent)

	Very important	Somewhat important	Not very important	Not at all important
Medicare				
1999[1]	80	17	2	1
2005[2]	83	14	1	1
2009[3]	77	19	1	1
Medicaid				
1999[1]	67	26	4	2
2005[2]	74	20	2	2

Note: "Don't know" responses not shown.

Question: I'm going to read you a list of federal government programs and for each one, please tell me how important you think this program is. (Medicaid/Medicare)? (1995, 2005)

Question: How important, if at all, is the Medicare program for the country as a whole? (2009)

Sources: [1]NPR/Kaiser Family Foundation/Kennedy School of Government, "National Survey of Americans on Social Security," May 20, 1999 (conducted March 4–24, 1999). [2]Kaiser Family Foundation, "National Survey of the Public's Views about Medicaid," June 2005 (conducted April 1–May 1, 2005). [3]Kaiser Family Foundation, "Kaiser Health Tracking Poll," April 2009 (conducted April 2–8, 2009).

Table 7-3 Americans' Views about Spending on Medicare and Medicaid, 1971–2009 (percent)

	Too little/Increase	Right amount/Keep the same	Too much/Decrease
Medicare			
1971[1]	55	34	4
1981[2]	57	39	3
1986[2]	63	33	4
1987[2]	74	22	3
1989[2]	72	25	2
1990[3]	56	35	7
1997[4]	44	44	8
2001[4]	70	26	2
2002[4]	63	31	3
2005[5]	54	34	6
2006[6]	61	30	6
2008[7]	43	51	6
2009[4]	53	37	6
Medicaid			
1972[8]	53	35	8
1981[2]	44	41	13
1986[2]	49	42	9
1987[2]	62	32	6
1989[2]	61	33	6

(Table continues)

Table 7-3 *Continued*

1998[9]	43	40	13
2005[5]	48	32	10
2006[6]	51	34	10
2008[7]	34	54	11

Note: "Don't know" responses not shown.

Question: Here is a list of various government programs. For each one would you tell me whether you think government spending should be kept at the present level, if spending should be increased, or if spending should be decreased . . . Medicare (1971)

Question: Now I'm going to read off the names of some programs the federal government in Washington is helping to finance. As I mention each program, please tell me whether you feel the amount of tax money now being spent for each should be increased, kept at the present level, or reduced, or ended altogether. . . . The Medicaid program to help low-income families pay their medical bills? (1972)

Question: Now I'd like to ask about some specific federal government programs. Again, for each, please tell me whether you feel spending for that program should be increased, decreased, or left about the same. . . . (Medicare which helps reduce health care costs for the elderly/Medicaid which provides free health care for the poor). (1981, 1986, 1987, 1989)

Question: Do you think that federal spending this year should be increased, decreased, or remain the same for each of the following? . . . Medicare (1990)

Question: Let's talk for a few minutes about government spending on various programs. I'm going to read you a list of programs. For each one just tell me, in your opinion, whether the federal government should spend more or should spend less on each program. (Even if your own taxes increase? . . . Medicare (1993)

Question: If you were making up the budget for the federal government this year, would you increase spending for Medicare, decrease spending for Medicare, or keep spending the same for this? (1997, 2001, 2002, 2009)

Question: In general would you say government spends too much, too little, or about the right amount on . . . Medicaid, the health insurance program for low-income families and children? (1998)

Question: In general, do you think the federal government spends too much, too little, or about the right amount of money on . . . (Medicare/Medicaid)? (2005)

Question: For each of the following budget items, please state whether you think the new budget should increase spending on this item from the previous budget, decrease spending on this item from the previous budget, or keep it the same . . . (Medicare/Medicaid). (2006)

Question: As you know, the federal government has a substantial budget deficit and there are many competing spending priorities facing the next president and Congress. Thinking about the federal budget, do you want to see the next president and Congress increase spending on . . . (Medicare, the program that provides health insurance primarily to people age 65 and older/Medicaid, the program that provides health insurance and long-term care to low-income families and people with disabilities), decrease spending, or keep it about the same? (2008)

Sources: [1]Opinion Research Corporation Poll (Storrs, Conn.: Roper Center for Public Opinion Research, May 7–25, 1971). [2]ABC News/*Washington Post* polls (Storrs, Conn.: Roper Center for Public Opinion Research, February 19–20, 1981; February 6–12, 1986; January 13–19, 1987; August 17–21, 1989). [3]Marist College Institute for Public Opinion Poll (Storrs, Conn.: Roper Center for Public Opinion Research, January 29–31, 1990); [4]Pew Research Center for the People and the Press polls (Storrs, Conn.: Roper Center for Public Opinion Research, May 15–18, 1997; April 18–22, 2001; February 12–18, 2002; May 1–June 14, 2009). [5]Kaiser Family Foundation, "National Survey of the Public's Views about Medicaid," June 2005 (conducted April 1–May 1, 2005). [6]AARP Poll (Storrs, Conn.: Roper Center for Public Opinion Research, January 4–9, 2006). [7]Kaiser Family Foundation/Harvard School of Public Health, "The Public's Health Care Agenda for the New President and Congress," January 2009 (conducted December 4–14, 2008). [8]Gallup/Potomac Associates Poll (Storrs, Conn.: Roper Center for Public Opinion Research, May 1972); [9]Harris Poll (Storrs, Conn.: Roper Center for Public Opinion Research, April 22–27, 1998).

Table 7-4 Opinions on Medicare and Medicaid Spending, by Party Identification, Ideology, and Age (percent)

	Increase	Keep the same	Decrease
Medicare			
Total	43	51	6
By party identification			
Democrat	53	43	2
Independent	43	51	5
Republican	31	61	8
By political ideology			
Liberal	53	43	2
Moderate	40	54	5
Conservative	39	53	8
By age			
18–39	42	50	8
40–49	40	54	3
50–64	51	42	6
65+	36	59	3
Medicaid			
Total	34	54	11
By party identification			
Democrat	45	47	7
Independent	34	53	10
Republican	18	68	14
By political ideology			
Liberal	43	46	10
Moderate	34	56	7
Conservative	30	55	15
By age			
18–39	33	51	15
40–49	32	55	12
50–64	42	52	4
65+	32	58	9

Note: "Don't know" responses not shown

Question: As you know, the federal government has a substantial budget deficit and there are many competing spending priorities facing the next president and Congress. Thinking about the federal budget, do you want to see the next president and Congress increase spending on (Medicare, the program that provides health insurance primarily to people age 65 and older/Medicaid, the program that provides health insurance and long term care to low-income families and people with disabilities), decrease spending, or keep it about the same?

Source: Kaiser Family Foundation/Harvard School of Public Health, "The Public's Health Care Agenda for the New President and Congress," January 2009 (conducted December 4–14, 2008).

Table 7-5 Americans' Attitudes about Cutting Medicaid Spending in Their State (percent)

Making some cuts to Medicaid program in your state to help balance state budget	
Strongly support	5
Somewhat support	17
Somewhat oppose	22
Strongly oppose	52
Don't know	4
Best way for your state to reduce its budget problems	
The state should cut funding for programs other than Medicaid such as education, the prison system, and transportation	24
The state should raise taxes	21
The state should cut funding for the Medicaid program	21
Some other way (vol.)	15
None (vol.)	8
Don't know	11

Note: (vol.) = volunteered response

Question: As you may know, many states are thinking about cutting back their Medicaid program in order to help balance their state budget. Would you support or oppose making some cuts to the Medicaid program in your state?

Question: In your opinion, which one of the following is the best way for your state to reduce its budget problems?

Source: Kaiser Family Foundation, "National Survey of the Public's Views about Medicaid," June 2005 (conducted April 1–May 1, 2005).

Table 7-6 Attitudes about Expanding Medicare and Medicaid to Cover More People, 1999–2009 (percent)

	Expanding Medicare to cover people between the ages of 55 and 64 who do not have health insurance			Expanding state government programs for low-income people, such as Medicaid and the Children's Health Insurance Program, to the provide coverage for people without health insurance		
	Favor	Oppose	Don't know	Favor	Oppose	Don't know
December 1999	57	34	9	70	23	7
January 2000	67	31	2	78	21	1
November 2000	76	20	4	81	15	4
May 2002				84	15	1
November 2004	74	23	2	80	18	2
September 2008	70	24	5	72	21	6
December 2008	76	22	2	73	25	2
April 2009	79	18	3	77	20	2
June 2009	75	22	2	75	22	3
July 2009	77	21	2	74	22	3
August 2009	75	22	3	79	17	4

Question: I'm going to read you some different ways to increase the number of Americans covered by health insurance. As I read each one, please tell me whether you would favor it or oppose it. (Expanding Medicare to cover people between the ages of 55 and 64 who do not have health insurance/ Expanding state government programs for low-income people, such as Medicaid or the State Children's Health Insurance Program) Do you favor or oppose this?

Sources: Kaiser Family Foundation/Harvard School of Public Health Poll (Storrs, Conn.: Roper Center for Public Opinion Research, December 3–13, 1999); *NewsHour with Jim Lehrer*/Kaiser Family Foundation, "National Survey on the Uninsured," April 2000 (conducted January 10–February 9, 2000); Kaiser Family Foundation/Harvard School of Public Health, "Post-Election Survey: The Public and the Health Care Agenda for the New Administration and Congress," January 2001 (conducted November 13–December 13, 2000); NPR/Kaiser Family Foundation/Kennedy School of Government Poll (Storrs, Conn.: Roper Center for Public Opinion Research, March 28–May 1, 2002); Kaiser Family Foundation/Harvard School of Public Health, "Health Agenda for the New Congress," January 2005 (conducted November 4–28, 2004); Kaiser Family Foundation, "Kaiser Health Tracking Poll: Election 2008," October 2008 (conducted September 8–13, 2008); Kaiser Family Foundation/Harvard School of Public Health, "The Public's Health Care Agenda for the New President and Congress," January 2009 (conducted December 4–14, 2008); Kaiser Family Foundation polls (Storrs, Conn.: Roper Center for Public Opinion Research, April 2–8, 2009; June 1–5, 2009; July 7–14, 2009; August 4–11, 2009).

Table 7-7 Public Perception of Medicare and Medicaid, 1996–2007 (percent)

Medicare	Very favorable	Mostly/ Somewhat favorable	Half-and-half	Mostly/ Somewhat unfavorable	Very unfavorable	Don't know
March 1996	30	31	23	7	6	3
June 1996	39	33	16	6	3	3
May 2000	29	41	NA	16	12	3
August 2007	29	35	18	8	3	7

Medicaid	Very favorable	Mostly/ Somewhat favorable	Half-and-half	Mostly/ Somewhat unfavorable	Very unfavorable	Don't know
March 1996	21	28	27	13	7	5
June 1996	30	28	20	7	3	12
August 2007	20	30	22	9	5	14

Note: "NA" = not offered as a response category

Question: I would like to ask your opinion of various government programs. As I read each one, please tell me if your opinion is very favorable, mostly favorable, half-and-half, mostly unfavorable, or very unfavorable. (Medicare/Medicaid). (1996)

Question: I am going to read you a list of federal government programs. For each one please tell me if you have a favorable or an unfavorable opinion of that program. How about . . . Medicare? Do you have a favorable or an unfavorable opinion? (If favorable/unfavorable, ask:) Is that a very favorable or somewhat favorable/very unfavorable or somewhat unfavorable opinion? (2000)

Question: Now, I am going to read you a list of various health care programs. Please tell me, as I read each one is your opinion of that program: very favorable, mostly favorable, half-and-half, mostly unfavorable, or very unfavorable. If I mention one that you are unfamiliar with just tell me and we'll move on to the next one. . . . (Medicare/Medicaid). (2007)

Sources: Cato Institute/Public Opinion Strategies Poll (Storrs, Conn.: Roper Center for Public Opinion Research, March 27–31, 1996); Cato Institute/Public Opinion Strategies Poll (Storrs, Conn.: Roper Center for Public Opinion Research, June 12–16, 1996); NPR/Kaiser Family Foundation/Kennedy School of Government, "Attitudes toward Government," May 26–June 25, 2000; Robert Wood Johnson Foundation/Public Opinion Strategies Poll (Storrs, Conn.: Roper Center for Public Opinion Research, August 4–7, 2007).

Table 7-8 Americans' Knowledge about Medicare and Medicaid (percent)

	1995	1997	2000	2003	2005	2009
Medicare is primarily . . .						
Federal government program	77	74	75	74		
State government program	13	17	16	16		
Private insurance program	4	7	5	2		
Don't know	6	2	4	7		
Who currently funds Medicaid program						
Federal government					21	
State government					10	
Both federal and state government					53	
Don't know					15	
Two largest areas of federal spending						
Defense and military spending					73	54
Foreign aid					49	45
Social Security					26	33
Medicare					20	33
Food stamps					10	17
Don't know					2	4

Question: To the best of your knowledge, is Medicare primarily a federal government program, a state government program, or a private insurance program?

Question: Who currently funds the Medicaid program: the federal government, state governments, or both federal and state governments?

Question: Which of the items on this list would you say are the two largest areas of spending by the federal government? . . . Defense and military spending, food stamps, foreign aid, Medicare, Social Security.

Sources: Kaiser Family Foundation/Harvard School of Public Health Poll (Storrs, Conn.: Roper Center for Public Opinion Research, May 31–June 5, 1995); *Washington Post*/Kaiser Family Foundation/Harvard University, "Survey of Americans' Knowledge and Attitudes about Entitlements," March 1997; *Washington Post*/Kaiser Family Foundation/Harvard University, "Issues in the 2000 Election: Health Care," July 2000; Kaiser Family Foundation/Harvard School of Public Health, "National Survey of the Public's Views on Medicare," April 25–June 1, 2003; Kaiser Family Foundation, "National Survey of the Public's Views about Medicaid," June 2005 (conducted April 1–May 1, 2005); *Washington Post*/Kaiser Family Foundation/Harvard University, "Survey on Social Security," February 2005; Kaiser Family Foundation "Survey of Americans on the U.S. Role in Global Health," May 2009.

Table 7-9 Americans' Views about Seriousness of Problems Facing Medicare, 1995–2009 (percent)

Condition of Medicare	Crisis	Major problems, not in crisis	Minor problems	No problems
September 1995	23	58	15	2
March 1997	21	54	19	3
January 1998	25	46	24	2
August 2002	10	47	33	3
January 2003	18	52	23	2
January 2005	12	52	29	2
Financial condition of Medicare	**Financial crisis**	**Major problems, not in crisis**	**Minor problems**	**No problems**
April 2009	30	44	17	4

Note: "Don't know" responses not shown.

Question: Which of these statements do you think best describes the Medicare system today: Medicare is in a state of crisis, it has major problems, it has minor problems, or it does not have any problems? (1995, 2005)

Question: Which of the following four statements comes closest to your own view of the Medicare program: the program is in crisis, the program has major problems but is not in crisis, the program has minor problems, or the program has no problems? (1997, 1998)

Question: Now I have a few questions about Medicare, the government program that provides health insurance for seniors and some disabled people. . . . Please tell me which one of the following four statements comes closest to your view of the Medicare program. Would you say . . . the program is in crisis, the program has major problems, but is not in crisis, the program has minor problems, or the program has no problems? (2002, 2003)

Question: Which of the following statements comes closest to your own view of the . . . Medicare program? The program is in financial crisis, the program has major problems, but is not in financial crisis, the program has minor problems, or the program has no problems? (2009)

Sources: Gallup/CNN/*USA Today* Poll (Storrs, Conn.: Roper Center for Public Opinion Research, September 22–24, 1995); *Washington Post*/Kaiser Family Foundation/Harvard University Poll, March 13–23, 1997; Kaiser Family Foundation/Harvard School of Public Health Poll, August 14–September 20, 1998; *Washington Post*/Kaiser Family Foundation/Harvard University Poll, August 2–September 1, 2002; ABC News/*Washington Post* Poll (Storrs, Conn.: Roper Center for Public Opinion Research, January 30–February 1, 2003); Quinnipiac University Poll (Storrs, Conn.: Roper Center for Public Opinion Research, January 25–31, 2005); Kaiser Family Foundation, "Kaiser Health Tracking Poll," April 2009.

Table 7-10 Confidence That Medicare Will Continue to Provide Benefits of at Least Equal Value to Benefits Received by Retirees Today, 1992–2009 (percent)

	Very confident	Somewhat confident	Not too confident	Not at all confident
Workers				
1992	1	26	45	25
1993	3	21	43	30
1998	4	24	34	36
2003	5	34	36	25
2004	6	31	35	26
2005	7	30	33	28
2006	5	29	36	28
2007	6	30	33	28
2008	4	30	35	29
2009	5	33	35	26
Retirees				
1992	10	28	39	17
1993	12	32	32	14
1998	12	35	39	11
2003	19	44	26	8
2004	16	37	31	11
2005	20	42	24	9
2006	12	50	26	10
2007	15	44	22	13
2008	8	44	32	13
2009	9	50	26	13

Note: "Don't know" responses not shown.

Question: How confident are you that the Medicare system will continue to provide benefits of at least equal value to the benefits received by retirees today? Would you say that you are very confident, somewhat confident, not too confident, or not at all confident?

Source: Employee Benefit Research Institute, "The 2009 Retirement Confidence Survey: Economy Drives Confidence to Record Lows; Many Looking to Work Longer," Issue Brief no. 328, April 2009.

Table 7-11 Americans' Concerns about Receiving Medicare Benefits When They Retire, 2003 and 2009 (percent)

		Very concerned	Somewhat concerned	Not too concerned	Not at all concerned
That you will not continue to receive the current level of Medicare benefits you now received (among those now on Medicare)	2003	50	25	11	11
That benefits seniors have today will not be available to you when you retire (2003 among those not on Medicare; 2009 among those under age 65)	2003	58	27	7	7
	2009	58	27	9	5

Note: "Don't know" responses not shown.

Question: (Asked of those who said Medicare is their main source of health insurance coverage) How concerned are you that, in the future, you will not continue to receive the current level of Medicare benefits you now receive?

Question: (Asked of those who did not say Medicare is their main source of health insurance in 2003; asked of those under age 65 in 2009) How concerned are you that the Medicare benefits seniors have today will not be available for you when you retire?

Sources: Kaiser Family Foundation/Harvard School of Public Health, "National Survey of the Public's Views on Medicare," April 25–June 1, 2003; Kaiser Family Foundation, "Kaiser Health Tracking Poll," April 2009.

Table 7-12 Social Security and Medicare as Priorities for Using the Federal Budget Surplus, 1998–2001 (percent)

Money from the federal budget deficit should be used . . .	January 1998	June 1998	August 1998	January 1999	February 2000	February 2001
To help make the Social Security and Medicare programs financially sound	32	44	39	50	44	37
For increased spending on domestic programs such as health, education, and the environment	33	28	29	21	24	23
For a tax cut	11	9	10	14	12	19
To pay off the national debt more quickly	22	17	19	12	18	17

Note: "Don't know" responses not shown.

Question: (If it turns out that the federal government has/As you may know, the federal government now has) a budget surplus. In your opinion, which one of the following should be done with the available money? Should the money be used for a tax cut; to pay off the national debt more quickly; for increased spending on domestic programs such as health, education, and the environment; or to help make the Social Security and Medicare programs financially sound?

Source: Pew Research Center for the People and the Press, "February 2001 News Interest Index: Final Topline."

Table 7-13 Ways to Make Medicare More Financially Sound (percent)

	2008		2009	
	Favor	Oppose	Favor	Oppose
Allowing the federal government to use its buying power to negotiate with drug companies to try to get a lower price for prescription drugs under Medicare[1]	90	9	86	12
Having Medicare pay for new treatments and technologies only if they provide better results than current treatments	NA	NA	75	21
Reducing Medicare payments to HMOs and other private insurers	46	46	66	29
Reducing payments to doctors and hospitals for treating people covered by Medicare	57	41	65	31
Requiring higher-income seniors to pay higher Medicare premiums	51	47	53	45
Increasing the payroll taxes workers and employers now pay to help fund the Medicare program	47	49	45	50
Gradually raising the age of eligibility for Medicare from 65 to 67 for future retirees	34	66	41	57
Requiring all seniors to pay a larger share of Medicare costs out of their own pocket	11	88	20	79
Rolling back tax cuts for upper-income Americans	46	51	NA	NA
Turning Medicare into a program that only serves low-income seniors instead of serving all seniors	26	73	NA	NA
Cutting back the Medicare drug benefit to save money	23	74	NA	NA

Note: "Don't know" responses not shown.

[1]Wording in 2009 was "Allowing the federal government to negotiate with drug companies to try to get lower drug prices for seniors"

Question: I'm going to read you some proposals to keep the Medicare program financially sound in the future. Please tell me whether you would generally favor or oppose each one. Would you favor or oppose (insert each item)? (2008)

Question: I'm going to read you some proposals that could help keep Medicare financially sound in the future. Please tell me whether you would generally favor or oppose each one. Would you favor or oppose (insert each item)? (2009)

Sources: Kaiser Family Foundation/Harvard School of Public Health, "The Public's Health Care Agenda for the New President and Congress," January 2009 (conducted December 4–14, 2008); Kaiser Family Foundation, "Kaiser Health Tracking Poll," April 2009 (conducted April 2–8, 2009).

Table 7-14 Americans' Views on How to Deal with Medicaid's Financial Problems (percent)

Medicaid program . . .			
Is in financial crisis	22		
Has major problems, but not in crisis	39		
Has minor problems	27		
Has no problems	3		
Don't know	9		

	Favor	Oppose	Don't know
Ways to deal with Medicaid's financial problems			
Reducing the number of people who qualify for Medicaid	44	49	6
Lowering the amount Medicaid pays for prescription drugs	42	54	5
Lowering the amount Medicaid pays for doctor and hospital fees	41	54	5
Increasing the co-payments and deductibles that people on Medicaid have to pay for services such as doctor visits	41	54	5
Eliminating the ability of middle class elderly to transfer their assets to their children in order to qualify for Medicaid	37	55	8
Limiting which prescription drugs Medicaid will pay for	32	65	3

Question: Which of the following four statements comes closest to your own view of the Medicaid program—the program is in a financial crisis, the program has major problems but is not in a financial crisis, the program has minor problems, or the program has no problems?

Question: I am going to read you a list of some ways that have been suggested to deal with the financial problems of Medicaid. For each one, please tell me if you would favor or oppose such a proposal.

Source: Kaiser Family Foundation, "National Survey of the Public's Views about Medicaid," June 2005 (conducted April 1–May 1, 2005).

Table 7-15 Americans' Views about Medicaid Benefits (percent)

In order to receive federal funding for Medicaid . . .	
States should be required to offer the same set of core health care benefits	58
States should be able to decide what benefits they want to offer in their own states	39
Don't know	3

How essential that Medicaid coverage includes . . .	Essential for Medicaid to cover	Should pay for on their own	Don't know
Prescription drugs	87	10	2
Hospital stays	87	11	2
Medical equipment like wheelchairs and artificial limbs	85	13	2
Mental health services	83	13	4
Emergency room visits	82	15	3
Nursing home care	82	15	4
Physical therapy	81	15	3
Doctor visits	81	16	3
Chiropractor visits	43	52	5
Travel to and from doctor visits	38	57	5

Question: In order to receive federal funding for the Medicaid program, should all states be required to offer the same set of core health care benefits, or should states be able to decide what benefits they want to offer in their own states?

Question: I would like to ask you about the services offered through the Medicaid program. Do you think it is essential that health insurance offered through Medicaid include coverage for (prescription drugs/doctor visits/nursing home care/hospital stays/emergency room visits/physical therapy/mental health services/chiropractor visits/travel to and from doctor visits/medical equipment like wheelchairs and artificial limbs), or is this something people should pay for on their own?

Source: Kaiser Family Foundation, "National Survey of the Public's Views about Medicaid," June 2005 (conducted April 1–May 1, 2005).

Table 7-16 Americans' Views about Medicare versus Private Insurance, by Age (percent)

	Total	Age 18–64	Age 65+
Trust more to provide health insurance for seniors . . . [1]			
The current government-run Medicare program	36	32	57
Plans offered through the private health care industry	40	45	19
Neither (vol.)	4	5	3
Both equally (vol.)	4	3	6
Don't know	16	15	15
Trust more to provide health insurance for seniors . . . [1]			
The current Medicare program	42	38	60
Private health insurance plans	40	46	14
Neither (vol.)	2	3	*
Both equally (vol.)	5	3	11
Don't know	11	10	15
Trust more to provide better health care . . . [2]			
Government's Medicare program	39		
Private insurance industry's health maintenance organizations	41		
Not sure	20		
Preference as way to get Medicare benefits[3]			
Current governmnent Medicare program	36	31	63
Private health plan, such as PPOs or HMOs	49	56	19
Don't know	14	13	17
Offers more generous benefits[3]			
Medicare	14	14	17
Private plans	41	46	16
About equal	31	28	45
Don't know	14	12	22
Offers more choice of doctors/hospitals[3]			
Medicare	20	18	27
Private plans	38	41	20
About equal	30	29	38
Don't know	12	11	15
Medicare compared with private insurance plans[1]			
More fraud and abuse	37	37	33
Less fraud and abuse	6	6	6
About the same amount	51	52	49
Don't know	6	5	12

Note: (vol.) = volunteered response

Question: Which do you trust more to provide health insurance to seniors: the current government-run Medicare program or plans offered through the private health care industry?

Question: Which do you trust more to provide health insurance to seniors: the current Medicare program or private insurance industry's health maintenance organizations?

Question: Who do you trust more to provide better health care? The government's Medicare program or the private insurance industry's health maintenance organizations?

Question: (When you retire) If you had a choice, would you prefer to get your Medicare health insurance benefits from the current government Medicare program, or from a private health plan, such as PPOs or HMOs?

Question: Which do you think offers more generous health benefits, Medicare or private health plans, such as PPOs and HMOs, that people get through their jobs, or do you think they both offer benefits that are about equally generous?

Question: Which do you think offers more choice among doctors and hospitals: Medicare or private health plans that people get through their jobs, or do you think they both offer about the same amount of choice among doctors and hospitals?

Question: Compared to most private health insurance plans, do you think there is more fraud and abuse in the Medicare program, less fraud and abuse, or about the same amount?

Sources: [1]Kaiser Family Foundation/Harvard School of Public Health, "National Survey on Medicare Policy Options," August 14–September 20, 1998. [2]*Time*/CNN/Yankelovich Partners Poll (Storrs, Conn.: Roper Center for Public Opinion Research, September 6–7, 2000). [3]Kaiser Family Foundation/ Harvard School of Public Health, "National Survey of the Public's Views on Medicare," April 25–June 1, 2003.

Table 7-17 Public Support for Addition of Prescription Drug Benefit to Medicare, 1994–2003 (percent)

	Favor	Oppose	Don't know
1994	88	10	3
1999	86	12	3
2000	85	12	3
2001	89	8	3
2003	80	16	4

Question: President Clinton's (health care reform) plan calls for a new Medicare benefit, so that the elderly will have most of the cost of their prescription drugs paid for. Do you favor or oppose this? (1994)

Question: The Medicare program pays for all or part of the costs of hospitals and doctors for people over 65 and people with disabilities, but it does not cover prescription drug costs. Do you favor or oppose adding a new Medicare drug benefit to cover part of the cost of prescription drugs? (1999)

Question: As you may know, Medicare does not currently pay for prescription drugs. Would you favor or oppose a proposal to guarantee prescription drug coverage to everyone on Medicare? (2000)

Question: I'd like your opinion of some programs and proposals being discussed in this country today. Please tell me if you strongly favor, favor, oppose, or strongly oppose each one. . . . Making prescription drug benefits part of the Medicare system. (2001)

Question: From what you have heard or read, do you favor or oppose expanding Medicare to partially pay for prescription drugs for Americans 65 or older? (2003)

Sources: New York Times Poll (Storrs, Conn.: Roper Center for Public Opinion Research, March 8–11, 1994); Harris Poll (Storrs, Conn.: Roper Center for Public Opinion Research, September 17–21, 1999); *NewsHour with Jim Lehrer*/Kaiser Family Foundation, "National Survey on the Uninsured," April 2000 (conducted January 10–February 9, 2000); Pew Research Center for the People and the PressPoll (Storrs, Conn.: Roper Center for Public Opinion Research, June 13–17, 2001; *Time*/CNN/Harris Interactive Poll (Storrs, Conn.: Roper Center for Public Opinion Research, July 16–17, 2003).

Table 7-18 Americans' Preference for How to Help Seniors Pay Prescription Drug Costs, 2000–2003 (percent)

What federal government should do to help people age 65+ pay for prescription drug costs	November–December 2000	March–May 2002	August–September 2002	February 2003
Expand Medicare to pay directly for prescription drug costs	56	67	55	53
Help them buy private health insurance plans that would pay part of their prescription drug costs	32	26	36	35
Keep things as they are now	6	6	5	4

Note: "Don't know" responses not shown.

Question: As you may know, Medicare does not currently pay for prescription drugs. Which one of the following three statements comes closest to your own opinion about what the federal government should do to help people age 65 and over pay for prescription drugs? Do you think the federal government should . . . keep things as they are now: the Medicare program should not pay for prescription drugs, expand Medicare to pay directly for part of prescription drug costs, or help seniors buy private health insurance plans that would pay part of their prescription drug costs?

Sources: Kaiser Family Foundation/Harvard School of Public Health, "Post-Election Survey: The Public and the Health Care Agenda for the New Administration and Congress," January 2001 (conducted November 13–December 13, 2000); NPR/Kaiser Family Foundation/Kennedy School of Government Poll (Storrs, Conn.: Roper Center for Public Opinion Research, March 28–May 1, 2002); *Washington Post*/Kaiser Family Foundation/Harvard University Poll (Storrs, Conn.: Roper Center for Public Opinion Research, August 2–September 1, 2002); Kaiser Family Foundation/Harvard School of Public Health Poll (Storrs, Conn.: Roper Center for Public Opinion Research, February 6–10, 2003).

Table 7-19 Seniors' Impressions of Medicare Prescription Drug Benefit, 2004–2006 (percent)

	Favorable	Unfavorable	Neither/Neutral/ Don't know
2004			
February[1]	17	55	28
April[1]	24	47	29
June[1]	24	45	31
October[1]	27	44	29
December[1]	25	42	33
2005			
April[1]	21	34	45
August[1]	32	32	36
October[1]	31	37	32
December[1]	28	50	22
2006			
February[1]	23	45	32
April[1]	30	46	24
June[1]	32	30	38
November total[2]	42	34	24
Responses of those . . .			
Enrolled in Medicare prescription drug plan	56	33	11
Not enrolled	32	36	31

Question: Given what you know about it, in general, do you have a favorable or unfavorable impression of the new Medicare prescription drug (law/benefit)?

Sources: [1]Kaiser Family Foundation, "The Public on Medicare Part D—The Medicare Prescription Drug Benefit," Kaiser Public Opinion Spotlight, April 2006. [2]Kaiser Family Foundation/Harvard School of Public Health, "The Public's Health Care Agenda for the New Congress and Presidential Campaign," December 2006 (conducted November 9–19, 2006).

Table 7-20 Satisfaction with Medicare Part D Prescription Drug Plans among Seniors Who Are Enrolled, 2006–2008 (percent)

	Very positive	Somewhat positive	Somewhat negative	Very negative	Don't know
Experiences with your drug plan (2006)	46	30	12	7	5

Satisfaction with drug plan	Extremely satisfied	Very satisfied	Somewhat satisfied	Not very satisfied	Not at all satisfied	Don't know
2007[1]	17	42	26	6	4	4
2008[2]	23	44	19	6	7	1
Satisfaction with premium						
2007[1]	17	32	31	9	5	6
2008[2]	19	35	31	7	7	1

Question: All in all, have your experiences using your plan been very positive, somewhat positive, somewhat negative, or very negative?

Question: In general, how satisfied are you with the Medicare prescription drug plan you are enrolled in now? How satisfied are you with the amount of the monthly premium that you pay for your (Medicare) prescription drug coverage?

Sources: [1]Kaiser Family Foundation/Harvard School of Public Health, "The Public's Health Care Agenda for the New Congress and Presidential Campaign," December 2006 (conducted November 9–19, 2006). [2]AARP Polls (Storrs, Conn.: Roper Center for Public Opinion Research, October 5–26, 2007; November 8–20, 2008).

Table 7-21 Effect of Medicare Part D Plans on Prescription Drug Costs among Seniors Enrolled in a Plan (percent)

Compared to what you paid for prescriptions last year*[1]	
Saving money now	52
Paying about the same now	31
Paying more now	14
Don't know	4
Under Medicare Part D[2]	
I think prescription drugs are much more affordable	20
I think prescription drugs are somewhat more affordable	24
I think prescription drugs are just as affordable as before	19
I think prescription drugs are somewhat less affordable	8
I think prescription drugs are much less affordable	6
Don't know	23
Compared to last year . . .[2]	
I have saved a great deal of money	19
I have saved some money	32
I have saved very little money	16
I have saved no money	16
Don't know	18

Note: * = Seniors who have enrolled and filled a prescription under their Part D plan

Question: Compared to what you paid for prescriptions last year, are you now saving money, paying more, or paying about the same overall for your prescriptions?

Question: What do you think about the price of prescription drugs under Medicare Part D?

Question: Compared to last year, how much do you think you have saved on prescription drugs since you enrolled in the new (Medicare drug) plan?

Sources: [1]Kaiser Family Foundation/Harvard School of Public Health, "The Public's Health Care Agenda for the New Congress and Presidential Campaign," December 2006 (conducted November 9–19, 2006). [2]AARP Poll (Storrs, Conn.: Roper Center for Public Opinion Research, October 5–26, 2007).

Table 7-22 Seniors' Views about Medicare Part D Being Too Complicated, 2004–2006 (percent)

Medicare prescription drug benefit is too complicated	Agree	Disagree	Don't know
November 2004	81	13	7
December 2005	73	15	12
January 2006	77	13	10
April 2006	69	19	12
November 2006	71	16	12

Question: I'm going to read you a list of things some people say are problems with the new Medicare law that need to be fixed. Please tell me if you agree or disagree with each. Some people have said the new law is too complicated for people on Medicare to understand. (November 2004)

Question: I'm going to read you several things that some people have said about the new Medicare prescription drug plan. For each one please tell me whether you agree or disagree with that statement. . . . It is too complicated and confusing. (December 2005–April 2006)

Question: I'm going to read you some things some people have said about the Medicare prescription drug benefit, and I'd like you to tell me how much you agree or disagree with each. Do you agree or disagree that the Medicare prescription drug benefit is too complicated? (November 2006)

Sources: Kaiser Family Foundation/Harvard School of Public Health, "Health Agenda for the New Congress," January 2005 (conducted November 4–28, 2004); NBC News/*Wall Street Journal* Poll (Storrs, Conn.: Roper Center for Public Opinion Research, December 9–12, 2005); NBC News/*Wall Street Journal* Poll (Storrs, Conn.: Roper Center for Public Opinion Research, January 26–29, 2006); NBC News/*Wall Street Journal* Poll (Storrs, Conn.: Roper Center for Public Opinion Research, April 21–24, 2006); Kaiser Family Foundation/Harvard School of Public Health, "The Public's Health Care Agenda for the New Congress and Presidential Campaign," December 2006 (conducted November 9–19, 2006).

Table 7-23 Seniors' Understanding of Personal Impact of Medicare Prescription Drug Benefit, 2005–2006 (percent)

	Yes, have enough information	No	Don't know
2005			
April	27	66	7
August	33	62	5
October	36	58	6
December	40	54	6
2006			
February	45	49	6
April	47	46	7

Question: Do you feel you have enough information about the new Medicare prescription drug benefit to understand how it will impact you personally or not?

Source: Kaiser Family Foundation, "The Public on Medicare Part D—The Medicare Prescription Drug Benefit," Kaiser Public Opinion Spotlight, April 2006.

Table 7-24 Seniors' Satisfaction with the Choice They Made of Prescription Drug Plans, 2006–2008 (percent)

	2006	2007	2008
I made a good choice	74	78	77
I'd be better off with a different plan	8	6	8
Don't know	18	15	15

Question: Overall, do you think you made a good choice in selecting your Medicare prescription drug plan, or do you think you would have been better off with a different plan?

Sources: Kaiser Family Foundation, "May/June 2006 Kaiser Family Health Poll Report Survey: Selected Findings on Health Care," July 2006 (conducted June 12–19, 2006); AARP Polls (Storrs, Conn.: Roper Center for Public Opinion Research, October 5–26, 2007; November 8–20, 2008).

Table 7-25 Support for Increased Spending to Get Rid of the "Doughnut Hole" in the Medicare Drug Benefit, 2006–2008 (percent)

	Total public	Seniors
2006		
Strongly favor	49	46
Somewhat favor	22	19
Somewhat oppose	8	9
Strongly oppose	15	14
Don't know	6	12
2008		
Strongly favor	53	
Somewhat favor	24	
Somewhat oppose	9	
Strongly oppose	11	
Don't know	1	

Question: Do you favor or oppose spending more federal money to get rid of the existing coverage gap—or doughnut hole—so that seniors will not have a period where they are responsible for paying the full cost of their medicines? Is that strongly or just somewhat?

Question: The way the Medicare prescription drug benefit currently works, some seniors with high drug costs hit a coverage gap where they have to pay the full costs of their medications out of their own pockets, up to several thousand dollars for some people. Would you favor or oppose spending more federal money to expand the Medicare prescription drug benefit to help pay the prescription costs for seniors in this situation? Is that strongly or somewhat favor/oppose?

Sources: Kaiser Family Foundation/Harvard School of Public Health, "The Public's Health Care Agenda for the New Congress and Presidential Campaign," December 2006 (conducted November 9–19, 2006); Kaiser Family Foundation/Harvard School of Public Health, "The Public's Health Care Agenda for the New President and Congress," January 2009 (conducted December 4–14, 2008).

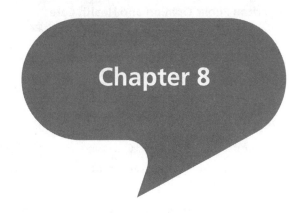

Chapter 8

PUBLIC OPINION ON PRESCRIPTION DRUGS

Claudia Deane and Mollyann Brodie

O f all the health care products and services consumed by the American public, prescription drugs are perhaps the most omnipresent. One in every two American adults reports taking a prescription medicine every single day, which translates into frequent trips to the local pharmacy and frequent opportunities to be reminded of cost and coverage issues. And because the nation's senior citizens are both the most likely people to be taking prescription drugs and the most likely to vote, the issue also has the potential to pack a real punch at the ballot box.

In 2006 the United States spent $216.7 billion on prescription medicines, up from $40.3 billion in 1990.[1] This spending boom is being driven by three important trends. First is the rise in the use of prescription drugs. Over a ten-year period, the number of prescriptions purchased went up 72 percent, to 3.8 billion in 2007, while the U.S. population grew by only 11 percent.[2] Second is the increase in the cost of prescription drugs from an average of $35.72 per prescription in 1997 to $69.91 in 2007, a 6.9 percent annual increase when the average annual inflation rate was 2.6 percent.[3] Third is the continuing introduction of new, more expensive or more widely used medications.

Although massive, prescription drug spending remains a relatively small share of U.S. spending on health overall—roughly 10 percent—dwarfed by the amount of money Americans and their insurers are spending on doctors and hospitals.[4] But the cost of medications has grabbed public attention because of its rapid and dramatic growth, particularly in the late 1990s when spending on prescription drugs was rising at double digit rates, and because consumers are so aware of these costs.

In addition, the role of a federal agency—the Food and Drug Administration (FDA)—in regulating issues of drug safety and efficacy puts prescription drug policy on the agenda of many policymakers in Washington. Understanding the public's views toward prescription drugs and their availability and coverage, therefore, is particularly important to understanding how proposals are being shaped, introduced, ignored, and publicized.

This chapter examines the public's views on prescription drugs themselves—their usefulness and their safety—and measures Americans' concern about rising drug costs, their evaluations of the pharmaceutical manufacturers who produce these vital products, and how the burgeoning use of prescription drug advertising is affecting consumer behavior.

Widespread Prescription Drug Usage

Part of understanding and predicting public opinion on any topic is getting a sense of the size of the constituency that would be affected by changes in policy. When it comes to prescription drugs, that constituency is enormous, and the opinions—if not different—tend to be more intense.

About eight in ten Americans say that if you open their medicine cabinets, you will find at least one bottle of prescription drugs.[5] A 2008 survey found that half of American adults report taking prescription medicine on a *daily* basis. This proportion rises to a striking 83 percent of those sixty-five and older, a group known for turning out in force at the polls each election cycle. Overall, roughly one in five adults (19 percent) reported taking at least four different prescription drugs (**Table 8–1**).[6]

According to the National Center for Health Statistics (NCHS), use of medications has risen in all age groups since the early 1990s.[7] One reason for the rise in usage is that health insurers are more likely than in the past to cover prescription drugs. Currently, nearly all covered workers in employer-sponsored plans have a prescription drug benefit.[8] The NCHS report also pointed to the discovery of useful new medications as a reason for the growth in prescription drug usage, as well as changes in clinical practice that encourage doctors to prescribe medication as one way of treating widespread conditions such as high cholesterol.

Perceived Value of Prescription Drugs

As a product, separate from their manufacturers, prescription drugs themselves are widely seen as highly valuable. Nearly three in four Americans say the medicines developed over the past twenty years have had a positive impact on the nation's health and quality of life.[9]

These drugs are most widely seen as making a "big difference" in the lives of those with heart disease (72 percent) and cancer (63 percent), and a narrow majority (52 percent) also sees them as positively impacting those with HIV/AIDS. Americans are less sure that prescription medicines are making a major impact on the lives of those suffering from mental illness (although 42 percent do see an effect) and least sure that drugs are helping those fighting obesity (18 percent see a big difference).[10]

Americans also see prescription medicines making a difference in their own lives, with just over six in ten saying that these products have made their lives, and the lives of their family members, better over the past twenty years (**Table 8–2**).[11]

Cautious Approval of Drug Safety

Prescription drugs for sale in the United States are seen as valuable, but are they seen as safe? This question has particular resonance in the wake of the dramatic 2004 recall of Merck's popular arthritis medicine, Vioxx, a drug for which more than 84 million prescriptions had been written and that racked up $2.5 billion in worldwide sales in 2003.

The recall was triggered by new evidence that prolonged use of the drug elevated the risk of heart attack, and it became the largest voluntary drug withdrawal in U.S. history.[12] The combination of adverse health effects and financial catastrophe grabbed headlines: two in three Americans said they were closely following the Vioxx story in the months after it broke.[13] Its aftermath continues to be felt in lawsuits and in persistent questions about the FDA's effectiveness in monitoring drug safety.

American consumers, looking for relief from myriad symptoms, vote on the safety question with their wallets (or those of their insurance plans), and sales figures suggest that belief in drug safety is robust. Public opinion data backs that answer, but suggests that the vote of confidence is somewhat more hedged.

In a survey conducted in February 2005, several months after the Vioxx recall, 80 percent of the public said they were at least "somewhat confident" in the safety of prescription drugs sold in the United States, but many fewer—28 percent—said they were "very confident." An early 2008 survey found similar numbers, suggesting that these opinions have been fairly stable.[14] Virtually identical proportions said they were "very" (22 percent) and "somewhat" (55 percent) confident in the FDA's ability to make sure that the drugs we buy at the pharmacy are safe.[15] Despite the Vioxx scare and other controversies, more than half the public (55 percent) thinks that pharmaceutical companies do enough to test and monitor the safety of their drugs, and the same share trusts the companies at least somewhat to alert them promptly if safety concerns are uncovered.[16] A considerable share of the American public—about four in ten—believe that drugs that are manufactured outside the United States are less safe than those made within the country's borders. About half believe that these drugs are just as safe.[17]

Although incidents such as the Vioxx recall may not have a permanent depressing effect on overall views of safety, they do seem to influence the public's views about the need for more drug safety regulation. Between 2000 and 2005 the proportion of Americans who thought there was not enough government regulation to make sure prescription drugs are safe rose from 36 percent to 50 percent.[18] By 2008 the desire for regulation had modulated a bit, settling at 44 percent, which is in line with public attitudes about drug safety regulation during the 1970s and 1980s (**Table 8–3**).[19] Similarly, the overall rating of the FDA declined from 67 percent excellent or good in 2001 to 58 percent in 2005 among those who said they knew what the FDA does (**Table 8–4**).[20]

Shortly after the 2006 elections, a majority (53 percent) of the public thought the president and the new Congress should do more to strengthen the FDA's ability to ensure the safety of prescription drugs, and 43 percent believed that the FDA was doing a good job as it was.[21] Although some individuals have accused the drug companies of attempting to unduly influence the FDA's approval process in this regard, their accusation does not resonate with a majority of the public.

About half say that pharmaceutical companies have too little (17 percent) or about the right amount (34 percent) of influence over which drugs are approved by the FDA, compared with 42 percent who say they have too much.[22]

Brand Names versus Generics

It is impossible to understand the prescription drug industry without understanding the difference between brand name drugs and their generic versions. This difference is less in the drugs' actual makeup—they have the same active ingredients—than in the patent laws that drive their pricing structures.

Manufacturers who discover new chemical compounds and new medications get a form of legal protection through a patent, which gives them the right to be the only entity selling that product for up to twenty years from the application filing date. This exclusivity is intended to give manufacturers an incentive to spend the large sums necessary to research and develop new cures by guaranteeing them the opportunity to be the only seller in the market, which allows them to charge relatively high prices. When drugs come "off patent," other manufacturers can duplicate the compound, and the competition drives prices down dramatically. In fact, the Congressional Budget Office estimates that buying generics rather than brand name prescriptions saves the American consumer up to $10 billion a year.[23]

Given Americans' heightened concern about the prices of medicines (discussed in the next section) and that the government, via the FDA, controls the speed at which consumers have access to generic drugs, understanding the public's views about brand names versus generics is important. As long as people consider generics to be just as good as brand names, and they are significantly cheaper, the public could pressure the government and private insurers to do more to promote their use.

Overall, nearly all American consumers are aware of the existence of generic drugs—96 percent in a 2003 survey.[24] And a substantial majority say that they see the two types of drugs as essentially equivalent: eight in ten said brand name medicines are about the same in quality as generic prescription drugs, while 13 percent see brand names as better and 2 percent as worse (**Table 8–5**).[25]

A survey of Americans aged fifty and older found a slightly higher percentage—25 percent—saying that they saw the two products as different. When researchers followed up to ask that quarter of respondents how generics differed, 57 percent of them said generics might be less effective or of poorer quality, while others pointed to positive or neutral traits (21 percent mentioned lower costs, and 12 percent pointed out the inclusion of different inactive ingredients). Still, overall, roughly two in three of the fifty and older respondents perceived the two products as equivalent.[26]

This perceived lack of difference is reflected in the fact that relatively few Americans worry about whether they might receive a generic drug rather than a brand name when they go to the pharmacy. Although health consumers in general are concerned about how their own health plan may change their drug coverage, seven in ten said they were not particularly worried that their health plan might require them to switch to generics (**Table 8–6**). Among the 37 percent who had actually gone to a doctor or pharmacist expecting to get a brand name prescription only to be given a generic, two in three (65 percent) said it did not matter to them, and a third reported they would have preferred the brand name.[27] In fact, just over half of Americans report they have done the reverse: asked for a generic drug when they had been prescribed a brand name medication.[28] An even larger proportion of adults aged forty-five and over report they "always" ask their doctor if there is generic version of any new prescription they might receive (58 percent, with another 6 percent saying their doctor automatically prescribes them generics).[29]

Despite this endorsement of generics, the public is more divided about whether health plans should have to pay for a brand name drug if a patient or doctor specifically requests it. Half say the patient should have the right to get a brand name when they want one, and the other half say that if a generic is available the plan should not have to cover the more costly version. Slightly more preference is given to doctor requests: roughly two in three (64 percent) say the insurance company should honor a doctor's request for a brand name. Majorities flip against mandatory coverage of brand names when told this might mean they have to pay higher health insurance premiums.[30]

It is costs that make the most important difference in the public's views of generics versus brand names. In an era when retail giant Wal-Mart has begun selling hundreds of generic drugs for $4 per prescription, most Americans (76 percent) say that generic drugs are reasonably priced compared to other things they buy, and an overwhelming 83 percent say brand name drugs are unreasonably expensive.[31] This differentiation plays into one of the most significant strands of public opinion on prescription drugs: concern about their prices.

Drug Costs a Major Concern

As noted, the cost of medication is indeed on the rise. And most Americans are very aware of this phenomenon: a 2000 survey, taken when drug prices were rising by double digits, found that 62 percent of the public, and 80 percent of those over age sixty-five, thought that the price of prescription drugs "has risen faster than most other things."[32] Concerns about rising prescription drug prices are near the top of the list of Americans' personal worries, with half of Americans (52 percent) saying they are at least somewhat worried about not being able to afford the prescription drugs they need, a number comparable to the percentage of employed Americans who were worried about losing their job in the midst of the 2009 recession.[33]

Concerns about rising costs are far more than idle worries for many Americans, who are finding paying for their medications so difficult that they are either not able to buy the basic necessities of daily life or are modifying their prescribed dosages to make the drugs last longer. A 2008 survey found that over a two-year period roughly three in ten Americans had not filled a prescription because of the cost, and just over two in ten said they had cut pills in half or skipped doses to make a medication last longer. These percentages were significantly higher among the lower-income population and among those without health insurance.[34] A previous survey found that half of those who had taken either of these steps reported that their condition had gotten worse as a result (**Table 8–7**).[35]

A survey conducted in 2000 found that including people who had difficulty paying for their medications along with those who failed to fill a prescription because of cost concerns brought the total affected to 47 percent of the public.[36] Among those, slightly more than half (54 percent)—or about one in four of all Americans—said they had to give up on other things to afford their medicines. For nearly one in ten individuals, this meant cutting back on a necessity such as food or clothing. Six in ten Americans say they have heard of the existence of pharmaceutical company programs that provide free or discounted drugs to a select number of people who cannot afford them, but two in three among this group said the programs do not go far enough.[37]

Americans' frustrations with drug costs are likely fueled by their feelings that the prices are not justified. Eight in ten say the prices of brand name drugs are unreasonable; six in ten say they do not trust pharmaceutical companies to price their products fairly; and two in three say that prescription drugs in general only give "fair" or "poor" value for the dollar.[38] Three in four believe that people in Canada, Mexico, and Western Europe are paying less for the same medicines.[39]

Although the pharmaceutical industry points to the high cost of research and development (R and D) for new medicines, the public does not see R and D as the only reason for high prices. Instead, many see the problem as greed. Overall, eight in ten say drug costs are unjustified because drug companies charge more than they need to, and only 14 percent agree that prices are "usually justified" because of development costs.[40] Overall, pharmaceutical company profits top the list of culprits as the biggest driver of the cost of drugs: 79 percent say this is a "major" factor, compared with 72 percent who name the cost of medical research, 62 percent who name the cost of advertising, and 56 percent the cost of lawsuits (**Table 8–8**).[41]

Aside from the personal impact of paying high prices at the pharmacy, Americans are susceptible to believing that rising prices are having an impact on the nation's health care system overall. On the one hand, a majority of the public (59 percent) believes that prescription drugs reduce the need for more expensive medical procedures by dealing with health problems before they call for more invasive actions.[42] On the other hand, most Americans still believe that the high price of prescription drugs has raised aggregate health spending. Putting the two concepts head-to-head, six in ten (59 percent) agree that prescription drugs are more likely to increase overall medical spending because they are so expensive, and 23 percent believe they are more likely to decrease overall costs by reducing the need for costly medical procedures.[43]

For all these reasons, the public demonstrates a significant appetite for congressional and executive branch action on drug costs. In 2005, eight in ten said lowering the cost of drugs was a "very important" issue for the president and Congress to address.[44] In a survey conducted four years later, 52 percent said the government was not doing enough to regulate the price of prescription drugs.[45] The pharmaceutical industry strongly argues that any government interference in price setting would inevitably hamper the amount of money they could invest in R and D and limit the potential for discovering new drugs. When respondents to the 2005 survey were pressed with this argument, support for government price regulation dropped by 16 points, but 48 percent continued to support cost controls.[46] Although arguments about the consequences for R and D do resonate with some price control supporters, only a minority of Americans (33 percent) currently believe that cost controls would in fact reduce the number of new products on the market (**Table 8–9**).[47]

Skepticism about the Pharmaceutical Industry

In general, drug companies have an image problem in the United States. Two different surveys have compared general perceptions of the pharmaceutical industry with perceptions of other major industries over time—health care–related and not—and found that drugmakers do not fare very well. In both surveys, pharmaceutical companies are among the lower ranked, and less than half of the public has a favorable or positive opinion of the industry (**Table 8–10**).[48] One of the surveys, conducted annually, found that drugmakers saw a decline in their overall positive ratings in 2004 (31 percent) and 2005 (29 percent) during debate about the Medicare prescription drug benefit. That rating blipped up to 39 percent in 2006, but dropped back down to 33 percent in 2007 and remained at 31 percent in 2008 and 2009, as debate over health care reform heated up. The otherwise cruel economic recession of 2009 did have one positive impact on drugmakers' reputations, however: the comparatively greater troubles of the banking, real estate, and automobile industries meant that those industries joined the federal government and the oil companies at the bottom of the public's popularity lists, displacing pharmaceutical companies.[49]

Drugmakers also have had issues with their customer service ratings. In an extensive series of polls by Harris Interactive, pharmaceutical companies were ranked fifteenth out of twenty-one industries measured on this dimension in 2009. Overall, 54 percent said drug companies do a "good job of serving their consumers," and 45 percent said they do a bad job. The positive to negative balance on this question has dropped more for drug companies and oil companies over the twelve years this question has been asked than for any of the other industries studied over the time period (**Table 8–11**).[50]

These general ratings mask the fact that the public does hold some positive views of the industry. Six in ten say that drugmakers make a "very important" contribution by developing new drugs and treatments. But even this positive rating has a dark side: although most people appreciate the contribution pharmaceutical manufacturers are making, they see that contribution being made for profits rather than the public good. Only one in four (24 percent) agree that drugmakers' primary concern is saving lives rather than making money, while seven in ten say pharmaceutical companies "put profits ahead of people."[51] And although advocates of the industry say it holds a special place in society because of the life-saving products it makes, most Americans (56 percent) say that pharmaceutical companies deserve neither more nor less credit than any other company producing goods for sale in the marketplace.[52]

The profits question clearly resonates with the public, and with some reason. From the mid-1990s through 2002, pharmaceutical manufacturers were the country's most profitable industry. They dropped to third most profitable in 2003 and remained at roughly that rank through 2008, when their profits were 19.3 percent of revenues compared to 2.4 percent for medical facilities and 1.5 percent for food and drug stores.[53] This position of relative affluence is reflected in Americans' opinions. Three in four say that drug companies are making too much profit, putting them in the top tier of industries seen as too grasping along with oil and tobacco (75 percent and 76 percent, respectively). In comparison, 46 percent say hospitals are making too much money, and 33 percent say the same about airlines.[54]

Americans see these high profits as affecting the health care system in general. "Drug and insurance companies making too much money" is the most popular choice when Americans are asked to evaluate a list of nine possible reasons why health care costs are rising, chosen by 50 percent of the public.[55]

In contrast, although the pharmaceutical industry may not be well regarded, the men and women who dispense their products are. Two in three Americans rank the honesty and ethical standards of pharmacists as "very high" or "high," making pharmacy one of the best-regarded professions.[56]

Who Should Be Responsible for Developing New Drugs?

Americans are most likely to point to for-profit pharmaceutical companies as the primary researchers for new drugs (75 percent say they have a major role), followed by universities (60 percent), and then the federal government (49 percent). But surveys find far less agreement as to which of these bodies *should* be responsible for development, with roughly equal shares choosing pharmaceutical companies (28 percent) and universities (27 percent), and somewhat smaller shares choosing the federal government (16 percent) and nonprofit organizations (11 percent) (**Table 8–12**).[57]

On the more difficult issue of so-called orphan drugs—medicines that treat the relatively small numbers of people suffering from rare diseases—the public shifts the balance of responsibility to the federal government, with 48 percent choosing the government compared to 27 percent choosing the pharmaceutical industry. A similar pattern is found when the public is asked about responsibility for developing medicinal cures for diseases that are particularly severe in poorer countries, but here the plurality (42 percent) would put the main responsibility on international nonprofit organizations or charities.[58]

The desire to shift some development responsibilities to other entities may be related in part to concerns about the drug companies' priorities. Just over half the public says pharmaceutical manufacturers spend too much money researching "lifestyle" drugs such as Viagra and Botox at the expense of cures for more serious conditions.[59]

Direct-to-Consumer Prescription Drug Advertising

Like all industries intent on selling a product and making a profit, drugmakers spend a lot of time, money, and effort marketing their wares. Traditionally, much of this marketing was aimed at physicians, the gatekeepers between the prescription drug and the patient. Although the bulk of marketing money is still spent in wooing physicians, pharmaceutical companies have learned the benefits of advertising their products to the public. Their spending on so-called direct-to-consumer (DTC) advertising has skyrocketed from $166 million in 1993 to $4.2 billion in 2005.[60]

The explosion of prescription drug advertising on television came after a 1997 FDA ruling that relaxed restrictions on the type of cautionary information that had to be included in broadcast advertising. More specifically, the "Draft Guidance for Industry: Consumer-Directed Broadcast Advertisements" said drug companies could refer viewers to a toll-free number, a print ad, a

Web site, or even their own physician for more information on the drug and its side effects, rather than including all this information in the television ad itself.[61]

The growth in DTC advertising is not without controversy. Opponents say that commercials create a false need for prescription drugs in general, and in particular those that may be more expensive than other viable alternatives. They also claim that doctors could be burdened by patients who have unrealistic expectations about clearly inappropriate treatments. Proponents point to the educational value of the ads, which often discuss not only medications but also the diseases they are intended to treat. They argue that because these drugs cannot be obtained without a prescription, the danger of misuse is small.

Survey researchers, in the meantime, have been busy attempting to measure whether the ads are widely viewed, if the public trusts the information they see in them, if they are in fact learning from advertising, and if these commercials are translating into patient-doctor conversations about specific products. Public opinion data suggest that the ads are indeed widely viewed. A 2008 survey found that 91 percent of Americans had "seen or heard" an advertisement for prescription drugs, up from 76 percent in 2000 and 63 percent in 1997.[62]

The big-picture views on this advertising are decidedly mixed. Speaking most broadly, a narrow majority of Americans (53 percent) say that prescription drug advertising is "mostly a good thing," with a minority of four in ten saying it is "mostly a bad thing." At the same time that positive views outweigh negative views at the general level, two in three complain that there are too many such ads on television, and an even larger majority (77 percent) say that the cost of creating and airing these commercials is further driving up the price of medicines. Two in three agree with those critics who say the ads encourage people to take medicines they do not need.[63]

Still, many people believe they are gaining valuable information from the commercials. Overall, two in three say prescription drug ads "educate people about available treatments" and possible conditions. Just over half rate the job commercials do in these regards as excellent or good. Fewer (45 percent) say commercials do a good job explaining the side effects of their products.

Doctors and pharmacists are in no danger of being supplanted as information sources, however. Ads are the public's least-trusted source for accurate information about prescription medicines, with about one in four saying they rely on advertising to provide accurate information "a lot" or "somewhat," compared to upwards of eight in ten who trust doctors, pharmacists, or the literature that comes with the prescription.[64]

There is one important, and interesting, caveat to these findings: an experiment conducted online showed respondents actual television ads for popular drugs and found that people's reactions to a specific ad were significantly more trusting than when they talked about drug advertising in general. Sixty-four percent of those who had seen an ad said they trusted the information provided about the condition, compared to 33 percent of nonviewers asked about prescription ads in general.[65]

The evidence is also somewhat mixed as to whether, as proponents of DTC advertising claim and as viewers' evaluations of these commercials might suggest, viewers are actually learning a lot about diseases, their pharmaceutical treatments, or the side effects of those products. The above-mentioned experimental study showed a randomly selected group of respondents three different drug ads and then asked them specific questions to test their knowledge. This kind of study offers a more direct way to measure knowledge, but again the findings were mixed. Respondents who viewed an ad about a prescription drug to treat asthma were more likely than nonviewers to know that "there are pills that people with asthma can take to prevent or limit the number of asthma attacks they have." But in the other two cases, the public was already so knowledgeable about the conditions in question (high cholesterol and acid reflux) that no additional learning was measured. In contrast, most respondents reported that they did not *feel* they had learned much from watching the ads: 70 percent said they knew at best only a little more about the condition after seeing the commercial, and 59 percent said they knew at best only a little more about the medicine. Despite these findings—and suggesting why marketing research is so difficult—viewers overwhelmingly reported that the ad did an excellent or good job telling them about the condition.[66]

When it came to side effects, most of those who had seen the ads were not able to identify correctly potential side effects, even after having just viewed the commercial. Nor were they particularly successful in learning where they could go to get more information. They were, however, more likely than nonviewers to perceive the side effects of the various drugs as serious.

In addition to testing the learning claims made by proponents of DTC, surveys have tested claims by detractors that this kind of advertising encourages patients to take time during already brief doctors' appointments to raise questions about medications they had seen on television. In fact, evidence suggests a fair number of people are motivated by ads to talk to their doctor about specific drugs. Although the percentage varies across surveys, roughly three in ten people said they had followed up with their doctor about something they had seen.[67] Slightly more in the study that showed respondents actual TV commercials said they would talk to their doctor either about the condition itself (40 percent) or the particular medicine they saw advertised (37 percent).[68]

A 2008 survey found that among the 32 percent who spoke to their doctor about a drug they had seen advertised, 44 percent received a prescription for that medicine. Just over half in this group had a doctor recommend an alternate drug, and an equally large portion reported that the doctor had suggested behavioral or lifestyle changes (**Table 8–13**).[69]

Data collected from doctors confirm the reports of their patients, at least about how often they are asked to discuss things these patients saw on television or heard on the radio. According to one nationwide survey, the percentage of physicians who say their patients frequently bring up diseases and treatments they heard about from drug ads is on the rise. In 2006, 28 percent of doctors reported hearing about drug ads frequently in conversations with their patients, up from 17 percent in 2001. This put advertising in a tie with "general news media" for second-most popular source of references, after the most popular way Americans hear about new drugs, from their friends or family (37 percent).[70]

Few doctors (5 percent), however, said that they "frequently" give patients the prescription they heard about in the media. Half (52 percent) say this happens "sometimes."[71]

In addition to the public's self-reported behaviors, economic analysis suggests that drug ads generate additional prescription activity. A 2003 study found that increases in DTC advertising were linked to higher sales. Specifically, each additional dollar spent on DTC advertising in 2000 yielded $4.20 in additional pharmaceutical sales.[72] In other words, although DTC advertising is not the most important driver of spending growth, it definitely works as intended.

The public shows some interest in having the government continue to regulate this potent form of advertising, but the desire for more regulation does not have majority support. About four in ten (43 percent) said that the government was not currently doing enough to make sure that "statements about benefits and possible side effects made in advertisements for prescription drugs are not misleading"; only 6 percent thought there was too much regulation of advertising, and 48 percent thought the regulatory climate was about right.[73]

Prescription Drugs and the Policy Agenda

Given the FDA's responsibility to oversee the introduction and monitoring of prescription drugs and the amount of money spent on medicines in the United States, prescription drugs are destined to be a permanent part of the public debate in Washington. Over the past few years, several prescription drug policy issues in particular have been discussed in Congress, in statehouses, and in the health care community. Among these issues are importation, or reimportation, of drugs from Canada and other countries, changes to the Medicare prescription drug benefit, and state debates over conscience clauses for pharmacists.

Importing Drugs from Canada

Prices for common brand name drugs are significantly lower in Canada and several other developed economies than they are in the United States because those countries' governments are directly involved in establishing drug prices and regulating the industry's profits. But with certain minor exceptions, it is currently illegal for individuals, pharmacies, or wholesalers in the United States to buy medicines from other countries.[74] This situation has led many policymakers to advocate a change in the law. The bills they have introduced vary in terms of the countries and medicines included and the safety standards and regulatory requirements imposed. On several occasions the Senate has voted to allow the importing of drugs from Canada, but no bill has been enacted into law.

Supporters say loosening restrictions would lower health costs for individuals and drive down prices nationwide. Opponents, including the pharmaceutical industry, say any such law would raise serious safety concerns and that the cost savings could be short-lived if other countries decided to curtail their exports or drug companies began limiting sales to nations that then reexported their products.

The public, at least so far, has been firmly on the supporters' side. At the time of the 2008 presidential election, roughly seven in ten Americans, including robust majorities of Republicans, Democrats, and independents, said they would support Congress changing the law to allow consumers to buy prescription drugs from Canada.[75] Roughly eight in ten (79 percent) in a 2005 survey said such a change in policy would go at least part way to a meaningful reduction in drug prices.[76] As noted earlier, three in four say Americans are paying higher prices "than people in Canada, Mexico, and Western Europe pay for the same prescription drug."[77]

And in general, Americans are skeptical about the arguments being made against reimportation. Roughly two in three reject the idea that allowing Americans to buy Canadian products will expose consumers to unsafe products, and slightly more say they do not believe this change would decrease R and D efforts in the United States (**Table 8–14**).[78] If they were presented with evidence that research into new drugs *would* suffer, however, enthusiasm for reimportation would likely dim. A survey fielded in 2000 pushed supporters on this point, asking "what if you heard that importing lower priced prescription drugs might lead to less research and development of new drugs since drug companies would be making smaller profits." Supporters dropped from 79 percent of the population to 50 percent.[79]

Changes to the Medicare Prescription Drug Benefit

In 2003 President George W. Bush and the U.S. Congress enacted a groundbreaking change in the law governing Medicare by expanding the program to help pay for prescription drugs. As of January 2006, all 47 million elderly and disabled beneficiaries have the opportunity to purchase subsidized prescription drug coverage from a large number of government-approved private plans. By 2009, roughly 26.7 million beneficiaries had chosen to enroll in the so-called "Part D" benefit.[80] (See Chapter 7 for more details about Medicare Part D.)

Although the legislation has been enacted and implemented, lawmakers are still discussing ways to modify the program. At the top of the Democrats' list of proposed changes is a plan to change the section of the law that prohibits the federal government from inserting itself into negotiations between the various private drug plans and the drug manufacturers that supply them.

Surveys have found that most Americans are in favor of giving the federal government negotiating power for Medicare Part D. In 2008 roughly nine in ten voters (89 percent), including large majorities in each political party, said they backed the proposal to give the federal government direct negotiating power, even though previous surveys found that roughly six in ten see such a plan as "government price controls."[81] Majorities were receptive to proponents' arguments regarding the government's existing role negotiating for members of the military and veterans, and saw the plan as a way to reduce costs overall and make drugs more affordable for Medicare recipients. Fewer (31 percent) accepted opponents' claim that the policy change would "lead U.S. drug companies to do less research and development" (**Table 8–15**).[82]

Conscience Clause Debates

Prescription drugs have also become enmeshed in the debate over whether individual health care providers, in this case pharmacists, can be required by their employers to dispense products of which they morally disapprove. This debate brings into sharp conflict two American traditions: freedom of religion and patients' rights. The current clashes have often involved the morning-after pill, a form of emergency contraception.

Congress, along with a growing minority of states, is considering laws on both sides of the issue. Some, often called "right of conscience" proposals, would give health professionals the right to withhold certain pharmaceutical products; others would make clear those rights do not exist.[83]

The public and pharmacists seem to differ in their response to this issue. Asked about the particular case of birth control pills, the large majority of Americans (80 percent) say that pharmacists should not be able to refuse to dispense birth control pills.[84] Asked about the issue more generally, half of pharmacists say that they should have the right to turn down patients who ask for prescriptions that they object to on moral or religious grounds. This belief was more common among independent pharmacists than among those working in chain drugstores.[85] On the other hand, 36 percent of pharmacists say they should be required to fill all requested prescriptions.

Although most Americans believe pharmacists should be required to dispense birth control regardless of their beliefs, a 2004 survey of voters suggests that they are considerably more divided as to whether health insurance plans should be required to cover the cost of these prescriptions, with 44 percent saying the federal government should mandate that all plans cover contraception, and 49 percent saying this kind of mandate should be decided on a state-by-state basis (**Table 8–16**).[86]

Conclusion

Although spending on prescription drugs remains a relatively small fraction of health spending overall, the rapid and enormous increase in sales of these drugs and the dramatic uptick in their prices make them a flashpoint in American opinion on the health care system. And, as a consumer product, prescription drugs are omnipresent: a large majority of Americans report having at least one prescription medicine in their medicine cabinet, and the nation's growing and politically active senior population is particularly likely to be taking such drugs on a daily basis. These medications are also valued, with most people telling survey researchers that drugs developed in recent decades have improved Americans' quality of life. Neither their indispensability nor their perceived value is likely to change in the near future, meaning that intense public support for their availability will continue.

The cost of prescription drugs has preoccupied the public more than safety issues in recent years, although this could change. Currently, most Americans report being fairly satisfied that the prescription drugs they take are safe. A large portion of the public would like to see the president and Congress do more to strengthen the FDA, but the support has not necessarily translated into public pressure, and the topic does not rank highly on the public's laundry list of health issues for the government to address. This aspect of public opinion is fluid, however, and one question for opinion watchers is how another safety scandal might catalyze the public's demand for more action on this front.

Concerns about health care costs, including the cost of prescription drugs, have been at the top of Americans' list of personal worries for years, and these worries are unlikely to evaporate in the near future. The extent to which they spur anger or a desire for change will be influenced by a number of factors, including the way the health insurance industry provides coverage for prescriptions, the speed at which prices rise, the availability and popularity of generic alternatives, and the extent to which manufacturers can convince a skeptical public that higher prices derive from higher R and D costs rather than excessive greed for profits. Together, these and other currents will influence the extent to which Americans pressure the executive and legislative branches to take action on costs. Opinion watchers will want to be attentive not only to the way prescription drug costs and coverage change over the next decade, but also to the even more complex question regarding what the public wants the government to do—if anything—to rein in these costs.

Several more specific policy issues involving prescription drugs bear watching. First among these are legislative attempts to expand Americans' ability to import prescription drugs, a proposal that is popular with the public but faces real resistance from drug manufacturers and powerful political forces. The public is also receptive to the idea of allowing the federal government to negotiate prices directly with pharmaceutical manufacturers. Finally, a complex and divisive swirl of issues surrounds so-called conscience clause debates, which center around pharmacists' rights to withhold products such as contraceptives with which they morally disagree.

Notes

[1] Aaron Catlin, Cathy Cowan, Micah Hartman, Stephen Heffler, and the National Health Expenditure Accounting Team, "National Health Spending in 2006," *Health Affairs* 27 (January/February 2008): 14–29; Kaiser Family Foundation, "Prescription Drug Trends," September 2008, http://www.kff.org/rxdrugs/3057.cfm.

[2] Kaiser Family Foundation, "Prescription Drug Trends," September 2008.

[3] Ibid.

[4] Ibid.

[5] *NewsHour*/Kaiser Family Foundation/Harvard School of Public Health Poll (Storrs, Conn.: Roper Center for Public Opinion Research, July 26–September 5, 2000).

[6] *USA Today*/Kaiser Family Foundation/Harvard School of Public Health, "The Public on Prescription Drugs and Pharmaceutical Companies," March 2008, http://www.kff.org/kaiserpolls/upload/7747.pdf.

[7] Robert Pear, "Americans Relying More on Prescription Drugs, Report Says," *New York Times*, December 3, 2004, A3.

[8] Kaiser Family Foundation/Health Research and Educational Trust, "Employer Health Benefits 2009 Annual Survey," http://ehbs.kff.org/pdf/2009/7936.pdf.

[9] *USA Today*/Kaiser Family Foundation/Harvard School of Public Health, "The Public on Prescription Drugs and Pharmaceutical Companies," March 2008.

[10] Kaiser Family Foundation, "Health Poll Report Survey," January/February 2005, http://www.kff.org/kaiserpolls/upload/January-February-2005-Health-Poll-Report-Survey-Toplines.pdf.

[11] *USA Today*/Kaiser Family Foundation/Harvard School of Public Health, "The Public on Prescription Drugs and Pharmaceutical Companies," March 2008.

[12] Brooke A. Masters, "Stock Price Falls 27% after Drug Firm Withdraws Vioxx," *Washington Post*, October 1, 2004, E1.

[13] Kaiser Family Foundation, "Health Poll Report Survey," November/December 2004, http://www.kff.org/kaiserpolls/upload/The-Kaiser-Family-Foundation-Health-Poll-Report-Survey-Selected-Findings-on-the-New-Medicare-Drug-Law.pdf.

[14] *USA Today*/Kaiser Family Foundation/Harvard School of Public Health, "The Public on Prescription Drugs and Pharmaceutical Companies," March 2008.

[15] Kaiser Family Foundation, "Health Poll Report Survey," January/February 2005.

[16] *USA Today*/Kaiser Family Foundation/Harvard School of Public Health, "The Public on Prescription Drugs and Pharmaceutical Companies," March 2008.

[17] Ibid.

[18] *NewsHour*/Kaiser Family Foundation/Harvard School of Public Health Poll, July 26–September 5, 2000; Kaiser Family Foundation, "Health Poll Report Survey," January/February 2005.

[19] Roper Organization, Roper Reports (Storrs, Conn.: Roper Center for Public Opinion Research, February 21–March 2, 1974; February 15–March 1, 1975; February 12–26, 1977; February 10–24, 1979; February 9–23, 1980; February 12–27, 1982; February 11–25, 1984; February 8–22, 1986); Kaiser Family Foundation/Harvard School of Public Health Poll (Storrs, Conn.: Roper Center for Public Opinion Research, November 13–December 13, 2000); Harvard School of Public Health Poll (Storrs, Conn.: Roper Center for Public Opinion Research, March 29–April 2, 2007); *USA Today*/Kaiser Family Foundation/Harvard School of Public Health, "The Public on Prescription Drugs and Pharmaceutical Companies," March 2008.

[20] Harris Interactive Poll (Storrs, Conn.: Roper Center for Public Opinion Research, September 19–24, 2001); Harvard School of Public Health Poll (Storrs, Conn.: Roper Center for Public Opinion Research, June 23–28, 2005).

[21] Kaiser Family Foundation/Harvard School of Public Health, "The Public's Health Care Agenda for the New Congress and Presidential Campaign," December 2006, http://www.kff.org/kaiserpolls/upload/7598.pdf.

[22] *USA Today*/Kaiser Family Foundation/Harvard School of Public Health, "The Public on Prescription Drugs and Pharmaceutical Companies," March 2008.

[23] Food and Drug Administration, "FDA-Approved Bargain Drugs," December 2003, http://www.fda.gov/Drugs/EmergencyPreparedness/BioterrorismandDrugPreparedness/ucm134212.htm.

[24] Employee Benefit Research Institute/Consumer Health Education Council/Mathew Greenwald and Associates Poll (Storrs, Conn.: Roper Center for Public Opinion Research, April 24–May 24, 2003).

[25] *USA Today*/Kaiser Family Foundation/Harvard School of Public Health, "The Public on Prescription Drugs and Pharmaceutical Companies," March 2008.

[26] AARP Poll (Storrs, Conn.: Roper Center for Public Opinion Research, October 7–18, 2004).

[27] *NewsHour*/Kaiser Family Foundation/Harvard School of Public Health Poll, July 26–September 5, 2000.

[28] *USA Today*/Kaiser Family Foundation/Harvard School of Public Health, "The Public on Prescription Drugs and Pharmaceutical Companies," March 2008.

[29] AARP Poll (Storrs, Conn.: Roper Center for Public Opinion Research, November 8–20, 2008).

[30] *NewsHour*/Kaiser Family Foundation/Harvard School of Public Health Poll, July 26–September 5, 2000.

[31] Kaiser Family Foundation/Harvard School of Public Health, "The Public's Health Care Agenda for the New Congress and Presidential Campaign," December 2006.

[32] *NewsHour*/Kaiser Family Foundation/Harvard School of Public Health Poll, July 26–September 5, 2000.

[33] Kaiser Family Foundation, "Kaiser Health Tracking Poll: July 2009," http://www.kff.org/kaiserpolls/7943.cfm.

[34] *USA Today*/Kaiser Family Foundation/Harvard School of Public Health, "The Public on Prescription Drugs and Pharmaceutical Companies," March 2008.

[35] *USA Today*/Kaiser Family Foundation/Harvard School of Public Health Poll (Storrs, Conn.: Roper Center for Public Opinion Research, April 25–June 9, 2005).

[36] *NewsHour*/Kaiser Family Foundation/Harvard School of Public Health Poll, July 26–September 5, 2000.

[37] *USA Today*/Kaiser Family Foundation/Harvard School of Public Health, "The Public on Prescription Drugs and Pharmaceutical Companies," March 2008.

[38] Kaiser Family Foundation/Harvard School of Public Health, "The Public's Health Care Agenda for the New Congress and Presidential Campaign," December 2006; *USA Today*/Kaiser Family Foundation/Harvard School of Public Health, "The Public on Prescription Drugs and Pharmaceutical Companies," March 2008; Kaiser Family Foundation, "Health Poll Report Survey," January/February 2005.

[39] *USA Today*/Kaiser Family Foundation/Harvard School of Public Health, "The Public on Prescription Drugs and Pharmaceutical Companies," March 2008.

[40] CBS News Poll (Storrs, Conn.: Roper Center for Public Opinion Research, September 20–22, 2004).

[41] *USA Today*/Kaiser Family Foundation/Harvard School of Public Health, "The Public on Prescription Drugs and Pharmaceutical Companies," March 2008.

[42] Ibid.

[43] Ibid.

[44] Kaiser Family Foundation, "Health Poll Report Survey," January/February 2005.

[45] Kaiser Family Foundation/Harvard School of Public Health, "The Public's Health Care Agenda for the New President and Congress," January 2009, http://www.kff.org/kaiserpolls/upload/7853.pdf.

[46] Kaiser Family Foundation, "Health Poll Report Survey," January/February 2005.

[47] Harris Interactive Poll, August 10–15, 2004.

[48] *USA Today*/Kaiser Family Foundation/Harvard School of Public Health, "The Public on Prescription Drugs and Pharmaceutical Companies," March 2008; Kaiser Family Foundation, "Health Poll Report Survey," January/February 2005; Gallup Poll (Storrs, Conn.: Roper Center for Public Opinion Research, August 6–9, 2009).

[49] Gallup Polls (Storrs, Conn.: Roper Center for Public Opinion Research, August 4–6, 2003; August 9–11, 2004; August 8–11, 2005; August 7–10, 2006; August 13–16, 2007; August 7–10, 2008; August 6–9, 2009). Gallup Poll, "Automobile, Banking Industry Images Slide Further," August 17, 2009, http://www.gallup.com/poll/122342/Automobile-Banking-Industry-Images-Slide-Further.aspx.

[50] Harris Polls (Storrs, Conn.: Roper Center for Public Opinion Research, February 19–23, 1997; March 11–18, 1998; April 8–13, 1999); Harris Interactive Polls (Storrs, Conn.: Roper Center for Public Opinion Research, April 7–10, 2000; April 26–May 5, 2001; May 22–28, 2002; April 10–15, 2003; April 8–15, 2004; April 5–10, 2005; April 4–10, 2006; July 10–16, 2007; July 8–13, 2008; July 8–13, 2009). Over time trend reference from Harris Interactive Poll, August 18, 2009, http://www.harrisinteractive.com/harris_poll/pubs/Harris_Poll_2009_08_18.pdf.

[51] Kaiser Family Foundation, "Health Poll Report Survey," January/February 2005.

[52] *USA Today*/Kaiser Family Foundation/Harvard School of Public Health, "The Public on Prescription Drugs and Pharmaceutical Companies," March 2008.

[53] Kaiser Family Foundation, "Prescription Drug Trends," September 2008; Fortune 500, "Top Industries: Most Profitable," May 2009, http://money.cnn.com/magazines/fortune/fortune500/2009/performers/industries/profits.

[54] *NewsHour*/Kaiser Family Foundation/Harvard School of Public Health Poll, July 26–September 5, 2000; *USA Today*/Kaiser Family Foundation/Harvard School of Public Health, "The Public on Prescription Drugs and Pharmaceutical Companies," March 2008.

[55] ABC News/Kaiser Family Foundation/*USA Today*, "Health Care in America 2006 Survey," October 2006, http://www.kff.org/kaiserpolls/upload/7573.pdf.

[56] Gallup data, published in Robert J. Blendon, Mollyann Brodie, John M. Benson, Drew E. Altman, and Tami Buhr, "Americans' Views about Health Care Costs, Access, and Quality," *Milbank Quarterly* 84 (December 2006): 623–657.

[57] *USA Today*/Kaiser Family Foundation/Harvard School of Public Health, "The Public on Prescription Drugs and Pharmaceutical Companies," March 2008.

[58] Ibid.

[59] Ibid.

[60] Julie Donohue, "A History of Drug Advertising: The Evolving Roles of Consumers and Consumer Protection," *Milbank Quarterly* 84 (December 2006): 659–699.

[61] Ibid., 685.

[62] *USA Today*/Kaiser Family Foundation/Harvard School of Public Health, "The Public on Prescription Drugs and Pharmaceutical Companies," March 2008; Kaiser Family Foundation/ Agency for Health Care Research and Quality, "National Survey on Americans as Health Care Consumers: An Update on the Role of Quality Information," December 2000, http://www.kff .org/kaiserpolls/loader.cfm?url=/commonspot/security/getfile.cfm&PageID=13571. For 1997, *Prevention Magazine* poll data, published in Kaiser Family Foundation, "Impact of Direct-to-Consumer Advertising on Prescription Drug Spending," June 2003, page 5, http://www.kff.org/ rxdrugs/loader.cfm?url=/commonspot/security/getfile.cfm&PageID=14378.

[63] *USA Today*/Kaiser Family Foundation/Harvard School of Public Health, "The Public on Prescription Drugs and Pharmaceutical Companies," March 2008.

[64] Ibid.

[65] Kaiser Family Foundation, "Understanding the Effects of Direct-to-Consumer Prescription Drug Advertising," November 2001, http://www.kff.org/rxdrugs/upload/Understanding-the-Effects-of-Direct-to-Consumer-Prescription-Drug-Advertising-Report.pdf.

[66] Ibid.

[67] *USA Today*/Kaiser Family Foundation/Harvard School of Public Health, "The Public on Prescription Drugs and Pharmaceutical Companies," March 2008.

[68] Kaiser Family Foundation, "Understanding the Effects of Direct-to-Consumer Prescription Drug Advertising," November 2001.

[69] *USA Today*/Kaiser Family Foundation/Harvard School of Public Health, "The Public on Prescription Drugs and Pharmaceutical Companies," March 2008.

[70] Kaiser Family Foundation, "Prescription Drugs: Advertising, Out-of-Pocket Costs, and Patient Safety from the Perspective of Doctors and Pharmacists," November 2006, http://www.kff.org/ kaiserpolls/upload/7583.pdf.

[71] Ibid.

[72] Meredith B. Rosenthal, Ernst R. Berndt, Julie M. Donohue, Arnold M. Epstein, and Richard G. Frank, "Demand Effects of Recent Changes in Prescription Drug Promotion," June 2003, pages 18–19, http://www.kff.org/rxdrugs/upload/Demand-Effects-of-Recent-Changes-in-Prescription-Drug-Promotion-Report.pdf.

[73] *USA Today*/Kaiser Family Foundation/Harvard School of Public Health, "The Public on Prescription Drugs and Pharmaceutical Companies," March 2008.

[74] The 2007 Homeland Security appropriations bill did contain language that allows individuals to bring in from Canada a 90-day supply of prescription drugs for personal use without fear of confiscation. Barbara Kermode-Scott, "US Eases Its Restrictions on Prescription Drugs from Canada," *BMJ* [*British Medical Journal*] 333 (October 21, 2006): 824.

[75] Kaiser Family Foundation/Harvard School of Public Health, "The Public's Health Care Agenda for the New President and Congress," January 2009.

[76] Kaiser Family Foundation, "Health Poll Report Survey," January/February 2005.

[77] *USA Today*/Kaiser Family Foundation/Harvard School of Public Health, "The Public on Prescription Drugs and Pharmaceutical Companies," March 2008.

[78] Ibid.

[79] *NewsHour*/Kaiser Family Foundation/Harvard School of Public Health Poll, July 26–September 5, 2000.

[80] Patricia Neuman and Juliette Cubanski, "Medicare Part D Update—Lessons Learned and Unfinished Business," *New England Journal of Medicine* 361 (July 23, 2009): 406–414, http://content.nejm.org/cgi/content/full/361/4/406.

[81] Kaiser Family Foundation/Harvard School of Public Health, "Pre-Election Poll: Voters, Health Care and the 2008 Election," October 2008, based on self-identified registered voters, http://www.kff.org/kaiserpolls/upload/7829.pdf; Kaiser Family Foundation/Harvard School of Public Health, "The Public's Health Care Agenda for the New Congress and Presidential Campaign," December 2006.

[82] Overall cost reduction data from Kaiser Family Foundation, "Health Poll Report Survey," April 2005; others from Kaiser Family Foundation/Harvard School of Public Health Poll, "The Public's Health Care Agenda for the New Congress and Presidential Campaign," December 2006.

[83] Rob Stein, "A Medical Crisis of Conscience; Faith Drives Some to Refuse Patients Medication or Care," *Washington Post*, July 16, 2006, A1.

[84] Pew Research Center for the People and the Press/Pew Forum on Religion and Public Life Poll, August 3, 2006, http://pewforum.org/docs/index.php?DocID=150.

[85] Kaiser Family Foundation, "National Survey of Pharmacists," November 2006, http://www.kff.org/kaiserpolls/upload/7585.pdf.

[86] Stony Brook University Center for Survey Research Poll (Storrs, Conn.: Roper Center for Public Opinion Research, September 13–29, 2004).

Table 8-1 Reported Prescription Drug Use, by Age (in percent)

	Total	Under 65	65 and over
Yes	54	48	86
No	45	52	14

Note: "Don't know" responses not shown.

Question: Do you currently take any prescription medicine or not?

Source: USA Today/Kaiser Family Foundation/Harvard School of Public Health, "The Public on Prescription Drugs and Pharmaceutical Companies," March 2008.

Table 8-2 Perceived Impact of Prescription Drugs (in percent)

	Better	Worse	Haven't made much difference
Impact of new prescription drugs developed over past 20 years on:[1]			
The lives of people in the U.S.	73	10	14
Your own life and your family members' lives	63	4	31
Percent who say prescription drugs have made a "big difference" in:[2]			
The life of the average person	58		
The lives of people with . . .			
Heart disease	72		
Cancer	63		
HIV	52		
Mental illness	42		
Obesity	18		

Note: "Don't know" responses not shown.

Question: Do you think prescription drugs developed over the past 20 years have generally made the lives of people in the United States better, worse, or haven't they made much difference?

Question: Do you think prescription drugs developed over the past 20 years have generally made your own life and the lives of your family members better, worse, or haven't they made much difference?

Question: Do you think prescription drugs developed over the past 20 years have made a big difference, a small difference, or no difference in the life of the average person? In the lives of people with (heart disease/cancer/HIV/mental illness/obesity)?

Sources: [1]*USA Today*/Kaiser Family Foundation/Harvard School of Public Health, "The Public on Prescription Drugs and Pharmaceutical Companies," March 2008. [2]Kaiser Family Foundation, "Health Poll Report Survey," January/February 2005.

Table 8-3 Americans' Views on Prescription Drug Safety (in percent)

Confidence in . . .	Safety of prescription drugs[1]	FDA's ability to make sure drugs are safe[2]
Very confident	27	22
Somewhat confident	51	55
Not too confident	15	15
Not at all confident	6	7

Government regulation to make sure prescription drugs are safe for people to use	Not enough	About right	Too much
2000[3]	36	48	12
2005[2]	50	39	8
2008[1]	44	47	8

Government regulation of the safety of prescription drugs[4]	Not enough	About right	Too much
1974	44	45	3
1975	42	44	4

(Table continues)

Table 8-3 *Continued*

1977	48	39	5
1979	48	38	7
1980	51	38	6
1982	48	43	5
1984	47	46	3
1986	45	45	4
2000	34	49	11
2007	43	40	13

Note: "Don't know" responses not shown.

Question: Overall, how confident are you that prescription drugs sold in the United States are safe? Would you say you are very confident, somewhat confident, not too confident, or not at all confident?

Question: How confident are you in the Food and Drug Administration's ability to make sure prescription drugs for sale in the United States are safe? Very confident, somewhat confident, not too confident, or not at all confident?

Question: I'd like your opinion of current government regulation of prescription drugs in some different areas. Is there too much regulation in this area, not as much as there should be, or about the right amount of regulation. . . . Making sure prescription drugs are safe for people to use.

Question: I'm going to name some things, and for each one would you tell me whether you think there is too much government regulation of it now, or not enough government regulation now, or about the right amount of government regulation now? . . . The safety of prescription drugs. (1974–1986, 2007)

Question: As I read each of the following, please tell me whether you think there is too much government regulation in this area, not enough regulation, or about the right amount. . . . The safety of prescription drugs. (2000)

Sources: [1] *USA Today*/Kaiser Family Foundation/Harvard School of Public Health, "The Public on Prescription Drugs and Pharmaceutical Companies," March 2008. [2] Kaiser Family Foundation, "Health Poll Report Survey," January/February 2005. [3] *NewsHour*/Kaiser Family Foundation/Harvard School of Public Health Poll (Storrs, Conn.: Roper Center for Public Opinion Research, July 26–September 5, 2000). [4] Roper Organization, Roper Reports (Storrs, Conn.: Roper Center for Public Opinion Research, February 21–March 2, 1974; February 15–March 1, 1975; February 12–26, 1977; February 10–24, 1979; February 9–23, 1980; February 12–27, 1982; February 11–25, 1984; February 8–22, 1986); Kaiser Family Foundation/Harvard School of Public Health Poll (Storrs, Conn.: Roper Center for Public Opinion Research, November 13–December 13, 2000); Harvard School of Public Health Poll (Storrs, Conn.: Roper Center for Public Opinion Research, March 29–April 2, 2007).

Table 8-4 Americans' Views of the Food and Drug Administration (in percent)

	Excellent/pretty good	Only fair/poor
The job the FDA does overall (among those say they know what the FDA does)		
2001[1]	67	32
2005[2]	58	38
The amount of influence pharmaceutical companies have over which drugs are approved by the FDA[3]		
Too much	42	
About the right amount	34	
Too little	17	

Note: "Don't know" responses not shown.

Question: Overall, how would you rate the job the Food and Drug Administration, or FDA, does—excellent, pretty good, only fair, or poor?

Question: Do you think pharmaceutical companies have too much, too little, or about the right amount of influence on which drugs are approved by the FDA?

Sources: [1] Harris Interactive Poll (Storrs, Conn.: Roper Center for Public Opinion Research, September 19–24, 2001). [2] Harvard School of Public Health Poll (Storrs, Conn.: Roper Center for Public Opinion Research, June 23–28, 2005). [3] *USA Today*/Kaiser Family Foundation/Harvard School of Public Health, "The Public on Prescription Drugs and Pharmaceutical Companies," March 2008.

Table 8-5 Americans' Overall Assessment of Generic Drugs (in percent)

Brand name drugs are . . .	2000	2008
Better than generic drugs	14	13
About the same	80	81
Worse than generic drugs	3	2

Note: "Don't know" responses not shown.

Question: In most cases, do you think brand name prescription drugs are better, worse, or about the same in quality as generic prescription drugs?

*Sources: NewsHour/*Kaiser Family Foundation/Harvard School of Public Health Poll (Storrs, Conn.: Roper Center for Public Opinion Research, July 26–September 5, 2000); *USA Today/*Kaiser Family Foundation/Harvard School of Public Health, "The Public on Prescription Drugs and Pharmaceutical Companies," March 2008.

Table 8-6 Americans' Attitudes about Generic Drugs (in percent)

Worried that your health plan might require your family to use generic drugs instead of brand name drugs (Among those with prescription drug coverage)[1]		
Very worried	11	
Somewhat worried	17	
Not very worried	31	
Not at all worried	41	

Asked for a generic drug when prescribed a brand name[2]		
Yes, have	54	
No, have not	46	

Should health plan pay for brand name even if cheaper generic drug is available . . .[1]	Yes	No
When patient requests	50	47
When doctor requests	64	32

Even if it meant you would pay higher insurance premium[1]	Yes	No
When patient requests	28	67
When doctor requests	40	55

Reasonableness of prices of . . .[3]	Reasonable	Unreasonable
Brand name prescription drugs	13	83
Generic prescription drugs	76	20

Note: "Don't know" responses not shown.

Question: How worried are you that in the near future . . . your health plan might require that you or your family use generic drugs instead of brand name drugs? Would you say very worried, somewhat worried, not very worried, or not at all worried?

Question: In the last two years, have you asked for a generic drug when you were prescribed a brand name, or not?

Question: Do you think health plans should pay for brand name prescription drugs when a (patient/doctor) requests them, even if a cheaper generic drug is available, or not?

Question: Would you still favor this if it meant that you would have to pay higher health insurance premiums?

Question: Compared to other goods and services you purchase, how reasonable or unreasonable do you think the prices of the following items are? (Brand name prescription drugs/Generic prescription drugs)

Sources: [1]*NewsHour/*Kaiser Family Foundation/Harvard School of Public Health Poll (Storrs, Conn.: Roper Center for Public Opinion Research, July 26–September 5, 2000). [2]*USA Today/*Kaiser Family Foundation/Harvard School of Public Health, "The Public on Prescription Drugs and Pharmaceutical Companies," March 2008. [3]Kaiser Family Foundation/Harvard School of Public Health, "The Public's Health Care Agenda for the New Congress and Presidential Campaign," December 2006.

Table 8-7 Reported Skipping of Prescriptions or Doses Because of Drug Costs, by Health Insurance Status (in percent)

Have not filled a prescriptions because of the cost	
Total	29
Insured	26
Uninsured	43
Have cut pills in half or skipped doses because of the cost	
Total	23
Insured	22
Uninsured	29

Note: "Don't know" responses not shown.

Question: In the last two years, have you not filled a prescription because of the cost?

Question: In the last two years, have you ever cut pills in half, or skipped doses in order to make a medicine last longer, or not?

Source: USA Today/Kaiser Family Foundation/Harvard School of Public Health, "The Public on Prescription Drugs and Pharmaceutical Companies," March 2008.

Table 8-8 Perceived Reasons for High Drug Costs (in percent)

Prescription and over the counter drug costs are . . .[1]	
Not usually justified because companies charge more than necessary	81
Usually justified because companies need a lot of money to research and develop new drugs	14
Which are major factors contributing to the price of prescription drugs[2]	
Profits made by pharmaceutical companies	79
The cost of medical research	72
The cost of marketing and advertising	62
The cost of lawsuits against pharmaceutical companies	56

Note: "Don't know" responses not shown.

Question: Which of these statements comes closer to your opinion: prescription and over the counter drug costs are not usually justified because companies charge more than necessary or usually justified because companies need a lot of money to research and develop new drugs?

Question: I'm going to read you some factors that some people say contribute to the price of prescription drugs. For each, I'd like you to tell me if this is a major factor, a minor factor, or not a factor contributing to the price of prescription drugs. What about (the cost of medical research), (the cost of marketing and advertising), (profits made by pharmaceutical companies), (the cost of lawsuits against pharmaceutical companies).

Sources: [1]CBS News Poll (Storrs, Conn.: Roper Center for Public Opinion Research, September 20–22, 2004). [2]USA Today/Kaiser Family Foundation/Harvard School of Public Health, "The Public on Prescription Drugs and Pharmaceutical Companies," March 2008.

Table 8-9 Americans' Attitudes about Government Regulation of Prescription Drug Prices (in percent)

Perceived amount of government regulation of prescription drug prices[1]	
Too much	23
Not enough	52
About right	21

(Table continues)

Table 8-9 *Continued*

Effect of government price controls on new drugs. Drug industry would develop . . . [2]

More new drugs	12
Less	33
About the same	50

Note: "Don't know" responses not shown.

Question: Overall, do you think there is too much, not enough, or about the right amount of government regulation of the price of prescription drugs?

Question: If the government controlled the prices of prescription drugs, do you think the pharmaceutical industry would develop more, less, or about the same number of valuable new drugs?

Sources: [1]Kaiser Family Foundation/Harvard School of Public Health, "The Public's Health Care Agenda for the New President and Congress," January 2009. [2]Harris Interactive Poll (Storrs, Conn.: Roper Center for Public Opinion Research, August 10–15, 2004).

Table 8-10 Americans' Views about Various Groups and Companies (in percent)

	Very favorable	Somewhat favorable	Somewhat unfavorable	Very unfavorable	Don't know	Refused
Doctors	44	37	8	7	3	1
Banks	27	42	16	7	5	2
Food manufacturers	24	47	12	8	1	1
Airlines	21	40	15	8	1	1
Pharmaceutical or drug companies	15	32	21	23	7	1
Health insurance companies	13	27	25	29	5	1
Oil companies	9	20	17	46	7	1

Question: I am going to read you a list of companies and groups. For each one, please tell me if you have a favorable or unfavorable opinion of each. (Doctors/banks/food manufacturers/airlines/pharmaceutical or drug companies/health insurance companies/oil companies).

Source: USA Today/Kaiser Family Foundation/Harvard School of Public Health, "The Public on Prescription Drugs and Pharmaceutical Companies," March 2008.

Table 8-11 Americans' Consumer Ratings of Pharmaceutical Companies (in percent)

	Good job	Bad job	Don't know
1997	79	19	2
1998	73	23	4
1999	66	30	4
2000	59	35	7
2001	57	37	6
2002	59	29	12
2003	49	45	6
2004	44	48	8
2005	56	43	1
2006	61	36	3
2007	60	39	<1
2008	56	41	3
2009	54	45	1

Question: Do you think pharmaceutical and drug companies generally do a good job or bad job serving their consumers?

Sources: Harris Polls (Storrs, Conn.: Roper Center for Public Opinion Research, February 19–23, 1997; March 11–18, 1998; April 8–13, 1999); Harris Interactive Polls (Storrs, Conn.: Roper Center for Public Opinion Research, April 7–10, 2000; April 26–May 5, 2001; May 22–28, 2002; April 10–15, 2003; April 8–15, 2004; April 5–10, 2005; April 4–10, 2006; July 10–16, 2007; July 8–13, 2008; July 8–13, 2009).

Table 8-12 Americans' Views on Who Is and Should Be Responsible for Doing Research (in percent)

	For–profit pharmaceutical companies	Universities	The federal government	Nonprofit or charity organizations	Some combination (vol.)
How big a role each plays in researching and developing new prescription drugs					
Major role	75	60	49	24	NA
Minor role	19	31	39	52	NA
No role	3	4	9	18	NA
Who *should* be primarily responsible for developing new drugs	28	27	16	11	13
Who should be responsible for making sure research is conducted on drugs that could make a big difference and save lives, but the medical conditions mainly affect . . .					
a small number of people	27	NA	48	17	5
people in poorer countries who cannot afford to pay a lot for drugs	19	NA	25	42*	9

Note: "Don't know" responses not shown; (vol.) = volunteered response; NA = not a response category for this questions. *For the "people in poorer countries" question, "international nonprofit or charity organizations."

Question: How big a role do you think each of the following play in researching and developing new prescription drugs? What about (universities/the federal government/non-profit or charity organizations/for-profit pharmaceutical companies)? Do they play a major role, a minor role, or no role in researching new drugs?

Question: Who do you think *should* be primarily responsible for developing new drugs—universities, the federal government, nonprofit or charity organizations, or for-profit pharmaceutical companies?

Question: There are some serious medical conditions for which new prescription drugs could potentially make a big difference and save lives, but these conditions affect a relatively small number of people. Who do you think should be responsible for making sure research is conducted on drugs for these conditions—the federal government, non-profit or charity organizations, or pharmaceutical companies?

Question: There are some serious medical conditions for which new prescription drugs could potentially make a big difference and save lives, but these conditions mainly affect people in poorer countries around the world who cannot afford to pay a lot for drugs. Who do you think should be responsible for making sure research is conducted on drugs for these conditions—the federal government, international nonprofit or charity organizations, or pharmaceutical companies?

Source: USA Today/Kaiser Family Foundation/Harvard School of Public Health, "The Public on Prescription Drugs and Pharmaceutical Companies," March 2008.

Table 8-13 Americans Talking to a Doctor as a Result of Prescription Drug Ads (in percent)

As a result of seeing a prescription drug ad, talked with doctor about that specific medicine	32

Outcome of talking to doctor (Among the 32 percent who have talked to a doctor as a result of seeing an ad)

The doctor did one or more of the following . . .	
Recommended lifestyle changes	57
Recommended a different prescription	54
Gave you a prescription for the drug you asked for	44
Recommended an over-the-counter drug	30

Question: As a result of seeing an ad for a prescription medicine, have you ever talked with a doctor about the specific medicine you saw or heard advertised, or not?

Question: (If talked with a doctor about the specific medicine) When you talked to your doctor about a prescription medicine you saw advertised, please tell me if your doctor did any of the following things. Did your doctor (give you the prescription drug you asked about/recommend a different prescription drug/recommend an over-the-counter drug/recommend that you make changes in your behavior or lifestyle)? (Yes/no to each)

Source: USA Today/Kaiser Family Foundation/Harvard School of Public Health, "The Public on Prescription Drugs and Pharmaceutical Companies," March 2008.

Table 8-14 Americans' Views about Importation of Prescription Drugs from Canada (in percent)

Changing the law to allow Americans to buy prescription drugs from Canada[1]	
Favor	69
Oppose	27

Changing the law to allow Americans to buy prescription drugs from Canada would help reduce drug costs . . .[2]	
A lot	42
Some	37
Not much	9
Not at all	9

Allowing Americans to buy prescription drugs imported from Canada . . .[2]	Agree	Disagree
Will make medicines more affordable without sacrificing safety or quality	70	24
Will expose Americans to unsafe medicines from other countries	30	65
Will lead U.S. drug companies to do less research and development	26	70

Note: "Don't know" responses not shown.

Question: Do you favor or oppose the president and Congress changing the law to allow Americans to buy prescription drugs imported from Canada?

Question: If Congress changed the law to allow Americans to buy prescription drugs imported from Canada, how much do you think this would help in reducing prescription drug costs in the United States? Would it help a lot, some, not much, or not at all?

Question: I'm going to read you a list of things some people have said about allowing Americans to buy prescription drugs imported from Canada, and I'd like you to tell me whether you agree or disagree with each of these statements. Some people say that allowing Americans to buy prescription drugs imported from Canada will make medicines more affordable without sacrificing safety or quality/will expose Americans to unsafe medicines from other countries/will lead U.S. drug companies to do less research and development.

Sources: [1]Kaiser Family Foundation/Harvard School of Public Health, "The Public's Health Care Agenda for the New President and Congress," January 2009. [2]Kaiser Family Foundation, "Health Poll Report Survey," January/February 2005.

Table 8-15 Americans' Views about Government Negotiation of Prescription Drug Prices (in percent)

Allowing the federal government to use its buying power to negotiate with drug companies to try to get lower price for Medicare prescription drugs[1]	
Favor	89
Oppose	10

If Congress allowed government price negotiation for prescription drugs for people in Medicare, how much would it help in reducing prescription drug prices in the U.S.[2]	
A lot	31
Some	48
Not much	12
Not at all	6

(Table continues)

Table 8-15 *Continued*

Government price negotiations for prescription drugs for people on Medicare . . .[3]	Agree	Disagree
Will make medicines more affordable for people on Medicare	81	15
Makes sense because the government already negotiates lower prices for members of the military and veterans	80	16
Will lead to government price controls on prescription drugs	60	34
Will lead U.S. drug companies to do less research and development	31	64

Note: "Don't know" responses not shown.

Question: Do you favor or oppose changing the law to allow the federal government to use its buying power to negotiate with drug companies to try to get a lower price for prescription drugs for people on Medicare?

Question: If Congress changed the law to allow the federal government to negotiate with drug companies to try to get a lower price on prescription drugs for people on Medicare, how much do you think this would help in reducing prescription drug costs in the United States? Would it help a lot, some, not much, or not at all?

Question: I'm going to read you a list of things some people have said about allowing the federal government to use its buying power to negotiate with drug companies to try to get a lower price for prescription drugs for people on Medicare, and I'd like you to tell me whether you agree or disagree with each of these statements. Some people say that allowing the federal government to negotiate with drug companies for lower prices (will lead to government price controls on prescription drugs/will make medicines more affordable for people on Medicare/makes sense because the government already negotiates lower prices for members of the military and veterans/will lead U.S. drug companies to do less research and development). Do you agree or disagree?

Sources: [1]Kaiser Family Foundation/Harvard School of Public Health, "Pre-Election Poll: Voters, Health Care and the 2008 Election," September 2008. Based on registered voters. [2]Kaiser Family Foundation, "Health Poll Report Survey," April 2005. [3]Kaiser Family Foundation/Harvard School of Public Health "Health Care Agenda for the New Congress and Presidential Campaign," December 2006.

Table 8-16 Attitudes about Conscience Clauses (in percent)

Pharmacists personally opposed to birth control for religious reasons . . .[1]	General public
Should be able to refuse to sell birth control pills	17
Should not be able to refuse to sell birth control pills	80

Pharmacists . . .[2]	All pharmacists	Independent pharmacists	Chain pharmacists
Should be allowed to refuse to fill prescriptions	50	61	47
Should be required to fill all prescriptions	36	29	38
Depends (vol.)	6	6	6

Federal government requirement to cover costs of contraceptives[3]	General Public
Federal government should require all health insurance plans to cover contraceptives	44
Federal government should leave this up to individual states	49
Neither (vol.)	4

Note: "Don't know" responses not shown; (vol.) = volunteered response.

Question: Should pharmacists who personally oppose birth control for religious reasons be able to refuse to sell birth control pills to women who have a prescription for them, or shouldn't pharmacists be able to refuse to sell birth control pills?

Question: Do you think pharmacists should be allowed to refuse to fill prescriptions that they object to on moral or religious grounds, such as emergency contraception or Plan B, or should pharmacists be required to fill all prescriptions?

Question: Some private health insurance plans do not include the cost of contraceptives as part of their prescription drug plans. Do you think the federal government should require all health insurance plans to cover the cost of contraceptives as has occurred in several states already? Or should the federal government leave this up to individual states?

Sources: [1]Pew Research Center for the People and the Press/Pew Forum on Religion and Public Life Poll, August 3, 2006. [2]Kaiser Family Foundation, "National Survey of Pharmacists," November 2006. [3]Stony Brook University Center for Survey Research Poll (Storrs, Conn.: Roper Center for Public Opinion Research, September 13–29, 2004).

Chapter 9

QUALITY OF CARE AND MEDICAL ERRORS

Mollyann Brodie, Elizabeth C. Hamel, Claudia Deane, and John M. Connolly

The quality of health care in the United States has become one of the most talked about issues in health policy circles, and at times it has even successfully competed for attention against high profile topics such as coverage and cost. We often hear assertions that even though the United States spends more on health care per capita than any other industrialized nation, it ranks lower on many health outcome measures. Stories about quality of care issues, particularly if they involve dramatic medical errors, are reported by the news media. This attention, along with people's own experiences within the health care system, makes quality an issue of concern for many Americans.

The field of health care quality is broad and diffuse, encompassing topics from evidence-based medicine, that is, making treatment decisions based on the best available scientific evidence, to how health information technology can improve care to coordination of services. But medical errors seem to garner the most attention. One of the landmarks in documenting problems on this front was the 1999 release of the Institute of Medicine's (IOM) report *To Err Is Human: Building a Safer Health System*. The report concluded that 44,000 to 98,000 people die each year in hospitals due to preventable medical errors, more than die of breast cancer, AIDS, or motor vehicle accidents.[1] These findings grabbed the attention of the American public and became the most closely followed health policy story of that year.[2]

The IOM report and subsequent research, in particular a large 2003 study focusing on ambulatory care that suggested American adults receive evidence-based care only about half of the time they seek treatment for the most common chronic conditions,[3] prompted public and private organizations to focus their attention once again on improving the quality of health care in the United States. This movement, spearheaded at the federal level by the Agency for Healthcare Research and Quality (AHRQ) in the Department of Health and Human Services, attempts not only to educate providers about the best ways to deliver higher quality health care, but also to enable Americans as consumers to recognize and seek it out.

Despite popular concern about quality, particularly surrounding errors made by doctors and hospitals, Americans' views concerning this issue do not always match those of health policy experts. In this chapter, we look at Americans' big picture views about the quality of care in the United States, their feelings and experiences about their own care, and the way they define the amorphous term *quality* for themselves. We pay particular attention to people's views about medical errors, and how these views have become incorporated into broader assessments of health care quality.

Concerns about Quality

Perhaps as a result of what they have heard in the media or from friends and acquaintances, roughly half of Americans say they are generally concerned about the quality of U.S. health care in general. Between 1993 and 2009 the share of the public saying they were dissatisfied with the nation's quality of care bounced between 43 percent and 66 percent. In 2009, 48 percent said they were dissatisfied, and 48 percent said they were satisfied (**Table 9–1**).[4] On a different measure, 42 percent of Americans in 2008 rated the quality of health care nationally as only fair or poor, and 57 percent said it was excellent or good. These figures have varied within a narrow range since 2001, with between 40 percent and 47 percent giving only fair or poor ratings.[5]

But when people rate the quality of the health care they themselves receive, a large majority of Americans say they are generally pleased. In a 2009 survey, 77 percent of Americans reported that they were satisfied with the quality of care they have experienced.[6] In 2008, 83 percent rated the quality of care they received the last time they visited a doctor as excellent or good.[7]

The difference between personal ratings and more general ratings is a common finding in public opinion research, with individuals tending to rate institutions and experiences in their own environment positively—be it health care, public schools, or their member of Congress—while expressing unhappiness with the same subjects at the system level.[8] The high level of personal satisfaction with individual quality of care may also suggest that people's problems with the health care system have not been so common as to have spurred widespread discontent about personal care, or that expert-identified quality issues do not factor highly in the average American's judgment of quality, an issue we explore in more depth below.

Americans' reported satisfaction with the quality of their own personal health care is not without nuance. The most important additional piece of information is this: people feel they are being treated well at present, but many worry that care will deteriorate over time. Surveys have found consistently that about six in ten adults say they are worried about the quality of health care services they receive getting worse, including about three in ten who say they are "very" worried (**Table 9–2**).[9] This undercurrent of worry about the future likely undermines people's current satisfaction, making them both more interested in, and more concerned about, change.

A related issue is how safe people feel when they are treated in the American health care system. In 2004 nearly half (48 percent) of the public said they were "very" or "somewhat" worried about the "safety of medical care you and your family receive."[10] This safety concern is another subtext worry that factors into public opinion on health care quality.

Reported Problems with Specific Aspects of Quality of Care

Even though most Americans report they are satisfied with the quality of care they receive, surveys also suggest that many people experience the kinds of problems that experts would say signal quality issues. In particular, majorities say they have experienced some sort of problem with coordination of care, and a sizable minority report personal experience with a preventable medical error.

As the term suggests, coordination of care refers to a broad spectrum of efforts to make sure that information garnered about a patient's condition or needs is shared among all the people or institutions dealing with that patient's health. Overall, four in ten people believe that coordination among all of their different health professionals is a problem, including almost a fifth (17 percent) who say it is a "major" problem.[11] Many people also report specific problems with coordination of care, including having to wait for test results longer than they thought appropriate (54 percent), seeing a health care professional who did not have all of their medical information (51 percent), having to wait for a health professional or make another appointment because he or she did not have the appropriate medical information (32 percent), and being sent for duplicate medical tests (26 percent) (**Table 9–3**).[12]

Furthermore, after being read a common definition of medical errors, an alarming share of Americans (34 percent) say that at some point in their life, they have experienced a serious medical error in their own care or that of a family member. Most of these people say the errors caused serious health consequences. Small but noteworthy shares say that the error in their own or a family member's care resulted in severe pain (16 percent), significant loss of time at important life activities (16 percent), temporary disability (12 percent), long-term disability (11 percent), or death (8 percent) (**Table 9–4**).[13]

Worry about the possibility of experiencing such an error spreads beyond those who actually have had such an incident in their immediate family circle. Those with the most constant exposure to the medical system are, not surprisingly, the most concerned. Nearly six in ten (57 percent) of those with chronic illnesses or disabilities say they are "very concerned" about errors or mistakes. And even among those who do not fall into either of these categories—the relatively healthy—45 percent are very concerned.[14]

Nevertheless, a majority of Americans (55 percent) believe that the quality of health care patients receive in the U.S. health care system is better than that in countries such as Canada, Great Britain, and France. Only 16 percent think the U.S. system is worse. (One in five say they do not know if the U.S. system is better or worse, and 6 percent volunteer the opinion that it is about the same.)[15]

In a 2007 international study based on reports by the public and physicians in six advanced industrialized countries, however, the United States did not fare well on quality of care. The public and physicians were asked several specific questions about their own or their patients' experiences in four broad areas considered important in judging quality: care that is effective or "right," safe, coordinated, and patient-centered. The United States ranked first in effective care, but no higher than fifth on any of the other three aspects of quality. In the aggregate, the United States ranked fifth of the six countries on the study's quality of care score. On two other measures that could be considered part of quality—efficiency and equity—the United States ranked last.[16]

What Does Quality of Care Mean to People?

Why do a number of Americans report the type of quality of care experiences that experts have identified as problems, but also say their own health care quality is satisfactory? Answering that question requires looking into how Americans define the concept of quality health care and whether their views agree with what the evidence suggests is superior care. This exercise, however, turns out to be imprecise.

Overall, surveys find no broad public consensus on what produces care of a high quality, which is perhaps not surprising given the complexity of the issue and that experts themselves struggle with how to measure quality. When people were asked in an open-ended question to name the most important factor in determining the quality of health care, their most frequent response—named by only 14 percent—had to do with the affordability or cost of health care. Two additional access-related factors were in the top four: availability of care for everyone (9 percent) and insurance coverage of care and procedures (8 percent). The second most mentioned response about which single factor most impacts quality was doctors' qualifications and experience (13 percent).[17] Quality, which is seen in health policy as something separate from studies of cost and coverage, is clearly not seen as a discrete topic by most Americans (**Table 9–5**).

Greater consensus appears when Americans are posed a more concrete question: Which qualifications would help them the most if they were trying to decide between the quality of care provided by different doctors, hospitals, or health care plans? Here the public often places appropriately high levels of attention on factors, such as experience, that experts say do make a difference in improving quality. At the same time, however, the public overemphasizes certain types of information as barometers of quality, such as the much-discussed topics of medical errors and malpractice suits.

When people were asked how much each type of information would tell them about the quality of a doctor if they were trying to choose among physicians, three traits stood out as having the strongest appeal: a physician's experience with a particular procedure (named by 66 percent as telling them "a lot"), whether the doctor is board certified (65 percent), and the number of malpractice suits filed against the doctor (64 percent). When comparing hospitals in a similar question, information on medical error rates ranked first (70 percent said it would tell them "a lot"), followed by experience performing particular procedures (65 percent) (**Tables 9–6 and 9–7**).[18]

In both cases, according to experts, respondents were more correct in placing a heavy emphasis on experience than on malpractice and reports of medical errors. The public also appropriately placed little credence in factors such as how much a doctor charges when trying to ascertain quality; experts say there is little correlation between price and quality in health care, and the public put this item last on their list of eight possible factors. When comparing health plans, people focused on a larger number of factors, but information about complaints and medical errors of doctors and hospitals that participated in the plan again were among their top choices (**Table 9–8**).[19]

It is clear that the public correctly sees a variety of factors as impacting quality, and given the evidence of the open-ended question above, is not particularly focused on any one measure. To the extent that there was any focus in responses to that question, it tended to be more about access to care. It is also clear that the attention of the media and the policymakers to medical errors has affected the public's evaluation of what defines quality care. In the next section, we turn more specifically to the public's views on this high-profile topic.

Perceptions of the Frequency of Medical Errors

Surveys confirm that many Americans place a heavy emphasis on reports of medical errors when judging doctors and hospitals. Public opinion data suggest several reasons for this finding. First, as discussed above, is personal experience: about one in three Americans reports either suffering a preventable medical error themselves or having this happen to a family member. Worry about experiencing such a mistake is even more widespread. In addition, the media paid a great deal of attention to the IOM report on the prevalence of medical errors, and the public followed the story closely. As affirmation of the power of the media to publicize this topic, most Americans say they have derived their information on medical errors from the media (61 percent), compared to 15 percent who say their views come from personal experience, and 18 percent who say they come from the experiences of friends or family.[20]

Driven by the media's and policymakers' attention to this issue, awareness of medical errors is on the rise, such that these mistakes have become symbolic of problems with the quality of care. In fact, the share of the public saying they know what the term "medical error" means rose steadily from three in ten in 2002 to roughly four in ten in 2004, and more than half (55 percent) in 2006.[21]

Americans also view these errors as widespread. In a series of surveys beginning in 2002, respondents were read a common definition of preventable medical errors and asked how often they think such errors are made when people seek care. Around one in ten consistently have said such errors are made "very often," and between three and four in ten have said they are made "somewhat often." The combined share of the public saying that preventable errors occur very or somewhat often was at its highest—nearly half (49 percent)—in 2002, decreased to just over a third (36 percent) in 2004, and increased again to 43 percent in 2006 (**Table 9–9**).[22]

When asked directly about the number of people who die each year in hospitals from preventable medical errors, however, Americans typically underestimate the fatality of such mistakes. In 2004 about half the public (49 percent) said they thought 5,000 or fewer deaths occur in hospitals each year due to medical errors, much lower than the 1999 IOM estimate of between 44,000 and 98,000.[23]

Likely adding to their feelings of frustration over the issue, the large majority of Americans believe that at least half of the deaths caused by medical errors could have been prevented.[24]

Perceived Causes of Medical Errors and Possible Solutions

Before looking at the public's views of possible solutions to the problem of preventable medical errors, we should understand people's views about the source of such problems. Here, contrary to the belief of most health policy experts, the public is more likely to blame individual health professionals for causing medical errors than the institutions where those professionals work. In 2006 nearly half (48 percent) of the public said that mistakes made by individual health professionals were more important in causing preventable medical errors, compared to just over a third (36 percent) who believed that mistakes by institutions were the bigger problem.[25] In contrast with the public's general tendency to focus on individual care providers, health services experts often emphasize system-level flaws as being the most important contributors to suboptimal care. In fact, according to the administrator of AHRQ, the main point of the IOM report and its sequel, *Crossing the Quality Chasm,* can be summed up simply as: "It's the system."[26]

In a more detailed question, the public was provided with nine possible causes of medical errors that result in serious harm to the patient. Here the public correctly put a systems-level problem at the top of the list, with 74 percent saying "overwork, stress, or fatigue of health professionals" was "very important" in causing errors.[27] In fact, studies have shown that fewer errors occur when health professionals work shorter hours.[28] Other potential causes that a majority of the public identified as very important included: doctors not having enough time with patients, too few nurses in hospitals, and health professionals not working together (**Table 9–10**).[29]

On the other hand, the public has not yet recognized some systems-level problems that experts say are possible causes of preventable medical errors. Studies have shown that having physicians enter their prescriptions via computer can greatly reduce prescription errors, but poor handwriting by health professionals ranked relatively low on the public's list of causes.[30] Similarly, the least popular choice among the public as a cause of medical errors was "lack of computerized medical records," a factor that experts have shown to be vitally important to improve quality.[31]

Consistent with the opinions of the public as a whole, those who have experienced a serious error in their own or a family member's care are most likely to place responsibility for the error on the physician involved. Few, however, report pursuing medical malpractice lawsuits. Among the 34 percent of the public who said they or a family member experienced a medical error, a substantial majority (72 percent) said the doctor involved had a lot of responsibility for the error, and far fewer said the same about the institution (39 percent), nurses (28 percent), or other health care professionals (27 percent). Just over one in ten (11 percent) of those who reported having experience with a medical error said they or their family member sued a health care professional for malpractice. This share was not significantly higher (14 percent) among those who said the medical error they or their family member experienced had serious health consequences.[32]

Even though many Americans worry about the possibility of a medical error and believe the fault is usually with the individual practitioner handling the treatment, a majority believe their own doctor would tell them if a preventable medical error occurred in the course of their treatment. This is yet another example of the phenomenon of individuals trusting their *own* doctors, or rating their *own* quality of care highly, while having more doubts about the wider system. Asked how likely it was that their doctor would tell them if a preventable error had resulted in their experiencing serious harm, more than half said they thought it very likely (23 percent) or somewhat likely (31 percent).[33] Even more (68 percent) agreed with the more general statement: "I trust my doctor to tell me if a mistake was made about my treatment."[34]

Nevertheless, a considerable minority of the public has experienced a situation in which a physician did not inform them of an error in either their treatment or that of a family member. Of the 34 percent of the public who said they or a family member experienced a medical error, seven in ten (70 percent) said the health professional involved did *not* tell them that a mistake had been made. Three in ten (28 percent) said they were told.[35] These findings accord with at least one study that showed an official from the medical facility reported telling patients or families about serious medical errors in less than one-fourth of the cases studied.[36]

Based on their views about the individual-level causes of preventable errors, it is not surprising that people's top solution to this type of problem is increasing the amount of time doctors are able to spend with their patients. Asked about twelve possible strategies for reducing serious preventable medical errors, 79 percent said "giving doctors more time to spend with patients" would be "very effective."[37] Although more time is clearly something that the average health care consumer would value, research studies have not been able to show that extra time actually increases quality of care.[38] Two-thirds or more of the public thought other solutions would be very effective in reducing medical errors: better training of health practitioners, requiring hospitals to develop error-prevention systems, requiring hospitals to report errors to a state agency, increasing the number of hospital nurses, reducing residents' work hours, and using only intensive care medicine specialists in ICUs (**Table 9–11**).[39]

The solutions most often cited by medical experts, such as the use of computerized medical records, concentrating high-risk procedures at certain hospitals, and having hospital patients taken care of by hospital doctors rather than their regular doctors, ranked farther down on the public's list. Only two in ten Americans see substituting hospital physicians for patients' personal physicians as a "very effective" solution.[40]

Public Support for the Reporting of Errors

Another contentious policy debate centers around whether errors should be publicly reported. Those who advocate mandatory public disclosure say it would increase the public's information about hospital quality, boost their faith in the transparency of the system, and give providers an incentive to work harder to reduce errors.[41] Those who oppose disclosure, including organizations representing doctors and hospitals, say it will increase the number of lawsuits, lead to higher insurance premiums for medical providers, and discourage honest reporting.[42]

The public comes down firmly on the disclosure side of this argument: Regardless of their trust in physicians, most people believe that doctors should be required to inform them of preventable errors made in the course of their treatment and to publicly report these errors. A large majority (87 percent) say that doctors should be required to tell their patients if a serious error is made in their care, and the same share believes that public reporting of preventable errors in general should be mandatory, not voluntary. In fact, nearly two-thirds (63 percent) believe that information about medical errors should be released to the public, and about three in ten (29 percent) say such information should be confidential and used only to learn how to prevent future mistakes.[43]

Quality Information and Individual Decision Making

Experts believe that improving health care quality depends not only on changing the behavior of health care providers, but also on changing consumer behavior and empowering individuals to seek out and demand better care. It is particularly important, therefore, to understand whether published information about quality matters in the public's decisions about their health care.

Despite the importance of quality information in making good choices about personal health care, most people either do not see it or do not use it. Instead, they are more likely to turn to someone they know to help them with health care decisions. In many ways, this behavior is understandable, given that quality information is not always available—particularly regarding individual doctors—even for those with the interest and skills to search for it.

In 2008 almost a third (30 percent) of the public said that in the past year they had seen information comparing the quality of different health plans, hospitals, or doctors. People were almost twice as likely to say they saw information comparing the quality of health plans (22 percent) and hospitals (20 percent) as to have seen information comparing the quality of doctors (12 percent). About half of those who have seen quality information, or 14 percent of all Americans, said they used this information to make a decision about their care (**Table 9–12**).[44]

A 2004 study found those who saw health quality information on hospitals or health plans and chose not to use it were most likely to say the reason was that they did not need to make a decision about their care at the time, or that the information they saw was not specific to their health concerns.[45]

Aside from published quality information and ratings, consumers cite a variety of factors that affect how they choose different doctors, hospitals, or health plans, and they turn to a variety of sources to get information about each. The Internet became a more frequent source of quality information between 2000 and 2004, but Americans are still more likely to say they would seek such information from people they know, including not only their inner circle of family members and friends but also their own doctors and nurses, rather than contacting official groups or looking for printed or online information.[46]

When it comes to selecting a hospital, familiarity is more important than expert ratings, even if those ratings are likely to be a more reliable guide to quality of care. Consistently between 1996 and 2008, far more people said that they would choose a hospital they and family members had used for many years without problems rather than one with a higher quality rating by experts (**Table 9–13**).[47]

The picture changes when the choice is between two surgeons at a hospital. In 2008 the public was almost evenly split between a surgeon who had treated a friend or family member without problems, but whose ratings were not as high as others at the hospital, and a surgeon whose ratings were higher, but who had not had as a patient anyone they knew personally.

Prior to 2008, the public was almost evenly split between favoring health plans that family and friends recommend and those that experts rate more highly. Recently, surveys show a movement toward expert ratings—a hopeful sign to advocates of the importance of transparency and consumerism in driving quality improvement. It is worth noting here that quality ratings of health plans have been in existence longer than ratings of doctors and hospitals, giving the public a greater chance to encounter, use, and trust such information.[48]

Although most Americans rely on their employers to provide health insurance, in general people do not trust their employers to give them good information as to the quality of various health plans. In 2008 about half said they did not trust what employers said about health plans, believing that employers' main concern is saving money on health benefits, and a little over a third said that employers are a good source of information because they examine plans closely when deciding which to offer (**Table 9–14**).[49]

In addition to seeking out quality information before choosing a health care provider, consumers have other ways to try and improve the quality of care they receive. The U.S. Department of Health and Human Services, in partnership with the American Hospital Association and the American Medical Association, has produced a list of specific recommendations entitled "Five Steps to Safer Health Care."[50] Surveys show that many Americans are beginning to take these steps, either because they have heard of the recommendations or because of their own common sense. The steps taken most often were: asking their doctor questions about their health or prescribed treatments (83 percent), checking the medication they got from a pharmacist against the prescription their doctor wrote (70 percent), talking to a surgeon about the details of surgery (67 percent), calling to check on the results of medical and laboratory tests (64 percent), and bringing a list of all of their medications to an appointment with a doctor (59 percent, up from 48 percent in 2004).[51] A little over a third of the public also reports that they have created their own set of medical records to ensure that their health care providers have all of their information.

Quality as a Priority for Government and for Voters

Although undeniably important to Americans, particularly on a personal level, quality issues have not been at the top of the public's agenda for government action in recent years. When the public is asked to rank their priorities, health care quality consistently ranks behind other health issues—such as cost, the uninsured, and health care for seniors.

Making affordable coverage more available was clearly a higher priority for the public than improvement in the quality of care in the 2008 presidential election. Making "health insurance more affordable" was ranked as the most important issue in the vote for president, while "improving quality of care and reducing medical errors" was ranked third on a list of five issues.[52] The pattern was similar in the November 2006 election; "problems with health care quality" ranked fifth on a list of eight different health care issues in terms of the share of the public saying it would be "extremely important" to their vote for Congress. In a survey just *after* the 2006 election, "improving the quality of care and reducing errors" ranked fourth on a list of five issues when respondents were asked to choose one health issue for the president and Congress to work on in the coming year (**Table 9–15**).[53]

Conclusion

Understanding what Americans think about the quality of their own health care and of health care in the country more generally is almost as difficult as the task experts face in defining high quality care and striving to attain it. People express satisfaction with the quality of their own care, and at the same time report the kinds of problems that experts say indicate poor quality. And despite their personal satisfaction, many think poorly of the quality of care in the country in general. These discrepancies may stem from the difficulty of evaluating quality. Like the proverbial blind men describing an elephant, everyone may be experiencing a different part of the health care system when they respond to surveys.

Several aspects of public opinion on quality of care, however, have relevance for future policy debates. First, Americans' basic satisfaction with their personal quality of care, and their disinclination to prioritize this issue in terms of government action, suggest that it might be challenging to mobilize public opinion for efforts on this front. Second, and somewhat contradictory to the first point, the public seems ready to focus on comparatively dramatic—and negative—events in health care, particularly reports of preventable medical errors and malpractice lawsuits. Motivating people by fear of error, however, may be a politically difficult way to move forward. Third, people tend to believe that medical errors stem from individual mistakes, rather than looking to systemwide failures. Experts, on the other hand, might agree that individuals make mistakes but would also assert that the best solution to the problem of medical errors lies in creating and maintaining systems that can catch these all-too human errors.

The learning curve about quality persists. But, although still not a majority, many people are beginning to seek out quality information, to use that information, and to try to improve the quality of their own care by taking steps such as creating copies of their own medical records. These efforts may multiply on their own, as Americans follow their tendency to consult their family, friends, and their own physicians about quality, and are urged by others to adopt these practices.

Notes

[1] Linda T. Kohn, Janet M. Corrigan, Molla S. Donaldson, and the Committee on Quality of Health Care in America, Institute of Medicine, *To Err Is Human: Building a Safer Health System* (Washington, D.C.: National Academy Press, 1999). See also Drew Altman, Carolyn Clancy, and Robert J. Blendon, "Improving Patient Safety—Five Years after the IOM Report," *New England Journal of Medicine* 351 (November 11, 2004): 2041–3.

[2] Kaiser/Harvard Health News Interest Index project. Altman, Clancy, and Blendon. "Improving Patient Safety—Five Years after the IOM Report," *New England Journal of Medicine*, 2004.

[3] Elizabeth A. McGlynn, Steven M. Asch, John Adams, Joan Keesey, Jennifer Hicks, Alison DeCristofaro, and Eve A. Kerr, "The Quality of Health Care Delivered to Adults in the United States," *New England Journal of Medicine* 348 (June 26, 2003): 2635–45.

[4] Gallup/CNN/*USA Today* Poll (Storrs, Conn.: Roper Center for Public Opinion Research, May 10–12, 1993); Gallup Poll (Storrs, Conn.: Roper Center for Public Opinion Research, September 11–13, 2000); ABC News/*Washington Post* Poll (Storrs, Conn.: Roper Center for Public Opinion Research, October 9–13, 2003); Kaiser Family Foundation polls (Storrs, Conn.: Roper Center for Public Opinion Research, June 4–8, 2004; October 14–17, 2004); Kaiser Family Foundation/Agency for Healthcare Research and Quality/Harvard School of Public Health Poll (Storrs, Conn.: Roper Center for Public Opinion Research, July 7–September 5, 2004); ABC News/Kaiser Family Foundation/*USA Today*, "Health Care in America 2006 Survey," October 2006, http://www.kff.org/kaiserpolls/upload/7573.pdf; CBS News/*New York Times* Poll (Storrs, Conn.: Roper Center for Public Opinion Research, February 23–27, 2007); CBS News Poll (Storrs, Conn.: Roper Center for Public Opinion Research, September 14–16, 2007); CBS News/*New York Times* Poll (Storrs, Conn.: Roper Center for Public Opinion Research, June 12–16, 2009).

[5] Gallup Poll, "Healthcare System," 2008, http://www.gallup.com/poll/4708/Healthcare-System.aspx.

[6] CBS News/*New York Times* Poll, June 12–16, 2009.

[7] Harvard School of Public Health/Robert Wood Johnson Foundation Poll (Storrs, Conn.: Roper Center for Public Opinion research, March 26–30, 2008).

[8] David Whitman, *The Optimism Gap* (New York: Walker and Co., 1998); Robert Blendon and John Benson, "How Americans View Their Lives: An Annual Survey," *Challenge: The Magazine of Economic Affairs* 47 (May-June 2004): 2–26.

[9] Kaiser Family Foundation, "Kaiser Health Tracking Poll—July 2009," http://www.kff.org/kaiserpolls/posr072309pkg.cfm.

[10] Kaiser Family Foundation/Agency for Healthcare Research and Quality/Harvard School of Public Health, "National Survey on Consumers' Experiences with Patient Safety and Quality Information," November 2004, http://www.kff.org/kaiserpolls/7210.cfm.

[11] NPR/Kaiser Family Foundation/Harvard School of Public Health, "The Public and the Health Care Delivery System," April 2009, http://www.kff.org/kaiserpolls/posr042209pkg.cfm.

[12] Kaiser Family Foundation, "2008 Update on Consumers' Views of Patient Safety and Quality Information," October 2008, http://www.kff.org/kaiserpolls/posr101508pkg.cfm.

[13] Kaiser Family Foundation/Agency for Healthcare Research and Quality/Harvard School of Public Health, "National Survey on Consumers' Experiences with Patient Safety and Quality Information," November 2004.

[14] Kaiser Family Foundation/Agency for Healthcare Research and Quality, "National Survey on Americans as Health Care Consumers: An Update on the Role of Quality Information," December 2000, http://www.kff.org/kaiserpolls/upload/National-Survey-on-Americans-as-Health-Care-Consumers-An-Update-on-the-Role-of-Quality-Information-Toplines-Survey.pdf.

[15] Harvard School of Public Health/Harris Interactive Poll (Storrs, Conn.: Roper Center for Public Opinion Research, March 5–8, 2008).

[16] The five other countries were Australia, Canada, Germany, New Zealand, and the United Kingdom. Karen Davis, Cathy Schoen, Stephen C. Schoenbaum, Michelle M. Doty, Alyssa L. Holmgren, Jennifer L. Kriss, and Katherine K. Shea, "Mirror, Mirror on the Wall: An International Update on the Comparative Performance of American Health Care," May 2007, http://www.commonwealthfund.org/usr_doc/1027_Davis_mirror_mirror_international_update_final.pdf?section=4039.

[17] Kaiser Family Foundation/Agency for Healthcare Research and Quality/Harvard School of Public Health, "National Survey on Consumers' Experiences with Patient Safety and Quality Information," November 2004.

[18] Ibid.

[19] Ibid.

[20] Kaiser Family Foundation/Agency for Healthcare Research and Quality/Harvard School of Public Health, "National Survey on Consumers' Experiences with Patient Safety and Quality Information," November 2004.

[21] Kaiser Family Foundation/Harvard School of Public Health, "Medical Errors: Practicing Physician and Public Views," 2002, http://www.kff.org/insurance/loader.cfm?url=/commonspot/security/getfile.cfm&PageID=14099; Kaiser Family Foundation/Agency for Healthcare Research and Quality/Harvard School of Public Health, "National Survey on Consumers' Experiences with Patient Safety and Quality Information," November 2004; Kaiser Family Foundation/Agency for Healthcare Research and Quality, "2006 Update on Consumers' Views of Patient Safety and Quality Information," September 2006.

[22] Ibid.

[23] Kaiser Family Foundation/Agency for Healthcare Research and Quality/Harvard School of Public Health, "National Survey on Consumers' Experiences with Patient Safety and Quality Information," November 2004; Kohn et al., *To Err Is Human*.

[24] Kaiser Family Foundation/Agency for Healthcare Research and Quality/Harvard School of Public Health, "National Survey on Consumers' Experiences with Patient Safety and Quality Information," November 2004.

[25] Kaiser Family Foundation/Agency for Healthcare Research and Quality, "2006 Update on Consumers' Views of Patient Safety and Quality Information," September 2006.

[26] Carolyn M. Clancy, "Testimony on Patient Safety: Supporting a Culture of Continuous Quality Improvement in Hospitals and Other Health Care Organizations, before the Senate Permanent Subcommittee on Investigations, Committee on Governmental Affairs, June 11, 2003," http://www.ahrq.gov/news/tst61103.htm; Committee on Quality of Health Care in America, Institute of Medicine, *Crossing the Quality Chasm: A New Health System for the 21st Century* (Washington, D.C.: National Academy Press, 2001).

[27] Kaiser Family Foundation/Agency for Healthcare Research and Quality/Harvard School of Public Health, "National Survey on Consumers' Experiences with Patient Safety and Quality Information," November 2004.

[28] C. P. Landrigan, J. M. Rothschild, J. W. Cronin, R. Kaushal, E. Burdick, J. T. Katz et al., "Effect of Reducing Interns' Work Hours on Serious Medical Errors in Intensive Care Units," *New England Journal of Medicine* 351 (October 28, 2004): 1838–48.

[29] Kaiser Family Foundation/Agency for Healthcare Research and Quality/Harvard School of Public Health, "National Survey on Consumers' Experiences with Patient Safety and Quality Information," November 2004.

[30] D. W. Bates, L. L. Leap, D. J. Cullen, N. Laird, L. A. Petersen, J. M. Teich et al., "Effect of Computerized Physician Order Entry and a Team Intervention on Prevention of Serious Medication Errors," *JAMA: Journal of the American Medical Association* 280 (October 21, 1998): 1311–6.

[31] Kaiser Family Foundation/Agency for Healthcare Research and Quality/Harvard School of Public Health, "National Survey on Consumers' Experiences with Patient Safety and Quality Information," November 2004.

[32] Ibid.

[33] Ibid.

[34] James A. Davis, Tom W. Smith, and Peter V. Marsden, *General Social Surveys, 1972–2006* (Chicago: National Opinion Research Center, 2007).

[35] Kaiser Family Foundation/Agency for Healthcare Research and Quality/Harvard School of Public Health, "National Survey on Consumers' Experiences with Patient Safety and Quality Information," November 2004.

[36] A. W. Wu, S. Folkman, S. J. McPhee, and B. Lo, "Do House Officers Learn from Their Mistakes?" *JAMA* 265 (April 24, 1991): 2089–94.

[37] Kaiser Family Foundation/Agency for Healthcare Research and Quality/Harvard School of Public Health, "National Survey on Consumers' Experiences with Patient Safety and Quality Information," November 2004.

[38] Robert H. Brook, Elizabeth A. McGlynn, and Paul G. Shekelle, "Defining and Measuring Quality of Care: A Perspective from US Researchers," *International Journal for Quality in Health Care* 12 (August 2000): 281–295.

[39] Kaiser Family Foundation/Agency for Healthcare Research and Quality/Harvard School of Public Health, "National Survey on Consumers' Experiences with Patient Safety and Quality Information," November 2004.

[40] David Blumenthal and John P. Glaser, "Information Technology Comes to Medicine." *New England Journal of Medicine* 356 (June 14, 2007): 2527–34; Kaiser Family Foundation/Agency for Healthcare Research and Quality/Harvard School of Public Health, "National Survey on Consumers' Experiences with Patient Safety and Quality Information," November 2004.

[41] Lynda Flowers and Trish Riley, "State-based Mandatory Reporting of Medical Errors: An Analysis of the Legal and Policy Issues," March 2001, National Academy for State Health Policy, http://www.nashp.org/Files/GNL_36_Reprint.pdf.

[42] Robert Pear, "Clinton to Order Steps to Reduce Medical Mistakes," *New York Times,* February 22, 2000, http://www.nytimes.com/2000/02/22/us/clinton-to-order-steps-to-reduce-medical-mistakes.html.

[43] Kaiser Family Foundation/Agency for Healthcare Research and Quality, "2006 Update on Consumers' Views of Patient Safety and Quality Information," September 2006.

[44] Kaiser Family Foundation, "2008 Update on Consumers' Views of Patient Safety and Quality Information," October 2008.

[45] Kaiser Family Foundation/Agency for Healthcare Research and Quality/Harvard School of Public Health, "National Survey on Consumers' Experiences with Patient Safety and Quality Information," November 2004.

[46] Kaiser Family Foundation/Agency for Healthcare Research and Quality, "National Survey on Americans as Health Care Consumers: An Update on the Role of Quality Information," December 2000; Kaiser Family Foundation/Agency for Healthcare Research and Quality/ Harvard School of Public Health, "National Survey on Consumers' Experiences with Patient Safety and Quality Information," November 2004; Kaiser Family Foundation, "2008 Update on Consumers' Views of Patient Safety and Quality Information," October 2008.

[47] Kaiser Family Foundation/Agency for Health Care Policy and Research Poll (Storrs, Conn.: Roper Center for Public Opinion Research, July 26–September 5, 1996); Kaiser Family Foundation/Agency for Healthcare Research and Quality, "National Survey on Americans as Health Care Consumers: An Update on the Role of Quality Information," December 2000; Kaiser Family Foundation/Agency for Healthcare Research and Quality/Harvard School of Public Health, "National Survey on Consumers' Experiences with Patient Safety and Quality Information," November 2004; Kaiser Family Foundation, "2008 Update on Consumers' Views of Patient Safety and Quality Information," October 2008.

[48] Ibid.

[49] Kaiser Family Foundation, "2008 Update on Consumers' Views of Patient Safety and Quality Information," October 2008.

[50] U.S. Department of Health and Human Services, American Hospital Association, American Medical Association, "Five Steps to Safer Health Care," http://www.ahrq.gov/consumer/5steps .pdf.

[51] Kaiser Family Foundation/Agency for Healthcare Research and Quality/Harvard School of Public Health, "National Survey on Consumers' Experiences with Patient Safety and Quality Information," November 2004; Kaiser Family Foundation, "2008 Update on Consumers' Views of Patient Safety and Quality Information," October 2008.

[52] Kaiser Family Foundation, "Kaiser Health Tracking Poll: Election 2008," October 2008, http://www.kff.org/kaiserpolls/h08_posr102108pkg.cfm.

[53] Kaiser Family Foundation, "Health Poll Report Survey," October 2006, http://www.kff.org/ kaiserpolls/upload/7578.pdf.

Table 9-1 Satisfaction with the Quality of Health Care, 1993–2007 (in percent)

	Satisfied	Dissatisfied
Quality of health care in this country		
1993[1]	51	46
2000[2]	54	44
2003[3]	44	55
June 2004[4]	50	47
July 2004[5]	41	55
October 2004[6]	54	43
2006[7]	45	54
February 2007[8]	38	57
September 2007[9]	32	66
2009[10]	48	48
Quality of health care you receive		
2007[8]	77	20
2009[10]	77	20

Note: "Don't know" responses not shown.

Question: Thinking about health care in the country as a whole, are you generally satisfied or dissatisfied with the quality of health care in this country? (1993–2006)

Question: Thinking about the country as a whole, are you generally satisfied with the quality of health care in the country? (2007–2009)

Question: What about the health care you receive? Are you generally satisfied or dissatisfied with the quality of health care you receive?

Sources: [1]Gallup/CNN/*USA Today* Poll (Storrs, Conn.: Roper Center for Public Opinion Research, May 10–12, 1993); [2]Gallup Poll (Storrs, Conn.: Roper Center for Public Opinion Research, September 11–13, 2000); [3]ABC News/*Washington Post* Poll (Storrs, Conn.: Roper Center for Public Opinion Research, October 9–13, 2003); [4]Kaiser Family Foundation Poll (Storrs, Conn.: Roper Center for Public Opinion Research, June 4–8, 2004); [5]Kaiser Family Foundation/Agency for Healthcare Research and Quality/Harvard School of Public Health Poll (Storrs, Conn.: Roper Center for Public Opinion Research, July 7–September 5, 2004); [6]Kaiser Family Foundation Poll (Storrs, Conn.: Roper Center for Public Opinion Research, October 14–17, 2004); [7]ABC News/Kaiser Family Foundation/*USA Today*, "Health Care in America 2006 Survey," October 2006; [8]CBS News/*New York Times* Poll (Storrs, Conn.: Roper Center for Public Opinion Research, February 23–27, 2007); [9]CBS News Poll (Storrs, Conn.: Roper Center for Public Opinion Research, September 14-16, 2007); [10]CBS News/*New York Times* Poll (Storrs, Conn.: Roper Center for Public Opinion Research, June 12–16, 2009).

Table 9-2 Americans' Worries about the Quality of Health Care Services They Receive Getting Worse, 2004–2009 (in percent)

	Very worried	Somewhat worried	Not too worried	Not at all worried
2004				
February	29	29	19	22
April	31	28	18	21
June	29	28	18	24
August	30	26	14	29
October	30	28	16	26
December	34	26	18	22
2005				
February	23	33	19	24
March-April	32	28	15	24
June	28	29	18	23
October	28	28	18	24
2006				
February	27	31	16	24
August	25	31	18	24
October	33	29	18	20
2007				
March	30	31	16	21
May-June	32	28	19	20
October	29	30	18	20
November-December	33	29	17	19
2008				
April	26	30	18	24
September	24	28	22	26
October	26	27	21	25
2009				
July	28	33	18	21

Note: "Don't know" responses not shown.

Question: I'm going to read you a list of things that some people worry about and others do not. I'd like you to tell me how worried you are about each of the following things. How worried are you about the quality of health care services you receive getting worse? Are you very worried, somewhat worried, not too worried, or not at all worried?

Sources: Kaiser Family Foundation polls (Storrs, Conn.: Roper Center for Public Opinion Research, February 4–8, 2004; April 1–5, 2004; June 4–8, 2004; August 5–8, 2004; October 14–17, 2004; December 2–5, 2004; February 3–6, 2005; March 31–April 3, 2005; June 2–5, 2005; October 4–9, 2005; February 2–7, 2006; August 3–8, 2006; October 5–10, 2006; March 8–13, 2007; May 31–June 5, 2007; October 1–10, 2007; November 28–December 9, 2007; April 3–13, 2008; September 8–13, 2008; October 8–13, 2008; July 7–14, 2009).

Table 9-3 Experience of Problems with Health Care Quality (in percent)

	2006[1]	2008[2]	2009[3]
Coordination among different health professionals is . . .			
Major problem	26	30	17
Minor problem	34	37	27
Not a problem at all	36	26	52
Don't know	4	7	3
Percent saying the following have ever happened to them . . . (2008)[2]			
Had to wait for test results longer than you thought appropriate			54
Seen a health care professional and noticed that they did not have all of your medical information			51
Had to wait for a health professional or had to come back for another appointment because they did not have your medical information available			32
Been told to get a test that you already had done in the past two weeks			26

Question: In general, do you think that coordination among all of the different health professionals that you see is a major problem, a minor problem, or not a problem at all?

Question: How often have you (had to wait for test results longer than you thought appropriate/seen a health care professional and noticed that they did not have all of your medical information/had to wait for a health professional or had to come back for another appointment because they did not have your medical information available/been told to get a test that you already had done in the past two weeks)? Has this happened to you very often, somewhat often, not too often, or has this never happened to you?

Sources: [1]Kaiser Family Foundation/Agency for Healthcare Research and Quality, "2006 Update on Consumers' Views of Patient Safety and Quality Information," September 2006; [2]Kaiser Family Foundation, "2008 Update on Consumers' Views of Patient Safety and Quality Information," October 2008; [3]Kaiser Family Foundation/NPR/Harvard School of Public Health, "The Public and the Health Care Delivery System," April 2009.

Table 9-4 Experience and Consequences of Medical Errors (in percent)

Percent who say they have personally been involved in a situation where a preventable medical error was made in their own or a family member's medical care (Net)	34
Percent saying an error resulted in serious health consequences (Subnet)	21
Consequences included severe pain	16
Consequences included significant loss of time at work, school, or other important life activities	16
Consequences included temporary disability	12
Consequences included long-term disability	11
Consequences included death	8
Percent saying the error resulted in minor health consequences or no health consequences	13

Question: Sometimes when people are ill and receive medical care, mistakes are made that result in serious harm, such as death, disability, or additional or prolonged treatment. These are called medical errors. Some of these errors are preventable, while other may not be. I'd like to ask some questions about preventable medical errors that result in serious harm. If for any of these questions, you feel you haven't heard enough to have an opinion, just say so. . . . Have you ever been personally involved in a situation where a preventable medical error was made in your own medical care or that of a family member?

Question: (If yes) Please think about the preventable medical error that occurred (to you or a family member) most recently. . . . Did the error have serious health consequences, minor health consequences, or no health consequences at all?

Question: (If had serious health consequences) Did these serious health consequences include any of the following? Severe pain/significant loss of time at work, school, or other important life activities/temporary disability/long-term disability/death? (Yes/No to each)

Source: Kaiser Family Foundation/Agency for Healthcare Research and Quality/Harvard School of Public Health, "National Survey on Consumers' Experiences with Patient Safety and Quality Information," November 2004.

Table 9-5 Americans' Views on What Determines the Quality of Health Care Patients Receive (in percent)

Health care affordability/cost	14
Doctor's qualifications and experience	13
Total access/availability for everyone	9
Type and range of insurance coverage	8
The cost and coverage for prescription medicines	3
Other staff qualified and courteous	3
Time doctor spends with patient	3
Low incidence of medical errors	2
Results/patient outcome	2
The availability of appointments	2
Ability to choose own doctor	2
Other responses (each mentioned by 1% or less of the public)	23
Don't know/Refused	16

Question: What specifically do you think is most important in determining the quality of health care patients receive? Just tell me the first thing that comes to mind.

Source: Kaiser Family Foundation/Agency for Healthcare Research and Quality/Harvard School of Public Health, "National Survey on Consumers' Experiences with Patient Safety and Quality Information," November 2004.

Table 9-6 What Information Americans Believe Tells Them about the Quality of Doctors When Comparing Two or More Doctors

Percent saying "a lot"

How many times a doctor has done a specific medical procedure	66
Whether a doctor is board certified, that is, has had additional training and testing in his or her area of specialty	65
How many malpractice suits a doctor has had filed against him or her	64
How patients who are surveyed rate how well the doctor communicates	52
Whether a doctor attended a well-known medical school or training program	37
Whether a doctor has admission privileges to send patients to a particular local hospital	35
Whether a doctor has been rated "the best" by a local newspaper or magazine	28
Whether a doctor charges more than other doctors do	18

Question: Please tell me how much you think each of the following kinds of information would tell you about the quality of a doctor, if you wanted to compare two or more doctors. (INSERT ITEM) Would this tell you a lot, something, only a little, or nothing about the quality of a doctor?

Source: Kaiser Family Foundation/Agency for Healthcare Research and Quality/Harvard School of Public Health, "National Survey on Consumers' Experiences with Patient Safety and Quality Information," November 2004.

Table 9-7 What Information Americans Believe Tells Them about the Quality of Hospitals When Comparing Two or More Hospitals

Percent saying "a lot"

Reports of medical errors or mistakes that lead to harm for patients, such as a wrong dose or kind of medicine being given or the wrong operation being done	70
How much experience the hospital has in performing a particular test or surgery you or your family may need	65

(Table continues)

Table 9-7 *Continued*

How many patients die after having surgery at the hospital	57
How patients who are surveyed rate the quality of care	52
Whether the hospital has passed a review and been accredited by an independent organization that evaluates hospitals	50
The number of patients who do NOT get the standard recommended treatments, such as aspirin after heart attack	47
How long it takes the hospital lab to get test results back to you	47
Whether the hospital is a teaching hospital and trains doctors, nurses, and other health professionals	44
Whether the hospital has been rated "the best" by a newspaper or magazine	28

Question: Please tell me how much you think each of the following kinds of information would tell you about the quality of a hospital, if you wanted to compare two or more hospitals. (INSERT ITEM) Would this tell you a lot, something, only a little, or nothing about the quality of a hospital?

Source: Kaiser Family Foundation/Agency for Healthcare Research and Quality/Harvard School of Public Health, "National Survey on Consumers' Experiences with Patient Safety and Quality Information," November 2004.

Table 9-8 What Information Americans Believe Tells Them about the Quality of Health Plans When Comparing Two or More Plans

Percent saying "a lot"

The number of complaints filed by health plan members against the plan	69
Whether the plan has programs to help people with chronic illnesses—such as diabetes, heart disease, or HIV—monitor their condition, and improve their health	67
The number of medical errors or mistakes by the plan's doctors and hospitals that lead to harm for patients	66
How easy it is for plan members to see specialists, such as orthopedists, allergists, and doctors who treat heart problems	65
The percentage of plan members who get preventive care for things like high blood pressure and breast cancer screening and well-baby care	62
The percentage of doctors in the plan who have had a complaint filed against them by patients or lost malpractice lawsuits	62
How quickly patients can get in to be seen by a doctor or get the laboratory tests that they need	61
How patients who are surveyed rate the quality of care	60
The range of health benefits available beyond basic medical coverage, such as prescription drugs, eye care, and dental care	58
Turnover rates of doctors in the plan, that is, the percentage of doctors who leave the plan each year	47
Whether the plan has passed a review and been accredited by an independent organization that evaluates plans	44
How much the health plan costs	40

Question: Please tell me how much you think each of the following kinds of information would tell you about the quality of a health plan, if you wanted to compare two or more health plans. (INSERT ITEM) Would this tell you a lot, something, only a little, or nothing about the quality of a health plan?

Source: Kaiser Family Foundation/Agency for Healthcare Research and Quality/Harvard School of Public Health, "National Survey on Consumers' Experiences with Patient Safety and Quality Information," November 2004.

Table 9-9 Perceived Frequency of Preventable Medical Errors, 2002–2006 (in percent)

	2002[1]	2004[2]	2006[3]
Frequency of medical errors			
Very often	10	7	9
Somewhat often	39	29	34
Not too often	37	44	37
Not often at all	8	8	9
Don't know/Refused	6	12	11
How many could have been prevented[2]			
All of them		11	
Three-quarters of them		25	
Half of them		40	
One-quarter of them		14	
None of them		1	
Don't know/Refused		9	

Question: Sometimes when people are ill and receive medical care, mistakes are made that result in serious harm, such as death, disability, or additional or prolonged treatment. These are called medical errors. Some of these errors are preventable, while others may not be. When people seek help from a health professional, how often do you think such preventable medical errors are made in their care?

Question: Realistically, about how many of these deaths [that occur in hospitals each year as a result of preventable medical errors] do you think could have been prevented?

Sources: [1]Kaiser Family Foundation/Harvard School of Public Health, "Medical Errors: Practicing Physician and Public Views," 2002. [2]Kaiser Family Foundation/Agency for Healthcare Research and Quality/Harvard School of Public Health, "National Survey on Consumers' Experiences with Patient Safety and Quality Information," November 2004. [3]Kaiser Family Foundation/Agency for Healthcare Research and Quality, "2006 Update on Consumers' Views of Patient Safety and Quality Information," September 2006.

Table 9-10 Perceived Causes of Medical Errors

Percent saying "very important"	
Overwork, stress, or fatigue of health professionals	74
Doctors not having enough time with patients	70
Not enough nurses in hospitals	69
Health professionals not working together or not communicating as a team	68
Poor training of health professionals	58
The influence of HMOs and other managed care plans on treatment decisions	55
Poor handwriting by health professionals	52
Medical care being very complicated	47
Lack of computerized medical records	46

Question: I'm going to read you a list of some things that could cause preventable medical errors that result in serious harm to the patient. For each one, please tell me how important each is as a cause of these medical errors. (READ ITEM) Is this a very important cause, somewhat important, not very important, or not important at all?

Source: Kaiser Family Foundation/Agency for Healthcare Research and Quality/Harvard School of Public Health, "National Survey on Consumers' Experiences with Patient Safety and Quality Information," November 2004.

Table 9-11 Perceived Effectiveness of Ways of Reducing Medical Errors

Percent saying "very effective"	
Giving doctors more time to spend with patients	79
Better training of health professionals	72
Requiring hospitals to develop systems to avoid medical errors	72
Requiring hospitals to report all serious medical errors to a state agency	71
Increasing the number of hospital nurses	67
Reducing the work hours of doctors in training to avoid fatigue	66
Using ONLY doctors specially trained in intensive care medicine on intensive care units	66
Fining and suspending the license of health professionals who make medical errors	54
More use of computerized medical records and computers instead of paper records for ordering of drugs and medical tests	51
Limiting certain high-risk medical procedures to hospitals that do a lot of these procedures	49
Including a pharmacist on hospital rounds when doctors review the progress of patients	42
Having hospitalized patients be taken care of by hospital doctors rather than their regular doctors	21
More lawsuits for malpractice	21

Question: Please tell me how effective you think each one of the following would be in reducing preventable medical errors that result in serious harm. (READ ITEM) Do you think this would be very effective, somewhat effective, not very effective, or not effective at all?

Source: Kaiser Family Foundation/Agency for Healthcare Research and Quality/Harvard School of Public Health, "National Survey on Consumers' Experiences with Patient Safety and Quality Information," November 2004.

Table 9-12 Use of Quality Information, 2000–2008 (in percent)

	2000[1]	2004[2]	2006[3]	2008[4]
Total saw any quality information in the past 12 months (Net)	27	35	36	30
Total used quality information to make a health care decision (Subnet)	12	19	20	14
Used quality information about doctors	4	6	7	6
Used quality information about hospitals	4	8	10	7
Used quality information about health plans	9	13	12	9
Saw information, but did not use it	15	16	16	16
Total did not see any quality information	73	65	64	70

Percent who say they would be "very likely" to do each of the following to try to find information about the quality of different doctors, hospitals, or health plans	2000[1]	2004[2]
Ask friends, family members, or co-workers who have had experience as patients for their recommendation	70	65
Ask YOUR doctor, nurse, or other health professionals you know for their recommendation	65	65

(Table continues)

Table 9-12 *Continued*

Go online to an Internet Web site that posts quality information	28	37
Contact someone at your health plan, or refer to materials provided by the plan for quality information	37	36
Order a printed booklet with quality information by phone, mail, or online	21	20
Contact a state agency for quality information	20	18
Refer to a section of a newspaper or magazine that lists quality information	17	16

Question: Did you see any information comparing the quality among different doctors, hospitals, or health insurance plans in the past 12 months, or not?

Question: Did you personally use the information you saw comparing quality among doctors in making any decisions about doctors, or not?

Question: Did you personally use the information you saw comparing quality among hospitals in making any decisions about hospitals, or not?

Question: Did you personally use the information you saw comparing quality among health insurance plans in making any decisions about health plans, or not?

Question: Suppose you wanted to find information comparing the quality of health care among different doctors, hospitals, or health plans. Please tell me how likely you would be to do each of the following to try to find the information about quality that you were looking for. How likely would you be to (INSERT ITEM)? Would you be very likely, somewhat likely, not too likely, or not likely at all to do this?

Sources: [1]Kaiser Family Foundation/Agency for Healthcare Research and Quality, "National Survey on Americans as Health Care Consumers: An Update on the Role of Quality Information," December 2000. [2]Kaiser Family Foundation/Agency for Healthcare Research and Quality/Harvard School of Public Health, "National Survey on Consumers' Experiences with Patient Safety and Quality Information," November 2004. [3]Kaiser Family Foundation/Agency for Healthcare Research and Quality, "2006 Update on Consumers' Views of Patient Safety and Quality Information," September 2006. [4]Kaiser Family Foundation, "2008 Update on Consumers' Views of Patient Safety and Quality Information," October 2008.

Table 9-13 How the Public Chooses among Health Care Providers, 1996–2008 (in percent)

	Choice between two hospitals				Choice between two surgeons at a hospital			Choice between two health plans			
	1996	2000	2004	2008	2000	2004	2008	1996	2000	2004	2008
Familiar	72	62	61	59	50	48	44	52	47	45	40
Higher-ranked	25	32	33	35	38	46	47	43	45	49	52
Don't know	3	6	6	6	11	7	9	5	8	6	8

Question: Suppose you had to choose between two different hospitals. The first one is the hospital you and your family have used for many years without any problems, but the second hospital is rated much higher in quality by the experts. Which hospital would you be more likely to choose?

Question: Suppose you had to choose between two surgeons at a hospital. The first surgeon has treated a friend or family member without any problems, but his ratings are not as high as those of other surgeons at the hospital. The second surgeon's ratings are much higher, but no one you know personally has ever been one of his patients. Which surgeon would you be more likely to choose?

Question: Suppose you had to choose between two health plans. The first one is strongly recommended to you by friends and family, but the second one is rated much higher in quality by independent experts who evaluate plans. If the two plans cost the same, which would you be more likely to choose?

Sources: Kaiser Family Foundation/Agency for Health Care Policy and Research Poll (Storrs, Conn.: Roper Center for Public Opinion Research, July 26–September 5, 1996); Kaiser Family Foundation/Agency for Healthcare Research and Quality, "National Survey on Americans as Health Care Consumers: An Update on the Role of Quality Information," December 2000; Kaiser Family Foundation/Agency for Healthcare Research and Quality/ Harvard School of Public Health, "National Survey on Consumers' Experiences with Patient Safety and Quality Information," November 2004; Kaiser Family Foundation, "2008 Update on Consumers' Views of Patient Safety and Quality Information," October 2008.

Table 9-14 Employers as Source of Quality Information about Health Plans, 1996–2008 (in percent)

	1996[1]	2000[2]	2004[3]	2008[4]
Employers are a good source of information about the quality of different health plans because employers examine plans closely when deciding which ones to offer	36	29	25	36
Don't trust what employers say because employers'main concern is saving the company money on health benefits	58	61	69	53
Don't know	6	10	7	11

Question: Some people think employers are a good source of information about the quality of different health plans because employers examine plans closely when deciding which ones to offer. Other don't trust what employers say because employers' main concern is saving the company money on health benefits. Which comes closer to your view?

Sources: [1]Kaiser Family Foundation/Agency for Health Care Policy and Research Poll (Storrs, Conn.: Roper Center for Public Opinion Research, July 26–September 5, 1996). [2]Kaiser Family Foundation/Agency for Healthcare Research and Quality, "National Survey on Americans as Health Care Consumers: An Update on the Role of Quality Information," December 2000. [3]Kaiser Family Foundation/Agency for Healthcare Research and Quality/Harvard School of Public Health, "National Survey on Consumers' Experiences with Patient Safety and Quality Information," November 2004. [4]Kaiser Family Foundation, "2008 Update on Consumers' Views of Patient Safety and Quality Information," October 2008.

Table 9-15 Importance of Various Health Care Issues in the 2006 and 2008 Elections

In 2006, percent saying "extremely important" in deciding vote for Congress[1]	
The cost of health care and health insurance	41
The number of Americans without health insurance	38
Prescription drug benefits for seniors	31
Medicare	29
Problems with health care quality	26
Abortion	21
Stem cell research	17
Medical malpractice	13

In 2008, most important health care issue in deciding vote for president (in percent)[2]	
Making health care and health insurance more affordable	50
Expanding health insurance coverage for the uninsured	25
Improving the quality of care and reducing medical errors	11
Reducing spending on government health programs like Medicare and Medicaid	7
Reducing the total amount the country spends on health care	6
None of these (vol.)	1

Question: I'm going to read you a list of specific health care issues. For each one, please tell me how important it will be in your vote for U.S. Congress this year. Will it be extremely important in deciding your vote, very important, somewhat important, or not important? (2006)

Question: Now thinking specifically about health care, which one of the following health care issues is most important in your vote for president?

Sources: [1]Kaiser Family Foundation, "Health Poll Report Survey," October 2006. [2] Kaiser Family Foundation, "Kaiser Health Tracking Poll: Election 2008," October 2008.

Chapter 10

ATTITUDES ABOUT HIV/AIDS

Mollyann Brodie, John M. Connolly, Claudia Deane, and
Elizabeth C. Hamel

On June 5, 1981, the U.S. Centers for Disease Control and Prevention (CDC) first reported the emergence of a rare form of pneumonia among a small group of young homosexual men in Los Angeles.[1] In the months that followed, medical and scientific professionals identified this rare pneumonia and other newly developing rare illnesses as part of a syndrome they later labeled acquired immune deficiency syndrome (AIDS). Since 1981 AIDS has become one of the most severe public health threats facing the United States and the world. As of 2009 more than 25 million people worldwide had died of AIDS, and another 33.4 million were estimated to be living with the human immunodeficiency virus (HIV), which causes AIDS.[2]

In the first year after the discovery of the disease, some media and health care professionals in the United States referred to the disease as GRID, or gay-related immune deficiency, which reflected the prevalence of the disease in gay men and the mistaken assumption that the syndrome was inherently linked to homosexuality. In 1982 the CDC formally established the term *AIDS* and noted that although the cause of the syndrome was unknown, there were four identified risk groups: male homosexuals, intravenous drug users, people of Haitian origin, and certain hemophiliacs.

Because the method of transmission remained unknown throughout the early 1980s, hysteria quickly erupted about contracting AIDS, and many feared that the disease could be spread through casual contact, such as touching and kissing, using the same toilet seat, or sharing a drinking glass. Persecution of people with AIDS was also reported. In 1987 arsonists in Florida burned down the home of nine-year-old Ricky Ray, a hemophiliac with HIV.

The authors would like to thank Jennifer Kates, vice president and director of HIV Policy at the Kaiser Family Foundation, for her contributions to this chapter.

In 1984 French scientist Luc Montagnier of the Pasteur Institute and Robert Gallo of the National Cancer Institute in the United States identified HIV as the cause of AIDS. Once the scientific community knew that a virus was causing the disease, public health officials could issue guidelines and regulations to help prevent its spread. In 1988 the U.S. surgeon general and the CDC mailed an informational brochure, "Understanding AIDS," to all U.S. households, the first and only national mailing of this nature.

As certain well-known individuals announced that they had contracted HIV, the public image of the disease and the people it affected began to change. In 1985 Rock Hudson, a popular American film star of the 1950s and 1960s, announced that he had AIDS. He died later that year. Ryan White, an Indiana teenager with hemophilia who was barred from attending school, captured national media attention in 1985. White's infection ran contrary to certain popular perceptions that AIDS was a disease that exclusively affected gay men, and he chose to speak publicly about his experiences as a person with AIDS. In 1991 basketball star Earvin "Magic" Johnson also announced that he was HIV-positive and retired from professional sports, which further changed the image of people with HIV in the United States.

Nevertheless, associations of HIV/AIDS with gay men and intravenous drug users served to make the disease an uncomfortable and controversial topic for many people, including political figures, which may have contributed to most elected officials remaining silent about AIDS in the 1980s. President Ronald Reagan did not mention AIDS in public until 1986, and he gave his first speech specifically addressing HIV/AIDS in 1987. In the latter part of the 1980s, however, Congress accelerated its response to the epidemic. In 1988 Congress passed the Health Omnibus Programs Extension Act (HOPE) to authorize the use of federal funds for AIDS prevention, education, and testing. Two years later Congress enacted the Ryan White Comprehensive AIDS Resources Act (CARE), which provides federal funds for community-based care and treatment services. Since its initial passage Congress has reauthorized this act four times: in 1996, 2000, 2006, and 2009. President Bill Clinton established the first White House Office of National AIDS policy in 1993 and the Presidential Advisory Council on HIV/AIDS in 1995.

In the 1990s AIDS became one of the gravest public health threats in the United States. By 1992 the disease had become the leading cause of death for all American men ages twenty-five to forty-four, and in 1994 it became the leading cause of death for all Americans in that age group and remained so in 1995. The rate of new HIV infections in the United States stabilized in the 1990s, and the demographic makeup of the population with HIV began to change. Although men who have sex with men continue to account for a large share of new AIDS cases, the disease now increasingly affects women and African Americans. In fact, African Americans currently make up roughly one-half of all new AIDS cases.[3] Women now account for 27 percent of new AIDS diagnoses, compared with just 8 percent in 1985.[4]

Scientific advances since the early 1990s have done a great deal to extend life expectancy for people with HIV and prevent perinatal transmission of HIV from mother to child. By 1997 the rate of AIDS-related deaths had decreased by more than 40 percent compared to the previous year, chiefly due to the widespread use of highly active antiretroviral therapy. Despite these advances, HIV has become a global problem, reaching virtually every region of the world. In fact, HIV is a leading cause of death worldwide, and the number one cause of death in Africa.[5] The spread of HIV has become especially devastating in sub-Saharan Africa, where access to new, effective treatments is limited, and AIDS has begun to cause life expectancies to drop in certain countries in this region. To combat the global spread of HIV, the Global Fund to Fight AIDS, Tuberculosis, and Malaria was established in 2002, and in 2003, President George W. Bush established the President's Emergency Plan for AIDS Relief, a five-year, $15 billion initiative to address HIV in particularly hard-hit countries. Congress reauthorized PEPFAR in 2008, including an additional $39 billion for global HIV through 2013.

In this chapter, we provide a summary of U.S. public opinion concerning HIV/AIDS both domestically and globally. We first present a general overview of broad public perceptions about HIV/AIDS and examine trends in knowledge and attitudes about the disease. The chapter then focuses on public opinion in three more specific areas: (1) opinion on domestic public policy and spending on HIV/AIDS; (2) the opinions and experiences of African Americans and Latinos living in the United States regarding HIV/AIDS; and (3) American opinions on the global epidemic.

General Perceptions and Trends

Views of AIDS have changed dramatically since its sudden emergence in 1981. Over time, as the epidemic changed, Americans have become significantly less alarmed about the extent to which AIDS is a domestic threat, with more now seeing it as an urgent problem globally rather than at home. Fear of contracting the disease also has dropped at the same time that a growing number of Americans report knowing someone personally affected by AIDS.

In 1987 a striking majority of the public, 68 percent, named AIDS as the most urgent health problem facing the nation. This easily pushed it to the top of the public's list of pressing health issues, a ranking it held throughout the 1990s. In 1991, with knowledge about AIDS on the rise, that number dropped to 45 percent, but still topped the list. In 2006, 17 percent named AIDS as the nation's most urgent health problem, placing it third behind the percentages naming cancer and heart disease. By 2009 the share had declined to 6 percent, ranking behind other diseases such as cancer (28 percent), heart disease (14 percent), obesity/nutrition disorders (14 percent), and diabetes (8 percent), as well as other health care–related concerns such as the uninsured (18 percent), health care costs (17 percent), and health care access (9 percent) as the most urgent health problem facing the nation (**Table 10–1**).[6]

In addition to the smaller shares of the public naming HIV/AIDS as the most important health problem facing the nation, a plurality of the public continues to believe that the country is making progress in its response to the domestic HIV/AIDS epidemic (45 percent in 2009, a share that has been fairly consistent since 1997). Moreover, the share of the public saying the United States is losing ground on the problem of HIV/AIDS has decreased (**Table 10–2**).[7]

Since 2000 Americans have been more likely to see HIV/AIDS as an urgent health problem for the world than for the nation. In 2009 more than three times as many named HIV/AIDS as the most urgent health problem facing the world (21 percent) as facing the nation (6 percent).[8]

Concern about becoming infected with HIV also has receded. Between 1997 and 2009 the share saying they were very concerned about becoming infected declined from 24 percent to 13 percent, and the share saying they were at least somewhat concerned about this possibility declined from 41 percent to 25 percent. In addition, in 1997, 52 percent of parents said they were very concerned about a son or daughter becoming infected; that figure fell to 33 percent in 2009. In the same time period, the share saying they were at least somewhat concerned about this possibility fell from 73 percent to 56 percent (**Table 10–3**).[9]

Over this period, the proportion of people saying they know someone with HIV/AIDS has increased. Between 1987 and 1991, that number rose from 9 percent to 17 percent.[10] The share continued to rise to around four in ten in 1995 and has remained about steady since then (**Table 10–4**).[11]

Knowledge about HIV

Understanding the level of public knowledge about HIV/AIDS and about which groups have been most affected by the disease is important because knowledge may influence the amount of risk that some individuals feel and how they view others who may be affected, and they may alter their behavior accordingly. Since the first few years of the U.S. epidemic, public knowledge about the disease has increased over time in many areas, but some significant misconceptions still remain.

At the most basic level, information serves a public health purpose: to slow transmission. The public needs to understand the disease and how it is transmitted to reduce risk. But because knowledge about the disease is also related to attitudes about relevant public policies, measuring misinformation has become a critical component of understanding public opinion on the topic.

In the 1980s a substantial minority of Americans held mistaken views about how HIV could be transmitted. In 1985, 37 percent of Americans said that you were at least somewhat likely to be at risk of contracting HIV by working near someone with the disease; this figure declined to 16 percent by 1987.[12] In 1987 a significant minority of Americans also incorrectly believed that you could get AIDS from mosquitoes (32 percent), from being coughed or sneezed on (25 percent), from a drinking fountain (22 percent), by sharing a swimming pool (21 percent), from sharing a telephone (12 percent), and by being touched by someone who has the disease (10 percent).[13]

Recent trends indicate that public knowledge has increased dramatically about how HIV/ AIDS is spread, but misconceptions remain. In 1985, 44 percent of Americans did not know that HIV cannot be transmitted through sharing a drinking glass; by 2009 the share had dropped to 27 percent. In the same time period, the proportion of the public that did not know that HIV cannot be transmitted through touching a toilet seat fell from 31 percent to 17 percent. Yet, since 1990 there has been almost no change in the share who do not know that HIV cannot be transmitted in these ways (**Table 10–5**).[14]

Other misconceptions about HIV transmission and treatment remain relatively common. In 2006 more than half of the public did not know that having another sexually transmitted disease, such as herpes or gonorrhea, can increase a person's risk of getting HIV (56 percent), and in 2009 a similar share did not know that a pregnant woman with HIV can take drugs to reduce the risk of her baby being infected (55 percent). Smaller shares in 2009 did not know that there is currently no cure for HIV (18 percent) and that medications can lengthen the lives of people with HIV (12 percent).[15]

The public also holds misconceptions about rates of HIV infection and which groups were most affected. African Americans made up approximately half (49 percent) of all new HIV diagnoses in the United States in 2005, and whites were 31 percent of new cases.[16] Nevertheless, two-thirds of Americans in 2006 believed that African Americans and whites are equally likely to become infected with HIV.[17]

The CDC reports major challenges in accessing HIV treatment in the United States, estimating that about half of those who need antiretrovirals are not getting them.[18] In 2006, seven in ten Americans believed that most people who need medication for HIV in the United States do not receive it; 17 percent said they believed that those who need medication received it; and 13 percent said they did not know.[19]

At the same time, 57 percent of the public in 2006 said that most people at high risk for HIV infection in the United States have access to needed prevention services, such as HIV education, testing, and counseling; 34 percent said they did not; and 9 percent said they did not know.[20] We have no clear data measuring what percentage of those needing preventive services actually get them, but because the CDC estimates that 21 percent of those who are HIV positive do not know it, and because there were more than 56,000 new infections in 2006, prevention is clearly not reaching all who need it.[21]

Perceptions, Stigma, and Discrimination

Because HIV/AIDS historically has affected marginalized groups in American society, such as gay men and intravenous drug users, certain types of stigma and discrimination have been associated with the disease. In fact, many Americans still associate HIV/AIDS primarily with these groups. In an open-ended question in 2006, a plurality (43 percent) named gay men as one of the two groups most likely to become infected, and one-third (33 percent) named drugs users.[22]

But as the demographics of the disease have changed and public knowledge has increased, many early perceptions have faded, and majorities of Americans have expressed tolerant and even compassionate views of those suffering from AIDS. Still, public opinion data show that a certain amount of stigma has persisted through recent years.

In the early years of the epidemic, many Americans expressed discomfort with being physically close to someone who had AIDS. In 1987, one in four adults reported that they would refuse to work alongside a person with AIDS, and 40 percent said they would be at least somewhat upset if a treatment or housing center for patients with AIDS were located in their neighborhood.[23] A 1989 survey asked the public to rank a list of facilities that they would welcome in their neighborhood, and group homes for AIDS patients ranked eleventh out of the fourteen facilities on that list, ahead of only factories, garbage landfills, and prisons.[24]

A notable minority of Americans also showed signs of hostility or intolerance toward people with AIDS in the 1980s, especially those who contracted the disease through sexual practices or drug use rather than through blood transfusions or perinatally. In a 1990 survey, 27 percent of the public disagreed with the statement that people who contracted HIV through homosexual activity should be treated with compassion, and 30 percent disagreed if transmission occurred through illegal drug use, while just 3 percent would withhold compassion if the transmission resulted from a blood transfusion.[25]

At the same time, a majority of Americans were sensitive to the existence of these feelings of intolerance. Six in ten Americans in 1990 reported that they believed AIDS had caused unfair discrimination against homosexuals, up from 49 percent in 1987.[26]

Over the last two decades, public attitudes appear to have become more sympathetic to people with HIV, although stigma and discomfort do remain. The public has become less likely to believe that it is someone's own fault if they contract HIV. In 1987, 51 percent agreed with a statement that if a person became infected, it was his or her own fault; after falling to 33 percent in 1991, that figure stood at 40 percent in 2002.[27]

The proportion of Americans who say they would feel uncomfortable working with someone with HIV declined from 33 percent in 1997 to 23 percent in 2009. In 2009 nearly three-quarters said they would be very (44 percent) or somewhat comfortable (29 percent) (Table 10–6).[28]

Although majorities also felt at least somewhat comfortable having close relationships with someone who was HIV-positive, the overall comfort level with having these relationships was somewhat less than it was for working with someone with HIV. In 2009, 53 percent said they would be very or somewhat comfortable having a roommate who was HIV-positive, with 20 percent saying they would be very comfortable. Sixty-three percent of parents said they would be very or somewhat comfortable with their children having a teacher who was HIV-positive, with 17 percent saying they would be very comfortable. People were least likely to report being comfortable having their food prepared by someone who was HIV-positive, with 46 percent saying they would be comfortable, and 27 percent saying they would be very uncomfortable.[29]

Lingering misconceptions about how HIV is transmitted are potentially a contributing factor to prejudice against HIV-positive individuals. People who harbor such misconceptions are much more likely to express discomfort about working with someone who has HIV or AIDS than those who know that HIV cannot be transmitted in these ways. People who believe that HIV might be transmitted through sharing a drinking glass, touching a toilet seat, or swimming in a pool with someone who is HIV-positive are about three times as likely (43 percent) as those who do not believe HIV is transmitted in any of these ways (13 percent) to say they feel at least somewhat uncomfortable working with someone who has HIV or AIDS.[30]

Most Americans believe that prejudice and discrimination against people living with HIV and AIDS still exists in the United States, and these levels have remained relatively stable. Although questions have been worded somewhat differently, the share saying there is "a lot" of discrimination has remained fairly steady at around half since 1986 (Table 10–7).[31]

One concern about HIV-related stigma is whether it discourages people from getting tested for the disease. Public opinion data show that stigma is not a stated concern for most people, but for a minority of the public, HIV-related stigma may have some relation to the decision not to get tested. In 2000, 33 percent said they would be at least somewhat concerned that people would think less of them if they found out they had been tested for HIV; by 2009 the share had fallen to sixteen percent.[32]

In recent years, people also have said that the HIV/AIDS epidemic had an impact on behavior and culture in the United States. In 2006 almost six in ten (58 percent) said the epidemic has made people more likely to practice safe sex, a share that has remained relatively stable since 2004 (55 percent).[33] Nearly half (47 percent) also said that it has made people more likely to talk openly about sex, but half also thought that the epidemic has made people more likely to discriminate against gays and lesbians.[34]

Early HIV Policy Debates

Public health policies have been central to controlling HIV/AIDS since its emergence in the United States in 1981. As with other public health issues in a government controlled by popularly elected officials, public opinion about federal and state responses to HIV/AIDS may constrain, if not shape, policy options.

In the early years of the epidemic, it was not only the public that had little understanding of AIDS; public health and medical professionals also were struggling to identify the virus they suspected was behind the disease. Although the health community had a growing body of knowledge about how AIDS was being spread, it took three years after its discovery in the United States to identify HIV as its cause.

This lack of knowledge in the first several years of the epidemic caused much of the public debate around AIDS to focus on the issue of privacy, as substantial majorities of Americans tended to support aggressive policy measures that might sacrifice individual privacy to curtail the spread of AIDS. In 1987, 81 percent felt that controlling the spread of the disease should take precedence over concerns of personal privacy, and 74 percent felt that identifying those who were infected with HIV should take precedence over concern for personal privacy.[35] In addition, 29 percent supported the creation of a tattoo for persons who tested positive for the disease, which was an increase from 15 percent in 1985.[36] In 1991 about eight in ten favored mandatory HIV screening for people in high-risk groups, such as gay men and intravenous drug users.[37]

Early on, Americans were concerned about HIV-positive people in public professions, such as teaching and health care, and about HIV-positive visitors and immigrants to the United States. In 1987, 39 percent of Americans said that public school employees should be dismissed if they had AIDS. In 1991, nine in ten favored requiring all health care professionals to get tested for HIV and to reveal their HIV status to patients. Forty-nine percent felt health care workers should be prohibited from practicing if they tested positive for HIV, and nearly two-thirds said they would stop treatment with a health care provider if they found out that he or she had HIV.[38]

In 1985, 75 percent of Americans said they favored barring foreign visitors who were infected with HIV from entering the United States.[39] In 1990 that proportion dropped to 49 percent. Also in 1990 nearly six in ten believed that HIV-positive immigrants should be excluded from the country.[40] In 1993 nearly two out of three Americans said they were at least "somewhat concerned" about immigrants spreading AIDS.[41] HIV and immigration is still a policy issue today, and HIV remained grounds for inadmissibility of visitors and immigrants until January 2010, but no public opinion surveys have been fielded on this topic since the early 1990s.

Trends in Americans' policy preferences indicate that intolerance toward people with HIV/AIDS decreased in the latter part of the 1980s. Surveys found a sizable decrease between 1987 and 1991 in the share of people who said they would refuse to work alongside a person with AIDS, from 25 percent to 16 percent. Similarly, the share saying that children with AIDS should not be allowed to attend school decreased from 39 percent in 1985 to 9 percent in 1991. The proportion of Americans favoring quarantine or isolation measures declined from 20 percent to 10 percent between 1987 and 1991. The proportion supporting a landlord's right to evict a tenant with AIDS declined from 17 percent to 10 percent in same period. But the proportion of Americans who thought that employers should have the right to fire a worker with AIDS was little changed from 1987 (25 percent) to 1991 (21 percent).[42]

Spending on HIV/AIDS

Throughout the epidemic, Americans have been supportive of government spending on HIV/AIDS. In the 1980s most Americans supported increasing the level of government funding devoted to combating the AIDS epidemic. In 1987 more than two-thirds (69 percent) of Americans favored increased federal spending for AIDS research.[43] In 1991 six in ten Americans believed the government was not doing enough about AIDS.[44]

Since 1997 a majority of the public usually has said the federal government spends too little on HIV/AIDS in the United States, a share that rose from 52 percent in 2004 to 63 percent in 2006, and fell back to 50 percent in 2009 as the economic recession set in. During this time, less than one in ten thought that the federal government was spending too much on HIV/AIDS (Table 10–8).[45] In response to a similar question, about federal spending on HIV in comparison to other diseases, about a third (35 percent) of Americans in 2009 said that spending was too low, and a similar share (36 percent) said it was about right. Only 7 percent thought it was too high (Table 10–9).[46]

The widespread interest in increasing federal spending may be linked to Americans' optimism that putting more resources into the fight against AIDS would make a real difference. In 2009, six in ten said that spending more money on HIV/AIDS prevention would lead to meaningful progress in slowing the epidemic in the United States, and nearly half (48 percent) said that spending more money on HIV/AIDS treatment would lead to progress. Smaller shares said that spending more money on either prevention (31 percent) or treatment (38 percent) would not make much difference in controlling the epidemic (Table 10–10).[47]

Policy Issues from 1990 to the Present

As the HIV/AIDS epidemic developed in the United States, the nature of the policy debates began to shift toward issues other than spending and privacy. Understanding about HIV transmission and treatment became more sophisticated, which caused public discussions about HIV/AIDS to focus on preventive measures, public education, and testing, as well as treatment and vaccine research.

Education

Americans have consistently supported widespread education about AIDS. In 1990 the vast majority, 94 percent, supported education about AIDS in the schools, and roughly eight out of ten wanted that education to include information about condoms as a preventive measure. About the same proportion felt that AIDS education should begin in elementary school, with roughly 40 percent saying it is acceptable to teach school-age children about condoms.[48] Close to four in ten (37 percent) also supported the distribution of condoms in public high schools, and 70 percent found condom advertisements acceptable on television.[49] Although 52 percent felt that mandatory testing would reduce the spread of AIDS, 72 percent believed that education would be a more effective method.[50]

Public support for the inclusion of condom education has remained strong. In 2004, 74 percent said that government should fund programs that emphasize condoms as the best method of protection against HIV/AIDS.[51] In 2006 strong majorities of the public identified increasing the use of condoms (83 percent), more education about abstinence for young people (82 percent), and getting more people tested for HIV (72 percent) as very important priorities for HIV/AIDS prevention in the United States. When people were forced to choose one of these approaches as the most important, more than half chose abstinence education; almost a quarter chose condom use; 9 percent said testing; and 13 percent said all of these measures were equally important. When offered as an explicit option, comprehensive programs are even more popular. Three-quarters believed that the focus of HIV prevention programs for youth should combine education about abstinence, being faithful to one partner, and using condoms. One in ten said programs should focus mainly on abstinence, and 13 percent said they should focus on condom use.[52]

Needle Exchange

The use of federal funds for programs that provide clean needles to intravenous drug users as a means of preventing the spread of HIV has been a controversial topic since the late 1980s, and there was a ban on such funding from 1988 until 2009, when President Obama lifted it. As the course of the epidemic wore on, however, Americans became more supportive of needle exchange programs to prevent the spread of HIV among intravenous drug users. From 1988 to 1990 the level of public support for the distribution of free, clean needles to drug users as a way to prevent the spread of AIDS increased from 40 percent to 51 percent.[53] In 2000 the share stood at 58 percent.[54]

Testing

Americans have also seen testing as a critical tool for controlling the spread of HIV. In 2009 nearly half (47 percent) of Americans said they had been tested for HIV at some point, including 16 percent who said they had been tested in the past year. People ages eighteen to twenty-nine (54 percent) and thirty to forty-nine (61 percent) were more likely to say they had been tested than those age fifty to sixty-four (40 percent) and those sixty-five and older (16 percent). In addition, the share of non-elderly adults who said they had been tested for HIV increased slowly but steadily from 1997 to 2004, and has since leveled off at just over half (53 percent in 2009).[55]

A majority of the public has supported measures that would make HIV testing more frequent and widespread in the United States. In 2004 about two-thirds (65 percent) said that their communities would benefit from free and confidential HIV testing and counseling.[56] In 2006 about two-thirds (65 percent) said that HIV testing should be treated just like routine screening for other diseases, and about a quarter (27 percent) said it should require special procedures, such as written permission from the patient. The CDC now recommends routine HIV screening for everyone ages thirteen to sixty-four in health care settings. A majority of the public (65 percent) also thought rapid home HIV-testing was a good idea, but when asked their personal preference, most (62 percent) still preferred to get tested in a doctor's office rather than use a home test.[57]

Vaccine

A large share of Americans support vaccine research as a major tool in the fight against the AIDS epidemic. In 2003, 63 percent said that a vaccine would be the best hope for controlling AIDS, and 82 percent said that research to develop an HIV vaccine is just as important as programs to educate the public about HIV prevention. At the same time, certain disproportionately affected groups have doubts about the safety of HIV vaccine trials and the government's handling of an HIV vaccine. Seventy-eight percent of African Americans and 56 percent of Latinos either incorrectly believed that the vaccines being tested could cause HIV infection or did not know whether or not the vaccines would do so. Perhaps as a reflection of that belief, only 35 percent of African Americans (and 29 percent of the general population) are supportive of someone they know volunteering for an HIV vaccine trial. In addition, approximately 47 percent of African Americans and 27 percent of Latinos believed an HIV vaccine already exists and is being kept secret.[58]

African American and Latino Attitudes and Experiences with HIV

African Americans and Latinos have been disproportionately affected by the HIV/AIDS epidemic in the United States. In 2008 the CDC estimated that the rate of new HIV infections among African Americans was seven times that of whites, and the rate for Latinos was three times higher.[59] Moreover, this impact appears to be reflected in both groups' attitudes and perceptions.

Since 1995 African Americans and Latinos have consistently been more likely than whites to name HIV as the most urgent health problem facing the nation (**Table 10–11**). African Americans and Latinos are also more likely than whites to say the United States is losing ground in its efforts to control the spread of HIV/AIDS (**Table 10–12**).[60]

Although personal concern about becoming infected with HIV has decreased over time for all racial groups, larger proportions of African Americans and Latinos than whites said they were concerned about becoming infected with HIV, as well as having a child become infected. In 2009 only 6 percent of whites said they were very concerned about becoming infected with the disease, but 38 percent of African Americans and 25 percent of Latinos said they were very concerned (**Table 10–13**).[61] About a quarter of white parents said they were very concerned about the possibility of a child becoming infected, but this was true of 68 percent of African American parents and 39 percent of Latino parents (**Table 10–14**).[62]

African Americans (58 percent) were also considerably more likely than whites (43 percent) and Latinos (37 percent) to say that they knew someone who has AIDS, died from AIDS, or has HIV (**Table 10–15**). In addition, African Americans (40 percent) and Latinos (35 percent) were far more likely than whites (10 percent) to say that HIV/AIDS has become a more urgent problem in their local communities than it was a few years ago (**Tables 10–16**).[63]

More than other racial and ethnic groups, African Americans seem to have embraced the message that testing is important. In 2009 African Americans under age sixty-five were more likely than whites and Latinos in this age range to say they had been tested for HIV in the last year.[64] In 2006 African Americans were also more likely than whites to say that getting more people tested for HIV should be a very important priority for HIV prevention and spending more money on HIV testing would lead to meaningful progress in slowing the epidemic in the United States.[65]

Views on the Global HIV Epidemic

Over the last two decades, the rate of domestic infection has leveled off, and the availability of effective treatments for Americans with HIV/AIDS has increased markedly, but HIV has been exploding in other parts of the world, particularly in developing countries in sub-Saharan Africa. As the situation worsened, the eyes of governments, activists, and the media turned to the global epidemic, rather than HIV/AIDS in the United States.[66] In light of this development, public opinion surveys have begun asking Americans' opinions about HIV in the developing world and how the U.S. government ought to respond to it.

Between 2000 and 2006, roughly one in three Americans named HIV/AIDS as the most urgent health problem facing the world. That share fell to 21 percent in 2009, ranking HIV second behind cancer (31 percent) in the share perceiving it as the world's most urgent health problem. As more attention has been given to the global epidemic, Americans have expressed divided assessments of the progress being made. In three surveys fielded between 2002 and 2006 about a third said the world is making progress in fighting HIV/AIDS, while between four and five in ten said they believed that the world was losing ground. Between 2006 and 2009, however, the share saying "making progress" increased from 36 percent to 46 percent; the share saying "losing ground" decreased from 40 percent to 32 percent; and for the first time, more people felt the world was making progress in fighting the disease than felt it was losing ground (**Table 10–17**).[67]

In 2009 large majorities believed that developing countries had an inadequate level of care and prevention services. Eighty-nine percent said they believed that most people in developing countries who needed medication for HIV did not get it, and 72 percent said that most people at high risk for HIV in developing countries did not have access to necessary prevention services, such as HIV education, testing, and counseling.[68]

A majority of Americans also placed blame for this perceived shortfall on many different types of organizations and leaders. In 2006, 76 percent said the governments in developing countries hardest-hit by HIV were not doing enough to fight the disease; 64 percent cited pharmaceutical companies; 62 percent, President Bush and his administration; 61 percent, the United Nations; 61 percent, the U.S. government; and 54 percent, governments of developed nations other than the United States. Forty-six percent said that international nonprofit organizations and foundations were not doing enough to combat the global HIV epidemic[69] (**Table 10–18**).

The public has been generally supportive of foreign aid for HIV; in fact, people are more in favor of this type of spending than they are of foreign aid in general. In 2009 more than half of Americans (52 percent) felt that the United States was spending too much on foreign aid. The same survey, however, found that about two-thirds said the amount the United States was spending to deal with the problem of HIV/AIDS in developing countries was either too little (37 percent) or the right amount (29 percent), and just 16 percent said that the United States was spending too much.[70] Similar to views of spending on the domestic epidemic, trend data indicate that Americans' willingness to have the federal government spend money on the global epidemic increased between 2002 and 2006, and decreased somewhat as the recession hit in 2009. The share of the public saying the United States is spending too little on HIV/AIDS in developing countries increased from 31 percent in 2002 to 56 percent in 2006, and stood at 37 percent in 2009 (**Table 10–19**).[71]

A similar trend is evident in the share of the public that feels the United States has a responsibility to contribute to the fight against HIV/AIDS in developing countries. The percentage that said they agreed that the United States had such a responsibility to spend more money on the epidemic increased steadily from 44 percent in 2002 to 60 percent in 2006, and fell back to 49 percent in 2009. At the same time, the proportion saying they agree that the country should address problems at home rather than spend more money to deal with the HIV/AIDS epidemic in developing countries fell from 78 percent in 2002 to 67 percent in 2006, and increased again to 76 percent in 2009.[72]

When forced to choose between addressing domestic problems before spending money on the global HIV/AIDS epidemic or accepting responsibility as a global leader for fighting HIV/AIDS overseas, 69 percent in a 2009 survey said the United States should focus its attention at home, while 23 percent said it has a responsibility to spend more money to fight the global epidemic (**Table 10–20**).[73]

Americans also have clear priorities for how the U.S. government ought to contribute to the fight against global HIV/AIDS. In 2009, 59 percent said the government's top priority should be spending for prevention and education; 15 percent said spending for treatment and care; and 18 percent said reducing the amount of money that developing countries owe so they can do more to fight the epidemic themselves. The majority of the public also believes that U.S. spending on HIV/AIDS will have a positive effect in the fight against the epidemic, with 56 percent saying that spending more money on HIV prevention in developing countries would lead to meaningful progress in slowing the epidemic; 36 percent said that it would not make much difference.[74]

When asked why it has been difficult to control the spread of HIV/AIDS in developing countries, large majorities said the major reasons were the unwillingness of people in these countries to change their unsafe sexual practices (79 percent), developing countries' governments not doing enough themselves (78 percent), poverty (72 percent), corruption and misuse of funds (69 percent), and lack of effective programs (66 percent). Thirty-four percent said that a lack of money from the U.S. government and other developed nations to fund prevention and treatment was a major reason. When forced to choose the most important reason, about three in ten (31 percent) said unwillingness of people in developing countries to change their unsafe sexual practices; 17 percent each said widespread poverty and corruption and misuse of funds; 15 percent cited the lack of action from governments of developing countries; 13 percent said lack of effective programs; and 3 percent chose a lack of money from the United States and other developed countries.[75]

Conclusion

Since 1981 much about HIV/AIDS and public opinion on the epidemic has changed. Although the disease initially affected a mostly white population of gay men and intravenous drug users in the United States, it has now become a major challenge for the African American community and women as well. Moreover, the epidemic has become more global. As the rate of new infections stabilized in the United States, the spread of HIV in sub-Saharan Africa has become so devastating that the life expectancy in some countries is falling. New hotspots are coming to the world's attention: the Caribbean now follows sub-Saharan Africa as the region with the highest percentage of its population infected with HIV. China and India have relatively low prevalence rates, but their large populations translate into substantial numbers of people living with HIV. Parts of Eastern Europe and Central Asia are also areas of concern.

Public attitudes and knowledge about HIV/AIDS in the United States have changed a great deal since the 1980s. Americans are now more likely to see the disease as an urgent problem for the world than for the United States, and they are less likely to express personal concern about becoming infected with HIV. In addition, more of the public now feels comfortable being around, and having personal relationships with, people with HIV/AIDS. The public is more knowledgeable about how the disease is spread, although a lack of knowledge about transmission persists among small shares of the public.

As Americans have seen HIV/AIDS become a global problem, they became more supportive of foreign aid for HIV/AIDS prevention and treatment efforts in developing countries between 2002 and 2006. When the global economic recession took hold in 2009, however, public opinion began to shift back toward addressing problems at home first rather than spending more to fight HIV in developing countries.

What happens on the global front will be determined largely by how the epidemic evolves in sub-Saharan Africa, China, India, and Russia. It remains uncertain how long the devastation will continue in Africa. Moreover, China and India, the world's two most populous countries, have only recently begun to grapple with the challenges of this disease. The United States has not succeeded in reducing its infection rate, and the epidemic has morphed so that members of racial and ethnic minority groups now represent the majority of those living with the disease. Both a cure and a vaccine for HIV/AIDS continue to elude scientists at the present time. Even if these life-saving technologies become available, ensuring access to them in many poor and politically unstable regions that have been most affected by the epidemic will present another set of immense challenges. Consequently, it seems clear that this disease will continue to be an extremely important national and global health problem for the foreseeable future.

Notes

[1] Except where noted, the historical overview in this chapter is based on Kaiser Family Foundation "The Global HIV/AIDS Timeline," http://www.kff.org/hivaids/timeline/hivtimeline.cfm.

[2] Kaiser Family Foundation, "The HIV/AIDS Epidemic in the United States," HIV/AIDS Policy Fact Sheet, September 2009, http://www.kff.org/hivaids/upload/3029–10.pdf.

[3] Kaiser Family Foundation, "Black Americans and HIV/AIDS," HIV/AIDS Policy Fact Sheet, September 2009, http://www.kff.org/hivaids/upload/6089–07.pdf.

[4] Kaiser Family Foundation, "Women and HIV/AIDS in the United States," HIV/AIDS Policy Fact Sheet, September 2009 http://www.kff.org/hivaids/upload/6092–07.pdf.

[5] Kaiser Family Foundation, "The Global HIV/AIDS Epidemic," U.S. Global Health Policy Fact Sheet, April 2009, http://www.kff.org/hivaids/upload/3030–13.pdf.

[6] Gallup polls (Storrs, Conn.: Roper Center for Public Opinion Research, October 23–26, 1987; May 2–5, 1991; March 26–29, 1992); *Los Angeles Times* Poll (Storrs, Conn.: Roper Center for Public Opinion Research, January 21–24, 1990); Kaiser Family Foundation polls (Storrs, Conn.: Roper Center for Public Opinion Research, November 27–December 17, 1995; September 17–October 19, 1997; August 14–October 26, 2000; March 15–May 11, 2004; October 4–9, 2005; March 24–April 18, 2006, January 26–March 8, 2009); *Washington Post*/Kaiser Family Foundation/Harvard University Poll (Storrs, Conn.: Roper Center for Public Opinion Research, June 13–23, 2002).

[7] Kaiser Family Foundation trend data in "Kaiser Family Foundation 2009 Survey of Americans on HIV/AIDS: Summary of Findings on the Domestic Epidemic," April 2009, http://www.kff .org/kaiserpolls/upload/7889.pdf.

[8] Kaiser Family Foundation polls, August 14–October 26, 2000; March 15–May 11, 2004; October 4–9, 2005; March 24–April 18, 2006; January 26–March 8, 2009; *Washington Post*/ Kaiser Family Foundation/Harvard University Poll, June 13–23, 2002.

[9] Kaiser Family Foundation polls, September 17–October 19, 1997; August 14–October 26, 2000; March 15–May 11, 2004; October 4–9, 2005; March 24–April 18, 2006; January 26–March 8, 2009; *Washington Post*/Kaiser Family Foundation/Harvard University Poll, June 13–23, 2002.

[10] Robert J. Blendon, Karen Donelan, and Richard A. Knox, "Public Opinion and AIDS: Lessons for the Second Decade," *JAMA: Journal of the American Medical Association* 267 (February 19, 1992): 981–986.

[11] Kaiser Family Foundation trend data in "Kaiser Family Foundation 2009 Survey of Americans on HIV/AIDS: Summary of Findings on the Domestic Epidemic," April 2009.

[12] Harris Poll (Storrs, Conn.: Roper Center for Public Opinion Research, September 5–8, 1985); National Center for Health Statistics Poll (Storrs, Conn.: Roper Center for Public Opinion Research, December 1987).

[13] Gallup Poll, October 23–26, 1987.

[14] The figures presented here include those who thought HIV/AIDS could be transmitted in each of these ways, plus those who did not know if it could. ABC News/*Washington Post* polls (Storrs, Conn.: Roper Center for Public Opinion Research, September 19–23, 1985; March 5–9, 1987); ABC News Poll (Storrs, Conn.: Roper Center for Public Opinion Research, June 15–19, 1990); Kaiser Family Foundation polls, August 14–October 26, 2000; March 15–May 11, 2004; March 24–April 18, 2006; January 26–March 8, 2009.

[15] Kaiser Family Foundation polls, March 24–April 18, 2006; January 26–March 8, 2009.

[16] Centers for Disease Control and Prevention, "HIV/AIDS and African Americans," http://www.cdc.gov/hiv/topics/aa/index.htm.

[17] Kaiser Family Foundation trend data in "2006 Kaiser Family Foundation Survey of Americans on HIV/AIDS," May 2006, http://www.kff.org/kaiserpolls/upload/Chartpack–2006-Survey-of-Americans-on-HIV-AIDS.pdf.

[18] Eyasu Teshale, L. Kamimoto, N. Harris, J. Li, H. Wang, and M. McKenna, "Estimated Number of HIV-infected Persons Eligible for and Receiving HIV Antiretroviral Therapy, 2000—United States," 12th Conference on Retroviruses and Opportunistic Infections, February 2005, http://www.retroconference.org/2005/CD/Abstracts/24468.htm.

[19] Kaiser Family Foundation trend data in "2006 Kaiser Family Foundation Survey of Americans on HIV/AIDS," May 2006.

[20] Ibid.

[21] Kaiser Family Foundation, "The HIV/AIDS Epidemic in the United States."

[22] Kaiser Family Foundation trend data in "2006 Kaiser Family Foundation Survey of Americans on HIV/AIDS," May 2006.

[23] Gallup Poll, October 23–26, 1987; Metropolitan Life/Paul Loewenwarter Productions/Louis Harris and Associates Poll (Storrs, Conn.: Roper Center for Public Opinion Research, July 29–August 10, 1987).

[24] Andrew B. Borinstein, "Public Attitudes Toward Persons with Mental Illness," *Health Affairs* 11 (Fall 1992): 186–196.

[25] Blendon, Donelan, and Knox, "Public Opinion and AIDS: Lessons for the Second Decade."

[26] Ibid.

[27] Gallup polls, October 23–26, 1987; May 2–5, 1991; *Washington Post*/Kaiser Family Foundation/Harvard University Poll, June 13–23, 2002.

[28] Kaiser Family Foundation polls, September 17–October 19, 1997; August 14–October 26, 2000; March 15–May 11, 2004; March 24–April 18, 2006; January 26–March 8, 2009.

[29] Kaiser Family Foundation, "Kaiser Family Foundation 2009 Survey of Americans on HIV/AIDS: Summary of Findings on the Domestic Epidemic," April 2009.

[30] Ibid.

[31] CBS News Poll (Storrs, Conn.: Roper Center for Public Opinion Research, October 14–16, 1986); CBS News/*New York Times* polls (Storrs, Conn.: Roper Center for Public Opinion Research, May 22–24, 1990; June 3–6, 1991); Kaiser Family Foundation polls, August 14–October 26, 2000; March 15–May 11, 2004; March 24–April 18, 2006.

[32] Kaiser Family Foundation polls, August 14–October 26, 2000; March 24–April 18, 2006; January 26–March 8, 2009.

[33] Associated Press/IPSOS Public Affairs Poll (Storrs, Conn.: Roper Center for Public Opinion Research, July 19–21, 2004); Kaiser Family Foundation, "2006 Kaiser Family Foundation Survey of Americans on HIV/AIDS," May 2006.

[34] Kaiser Family Foundation trend data in "2006 Kaiser Family Foundation Survey of Americans on HIV/AIDS," May 2006.

[35] ABC News/*Washington Post* Poll, March 5–9, 1987; Metropolitan Life/Paul Loewenwarter Productions/Louis Harris and Associates Poll, July 29–August 10, 1987.

[36] *Los Angeles Times* Polls (Storrs, Conn: Roper Center for Public Opinion Research, December 5–12, 1985; July 24–28, 1987).

[37] Blendon, Donelan, and Knox, "Public Opinion and AIDS: Lessons for the Second Decade."

[38] Ibid.

[39] Robert J. Blendon and Karen Donelan, "Discrimination against People with AIDS: The Public's Perspective." *New England Journal of Medicine* 319 (October 13, 1988): 1022–6.

[40] Blendon, Donelan, and Knox, "Public Opinion and AIDS: Lessons for the Second Decade."

[41] *Newsweek*/Princeton Survey Research Associates Poll (Storrs, Conn.: Roper Center for Public Opinion Research, July 29–30, 1993).

[42] Blendon, Donelan, and Knox, "Public Opinion and AIDS: Lessons for the Second Decade."

[43] Gallup/Times Mirror Poll (Storrs, Conn.: Roper Center for Public Opinion Research, April 25–May 10, 1987).

[44] Gallup Poll, May 2–5, 1991.

[45] Kaiser Family Foundation trend data in "Kaiser Family Foundation 2009 Survey of Americans on HIV/AIDS: Summary of Findings on the Domestic Epidemic," April 2009; *Washington Post*/Kaiser Family Foundation/Harvard University Poll, June 13–23, 2002.

[46] Kaiser Family Foundation trend data in "Kaiser Family Foundation 2009 Survey of Americans on HIV/AIDS: Summary of Findings on the Domestic Epidemic," April 2009.

[47] Ibid.

[48] Blendon, Donelan, and Knox, "Public Opinion and AIDS: Lessons for the Second Decade."

[49] *Parents Magazine*/Kane, Parsons, and Associates Poll (Storrs, Conn: Roper Center for Public Opinion Research, January 15–27, 1998); Gallup Poll (Storrs, Conn: Roper Center for Public Opinion Research, November 14–18, 1991).

[50] ABC News Poll, June 15–19, 1990.

[51] Stony Brook University Center for Survey Research Poll (Storrs, Conn.: Roper Center for Public Opinion Research, September 13–29, 2004).

[52] Kaiser Family Foundation trend data in "2006 Kaiser Family Foundation Survey of Americans on HIV/AIDS," May 2006.

[53] Blendon, Donelan, and Knox, "Public Opinion and AIDS: Lessons for the Second Decade."

[54] Kaiser Family Foundation Poll, August 14–October 26, 2000.

[55] Kaiser Family Foundation trend data in "Kaiser Family Foundation 2009 Survey of Americans on HIV/AIDS: Summary of Findings on the Domestic Epidemic," April 2009.

[56] Research!America/American Public Health Association/Harris Interactive poll (Storrs, Conn.: Roper Center for Public Opinion Research, October 1–10, 2004).

[57] Kaiser Family Foundation poll, March 24–April 18, 2006.

[58] M. A. Allen, T. S. Liang, T. La Silva, B. Tjugum, R. J. Gulakowski, and M. Murguía, "Assessing the Attitudes, Knowledge, and Awareness of HIV Vaccine Research among Adults in the United States," *Journal of Acquired Immune Deficiency Syndromes* 40 (December 15, 2005): 617–624.

[59] Centers for Disease Control and Prevention, "Fact Sheet: Estimates of New HIV Infections in the United States," August 2008, http://www.cdc.gov/hiv/topics/surveillance/resources/factsheets/incidence.htm.

[60] Kaiser Family Foundation, "Kaiser Family Foundation 2009 Survey of Americans on HIV/AIDS: Summary of Findings on the Domestic Epidemic," April 2009.

[61] Ibid.

[62] Ibid.

[63] Ibid.

[64] Ibid.

[65] Kaiser Family Foundation Poll, March 24–April 18, 2006.

[66] Mollyann Brodie, Elizabeth Hamel, Lee Ann Brady, Jennifer Kates, and Drew E. Altman, "AIDS at 21: Media Coverage of the HIV Epidemic 1981–2002," *Columbia Journalism Review* 42 (Supplement, March/April 2004): 1–8.

[67] Kaiser Family Foundation trend data in "Kaiser Family Foundation Survey of Americans on the U.S. Role in Global Health," May 2009, http://www.kff.org/kaiserpolls/upload/7894.pdf.

[68] Kaiser Family Foundation, "Kaiser Family Foundation Survey of Americans on the U.S. Role in Global Health," May 2009.

[69] Kaiser Family Foundation, "2006 Kaiser Family Foundation Survey of Americans on HIV/AIDS," May 2006.

[70] Kaiser Family Foundation, "Kaiser Family Foundation Survey of Americans on the U.S. Role in Global Health," May 2009.

[71] Kaiser Family Foundation trend data in "Kaiser Family Foundation Survey of Americans on the U.S. Role in Global Health," May 2009.

[72] *Washington Post*/Kaiser Family Foundation/Harvard University Poll, June 13–23, 2002; Kaiser Family Foundation polls, March 15–May 11, 2004; March 24–April 18, 2006; January 26–March 8, 2009.

[73] Kaiser Family Foundation, "Kaiser Family Foundation Survey of Americans on the U.S. Role in Global Health," May 2009.

[74] Ibid.

[75] Ibid.

Table 10-1 Americans' Views about Most Urgent Health Problem Facing the Country and the World

	Percent naming HIV/AIDS (rank in parentheses)	
	Facing the country	Facing the world
1987	68 (1)	
1990	49 (1)	
1991	45 (1)	
1992	41 (1)	
1995	44 (1)	
1997	38 (1)	
2000	26 (2)	37 (1)
2002	17 (4)	33 (2)
2004	21 (2)	NA
2005	16 (2)	36 (2)
2006	17 (3)	34 (2)
2009	6 (8)	21 (2)

Note: In 1990 respondents could give up to two answers. In 1995–2009, respondents could give up to three answers, although most did not. NA = not asked.

Question: What would you say is the most urgent health problem facing this country at the present time? (1987, 1991, 1992)

Question: What do you think is the most urgent health problem facing this nation today? Is there another health problem you think is almost as urgent? (1990, 1995–2009)

Sources: Gallup polls (Storrs, Conn.: Roper Center for Public Opinion Research, October 23–26, 1987; May 2–5, 1991; March 26–29, 1992); *Los Angeles Times* Poll (Storrs, Conn.: Roper Center for Public Opinion Research, January 21–24, 1990); Kaiser Family Foundation polls (Storrs, Conn.: Roper Center for Public Opinion Research, November 27–December 17, 1995; September 17–October 19, 1997; August 14–October 26, 2000; March 15–May 11, 2004; October 4–9, 2005; March 24–April 18, 2006; January 26–March 8, 2009); *Washington Post*/Kaiser Family Foundation/Harvard University Poll (Storrs, Conn.: Roper Center for Public Opinion Research, June 13–23, 2002).

Table 10-2 Americans' Views on Progress with HIV/AIDS in the United States, 1995–2009 (in percent)

	Making progress	About the same	Losing ground	Don't know
1995	32	15	48	5
1997	52	14	27	7
2002	49	20	26	5
2003	40	21	30	9
2004	47	13	36	4
2006	40	22	29	10
2009	45	18	22	14

Question: Thinking about the way the problem of HIV/AIDS affects the United States today, do you think the problem is about the same as it has been, that the United States today is making progress in this area, or that the United States today is losing ground?

Source: Kaiser Family Foundation trend data in "Kaiser Family Foundation 2009 Survey of Americans on HIV/AIDS: Summary of Findings on the Domestic Epidemic," April 2009.

Table 10-3 Americans' Concern about Becoming Infected with HIV/AIDS

	Percent at least somewhat concerned (Percent very concerned in parentheses)	
	Personal concerns about becoming infected	Parents' concern about children becoming infected
1997	41 (24)	73 (52)
2000	37 (19)	71 (44)
2001	41 (26)	NA
2002	33 (18)	NA
2004	31 (17)	68 (36)
2006	29 (15)	60 (32)
2009	25 (13)	56 (33)

Note: NA = not asked.

Question: Bearing in mind the different ways people can be infected with HIV, the virus that causes AIDS, how concerned are you personally about becoming infected with HIV? Are you very concerned, somewhat concerned, not too concerned, or not at all concerned?

Question: (Asked of parents of children aged 21 or younger) How concerned are you about a son or daughter becoming infected with HIV? Are you very concerned, somewhat concerned, not too concerned, or not at all concerned?

Sources: Kaiser Family Foundation polls (Storrs, Conn.: Roper Center for Public Opinion Research, September 17–October 19, 1997; August 14–October 26, 2000; March 15–May 11, 2004; October 4–9, 2005; March 24–April 18, 2006; January 26–March 8, 2009); *Washington Post*/Kaiser Family Foundation/Harvard University Poll (Storrs, Conn.: Roper Center for Public Opinion Research, June 13–23, 2002).

Table 10-4 Americans Who Say They Know Someone with or Tested Positive for HIV/AIDS (in percent)

1983	2
1987	9
1991	17
1995	39
1997	35
2000	43
2004	44
2006	42
2009	43

Question: Have you heard or read anything about a new disease called AIDS, which stands for Acquired Immune Deficiency Syndrome? (If yes) Do you know anyone who suffers from AIDS? (1983)

Question: Do you personally know anyone who has contracted AIDS? (1987, 1991)

Question: Do you personally know anyone who now has AIDS, has died from AIDS, or has tested positive for HIV? (1995–2009)

Sources: For 1983–1991, Robert J. Blendon, Karen Donelan, and Richard A. Knox, "Public Opinion and AIDS: Lessons for the Second Decade," *JAMA: Journal of the American Medical Association* 267 (February 19, 1992): 981–986. For 1995–2009, Kaiser Family Foundation trend data in "Kaiser Family Foundation 2009 Survey of Americans on HIV/AIDS: Summary of Findings on the Domestic Epidemic," April 2009.

Table 10-5 Americans' Beliefs about Ways of Contracting HIV/AIDS, 1985–2009

	Percent who believe someone can get HIV/AIDS by . . .			
	Yes	No	Don't know/Refused	Yes + Don't know
Kissing				
1985	50	36	14	64
1987	27	60	13	40
1990	24	63	13	37
2000	31	62	8	39
2004	32	62	6	38
2006	29	63	8	37
Sharing a drinking glass				
1985	28	55	16	44
1987	17	74	9	26
1990	12	75	12	24
2000	15	77	7	22
2004	19	76	6	25
2006	16	77	6	22
2009	20	73	7	27
Touching a toilet seat				
1985	16	69	15	31
1987	12	81	7	19
1990	7	84	9	16
2000	10	84	6	16

(Table continues)

Table 10-5 *Continued*

2004	12	82	6	18
2006	10	84	6	16
2009	12	83	5	17

Swimming in a pool with someone who is HIV-positive

2009	7	86	7	14

Question: I'm going to read you a list. For each item please tell me if you think that it is or is not a way for someone to catch AIDS from someone who has it. If you are not sure, please tell me. Can you catch AIDS from . . . kissing/using the same drinking glass/sitting on a toilet seat (1985–1990).

Question: As I read each of the following, please tell me if a person can become infected with HIV this way or not . . . kissing/sharing a drinking glass/touching a toilet seat (2000).

Question: As I read each of the following, please tell me if, as far as you know, a person can become infected with HIV this way or not . . . kissing/sharing a drinking glass/touching a toilet seat/swimming in a pool with someone who is HIV-positive (2004, 2006, 2009).

Sources: ABC News/*Washington Post* polls (Storrs, Conn.: Roper Center for Public Opinion Research, September 19–23, 1985; March 5–9, 1987); ABC News Poll (Storrs, Conn.: Roper Center for Public Opinion Research, June 15–19, 1990); Kaiser Family Foundation polls (Storrs, Conn.: Roper Center for Public Opinion Research, August 14–October 26, 2000; March 15–May 11, 2004; March 24–April 18, 2006; January 26–March 8, 2009).

Table 10-6 Americans' Comfort Level with Having a Colleague with HIV/AIDS in the Workplace, 1997–2009 (in percent)

	1997	2000	2004	2006	2009
Comfortable (net)	65	68	70	71	73
Very	32	33	35	41	44
Somewhat	33	35	35	30	29
Uncomfortable (net)	33	28	28	21	23
Somewhat	21	20	18	13	15
Very	12	8	10	8	8
Don't know/Refused	2	4	3	8	4

Question: In general, how comfortable would you be, personally, working with someone who has HIV or AIDS—very comfortable, somewhat comfortable, or very comfortable?

Sources: Kaiser Family Foundation polls (Storrs, Conn.: Roper Center for Public Opinion Research, September 17–October 19, 1997; August 14–October 26, 2000; March 15–May 11, 2004; March 24–April 18, 2006; January 26–March 8, 2009).

Table 10-7 Perceptions of Prejudice and Discrimination against People with HIV/AIDS, 1986–2006 (in percent)

	1986	1990	1991	2000	2004	2006
A lot	50	51	57	51	45	45
Some	NA	NA	NA	33	38	36
Only a little/None	NA	NA	NA	10	11	14
Treated appropriately	34	37	35	NA	NA	NA
Don't know/Refused	16	12	8	6	5	5

Note: NA = not asked.

Question: Do you think there has been a lot of discrimination against people with AIDS, or do you think their treatment has been generally appropriate? (1986–1991)

Question: How much prejudice and discrimination do you think there is against people living with HIV and AIDS in this country? (2000–2006)

Sources: CBS News Poll (Storrs, Conn.: Roper Center for Public Opinion Research, October 14–16, 1986); CBS News/*New York Times* polls (Storrs, Conn.: Roper Center for Public Opinion Research, May 22–24, 1990; June 3–6, 1991); Kaiser Family Foundation polls (Storrs, Conn.: Roper Center for Public Opinion Research, August 14–October 26, 2000; March 15–May 11, 2004; March 24–April 18, 2006).

Table 10-8 Opinions on Government Spending on HIV/AIDS, 1997–2009 (in percent)

	1997	2000	2002	2004	2006	2009
Too much	8	5	7	5	7	5
About right	32	25	39	36	17	28
Too little	51	55	39	52	63	50
Don't know/Refused	9	15	15	8	14	17

Question: In general, do you think the federal government spends too much money on HIV/AIDS, too little money on HIV/AIDS, or about the right amount?

Sources: For 1997–2000, 2004, 2006, 2009, Kaiser Family Foundation trend data in "Kaiser Family Foundation 2009 Survey of Americans on HIV/AIDS: Summary of Findings on the Domestic Epidemic," April 2009. For 2002, *Washington Post*/Kaiser Family Foundation/Harvard University Poll (Storrs, Conn.: Roper Center for Public Opinion Research, June 13–23, 2002).

Table 10-9 Opinions on Government Spending on HIV/AIDS Compared with Other Health Problems, 2000–2009 (in percent)

	2000	2002	2004	2006	2009
Too high	8	11	6	7	7
About right	30	42	40	24	36
Too low	43	29	42	48	35
Don't know/Refused	19	18	12	21	23

Question: Compared with the amount of money the federal government spends on other health problems, such as heart disease and cancer, do you think federal spending on HIV/AIDS is too high, too low, or about right?

Source: Kaiser Family Foundation trend data in "Kaiser Family Foundation 2009 Survey of Americans on HIV/AIDS: Summary of Findings on the Domestic Epidemic," April 2009.

Table 10-10 Opinions on Government Spending and Progress on the HIV/AIDS Epidemic, 2004–2009 (in percent)

	2004	2006	2009
Will lead to meaningful progress	57	62	60
Won't make much difference	34	30	31
It depends (vol.)	3	5	2
Don't know/Refused	7	4	8

Note: (vol.) = volunteered response.

Question: In general, do you think that spending more money on HIV/AIDS prevention in the United States will lead to meaningful progress in slowing the epidemic, or that spending more money won't make much difference?

Sources: Kaiser Family Foundation polls (Storrs, Conn.: Roper Center for Public Opinion Research, March 15–May 11, 2004); Kaiser Family Foundation, "2006 Kaiser Family Foundation Survey of Americans on HIV/AIDS," May 2006; Kaiser Family Foundation, "Kaiser Family Foundation 2009 Survey of Americans on HIV/AIDS: Summary of Findings on the Domestic Epidemic," April 2009.

Table 10-11 HIV/AIDS as the Most Urgent Health Problem Facing the Nation, by Race/Ethnicity, 1995–2009

	Percent naming HIV/AIDS						
	1995	1997	2000	2002	2004	2006	2009
Total	44	38	26	17	21	17	6
African American	56	52	41	35	43	39	22
Latino	51	50	40	30	31	23	9
White	42	35	23	23	17	13	2

Note: Respondents could give up to three answers, although most did not.

Question: What do you think is the most urgent health problem facing the nation today? Is there another problem you think is almost as urgent?

Source: Kaiser Family Foundation trend data in "Kaiser Family Foundation 2009 Survey of Americans on HIV/AIDS: Summary of Findings on the Domestic Epidemic," April 2009.

Table 10-12 Opinions about Overall Progress on HIV/AIDS in the United States, by Race/Ethnicity, 2009 (in percent)

	Making progress	About the same	Losing ground	Don't know
Total	45	18	22	14
African American	41	14	34	11
Latino	44	14	30	12
White	45	20	19	16

Question: Thinking about the way the problem of HIV/AIDS affects the United States today, do you think the problem is about the same as it has been, that the United States today is making progress in this area, or that the United States today is losing ground?

Source: Kaiser Family Foundation, "Kaiser Family Foundation 2009 Survey of Americans on HIV/AIDS: Summary of Findings on the Domestic Epidemic," April 2009.

Table 10-13 Level of Concern about Becoming Infected with HIV, by Race/Ethnicity, 1997–2009

	Percent very concerned					
	1997	2000	2002	2004	2006	2009
Total	24	19	18	17	15	13
African American	50	37	43	43	34	38
Latino	46	34	32	30	31	25
White	16	14	11	10	9	6

Question: How concerned are you personally about becoming infected with HIV? Are you very concerned, somewhat concerned, not too concerned, or not at all concerned?

Source: Kaiser Family Foundation trend data in "Kaiser Family Foundation 2009 Survey of Americans on HIV/AIDS: Summary of Findings on the Domestic Epidemic," April 2009.

Table 10-14 Parents' Concern about Children Becoming Infected with HIV, by Race/Ethnicity, 2009 (in percent)

	Very concerned	Somewhat concerned	Not too concerned	Not at all concerned
Total	33	23	24	19
African American	68	12	7	13
Latino	39	22	15	24
White	24	26	30	19

Note: "Don't know" responses not shown.

Question: (Asked of parents of children aged 21 or younger) How concerned are you about a son or daughter becoming infected with HIV? Are you very concerned, somewhat concerned, not too concerned, or not at all concerned?

Source: Kaiser Family Foundation, "Kaiser Family Foundation 2009 Survey of Americans on HIV/AIDS: Summary of Findings on the Domestic Epidemic," April 2009.

Table 10-15 Americans Who Say They Know Someone with HIV/AIDS, by Race/Ethnicity, 2009 (in percent)

Total	43
African American	58
Latino	37
White	43

Question: Do you personally know anyone who now has AIDS, has died from AIDS, or has tested positive for HIV?

Source: Kaiser Family Foundation, "Kaiser Family Foundation 2009 Survey of Americans on HIV/AIDS: Summary of Findings on the Domestic Epidemic," April 2009.

Tables 10-16 Perception of HIV/AIDS as a Problem in Local Community, by Race/Ethnicity, 2009 (in percent)

	More urgent	About the same	Less urgent	Never been a problem
Total	17	31	12	29
African American	40	25	10	17
Latino	35	29	8	19
White	10	33	13	34

Note: "Don't know" responses not shown.

Question: Thinking about the way the problem of AIDS is affecting your local community today, do you think AIDS is a more urgent problem for your community than it was a few years ago, a less urgent problem, is it about the same, or has AIDS never been a problem in your community?

Source: Kaiser Family Foundation, "Kaiser Family Foundation 2009 Survey of Americans on HIV/AIDS: Summary of Findings on the Domestic Epidemic," April 2009.

Table 10-17 Perceptions of Progress on Global HIV/AIDS, 2002–2009 (in percent)

	2002	2004	2006	2009
Making progress	35	38	36	46
About the same	15	9	16	14
Losing ground	45	49	40	32
Don't know	5	4	8	8

Question: Thinking about the way the problem of HIV/AIDS affects the world today do you think the problem is about the same as it has been, that the world today is making progress in this area, or that the world today is losing ground?

Source: Kaiser Family Foundation trend data in "Kaiser Family Foundation Survey of Americans on the U.S. Role in Global Health," May 2009.

Table 10-18 Views on Who Is Doing Enough to Solve the Problem of AIDS in Developing Countries (in percent)

	Doing enough	Not doing enough	Don't know
Governments of developing countries hardest hit by HIV	14	76	10
Pharmaceutical companies	19	64	16
President Bush and his administration	22	62	15
United Nations	16	61	22
U.S. government	27	61	11
Governments of developed nations other than the U.S.	15	54	30
International nonprofit organizations/ foundations	36	46	18

Question: When it comes to the problem of AIDS in developing countries, would you say the following are doing enough to help solve the problem of AIDS in developing countries, or are they not doing enough?

Source: Kaiser Family Foundation, "2006 Kaiser Family Foundation Survey of Americans on HIV/AIDS," May 2006.

Table 10-19 Views on U.S. Spending on HIV/AIDS in Developing Countries, 2002–2009 (in percent)

	2002	2006	2009
Too much	16	13	16
Right amount	34	13	29
Too little	31	56	37
Don't know/Refused	20	18	18

Question: Do you think the United States is now spending too much, too little, or about the right amount to deal with the HIV/AIDS problem in developing countries?

Source: Kaiser Family Foundation trend data in "Kaiser Family Foundation Survey of Americans on the U.S. Role in Global Health," May 2009.

Table 10-20 The Public's Government Spending Priorities: Domestic versus
International HIV/AIDS, 2002–2009 (in percent)

	The United States should address problems at home first rather than spending more money to deal with the HIV/AIDS epidemic in developing countries.			The United States is a global leader and has a responsibility to spend more money to help fight the HIV/AIDS epidemic in developing countries.	
	Agree	Disagree		Agree	Disagree
2002	78	18	2002	44	51
2004	71	25	2004	53	42
2006	67	28	2006	60	33
2009	76	19	2009	49	46
When forced to choose between the statements					
2002	71			22	
2004	62			30	
2006	55			34	
2009	69			23	

Note: "Don't know" responses not shown. The forced choice question was asked of those who agreed with both statements. The share who agreed with only one statement is included in the percentage for that statement in the forced choice. The share who disagreed with both statements is not shown.

Question: I'm going to read you two statements and ask whether you agree with each. The United States should address problems at home first rather than spending more money to deal with the HIV/AIDS epidemic in developing countries. The United States is a global leader and has a responsibility to spend more money to help fight the HIV/AIDS epidemic in developing countries. Do you agree or disagree?

Question: Which of these two statements do you agree with more strongly?

Source: Kaiser Family Foundation trend data in "Kaiser Family Foundation Survey of Americans on the U.S. Role in Global Health," May 2009.

Chapter 11

ATTITUDES ABOUT ABORTION

Gillian K. SteelFisher and John M. Benson

For nearly four decades, the issue of abortion has played an important part in U.S. political life.[1] Demonstrations by "pro-choice" and "pro-life" activists have provided the media with headlines and photo opportunities; politicians have used abortion to challenge opponents or claim supporters in elections at every level; and relevant legislation and court rulings have come forth in every decade since the 1973 Supreme Court decision in *Roe v. Wade*.[2] In the midst of all this attention, it may seem that legalized abortion is one of the most politicized and polarized health issues of our time. But organized interests, politicians, and the media do not always accurately portray the attitudes and perspectives of the broader public. Insofar as the public shapes the behaviors of politicians and the direction of legislation, understanding the true public perspective—as opposed to that presented by interest groups—is critical to evaluating the future of this issue. To begin the discussion, it is helpful to review briefly the basic facts about abortion, including its prevalence, history, and related policies.

According to the Guttmacher Institute, approximately 1.2 million women in the United States had an abortion in 2005, or 19.4 per thousand women aged fifteen to forty-four.[3] Although the U.S. rate is higher than in some European countries, it has gone down since 1980.[4] The decline is due in large part to increased contraceptive use and lower rates of unintended pregnancy.[5] Because of improved technologies, women are also more likely to have an abortion early in pregnancy, when the procedure is safest for the woman. In 1973, 38 percent of abortions occurred within eight weeks gestation age; in 2006, 62 percent of abortions occurred within this window.[6] Although women who have abortions span the full spectrum of demographics, the rates of abortion are highest among certain groups, including women who are younger, unmarried, lower income, and of color.[7]

The recent history of abortion has been largely shaped by the court system, with a focus on three major rulings. The best known case is *Roe v. Wade,* which legalized abortion in 1973 at the federal level by stating that the Constitution's implicit right to privacy protects a woman's right to abortion, in consultation with her physician.[8] The right to privacy, however, is not absolute and is limited by a "compelling state interest" in the fetus after it reaches "viability," which is defined as the potential to live outside the mother's womb. States may not restrict abortion during the first trimester, but may provide minimal restrictions in the second and "even proscribe abortion except where it is necessary, in appropriate medical judgment, for the preservation of the life or health of the mother" in the third.[9] *Roe* was the culmination of efforts by people who were frustrated with the health problems associated with illegal abortions. These included many in the medical community, some religious organizations, and women's groups, who subsequently became known as pro-choice advocates.

Roe v. Wade also awakened groups that later became know as pro-life activists, including organized religious groups, such as the Roman Catholic Church and the Christian evangelical movement.[10] None of their efforts was particularly successful until *Planned Parenthood of Southeastern Pennsylvania v. Casey* in 1992. Although still affirming a woman's right to choose, the Supreme Court allowed further restrictions on abortion if they did not impose an "undue burden." An undue burden was defined as a "substantial obstacle in the path of a woman seeking an abortion of a nonviable fetus." *Casey* allowed states to pass additional restrictions on abortion, such as a twenty-four-hour waiting period, informed consent, and parental consent with a judicial waiver.[11]

The most recent history of abortion legislation has focused on additional restrictions, particularly for late-term procedures. Several attempts were made to ban abortions using a specific procedure, intact dilation and extraction (or D and X), referred to by opponents as "partial-birth" abortion. President George W. Bush signed the Partial-Birth Abortion Ban Act in October 2003, and in April 2007 the Court upheld the law in *Gonzales v. Carhart*. The immediate impact of the ban was to make the specific procedure illegal in all stages of gestation.[12]

Few abortions are funded by the government. In 1976 Congress passed the Hyde Amendment, which banned federal Medicaid funding for abortions "except to save the mother's life as well as in cases of rape and incest."[13] The restriction also made it difficult for states to fund abortions.[14] As of 2008, only seventeen states used their own Medicaid funding to cover abortions for low-income women.[15]

As part of an effort to expand health insurance coverage to more Americans, the health care reform law enacted in 2010 created state-based exchanges through which people will be able to buy private insurance coverage. Abortion played an important part in the congressional debate because there was a chance that pro-life Democrats would not vote for the law without restrictions on federal funding of abortion in these exchanges.[16] The legislation that passed restricts the use of federal premium or cost-sharing subsidies; they cannot be used for abortion coverage that extends beyond saving the life of the mother or in cases of rape or incest. This provision is consistent with the Hyde Amendment. Health insurance companies offering plans through the new exchanges must offer separate plans for abortion under other circumstances, and anyone who receives federal assistance and wants to purchase insurance that covers abortion under other circumstances must pay for it separately.[17]

The U.S. government also has imposed significant restrictions on federal funding of abortion services to developing nations receiving U.S. aid. In August 1984 President Ronald Reagan announced what became known as the Mexico City policy, which prevents the United States from funding family planning services to any organization that provides abortion services, even with separate, non-U.S. funds. The policy was rescinded in 1993 by President Bill Clinton and reinstated in 2001 by President Bush. On January 23, 2009, President Barack Obama signed an executive order overturning the Mexico City policy.[18]

To better understand how public opinion has shaped and will shape abortion policy in future years, this chapter begins with a focus on the importance of abortion to the public. It then reviews opinions about the central policy question of legality, as well as secondary policy questions related to funding and the rights of those involved in the debate. Finally, to help assess where abortion policy might go in the future, the chapter reviews policies related to new technologies, including RU-486 and emergency contraception.

Importance of Abortion as an Issue

Abortion is one of a set of issues many people think about in the policy and electoral context, but for most Americans it is not the most pressing issue. In 2009, 15 percent said abortion was "a critical issue facing the country," and 33 percent said it is "one among many important issues," a sharp drop from 2006, when 28 percent considered abortion a critical issue. In 2009 those who believed that abortion should be illegal in all or most cases were more than four times as likely to see the issue as critical than those who thought it should be legal in all or most cases (27 percent to 6 percent).[19]

Only a small percentage of the general public makes up the single-issue abortion voters, but those voters can be important in close elections. Asked in May 2008 about how the abortion issue might affect their vote for major offices, 13 percent of the public said they would only vote for a candidate who shares their views on abortion, and 49 percent said it was just one of many important factors.[20] When it comes to activism on abortion, 13 percent of the public said in 2006 that they had done something in the past year "to express [their] views on abortion, such as by donating money to groups, participating in marches or meetings, or writing letters to the news media or [their] representatives."[21]

Although abortion was not a prominent issue in the 2008 presidential election, it has been important in several other recent presidential elections.[22] In 1992 abortion ranked as the fourth most important issue to voters in deciding their choice for president.[23] Abortion has generally been a more important voting issue for Republicans than for Democrats. Shortly before the 2004 presidential election, 30 percent of Republican registered voters, compared with 18 percent of Democratic registered voters, said that abortion was an extremely important issue in their voting decision.[24] In addition, those who cite abortion as one of the most important voting issues, including single-issue abortion voters, have are more likely to hold pro-life views than the public as a whole.[25]

Elections are where differences in attitudes about abortion are at their strongest and most visible. Democratic and Republican voters in presidential elections, and particularly those who vote in their party's presidential primaries, tend to hold strongly contrasting views. This division was apparent in the 2008 election. In a poll conducted shortly before election day, 72 percent of registered voters who said they intended to vote for Democrat Barack Obama said abortion should be legal in all or most cases. Sixty percent of Republican John McCain's voters thought it should be illegal in all or most cases.[26]

Single-issue abortion voters can be particularly influential in presidential primaries, where the turnout is lower than in the general election. In a survey of likely voters in states that held presidential primaries or caucuses in 2008, just over a fourth of Republican (29 percent) and Democratic (26 percent) likely voters said they could not vote for a candidate who did not share their views on abortion. Among these voters, Democrats and Republicans differed sharply in their views. A large majority (73 percent) on the Democratic side believed that abortion should be legal in all or most cases, and a large majority (82 percent) of the Republican side believed that abortion should be illegal in all or most cases.[27]

Views on Legality

The central policy question regarding abortion is legality: Should abortion ever be legal? If so, should it always be legal or only under certain circumstances? The media often portray viewpoints on this issue as strongly divided and diametrically opposed to one another. One reason for this may be the sharp contrast between Democratic and Republican candidates and voters in major elections; another may be the attention the media pays to the perspectives of interest groups and activists, who are much more divided than the general public. In fact, most data point to a broad middle ground in public opinion concerning abortion.

General Support and Opposition

Part of the reason Americans appear deeply divided on abortion may come from the public's willingness to self-identify as pro-choice or pro-life. About half (46 percent) consider themselves pro-life, and about an equal proportion (45 percent) consider themselves pro-choice (**Table 11–1**).[28] When we look at the specifics of public support for legal abortion, however, the picture is not so simple, and the data suggest that the public's labels do not align with the interest group definitions.[29]

When offered three choices—legal under any circumstances, legal only under certain circumstances, and illegal in all circumstances—a majority of Americans choose the middle ground. In 2010, 21 percent said that abortion should be legal under all circumstances, and 22 percent believed it should be illegal under all circumstances. The middle position was held by just over half (56 percent) of the population (**Table 11–2**).[30] These proportions have varied somewhat over time. Most recently, the proportion saying that abortion should be legal under any circumstances has fallen from 30 percent in 2006 to 21 percent in 2010. But given the changes in technology, politics, and even demographics, it is surprising that opinions about abortion have remained relatively consistent since the 1970s.[31] The major point of consistency is that the middle proportion has stayed largely the same—at 49 percent to 63 percent—since 1975, just two years after *Roe v. Wade*.[32]

Looking at the same data another way, the public generally agrees that abortion should be legal under at least some circumstances. In 2010, 77 percent felt that way. Even within this group of supporters, however, the position on abortion is relatively conservative. In a follow-up question, more than three-fourths of those who choose the middle ground (legal only under certain circumstances) said they thought that abortion should be legal only in a few circumstances rather than in most. That result means that more than half of those who thought that abortion should be legal under at least some circumstances (42 percent of the total public) believe that abortion should be legal under only a few circumstances.[33]

The picture is slightly different when the public is offered four options about the legality of abortion—that it should be legal in all cases, legal in most cases, illegal in most cases, or illegal in all cases. One way to look at the results from this question is to say that in 2010 the public is divided between the 52 percent who say abortion should be legal in all (17 percent) or most cases (35 percent) and the 45 percent who believe it should be illegal in all (18 percent) or most cases (27 percent). Looked at in another way, the data show that most Americans (79 percent) prefer abortion to be legal in at least some cases, but a majority (62 percent) wants abortion to be legal in some but not all cases (**Table 11–3**).[34]

Finally, it is worth noting that opinion on this issue seems relatively stable at the individual level. Nearly two-thirds (66 percent) say they never question whether their position on abortion is the right one.[35] And yet, 60 percent believe the country needs to find some middle ground on the related laws, while only 29 percent believe there is no room for compromise.[36]

Attitudes about Legal Abortion under Specific Circumstances

To understand this "middle ground," we turn to questions about the specific conditions under which the public feels abortion should be legal and those conditions where it does not. The take away from these questions is that the public feels differently about abortion under different circumstances. In particular, a strong majority of the public believes abortion should be available when there are medical reasons for a woman to terminate a pregnancy or when the woman was a victim of rape or incest and became pregnant.[37] The public is much less supportive in several other circumstances that might drive the decision, such as poverty or a desire to have no more children. The best-known data in this area come from the General Social Survey (GSS), which began tracking opinions on the legality of abortion even before 1973.[38] The questions focus on seven scenarios (**Table 11–4**). In addition, other organizations have asked questions about slightly different circumstances (although not as routinely), which help flesh out the public perspective.

In general, the public supports access to legal abortion when significant medical issues are present, and particularly when the woman is at risk. In the 2008 GSS, 85 percent of the population supported legal abortion when "the mother's own health is seriously endangered by the pregnancy."[39] Data from other surveys show similar results for cases "when the woman's life is endangered" (88 percent think abortion should be legal in that situation) or "when the woman's physical health is endangered" (77 percent to 82 percent).[40] Support drops to 63 percent "when the woman's mental health is endangered."[41]

A large majority also supports legal abortion when the fetus is at medical risk. Seventy percent of the population believes abortion should be legal if "there is a strong chance of a serious defect in the baby."[42] When questions are more explicit about what this defect is, however, support drops. Support for legal abortion is 56 percent when "there is evidence that the baby may be physically impaired." Support is about the same level (55 percent) when "the baby may be mentally impaired."[43] It may be that support drops because the explicit explanation—physical or mental impairment—sounds less threatening than the more nebulous "serious defect," but this reasoning has not been evaluated through additional testing.

Support is widespread for legal abortion in the case of rape or incest. In 2008, 72 percent supported legal abortion if the woman "became pregnant as a result of rape."[44] The percentage was roughly the same (70 percent) when another survey's question was about "rape or incest."[45]

For the other reasons that women seek abortions (and for which we have reasonable polling data), the American public is much less supportive: none of the other circumstances in the GSS receives majority support. Support for legal abortion when the "family has a very low income and cannot afford any more children" is 41 percent. Nearly the same proportion supports legal abortion if the woman seeking an abortion when she is not married and does not want to marry the father (39 percent), or if she is married and does not want any more children (43 percent).[46] Notably, the public is especially disapproving when a woman would seek an abortion because the pregnancy "would force a professional woman to interrupt her career." Only 25 percent of the public believes it should be possible to obtain a legal abortion in this case.[47]

Finally, when asked whether it should be possible to obtain a legal abortion "if the woman wants it for any reason," 40 percent of the public expressed support in 2008. This percentage is about the same as for three of the four reasons just discussed, but higher than the 25 percent who support having an abortion for career reasons.[48] This seeming inconsistency likely arises because the respondents are not thinking of *all* the specific circumstances that would constitute "any reason" for seeking an abortion. Instead, they may be focused on the collection of social reasons—like poverty or single motherhood—so often presented in the media. Therefore, the support "for any reason" can be higher than for isolated reasons.

Given that the public shows varying support for abortion under different circumstances, it may be helpful to consider whether there is a pattern that helps explain more generally when the public believes abortion should be legal and when it does not. One possibility is that people may be weighing the rights of the mother against the rights of the fetus in deciding whether abortion should be legal under any given circumstance.[49] People generally conclude that, under some circumstances, such as when a woman's health is at serious risk from the pregnancy or when she did not have a say in whether or not she became pregnant, the rights of the mother outweigh the rights of the fetus. Under other circumstances, such as when the mother is single or poor, they generally conclude that the rights of the fetus outweigh the rights of the mother.

The overall patterns evident in these questions are long-standing. Support for any of the specific circumstances asked about in the GSS trend series has not changed much since the 1970s. Support for legal abortion when the woman's health is seriously endangered has hovered between 83 percent and 91 percent. Still, some general trends become evident if one combines the questions into a composite measure, as several analysts have done.[50] In the 1970s support increased, and in the early 1980s declined a little bit. Support began to rise again in the 1980s and reached a peak in the early 1990s. Since then, it has declined again. These numbers reveal that the mood on abortion changes over time, but the changes are relatively small. The overall sense is that opinions on the legality of abortion have remained more consistent since the 1970s than one might have expected, given the developments in legislation, technology, and demographics.

Abortion in the Third Trimester

Public support for legal abortion drops dramatically over the course of a pregnancy.[51] Sixty percent of the public support legal abortion "in general" during the first three months, but support drops to 26 percent in the second three months, and 12 percent in the last three months (**Table 11–5**).[52]

When the public is provided with some explanations of why a woman would have an abortion late in pregnancy, support goes up. Seventy-five percent say it should be legal to have an abortion during the third trimester if the woman's life is in danger.[53] This percentage is substantially higher than the 12 percent support for abortion in the last three months generally, but lower than the 85 percent who support legal abortion if the woman's health is seriously endangered and no time frame is specified.[54] About six in ten (59 percent) support legal abortions during the third trimester when the pregnancy resulted from rape or incest.[55] Again, this result is dramatically higher than support for abortion in the last three months generally, but lower than the 70 percent who support abortion when the pregnancy was caused by rape or incest and no time frame is specified.[56] And finally, 38 percent of the public supports abortion in the third trimester when the child would be born mentally disabled, as compared to 55 percent when no time frame is specified.[57]

In April 2007 the Supreme Court upheld a ban on a late-term procedure that opponents call partial-birth abortion. Not surprisingly, given the procedure's association with abortion in the later stages of pregnancy, a large majority (66 percent to 75 percent) believes it should be illegal, but arguments involving the woman's health affect the public's views.[58] In a 2003 poll, 74 percent thought the late-term procedure should be illegal, and 33 percent still thought it should be illegal if the pregnancy would present a "serious threat to the woman's health."[59]

Restrictions

Given the public's general view that abortion should be legal only under certain circumstances, it is perhaps not surprising that support for restrictions on the legal availability of abortion is fairly broad. Eighty-one percent support requiring a woman to have counseling about the dangers of and alternatives to abortion.[60] About three-fourths (78 percent) support requiring that parents of teenagers be notified, and 76 percent favor requiring that those under eighteen get parental consent to get an abortion.[61] Seventy-one percent support requirements for a twenty-four-hour waiting period, and about two-thirds of the public (64 percent) also supports notification of a married woman's husband.[62] Perhaps because some respondents are thinking of unmarried women, the support for requiring consent from biological fathers is 49 percent.[63] An interesting note is that far fewer Americans favor restrictions when they are described as means to "make it more difficult for a woman to get an abortion." Only 41 percent of Americans would back such efforts.[64] The public is comfortable with restrictions, but not if they make obtaining an abortion more difficult (**Table 11–6**).

Roe v. Wade

Another marker of support for legalized abortion is how the public feels about *Roe v. Wade*. Support for the Court's opinion is not equivalent to support for legalized abortion because some people feel abortion should be legal, but for reasons different from those written into *Roe v. Wade*. Others feel abortion should be legal, but with many more restrictions than *Roe* encompassed. Still, this opinion has served as important fuel for interest groups and politicians on both sides of the debate.[65]

Only about three in ten Americans (29 percent) favor overturning this 1973 decision.[66] Six in ten (60 percent) say they agree with the *Roe v Wade* decision "that established a woman's right to an abortion."[67] In 2005, 61 percent said they would want any new justices on the Court to uphold *Roe v. Wade*, and 61 percent oppose a constitutional amendment to ban abortions in all circumstances except to save the mother's life (**Table 11–7**).[68] These data indicate only limited support for a complete overhaul of existing policies, but considerable support for measures restricting the availability of abortion.

Moral Dimensions

It is important to distinguish legal from moral support, because people do not always agree that abortion is morally acceptable, even if they think it should be legal. When asked directly if they think having an abortion is wrong, 60 percent say it is.[69] Given the choice between wrong and acceptable, 50 percent say that abortion is morally wrong, and 38 percent believe it is morally acceptable.[70]

Judgments about whether abortion is wrong, however, depend on the circumstances. Although about one-fourth of the public thinks that having an abortion is morally wrong in nearly all circumstances (24 percent), and an equal proportion believes it is not a moral issue, the plurality (49 percent) takes the middle position—that having an abortion is morally wrong in "some" circumstances.[71] Americans have very different views about the morality of having an abortion when there is a strong chance of a serious defect in the baby (51 percent say it is not wrong at all, and 23 percent believe it is always wrong) than they do in a situation where the family has a very low income and cannot afford any more children (28 percent say it is not wrong at all, and 50 percent believe it is always wrong) (**Table 11–8**).[72]

Nearly half (46 percent) of the public believes that abortion is "an act of murder."[73] Because about three-fourths of the public thinks that abortion should be legal under at least some circumstances, simple math would suggest that some people believe both that abortion should be legal and that it is murder. In spite of their misgivings, nearly six in ten Americans (58 percent) agree with the statement that "abortion is sometimes the best course in a bad situation."[74] A 1995 poll made this choice explicit: 50 percent of people who said abortion is the same thing as murdering a child also agreed that "abortion is sometimes the best course in a bad situation."[75]

For most Americans, the issue of abortion is a morally tense one, with legality and morality being somewhat distinct. But, the American public also is reluctant to place their moral values on others, through law or otherwise. A 2000 poll showed that 68 percent of the public agrees that "No matter how I feel about abortion, I believe it is a decision that has to be made by a woman and her doctor."[76]

Diversity of Americans' Views on Abortion

Support for and opposition to abortion varies significantly between different groups in American society. To examine these differences, this section provides an in-depth look at the GSS data concerning who said what about abortion in seven different circumstances (**Table 11–9**).[77]

Sex

Although one can argue that abortion affects women in dramatically different ways from how it affects men, both sexes have quite similar policy views. In none of the different circumstances do the views of women and men differ by more than six percentage points.[78] Other data show that although the views of women and men are similar overall, the issue is more important to women than to men. In a 2004 poll of registered voters, 27 percent of women, compared with 17 percent of men, said that abortion would be an extremely important issue in their presidential voting decision.[79]

Age

Differences in abortion attitudes by age are modest. In general, the oldest group (age 65+) is more likely than the youngest (18–29) to oppose legal abortion in various circumstances. The largest differences are seen in two circumstances: when the family has a very low income and cannot afford more children and if the woman wants an abortion for any reason. No age group has a majority supporting legal abortion in these two situations.[80]

Race

Since 1994 whites and African Americans have held similar views about abortion using the GSS measures.[81] Going back to 1974, the difference between the groups was larger, with whites being generally more in favor of legal abortion; and in 1984 the gap was somewhat smaller, but still evident. Although some researchers have used complex modeling to suggest otherwise, a rough cut of the data suggests that whites and African Americans converged in their opinions at least to a small degree—particularly in the 1970s and 1980s. Specifically, support among African Americans has increased, and support among whites has stayed roughly the same.[82]

Education

Higher levels of education are associated with more support for legal abortion under all circumstances. In the example of a married woman who does not want any more children, support for legal abortion among those with a high school education or less is 33 percent, but 54 percent among college graduates, including 61 percent of those who have had more than four years of college. A majority of college graduates support legal abortion in all seven circumstances.[83]

Income

Relatively little difference of opinion is found between income groups, except that people in the highest income bracket ($75,000 or more per year) are more likely than others to support abortion being legal. In the responses of the lowest-income group (less than $25,000 per year) compared to the highest, differences range from eight to twenty percentage points.[84]

Region

The biggest contrast in abortion views by region is between residents of the Northeast and the South. Support for legal abortion is higher in the Northeast than it is in the South in cases where a woman is married but does not want more children (55 percent to 33 percent); where the family has a low income and cannot afford more children (51 percent to 32 percent); or when a woman does not want to marry the father (50 percent to 28 percent).[85]

Party Identification

Data presented above show that voters in presidential elections—particularly, presidential primaries—tend to be sharply divided along partisan lines on the legality of abortion. When it comes to whether abortion should be legally available in particular circumstances, the partisan division is still present but is less extreme.

Democrats are substantially more likely to support legal abortion than their Republican counterparts, across the board, with differences ranging from nine to sixteen percentage points. The greatest difference is in the circumstance when the family has a very low income and cannot afford any more children: 49 percent of Democrats think abortion should be legal, compared with 33 percent of Republicans. Independents' viewpoints tend to parallel Republican views in the different circumstances.[86]

Marital Status

In general, married people are less likely to support legal abortion than those who have never been married or are separated or divorced.[87]

Religious Identification

Religion is more important in the day-to-day lives of Americans than it is for citizens of other industrialized countries.[88] In addition, a substantial minority of Americans (40 percent in 2005, but only 27 percent in 2007) think political leaders should rely on their religious beliefs in making policy decisions.[89] This desire for more religion-based public decision making has led a number of large church and religious organizations to become more active in American politics with the aim of electing candidates who will make policy decisions based on their religious teachings.[90] The health care issues that have been the focus for many of these groups, including evangelical Christian churches and the Catholic Church, have included opposition to the following: abortion, contraceptive education for teenagers, embryonic stem cell research, euthanasia, physician-assisted suicide, and the discontinuance of support care for terminally ill and comatose patients.[91]

Some of the most talked about divisions related to abortion have to do with religion. Given the prominence of the Catholic Church in the abortion debate, one might expect U.S. Catholics to be more conservative on abortion than Protestants, but surveys show virtually no difference between the two.[92] Moreover, classifying Christian religious identification into Catholics and Protestants can disguise important differences within the two groups, as the views of evangelical Christians on abortion are much more conservative than the views of mainline Protestants.[93]

The opinions of Catholics and Protestants differ sharply from those who do not identify with any religion. On every one of the GSS measures, a majority of those with no religious affiliation favor legal abortion.[94] Most public opinion polls do not have enough people of other faiths, such as Judaism or Islam, for analysis on these questions.

Religiosity

Across religions and denominations, the *strength* of one's religious beliefs and how important they are in daily life correlate to large differences in support for legal abortion.[95] Among many measures used to assess religiosity, this analysis of the GSS data focuses on frequency of attendance at religious services, which partly reflects active participation in a religious organization as well as differences in beliefs.

Support for legal abortion in the various circumstances falls dramatically with increased religious attendance. People who attend religious services once a week or more still support abortion when the mother's life/health is in danger (73 percent), and about half say that abortion should be legally available if there is a strong chance of a serious defect in the baby (51 percent) and in the case of rape (48 percent). In the four remaining circumstances, support for abortion is less than one in five. As religious attendance falls, support climbs linearly. A majority of those who never attend support abortion being legally available in all seven circumstances.[96]

Government Funding of Abortion

Perhaps because of the many restrictions on funding abortions in the United States and abroad (through U.S. funds), few questions have been asked about this issue. During the debate leading up to passage of the 2010 health care reform law, funding of abortion became an issue of considerable controversy. About six in ten (61 percent) thought that private health insurance bought with government assistance should not be allowed to include coverage for abortions.[97] In 2003 the country was divided almost evenly—47 percent in favor, 51 percent opposed—on funding abortions for poor women in the United States.[98]

Public opinion on funding overseas is also divided. In 2003, 45 percent of the public supported U.S. aid programs contributing to "voluntary, safe abortions as part of reproductive health care in developing nations that request it," and 52 percent were opposed. At the same time, 47 percent of the public supported legislation to "prevent the United States from funding family planning services in health care organizations overseas if those organizations also happen to perform abortions with other, non-U.S. funding," and 44 percent were opposed.[99]

At the time of President Bush's executive order blocking all U.S. funding to overseas family planning groups that offered abortion counseling, 42 percent approved of the order, 50 percent disapproved.[100] In 2008, when respondents were read a long description of the Bush policy, they were almost evenly divided, with 47 percent in favor, 48 percent opposed.[101]

Rights of Protesters

A major part of the activism of pro-life groups is conducting demonstrations at health clinics that provide abortion counseling and services. In addition, extremists within the pro-life movement have targeted clinics and the professionals who work in them with violence. For the most part, the public supports the right of pro-life groups to demonstrate near clinics, but has some concern about protests that are physically too close to the clinics and their clients. A 2002 survey showed that 73 percent of the public believes antiabortion protesters have the right to hold a peaceful demonstration across the street from a family planning clinic where abortions take place, but only 17 percent think these protestors may stand next to the entrance.[102] This difference in support may stem from believing that close proximity will cause an "undue burden" on the women seeking services or the providers or that violence could erupt in this setting.

The public also disapproves of violent "protest." In the late 1990s several clinics were bombed and a doctor was murdered by antiabortion groups. The vast majority of the public (88 percent) did not feel that using force to prevent abortion was justifiable, and only 8 percent felt it was.[103] In fact, in 1998 at the time of the attacks, 76 percent of the public felt "the government should be doing more to investigate and identify individuals or groups who might commit acts of violence against abortion providers," and 63 percent felt the government should do more to protect abortion providers from physical violence.[104] Violence directed against health care workers who provide abortions now includes listing doctors and their families on Web sites. Again, the public disapproves, with 89 percent saying such actions go beyond antiabortion protestors' rights.[105]

New Technologies

Many have claimed the dynamics of the abortion debate would be very different if most abortions were nonsurgical and therefore did not necessitate visits to specialty clinics. Approval of mifepristone (RU-486), a prescription drug used as an abortifacient, therefore, had the potential to change this aspect of the debate. At the time RU-486 was approved, in September 2000, 50 percent of the public agreed with this decision.[106]

"Emergency contraception" (EC), "the morning-after pill," and "Plan B" are all names for a hormone-based drug combination that works by preventing sperm from reaching an egg, by preventing an egg from being released, and/or by preventing a fertilized egg from implanting. Technically, the drug is not an abortifacient because it is designed to work prior to implantation.[107] But because it *can* prevent implantation of a fertilized egg—and because contraception itself can be part of the abortion debate—this drug is linked in with abortion policy.

In fact, how people understand how EC works is a pivotal part of the debate. A 2004 poll of women found that nearly two-thirds (64 percent) of women of reproductive age correctly said that there is something a woman can do to prevent pregnancy following sexual intercourse. But a 2003 poll found that only one in four women in California knew that EC pills were different from the medical abortion drug, RU-486.[108]

A 2002 poll provided a description that did not include information about preventing implantation: "Emergency contraception—sometimes called the morning-after pill—is a higher dose of ordinary birth control pills that significantly reduces unintended pregnancy if taken within seventy-two hours of unprotected sex or contraceptive failure. These pills have been approved by the U.S. Food and Drug Administration as safe and effective." After hearing this information a plurality (43 percent) said they thought of EC as a form of contraception that prevents pregnancy from occurring; 26 percent thought it was a form of abortion; and 31 percent were not sure.[109] They may not have been sure because this description did not include the mechanism of action, or they may not have been sure even if they did have a more complete description. Depending on what information gets out to the public, perceptions of this dimension may change and have an impact on support.

In the meantime, the debate focused on whether emergency contraception should be allowed without a doctor's prescription. Some have argued that this drug should be available immediately to women because it is effective only if used within seventy-two hours of unprotected intercourse, and it works best within twenty-four hours. Others argue that widespread availability will encourage young people to have sex. As of 2006, 48 percent favored allowing women (age not specified) to get the morning-after pill without a doctor's prescription, and 41 percent were opposed.[110] At the same time, 53 percent of Americans favored allowing *adult* women, eighteen and older, to get the morning-after pill without a prescription. Support dropped to 24 percent when the question was asked about women under eighteen. The public was almost evenly divided on the question of whether making the morning-after pill available without a prescription would lead to more sexual promiscuity: 46 percent thought it would, 47 percent that it would not (**Table 11–10**).[111]

The Future of Abortion Politics and Public Opinion

This chapter describes American public opinion on abortion. The media and politicians present the image of passionate, polarized citizens who take this issue to heart every time they vote. The data show a more nuanced picture.

Abortion sometimes figures prominently in elections for president and other major offices, and single-issue abortion voters tend to participate in strong numbers in presidential primaries and caucuses. But abortion is just one of several issues very important to the public, and for most people it is not the single most important issue.

The majority of Americans agree in broad terms that abortion should be legal, but with significant restrictions—especially when medical and other dire circumstances are not present—to ensure that the decision is not made lightly. Further, support for abortion decreases over the course of a pregnancy, as the fetus develops. This general outline has held true for more than three decades.

But the existence of this "middle ground" does not mean that political and social divisions about abortion will go away. The issue involves a conflict of deeply held values, and polls find large differences of opinion between groups within American society: support for legal abortion is higher among those with higher education and higher income, and opposition is significantly higher among the more religious. The public is also divided on policies less directly related to the legality of abortion, such as public funding for abortion domestically and overseas, RU-486 (at least at the time of its approval), and the availability of emergency contraception without a doctor's prescription.

Public policy is not dictated purely by the public. But insofar as public opinion helps set the direction or limits of policy, one can outline some possible directions for the future based on these findings. Unlike the elected branches of government, the Supreme Court is free to ignore public opinion, which currently shows little support for a complete overhaul of *Roe v. Wade*. That said, support does exist for increasing various restrictions, particularly later in a pregnancy. And, one may expect additional state or federal restrictions like waiting periods and parental notification laws.

There is perhaps some room for policy change in the realm of emergency contraception. At this point, the public is divided and not very well informed. If emergency contraception is framed and understood as a means to prevent abortion, or as contraception, support may increase. If it is framed as an abortificient in the hands of young women, support may stagnate or decline. Even then, however, these issues are unlikely to be decisive in the voting booth for most of the public.

Setting aside future decisions by the Court, abortion policy is unlikely to change dramatically in the short run, given the relative stability of public opinion on abortion. Even the partial-birth abortion ban ruling was a targeted decision that focused on a rarely used procedure. Still, a lot of policy changes around the edges could significantly alter the health service landscape. Providers, access, and related services may become even scarcer than now across regions and states with additional restrictions put in place.

Abortion is not a top issue for most voters, but it can affect close elections. Moreover, although we focus on the perceptions of the public at large in this chapter, additional analyses suggest that most single-issue voters on abortion are pro-life. Therefore, in some elections the abortion issue is one not to be ignored, especially as attitudes about abortion may impact perceptions of other related health policy issues, such as stem cell research and end-of-life care.

Notes

[1] Technically the term "abortion" includes both miscarriages and intended pregnancy terminations. In the political context, and in this text, it refers exclusively to intended pregnancy termination.

[2] Both sides of the debate have adopted different terms over time in an attempt to clarify their positions and gain increased public support. Because the terms *pro-life* and *pro-choice* have been used historically and are consistent with polling questions, we continue to use these terms, as other academics have done. See, for example, Barbara Hinkson Craig and David M. O'Brien, *Abortion and American Politics* (Chatham, N.J.: Chatham House, 1993); Elizabeth Adell Cook,

Ted G. Jelen, and Clyde Wilcox, *Between Two Absolutes: Public Opinion and the Politics of Abortion* (Boulder, Colo.: Westview Press, 1992).

[3] Guttmacher Institute, "Facts on Induced Abortion in the United States," May 2010, http://www.guttmacher.org/pubs/fb_induced_abortion.html. Note that this figure is higher than the estimate by the Centers for Disease Control and Prevention (839,226): Lilo T. Strauss, Sonya B. Gamble, Wilda Y. Parker, Douglas A. Cook, Suzanne B. Zane, and Saeed Hamdan, "Abortion Surveillance—United States 2004," *MMWR Surveillance Summaries* 56 (November 23, 2007): 1–33, http://www.cdc.gov/mmwr/preview/mmwrhtml/ss5609a1.htm.

[4] Heather D. Boonstra, Rachel Benson Gold, Cory L. Richards, and Lawrence B. Finer, *Abortion in Women's Lives* (New York: Guttmacher Institute, 2006), 30; Guttmacher Institute, "Facts on Induced Abortion in the United States."

[5] Boonstra et al., *Abortion in Women's Lives*, 15.

[6] S. K. Henshaw and J. Van Vort, *Abortion Factbook, 1992 Edition: Readings, Trends, and State and Local Data to 1988* (New York: Guttmacher Institute, 1992); Guttmacher Institute, "Facts on Induced Abortion in the United States."

[7] Kaiser Family Foundation, "Abortion in the U.S.: Utilization, Financing, and Access," June 2008, http://www.kff.org/womenshealth/upload/3269–02.pdf.

[8] Karen J. Lewis and Jon O. Shimabukuro, "Abortion Law Development: A Brief Overview," Congressional Research Service, Almanac of Policy Issues, 2001, http://www.policyalmanac.org/culture/archive/crs_abortion_overview.shtml.

[9] Ibid.

[10] N. E. H. Hull and Peter Charles Hoffer, *Roe v. Wade: The Abortion Rights Controversy in American History* (Lawrence: University Press of Kansas, 2001), 185–187.

[11] Lewis and Shimabukuro, "Abortion Law Development."

[12] Linda Greenhouse, "Justices Back Ban on Method of Abortion," *New York Times*, April 19, 2007, http://www.nytimes.com/2007/04/19/washington/19scotus.html?ei=5090&en=5666b2d5 5ee42dbd&ex=1334635200&pagewanted=print.

[13] Hull and Hoffer, *Roe v. Wade*, 190.

[14] Heather D. Boonstra, "The Heart of the Matter: Public Funding of Abortion for Poor Women in the United States," *Guttmacher Policy Review* 10 (Winter 2007): 12–16.

[15] Kaiser Family Foundation, "Abortion in the U.S.: Utilization, Financing, and Access."

[16] Ed Hornick, "Abortion Issue Seen as Key to Health Care Reform Passage," CNN Politics, March 22, 2010, http://www.cnn.com/2010/POLITICS/03/22/abortion.health.care.vote/index .html"\t"_blank.

[17] Kaiser Family Foundation, "Summary of New Health Reform Law," April 21, 2010, http://sz0158.wc.mail.comcast.net/service/home/~/Kasier%20Summary_April%2021%2C%202010 .pdf?auth=co&loc=en_US&id=52263&part=2.

[18] George W. Bush, "Memorandum: Restoration of the Mexico City Policy," January 2001, http://web.archive.org/web/20010604032136/http://www.whitehouse.gov/news/releases/20010123–5. html. Barack Obama, "Statement Released after the President Rescinds 'Mexico City Policy,' " January 2009, http://www.whitehouse.gov/statement-released-after-the-president-rescinds;

ABC News, "Obama Overturns 'Mexico City Policy' Implemented by Reagan," January 23, 2009, http://www.abcnews.go.com/Politics/International/story? id=6716958&page=1.

[19] Pew Research Center for the People and the Press Poll (Storrs, Conn.: Roper Center for Public Opinion Research, March 8–12, 2006); Pew Research Center for the People and the Press/ Pew Forum on Religion and Public Life Poll (Storrs, Conn.: Roper Center for Public Opinion Research, August 20–27, 2009).

[20] Gallup Poll (Storrs, Conn.: Roper Center for Public Opinion Research, May 8–11, 2008).

[21] Ibid.

[22] The 2008 presidential election was dominated by concerns about the economy. When respondents were asked a month before the general election to rate the importance of thirteen issues in deciding their vote, abortion ranked twelfth in the percentage that said it was very important. Pew Research Center for the People and the Press Poll (Storrs, Conn.: Roper Center for Public Opinion Research, October 16–19, 2007).

[23] Voter Research and Surveys, National Election Day Exit Poll (Storrs, Conn.: Roper Center for Public Opinion Research, November 3, 1992).

[24] Robert J. Blendon, Mollyann Brodie, Drew E. Altman, John M. Benson, and Elizabeth C. Hamel, "Voters and Health Care in the 2004 Election," *Health Affairs* 24 (Suppl. 1; March 1, 2005): 86–96. In the 2004 election, President Bush won 74 percent of those who believed abortion should be mostly illegal or outlawed completely.

[25] Robert J. Blendon, John M. Benson, and Karen Donelan, "The Public and the Controversy over Abortion," *JAMA: The Journal of the American Medical Association* 270 (December 15, 1993): 2871–5; Robert J. Blendon, Drew E. Altman, John M. Benson, Mollyann Brodie, Tami Buhr, Claudia Deane, and Sasha Buscho, "Voters and Health Reform in the 2008 Presidential Election," *New England Journal of Medicine* 359 (November 6, 2008): 2050–61; Lydia Saad, "Public Opinion about Abortion—An In-depth Review," Gallup Poll News Service, January 22, 2002, http://www.gallup.com/poll/9904/Public-Opinion-About-Abortion-InDepth-Review .aspx#1; Craig and O'Brien, *Abortion and American Politics*, 46; Cook, Jelen, and Wilcox, *Between Two Absolutes*, 183.

[26] Blendon et al., "Voters and Health Reform in the 2008 Presidential Election."

[27] Robert J. Blendon, Drew E. Altman, Claudia Deane, John M. Benson, Mollyann Brodie, and Tami Buhr, "Health Care in the 2008 Presidential Primaries," *New England Journal of Medicine* 358 (January 24, 2008): 414–422.

[28] Gallup polls (Storrs, Conn.: Roper Center for Public Opinion Research, July 26–28, 1996; May 6–9, 2002; October 14–16, 2004; May 8–11, 2006; June 11–14, 2007; May 8–11, 2008). Gallup/CNN/*USA Today* polls (Storrs, Conn.: Roper Center for Public Opinion Research, November 6–9, 1997; January 16–18, 1998; April 30–May 2, 1999; July 14–16, 2000; August 10–12, 2001; October 24–26, 2003; July 22–24, 2005; July 17–19, 2009). Gallup/*USA Today* Poll (Storrs, Conn.: Roper Center for Public Opinion Research, March 26–28, 2010). At several times in this trend, most recently in 2004–2007, significantly more Americans identified as pro-choice than pro-life. Whether the change in 2009 and 2010 to a nearly even balance is part of a longer-term conservative trend is unclear.

[29] A similar point is made by Saad, "Public Opinion about Abortion," 7.

[30] Gallup Poll, "U.S. Abortion Attitudes Closely Divided," August 4, 2009, http://www .gallup.com/poll/122033/U.S.-Abortion-Attitudes-Closely-Divided.aspx; CNN/Opinion

Research Corporation Poll (Storrs, Conn.: Roper Center for Public Opinion Research, April 9–11, 2010).

[31] Jennifer Strickler and Nicholas L. Danigelis, "Changing Frameworks in Attitudes Toward Abortion," *Sociological Forum* 17 (June 2002): 187–201.

[32] Gallup Poll, "U.S. Abortion Attitudes Closely Divided." CNN/Opinion Research Corporation Poll, April 9–11, 2010.

[33] CNN/Opinion Research Corporation Poll, April 9–11, 2010.

[34] ABC News/*Washington Post*, June 22, 2009, http://www.washingtonpost.com/wp–srv/politics/polls/postpoll_062209.html; Pew Research Center for the People and the Press, "Public Takes Conservative Turn on Gun Control, Abortion," April 30, 2009, http://people-press.org/report/513/; *Washington Post* Poll (Storrs, Conn.: Roper Center for Public Opinion Research, March 23–26, 2010).

[35] Pew Research Center for the People and the Press/Pew Forum on Religion and Public Life Poll, August 20–27, 2009.

[36] Pew Research Center for the People and the Press/Pew Forum on Religion and Public Life Poll (Storrs, Conn.: Roper Center for Public Opinion Research, August 11–17, 2009).

[37] Cook, Jelen, and Wilcox, *Between Two Absolutes*, 33 and note.

[38] James A. Davis, Tom W. Smith, and Peter V. Marsden, *General Social Surveys, 1972–2008* (Chicago: National Opinion Research Center, 2009).

[39] Ibid.

[40] Gallup/CNN/*USA Today* Poll (Storrs, Conn.: Roper Center for Public Opinion Research, January 10–12, 2003); ABC News/*Washington Post* Poll (Storrs, Conn.: Roper Center for Public Opinion Research, January 16–20, 2003).

[41] Gallup/CNN/*USA Today* Poll, January 10–12, 2003.

[42] Davis, Smith, and Marsden, *General Social Surveys, 1972–2008*.

[43] Gallup/CNN/*USA Today* Poll, January 10–12, 2003.

[44] Davis, Smith, and Marsden, *General Social Surveys, 1972–2008*.

[45] Fox News/Opinion Dynamics Poll (Storrs, Conn.: Roper Center for Public Opinion Research, October 23–24, 2007).

[46] Davis, Smith, and Marsden, *General Social Surveys, 1972–2008*.

[47] CBS News/*New York Times* Poll (Storrs, Conn.: Roper Center for Public Opinion Research, January 10–12, 1998).

[48] Davis, Smith, and Marsden, *General Social Surveys, 1972–2008*.

[49] A similar argument is made by Ladd and Bowman, that people are balancing the preciousness of human life and the need to respect individual choice. See Everett Carll Ladd and Karlyn H. Bowman, *Public Opinion about Abortion*, 2nd ed. (Washington, D.C.: AEI Press, 1999), 3. See also Saad, "Public Opinion about Abortion."

[50] Cook, Jelen, and Wilcox, *Between Two Absolutes;* Clyde Wilcox and Barbara Norrander, "Of Moods and Morals: The Dynamics of Opinion on Abortion and Gay Rights," in *Understanding Public Opinion,* 2nd ed., ed. Barbara Norrander and Clyde Wilcox, (Washington, D.C.: CQ Press, 2002), 127.

[51] While there is no direct evidence for a rights-based consideration framework, the evidence is consistent with the idea that the rights of the fetus grow relative to the mother as the fetus develops, discussed previously.

[52] Harris Interactive Poll (Storrs, Conn.: Roper Center for Public Opinion Research, February 8–13, 2005).

[53] Gallup Poll (Storrs, Conn.: Roper Center for Public Opinion Research, May 19–21, 2003).

[54] Davis, Smith, and Marsden, *General Social Surveys, 1972–2008.*

[55] Gallup Poll, May 19–21, 2003.

[56] Fox News/Opinion Dynamics Poll, October 23–24, 2007.

[57] Gallup Poll, May 19–21, 2003; Gallup/CNN/*USA Today* Poll, January 10–12, 2003.

[58] Pew Research Center for the People and the Press/Pew Forum on Religion and Public Life Poll (Storrs, Conn.: Roper Center for Public Opinion Research, August 1–18, 2007); Gallup Poll (Storrs, Conn.: Roper Center for Public Opinion Research, May 10–13, 2007); CNN/Opinion Research Corporation Poll (Storrs, Conn.: Roper Center for Public Opinion Research, May 4–6, 2007).

[59] ABC News Poll (Storrs, Conn.: Roper Center for Public Opinion Research, July 16–20, 2003).

[60] *Newsweek*/Princeton Survey Research Associates Poll (Storrs, Conn.: Roper Center for Public Opinion Research, November 10–11, 2005).

[61] Ibid. Pew Research Center for the People and the Press/Pew Forum on Religion and Public Life Poll, August 11–17, 2009.

[62] *Newsweek*/Princeton Survey Research Associates Poll, November 10–11, 2005; Gallup/CNN/*USA Today* Poll (Storrs, Conn.: Roper Center for Public Opinion Research, November 11–13, 2005).

[63] *Los Angeles Times* Poll (Storrs, Conn.: Roper Center for Public Opinion Research, June 8–13, 2000).

[64] Pew Research Center for the People and the Press/Pew Forum on Religion and Public Life Poll, August 11–17, 2009.

[65] Asking about specific legislation/court rulings is difficult. Many polling questions about support for *Roe v. Wade* have been criticized because they describe the ruling. This description can influence responses and may not represent actual support if it differs from the actual ruling. Therefore, this discussion reviews only those questions that do not include such a description. The solution is not perfect because it is not clear how much respondents know about the ruling, but it does give a better snapshot of support "today" if there was no renewed public debate.

[66] CBS News/*New York Times* Poll (Storrs, Conn.: Roper Center for Public Opinion Research, June 12–16, 2009).

[67] Quinnipiac University Poll (Storrs, Conn.: Roper Center for Public Opinion Research, April 14–19, 2010).

[68] Gallup/CNN/*USA Today* Poll (Storrs, Conn.: Roper Center for Public Opinion Research, June 24–26, 2005); Gallup/CNN/*USA Today* Poll, November 11–13, 2005.

[69] CNN/Opinion Research Corporation Poll (Storrs, Conn.: Roper Center for Public Opinion Research, October 12–14, 2007).

[70] Gallup Poll (Storrs, Conn.: Roper Center for Public Opinion Research, May 3–6, 2010).

[71] Pew Research Center for the People and the Press/Pew Forum on Religion and Public Life Poll, July 6–19, 2006.

[72] Davis, Smith, and Marsden, *General Social Surveys, 1972–2008.*

[73] *Time*/CNN/Harris Interactive Poll (Storrs, Conn.: Roper Center for Public Opinion Research, January 15–16, 2003).

[74] CBS News/*New York Times* Poll (Storrs, Conn.: Roper Center for Public Opinion Research, January 10–12, 1998).

[75] CBS News Poll (Storrs, Conn.: Roper Center for Public Opinion Research, January 2–3, 1995).

[76] *Los Angeles Times* Poll, June 8–13, 2000.

[77] The literature about support for legal abortion frequently debates these differences. Part of the debate stems from different statistical analyses or models used. We stick here to basic cross-tabulations to look at these groups over time, which offers a slightly different perspective from some of the literature on this same topic.

[78] Davis, Smith, and Marsden, *General Social Surveys, 1972–2008.*

[79] Robert J. Blendon, Drew E. Altman, John M. Benson, and Mollyann Brodie, "Health Care in the 2004 Presidential Election," *New England Journal of Medicine* 351 (September 23, 2004): 1314–22.

[80] Davis, Smith, and Marsden, *General Social Surveys, 1972–2008.*

[81] Ibid.

[82] Michael W. Combs and Susan Welch, "Blacks, Whites, and Attitudes toward Abortion," *Public Opinion Quarterly* 46 (Winter 1982): 510–520; Elaine J. Hall and Myra Marx Ferree, "Race Differences in Abortion Attitudes," *Public Opinion Quarterly* 50 (Summer 1986): 193–207; Clyde Wilcox, "Race Differences in Abortion Attitudes: Some Additional Evidence," *Public Opinion Quarterly* 54 (Summer 1990): 248–255.

[83] Davis, Smith, and Marsden, *General Social Surveys, 1972–2008.*

[84] Ibid.

[85] Ibid.

[86] Ibid. Using other questions about abortion, including that from American National Election Studies, independents hold a position that is more directly in the middle of Republicans and Democrats. American National Election Studies, "Abortion (2), by Law 1980–2004," The ANES Guide to Public Opinion and Electoral Behavior, http://www.electionstudies.org/nesguide/2ndtable/t4c_2b_4.htm.

[87] Davis, Smith, and Marsden, *General Social Surveys, 1972–2008.*

[88] Pew Research Center for the People and the Press, "Among Wealthy Nations, U.S. Stands Alone in its Embrace of Religion," December 19, 2002, http://pewglobal.org/reports/pdf/167.pdf.

[89] ABC News/*Washington Post* polls (Storrs, Conn.: Roper Center for Public Opinion Research, April 21–24, 2005; December 6–8, 2007).

[90] Kraig Beyerlein and Mark Chaves, "The Political Activities of Religious Congregations in the United States," *Journal for the Scientific Study of Religion* 42 (June 2003): 229–246;

Lyman A. Kellstedt, John C. Green, James L. Guth, and Corwin E. Smith, "Grasping the Essentials: The Social Embodiment of Religion and Political Behavior," in *Religion and the Culture Wars,* ed. Lyman A. Kellstedt, John C. Green, James L. Guth, and Corwin E. Smith (Lanham, Md.: Rowman and Littlefield, 1996), 267–290; Anna Greenberg, "The Church and the Revitalization of Politics and Community," *Political Science Quarterly* 115 (Fall 2000): 377–394.

[91] Robert J. Blendon, John M. Benson, and Melissa J. Herrmann, "The American Public and the Terri Schiavo Case," *Archives of Internal Medicine* 165 (December 12/26, 2005): 2580–4.

[92] Davis, Smith, and Marsden, *General Social Surveys, 1972–2008.*

[93] A majority (54 percent) of white mainline Protestants believe that abortion should be legal in all or most cases, compared with 23 percent of white evangelical Protestants. Pew Research Center for the People and the Press, "Public Takes Conservative Turn on Gun Control, Abortion."

[94] Davis, Smith, and Marsden, *General Social Surveys, 1972–2008.*

[95] As early as 1991, James D. Hunter, *Culture Wars: The Struggle to Define America* (New York: Basic Books, 1991), argued that there was a moral coalition of religious conservatives across denominations, advancing a traditionalist view of the sanctity of life against a more secularized and individualistic view of the variable value of life. Using a variety of definitions of "religiosity," John M. Benson and Melissa J. Herrmann, "Right to Die or Right to Life? The Public on Assisted Suicide," *Public Perspective* 10 (June/July 1999): 15–19, concluded that the main division on abortion and other right-to-life issues "is not between Protestants and Catholics, but between those who might be termed highly religious and those who are more secular in their orientation."

[96] Davis, Smith, and Marsden, *General Social Surveys, 1972–2008.*

[97] ABC News/*Washington Post* Poll (Storrs, Conn.: Roper Center for Public Opinion Research, November 12–15, 2009).

[98] Clifford Grammich, Julie DaVanzo, and Kate Stewart, "Changes in American Opinion about Family Planning," *Studies in Family Planning* 35 (September 2004): 197–206.

[99] Ibid.

[100] *Newsweek*/Princeton Survey Research Associates Poll (Storrs, Conn.: Roper Center for Public Opinion Research, February 8–9, 2001).

[101] *Religion and Ethics Newsweekly*/United Nations Foundation/Greenberg Quinlan Rosner Research Poll (Storrs, Conn.: Roper Center for Public Opinion Research, September 4–21, 2008).

[102] National Constitution Center/Public Agenda Foundation Poll (Storrs, Conn.: Roper Center for Public Opinion Research, July 10–24, 2002).

[103] *Time*/CNN/Yankelovich Partners Poll (Storrs, Conn.: Roper Center for Public Opinion Research, January 5, 1995).

[104] *Newsweek*/Princeton Survey Research Associates Poll (Storrs, Conn.: Roper Center for Public Opinion Research, October 29–30, 1998).

[105] Freedom Forum/Center for Survey Research and Analysis, University of Connecticut Poll (Storrs, Conn.: Roper Center for Public Opinion Research, February 26–March 24, 1999).

[106] Gallup Poll (Storrs, Conn.: Roper Center for Public Opinion Research, October 6–9, 2000).

[107] Kaiser Family Foundation, "Emergency Contraception," November 2005, http://www.kff.org/womenshealth/upload/3344-03.pdf.

[108] Ibid.

[109] Reproductive Health Technologies Project/Peter D. Hart Research Associates Poll (Storrs, Conn.: Roper Center for Public Opinion Research, July 11–14, 2002).

[110] Pew Research Center for the People and the Press/Pew Forum on Religion and Public Life Poll, July 6–19, 2006.

[111] *Newsweek*/Princeton Survey Research Associates Poll (Storrs, Conn.: Roper Center for Public Opinion Research, August 24–25, 2006).

Table 11-1 Pro-Choice or Pro-Life: Americans Describe Themselves, 1996–2010 (in percent)

	Pro-Choice	Pro-Life	Mixed/Neither (vol.)
1996	49	40	4
1997	51	40	3
1998	48	45	4
1999	48	42	3
2000	50	40	4
2001	46	46	3
2002	47	46	3
2003	48	45	2
2004	52	41	2
2005	51	42	3
2006	53	42	1
2007	51	43	2
2008	50	44	1
2009	46	47	3
2010	45	46	4

Note: In years when more than one poll was conducted, results are shown for the latest poll conducted entirely within that year. "Don't know" responses not shown. (vol.) = volunteered response.

Question: With respect to the abortion issue, would you consider yourself to be pro-choice or pro-life?

Sources: Gallup polls (Storrs, Conn.: Roper Center for Public Opinion Research, July 26–28, 1996; May 6–9, 2002; October 14–16, 2004; May 8–11, 2006; June 11–14, 2007; May 8–11, 2008). Gallup/CNN/*USA Today* polls (Storrs, Conn.: Roper Center for Public Opinion Research, November 6–9, 1997; January 16–18, 1998; April 30–May 2, 1999; July 14–16, 2000; August 10–12, 2001; October 24–26, 2003; July 22–24, 2005; July 17–19, 2009). Gallup/*USA Today* Poll (Storrs, Conn.: Roper Center for Public Opinion Research, March 26-28, 2010).

Table 11-2 Americans' Preferences on the Legality of Abortion, 1975–2010 (in percent)

	Legal under any circumstances	Legal only under certain circumstances	Illegal in all circumstances
1975	21	53	23
1977	22	55	19
1978	13	63	19
1979	22	54	19
1980	25	53	18
1983	23	58	16
1985	21	55	21
1988	24	54	17
1989	29	51	18
1990	29	56	14
1991	33	49	14
1992	31	53	14
1993	32	51	13
1994	33	52	15
1995	31	54	12
1996	24	52	17
1997	26	55	17
1998	23	58	17
1999	27	54	16
2000	28	51	19
2001	26	56	17
2002	25	57	22
2003	26	55	17
2004	24	55	19
2005	26	56	16
2006	30	52	15
2007	26	55	18
2008	28	53	17
2009	21	55	18
2010	21	56	22

	Legal under any circumstances	Legal in most circumstances	Legal in only a few circumstances	Illegal in all circumstances
2010	21	13	42	22

Note: In years when more than one poll was conducted, results are shown for the latest poll conducted entirely that year. "Don't know" response not shown.

Question: Do you think abortions should be legal under any circumstances, legal only under certain circumstances, or illegal in all circumstances? (If legal only under certain circumstances, ask) Do you think abortion should be legal in most circumstances or only in a few circumstances?

Source: Gallup Poll, "U.S. Abortion Attitudes Closely Divided," August 4, 2009. CNN/Opinion Research Corporation Poll (Storrs, Conn.: Roper Center for Public Opinion Research, April 9–11, 2010).

Table 11-3 Americans' Preferences on the Legality of Abortion, 1995–2010 (in percent)

	Legal in all cases	Legal in most cases	Illegal in most cases	Illegal in all cases
1995				
July[1]	27	32	26	14
September[1]	24	36	25	11
October[1]	26	35	25	12
1996				
June[1]	24	34	25	14
August[1]	22	34	27	14
1998				
July[1]	19	35	29	13
1999				
March[1]	21	34	27	15
September[1]	20	37	26	15
2000				
July[1]	20	33	26	17
2001				
January[1]	21	38	25	14
August[1]	22	27	28	20
2003				
January[1]	23	34	25	17
2004				
May[1]	23	31	23	20
December[1]	21	34	25	17
2005				
April[1]	20	36	27	14
December[1]	17	40	27	13
2007				
February[1]	16	39	31	12
July[1]	23	34	28	14
August[2]	17	37	26	15
October[2]	21	32	24	15
November[2]	18	33	29	15
December[1]	20	35	25	18
2008				
January[1]	22	36	25	15
June[2]	19	38	24	13
August[1]	22	32	26	18
October[2]	18	35	24	16
2009				
March-April[2]	18	28	28	16
June[1]	20	35	26	17
August[2]	17	32	27	18
2010				
March[3]	17	35	27	18

Note: In months when more than one poll was conducted, results are shown for the latest poll conducted entirely within that month. "Don't know" responses not shown.

Question: Do you think abortion should be legal in all cases, legal in most cases, illegal in most cases, or illegal in all cases?

Sources: [1]ABC News/*Washington Post,* June 22, 2009. [2]Pew Research Center for the People and the Press/Pew Forum on Religion and Public Life, "2009 Religion & Public Life Survey." [3]*Washingon Post* Poll (Storrs, Conn.: Roper Center for Public Opinion Research, March 23–26, 2010).

Table 11-4 Americans' Attitudes about Abortion under Various Circumstances, 1972–2008

Percent saying it should be possible to get legal abortion

	Woman's health	Defect	Rape	Low income	Married and wants no more	Not married	Any reason
1972	83		75		38	41	
1973	91		81		46	47	
1974	90		83		45	48	
1975	88		80	51	44	46	
1976	89		81	51	45	48	
1977	89		81	52	45	48	
1978	88	80	81	46	39	40	32
1980	88	80	80	50	45	46	39
1982	90	81	83	50	46	47	39
1983	87	76	80	42	39	38	33
1984	88	78	77	45	41	43	38
1985	87	76	78	42	39	40	36
1987	86	77	78	44	40	40	38
1988	86	76	77	41	39	38	35
1989	88	79	80	46	43	43	39
1990	89	78	81	46	43	43	43
1991	89	80	83	47	43	43	41
1993	86	79	79	48	45	46	43
1994	88	80	81	49	47	46	45
1996	89	79	81	45	45	43	43
1998	84	75	77	42	40	40	39
2000	85	75	76	40	39	37	38
2002	90	76	78	43	43	41	42
2004	83	69	73	39	39	40	38
2006	84	70	74	41	40	37	38
2008	85	70	72	41	43	39	40

Question: Please tell me whether or not you think it should be possible for a pregnant woman to obtain a legal abortion. (If the woman's own health is seriously endangered by the pregnancy/If there is a strong chance of serious defect in the baby/If she became pregnant as result of rape/If the family has a very low income and cannot afford any more children/If she is married and does not want any more children/If she is not married and does not want to marry the man/If the woman wants it for any reason.)

Source: James A. Davis, Tom W. Smith, and Peter V. Marsden, *General Social Surveys, 1972–2008* (Chicago: National Opinion Research Center, 2009).

Table 11-5 Americans' Attitudes about Abortion in the Third Trimester (in percent)

	Yes	No
Abortion should be legal in the . . .[1]		
First three months	60	38
Second three months	26	72
Last three months	12	86
Abortion should be legal in the last three months if . . .[2]		
Woman's life is endangered	75	22
Pregnancy caused by rape or incest	59	39
Child would be born mentally disabled	38	56

Note: "Don't know" repsonses not shown.

Question: Thinking more generally, do you think abortion should be generally legal or generally illegal during each of the following stages of pregnancy? How about in the first three months of pregnancy? In the second three months of pregnancy? In the last three months of pregnancy?

Question: Now I am going to read some specific situations under which abortion might be considered in the last three months of pregnancy. Thinking specifically about the third trimester, please say whether you think abortion should be legal in that situation, or illegal. How about (when the woman's life is endangered/when the pregnancy was caused by rape or incest/when the child would be born mentally disabled)?

Sources: [1] Harris Interactive Poll (Roper Center for Public Opinion Research, February 8-13, 2005). [2] Gallup Poll (Roper Center for Public Opinion Research, May 19-21, 2003).

Table 11-6 Americans' Attitudes about Restrictions in Abortion (in percent)

Percent Favor	
Counseling about dangers and alternatives to abortion[1]	81
Parental notification[1]	78
Parental consent for women under 18[2]	76
24-hour waiting period[1]	71
Husband notification[3]	64
Biological father consent[4]	49
Making it more difficult[2]	35

Question: Please tell me if you would support or oppose each of the following restrictions on abortion that some state legislatures have considered. Would you support or oppose a law requiring (women seeking abortions to be counseled about the dangers and alternatives to abortion/that parents of teenagers must be notified/women seeking abortions wait 24 hours before having the procedure done)?

Question: Do you strongly favor, favor, oppose, or strongly oppose (requiring that women under the age of 18 get the consent of at least one parent before they are allowed to have an abortion/making it more difficult for a woman to get an abortion)?

Question: Do you favor or oppose each of the following proposals. How about a law requiring that the husband of a married woman be notified if she decides to have an abortion?

Question: Generally speaking, are you in favor of requiring a woman to get the consent of the biological father before having an abortion, or are you opposed to that?

Sources: [1]*Newsweek*/Princeton Survey Research Associates Poll (Roper Center for Public Opinion Research, November 10–11, 2005). [2]Pew Research Center for the People and the Press/Pew Forum on Religion and Public Life Poll (Roper Center for Public Opinion Research, August 11–17, 2009). [3]Gallup/CNN/*USA Today* Poll (Roper Center for Public Opinion Research, November 11–13, 2005). [4]*Los Angeles Times* Poll (Roper Center for Public Opinion Research, June 8–13, 2000).

Table 11-7 Americans' Views on *Roe v. Wade* and a Constitutional Amendment to Ban Abortion (in percent)

Overturn *Roe v. Wade*	2005[1]	2006[2]	2007[3]	2009[4]
Yes	30	25	35	29
No	65	66	53	64
Don't know	6	9	12	7

Agree with *Roe v. Wade*[5]	2003	2005	2007	2010
Yes	62	65	62	60
No	35	30	32	35
Don't know	3	6	6	5

Want justices to vote to overturn *Roe v. Wade*[6]	2005
Overturn	35
Uphold	61
Don't know	4

Constitutional Amendment to ban abortion, except for mother's life	1996[7]	2003[8]	2005[9]
Favor	38	38	37
Oppose	59	59	61
Don't know	3	3	2

Question: Would you like to see the Supreme Court overturn its 1973 *Roe v. Wade* decision concerning abortion or not?

Question: In general, do you agree or disagree with the 1973 *Roe v. Wade* Supreme Court decision that established a woman's right to an abortion?

Question: If one of the U.S. Supreme Court justices retired, would you want the new Supreme Court justice to be someone who would vote to overturn *Roe v. Wade*—the decision that legalized abortion—or vote to uphold it?

Question: Do you favor or oppose each of the following proposals? How about a constitutional amendment to ban abortion in all circumstances, except in cases necessary to save the life of the mother?

Sources: [1]Gallup/CNN/*USA Today* Poll (Storrs, Conn.: Roper Center for Public Opinion Research, July 7–10, 2005). [2]Gallup Poll (Storrs, Conn.: Roper Center for Public Opinion Research, May 8–11, 2006). [3]CNN/Opinion Research Corporation Poll (Storrs, Conn.: Roper Center for Public Opinion Research, May10–13, 2007). [4]CBS News/*New York Times* Poll (Storrs, Conn.: Roper Center for Public Opinion Research, June 12–16, 2009). [5]Quinnipiac University Polls (Storrs, Conn.: Roper Center for Public Opinion Research, February 2–March 3, 2003; July 21–25, 2005; August 7–13, 2007; April 14–19, 2010). [6]Gallup/CNN/*USA Today* Poll (Storrs, Conn.: Roper Center for Public Opinion Research, June 24–26, 2005). [7]Gallup Poll (Storrs, Conn.: Roper Center for Public Opinion Research, July 26–28, 1996). [8]Gallup/CNN/*USA Today* Poll (Storrs, Conn.: Roper Center for Public Opinion Research, January 10–12, 2003). [9]Gallup/CNN/*USA Today* Poll (Storrs, Conn.: Roper Center for Public Opinion Research, November 11–13, 2005).

Table 11-8 Americans' Views about the Morality of Abortion (in percent)

Having an abortion is wrong[1]	
Yes	60
No	36
Abortion is . . . [2]	
Morally wrong	50
Morally acceptable	38
Depends (vol.)	9
Having an abortion is morally wrong . . . [3]	
In nearly all circumstances	24
In some circumstances	49
Not a moral issue	24
Having an abortion if there is a strong chance of serious defect in the baby is . . . [4]	
Always wrong	23
Almost always wrong	9
Wrong only sometimes	15
Not wrong at all	51
Having an abortion if the family has a very low income and cannot afford any more children is . . . [4]	
Always wrong	50
Almost always wrong	10
Wrong only sometimes	10
Not wrong at all	28
Abortion is an act of murder[5]	
Yes	46
No	46
Abortion is sometimes the best course in a bad situation[6]	
Agree	58
Disagree	36

Note: "Don't know" responses not shown.

Question: Regardless of whether you think abortion should be allowed, do you personally believe having an abortion is wrong?

Question: I'm going to read you a list of issues. Regardless of whether or not you think it should be legal, for each one, please tell me whether you personally believe that in general it is morally acceptable or morally wrong. How about abortion?

Question: Regardless of whether or not you think abortion should be legal, do you personally believe that having an abortion is morally wrong in nearly all circumstances, morally wrong in some circumstances, or is it not a moral issue?

Question: Do you personally think it is wrong or not wrong for a woman to have an abortion (if there is a strong chance of serious defect in the baby/if the family has a very low income and cannot afford any more children)? Always wrong, almost always wrong, wrong only sometimes, not wrong at all.

Question: Some people say abortion is an act of murder, while other people disagree. What is your view—do you think abortion is an act of murder or don't you feel this way?

Question: Do you agree or disagree with the following statement: Abortion is sometimes the best course in a bad situation?

Sources: [1]CNN/Opinion Research Corporation Poll (Storrs, Conn.: Roper Center for Public Opinion Research, October 12–14, 2007). [2]Gallup Poll (Storrs, Conn.: Roper Center for Public Opinion Research, May 3–6, 2010). [3]Pew Forum on Religion and Public Life/Pew Research Center for the People and the Press Poll (Storrs, Conn.: Roper Center for Public Opinion Research, July 6–19, 2006). [4]James A. Davis, Tom W. Smith, and Peter V. Marsden, *General Social Surveys, 1972–2008* (Chicago: National Opinion Research Center, 2009). [5]*Time*/CNN/Harris Interactive Poll (Storrs, Conn.: Roper Center for Public Opinion Research, January 15–16, 2003). [6]CBS News/*New York Times* Poll (Storrs, Conn.: Roper Center for Public Opinion Research, January 10–12, 1998).

Table 11-9 Americans' Attitudes about Abortion under Various Circumstances, by
Subgroups, 2008

Percent saying it should be possible to get legal abortion	Woman's health	Defect	Rape	Low income	Married and wants no more	Not married	Any reason
By sex							
Women	85	69	70	40	40	37	39
Men	86	71	75	43	46	42	41
By age							
18–29	85	62	75	44	41	38	42
30–49	87	75	73	44	46	44	44
50–64	85	71	71	41	45	37	38
65+	83	68	69	32	32	33	32
By race							
White	85	71	74	42	43	40	42
Black	89	71	72	42	45	36	37
By education							
HS grad or less	80	64	66	33	33	30	33
Some college	90	73	79	43	45	41	41
College grad or more	89	79	78	53	54	55	53
By household income							
<$25K	80	67	67	36	36	30	30
$25–49.9K	89	70	70	38	40	34	37
$50–74.9K	85	66	69	34	35	36	37
$75K+	88	77	79	50	53	49	50
By region							
Northeast	83	77	78	51	55	50	56
Midwest	88	71	76	47	46	44	45
South	83	64	64	32	33	28	28
West	88	73	77	44	44	44	43
By party identification							
Democrat	91	75	79	49	48	45	45
Independent	81	65	65	35	39	33	35
Republican	81	66	66	33	36	33	34
By marital Status							
Married	84	70	71	38	40	37	37
Divorced/Separated	86	74	71	48	49	43	43
Never married	91	68	78	48	48	44	48

(Table continues)

Table 11-9 *Continued*

By religion							
Protestant	85	67	68	35	36	32	32
Catholic	79	67	66	33	34	31	36
None	93	84	90	68	70	69	66
By frequency of attending religious services							
Never	94	85	89	62	60	61	60
Less than once/year to several times/year	92	81	81	50	54	47	49
Once a month/Nearly every week	82	65	74	37	40	34	37
Every Week +	73	51	48	18	18	17	17

Question: Please tell me whether or not you think it should be possible for a pregnant woman to obtain a legal abortion. (If the woman's own health is seriously endangered by the pregnancy/If there is a strong chance of serious defect in the baby/If she became pregnant as result of rape/If the family has a very low income and cannot afford any more children/If she is married and does not want any more children/If she is not married and does not want to marry the man/If the woman wants it for any reason.)

Source: James A. Davis, Tom W. Smith, and Peter V. Marsden, *General Social Surveys, 1972–2008* (Chicago: National Opinion Research Center, 2009).

Table 11-10 Americans' Attitudes about Emergency Contraceptive ("Morning-After Pill") (in percent)

Allowing women to get "morning-after pill" without prescription[1]

Favor	48
Oppose	41
Don't know	11

Allowing adult women (age 18+) to get "morning-after pill" without prescription[2]

Favor	53
Oppose	38
Don't know	9

Allowing women under 18 to get "morning-after pill" without prescription[2]

Favor	24
Oppose	64
Don't know	12

Making "morning-after poll" available without prescription will lead to more sexual promiscuity[2]

Yes	46
No	47
Don't know	7

Question: All in all, do you strongly favor, favor, oppose, or strongly oppose allowing women to get the morning-after pill without a doctor's prescription?

Question: Do you favor or oppose allowing adult women, age 18 and over, to get the so-called "morning-after pill" without a doctor's prescription?

Question: Would you favor or oppose allowing women under 18 to get the "morning-after pill" without a doctor's prescription?

Question: In general, do you believe that making the "morning-after pill" available without a prescription will lead to more sexual promiscuity in this country, or not?

Sources: [1]Pew Forum on Religion and Public Life/Pew Research Center for the People and the Press Poll (Storrs, Conn.: Roper Center for Public Opinion Research, July 6–19, 2006). [2]*Newsweek*/Princeton Survey Research Associates Poll (Storrs, Conn.: Roper Center for Public Opinion Research, August 24–25, 2006).

Chapter 12

ATTITUDES ABOUT STEM CELL RESEARCH

Gillian K. SteelFisher and John M. Benson

The potential of stem cell research and the political responses to it have captured the public's attention. Because the technology connects the issues of basic research, medical treatment, fertility, and cloning, the public view reflects a combination of opinions about science, medicine, religion, and abortion. Moreover, the complex nature of the issue and developments in the research itself lead to changes in opinions over time. This chapter explores existing public opinion data to tease out the critical contours of the public's views today. To begin, the chapter reviews basic facts of stem cell research, its controversies, and its recent political history.

The goal of stem cell research is to treat a variety of diseases by replacing damaged cells with new cells. Although techniques have not yet been fully developed and few patients have benefited from the research so far, scientists are optimistic about one day being able to treat illnesses such as juvenile diabetes, Parkinson's, and spinal cord injuries.[1] Stem cell treatments would rely on the unique characteristic of stem cells that allows them to differentiate into many kinds of cells in the body. Four primary kinds of stem cells have different capacities for differentiation.[2] Embryonic stem (ES) cells come from early-stage embryos, and they can become any and every kind of cell in the body. Adults also have some stem cells ("somatic" or "adult" stem cells) in various organs and tissues, such as bone marrow and the brain, but they are generally limited to differentiating only into cells related to the part where they originated.[3] In addition, stem cells have been discovered in umbilical cord blood and in amniotic fluid, which appear to have certain medical advantages over embryonic cells, but perhaps more limited capacity for differentiation.[4] Finally, in a recent discovery, human skin cells have been "reprogrammed" to act like embryonic stem cells. These are called "induced pluripotent stem" (iPS) cells.[5]

Historical, Ethical, and Political Background

In late 1998 a team of researchers at the University of Wisconsin at Madison, led by Dr. James Thomson, successfully isolated embryonic stem cells.[6] These types of cells are found in early-stage embryos before they have developed a nervous system. Under correct stimulation, they have the potential to differentiate into any type of cell, such as skin, liver, or brain cells. Scientists are hopeful that they may be able to "train" these stem cells into growing into different organs and body parts and provide potential cures for diseases such as Parkinson's, Alzheimer's, and diabetes.[7] Researchers have two ways to obtain ES cells. The first, more common method, is to take embryos formed as by-products of in-vitro fertilization (IVF) procedures, which generate more embryos than are used. Because these unused embryos are later frozen and ultimately discarded, many argue that they would be put to better use through experimentation. The alternative approach actually creates embryos for the purposes of research. Therapeutic cloning, for which stem cells could one day be used, would involve creating a clone embryo of a person and using its stem cells to grow the necessary tissue. This method would avoid the problem of tissue rejection by the person's immune system.[8]

Many people, seeking alternatives to the use of embryonic stem cells, emphasize the versatility of adult stem cells, pertaining to particular types of tissue, which in rare cases have been shown to turn into other types of cells. In January 2002 University of Minnesota researchers found that cells taken from adult bone marrow "can match the ability of embryonic stem cells to turn into nerves, muscle, liver, and other specialized tissues."[9] Adult stem cells, however, may not be as versatile as ES cells in developing into various types of tissue, and the location and rarity of the adult stem cells make access to them difficult.[10]

The discovery of stem cells has sparked a fierce debate between those who voice concerns over the ethical implications of embryonic research and others who consider the potential medicinal value of stem cell research. The primary controversy is that harvesting ES cells kills human embryos. Typically, ES cells come from excess embryos created by couples seeking fertility treatment through IVF. Although the embryos would often be discarded anyway, some people oppose their purposeful destruction. A second controversy arises over the use of adult stem cells. Scientists want to create lines of stem cells that match the donor patient in hopes that the tissues and organs derived from these cells will not be rejected by the patient's immune system—a common problem with donated organs.[11] But creating these lines requires cloning. Although the goal is not to clone whole animals or humans, some people believe that permission to clone under these conditions opens the gates for other kinds of cloning; and other people believe that any kind of cloning is wrong. Additional ethical questions arise about all kinds of stem cell research, such as the absence of public review for research undertaken in the private sector.

Although the debate regarding stem cells has taken shape only in the last few years, the larger debate regarding embryonic research originated almost forty years ago. Since *Roe v. Wade* (1973), the groundbreaking Supreme Court decision that legalized abortion in the United States, abortion opponents have sought to end research they feel would justify abortion or increase their number. Only a year after *Roe v. Wade*, the 1974 National Research Act effectively halted federal funding for fetal research, a decision that was further amended in 1975 to severely limit research that posed more than a "minimal risk" to a fetus. In the late 1970s, the Ethical Advisory Board was created for the purpose of reviewing research proposals that requested government funding. Although the board ruled in 1979 that federal funds could be used for IVF research, it was disbanded the following year at the start of the Reagan administration before it could approve any specific research proposals.[12]

With the election of President Bill Clinton, certain restrictions were lifted. The 1993 National Institutes of Health Revitalization Act allowed government-funded research on fetal tissue transplantation according to specific restrictions, including research on embryos created as a by-product of IVF.[13] A year later, NIH proposed a set of rules regarding the use of human embryos in research based on the recommendations of an advisory panel. Among other suggestions, the panel permitted the "creation of a limited number of human embryos for research purposes."[14] This provision ignited concerns over human cloning, and the Clinton administration was quick to announce "that it would prohibit federal funding for creating human embryos solely for research purposes." Although this restriction did not yet preclude the use of unwanted human embryos, in a subsequent ruling in 1995 Congress banned all federal funding of research in which "human embryos are destroyed, discarded or knowingly subjected to serious risk."[15]

The scientific potential of stem cells became increasingly apparent in the late 1980s and early 1990s after several breakthroughs from the global research community.[16] These successes increased the pressure to conduct more research in the United States—both because the opportunities seemed more promising and because the United States competes for excellence in science with other countries. But the political history of stem cell research in the United States is largely about public funding, and significant legislative barriers arise because of the use of embryonic cells and cloning techniques.

Encouraged in part by mounting pressure from the scientific community after stem cells were isolated, in January 1999 the Department of Health and Human Services determined that the existing law, which prohibited federal research that harmed embryos, did not account for research into stem cell lines, which cannot grow into humans.[17] In September 1999 the National Bioethics Advisory Commission issued a report, *Ethical Issues in Human Stem Cell Research*, making its recommendations about federal funding for various types of stem cell research. The recommendations included: (1) Federal funding for the derivation and use embryonic stem cells should be limited to cadaveric fetal tissue and embryos remaining after infertility treatments. (2) Research involving the use of stem cells from embryos remaining after infertility treatments should be eligible for federal funding. (3) Federal agencies should not fund research involving the derivation of stem cells from embryos made solely for research purposes. (4) Federal agencies should not fund research involving the derivation or use of stem cells from embryos made by transferring the nucleus of an adult somatic cell into an oocyte (enucleated egg). (5) Prospective donors of embryos remaining after infertility treatments should receive timely and appropriate information to make informed and voluntary choices regarding disposition of the embryos. Prior to considering the potential research use of the embryos, a prospective donor should be presented with the option of storing the embryos, donating them to another woman, or discarding them. If the prospective donor chooses to discard the embryos, the option of donating them to research may then be presented. (6) Researchers may not promise donors that stem cells derived from their embryos will be used to treat patient-subjects specified by the donors. (7) Embryos and cadaveric fetal tissue should not be bought or sold. (8) The Department of Health and Human Services should establish a national oversight panel to ensure federally funded research involving embryonic stem cells is conducted in conformance with the ethical principles and recommendations of the report.[18]

The following year, in August 2000, President Clinton, weighing the potential benefits of increased research, established new guidelines as to what sort of research could be granted federal funding. Specifically, funding would be available only for research involving embryos created through IVF.[19]

This period of increased—albeit stringently controlled—research possibilities was short-lived. With the election of George W. Bush, and with antiabortion activists infuriated by what they saw as inadequate research restrictions, Bush attempted to take the middle ground on the issue. Rather than reinstate an outright ban on federal funding, in August 2001 the president determined that funding would be granted only to scientists working with stem cell lines that already had been discovered up to that point.[20] This material consisted of about seventy cell lines, fewer than twenty-five of which were located within the United States. In addition, federal funding for embryonic stem cell research still remained frozen at around $25 million per annum.[21] Many researchers stated that the existing lines were insufficient for successful medical research, and opponents stated that using lines derived from any embryos was still wrong, especially when medical research benefits were as yet unclear. Neither side was completely satisfied with the status quo, as reflected by numerous bills submitted to expand or restrict stem cell research after the 2001 announcement.[22]

In response to limited federal funds, several states with significant research capabilities, either in the private sector or in universities, began to fund research. California was first (in 2004) with Proposition 71, which put $3 billion into stem cell research. Five other states—Connecticut, Illinois, Maryland, Massachusetts, and New Jersey—also decided to provide money for stem cell research.[23] On the other hand, Nebraska and South Dakota restricted research funding at the state level.[24] Voters in Missouri (2006) and Michigan (2008) approved amendments to their state constitutions to allow stem cell research.[25] In 2007 New Jersey voters rejected a $450 million bond issue over the next ten years to fund stem cell research.[26]

Interest group alignments on this issue are somewhat consistent with their stances on abortion. The Catholic Church, as represented by the U.S. Conference of Catholic Bishops, opposes all forms of ES cell research.[27] The medical benefits of stem cell research and the murky definitions of embryos that exist outside the womb, however, have allowed influential pro-life conservatives to be "pro-stem cell research" without feeling they have betrayed their values. Traditionally conservative senators, including Orin Hatch (R-Utah) and the late Strom Thurmond (R-S.C), came out in favor of stem cell research.[28] Nancy Reagan became a leading voice in efforts to support stem cell research, noting her own experiences with her husband's Alzheimer's, one of the diseases that stem cell therapy might someday alleviate.[29] The questions about stem cell research create new alliances and political wedges that can change the policy landscape.

On July 19, 2006, President Bush vetoed a bill that would have eased his earlier restrictions on federal funding for stem cell research. The bill would have allowed federal funding for medical research using stem cells discarded by fertility clinics. Bush argued that the vetoed bill "would support the taking of innocent human life in the hope of finding medical benefits for others. . . . It crosses a moral boundary that our decent society needs to respect."[30]

In November 2007 two groups of researchers announced that they had "reprogrammed" skin cells to act like embryonic stem cells, with the hypothetical potential to mature into any other kind of cell in the body.[31] Many scientists believe that using these "induced pluripotent stem" (iPS) cells will solve the ethical problems some people have about embryonic stem cell research. Opponents of ES cell research argue that having an alternative like iPS will mean that ES cell research is no longer necessary or ethically justifiable. Others argue that research has not yet established that iPS cells have the full potential of ES cells and that scientists have yet to understand fully how DNA is programmed or reprogrammed for therapeutic use. They argue, therefore, that at least for now, both kinds of research should continue.[32]

On March 9, 2009, President Barack Obama issued an executive order lifting limits on federal funding of ES cell research. He left the task of deciding what kinds of studies would be eligible for federal funding to the National Institutes of Health.[33] A survey conducted later in the month showed that about six in ten Americans (61 percent) supported the executive order.[34]

Americans' Views about the Importance of the Stem Cell Issue

At the height of the debate about stem cell research in 2006, public interest was high, as more than two-thirds of adults (71 percent) said they were very or somewhat interested.[35] In 2006 about six in ten registered voters (64 percent) said that stem cell research was important to them personally.[36] This is virtually the same proportion of registered voters (63 percent) and the public as a whole (62 percent) saying that stem cell research was important in 2001, shortly before President Bush announced his federal funding policy.[37] Immediately after that announcement, 78 percent of the public said stem cell research was important.[38] The short-term shift is likely due to increased media attention, but the take-away message is clear: a majority of the public views the issue of stem cell research as important.

As an issue, however, stem cell research appears to be only moderately influential in voting decisions. Shortly before the 2004 election, slightly less than half of registered voters and of the public as a whole indicated it would be important issue in determining their vote for president.[39] Similarly, a month before the 2006 congressional elections, 45 percent of Americans said the issue of stem cell research was extremely or very important in their vote (**Table 12–1**).[40] This is still a sizable percentage, but not a majority.[41]

The critical factor is that very few people consider stem cell research to be the *most* important issue in their vote. Given a list of issues, only 2 percent of likely voters indicated shortly before the 2004 election that stem cell research would be the most important issue in their presidential vote. Similarly, in the days just before the 2006 elections, only 3 percent said the same regarding their congressional vote (**Table 12–2**).[42] Stem cell research was not an important issue in the 2008 presidential campaign and did not appear in preelection or exit poll questions that gave voters a list of issues to choose from that might be important in their presidential vote.

The issue is also not a top priority for policy action. Asked just before the 2006 elections to choose from a list of issues, only 14 percent of registered voters said that reopening federal funding for new stem cell research should be one of the top one or two priorities for new Congress.[43] When respondents were asked in February 2009 how important it was for the president and Congress to deal with each of twelve issues, stem cell research ranked last in the proportion that said it was extremely or very important (33 percent).[44]

Public Support for Stem Cell Research and Federal Funding

Overall, a majority of the American public supports stem cell research, including research using cells from human embryos (**Table 12–3**).[45] With some important exceptions, a majority also favors federal funding for stem cell research (**Table 12–4**).[46] Support for stem cell research and for federal funding depends, however, on the extent to which the description and the type of stem cell research connect with American values. In general, support declines as the questions become more specific about the use of human embryos: 76 percent favor the use of "stem cells" in medical research; 65 to 68 percent favor the use of "embryonic stem cells"; and 57 percent to 63 percent favor medical research using "stem cells from human embryos."[47] When asked about medical research that uses stem cells from sources that do not involve human embryos, 70 percent of the public favor such research.[48] In addition, in response to a 2004 question that emphasized specific potential benefits, such as developing treatments or preventing diabetes, Alzheimer's, and Parkinson's, a large majority of the public (73 percent) favored stem cell research.[49]

Experimental data concerning support for federal funding of stem cell research also suggest that different types of stem cell research garner varied support. An August 2001 poll showed that baseline support for federal funding of stem cell research—that is, without any description other than its name—was 55 percent, and a description that explained the most common scenario (extra IVF embryos are destroyed in search of medical treatments) garnered the same level of support. On the other hand, a description that discussed adult stem cell research and emphasized that no embryos are destroyed got much higher support at 68 percent. A description in which the embryo is created in a laboratory for the purposes of research (as opposed to an extra embryo created by a fertility clinic) received lower support at 46 percent, and a description in which the embryo is the result of cloning got very low support at 28 percent (**Table 12–5**).[50]

In 2006 about half (46 percent) of those who opposed using tax dollars for stem cell research said they did so because it conflicts with their religious and moral values, and half (49 percent) said it was because they did not think it was a good use of public money.[51] When Americans were asked in late 2008 what the level of future federal spending on stem cell research should be, 33 percent said it should be increased; 41 percent thought it should be kept the same; and 23 percent said it should be decreased (**Table 12–4**).[52]

Shortly before President Obama's executive order, respondents were asked to choose among four possible levels of federal funding. A plurality (38 percent) favored easing the Bush-era restrictions to allow more ES cell research, and 14 percent thought there should be no restrictions on government funding. On the other hand, 22 percent favored keeping the restrictions that were in place under the Bush policy, and 19 percent thought the federal government should not fund ES cell research at all.[53]

Six months after California passed Proposition 71, more than half (53 percent) of the national public felt that other states should follow California's lead, and 37 percent thought they should not.[54]

Moral Concerns

Despite overall public support, it remains true that many Americans are concerned about the morality of stem cell research. In 2001, 79 percent of the public said that the ethical concerns over ES cell research were very or somewhat serious.[55] In 2010, 59 percent saw ES cell research as morally acceptable, and 32 percent saw it as morally wrong. These proportions have fluctuated within a relatively narrow range since 2002 (**Table 12–6**).[56]

In deciding about support, the public appears to weigh two components of the ES cell research equation: the ethical implications of using human embryos and the potential for medical treatments of significant illnesses. When asked explicitly, a slight majority of the public seems to regard the potential of research as more important than the value of not destroying human embryos. In 2009, 54 percent of the public thought the potential of research was more important, as compared to 32 percent who considered not destroying the life of embryos more important. This split was 43 percent to 38 percent in 2002 (**Table 12–7**).[57] But support is not as solid as it might first appear. In 2002, 46 percent of those who thought the potential of research was more important said they could imagine thinking differently, while only 23 percent of those who were focused on the potential life of human embryos said the same thing.[58]

The complexity of public opinion is clear when the morality and perceived necessity of using human embryos for stem cell research are queried at the same time. In 2001, 49 percent of the public believed that ES cell research was "morally wrong," but this number included 31 percent who said it might also be "necessary."[59] This result suggests that if alternatives to ES cell research look promising, support for ES cell research may decline.

Existing data suggest different sources of information about stem cell research exert influence on supporters and opponents. For supporters, these sources include news/the media (cited by 28 percent), education (22 percent), and personal nonreligious beliefs (17 percent). The thematic finding here is that secular institutions have a major effect on supporters. Personal experience, family/friends, and religious beliefs are much less important (**Table 12–8**).[60]

For opponents of stem cell research, religious beliefs are the dominant influence. In 2001, 42 percent of opponents cited religious beliefs as having the greatest effect on their opinions. Personal nonreligious beliefs are the next largest source, alongside the news/media, but only 17 percent and 13 percent of opponents cited these sources as the strongest. Education (cited by 6 percent) and noninstitutionalized influences (family/friends and personal experiences) (3 percent) are dramatically less influential.[61] Religion appears to be a steady influence over time. A 2005 survey shows that 57 percent of opposition to stem cell research is based on "religious objections" rather than "other grounds."[62]

Competition with Other Countries

The news media have raised a potentially important issue that has not yet been explored in polling: the competitive advantage internationally that stem cell research brings (or will bring) to the country that pursues it. Nations around the world have responded in different ways to the ethical and policy issues posed by stem cell research. Some countries, such as China, Israel, Japan, Singapore, South Korea, and the United Kingdom, have pursued stem cell research vigorously. Others, such as Canada and Spain, have taken a moderate approach. Germany, Ireland, and Italy have placed strict constraints on stem cell research.[63]

Attitudes of Various Groups about Stem Cell Research

A majority of most demographic groups in the United States expresses support for embryonic stem cell research and federal funding for such research, with important exceptions. Highly religious Americans and those who oppose abortion are especially likely to oppose ES cell research.

As distinct groups, men and women, younger and older adults, whites and African Americans differ little in their level of support. Differences in support become apparent when answers are analyzed by political party, level of education, and religiosity. Democrats and independents are significantly more likely than Republicans to support embryonic stem cell research. College graduates are significantly more supportive than adults with a high school diploma or less, although on some questions a majority of the latter favor such research (**Table 12–9**).[64]

Those who say that religious beliefs provide a great deal or quite a bit of guidance in their day-to-day lives are among the least supportive of ES cell research, and a large majority of those who say religion provides little guidance or is not an important part of their lives support the research (**Table 12–10**).[65] This pattern is consistent with attitudes about abortion as well as other "life" issues such as physician-assisted suicide, where we find large differences in attitude between very religious and less religious Americans.[66]

In spite of the distinction that some leaders make between embryonic stem cell research and abortion, public attitudes about the two issues are highly correlated. In a 2008 poll, support for ES cell research was higher than three-fourths (79 percent) among those who thought that a woman should be able to get an abortion if she wants one, but only 20 percent among those who thought abortion should always be illegal.[67]

Most of these same demographic differences were also apparent at the voting booth, on state ballot measures in California (2004) and Missouri (2006). Three-fourths of Democratic voters supported these two stem cell research propositions, and a substantial majority of Republican voters opposed. In both states, seven in ten voters who said they attended religious services only a few times a year or never voted yes, and large majorities of voters who said they attended religious services weekly or more often voted no. More than eight in ten generally pro-choice voters in Missouri voted for their state's stem cell amendment, compared with only one-fourth of pro-life voters (**Table 12–11**).[68]

When the question about stem cell research specifies a source other than human embryos, differences in attitude between various groups either shrink or disappear (**Table 12–12**).[69]

Virtually identical proportions of Democrats, independents, and Republicans favor such research. Although those who have had at least some college education are still significantly more likely to favor the research than those who have not, nearly two-thirds (64 percent) of the latter favor stem cell research that does not use human embryos.

Similarly, if the question does not concern using human embryos, the gap shrinks dramatically between more religious and less religious Americans and between those with pro-life and pro-choice views on abortion. Nearly two-thirds of highly religious Americans (65 percent) and those who believe abortion should always be illegal (65 percent) favor medical research that uses stem cells that are not derived from human embryos.[70] This result is in sharp contrast with these groups' views about embryonic stem cell research.

Public Interest and Understanding

The public seems to be engaged in the stem cell issue, with more than half saying that they have followed news about this issue during peak times of debate.[71] In 2007, 45 percent of Americans said they had "heard a lot" about stem cell research, a significant increase over 2001, when only 27 percent had "heard a lot" (**Table 12–13**).[72]

Despite the interest and attention, factual understanding of the issues at stake is less clear. In August 2001 only about half of the population (51 percent) could explain that the primary point of debate was that embryos are destroyed in the research process.[73] Asked in 2009 which of three phrases described how stem cells differ from other cells, only about half (52 percent) correctly said that they can develop into many different types of cells.[74]

Apart from these points of confusion, 60 percent of the public claimed to have a good basic understanding of the stem cell issue at the time of President Bush's announcement in 2001.[75] In 2008 a similar proportion (64 percent) said they were very or somewhat clear about the differences between stem cells that come from human embryos, stem cells that come from adults, and stem cells that come from other sources.[76] It is hard to know whether these differences really are clear, because no factual questions are available to measure true knowledge of the substantive issues and policies.

As the debate moves forward, the public will likely get additional information and education about stem cell research from the news, including the Internet. In 2006, two-thirds of Americans said they had gotten most of their information about such research from television (42 percent) and newspapers (25 percent).[77] In the same survey, two-thirds (67 percent) of adults indicated they would turn to the Internet if they wanted to learn more about stem cell research.[78]

Public Attitudes about Cloning

Therapeutic cloning may be an important step in stem cell research efforts because it may enable scientists to develop stem cell lines that match an individual patient, which could create tissues and organs that a patient's immune system would not reject. Although cloning is not always used in the process today, and the goal is not to create fully grown animals or humans, discussion of cloning could nevertheless affect the public's perception of stem cell research overall. How the issue is presented may be critical, as support varies quite dramatically for cloning in different contexts.

The public's basic view of cloning is extremely negative. In 2001, 64 percent of the public believed that cloning of animals should not be allowed. Opposition to human cloning is even stronger: 89 percent of the public believed that cloning of humans should not be allowed (**Table 12–14**).[79]

Moral concerns are an important reason for public objections to cloning. About six in ten Americans (63 percent) believe that cloning animals is morally wrong, and nearly nine out of ten adults (88 percent) think that cloning humans is morally wrong. These evaluations have been consistent since at least 2001 (**Table 12–15**).[80] In 2001 the main reasons for opposition to human cloning were religious beliefs (34 percent), the belief that cloning could interfere with distinctiveness and individuality (22 percent), concern that it could be used for "questionable purposes" (22 percent), and concern that the technology is dangerous (14 percent).[81]

Nevertheless, the public's view of cloning is not fixed. Support for cloning is highest when the purpose of cloning is framed around medical research and does not emphasize embryos. Cloning of human organs or body parts for use in medical transplants garners 59 percent support. The public is nearly evenly divided on cloning adult human cells for medical research and using human cloning technology if it is used only to help medical research develop new treatments. If the description includes the cloning of human embryos specifically—even if the purpose is medical research—only one third (34 percent) of the public is in favor (**Table 12–16**).[82] This evidence suggests the public may be more or less receptive to cloning in the context of stem cell research depending on how it is described.

On the question of using human cloning technology to develop new treatments, we see once again a sharp difference of opinion between the highly religious and the less religious. Support is only 43 percent among those who say that religious beliefs provide a great deal or quite a bit of guidance in their day-to-day living. In contrast, support is more than two-thirds (70 percent) among those who say religion provides some guidance or is not an important part of their life. In addition, Democrats (62 percent) and independents (55 percent) are significantly more likely than Republicans (37 percent) to favor using human cloning technology in this circumstance (**Table 12–17**).[83]

One reason that public perception may be malleable, not only in surveys but also in real life, is that the public knows very little about cloning, especially in the context of embryonic stem cell research. In 2002, 90 percent of the public was aware that the cloning of animals is scientifically feasible. At the same time, however, 46 percent of the public believed that cloning of humans was also scientifically feasible, which it currently is not.[84] Moreover, the public does not yet have set definitions for the main terms in the debate. Nearly two-thirds (64 percent) of Americans admit that the difference between reproductive and therapeutic cloning is "not very" or "not at all" clear to them.[85] Therefore, the final contribution of cloning to the stem cell debate is still an open question to some extent.

The Future of Stem Cell Politics and Public Opinion

The basic contours of public opinion about the emerging field of stem cell research reflect a complex mix of views about medicine, technology, religion, science, and abortion. Views on this topic will likely evolve in response to changes in the research itself and the media's presentation of its components.

The American public is interested in stem cell research and perceives it to be important, at least in the abstract. Although they take the moral questions related to the destruction of embryos seriously, for a majority the promise of medical treatment for an array of illnesses currently outweighs the concerns they have. So for now, a majority of the American public is in favor of stem cell research, including embryonic stem cell research. Moreover, the American public generally supports federal funding of such research.

Stem cell research has not been very important in the voting booth, and did not determine the results of the 2008 presidential and congressional elections. The public's influence on this issue may therefore be limited, as politicians will feel few constraints from their constituencies and may be more compelled to pay attention to interest groups and to their own experiences with health issues that could be treated by future successes in stem cell research.

One of the most interesting things about this issue is that opinion may change if there are changes in the science itself. If adult stem cell and iPS cell research—which do not require the destruction of embryos—look promising, then support for stem cell research overall may rise, but support for *embryonic* stem cell research may fall. The controversy may then become cloning rather than the particular use of embryos, which will change the debate dramatically.

Notes

[1] National Institutes of Health, "Stem Cell Information: The Official National Institutes of Health Resource for Stem Cell Research," http://stemcells.nih.gov/staticresources/info/basics/StemCellBasics.pdf.

[2] For a discussion of the first three types, see Cynthia B. Cohen, *Renewing the Stuff of Life: Stem Cells, Ethics, and Public Policy* (Oxford, U.K.: Oxford University Press, 2007), Chapter 1.

[3] National Institutes of Health, "Stem Cell Information."

[4] Judith A. Johnson and Erin D. Williams, "Stem Cell Research: CRS Report for Congress," Congressional Research Service, January 11, 2006, http://fpc.state.gov/documents/organization/59923.pdf; Paolo De Coppi, Georg Bartsch Jr., M. Minhaj Siddiqui, et al., "Isolation of Amniotic Stem Cell Lines with Potential for Therapy," *Nature Biotechnology* 25 (January 2007): 100–106.

[5] "Human Skin Cells Reprogrammed to Act Like Stem Cells," CNN, November 20, 2007, http://edition.cnn.com/2007/HEALTH/11/20/stem.cells.skin/index.html; Bridget M. Kuehn, "Skin Cells Reprogrammed to Be Stem Cells," *JAMA: Journal of the American Medical Association* 299 (January 2, 2008): 26.

[6] J. A. Thomson, J. Itskovitz-Eldor, S. S. Shapiro, et al., "Embryonic Stem Cell Lines Derived from Human Blastocysts," *Science* 282 (November 6, 1998): 1145–7, http://www.sciencemag.org/cgi/content/full/282/5391/1145.

[7] Adriel Bettelheim, "Embryo Research," in *Issues in Health Policy: Selections from the CQ Researcher* (Washington, D.C.: CQ Press, 2001), 157–173.

[8] Andrew Pollack, "The Stem Cell Debate; Use of Cloning to Tailor Treatment Has Big Hurdles, Including Cost," *New York Times*, December 18, 2001, F1.

[9] John Carey and Ellen Licking, "The Stem-Cell Debate Just Got Thornier," *BusinessWeek*, February 11, 2002, http://www.businessweek.com/bwdaily/dnflash/feb2002/nf2002021_8062.htm.

[10] Johnson and Williams, "Stem Cell Research." National Institutes of Health, "Stem Cell Information."

[11] A stem cell line is a family of constantly dividing cells, the product of a single parent group of stem cells. Generally they have been cultured under in vitro conditions that allow proliferation without becoming specialized cells for months to years.

[12] Heather Boonstra, "Human Embryo and Fetal Research: Medical Support and Political Controversy," *Guttmacher Report on Public Policy,* February 2001, http://www.guttmacher.org/pubs/tgr/04/1/gr040103.html.

[13] Eliot Marshall, "Rules on Embryo Research Due Out," *Science* 265 (August 19, 1994): 1024–6.

[14] John Schwartz and Ann Devroy, "Clinton to Ban U.S. Funds for Some Embryo Studies," *Washington Post,* December 3, 1994, A1.

[15] Boonstra, "Human Embryo and Fetal Research."

[16] Ibid.

[17] Gretchen Vogel, "NIH Sets Rules for Funding Embryonic Stem Cell Research," *Science* 286 (December 10, 1999): 2050–1.

[18] National Bioethics Advisory Commission, *Ethical Issues in Human Stem Cell Research,* September 1999, http://www.bioethics.gov/reports/past_commissions/nbac_stemcell1.pdf.

[19] D. Ian Hopper, "U.S. Sets Funding Rules on Embryo Cell Research," *Chicago Sun-Times,* August 23, 2000, 1.

[20] Katharine Q. Seelye, "The President's Decision: The Overview; Bush Gives His Backing for Limited Research on Existing Stem Cells," *New York Times,* August 10, 2001, http://www.nytimes.com/2001/08/10/politics/10BUSH.html.

[21] Bill Schu, "Can Science Bridge the Stem Cell Divide?" *Drug Discovery and Development,* April 1, 2005, http://www.dddmag.com/bridging-the-stem-cell-divide.aspx?adcode=group=genpro.

[22] Sheryl Gay Stolberg, "Scientists Urge Bigger Supply Of Stem Cells," *New York Times,* September 11, 2001, A1; Robin Toner, "The President's Decision: The Reaction; Each Side Finds Something to Like, and Not," *New York Times,* August 10, 2001, A17.

[23] National Conference of State Legislatures, "Stem Cell Research," January 2008, http://www.ncsl.org/programs/health/genetics/embfet.htm; "Timeline of Stem Cell Debate," *Washington Post,* July 18, 2006, http://www.washingtonpost.com/wp–dyn/content/article/2005/07/28/AR2005072800843.html; Christine Vestal, "Embryonic Stem Cell Research Divides States," Stateline.org, June 21, 2007, http://www.stateline.org/live/details/story?contentId=218416.

[24] Ariana Eunjung Cha, "A Struggling Science Experiment: States Watch Closely California's Stem Cell Research Initiative," *Washington Post,* February 13, 2005, A1; Peter Slevin, "In Heartland, Stem Cell Research Meets Fierce Opposition," *Washington Post,* August 10, 2005, A1.

[25] Vestal, "Embryonic Stem Cell Research Divides States"; "Obama Wins Michigan; Sen. Levin Re-elected; Medical Marijuana, Stem-cell Research Measures Approved," *USA Today,* November 11, 2008, http://www.usatoday.com/news/politics/election2008/mi.htm.

[26] Daniel B. Wood, "State Initiatives: New Jersey Rejects Stem-cell Research, Utah Axes Vouchers," *Christian Science Monitor,* November 9, 2007, http://www.csmonitor.com/2007/1109/p02s01–uspo.html.

[27] United States Conference of Catholic Bishops, "Stem Cell Research and Human Cloning: Questions and Answers," http://www.usccb.org/prolife/issues/bioethic/stemcell/Q&ABulletin Insert09222004.pdf.

[28] Rick Weiss, "Hatch to Support Bill Allowing Stem Cell Study; Decision on Embryo Cloning Is a Setback for Conservatives," *Washington Post,* May 1, 2002, A02. Ceci Connolly, "Conservative Pressure for Stem Cell Funds Builds; Key Antiabortionists Join Push for Embryo Research," *Washington Post,* July 2, 2001, A1.

[29] Alessandra Stanley, "Nancy Reagan, in a Whisper, Fights Bush over Stem Cells," *New York Times,* September 29, 2002, A1.

[30] "Timeline of Stem Cell Debate," *Washington Post,* July 18, 2006; Charles Babington, "Stem Cell Bill Gets Bush's First Veto," *Washington Post,* July 20, 2006, http://www.washingtonpost.com/wp–dyn/content/article/2006/07/19/AR2006071900524.html.

[31] "Human Skin Cells Reprogrammed to Act Like Stem Cells," CNN, November 20, 2007; J. Yu, M. A. Vodyanik, K. Smuga-Otto, et al., "Induced Pluripotent Stem Cell Lines Derived from Human Somatic Cells," *Science* 318 (December 21, 2007): 1917–20; K. Takahashi, K. Tanabe, M. Ohnuki, et al., "Induction of Pluripotent Stem Cells from Adult Human Fibroblasts by Defined Factors," *Cell* 131 (November 30, 2007): 861–872.

[32] "Human Skin Cells Reprogrammed to Act Like Stem Cells," CNN, November 20, 2007; Josephine Johnston, "Reprogrammed Skin Cells and Other Monkey Business," Bioethics Forum, November 21, 2007, http://www.thehastingscenter.org/Bioethicsforum/Post.aspx?id=664& terms=reprogrammed+and+%23filename+*.html; Steven Reinberg, "Scientists Show Stem Cells Don't Cause Cancer," *U.S. News & World Report,* February 14, 2008, http://health.usnews.com/usnews/health/healthday/080214/scientists-show-stem-cells-don't-cause-cancer.htm; "Stem Cell Breakthrough; A New Technology Shows Promise," *Washington Post,* November 24, 2007, http://www.washingtonpost.com/wp-dyn/content/article/2007/11/23/AR2007112301519.html; Rick Weiss, "Advance May End Stem Cell Debate; Labs Create a Stand-in Without Eggs, Embryos," *Washington Post,* November 21, 2007, http://www.washingtonpost.com/wp-dyn/content/article/2007/11/20/AR2007112000546_pf.html; D. Cyranoski, "Stem Cells: 5 Things to Know Before Jumping on the iPS Bandwagon," *Nature* 452 (March 27, 2008): 406–408; Bernadette Tansey, "New Skin Stem Cell Tech No Blow to Existing Research," *San Francisco Chronicle,* November 22, 2007, http://www.sfgate.com/cgi-bin/article.cgi?f=/c/a/2007/11/22/BUJUTGUL2.DTL.

[33] Rob Stein, "Obama's Order on Stem Cells Leaves Key Questions to NIH," *Washington Post,* March 10, 2009, A1, http://www.washingtonpost.com/wp-dyn/content/story/2009/03/09/ST2009030901296.html?sid=ST2009030901296; Sheryl Gay Stolberg, "Obama Lifts Bush's Strict Limits on Stem Cell Research," *New York Times,* March 10, 2009, http://www.nytimes.com/2009/03/10/us/politics/10stem.html?hp.

[34] NBC News/*Wall Street Journal* Poll (Storrs, Conn.: Roper Center for Public Opinion Research, April 23–26, 2009).

[35] Pew Internet and American Life Project/Princeton Survey Research Associates Poll (Storrs, Conn.: Roper Center for Public Opinion Research, January 9–February 6, 2006).

[36] Fox News/Opinion Dynamics Poll (Storrs, Conn.: Roper Center for Public Opinion Research, August 8–9, 2006).

[37] Fox News/Opinion Dynamics Poll (Storrs, Conn.: Roper Center for Public Opinion Research, July 25–26, 2001); Gallup/CNN/*USA Today* Poll (Storrs, Conn.: Roper Center for Public Opinion Research, August 3–5, 2001).

[38] Gallup/CNN/*USA Today* Poll (Storrs, Conn.: Roper Center for Public Opinion Research, August 10–12, 2001).

[39] *Newsweek*/Princeton Survey Research Associates Poll (Storrs, Conn.: Roper Center for Public Opinion Research, October 14–15, 2004); Kaiser Family Foundation Poll (Storrs, Conn.: Roper Center for Public Opinion Research, October 14–17, 2004).

[40] Kaiser Family Foundation Poll (Storrs, Conn.: Roper Center for Public Opinion Research, October 5–10, 2006).

[41] In some surveys, the percentage saying that the issue is important in their vote is much higher, at 78 percent or 74 percent. See *Time*/Schulman, Ronca, and Bucuvalas Poll (Storrs, Conn.: Roper Center for Public Opinion Research, October 14–15, 2004); Pew Research Center for the People and the Press/Princeton Survey Research Associates Poll (Storrs, Conn.: Roper Center for Public Opinion Research, October 15–19, 2004). These surveys, however, ask less stringent questions and encourage participants to think about the issue's importance in general rather than as a determinant in their vote. Moreover, stem cell research still ranks relatively low as compared to other topics. In the second survey noted above, stem cell research ties for eleventh place (out of thirteen) with abortion.

[42] Fox News/Opinion Dynamics Poll (Storrs, Conn.: Roper Center for Public Opinion Research, October 30–31, 2004); *Newsweek*/Princeton Survey Research Associates Poll (Storrs, Conn.: Roper Center for Public Opinion Research, November 2–3, 2006).

[43] NBC News/*Wall Street Journal* Poll (Storrs, Conn.: Roper Center for Public Opinion Research, October 28–30, 2006).

[44] CNN/Opinion Research Corporation Poll (Storrs, Conn.: Roper Center for Public Opinion Research, February 16–19, 2009). Unfortunately, available polls asked only about legislation to increase funding for stem cell research and not about legislation to restrict funding, so the picture of public opinion pressure on Congress and the president was incomplete.

[45] Pew Internet and American Life Project/Princeton Survey Research Associates Poll, January 9–February 6, 2006; ABC News/*Washington Post* Poll (Storrs, Conn.: Roper Center for Public Opinion Research, April 12–15, 2007); CBS News Poll (Storrs, Conn.: Roper Center for Public Opinion Research, January 18–21, 2007); Fox News/Opinion Dynamics Poll, August 8–9, 2006; Virginia Commonwealth University Life Sciences/Center for Public Policy, "VCU Life Sciences Survey 2008," http://www.vcu.edu/lifesci/images2/survey2008.pdf.

[46] ABC News/*Washington Post* Poll, January 13–16, 2009; Bloomberg/*Los Angeles Times* Poll (Storrs, Conn.: Roper Center for Public Opinion Research, January 13–16, 2007); Kaiser Family Foundation/Harvard School of Public Health Poll (Storrs, Conn.: Roper Center for Public Opinion Research, November 9–19, 2006); CNN/Opinion Research Corporation Poll (Storrs, Conn.: Roper Center for Public Opinion Research, May 4–6, 2007); *Newsweek*/Princeton Survey Research Associates Poll (Storrs, Conn.: Roper Center for Public Opinion Research, August 24–25, 2006); Kaiser Family Foundation/Harvard School of Public Health Poll (Storrs, Conn.: Roper Center for Public Opinion Research, December 4–14, 2008).

[47] Pew Internet and American Life Project/Princeton Survey Research Associates Poll, January 9–February 6, 2006; ABC News/*Washington Post* Poll, April 12–15, 2007; CBS News Poll, January 18–21, 2007; Fox News/Opinion Dynamics Poll, August 8–9, 2006; Virginia Commonwealth University Life Sciences/Center for Public Policy, "VCU Life Sciences Survey 2008."

[48] Virginia Commonwealth University Life Sciences/Center for Public Policy, "VCU Life Sciences Survey 2008."

[49] Harris Interactive Poll, August 18, 2004, http://www.harrisinteractive.com/harris_poll/index.asp?PID=488.

[50] Gallup/CNN/*USA Today* Poll, August 3–5, 2001.

[51] *Newsweek*/Princeton Survey Research Associates Poll, August 24–25, 2006.

[52] Kaiser Family Foundation/Harvard School of Public Health Poll, December 4–14, 2008.

[53] Gallup Poll (Storrs, Conn.: Roper Center for Public Opinion Research, February 20–22, 2009).

54 *Time*/Schulman, Ronca, and Bucuvalas Poll (Storrs, Conn.: Roper Center for Public Opinion Research, May 10–12, 2005).

55 Virginia Commonwealth University Life Sciences/Center for Public Policy Poll (Storrs, Conn.: Roper Center for Public Opinion Research, August 23–September 2, 2001).

56 Gallup trend data in Gallup Poll, "Moral Issues," 2010, http://www.gallup.com/poll/1681/Moral–Issues.aspx.

57 Pew Research Center for the People and the Press and Pew Forum on Religion and Public Life, "August 2007 Religion and Public Life Survey," http://people-press.org/reports/questionnaires/353.pdf; Pew Research Center for the People and the Press, "March 2009 Political Survey: Final Topline," http://people-press.org/reports/questionnaires/500.pdf.

58 Pew Forum on Religion and Public Life/Pew Research Center for the People and the Press Poll (Storrs, Conn.: Roper Center for Public Opinion Research, February 25–March 10, 2002).

59 Gallup/CNN/*USA Today* Poll, August 10–12, 2001.

60 ABC News/Beliefnet Poll (Storrs, Conn.: Roper Center for Public Opinion Research, June 20–24, 2001).

61 Ibid.

62 *Parade Magazine*/Research!America/Charlton Research Poll (Storrs, Conn.: Roper Center for Public Opinion Research, June 4–9, 2005).

63 Cohen, *Renewing the Stuff of Life*, Chapter 6.

64 ABC News/*Washington Post* Poll, April 12–15, 2007; Kaiser Family Foundation/Harvard School of Public Health Poll, November 9–19, 2006.

65 Virginia Commonwealth University Life Sciences/Center for Public Policy, "VCU Life Sciences Survey 2008." It should be noted that on some questions that elicit widespread support, such as the one that places a heavy emphasis on the potential benefits of stem cell research (Harris Interactive Poll, August 18, 2004), majorities of Republicans and very religious Americans favor such research, although the differences by political party and religiosity are still large.

66 John M. Benson and Melissa J. Herrmann, "Right to Die or Right to Life? The Public on Assisted Suicide," *Public Perspective* 10 (June/July 1999): 15–19.

67 Virginia Commonwealth University Life Sciences/Center for Public Policy, "VCU Life Sciences Survey 2008."

68 CNN, "America Votes 2004: Ballot Measures/California Proposition 71/Exit Poll," http://www.cnn.com/ELECTION/2004//pages/results/states/CA/I/02/epolls.0.html; CNN, "America Votes 2006: Ballot Measures/Missouri Amendment 2/Exit Poll," http://www.cnn.com/ELECTION/2006//pages/results/states/MO/I/01/epolls.0.html.

69 Virginia Commonwealth University Life Sciences/Center for Public Policy, "VCU Life Sciences Survey 2008."

70 Ibid.

71 Kaiser Family Foundation/Harvard School of Public Health Poll (Storrs, Conn.: Roper Center for Public Opinion Research, August 2–5, 2001); Kaiser Family Foundation Poll (Storrs, Conn.: Roper Center for Public Opinion Research, August 4–8, 2005); Kaiser Family Foundation/Agency for Healthcare Research and Quality Poll (Storrs, Conn.: Roper Center for Public Opinion Research, August 3–8, 2006).

72 Pew Research Center for the People and the Press and Pew Forum on Religion and Public Life, "August 2007 Religion And Public Life Survey."

73 Kaiser Family Foundation/Harvard School of Public Health Poll, August 2–5, 2001.

74 Pew Research Center for the People and the Press/American Association for the Advancement of Science Poll (Storrs, Conn.: Roper Center for Public Opinion Research, June 18–21, 2009).

[75] ABC News Poll (Storrs, Conn.: Roper Center for Public Opinion Research, August 10–12, 2001).

[76] Virginia Commonwealth University Life Sciences/Center for Public Policy, "VCU Life Sciences Survey 2008."

[77] Pew Internet and American Life Project/ Princeton Survey Research Associates Poll, January 9–February 6, 2006.

[78] Ibid.

[79] Gallup Poll (Storrs, Conn.: Roper Center for Public Opinion Research, May 10–14, 2001).

[80] Gallup trend data in Gallup Poll, "Moral Issues," 2010.

[81] *Time*/CNN/Yankelovich Partners Poll (Storrs, Conn.: Roper Center for Public Opinion Research, February 7–8, 2001).

[82] Gallup Poll (Storrs, Conn.: Roper Center for Public Opinion Research, May 6–9, 2002); Virginia Commonwealth University Life Sciences/Center for Public Policy, "VCU Life Sciences Survey 2008."

[83] Virginia Commonwealth University Life Sciences/Center for Public Policy, "VCU Life Sciences Survey 2008."

[84] Genetics and Public Policy Center at Johns Hopkins University/Princeton Survey Research Associates Poll (Storrs, Conn.: Roper Center for Public Opinion Research, October 15–29, 2002).

[85] Virginia Commonwealth University Life Sciences/Center for Public Policy, "VCU Life Sciences Survey 2008." Therapeutic cloning, also known as somatic cell nuclear transfer, is the use of cloning to produce new body tissues from stem cells for use in the treatment of disease or injury. It involves replacing the nucleus of an egg cell with the nucleus from a cell from a patient's body and allowing it to develop. Reproductive cloning is the use of cloning to produce a new genetically identical human or animal from the cells of a(nother) human or animal.

Table 12-1 Stem Cell Research as a Voting Issue (in percent)

Importance of the issue in deciding your vote for . . .	Very/somewhat important	Not too/not at all important
President, 2004 (registered voters)[1]	44	53
	Extremely/very important	Somewhat/not important
President, 2004[2]	49	45
Congress, 2006[3]	45	50

Note: "Don't know" responses not shown.

Question: How important, if at all, will the issue of stem cell research be in determining your vote for president: very important, somewhat important, not too important, or not at all important?

Question: I'm going to read you a list of specific health care issues. For each one, please tell me how important it will be in your vote for (president this year [2004]/Congress this year [2006]). Will it be extremely important in deciding your vote, very important, somewhat important or not important? . . . Stem cell research

Sources: [1]*Newsweek*/Princeton Survey Research Associates Poll (Storrs, Conn.: Roper Center for Public Opinion Research, October 14–15, 2004).
[2]Kaiser Family Foundation/Princeton Survey Research Associates Poll (Storrs, Conn.: Roper Center for Public Opinion Research, October 14–17, 2004).
[3]Kaiser Family Foundation/Princeton Survey Research Associates Poll (Storrs, Conn.: Roper Center for Public Opinion Research, October 5–10, 2006).

Table 12-2 Most Important Issue in Presidential and Congressional Vote (in percent)

	October 2004	November 2006
	Vote for President (likely voters)	Vote for Congress (registered voters)
Terrorism[1]	25	12
The economy	21	19
Iraq	17	32
Health care[2]	7	11
Immigration	NA	10
Abortion	5	5
Social Security	5	NA
Education	5	NA
Taxes	3	NA
Stem cell research	2	3
Gay marriage	1	NA

Note: [1]"Terrorism/Homeland security" in 2004; [2]"Health care and Medicare" in 2004. Volunteered "Other," "None," and "Don't know" responses not shown.

Question: Which one of the following issues will be the most important to your vote for president? . . . Terrorism/homeland security, the economy, Iraq, health care and Medicare, Social Security, education, abortion, taxes, stem cell research, gay marriage.

Question: In deciding your vote for Congress this year, which one of the following issues is most important to you? . . . The situation in Iraq, the economy, terrorism, health care, immigration, abortion, stem cell research.

Sources: Fox News/Opinion Dynamics Poll (Storrs, Conn.: Roper Center for Public Opinion Research, October 30–31, 2004). *Newsweek*/Princeton Survey Research Associates Poll (Storrs, Conn.: Roper Center for Public Opinion Research, November 2–3, 2006).

Table 12-3 Public Attitudes about Stem Cell Research, 2006–2008 (in percent)

	Favor/ Approve	Oppose/ Disapprove
Use of stem cells in medical research[1]	76	9
Medical research that uses stem cells from sources that do not involve human embryos[2]	70	22
Embryonic stem cell research[3]	68	28
Medical research using embryonic stem cells[4]	65	25
Stem cell research, i.e., medical research using tissue from human embryos (among registered voters)[5]	63	24
Medical research that uses stem cells from human embryos[2]	57	36

Note: "Don't know" responses not shown.

Question: In general, do you favor or oppose the use of stem cells in medical research?

Question: Do you favor or oppose medical research that uses stem cells from sources that do not involve human embryos. Do you strongly favor, somewhat favor, somewhat oppose, or strongly oppose this?

Question: Do you support or oppose embryonic stem cell research?

Question: Do you approve or disapprove of medical research using embryonic stem cells?

Question: Do you approve or disapprove stem cell research; that is, medical research using tissue from human embryos?

Question: On the whole, how much do you favor or oppose medical research that uses stem cells: do you strongly favor, somewhat favor, somewhat oppose, or strongly oppose?

Sources: [1]Pew Internet and American Life Project/Princeton Survey Research Associates Poll (Storrs, Conn.: Roper Center for Public Opinion Research, January 9–February 6, 2006). [2]Virginia Commonwealth University Life Sciences/Center for Public Policy, "VCU Life Sciences Survey 2008." [3]ABC News/*Washington Post* Poll (Storrs, Conn.: Roper Center for Public Opinion Research, April 12–15, 2007). [4]CBS News Poll (Storrs, Conn.: Roper Center for Public Opinion Research, January 18–21, 2007). [5]Fox News/Opinion Dynamics Poll (Storrs, Conn.: Roper Center for Public Opinion Research, August 8–9, 2006).

Table 12-4 Public Attitudes about Federal Funding of Stem Cell Research, 2006–2009 (in percent)

	Favor/Approve	Oppose/Disapprove
Loosening current restrictions on federal funding of embryonic stem cell research[1]	59	35
Increasing federal funding for embryonic stem cell research (with arguments on both sides)[2]	59	32
New Congress expanding stem cell research by allowing federal funding for research that uses newly created stem cells obtained from human embryos[3]	57	39
Federal government funding research that would use newly created stem cells obtained from human embryos[4]	53	41
Using federal tax dollars to fund medical research using stem cells obtained from human embryos[5]	48	40

	Increased	Kept same	Decreased
Federal spending on stem cell research should be . . .[6]	33	41	23

Note: "Don't know" responses not shown.

Question: Do you support or oppose loosening the current restrictions on federal funding for embryonic stem cell research?

Question: As you may know, Congress is considering increasing federal funding for embryonic stem cell research. Supporters say stem cell research could lead to breakthrough cures for diseases such as Parkinson's and Alzheimer's. Opponents say that stem cell research crosses an ethical line by using cells from potentially viable human embryos. What do you think? Do you support or oppose increasing federal funding for embryonic stem cell research?

Question: President Bush has banned federal funding for medical research using stem cells from human embryos, except from a small number of existing stem cell lines. Do you favor or oppose the new Congress expanding stem cell research by allowing federal funding for research that uses newly created stem cells obtained from human embryos?

Question: Do you think the federal government should or should not fund research that would use newly created stem cells obtained from human embryos?

Question: Do you favor or oppose using federal tax dollars to fund medical research using stem cells obtained from human embryos?

Question: As you know, the federal government has a substantial budget deficit and there are many competing spending priorities facing the next president and Congress. Thinking about the federal budget, do you want to see the next president and Congress increase spending on . . . stem cell research, decrease spending, or keep it about the same?

Sources: [1]ABC News/*Washington Post* Poll (Storrs, Conn.: Roper Center for Public Opinion Research, January 13–16, 2009). [2]Bloomberg/*Los Angeles Times* Poll (Storrs, Conn.: Roper Center for Public Opinion Research, January 13–16, 2007). [3]Kaiser Family Foundation/Harvard School of Public Health Poll (Storrs, Conn.: Roper Center for Public Opinion Research, November 9–19, 2006). [4]CNN/Opinion Research Corporation Poll (Storrs, Conn.: Roper Center for Public Opinion Research, May 4–6, 2007). [5]*Newsweek*/Princeton Survey Research Associates Poll (Storrs, Conn.: Roper Center for Public Opinion Research, August 24–25, 2006). [6]Kaiser Family Foundation/Harvard School of Public Health Poll (Storrs, Conn.: Roper Center for Public Opinion Research, December 4–14, 2008).

Table 12-5 Support for Federal Government Funding of Stem Cell Research under Different Circumstances (in percent)

	Should	Should not	Depends (vol.)	No opinion/ Not sure
Overall support	55	29	3	13
Stem cells that come just from adults and do not come from embryos at all	68	36	1	5
Stem cells developed from the remaining embryos that fertility clinics usually discard	55	40	2	3
Stem cells developed from embryos produced by cloning cells from a living human being rather than by fertilizing a woman's egg	46	49	1	4
Stem cells developed from embryos that are created in laboratories specifically for the purpose of conducting this research and not help a woman have a child	28	66	5	1

Note: (vol.) = volunteered response.

Question: As you may know, the federal government is considering whether to fund certain kinds of medical research known as stem cell research. . . . Do you think the federal government should or should not fund this type of research or don't know enough to say?

Question: There is a kind of research using stem cells that come just from adults and do not come from embryos at all. The research results in no injury to the person from whom the stem cells are taken. Do you think the federal government should or should not fund research on this kind of stem cells?

Question: I would like to ask about a few specific types of research on stem cells developed from human embryos that have been created outside a woman's womb. This kind of stem cell research destroys the embryos but may help find treatments for major diseases. As you may know, fertility clinics increase a woman's chance to have a child by fertilizing several embryos, but only a few are implanted in her womb to enable her to have a baby. Some stem cells are developed from the remaining embryos that the fertility clinics usually discard. Do you think the federal government should or should not fund research on stem cells from this kind of embryo?

Question: Some stem cells may be developed from embryos produced by cloning cells from a living human being rather than by fertilizing a woman's egg. Do you think the federal government should or should not fund research on stem cells from this kind of embryo?

Question: Some stem cells are developed from embryos that are created in laboratories specifically for the purpose of conducting this research and not help a woman have a child. Do you think the federal government should or should not fund research on stem cells from this kind of embryo?

Source: Gallup/CNN/*USA Today* Poll (Storrs, Conn.: Roper Center for Public Opinion Research, August 3–5, 2001).

Table 12-6 Public Views of the Moral Acceptability of Medical Research Using Stem Cells Obtained from Human Embryos, 2002–2010 (in percent)

	Morally acceptable	Morally wrong
2002	52	39
2003	54	38
2004	54	37
2005	60	33
2006	61	30
2007	64	30
2008	62	30
2009	57	36
2010	59	32

Note: Volunteered responses of "Depends," "Not a moral issue," and "Don't know" not shown.

Question: Regardless of whether or not you think it should be legal, please tell me whether you personally believe that in general it is morally acceptable or morally wrong: Medical research using stem cells obtained from human embryos.

Source: Gallup trend data in Gallup Poll, "Moral Issues," 2010.

Table 12-7 The Public's Balance of Values in Stem Cell Research, 2002–2009 (in percent)

Which is more important?	Conducting stem cell research that might result in new medical cures	Not destroying the potential life of human embryos involved in stem cell research	Don't know
2002	43	38	19
2004	52	34	14
2005	57	30	13
2006	56	32	12
2007 Total	51	35	14
By party identification			
Democrat	60	26	14
Independent	55	32	13
Republican	37	50	13
By religion			
Unaffiliated*	68	21	11
White non-Hispanic Catholic	59	32	9
White mainline Protestant	58	28	14
Black Protestant	40	40	20
White evangelical	31	57	12
2009	54	32	14

Note: *Includes self-described atheists, agnostics, and those who say their religious affiliation is "nothing in particular."

Question: All in all, which is more important: conducting stem cell research that might result in new medical cures or not destroying the potential life of human embryos involved in this research?

Sources: For 2002–2007, Pew Research Center for the People and the Press/Pew Forum on Religion and Public Life trend data, "August 2007 Religion and Public Life Survey." For 2009, Pew Research Center for the People and the Press, "March 2009 Political Survey: Final Topline."

Table 12-8 Influences in Public Opinion about Stem Cell Research (in percent)

	Responses of	
	Supporters	Opponents
News/the media	28	13
Education	22	6
Personal nonreligious beliefs	17	17
Personal experience	8	9
Family/friends	6	3
Religious beliefs	3	42
Something else	13	9

Note: "Don't know" responses not shown.

Question: What's had the most influence on your opinion on the issue of stem-cell research: the opinions of your family and friends, things you've seen or read in the news, your education, your personal experience, your religious beliefs, your personal nonreligious beliefs, or something else?

Source: ABC News/Beliefnet Poll (Storrs, Conn.: Roper Center for Public Opinion Research, June 20–24, 2001).

Table 12-9 Support for Embryonic Stem Cell Research, by Subgroups (in percent)

	Support embryonic stem cell research[1]	Support allowing federal funding for research using newly created embryonic stem cells[2]
Total	68	57
By sex		
Male	67	56
Female	69	57
By age		
18–39	71	56
40–49	64	57
50–65	64	59
65+	73	54
By party identification		
Democrat	80	67
Independent	70	63
Republican	49	37
By education		
High school grad or less	63	50
Some college	67	58
College grad	76	66

Question: Do you support or oppose embryonic stem cell research?

Question: President Bush has banned federal funding for medical research using stem cells from human embryos, except from a small number of existing stem cell lines. Do you favor or oppose the new Congress expanding stem cell research by allowing federal funding for research that uses newly created stem cells obtained from human embryos?

Sources: [1]ABC News/*Washington Post* Poll (Storrs, Conn.: Roper Center for Public Opinion Research, April 12–15, 2007). [2]Kaiser Family Foundation/ Harvard School of Public Health Poll (Storrs, Conn.: Roper Center for Public Opinion Research, November 9–19, 2006).

Table 12-10 Support for Medical Research That Uses Stem Cells from Human Embryos, by Subgroups (in percent)

	Strongly favor	Somewhat favor	Somewhat oppose	Strongly oppose
Total	23	34	14	22
By education				
High school grad or less	17	35	17	21
Some college	25	34	9	27
College grad	31	32	12	19
By role of religion in your life				
Religious beliefs provide a great deal or quite a bit of guidance for your day-to-day living	15	30	17	31
Religion provides some guidance or is not an important part of your life	35	40	8	8
By attitudes about abortion				
Should always be illegal	9	11	12	61
Should only be legal in certain circumstances	14	37	18	23
Woman should be able to get abortion if she wants it	39	40	8	6
By age				
18–44	22	36	14	21
45–64	23	35	13	23
65+	26	29	14	21
By party identification				
Democrat	33	38	12	11
Independent	23	36	16	17
Republican	13	27	11	41

Note: "Don't know" responses not shown.

Question: On the whole, how much do you favor or oppose medical research that uses stem cells from human embryos? Do you strongly favor, somewhat favor, somewhat oppose, or strongly oppose this?

Source: Virginia Commonwealth University Life Sciences/Center for Public Policy, "VCU Life Sciences Survey 2008."

Table 12-11 Exit Poll Results for California and Missouri Stem Cell Research Propositions, 2004 and 2006, by Subgroups (in percent)

	Percent voting "Yes"	
	California 2004	Missouri 2006
Total voters	59	51
By party identification		
Democrat	80	76
Independent	60	55
Republican	36	24
By education		
No college degree	58	50
College degree	61	53
By religion		
Protestant	50	46
Catholic	63	45
Jewish	86	NA
None	68	82
By religious attendance		
Weekly or more	42	31
Monthly	60	61
Few times a year or more	70	72
By abortion views		
Always/mostly legal	NA	82
Always/mostly illegal	NA	25

Note: Responses of voters as they left voting booths. "Yes" vote is pro–stem cell research

Question: How did you vote in [California] Proposition 71, to fund stem cell research? (Yes/No)

Question: How did you vote today on [Missouri] Amendment 2, regulating stem cell research? (Yes/No)

Sources: CNN, "America Votes 2004: Ballot Measures/California Proposition 71/Exit Poll;" CNN, "America Votes 2006: Ballot Measures/Missouri Amendment 2/Exit Poll."

Table 12-12 Support for Medical Research That Uses Stem Cells from Sources That Do Not Involve Human Embryos, by Subgroups (in percent)

	Strongly favor	Somewhat favor	Somewhat oppose	Strongly oppose
Total	34	36	14	8
By education				
High school grad or less	26	32	20	12
Some college	36	43	9	7
College grad	47	36	8	3
By role of religion in your life				
Religious beliefs provide a great deal or quite a bit of guidance for your day-to-day living	30	35	16	12
Religion provides some guidance or is not an important part of your life	43	36	9	3
By attitudes about abortion				
Should always be illegal	28	37	11	17
Should only be legal in certain circumstances	33	34	17	8
Woman should be able to get abortion if she wants it	39	39	11	6
By age				
18–44	35	37	17	8
45–64	39	37	11	4
65+	25	31	14	17
By party identification				
Democrat	33	40	13	9
Independent	36	35	12	9
Republican	39	33	16	6

Note: "Don't know" responses not shown.

Question: Do you favor or oppose medical research that uses stem cells from sources that do not involve human embryos? Do you strongly favor, somewhat favor, somewhat oppose, or strongly oppose this?

Source: Virginia Commonwealth University Life Sciences/Center for Public Policy, "VCU Life Sciences Survey 2008."

Table 12-13 Public Awareness of Stem Cell Research, 2002–2007 (in percent)

	A lot	A little	Nothing at all
2002	27	52	20
2004	42	43	15
2005	48	42	10
2006	43	42	15
2007	45	43	12

Question: As you may know, the federal government has debated whether to fund certain kinds of medical research known as stem cell research. How much have you heard about this? A lot, a little, or nothing at all?

Source: Pew Research Center for the People and the Press/Pew Forum on Religion and Public Life trend data, "August 2007 Religion and Public Life Survey."

Table 12-14 Americans' Attitudes about Whether Cloning of Animals and Humans Should Be Allowed (in percent)

	Should be allowed	Should not be allowed
Animals	32	64
Humans	9	89

Note: "Don't know" responses not shown.

Question: Do you think the cloning of (animals/humans) should or should not be allowed?

Source: Gallup Poll (Storrs, Conn.: Roper Center for Public Opinion Research, May 10–14, 2001).

Table 12-15 Public Views of the Moral Acceptability of Cloning Animals and Humans, 2001–2010 (in percent)

	Cloning animals			Cloning humans	
	Morally acceptable	Morally wrong		Morally acceptable	Morally wrong
2001	31	63	2001	7	88
2002	29	66	2002	7	90
2003	29	68	2003	8	90
2004	32	64	2004	9	88
2005	35	61	2005	9	87
2006	29	65	2006	8	88
2007	36	59	2007	11	86
2008	33	61	2008	11	85
2009	34	63	2009	9	88
2010	31	63	2010	9	88

Note: Volunteered responses of "Depends," "Not a moral issue," and "Don't know" not shown.

Question: Regardless of whether or not you think it should be legal, please tell me whether you personally believe that in general it is morally acceptable or morally wrong: Cloning animals/cloning humans.

Source: Gallup trend data in Gallup Poll, "Moral Issues," 2010.

Table 12-16 Public Support for Various Types of Cloning (in percent)

	Favor	Oppose
Cloning of human organs or body parts that can then be used in medical transplants[1]	59	37
Using human cloning technology if it is used only to help medical research develop new treatments for disease[2]	52	45
Cloning of human cells from adults for use in medical research[1]	51	44
Cloning of human embryos for use in medical research[1]	34	61
Cloning that is designed specifically to result in the birth of a child[1]	8	90

Note: "Don't know" responses not shown.

Question: Do you favor or oppose each of the following: (Cloning of human organs or body parts that can then be used in medical transplants)?

Question: Do you favor or oppose using human cloning if it is used only to help medical research develop new treatments for disease?

Question: Do you favor or oppose each of the following: (Cloning of human cells from adults for use in medical research/Cloning that is designed specifically to result in the birth of a child/Cloning of human cells from adults for use in medical research)?

Sources: [1]Gallup Poll (Storrs, Conn.: Roper Center for Public Opinion Research, May 6–9, 2002). [2]Virginia Commonwealth University Life Sciences/Center for Public Policy, "VCU Life Sciences Survey 2008."

Table 12-17 Support for Using Human Cloning Technology if It Is Used Only to Help Medical Research Develop New Treatment for Disease (in percent)

	Favor	Oppose
Total	52	45
By education		
High school grad or less	53	46
Some college	51	47
College grad	54	43
By role of religion in your life		
Religious beliefs provide a great deal or quite a bit of guidance for your day-to-day living	43	55
Religion provides some guidance or is not an important part of your life	70	27
By age		
18–44	56	44
45–64	50	47
65+	52	44
By sex		
Men	56	40
Women	48	49
By party identification		
Democrat	62	36
Independent	55	44
Republican	37	60

Note: "Don't know" responses not shown

Question: Do you favor or oppose using human cloning technology if it is used only to help medical research develop new treatments for disease?

Source: Virginia Commonwealth University Sciences/Center for Public Policy, "VCU Life Sciences Survey 2008."

Chapter 13

END-OF-LIFE CARE

John M. Benson and Melissa J. Herrmann

In the words of the Institute of Medicine's 1997 report, *Approaching Death: Improving Care at the End of Life,* "Death is not what it used to be."[1] A century ago, most people died in their own homes, surrounded by family. Infectious diseases, such as pneumonia, influenza, and tuberculosis which were the leading causes of death in 1900, killed quickly. The infant mortality rate was extraordinarily high, and life expectancy was less than fifty years (**Table 13–1**).[2]

The nature of death and dying in America underwent sweeping changes during the twentieth century. Modern medicine has made it possible for millions of people to live longer, healthier lives. Infant mortality has declined by 95 percent since 1900, and life expectancy is now nearly eighty years. By 1980 nearly three-fourths of deaths in the United States occurred in institutions, such as hospitals and nursing homes, and only 20 percent at home. The leading causes of death are not infections, but heart disease and cancer, chronic diseases more prevalent among older people.

These changes are largely due to advances in pharmacology and in medical technology, such as respirators and feeding tubes. Many people who in earlier times might have died can be kept alive longer. But some of them are confined to bed, dependent on machines for months or years, and sometimes in extreme pain. Some comatose patients can be kept alive for many years. As a result, these same improvements in technology may force patients and their families to face hard decisions.

The past three decades have witnessed growing concern about end-of-life issues. Several initiatives have been launched across the nation to improve clinical care at the end of life.[3] In addition, a number of medical journal articles and books highlight the major areas for improvement.[4] The use of hospice services has grown dramatically. Efforts have been made, but with modest success, to expand the use of "living wills," in which people express their preferences for end-of-life care ahead of time, and to encourage people to name "health proxies" to represent their wishes.

Some of the more controversial public policy issues involving end-of-life decision making have sparked turbulent debate. The public has taken sides over legal cases about termination of life support for patients who have been in a prolonged coma or in a "persistent vegetative state" (PVS) that has lasted for years.[5] A "vegetative state" is a clinical condition of "complete unawareness of the self and the environment." In addition, such patients show "no evidence of sustained, reproducible, purposeful, or voluntary behavior, or voluntary behavioral responses to visual, auditory, tactile, or noxious stimuli," "show no evidence of language comprehension or expression," and "have bowel and bladder incontinence." A PVS is a vegetative state lasting at least one month.[6]

The case of Karen Ann Quinlan in the New Jersey Supreme Court set a legal precedent in 1976 when the Quinlan family became the first in the country to win the right to refuse extraordinary medical treatment for someone in a persistent vegetative state.[7] Concern over the Quinlan case led Congress to pass legislation establishing the President's Commission for the Study of Ethical Problems in Medicine and Biomedical and Behavioral Research.[8]

In 1990 the U.S. Supreme Court made its first decision in an end-of-life case, in *Cruzan v. Director, Missouri Department of Health*. Nancy Cruzan's parents sued the state to withdraw life support from their daughter, who was in a persistent vegetative state, and allow her die.[9]

The Terri Schiavo case came to national prominence in early 2005. It was the culmination of a long, drawn out legal battle between Schiavo's husband and her parents over whether her feeding tube should be removed after she had been in a coma-like or persistent vegetative state for several years. Several elected officials at the state and national level, as well as advocacy groups, became involved in this highly visible dispute about the legal and ethical issues involved. Polling about this case is discussed at greater length below.

Physician-assisted suicide also became a prominent issue in the 1990s, when Dr. Jack Kevorkian made news by assisting several terminally or chronically ill patients to commit suicide, thereby raising a number of important legal and ethical issues. During the 1990s, four states voted on ballot initiatives to legalize physician-assisted suicide. In 1994 Oregon voters approved an initiative that made it legal for a physician, at the request of a terminally ill patient, to prescribe a lethal dose of medication for administration by the patient, and in 1997 an initiative to repeal the act failed.[10] In 1997 the U.S. Supreme Court overturned two lower court rulings that had found a constitutional right to die.[11] In 2008 voters in Washington State approved a ballot initiative making physician-assisted suicide legal.

The right-to-life movement, which played an important role in end-of-life debates as far back as the *Cruzan* case, has begun to focus even more of its attention on the end of life.[12] Antiabortion forces have been in the forefront of opposition to physician-assisted suicide referenda and are the impetus for "lethal dose" legislation that would use federal drug-control laws to make it illegal for a doctor to prescribe enough painkillers to help a patient commit suicide. In addition, they have been pursuing laws that would limit the ability of relatives to halt the artificial feeding or life support of patients who cannot make such decisions themselves.

With the graying of the baby boom generation, end-of-life issues are likely to remain on the public stage for many years to come (**Table 13–1**).[13] One of the main policy concerns associated with the aging of this generation of Americans is the cost of end-of-life care for so many people. More than 80 percent of adults who die are covered by Medicare, the federal government medical program for seniors. Approximately one-fourth of Medicare outlays go to pay for the last year of life.[14]

This chapter examines public opinion about a broad range of end-of-life issues. Keep in mind that a large proportion of the polling on death and dying has addressed highly visible and controversial issues, such as physician-assisted suicide and ending life support for patients. Far fewer questions have been asked about other aspects of the broad range of end-of-life issues, such as palliative care, economic and psychological stresses on family members of the dying, and quality of care at the end of a patient's life. Nevertheless, this chapter will strive wherever possible to discuss these issues as well as the more controversial.

The Public on Brain Death and Persistent Vegetative State

Traditionally, death was considered to be the cessation of circulation and respiration. But advances in medical technology that make it possible to sustain breathing and heart function by mechanical means presented a new question—how to determine whether a patient with catastrophic cerebral injuries was dead or alive.

In 1968 an ad hoc committee at the Harvard Medical School attempted to define death in this new technological climate. The committee's criteria described determination of a condition called "brain death."[15] The Uniform Determination of Death Act (1980) has served as a model statute for state legislation that defines death.[16] The act asserts that a person who has sustained either "irreversible cessation of circulatory and respiratory function," or "irreversible cessation of all functions of the entire brain, including the brainstem," is dead.[17]

A substantial minority of the public does not accept this definition of death. About half (48 percent) said in a 2009 poll that in their view life ends when the brain ceases to function "even though the heart may continue to beat," but 43 percent said that life ends only when the heart ceases to beat.[18] Forty-eight percent had disagreed with the brain death definition in 1981, shortly after it was adopted (**Table 13–2**).[19]

The same 2009 poll asked respondents how often a doctor's diagnosis that a patient will not recover from "a persistent vegetative or coma-like state with no higher brain activity" is wrong and the patient ends up at least partially recovering awareness or consciousness. About half thought this rarely (42 percent) or never (4 percent) happens. Thirty-eight percent thought it sometimes happens, and 7 percent thought it often occurs.[20] This question should not be considered strictly a measure of knowledge, because the matter is complex. Among adults who are in a PVS for three months after a traumatic brain injury (such as an injury resulting from a concussion or a car accident), about one-third regain consciousness within a year of the injury. Recovery is much lower (7 percent) for nontraumatic brain injuries (such as those caused by stroke, tumors, meningitis, or drug abuse, as well as inherited brain or nervous system disorders). It is not clear that many doctors make a diagnosis after three months that a patient will not recover. Studies show that PVS can be considered permanent twelve months after either traumatic or nontraumatic brain injury, as recovery of consciousness after that point is extremely rare and almost always involves a severe disability.[21]

Americans' Worries about End-of-Life Care

In thinking about what might happen to them at the end of life, a majority of Americans worry about a number of issues having to do with medical care or the health care system. Nearly three-fourths (73 percent) say they would be worried about the possibility of being vegetative for some period of time before they die. About six in ten worry about the emotional burden their family might face making decisions for them at the end of life (62 percent) and the economic burden a terminal illness might cause their family (61 percent). A majority also say they would be worried about not having access to lifesaving medical technology (56 percent); that if they run out of money or health insurance, they would get second-class health care (55 percent); and not having access to their own physician or hospital (52 percent) (**Table 13–3**).[22]

In addition, two-thirds (67 percent) of Americans worry about the possibility of great physical pain before they die.[23] Many Americans are skeptical about the ability of health professionals to control pain when a patient is terminally ill with cancer. Only half believe their pain can be controlled all (16 percent) or most (34 percent) of the time; 38 percent believe such pain can be controlled some of the time, and 9 percent think it can rarely be controlled.[24]

More than eight in ten (84 percent) say that maintaining control of decisions being made about their care would be very important to them if they were terminally ill. More than one-fourth (28 percent) say they are not very or not at all confident that, if they were hospitalized in an unconscious state with a terminal illness, their wishes would be followed by their physician. About four in ten (41 percent) believe that when a person is terminally ill, physicians usually do not explain the treatment choices in a way the patient can understand.[25]

Choices at the End of Life

Over the years, in responding to public concerns about end-of-life care, professional and lay groups have proposed making various choices available. The public supports, at least in principle, the availability of a wide range of these choices, even though fewer Americans would advise others to opt for some of these choices in specific circumstances, and many do not themselves choose to exercise them.

The following section looks at public support for several end-of-life options. These options include palliative care, hospice care, forgoing life-sustaining treatment, "double-effect" administration of pain medication, voluntary active euthanasia, physician-assisted suicide, suicide not involving health professionals, spiritual comfort, herbal medicine, dietary supplements, experimental drugs, and medical marijuana.

Because prior polling has shown that people can have varying views depending on the specifics involved, researchers have developed vignettes that explore how people would react in different circumstances.[26] In a 1998 survey, each respondent was asked a series of questions about one of six hypothetical end-of-life vignettes. These vignettes describe a patient as having lung cancer that has begun to spread throughout the body, for whom radiation treatment does not seem to be working, and who can expect to get continually worse with more pain. The vignettes were varied by the gender and age (35 and 72 years) of the patient and his/her life expectancy (2 or 18 months).[27] In the following sections on choices at the end of life, we occasionally reference the public's responses to the circumstances presented in these vignettes.

Palliative Care

Palliative care seeks to "prevent, relieve, reduce, or soothe the symptoms of disease or disorder without effecting a cure."[28] The term is often confused with hospice care, which shares similar goals of symptom relief and pain management. Nonhospice palliative care, however, can be used for anyone with a serious illness, including those who are expected to recover fully or to live with a chronic illness. Hospice care is also palliative, but the term refers to care near the end of life.

When asked about the medical care they would want if they were terminally ill, 86 percent say they would prefer being kept as comfortable and pain-free as possible, even if means not living as long; 10 percent say they would prefer having their life extended as long as possible, even if it means more pain and discomfort.[29]

Patients often do not make the same choices in actual care as they do in hypothetical questions. In a 2006 poll, adults from households where they or a family member had been diagnosed with or treated for cancer during the previous five years were asked the same hypothetical question as the one above. About eight in ten (81 percent) said that if they were terminally ill, they would prefer being kept as comfortable and pain-free as possible. Only 12 percent said they would want to have their life extended. Yet among the 23 percent of these adults who said they had made the very difficult decision about whether they or their family member with cancer should undergo a treatment that would increase their chances of survival by only a small amount, but could potentially lead to severe side effects, about seven in ten (71 percent) said they chose the treatment.[30]

Hospice Care

Hospice care emphasizes comfort, pain relief, and emotional support for patients certified by a doctor as having six months or less to live. Patients receive comfort care and forgo curative treatments for their terminal disease. A hospice can be a discrete site in the form of an inpatient hospital or nursing home unit or a freestanding facility, but most hospice patients in the United States receive care at home. Hospice programs provide, arrange, and advise on a wide range of medical and supportive services for dying patients and their families and friends.[31] Hospice care has been available in the United States since the 1960s, but relatively few people—about 1,000 in 1975—were enrolled early on. In 1982 a hospice benefit was added to Medicare.[32] By 1997, 3,000 hospice programs were in operation in the United States.[33] According to National Hospice and Palliative Care Organization, nearly four in ten deaths in the United States in 2007 were under the care of hospice.[34]

Most people (77 percent) say they would seriously consider entering a hospice program if they were terminally ill.[35] When presented with the six hypothetical end-of-life vignettes described above, 79 percent to 83 percent said the patients in those vignettes should choose hospice services.[36]

Forgoing Life-sustaining Treatment

Major organizations of health care professionals make careful distinctions when discussing ethics in end-of-life care. The Council on Ethical and Judicial Affairs of the American Medical Association (AMA) endorses the duty of physicians to respect the wishes of competent patients to forgo life-sustaining treatment, as well as the practice of providing effective pain treatment even though it might hasten death. The council does not endorse voluntary active euthanasia or physician-assisted suicide.[37]

About three-fourths (67 percent) of Americans favor withdrawing life support systems, including food and water, from hopelessly ill or irreversibly comatose patients if they or their families request it (**Table 13–4**).[38] Told that in some states it is legal to stop medical treatment that is keeping a terminally ill patient alive, or never start the treatment, if that is what the patient wants, 84 percent approved of laws that let patients decide about being kept alive though medical treatment.[39]

When presented with the six hypothetical end-of-life vignettes, 92 percent to 96 percent said the patients in those vignettes have a right to refuse further treatment except for pain. The proportion who said that the patient should actually refuse treatment except for pain, however, ranged in the described circumstances from 65 percent to 76 percent, about 20 percentage points lower than their support for the availability of the option.[40]

Half of Americans say they would seriously consider refusing help from a breathing machine if they were terminally ill. Similarly, 47 percent say they would seriously consider refusing nutrition through a feeding tube.[41]

Double-Effect Administration of Pain Medication

The AMA considers it ethical for a physician to provide pain treatment even though it may hasten death.[42] This practice is sometimes called double effect.

A large majority of Americans (80 percent) support allowing physicians to administer drugs to reduce pain, even if the dose might shorten the patient's life (**Table 13–5**).[43] When presented with the six hypothetical end-of-life vignettes, 61 percent to 70 percent said the patients described should ask physicians to increase the use of pain medication, even if it might lead to premature death.[44]

Voluntary Active Euthanasia

Voluntary active euthanasia (VAE) differs from double effect in that, on request of the patient, the physician administers medication or treatment the *intent* of which is to end the patient's life. VAE is often confused with physician-assisted suicide (PAS) in news reports, making it difficult to distinguish support for one or the other. PAS differs from VAE in that the person takes his or her own life, assisted by the physician, who would typically give the patient a prescription for a lethal drug. The public is able make some distinction between VAE and PAS when the two acts are described. Neither practice is condoned by the AMA.

In surveys conducted from 2005 to the present, questions about VAE and PAS have specified three different circumstances: when a patient has an incurable disease, when a patient has a terminal illness or is dying; and when a patient has a degenerative disease. A terminal illness is one that can reasonably be expected to cause death in a relatively short period of time, whether or not medical care is received. An incurable disease is not necessarily terminal: certain chronic and degenerative diseases do not lead to imminent death but may not curable. When answering a question about an incurable disease, respondents may have in mind terminal, chronic, or degenerative diseases, or all three, not just terminal diseases.

The public generally expresses a higher level of support for VAE than it does for PAS. A majority support VAE in each of the three circumstances measured. When a patient has an incurable disease, public support ranges from 56 percent to 69 percent.[45] In the case of a patient who is dying, support is 70 percent.[46] In the case of degenerative disease, support is 58 percent.[47] Nearly three in ten Americans (28 percent), however, believe that a physician injecting a terminally ill patient with a lethal dose of drugs at the person's request is the same thing as murder.[48]

Trend data show a considerable rise in public support for VAE if a person has an incurable disease. In the longest trend series on the subject, support grew from 37 percent in 1947 to 53 percent in 1973, then to 60 percent or more starting in the 1980s (**Table 13–6**).[49]

Four hypotheses may help explain the growth in support for VAE. First, support started out low. In 1947 and 1950 people were still reeling from revelations about practices used by the Nazis in involuntary settings. A second hypothesis, which may explain changes in public opinion about VAE during the late 1970s, is that the Quinlan case helped crystallize the nation's consciousness on end-of-life matters.[50] A third hypothesis is that more Americans adopted what might be called a secular humanist view of compassion. Related to this is a fourth hypothesis, that the trend represents a desire by Americans for legislation that would permit more personal control over the quality of life and death when they are terminally ill.[51]

Opponents of VAE and PAS often make a "slippery slope" argument, that their availability will exert pressure on elderly or disabled patients to have their lives ended when they might otherwise have wanted to continue living. One survey showed that a significant proportion of Americans were wary of this potential problem. Respondents were asked to compare two concerns about VAE. Forty-four percent said they were more worried that if physicians are not allowed to end an incurably ill patient's life, patients who are terminally ill and in great pain would not have this choice available An equal proportion (44 percent) were more worried that if physicians are allowed to end an incurably ill patient's life, some elderly or disabled patients might feel pressured into asking to have their lives ended.[52]

More people favor the availability of VAE than would consider using that option themselves. Half (50 percent) of Americans say they could imagine a situation where they might want to ask their physician to end their life intentionally by some painless means.[53]

Physician-assisted Suicide

Public support for physician-assisted suicide when a patient has an incurable disease is 56 percent.[54] Trend data show that the proportion who believe PAS should be allowed in this circumstance has varied, but the level of support is almost the same as it was when this question was first asked in 1997 (**Table 13–7**).[55] In the case of terminal illness, support ranges from 47 percent to 48 percent, with about an equal proportion opposed (44 to 46 percent).[56] The longest trend series on this subject shows that the public has generally been divided in its opinion since 1993 (**Table 13–8**).[57] In the case of degenerative disease, support is 56 percent.[58]

When given three choices about the circumstances under which PAS should be legal, the public is closely divided. Thirty-three percent support making PAS legal under a wide variety of circumstances; 32 percent support it in a few cases, but oppose it in most; and 33 percent oppose making PAS legal for any reason.[59]

Again, more Americans favor the availability of PAS than would advise patients faced with extreme end-of-life situations to choose that option. When presented with the six hypothetical end-of-life vignettes, 28 percent to 35 percent said the patients in those vignettes should ask for PAS.[60]

The lower level of support for PAS (47 percent to 56 percent across various circumstances) than for VAE (56 percent to 70 percent) provides an interesting insight into some of the forces that undergird public opinion on end-of-life issues. One might have expected the public to have a more favorable view of a practice where the patient controls the timing and final administration of the life-ending act and the physician merely provides the means. But other considerations, such as an instinctive aversion to and religious proscriptions against suicide or fear that the suffering patient might act too rashly or botch the attempt, evidently affect the responses of many Americans.

The effect of the word *suicide* can be seen in a split-sample polling experiment performed in 2003. Significantly more people favored making it legal for doctors to "give terminally ill patients the means to end their lives" (54 percent) than favored making it legal for doctors to "assist terminally ill patients in committing suicide" (43 percent).[61]

A few caveats are in order when discussing public opinion data on withdrawal of care, VAE, and PAS. The available questions tend to imply that patients and/or their families have given unequivocal expression to their wishes. In real life, as the Schiavo case shows, circumstances are often more complex. Also, terminally ill patients sometimes change their minds about requesting withdrawal of treatment, VAE, or PAS. A recent study of patients identified by their physicians to be terminally ill (with any disease other than HIV) illustrates this point. And the study shows once again the difference between someone wanting an option to be available and actually choosing that option. Sixty percent of the patients said they favored either VAE or PAS, but only 11 percent of these terminally ill patients said they had considered either VAE or PAS. In follow-up interviews, half of those who had considered these options had changed their minds, and an almost equal number had begun to consider them. Only about 1 percent of the patients in the study died of VAE or PAS or tried to commit suicide.[62]

Suicide Not Involving Health Professionals

Currently a majority (59 percent) of Americans believe that a person with an incurable disease has a right to end his or her own life. This finding represents a significant change since the late 1970s, when only 38 percent supported a right to commit suicide in such a case (**Table 13–9**).[63]

About one-third (35 percent) of Americans say they would consider suicide in cases of terminal illness.[64] About an equal proportion (33 percent) say they could imagine, if someone they loved was suffering terribly from an illness that was terminal, killing that person or helping him or her commit suicide.[65]

Spiritual Comfort

About two-thirds (63 percent) of Americans think physicians should join their patients in prayer, asking for spiritual help in curing an illness, if the patient requests it.[66] Similarly, two-thirds (70 percent) say that, if they were dying, having a physician who is spiritually attuned to them would be very important.[67]

Herbal Medicines, Dietary Supplements, and Experimental Drugs

More than three-fourths (82 percent) of Americans say they would seriously consider trying alternative treatments like herbal medicines or alternative diets if they were terminally ill.[68] One-third (35 percent) believe that dietary supplements, other than conventional vitamins and minerals, can help people with cancer.[69] Two-thirds (67 percent) of Americans say they would seriously consider taking experimental (not fully tested) drugs if they were terminally ill.[70]

Medical Marijuana

Fewer than half (44 percent) of Americans favor legalizing marijuana generally.[71] But 74 percent favor allowing physicians to prescribe marijuana to seriously ill patients to reduce pain.[72] Only 20 percent would favor allowing prescription of marijuana if scientific research found its use ineffective for this purpose.[73]

Demographic Differences on End-of-Life Issues

In examining the results of these public opinion polls, we need to keep in mind that Americans are not homogeneous in their views, especially on controversial issues. The following analysis looks at the responses of major subgroups of the population to the latest asking of four measures: withdrawal of life support, double-effect administration of pain medication, VAE for a patient with an incurable disease, and PAS for a patient who is terminally ill and in great pain (**Tables 13–10, 13–11, 13–12, 13–13**).[74]

Across the four measures, differences are largest by race, attitude about abortion, and religiosity. Whites are more likely than African Americans, by a range of 19 to 32 percentage points, to support the four policies. Given the history of race relations in the United States, and, in particular, medically related ethical abuses such as the Tuskegee syphilis study, we should not be surprised that many African Americans are wary of policies that they may believe puts them at risk of discriminatory and possibly lethal treatment within the medical system.[75]

Those who are pro-choice are 17 to 41 percentage points more likely than those who are pro-life to express support on these four measures.[76] Less religious Americans are 15 to 39 percentage points more likely than more religious Americans to express support.[77] The division in terms of religiosity holds for both Protestants and Catholics. Highly religious Protestants and highly religious Catholics are more like each other in their views here than they are like the less religious of their own denominations.[78] Those who do not identify with any religion are among the most likely to support each measure.

One might have hypothesized that seniors would be less supportive of these policies, which might lead to earlier death. On none of the four measures, however, did the views of seniors differ significantly from those of adults aged eighteen to sixty-four. On two measures, VAE and PAS, men were more likely than women to be in favor, although in neither case was the difference more than eight percentage points.

Because end-of-life issues (like other "life" issues such as abortion and stem cell research) have sometimes been the subject of heated partisan debate, it may at first seem puzzling that differences by party identification on these four measures are modest. The overall picture does not, however, take into account that each party is a coalition whose members are not homogenous. Important parts of the Republican coalition are strongly pro-life, against PAS, very religious, and believe that religion should have influence on government, while other Republicans have more secular concerns such as keeping taxes low. And although Democrats tend to be more pro-choice than Republicans, certain groups in the Democratic Party, particularly African Americans, are wary of VAE and PAS.

Living Wills

Living wills, advance care directives, and health care powers of attorney (proxies) are the best-known forms of written instruction in cases where a patient is unconscious and suffering from a terminal illness.[79] The enactment in 1991 of the Patient Self-Determination Act was expected by its proponents to increase greatly the proportion of Americans who filled out these documents. The evidence from polling on this issue is inconclusive because of the lack of trend data. In the latest poll on the subject, only three in ten Americans said they have a living will.[80]

In 2009 a provision about advance care planning in the U.S. House version of health reform legislation sparked controversy. The section would have reimbursed doctors for giving Medicare patients end-of-life counseling every five years, sooner if the patient got a terminal diagnosis.[81] Even though the provision did not *require* such consultations, opponents believed it was a step toward euthanasia as elderly patients would feel coerced to end their own lives.[82] Data presented above show that a substantial number of Americans worry about a slippery slope from voluntary to more coercive practices.

Surveys of Family Members and Loved Ones

One important way of measuring the quality of end-of-life care is to interview those whose family members or other loved ones have recently died. Although most of these surveys are conducted in specific settings so that the results are not generalizable to the public as a whole in their experiences with a loved one's death, they provide important information for researchers and health professionals trying to improve end-of-life care.[83]

Occasionally, survey researchers screen a general population to find people who have had an experience with a loved one's death and been one of the main people consulted by medical personnel in the last days of the patient's life. Most of these respondents express satisfaction with their loved one's care at the end of life. In a 2000 poll of this group, however, 11 percent reported that medical staff had not followed the patient's wishes about care at the end of life, and 16 percent believed that the patient had not been given the chance to be as involved in medical decisions about care as he or she wanted to be. About two-thirds (65 percent) believed that their loved one's passing had been a "good death"; in other words, that it had gone about as well as a person could expect. Thirty percent said that things had happened that made it a "bad death."[84]

Jack Kevorkian

During the 1990s Dr. Jack Kevorkian publicly assisted several terminally or chronically ill patients to commit suicide. Euthanasia came into American homes on the evening of November 22, 1998, when the popular television news magazine *60 Minutes* broadcast a story containing excerpts from a video of Kevorkian administering lethal medication to a fifty-two-year-old man with Lou Gehrig's disease, amyotropic lateral schlerosis (ALS).

Public disapproval for Kevorkian's actions increased between 1993 and 1998. In early December 1993, a slight majority approved (52 percent, compared with 41 percent who disapproved) of his assisting people who were terminally ill and wanted to commit suicide. In the days after the *60 Minutes* broadcast, more Americans disapproved (49 percent) than approved (43 percent).[85]

Specific circumstances can alter the public's response on controversial end-of-life issues. Although a majority of Americans favor VAE, they were closely divided on whether Kevorkian did the right (38 percent) or wrong thing (41 percent) in the video shown on *60 Minutes*.[86]

The Terri Schiavo Case

The case of Terri Schiavo, a woman in a coma-like or persistent vegetative state, had been ongoing in Florida state courts for several years before it burst onto the national scene in early 2005. An effort by Schiavo's husband to have her feeding tube disconnected was opposed by other family members. Schiavo had not left a living will, so her wishes were unknown. State and national elected officials, as well as pro-life and disability rights groups, became involved in trying to prevent the disconnection (or order the reinsertion) of the feeding tube. Eventually Schiavo's feeding tube was removed, and she died on March 31, 2005. The discussion of public opinion data in this section draws extensively from an article published by the authors in *Archives of Internal Medicine* in 2005.[87]

The removal of Schiavo's feeding tube was a highly polarizing issue among the American public. Depending on how the circumstances of her case were described and when the polls were taken, a majority or plurality of between 49 percent and 66 percent of Americans supported removing her feeding tube, and a substantial minority (27 percent to 42 percent) opposed.[88]

One issue raised by the opposition was whether Schiavo's condition could have improved with continued use of the feeding tube. A majority of Americans (54 percent) believed there was no chance whatsoever that she would ever show significant improvement in brain activity if the feeding tube were reinserted permanently. One-third (33 percent) thought there was at least some chance that she would show improvement, including 13 percent who thought there was a good or very good chance.[89]

Another area of disagreement was whether a person in Schiavo's condition would feel pain or discomfort if the feeding tube were removed, meaning the person no longer received food or water. A plurality (48 percent) of Americans thought her condition was such that she did not feel pain and discomfort when the feeding tube was withdrawn. But about one-third (32 percent) thought she did feel pain and discomfort, and 20 percent said they did not know.[90]

Schiavo's death brought no majority consensus on what should have been done.[91] A plurality (49 percent) of Americans agreed with the decision to remove her feeding tube; 36 percent disagreed; and 15 percent had no opinion (**Table 13–14**).[92]

The groups in American society most likely to support removing the feeding tube were Protestants who did not consider themselves born-again or evangelical (66 percent), people who were pro-choice on abortion (65 percent), and less-religious Americans (those who said that religion was only somewhat or not important at all in their own lives, 60 percent).

A majority of three groups opposed removing the feeding tube: those who were pro-life on abortion (70 percent), born-again and evangelical Christians (53 percent), and highly religious Roman Catholics (52 percent).

A majority of whites (54 percent) agreed with the decision, but only 36 percent of African Americans agreed. A majority of Democrats supported the decision, and Republicans were nearly evenly divided.

Polling from 2005 showed that the majority of Americans opposed efforts by elected politicians to intervene in the Schiavo case.[93] The unpopularity of these efforts may make politicians less likely to intervene directly in individual cases in the future.[94] But issues involving withdrawal of treatment in cases where the patient has not left a written directive are not likely to disappear from the political agenda. Disagreement about the decision was most widespread among pro-life and particular religious groups of voters who make up a significant bloc within the Republican Party.

Immediately after the Schiavo case, lawmakers attempted to pass legislation placing limits on who can make choices when a patient is vegetative or comatose for a long period of time and has left no written directive, as well as what level of proof should be required before such choices can be implemented.[95] At the same time, efforts to place more restrictions on choices in cases similar to Schiavo's have prompted opposition from those who favor maintaining choices currently available or expanding them.[96]

Conclusions

Because of advances in medical technology, the process of dying may now take years and sometimes involves complicated decisions that will affect the quality and duration of the dying person's life. For most people in our society, the process of dying is an unfamiliar experience. Over the past century, the transformation in the age, place, and cause of death in the United States, combined with changes in living arrangements from extended families to nuclear families and increasing geographic mobility that keep younger people out of contact with older relatives, has meant that most Americans of the past five decades grew up having little contact with people nearing death.[97] Americans' unfamiliarity with dying often leaves them ill-equipped to deal the issues many people face at the end of life. Somewhere between 2020 and 2040, as the baby boom generation reaches the end of its lifespan and puts an enormous strain on our nation's medical and social support systems, Americans are likely to have quite a bit more personal contact with death.

Taken as a whole, the trend data on Americans' views about end-of-life care show a growth through the 1970s into the early 1980s in support for various consensual practices that result in the death of terminally ill patents. Public opinion has been rather stable since then. The public seems able to differentiate broadly among various end-of-life situations and among possible ways to die.[98]

A majority of the public supports in principle the availability of a wide range of choices at the end of life. Many Americans, however, do not recommend some of these choices in specific circumstances, nor do they themselves choose to exercise them. In addition, many Americans have misgivings about the potential of a "slippery slope" from choice to coercion.

What the majority of people want most from health professionals is a way to alleviate pain and to avoid being vegetative prior to death. At the moment, the public is divided over whether health professionals will be able to help them adequately with these problems.

Finally, there are important differences in attitudes about end-of-life decisions, particularly related to the importance of religion in the individual's life and the person's race or ethnicity. These differences need to be taken into account in public policy discussions and in the day-to-day patient care activities and medical education of health professionals.

Notes

[1] Committee on Care at the End of Life, Division of Health Care Services, Institute of Medicine, Marilyn J. Field and Christine K. Cassel, eds, *Approaching Death: Improving Care at the End of Life* (Washington, D.C.: National Academy Press, 1997), 33.

[2] National Center for Health Statistics, *Health, United States, 2008*, http://www.cdc.gov/nchs/data/hus/hus08.pdf; Field and Cassel, *Approaching Death*; Centers for Disease Control and Prevention, "Leading Causes of Death, 1990–1998," http://www.cdc.gov/nchs/data/dvs/lead1900_98.pdf.

[3] Field and Cassel, *Approaching Death*; SUPPORT Principal Investigators, "A Controlled Trial to Improve Care for Seriously Ill Hospitalized Patients: The Study to Understand Prognoses and Preferences for Outcomes and Risks of Treatments (SUPPORT)," *JAMA: Journal of the American Medical Association* 274 (November 22/29, 1995): 1591–8.

[4] Joanne Lynn, Janice Lynch Schuster, and Andrea Kabcenell, *Improving Care for the End of Life: A Sourcebook for Health Care Managers and Clinicians* (New York: Oxford University

Press, 2000); Kathleen M. Foley, "Competent Care for the Dying Instead of Physician-Assisted Suicide," *New England Journal of Medicine* 336 (January 2, 1997): 54–58; Michael W. Rabow, Grace E. Hardie, Joan M. Fair, and Stephen J. McPhee, "End-of-Life Care Content in 50 Textbooks from Multiple Specialties," *JAMA* 283 (February 9, 2000): 771–778; Joanne Lynn, Hal R. Arkes, Marguerite Stevens, Felicia Cohn, Barbara Koenig, Ellen Fox, Neal V. Dawson, Russell S. Phillips, Mary Beth Hamel, and Joel Tsevat, "Rethinking Fundamental Assumptions: SUPPORT's Implications for Future Reform," *Journal of the American Geriatrics Society* 48 (May 2000): S206–S213; F. Amos Bailey, Kathryn L. Burgio, Lesa L. Woodby, Beverly R. Williams, David T. Redden, Stacey H. Kovac, et al., "Improving Processes of Hospital Care during the Last Hours of Life," *Archives of Internal Medicine* 185 (August 8/22, 2005): 1722–7.

[5] Lawrence O. Gostin, "Deciding Life and Death in the Courtroom: From Quinlan to Cruzan, Glucksberg, and Vacco—A Brief History and Analysis of Constitutional Protection of the 'Right to Die,' " *JAMA* 278 (November 12, 1997): 1523–8.

[6] Multi-Society Task Force on PVS, "Medical Aspects of the Persistent Vegetative State—First of Two Parts," *New England Journal of Medicine* 330 (May 26, 1994): 1499–1508, http://content .nejm.org/cgi/content/full/330/21/1499.

[7] Marilyn Webb, *The Good Death: The New American Search to Reshape the End of Life* (New York: Bantam, 1997), Chapter 5; Gostin, "Deciding Life and Death in the Courtroom."

[8] President's Commission for the Study of Ethical Problems in Medicine and Biomedical and Behavioral Research, *Deciding to Forego Life-Sustaining Treatment: A Report on the Ethical, Medical, and Legal Issues in Treatment Decisions* (Washington, D.C.: U.S. Government Printing Office, 1983), http://web.archive.org/web/20070712235757/http://www.bioethics.gov/reports/ past_commissions/deciding_to_forego_tx.pdf.

[9] Webb, *The Good Death,* Chapter 6. The Supreme Court decided not to rule on whether Cruzan's feeding tube should be withdrawn. The majority did affirm the right of a patient to refuse unwanted medical treatment, including life-sustaining equipment like a feeding tube, but did not call it a "fundamental liberty." The case was remanded to the original Missouri state court, but eventually the legal battle was dropped and the treatment withdrawn.

[10] Joan Woolfrey and Courtney S. Campbell, "What Happens Now? Oregon and Physician-Assisted Suicide," *Hastings Center Report* 28 (May–June 1998): 9–17.

[11] Gostin, "Deciding Life and Death in the Courtroom."

[12] Amy Goldstein, "'Pro-Life' Activists Take on Death," *Washington Post,* November 10, 1998, A1.

[13] For 1900 and 1950, U.S. Census Bureau, "The 2009 Statistical Abstract: Historical Statistics, Table HS-3, Population by Age: 1900 to 2002," http://www.census.gov/statab/hist/HS-03 .pdf. For 2010 and 2050, U.S. Census Bureau, "Projections of the Population by Selected Age Groups and Sex for the United States: 2010 to 2050," http://www.census.gov/population/www/ projections/files/nation/summary/np2008-t2.xls.

[14] Christopher Hogan, June Lunney, Jon Gabel, and Joanne Lynn, "Medicare Beneficiaries' Costs of Care in the Last Year of life," *Health Affairs* 20 (July/August 2001): 188–195.

[15] Ad Hoc Committee of the Harvard Medical School to Examine the Definition of Brain Death, "A Definition of Irreversible Coma," *JAMA:* 205 (August 5, 1968): 337–340.

[16] Jacqueline Sullivan, Debbie L. Seem, and Franki Chabalewski, "Determining Brain Death," *Clinical Care Nurse* 19 (April 1999), http://classic.aacn.org/AACN/jrnlccn.nsf/0/5ebf8de743ead 0fa8825674e005a8950?OpenDocument.

[17] President's Commission for the Study of Ethical Problems in Medicine and Biomedical and Behavioral Research, *Defining Death: A Report on the Medical, Legal and Ethical Issues in the Determination of Death* (Washington, D.C.: U.S. Government Printing Office, 1981), http://web.archive.org/web/20041015083802/http://bioethics.gov/reports/past_commissions/defining_death.pdf. The concept and definition of brain death have not been without controversy. See R. D. Truog, "Is It Time to Abandon Brain Death?" *Hastings Center Review* 27 (January/February 1992): 29–37; Amir Halevy and Baruch Brody, "Brain Death: Reconciling Definitions, Criteria, and Tests," *Annals of Internal Medicine* 119 (September 15, 1993): 519–525.

[18] Harvard School of Public Health/Robert Wood Johnson Foundation/ICR Poll (Storrs, Conn.: Roper Center for Public Opinion Research, June 24–July 5, 2009).

[19] Roper Organization Poll (Storrs, Conn.: Roper Center for Public Opinion Research, October 24–31, 1981).

[20] Harvard School of Public Health/Robert Wood Johnson Foundation/ICR Poll, June 24–July 5, 2009.

[21] Multi-Society Task Force on PVS, "Medical Aspects of the Persistent Vegetative State—Second of Two Parts," *New England Journal of Medicine* 330 (June 2, 1994): 1572–9, http://content.nejm.org/cgi/content/short/330/22/1572. For traumatic and nontraumatic causes of PVS, see BrainandSpinalCord.org, "Permanent Vegetative State (PVS)," http://www.brainandspinalcord.org/recovery-traumatic-brain-injury/Vegetative-state-tbi.html.

[22] Gallup/Nathan Cummings Foundation/Fetzer Institute Poll (Storrs, Conn.: Roper Center for Public Opinion Research, May 1997); James A. Davis, Tom W. Smith, and Peter V. Marsden, *General Social Surveys, 1972–2008* (Chicago: National Opinion Research Center, 2009).

[23] Gallup/Nathan Cummings Foundation/Fetzer Institute Poll, May 1997.

[24] Harvard School of Public Health/Robert Wood Johnson Foundation/ICR Poll (Storrs, Conn.: Roper Center for Public Opinion Research, April 22–May 15, 1999).

[25] Ibid.

[26] Charles E. Denk, John M. Benson, John C. Fletcher, and Tina M. Reigel, "How Do Americans Want to Die? A Factorial Vignette Survey of Public Attitudes about End-of-Life Decision-Making," *Social Science Research* 26 (March 1997): 95–120. For a more general discussion of the use of vignettes, see Peter H. Rossi and Steven L. Nock, *Measuring Social Judgments* (Beverly Hills, Calif.: Sage Publications, 1982).

[27] Davis, Smith, and Marsden, *General Social Surveys, 1972–2008*.

[28] Field and Cassel, *Approaching Death*, 31.

[29] Harvard School of Public Health/Robert Wood Johnson Foundation/ICR Poll (Storrs, Conn.: Roper Center for Public Opinion Research, August 7–22, 2000).

[30] *USA Today*/Kaiser Family Foundation/Harvard School of Public Health Poll (Storrs, Conn.: Roper Center for Public Opinion Research, August 1–September 13, 2006).

[31] Field and Cassel, *Approaching Death*, 31.

[32] Beth Han, Robin H. Remsburg, William J. McAuley, Timothy J. Keay, and Shirley S. Travis, "National Trends in Adult Hospice Use: 1991–1992 to 1999–2000," *Health Affairs* 25 (May/June 2006): 792–799.

[33] Webb, *The Good Death*, 65.

[34] "NHPCO Reports Growth in Number of Hospice Patients Served, 1.4 Million, With a Wider Range of Illnesses Seen by Providers," Bio-Medicine, November 10, 2008, http://www .bio-medicine.org/medicine-news-1/NHPCO-Reports-Growth-in-Number-of-Hospice-Patients-Served—1–4-Million—With-a-Wider-Range-of-Illnesses-Seen-by-Providers-29275–1.

[35] Harvard School of Public Health/Robert Wood Johnson Foundation/ICR Poll, April 22–May 15, 1999.

[36] Davis, Smith, and Marsden, *General Social Surveys, 1972–2008*.

[37] American Geriatrics Society Ethics Committee, "The Care of Dying Patients: Position Statement," 2007, http://www.americangeriatrics.org/products/positionpapers/careofd .shtml; American Medical Association, Council on Ethical and Judicial Affairs, "Sedation to Unconsciousness in End-of-Life Care," 2008, http://www.ama-assn.org/ama1/pub/upload/ mm/369/ceja_5a08.pdf; American Medical Association, Council on Ethical and Judicial Affairs, "Medical Futility in End-of-Life Care," 1996, http://www.ama-assn.org/ama1/pub/upload/ mm/369/ceja_2i96.pdf; American Medical Association, Council on Ethical and Judicial Affairs, "Decisions to Forgo Life-Sustaining Treatment for Incompetent Patients," 1991, http://www .ama-assn.org/ama1/pub/upload/mm/369/ceja_da91.pdf. Several of the amicus briefs filed by medical groups in connection with right-to-die cases also made distinctions between forgoing life-sustaining treatment and physician-assisted suicide.

[38] Harvard School of Public Health/Robert Wood Johnson Foundation/ICR Poll, June 24–July 5, 2009.

[39] Pew Research Center for the People and the Press Poll (Storrs, Conn.: Roper Center for Public Opinion Research, November 9–27, 2005).

[40] Davis, Smith, and Marsden, *General Social Surveys, 1972–2008*.

[41] Harvard School of Public Health/Robert Wood Johnson Foundation/ICR Poll, April 22–May 15, 1999.

[42] American Medical Association, Council on Ethical and Judicial Affairs, "Decisions to Forgo Life-Sustaining Treatment for Incompetent Patients," 1991.

[43] Harvard School of Public Health/Robert Wood Johnson Foundation/ICR Poll, June 24–July 5, 2009. For trend data on this question, see John M. Benson, "The Polls—Trends: End-of-Life Issues," *Public Opinion Quarterly* 63 (Summer 1999): 263–277; Harvard School of Public Health/ICR Poll (Storrs, Conn.: Roper Center for Public Opinion Research, September 24–30, 1999).

[44] Davis, Smith, and Marsden, *General Social Surveys, 1972–2008*, 2009.

[45] Gallup Poll (Storrs, Conn.: Roper Center for Public Opinion Research, May 8–11, 2006); Davis, Smith, and Marsden, *General Social Surveys, 1972–2008;* Harvard School of Public Health/Robert Wood Johnson Foundation/ICR Poll, June 24–July 5, 2009.

[46] Harris Poll (Storrs, Conn.: Roper Center for Public Opinion Research, April 5–10, 2005).

[47] Harvard School of Public Health/Robert Wood Johnson Foundation/ICR Poll, June 24–July 5, 2009.

[48] CBS News Poll (Storrs, Conn.: Roper Center for Public Opinion Research, March 3–11, 2005).

[49] Benson, "The Polls—Trends: End-of-Life Issues;" Davis, Smith, and Marsden, *General Social Surveys, 1972–2008*.

[50] Webb (*The Good Death*) argues that "Karen's [Quinlan's] case was a national watershed" (128) and that during the legal battles, "public support for the Quinlans was tremendous" (148). For the impact of the Quinlan case, see also Peter G. Filene, *In the Arms of Others: A Cultural History of the Right-to-Die in America* (Chicago: Ivan R. Dee, 1998).

[51] Robert J. Blendon, Ulrike S. Szalay, and Richard A. Knox, "Should Physicians Aid Their Patients in Dying?" *JAMA* 267 (May 20, 1992): 2658–2662.

[52] Harvard School of Public Health/Robert Wood Johnson Foundation/ICR Poll (Storrs, Conn.: Roper Center for Public Opinion Research, October 1–5, 1999). The New York State Task Force on Life and the Law lists ten risks associated with legalization of PAS (which might also apply to VAE), including a sense of obligation to die, vulnerability of socially marginalized groups, devaluation of the lives of the disabled, and increasing financial incentives to limit care. New York State Task Force on Life and the Law, "When Death Is Sought: Assisted Suicide and Euthanasia in the Medical Context," April 1997 supplement, http://www.health.state.ny.us/nysdoh/taskfce/sought.pdf.

[53] Gallup/Nathan Cummings Foundation/Fetzer Institute Poll, May 1997.

[54] Gallup Poll (Storrs, Conn.: Roper Center for Public Opinion Research, May 10–13, 2007).

[55] Gallup/CNN/*USA Today* polls (Storrs, Conn.: Roper Center for Public Opinion Research, June 23–24, 1997; June 5–7, 1998; March 12–14, 1999); Gallup polls (Storrs, Conn.: Roper Center for Public Opinion Research, May 10–14, 2001; May 6–9, 2002; May 19–21, 2003; May 2–4, 2004; May 2–5, 2005; May 8–11, 2006; May 10–13, 2007).

[56] Harvard School of Public Health/ICR Poll (Storrs, Conn.: Roper Center for Public Opinion Research, August 16–20, 2006); Associated Press/Ipsos-Public Affairs Poll (Storrs, Conn.: Roper Center for Public Opinion Research, May 22–24, 2007).

[57] Benson, "The Polls—Trends: End-of-Life Issues;" *Washington Post*/Kaiser Family Foundation/Harvard University polls (Storrs, Conn.: Roper Center for Public Opinion Research, July 29–August 18, 1998; June 30–August 30, 1999); Harvard School of Public Health/Robert Wood Johnson Foundation/ICR Poll (Storrs, Conn.: Roper Center for Public Opinion Research, August 16–20, 2000); Harvard School of Public Health/ICR polls (Storrs, Conn.: Roper Center for Public Opinion Research, April 1–5, 2005; August 16–20, 2006).

[58] CBS News/*New York Times* Poll (Storrs, Conn.: Roper Center for Public Opinion Research, January 20–25, 2006).

[59] Gallup/Nathan Cummings Foundation/Fetzer Institute Poll, May 1997.

[60] Davis, Smith, and Marsden, *General Social Surveys, 1972–2008.*

[61] Pew Research Center for the People and the Press Poll (Storrs, Conn.: Roper Center for Public Opinion Research, June 24–July 8, 2003).

[62] E. J. Emanuel, D. L. Fairclough, and L. L. Emanuel, "Attitudes and Desires Related to Euthanasia and Physician-Assisted Suicide among Terminally Ill Patients and Their Caregivers," *JAMA* (November 15, 2000): 2460–8.

[63] Davis, Smith, and Marsden, *General Social Surveys, 1972–2008.*

[64] Associated Press/Ipsos-Public Affairs Poll, May 22–24, 2007.

[65] Pew Research Center for the People and the Press Poll (Storrs, Conn.: Roper Center for Public Opinion Research, November 9–27, 2005).

[66] CBS News Poll (Storrs, Conn.: Roper Center for Public Opinion Research, April 20–22, 1998).

[67] Gallup/Nathan Cummings Foundation/Fetzer Institute Poll, May 1997. For more about ways that doctors can discuss religious issue with patents, see Bernard Lo, Delaney Ruston, Laura

W. Kates, Robert M. Arnold, Cynthia B. Cohen, Kathy Faber-Langendoen et al., "Discussing Religious and Spiritual Issues at the End of Life: A Practical Guide for Physicians," *JAMA* 287 (February 13, 2002): 749–754.

[68] Harvard School of Public Health/Robert Wood Johnson Foundation/ICR Poll, April 22–May 15, 1999.

[69] NPR/Kaiser Family Foundation/Kennedy School of Government Poll (Storrs, Conn.: Roper Center for Public Opinion Research, February 19–25, 1999).

[70] Harvard School of Public Health/Robert Wood Johnson Foundation/ICR Poll, April 22–May 15, 1999.

[71] CBS News Poll (Storrs, Conn.: Roper Center for Public Opinion Research, March 29–April 1, 2010).

[72] Gallup Poll (Storrs, Conn.: Roper Center for Public Opinion Research, November 10–12, 2003).

[73] ABC News Poll (Storrs, Conn.: Roper Center for Public Opinion Research, May 27, 1997).

[74] For withdrawal of life support and double-effect, Harvard School of Public Health/ICR Poll, June 24–July 5, 2009. For VAE for a patient with an incurable disease, Davis, Smith, and Marsden, *General Social Surveys, 1972–2008*. For PAS for a patient who is terminally ill and in great pain, Harvard School of Public Health/ICR Poll, August 16–20, 2006.

[75] In the Tuskegee syphilis study, African American men in Alabama who did not know they were receiving placebo treatment for syphilis were tracked by the federal government to study the effects of untreated disease. Tuskegee University, "Research Ethics: The Tuskegee Syphilis Study," http://www.tuskegee.edu/Global/Story.asp?s=1207598; James H. Jones, *Bad Blood: The Tuskegee Syphilis Experiment* (New York: Free Press, 1981).

[76] For the relationship between abortion and end-of-life attitudes, see John M. Benson and Melissa J. Herrmann, "Right to Die or Right to Life? The Public on Assisted Suicide," *Public Perspective* 10 (June/July 1999): 15–19.

[77] Research has shown that religiosity is significantly associated with wanting all efforts to extend life. T. A. Balboni, L. C. Vanderwerker, S. D. Block, M. E. Paulk, C. S. Lathan, J. R. Pateet, and H. G. Prigerson, "Religiousness and Spiritual Support among Advanced Cancer Patients and Association with End-of-Life Treatment Preferences and Quality of Life," *Journal of Clinical Oncology* 25 (February 10, 2007): 555–560; Andrea C. Phelps, Paul K. Maciejewski, Matthew Nilsson, Tracy A. Balboni, Alexi A. Wright, M. Elizabeth Paulk et al., "Religious Coping and Use of Intensive Life-Prolonging Care Near Death in Patients with Advanced Cancer," *JAMA* 301 (March 18, 2009): 1140–7.

[78] As early as 1991 James D. Hunter argued that there was a moral coalition of religious conservatives across denominations, advancing a traditionalist view of the sanctity of life against a more secularized and individualistic view of the variable value of life. James D. Hunter, *Culture Wars: The Struggle to Define America* (New York: Basic Books, 1991).

[79] Healthopedia.com, "Advanced Care Directives," 2001, http://www.healthopedia.com/advanced-care-directives/

[80] Pew Research Center for the People and the Press Poll, November 9–27, 2005.

[81] U.S. House of Representatives, "HR 3200: America's Affordable Health Choices Act," .docstoc, http://www.docstoc.com/docs/8605755/Americas-Affordable-Health-Choices-Act-Complete-Bill-Text-(HR-3200).

[82] Charles Lane, "Undue Influence: Will Section 1233 Hasten Patient Deaths?" *Washington Post,* August 8, 2009, http://www.washingtonpost.com/wp-dyn/content/article/2009/08/07/AR2009080703043_pf.html.

[83] See, for example, R. Baker, A. W. Wu, J. M. Teno, B. Kreling, A. M. Damiano, H. R. Rubin et al., "Family Satisfaction with End-of-Life Care in Seriously Ill Hospitalized Adults," *Journal of the American Geriatrics Society* 48 (Suppl., May 2000): 561–569; Joan M. Teno, Brian R. Clarridge, Virginia Casey, Lisa C. Welch, Terrie Wetle, Renee Shield, and Vincent Mor, "Family Perspectives on End-of-Life Care at the Last Place of Care," *JAMA* 291 (January 7, 2004): 88–93.

[84] Harvard School of Public Health/Robert Wood Johnson Foundation/ICR Poll (Storrs, Conn.: Roper Center for Public Opinion Research, August 7–22, 2000). For results from an earlier, more detailed study using this methodology, see John M. Benson, Joel C. Cantor, Joanne Lynn, and Joan Teno, "National Perspective on Dying in America: Does Place of Death Matter?" *Journal of the American Geriatrics Society* 48 (Suppl., May 2000): S230–S231.

[85] CBS News polls (Storrs, Conn.: Roper Center for Public Opinion Research, December 5–7, 1993; November 23–24, 1998).

[86] CBS News Poll, November 23–24, 1998.

[87] Robert J. Blendon, John M. Benson, and Melissa J. Herrmann, "The American Public and the Terri Schiavo Case," *Archives of Internal Medicine* 165 (December 12/26, 2005): 2580–4.

[88] ABC News, "Poll: No Role for Government in Schiavo Case," March 21, 2005, http://abcnews.go.com/Politics/PollVault/story?id=599622&page=1; Gallup/CNN/*USA Today* Poll (Storrs, Conn.: Roper Center for Public Opinion Research, April 1–2, 2005); *Time*/Schulman, Ronca, and Bucuvalas Poll, March 22–24, 2005; Harvard School of Public Health/ICR Poll, April 1–5, 2005; CBS News Poll (Storrs, Conn.: Roper Center for Public Opinion Research, March 21–22, 2005); Gallup/CNN/*USA Today* Poll (Storrs, Conn.: Roper Center for Public Opinion Research, March 18–20, 2005); Gallup/CNN/*USA Today* Poll (Storrs, Conn.: Roper Center for Public Opinion Research, March 22, 2005).

[89] Gallup/CNN/*USA Today* Poll, March 22, 2005.

[90] Harvard School of Public Health/ICR Poll, April 1–5, 2005.

[91] Blendon, Benson, and Herrmann, "The American Public and the Terri Schiavo Case."

[92] Ibid.

[93] ABC News, "Poll: No Role for Government in Schiavo Case," March 21, 2005; Harris Poll, April 5–10, 2005.

[94] Blendon, Benson, and Herrmann, "The American Public and the Terri Schiavo Case."

[95] Shaila Dewan, "States Taking a New Look at End-of-Life Legislation: Schiavo Case Prompts Flurry of Activity," *New York Times,* March 31, 2005, A14; Sheryl Gay Stolberg, "Lawmakers Ready to Again Debate End-of-Life Issues," *New York Times,* March 28, 2005, A1, A14; Not Dead Yet, "What the Disability Rights Movement Wants: Eight Things that Need to Happen to Safeguard against Non-Voluntary Euthanasia in the U.S.," http://www.notdeadyet.org/docs/drmwants0305.html.

[96] Blendon, Benson, and Herrmann, "The American Public and the Terri Schiavo Case."

[97] John M. Benson, "Final Moments: Perspective on Death," *Public Perspective* 12 (March/April 2001): 8–12.

[98] Benjamin I. Page and Robert Y. Shapiro, *The Rational Public: Fifty Years of Trends in Americans' Policy Preferences* (Chicago: University of Chicago Press, 1992).

Table 13-1 Dying in the United States, Past and Present

	1900	1950	1980	2005
Life expectancy at birth (years)[1]	47	68	74	78
Death rate (age adjusted, per 100,000 population)[1]	—	1446	1039	799
Infant mortality (per 1,000 live births)	162[2]	29[1]	13[1]	7[1]
Percent who die in institutions[2]	50	—	74	—
Leading causes of death	1 Pneumonia/influenza[3] 2 Tuberculosis[3]			1 Heart disease[1] 2 Cancer[1]

	1900	1950	2010	2050 (projected)
Percent of population aged 65+[4]	4.1	8.1	13.0	20.0
Percent of population aged 85+[4]	0.2	0.4	1.9	4.3

Sources: [1]National Center for Health Statistics, *Health, United States, 2008.* [2]Committee on Care at the End of Life, Division of Health Care Services, Institute of Medicine, Marilyn J. Field and Christine K. Cassel, eds. *Approaching Death: Improving Care at the End of Life* (Washington, D.C.: National Academy Press; 1997). [3]Centers for Disease Control and Prevention, "Leading Causes of Death, 1990–1998." [4]For 1900 and 1950, U.S. Census Bureau, "The 2009 Statistical Abstract: Historical Statistics, Table HS-3, Population by Age: 1900 to 2002." For 2010 and 2050, U.S. Census Bureau, "Projections of the Population by Selected Age Groups and Sex for the United States: 2010 to 2050."

Table 13-2 Americans' Views of Brain Death and Likelihood of Recovery from a Persistent Vegetative State (in percent)

	1981[1]	2009[2]
Life ends . . .		
When the brain ceases to function, even though the heart may continue to beat	43	48
Only when the heart ceases to beat	48	43
Don't know	9	9
How often a doctor's diagnosis that a patient will not recover from PVS is wrong and the patient at least partially recovers awareness or consciousness[2]		
Never		4
Rarely		42
Sometimes		38
Often		7
Don't know		9

Note: PVS = persistent vegetative state.

Question: Is it your view that life ends when the brain ceases to function even though the heart may continue to beat, or that life ends only when the heart ceases to beat?

Question: Some patients have serious health events that lead them to be in a persistent vegetative or coma-like state with no higher brain activity. After some time, doctors may make a diagnosis that the patient will never recover. How often do you think doctors' diagnoses are wrong in these cases and the patient ends up at least partially recovering awareness or consciousness? Would you say never, rarely, sometimes, or often?

Sources: Roper Organization Poll (Storrs, Conn.: Roper Center for Public Opinion Research, October 24–31, 1981); Harvard School of Public Health/ Robert Wood Johnson Foundation/ICR Poll (Storrs, Conn.: Roper Center for Public Opinion Research, June 24–July 5, 2009).

Table 13-3 What Worries Americans about the Care They Will Receive at the End of Life (in percent)

Being vegetative[1]	73
Great physical pain[1]	67
Emotional burden on family in making end-of-life decisions for them[2]	62
Economic burden on family[2]	61
Not having access to life-saving medical technology[1]	56
Second-class health care if they run out of money or health insurance[2]	55
Not having access to their own physician or hospital[1]	52

Note: [1]Worry a great deal or somewhat. [2]Agree strongly or agree that this is a worry.

Question: Here are some medical matters. How much, if at all, does each of these medical matters worry you when you think about your own death . . . a great deal, somewhat, not much, or not at all? . . . (The possibility of being vegetable-like for some period of time/The possibility of great physical pain before you die/The possibility of not having access to life-saving medical technology/The possibility of not having access to your own doctor or hospital).

Question: I would like to talk about concerns you may have when considering what may happen at the end of your life. Please tell me how much you agree or disagree with each of these statements. . . . Strongly agree, agree, neither agree nor disagree, disagree, strongly disagree . . . (I worry about the emotional burden that my family might face making decisions for me at the end of life/I worry about the economic burden that a terminal illness might cause my family/I worry that if I run out of money or health insurance I will get second class health care).

Sources: [1]Gallup/Nathan Cummings Foundation/Fetzer Institute Poll, May 1997. [2]Data from 1998, James A. Davis, Tom W. Smith, and Peter V. Marsden, *General Social Surveys, 1972–2008* (Chicago: National Opinion Research Center, 2009).

Table 13-4 Americans' Attitudes about Withdrawing Life Support, 1986–2009 (in percent)

	Favor	Oppose	Don't know
1986[1]	73	15	12
1991[1]	76	15	10
1999[2]	76	20	4
2009[3]	67	24	9

Question: Would you favor or oppose withdrawing life support systems, including food and water, from hopelessly ill or irreversibly comatose patients if they or their families request it? (1986, 1999, 2009)

Question: Would you strongly favor, favor, oppose, or strongly oppose withdrawing life support systems, including food and water, from hopelessly ill or irreversibly comatose patients if they or their families request it? (1991)

Sources: [1]John M. Benson, "The Polls—Trends: End-of-Life Issues," *Public Opinion Quarterly* 63 (Summer 1999): 263–277. [2]Harvard School of Public Health/ICR Poll (Storrs, Conn.: Roper Center for Public Opinion Research, September 29–October 3, 1999). [3]Harvard School of Public Health/ICR Poll (Storrs, Conn.: Roper Center for Public Opinion Research, June 24–July 5, 2009).

Table 13-5 Americans' Attitudes about Double-Effect Administration of Pain Medication, 1982–2009 (in percent)

	Yes, should be	No, Should not be	Don't know
1982[1]	79	14	7
1987[1]	74	21	5
1999[2]	81	14	5
2009[3]	80	14	6

Question: Assume that a patient who is in severe pain and with no hope of recovery has asked the doctor to help ease the pain, knowing that it might (kill him [1982, 1987]/shorten his or her life [1999, 2009]). Under these circumstances should it be permissible for a doctor to administer drugs to reduce the pain, even if the dose required might shorten the patient's life?

Sources: [1]John M. Benson, "The Polls—Trends: End-of-Life Issues," *Public Opinion Quarterly* 63 (Summer 1999): 263–277. [2]Harvard School of Public Health/ICR Poll (Storrs, Conn.: Roper Center for Public Opinion Research, September 24–30, 1999). [3]Harvard School of Public Health/ICR Poll (Storrs, Conn.: Roper Center for Public Opinion Research, June 24–July 5, 2009).

Table 13-6 Americans' Attitudes about Voluntary Active Euthanasia for a Patient with an Incurable Disease, 1947–2008 (in percent)

	Should be allowed	Should not be allowed	Don't know
1947[1]	37	54	9
1950[1]	38	56	7
1973[1]	53	40	7
1977[2]	60	36	4
1978[2]	58	38	4
1982[2]	61	34	5
1983[2]	63	33	4
1985[2]	64	33	3
1986[2]	66	31	4
1988[2]	66	29	5
1989[2]	66	30	4
1990[2]	69	26	5
1991[2]	70	25	5
1993[2]	65	30	5
1994[2]	68	27	5
1996[2]	68	28	4
1998[2]	68	27	6
2000[2]	64	30	5
2002[2]	66	32	2
2004[2]	65	32	3
2006[2]	66	31	3
2008[2]	64	33	4

Question: When a person has a disease that cannot be cured, do you think doctors should be allowed by law to end the patient's life by some painless means if the patient and his family request it?

Sources: [1]John M. Benson, "The Polls—Trends: End-of-Life Issues," *Public Opinion Quarterly* 63 (Summer 1999): 263–277. [2]James A. Davis, Tom W. Smith, and Peter V. Marsden, *General Social Surveys, 1972–2008* (Chicago: National Opinion Research Center, 2009).

Table 13-7 Americans' Attitudes about Physician-assisted Suicide for a Patient with Incurable Disease and Living in Severe Pain, 1997–2007 (in percent)

	Should be allowed	Should not be allowed	Don't know
1997[1]	57	36	8
1998[1]	59	39	2
1999[1]	61	35	4
2001[2]	68	27	5
2002[2]	62	34	4
2003[2]	62	37	1
2004[2]	65	31	4
2005[2]	58	39	3
2006[2]	64	31	5
2007[2]	56	38	6

Question: When a person has a disease that cannot be cured and is living in severe pain, do you think doctors should or should not be allowed by law to assist the patient to commit suicide if the patient requests it?

Sources: [1]Gallup/CNN/*USA Today* polls (Storrs, Conn.: Roper Center for Public Opinion Research, June 23–24, 1997; June 5–7, 1998; March 12–14, 1999). [2]Gallup polls (Storrs, Conn.: Roper Center for Public Opinion Research, May 10–14, 2001; May 6–9, 2002; May 19–21, 2003; May 2–4, 2004; May 2–5, 2005; May 8–11, 2006; May 10–13, 2007).

Table 13-8 Americans' Attitudes about Physician-assisted Suicide for a Patient Who Is Terminally Ill and in Great Pain, 1993–2006 (in percent)

	Should be legal	Should not be legal	Don't know
1993[1]	50	47	3
1998[2]	52	44	4
1999[2]	53	43	4
2000[3]	50	43	7
2005[4]	42	47	10
2006[4]	47	46	6

Question: If someone is terminally ill, is in great pain, and wants to kill themselves, should it be legal for a doctor to help them them to commit suicide or not?

Source: [1]John M. Benson, "The Polls—Trends: End-of-Life Issues," *Public Opinion Quarterly* 63 (Summer 1999): 263–277. [2]*Washington Post*/Kaiser Family Foundation/Harvard University polls (Storrs, Conn.: Roper Center for Public Opinion Research, July 29–August 18, 1998; June 30–August 30, 1999). [3]Harvard School of Public Health/Robert Wood Johnson Foundation/ICR Poll (Storrs, Conn.: Roper Center for Public Opinion Research, August 16–20, 2000). [4]Harvard School of Public Health/ICR polls (Storrs, Conn.: Roper Center for Public Opinion Research, April 1–5, 2005; August 16–20, 2006).

Table 13-9 Americans' Attitudes about Whether Someone Who Has a Terminal Disease Has a Right to End His or Her Own Life, 1977–2008 (in percent)

	Yes	No	Don't know
1977	38	59	3
1978	38	58	3
1982	45	50	5
1983	48	48	4
1985	44	53	3
1986	52	45	3
1988	50	46	4
1989	47	49	5
1990	56	38	6
1991	57	40	3
1993	57	39	5
1994	62	34	5
1996	61	34	5
1998	61	35	5
2000	55	40	5
2002	58	40	2
2004	58	39	3
2006	60	37	3
2008	59	38	3

Question: Do you think a person has the right to end his or her own life if this person has an incurable disease?

Source: James A. Davis, Tom W. Smith, and Peter V. Marsden, *General Social Surveys, 1972–2008* (Chicago: National Opinion Research Center, 2009).

Table 13-10 Attitudes about Withdrawing Life Support, by Demographic and Religious Groups

	Percent favor
Total	67
By sex	
Men	69
Women	66
By age	
18–64	66
65+	68
By race/ethnicity	
White (non-Hispanic)	74
Black (non-Hispanic)	54
Hispanic	50
By party identification	
Democrat	64
Independent	72
Republican	67
By importance of religion (self-described)	
Most/very important	61
Somewhat/Not too important	77
By religious preference/importance of religion	
Protestant, most/very important	64
Catholic, most/very important	59
Protestant, somewhat/not too important	82
Catholic, somewhat/not too important	72
No religion	68
By race/born-again or evangelical	
White born-again/evangelical	73
Black born-again/evangelical	53
By abortion position	
Pro-choice	80
Pro-life	56

Note: Pro-choice = abortion should be available to those who want it or should be available but under stricter limits. Pro-life = abortion should not be permitted at all or should be against the law except in certain cases.

Question: Would you favor or oppose withdrawing life support systems, including food and water, from hopelessly ill or irreversibly comatose patients if they or their families request it?

Source: Harvard School of Public Health/ICR Poll (Storrs, Conn.: Roper Center for Public Opinion Research, June 24–July 5, 2009).

Table 13-11 Attitudes about Double-Effect Administration of Pain Medication, by Demographic and Religious Groups

Percent favor	
Total	80
By sex	
Men	80
Women	79
By age	
18–64	81
65+	73
By race/ethnicity	
White (non-Hispanic)	86
Black (non-Hispanic)	54
Hispanic	72
By party identification	
Democrat	75
Independent	84
Republican	83
By importance of religion (self-described)	
Most/very important	74
Somewhat/Not too important	89
By religious preference/importance of religion	
Protestant, most/very important	74
Catholic, most/very important	72
Protestant, somewhat/not too important	85
Catholic, somewhat/not too important	90
No religion	94
By race/born-again or evangelical	
White born-again/evangelical	83
Black born-again/evangelical	51
By abortion position	
Pro-choice	89
Pro-life	72

Note: Pro-choice = abortion should be available to those who want it or should be available but under stricter limits. Pro-life = abortion should not be permitted at all or should be against the law except in certain cases.

Question: Assume that a patient who is in severe pain and with no hope of recovery has asked the doctor to help ease the pain, knowing that it might shorten his or her life. Under these circumstances, should it be permissible for a doctor to administer drugs to reduce the pain, even if the dose required might shorten the patient's life?

Source: Harvard School of Public Health/ICR Poll (Storrs, Conn.: Roper Center for Public Opinion Research, June 24–July 5, 2009).

Table 13-12 Attitudes about Voluntary Active Euthanasia for a Patient with an Incurable Disease, by Demographic and Religious Groups, Combined 2006 and 2008

Percent favor	
Total	65
By sex	
Men	70
Women	62
By age	
18–64	66
65+	61
By race	
White	68
Black	49
By party identification	
Democrat	66
Independent	60
Republican	59
By religious attendance	
High	50
Low	78
By religious preference/attendance	
Protestant, high	47
Catholic, high	51
Protestant, low	74
Catholic, low	75
No religion	82
By race/born-again	
White born-again	51
Black born-again	44
By abortion (health of the mother)	
Pro-choice	72
Pro-life	31

Note: Pro-choice = those who think it should be possible for a pregnant woman to obtain a legal abortion if her own health is seriously endangered by the pregnancy. Pro-life = those who think it should not.

Question: When a person has a disease that cannot be cured, do you think doctors should be allowed by law to end the patient's life by some painless means if the patient and his family request it?

Source: James A. Davis, Tom W. Smith, and Peter V. Marsden, General Social Surveys, 1972–2008 (Chicago: National Opinion Research Center, 2009).

Table 13-13 Attitudes about Physician-assisted Suicide for a Patient Who Is Terminally Ill and in Great Pain, by Demographic and Religious Groups (in percent)

	Should be legal	Should not
Total	47	46
By sex		
Men	51	44
Women	43	49
By age		
18–64	48	45
65+	44	50
By race/ethnicity		
White (non-Hispanic)	50	43
Black (non-Hispanic)	24	62
By party identification		
Democrat	46	45
Independent	57	37
Republican	36	60
By importance of religion (self-described)		
Most/very important	31	61
Somewhat/Not too important	70	26
By religious preference/importance of religion		
Protestant, most/very important	28	63
Catholic, most/very important	42	55
Protestant, somewhat/not too important	68	27
Catholic, somewhat/not too important	65	32
No religion	69	25
By race/Born-again or evangelical		
White born-again/evangelical	28	64
Black born-again/evangelical	NA	NA
By abortion position		
Pro-choice	68	24
Pro-life	28	67

Note: "Don't know" responses not shown. NA = not available. Pro-choice = abortion should be available to those who want it or should be available but under stricter limits. Pro-life = abortion should not be permitted at all or should be against the law except in certain cases.

Question: If someone is terminally ill, is in great pain and wants to kill themselves, should it be legal for a doctor to help them to commit suicide or not?

Source: Harvard School of Public Health/ICR Poll (Storrs, Conn.: Roper Center for Public Opinion Research, August 16–20, 2006).

Table 13-14 Americans' Attitudes, after Terri Schiavo's Death, about the Decision to Remove Her Feeding Tube (in percent)

	Agree with decision to remove	Disagree with decision to remove	No opinion
Total	49	36	15
By race/ethnicity			
White (non-Hispanic)	54	32	14
Black (non-Hispanic)	36	46	18
By party ID			
Democrat	52	33	15
Independent	49	37	14
Republican	43	44	13
By religious preference			
Protestant, not born-again/evangelical	66	21	13
Catholic	44	39	17
Born-again/evangelical	37	53	10
By importance of religion in own life			
Most/extremely important	43	46	11
Somewhat/not at all important	60	25	15
By religious preference/importance of religion			
Protestants/other non-Catholic Christians, religion most/extremely important	44	46	10
Catholics, religion most/extremely important	38	52	11
Protestants/other non-Catholic Christians, religion somewhat/not at all important	67	18	15
Catholics, religion somewhat/not at all important	49	35	15
By position on abortion			
Pro-choice	65	22	13
Pro-life	33	56	11

Question: Terri Schiavo was in a coma-like state for 15 years. Her husband said that Terri would not have wanted to be kept alive artificially in this state. He asked that the feeding tube that kept her alive be removed. Her parents disagreed, saying that Terri would not have wanted to die this way and contended that her condition could be improved. A Florida judge upheld her husband's request to remove the feeding tube. Do you agree or disagree with the decision to remove her feeding tube?

Source: Robert J. Blendon, John M. Benson, and Melissa J. Herrmann, "The American Public and the Terri Schiavo Case," *Archives of Internal Medicine* 165 (December 12/26, 2005): 2580–4.

Chapter 14

PUBLIC OPINION AND OBESITY

Sara Bleich and Robert J. Blendon

Obesity has long been a matter of concern in the medical and public health communities, but it has not always received a prominent position on the policy agenda or in the minds of the American people. The American Heart Association identified obesity as a cardiac risk factor as early as 1952.[1] Research during the following decades associated obesity with several other health complications such as gall bladder disease, stroke, diabetes, heart disease. and hypertension.[2] In 1985 obesity was recognized as a disease.[3] In 2001 the U.S. surgeon general's report, which focused on excess body weight, declared that "overweight and obesity have reached nationwide epidemic proportions."[4] One year later the World Health Organization called obesity a "global epidemic."[5] Prior to the surgeon general's report, obesity-related media coverage was low, with fewer than a dozen articles appearing in major U.S. outlets during the final quarter of 1999. By the final quarter of 2002, the number of articles on obesity was over 1,200, and since then more than 1,000 stories per quarter have been published.[6] Today, the problem of obesity is a significant issue not only in the popular press but also in academic research.

Obesity is defined as a body mass index (BMI) of 30 or higher (**Table 14–1**). BMI is a measure of an individual's weight relative to their height (weight in kilograms divided by the square of height in meters). The levels of BMI that distinguish healthy weight from overweight and obesity are based on how much the risk of chronic disease and death goes up as weight increases.[7]

The prevalence of obesity has risen rapidly in the past three decades. Since 1980 the proportion of American adults who are obese has doubled to 32 percent (in 2004).[8] Over the same period, rates of overweight and obesity tripled for six- to nineteen-year-olds.[9] Given that overweight children and adolescents have a higher probability of becoming overweight and obese adults,[10] these trends foreshadow even greater rates of obesity to come, although most recent trends show some leveling in obesity prevalence among children and adolescents.[11] The trends also have strong implications for obesity-related diseases and health care spending.

Although obesity is rising in all segments of the U.S. population, some groups and regions are disproportionately affected. Adult obesity occurs at higher rates in racial/ethnic populations, and within these minority populations, women and individuals with low socioeconomic status are particularly affected.[12] A similar gender disparity exists among children and adolescents. Black girls have the highest rates of overweight followed by Mexican-American girls; both of these groups are more likely to be overweight than white girls.[13] Across the states, the rates of obesity vary significantly. The states with the lowest level of obesity prevalence are Colorado, Connecticut, Hawaii, and Massachusetts. The states with the highest level of obesity prevalence are Alabama, Mississippi, Tennessee, and West Virginia.[14]

The increasing recognition of obesity as a major public health problem is due not only to the disparities in prevalence but also to the significant co-morbidities (causes of ill health) associated with excess weight. Obesity greatly increases the risk of illness from many serious medical conditions, such as hypertension, cardiovascular disease, and type 2 diabetes (a disease associated with physical inactivity and obesity that accounts for 90 percent to 95 percent of all diabetes; the remainder is type 1 diabetes).[15] In addition, obesity is the second-leading cause of preventable death in the United States, after tobacco use. Obesity is estimated to have accounted for 385,000 such deaths in 2000.[16]

The adverse affects of obesity are not only medical: excess body weight has also been shown to affect quality of life in both adults and children.[17] Obesity and its associated conditions are estimated to cost $147 billion annually, approximately 9 percent of total national health expenditures in the United States.[18]

The rise in obesity has been paralleled by a proliferation of health-clubs, organic foods, diet programs, and athletic gear—all factors that signal an increasingly health conscious nation. That we spend $40 billion to $100 billion annually on the diet industry suggests that people are trying to lose weight. These trends imply that we should be a fitter nation, but on average we are not. So, what explains the rising prevalence of obesity?

Experts agree that genetics are insufficient to explain the rapid rise in obesity; rather, they say obesity is caused by an energy imbalance. In general, individuals who eat more calories than they expend gain weight.[19] Scientists do not, however, entirely understand the complex interaction of factors that cause this energy imbalance.[20] Research has linked obesity with a number of social, economic, and environmental determinants that have encouraged increased opportunities for eating. These include bigger portion size, greater food availability, higher consumption of sugar-sweetened beverages, lower food prices, and more snacking, as well as fewer opportunities for energy expenditure related to more time spent watching television and playing video games, labor saving technologies, and reductions in physical education in schools.[21] Despite our growing knowledge base about the factors involved, many unanswered questions remain about the drivers of the energy imbalance.

The rapid escalation of obesity, along with its related diseases and associated health care costs, has led policymakers to place obesity among the top issues on the legislative agenda. At the federal level, dozens of obesity-related bills have been introduced annually over the past few years. In 2004 Medicare reclassified obesity as an illness, allowing for the coverage of weight loss therapies. The federal government does not, however, require states to provide Medicaid benefits for obesity treatments such as bariatric surgery (which accounted for $948 million in hospital costs in 2002) or prescription drugs (which cost each user an average of $304 annually).[22]

At the state level, the number of obesity-related bills filed by lawmakers has more than doubled over the past few years. Many of these bills focus on five main objectives related to nutrition, health, and weight in school settings: establishing nutritional standards for foods and beverages sold in schools, restricting access to and sales of competitive foods and beverages (such as vending machines), setting physical education and activity requirements, educating children about nutrition and active living, and monitoring and reporting students' body mass index.[23] Legislative efforts focused on environmental changes to combat obesity have included calorie posting on menus and menu boards in chain restaurants. These rules have passed in several cities, such as New York and Seattle, and in the state of California, and are currently under consideration in more than twenty states, cities, and counties.[24] In addition, a tax on sugary beverages has been debated at the state and federal level.[25] Recent legislation contrasts with earlier policy recommendations by focusing on societal and environmental contributors to obesity rather than on individual solutions alone to combat weight gain.[26]

This chapter explores obesity from two perspectives: obesity as a national issue, and obesity as a personal issue. The first section synthesizes public attitudes about the seriousness and causes of obesity, as well as responsibility for obesity. It then discusses public attitudes toward a number of government, school, and food industry obesity policies. The second section examines the public's views on weight and weight-related behavior in their personal lives. The chapter concludes with a discussion of possible policy opportunities for the future.

Obesity as a National Issue

Obesity has become an increasingly salient topic for Americans. The public identifies obesity as an important health problem with serious consequences. Americans primarily view obesity as an individual issue rather than a societal one, but they also see a role for government in addressing the problem. The public strongly supports efforts to reduce the health effects of excess weight, especially those efforts that are consistent with their belief in individual responsibility.

Public Attitudes on the Seriousness of Obesity

A majority of the public sees obesity as a serious concern. In 2005, two-thirds (68 percent) of Americans believed that obesity was a very serious health problem for adults, an increase from 58 percent in 2003. Public concern about the seriousness of childhood and adolescent obesity is also high (61 percent in 2003; 66 percent in 2005) (**Table 14–2**).[27]

Asked in 2009 to name the diseases or health conditions they thought posed the greatest threats to Americans, the public ranked obesity sixth (named by 9 percent as one of the two greatest health threats), behind cancer (57 percent), heart disease (28 percent), HIV/AIDS (25 percent), influenza (17 percent), and diabetes (13 percent).[28] Research has shown that people take into account a number of factors when assessing health threats. Their perceptions are based not only on the number of deaths they think a disease or condition causes but also on media coverage, the rapidity with which a disease or condition spreads, uneasiness about the unknown origins or consequences of new diseases, and fear of the suffering a particular disease may inflict before it becomes fatal.[29]

Americans believe that the consequences of being overweight can be quite serious. More than eight in ten (83 percent) believe that maintaining a healthy weight can improve an individual's chances for a long and healthy life "a lot."[30] The same proportion believes that being significantly overweight is very harmful for adults.[31] Moreover, three-fourths (73 percent) of the public think that someone who is moderately overweight is more likely to develop a chronic disease, such as diabetes or high blood pressure. But only about half (51 percent) believe that someone who is moderately overweight is more likely to die prematurely.[32] This finding suggests that the public is more likely to associate excess weight with increased morbidity (illness) rather than increased mortality. On one hand, this belief may be due to a lack of public awareness that obesity is a leading cause of death.[33] On the other hand, the public may recognize that the impact of obesity on morbidity is higher than its impact on death (**Table 14–3**).

Public Attitudes about the Causes of Obesity

Most Americans believe that obesity has more to do with personal behavior than with the broader society or environment. When the public was asked to assess several possible causes of obesity by level of importance, insufficient physical exercise (86 percent) and poor eating habits (85 percent) topped the list as most important or very important. The marketing of sweets and other high-calorie foods to children (65 percent) and watching too much television (59 percent) ranked third and fourth, respectively. At the bottom of the list for most and very important causes of obesity were lack of information on good eating habits (45 percent), the cost of buying healthy food (45 percent), and lack of information about food content (37 percent) (**Table 14–4**).[34]

Asked specifically whether personal factors, such as overeating, lack of exercise, and watching too much television, or external factors, such as exposure to junk food advertising, lack of safe places for children to play, and limited availability of healthy foods in some neighborhoods, was the bigger cause of childhood obesity, 64 percent said personal factors were. About one in five (18 percent) thought external factors were the bigger cause, while 16 percent though both were equal (**Table 14–5**).[35]

Of the personal behaviors that have been related to obesity, Americans generally place more blame on poor eating habits than on lack of physical activity. About half of the public sees poor eating habits as the primary factor causing obesity in adults and children, and about three in ten think that not enough physical activity is the main factor. Only a small fraction of the public believes that genetics or family history is most to blame (**Table 14–6**).[36]

Public Attitudes about Responsibility for Obesity

Just as Americans think the causes of obesity are largely related to personal behavior, they also believe that individuals are more responsible for weight gain than society or the environment. When asked specifically about how responsible obese individuals are for their weight problems, most Americans (83 percent) believe that they are very or somewhat responsible.[37] Similarly, 87 percent believe that individual Americans, in their choice of diet and lack of exercise, bear a great deal or a good amount of responsibility for the nation's obesity problem.[38]

Although Americans predominately blame personal behavior for the obesity epidemic, they also identify other sources of responsibility. About six in ten Americans believe that fast-food restaurants (64 percent), schools that allow high-calorie snacks and sweets (64 percent), manufacturers of high-calorie packaged and processed foods (61 percent), and marketers and advertisers of high-calorie packaged and processed foods (60 percent) bear a great deal or a good amount of responsibility for the national obesity problem. Far fewer Americans place that level of responsibility for obesity on government policies and laws on food content and marketing (41 percent) (**Table 14–7**).[39]

When asked who, aside from parents, should have the main responsibility for teaching children to avoid becoming overweight, a majority believe the task should fall to schools (55 percent). Few Americans think the media (13 percent), food providers such as restaurants (11 percent), or health care providers (10 percent) should be primarily responsible for helping children avoid becoming overweight (**Table 14–8**).[40]

Public Attitudes about Obesity Policies

Although Americans tend to identify obesity as a personal responsibility, they nevertheless see a role for government in addressing the problem. Similar to their view about the most serious health threats, the public in 2007 ranked obesity as the fifth most important disease or health condition for government to address, after cancer, HIV/AIDS, heart disease, and diabetes. College graduates are significantly more likely than individuals with less education to view obesity as one of the most important health conditions for government to address.[41]

In general, a slight majority (53 percent) of the public believes that the federal government is doing too little to address the problem of obesity; 35 percent think the government is doing the right amount; and 8 percent that it is doing too much. A larger majority (62 percent) believes that the government is doing too little about childhood obesity.[42] Americans support a series of government, school, and food industry actions that might help address the problem of excess weight (**Table 14–9**).

About three-fourths (73 percent) of the public favor government-funded advertising campaigns that promote eating right and exercising. Nearly two-thirds (64 percent) favor having programs such as Medicare and Medicaid cover the cost of nutrition counseling for overweight patients, and about half (52 percent) favor having those programs subsidize the cost of fitness programs for overweight patients. About half (53 percent to 55 percent) favor government placing limits on television advertising for "junk food" and fast food aimed at children.[43]

In 2005 a majority (56 percent) opposed putting a special tax on junk food, but the proportion favoring such a tax has increased from 26 percent in 2003 to 41 percent in 2005.[44] Only about four in ten (41 percent) would be willing to pay more in taxes to support government-funded public education campaigns to promote healthy eating and physical activity.[45]

In the school environment, Americans favor programs aimed at more exercise and a healthy diet and oppose policies that increase consumption of unhealthy foods. The vast majority

(93 percent) of Americans favor mandatory physical education. A majority (59 percent) say they are willing to pay higher taxes to cover the cost of more nutritious school lunch programs in public schools. More than three-fourths of the public oppose installing vending machines in school as a way to raise funds (79 percent) and disapprove of teachers using food, such as candy and gum, to encourage students to perform well (78 percent).[46]

The public's attitudes about regulating the food industry reflect the belief that obesity is largely an individual responsibility. A majority of Americans support increased dietary information for the consumer, but oppose direct regulation of the food industry. About two-thirds of Americans believe that fast-food restaurants should be required by law to list nutritional information (70 percent) and that packaged food should have warning labels about the risks of being overweight (66 percent).[47] More than eight in ten Americans (83 percent), however, oppose legislation that would require food manufacturers to reduce serving sizes and fat and sugar content to make their products healthier, and instead think that it is up to the individual consumer to choose healthy products. Similarly, 84 percent do not believe the government should restrict the sale of unhealthy foods (described as foods that have little nutritional value and may contribute to obesity) to adults.[48] Most of the public (84 percent) also opposes allowing parents to sue soft drink and snack food companies if they believe their child is obese from eating junk food.[49]

Obesity as a Personal Issue

Weight is an important personal issue for the public. A majority of Americans (60 percent) are very or somewhat concerned about their own weight, and 41 percent of parents are very or somewhat concerned about their children's weight (**Table 14–10**).[50] Public concern about weight has increased significantly over time. In 2005 nearly half of the public (49 percent) worried about their weight all or some of the time, compared to about one-third (34 percent) in 1990.[51]

Prevalence and Seriousness of Overweight in the Family and Community

About four in ten (43 percent) report that someone in their own household is overweight. About half of those respondents (21 percent of the total population) say they are very concerned that this overweight household member could develop health problems.[52] More than one-fourth (28 percent) of Americans report that obesity has been a cause of serious health problems in their family.[53] Nearly two-thirds say that most children in their community are very (11 percent) or a little (53 percent) overweight (**Table 14–11**).[54]

Americans' Perceptions of Their Weight

Despite this level of concern about personal weight, many Americans who fit the definition of overweight or obese do not see themselves that way. Approximately two-thirds (66 percent) of U.S. adults are overweight or obese.[55] Yet a minority of Americans (41 percent) describe themselves as being overweight, and half (53 percent) believe that their weight is about right.[56] Public perceptions of personal weight vary quite a bit by demographic group. Men are significantly less likely than women (35 percent to 47 percent) to view themselves as overweight, even though the actual prevalence of overweight and obesity is higher for men (71 percent) than for women (62 percent). Younger adults (ages 18 to 29) are significantly less likely than adults thirty and over to consider themselves overweight, and, in fact, younger adults are less likely to be overweight.[57] Black and white Americans are significantly more likely than Hispanics to view themselves as overweight. For blacks, this self-image could be related to heavier body image ideals or relatively lower societal pressure to lose weight.[58] For whites, this self-image could be related to evidence suggesting that of all racial/ethnic groups, white women are most likely to report being overweight.[59] The real prevalence of overweight and obesity is higher among blacks and Hispanics than among whites. An important point to bear in mind is that all groups underestimate their true prevalence of overweight and obesity.[60] More specifically, women tend to underestimate their weight and men tend to overestimate their height (**Table 14–12**).[61]

Personal Dietary Behaviors

The public is about evenly divided in their perception of the nutritional value of their own diet. Half of Americans consider their diet to consist of mostly nutritious, healthy foods (49 percent), and the other half believes that their diet is made up of some, but not nearly enough, nutritious and healthy foods (48 percent) or almost none (2 percent).[62]

When it comes to watching their diet, most Americans do not closely track important aspects of the food they eat. Only about one-fifth of Americans report that they closely track the fat content (22 percent) and number of servings of fruits and vegetables (21 percent) in their daily diet. About one-sixth say they closely track the amount of carbohydrates (16 percent) and calories (14 percent). Women are significantly more likely than men to say they closely track all four elements. Young adults are less likely than those age thirty and over to report that they closely track their daily fat intake. College graduates are more likely than individuals with a high school education or less to closely track the fat, carbohydrates, and fruit and vegetables they eat. Blacks are significantly more likely than whites and Hispanics to report closely tracking their carbohydrates (**Table 14–13**).[63]

Personal Exercise Behaviors

With respect to exercise, only about one-third (34 percent) of Americans report getting as much physical exercise as they should. Men are significantly more likely than women to believe they get as much exercise as they should, and young adults (18 to 29) are significantly more likely than older adults (30 to 64) (**Table 14–14**). [64]

Americans see a strong connection between exercise and weight. When asked to assess the importance of different ways to maintain a healthy weight, more than half the public (52 percent) said that increasing your level of physical activity is extremely important. In comparison, a minority (38 percent) thought that controlling the size of the portions you eat or increasing the amount of fruit and vegetables you eat (30 percent) was extremely important to maintaining a healthy weight (**Table 14–15**).[65]

Attempts to Lose Weight

Three in ten Americans (30 percent) reported in 2008 that they were seriously trying to lose weight. A Gallup trend starting in 1990 shows that the proportion who report trying to lose weight has varied over time but has generally gone up (**Table 14–16**).[66] Moreover, the reported frequency of diet attempts has increased considerably. In 1990 only 23 percent of the public reported having tried three or more times to lose weight, compared to 39 percent in 2005. In addition, the number of Americans who reported never having been on a diet declined from 44 percent in 1990 to 34 percent in 2005.[67]

Of the various weight loss schemes available in the marketplace, low-carbohydrate diets have soared in popularity and been shown to be most effective in the short-term (about a year).[68] The evidence is, however, insufficient for the scientific or medical community to recommend use or discontinuation of these diets.[69] What evidence is available suggests that adverse effects are not apparent during a one-year study period. Long-term evidence about safety is not currently available. This lack of information regarding possible adverse effects is concerning given the large number of Americans who rely on a low-carbohydrate approach to weight loss or weight maintenance.

Conclusion

Americans see obesity as a serious issue and rank it among the top five diseases or health conditions the government should address. Moreover, most Americans view obesity as a serious problem for both adults and children and believe that excess weight can lead to negative health consequences.

The public continues to place most of the blame for obesity on personal behaviors, but also considers obesity a problem that society and government can help solve. Still, Americans view the government's role as a complement to an individual's responsibility for maintaining a healthy weight.

As a public policy issue, obesity has an important personal component. Many Americans see themselves as overweight and are trying to lose weight. In fact, public concern about weight gain has risen over time, and a greater number of people are trying to lose weight.

Efforts to encourage weight loss and weight maintenance should be tempered not only by the realities of political feasibility, but also by evidence of efficacy. Unfortunately, evidence regarding the effectiveness of prevention and intervention strategies to reduce the obesity epidemic is limited.[70]

For those people interested in reducing the burden of obesity, there is some "low hanging fruit" that receives considerable public support. The public favors institutionally oriented and education-based policies that may increase physical activity or reduce consumption. But it is important to bear in mind that the public is quite resistant to some policy options. Americans strongly oppose policies that may limit their choices or that call for heavy regulation of the food industry.

Notes

[1] Marion Nestle and Michael F. Jacobson, "Halting the Obesity Epidemic: A Public Health Policy Approach," *Public Health Reports* 115 (January/February 2000): 12–24.

[2] Gina Bari Kolata, "Obesity: A Growing Problem," *Science* 198 (December 2, 1977): 905–906.

[3] Gina Kolata, "Obesity Declared a Disease," *Science* 227 (March 1, 1985): 1019–20.

4 U.S. Department of Health and Human Services, "The Surgeon General's Call to Action to Prevent and Decrease Overweight and Obesity," 2001, http://www.surgeongeneral.gov/topics/obesity.

5 World Health Organization/Food and Agriculture Organization of the United Nations, "Diet, Nutrition, and the Prevention of Chronic Diseases: Report of a Joint WHO/FAO Expert Consultation," 2003, http://www.who.int/hpr/NPH/docs/who_fao_expert_report.pdf.

6 International Food Information Council, "Trends in Obesity-Related Media Coverage," January 2008, http://www.ific.org/research/obesitytrends.cfm.

7 Centers for Disease Control and Prevention, "BMI—Body Mass Index," 2007, http://www.cdc.gov/nccdphp/dnpa/bmi/adult_BMI/about_adult_BMI.htm#Definition.

8 C. L. Ogden, M. D. Carroll, L. R. Curtin, M. A. McDowell, C. J. Tabak, and K. M. Flegal, "Prevalence of Overweight and Obesity in the United States, 1999–2004," *JAMA: Journal of the American Medical Association*, 295 (April 5, 2006): 1549–15.

9 Ogden et al., "Prevalence of Overweight and Obesity in the United States, 1999–2004"; National Center for Health Statistics, "Prevalence of Overweight among Children and Adolescents: United States: 2003–2004," http://www.cdc.gov/nchs/products/pubs/pubd/hestats/overweight/overwght_child_03.htm.

10 S. S. Guo, W. Wu, W. C. Chumlea, and A. F. Rocher, "Predicting Overweight and Obesity in Adulthood from Body Mass Index Values in Childhood and Adolescence," *American Journal of Clinical Nutrition* 76 (September 2002): 653–658; W. H. Dietz and T. N. Robinson, "Clinical Practice: Overweight Children and Adolescents," *New England Journal of Medicine* 352 (May 19, 2005): 2100–9.

11 C. L. Ogden, M. D. Carroll, and K. M. Flegal, "High Body Mass Index for Age among US Children and Adolescents, 2003–2006," *JAMA* 299 (May 28, 2008): 2401–5.

12 Ogden et al., "Prevalence of Overweight and Obesity in the United States, 1999–2004"; National Center for Health Statistics, "Health, United States, 2006," Table 73, http://www.cdc.gov/nchs/data/hus/hus06.pdf.

13 Ogden et al., "Prevalence of Overweight and Obesity in the United States, 1999–2004."

14 Centers for Disease Control and Prevention, Behavioral Risk Factor Surveillance System, "2008 State Obesity Rates," http://www.cdc.gov/obesity/data/trends.html.

15 D. B. Allison, K. R. Fontaine, J. E. Manson, J. Stevens, and T. B. VanItallie, "Annual Deaths Attributable to Obesity in the United States," *JAMA* 282 (October 27, 1999): 1530–8.

16 A. H. Mokdad, J. S. Marks, D. F. Stroup, and J. L. Gerberding, "Actual Causes of Death in the United States, 2000," *JAMA* 291 (March 10, 2004): 1238–45. There are two methods for calculating causes of death. By the traditional method, based on the proximate cause of death, heart disease and cancer are the two leading causes of death. Because diseases and injuries have multiple potential causes, and several factors may contribute to a single death, a second method has been developed that measures "actual causes" of death, or "external modifiable factors" contributing to death. By this method, tobacco use is the leading "actual cause" of death (an estimated 435,000 deaths in 2000) in the United States, followed by poor diet and physical activity (400,000 deaths). Obesity accounts for the vast majority (385,000) of the latter, which would still rank obesity well ahead of the third-leading "actual cause," alcohol consumption (85,000 deaths).

17 J. Williams, M. Wake, K. Hesketh, E. Maher, and E. Waters, "Health-related Quality of Life of Overweight and Obese Children," *JAMA* 293 (January 5, 2005): 70–76; K. R. Fontaine and I. Barofsky, "Obesity and Health-related Quality of Life," *Obesity Reviews* 2 (August 2001):

173–182; M. E. Lean, T. S. Han, and J. C. Seidell, "Impairment of Health and Quality of Life Using New U.S. Federal Guidelines for the Identification of Obesity," *Archives of Internal Medicine* 159 (April 26, 1999): 837–843.

[18] Eric A. Finkelstein, Justin G. Trogdon, Joel W. Cohen, and William Dietz, "Annual Medical Spending Attributable to Obesity: Payer- and Service-Specific Estimates," *Health Affairs* 28 (Web exclusive, July 27, 2009): w822–w831.

[19] E. Jéquier and L. Tappy, "Regulation of Body Weight in Humans," *Physiological Reviews* 79 (April 1999): 451–480.

[20] P. G. Kopelman, "Obesity as a Medical Problem," *Nature* 404 (April 6, 2000): 635–643.

[21] David M. Cutler, Edward L. Glaeser, and Jesse M. Shapiro, "Why Have Americans Become More Obese?" *Journal of Economic Perspectives* 17 (Fall 2003): 93–118; D. S. Ludwig, K. E. Peterson, and S. L. Gortmaker, "Relation Between Consumption of Sugar-Sweetened Drinks and Childhood Obesity: A Prospective, Observational Analysis," *Lancet* 357 (February 17, 2001): 505–508; M. B. Schulze, J. E. Manson, D. S. Ludwig, G. A. Colditz, M. J. Stampfer, W. C. Willett, and F. B. Hu, "Sugar-sweetened Beverages, Weight Gain, and Incidence of Type 2 Diabetes in Young and Middle-aged Women," *JAMA* 292 (August 25, 2004): 927–934; C. S. Berkey, H. R. Rockett, A. E. Field, M. W. Gillman, and G. A. Colditz, "Sugar-added Beverages and Adolescent Weight Change," *Obesity Research* 12 (May 2004): 778–788; Sara Bleich, David M. Cutler, Christopher J. Murray, and Alyce Adams, "Why is the Developed World Obese?" *Annual Review of Public Health* 29 (2008), http://www.nber .org/papers/w12954.pdf: F. B. Hu, T. Y. Li, G. A. Colditz, W. C. Willett, and J. E. Manson, "Television Watching and Other Sedentary Behaviors in Relation to Risk of Obesity and Type 2 Diabetes Mellitus in Women," *JAMA* 289 (April 9, 2003): 1785–91; Carlos J. Crespo, Ellen Smit, Richard P. Troiano, Susan J. Bartlett, Caroline A. Macera, and Ross E. Andersen, "Television Watching, Energy Intake, and Obesity in US Children: Results from the Third National Health and Nutrition Examination Survey, 1988–1994," *Archives of Pediatric and Adolescent Medicine* 155 (March 2001): 360–365; E. A. Vandewater, M. S. Shim, and A. G. Caplovitz, "Linking Obesity and Activity Level with Children's Television and Video Game Use," *Journal of Adolescence* 27 (February 2004): 71–85.

[22] W. E. Encinosa, D. M. Bernard, C. A. Steiner, and C. C. Chen, "Use and Costs of Bariatric Surgery and Prescription Weight-Loss Medications," *Health Affairs* 24 (July/August 2005): 1039–46.

[23] NetScan's Health Policy Tracking Service, "State Actions to Promote Nutrition, Increase Physical Activity and Prevent Obesity: A 2006 First Quarter Legislative Overview," 2006, http:// www.rwjf.org/files/research/NCSL%20FinalApril%202006%20Report.pdf.

[24] Robert Wood Johnson Foundation, *State Action to Promote Nutrition, Increase Physical Activity and Prevent Obesity* (Princeton, N.J.: Robert Wood Johnson Foundation, 2008).

[25] Janet Adamy, "Soda Tax Weighed to Pay for Health Care," *Wall Street Journal,* May 12, 2009, A4.

[26] Nestle and Jacobson, "Halting the Obesity Epidemic."

[27] Stony Brook University Center for Survey Research Poll (Storrs, Conn.: Roper Center for Public Opinion Research, July 22–August 12, 2003); Stony Brook University Center for Survey Research Poll (Storrs, Conn.: Roper Center for Public Opinion Research, September 1–25, 2005).

[28] Harvard School of Public Health/Robert Wood Johnson Foundation Poll (Storrs, Conn.: Roper Center for Public Opinion Research, June 24–28, 2009).

[29] Vincent T. Covello, Richard G. Peters, Joseph G. Wojtecki, and Richard C. Hyde, "Risk Communication, the West Nile Virus Epidemic, and Bioterrorism: Responding to the Communication Challenges Posed by the Intentional or Unintentional Release of a Pathogen in an Urban Setting," *Journal of Urban Health* 78 (June 2001): 382–391; Paul Slovic, "Perception of Risk," *Science* 236 (April 17, 1987): 280–285.

[30] Pew Research Center for the People and the Press Poll (Storrs, Conn.: Roper Center for Public Opinion Research, February 8–March 7, 2006).

[31] Gallup Poll (Storrs, Conn.: Roper Center for Public Opinion Research, July 12–15, 2007).

[32] Harvard School of Public Health Poll (Storrs, Conn.: Roper Center for Public Opinion Research, June 23–28, 2005).

[33] J. Eric Oliver and Taeku Lee, "Public Opinion and the Politics of Obesity in America," *Journal of Health Politics, Policy and Law* 30 (October 2005): 923–955; Mokdad et al., "Actual Causes of Death in the United States, 2000."

[34] ABC News/*Time* Poll (Storrs, Conn.: Roper Center for Public Opinion Research, May 10–16, 2004).

[35] Harvard School of Public Health/Robert Wood Johnson Foundation Poll, April 2–7, 2008.

[36] Stony Brook University Center for Survey Research Poll, July 22–August 12, 2003; Stony Brook University Center for Survey Research Poll, September 1–25, 2005.

[37] Stony Brook University Center for Survey Research Poll, July 22–August 12, 2003.

[38] ABC News/*Time* Poll, May 10–16, 2004.

[39] Ibid.

[40] Stony Brook University Center for Survey Research Poll, September 1–25, 2005.

[41] Harvard School of Public Health/Robert Wood Johnson Foundation Poll (Storrs, Conn.: Roper Center for Public Opinion Research, April 11–15, 2007).

[42] ABC News/*Time* Poll, May 10–16, 2004.

[43] *San Jose Mercury News*/Kaiser Family Foundation, "Survey on Childhood Obesity," March 2004, http://www.kff.org/kaiserpolls/upload/Survey-on-Childhood-Obesity-Toplines.pdf; Stony Brook University Center for Survey Research Poll, September 1–25, 2005.

[44] Stony Brook University Center for Survey Research Poll, July 22–August 12, 2003; Stony Brook University Center for Survey Research Poll, September 1–25, 2005.

[45] Harvard School of Public Health Poll, June 23–28, 2005.

[46] Stony Brook University Center for Survey Research Poll, September 1–25, 2005.

[47] *San Jose Mercury News*/Kaiser Family Foundation, "Survey on Childhood Obesity," March 2004.

[48] CNN/Opinion Research Corporation Poll (Storrs, Conn.: Roper Center for Public Opinion Research, August 6–8, 2007).

[59] Stony Brook University Center for Survey Research Poll, July 22–August 12, 2003.

[50] Stony Brook University Center for Survey Research Poll, September 1–25, 2005.

[51] Gallup Polls (Storrs, Conn.: Roper Center for Public Opinion Research, October 18–21, 1990; July 7–15, 2005).

[52] Harvard School of Public Health/Robert Wood Johnson Foundation Poll, April 2–7, 2008.

[53] Gallup Poll, July 12–15, 2007.

[54] Harvard School of Public Health/Robert Wood Johnson Foundation Poll, April 2–7, 2008.

[55] Ogden et al., "Prevalence of Overweight and Obesity in the United States, 1999–2004."

[56] Harvard School of Public Health Poll, June 23–28, 2005.

[57] Ogden et al., "Prevalence of Overweight and Obesity in the United States, 1999–2004."

[58] K. J. Flynn and M. Fitzgibbon, "Body Images and Obesity Risk among Black Females: A Review of the Literature," *Annals of Behavioral Medicine* 20 (Winter 1998): 13–24; S. Kumanyika, J. F. Wilson, and M. Guilford-Davenport, "Weight-related Attitudes and Behaviors of Black Women," *Journal of the American Dietetic Association* 93 (April 1993): 416–422; R. H. Striegel-Moore, D. E. Wilfley, M. B. Caldwell, M. L. Needham, and K. D. Brownell, "Weight-related Attitudes and Behaviors of Women Who Diet to Lose Weight: A Comparison of Black Dieters and White Dieters," *Obesity Research* 4 (March 1996): 109–116.

[59] S. Paeratakul, M. A. White, D. A. Williamson, D. H. Ryan, and G. A. Bray, "Sex, Race/ethnicity, Socioeconomic Status, and BMI in Relation to Self-perception of Overweight," *Obesity Research* 10 (May 2002): 345–350.

[60] Harvard School of Public Health Poll, June 23–28, 2005; Ogden et al., "Prevalence of Overweight and Obesity in the United States, 1999–2004."

[61] M. Ezzati, H. Martin, S. Skjold, S. Vander Hoorn, and C. J. Murray, "Trends in National and State-level Obesity in the USA after Correction for Self-report Bias: Analysis of Health Surveys," *Journal of the Royal Society of Medicine* 99 (May 2006): 250–257.

[62] Stony Brook University Center for Survey Research Poll, September 1–25, 2005.

[63] Harvard School of Public Health Poll, June 23–28, 2005.

[64] Ibid.

[65] Ibid.

[66] Gallup Polls (Storrs, Conn.: Roper Center for Public Opinion Research, October 18–21, 1990; February 23–25, 1996; July 22–25, 1999; July 19–22, 2001; November 11–14, 2002; November 3–5, 2003; November 7–10, 2004; November 7–10, 2005; November 9–12, 2006; November 11–14, 2007; November 13–16, 2008).

[67] Gallup Polls, October 18–21, 1990; July 7–15, 2005.

[68] Christopher D. Gardner, Alexandre Kiazand, Sofiya Alhassan, Soowon Kim, Randall S. Stafford, Raymond R. Balise, Helena C. Kraemer, and Abby C. King, "Comparison of the Atkins, Zone, Ornish, and LEARN Diets for Change in Weight and Related Risk Factors among Overweight Premenopausal Women: The A TO Z Weight Loss Study: A Randomized Trial," *JAMA* 297 (March 7, 2007): 969–977.

[69] Dena M. Bravata, Lisa Sanders, Jane Huang, Harlan M. Krumholz, Ingram Olkin, Christopher D. Gardner, and Dawn M. Bravata, "Efficacy and Safety of Low-carbohydrate Diets: A Systematic Review," *JAMA* 289 (April 9, 2003): 1837–50.

[70] K. Campbell, E. Waters, S. O'Meara, and C. Summerbell, "Interventions for Preventing Obesity in Children: A Systematic Review," *Obesity Reviews* 2 (August 2001): 149–157.

Table 14-1 Definition of Overweight and Obese by Body Mass Index (BMI)

Weight rating	BMI
Underweight	below 18.5
Healthy weight	18.5 to 24.9
Overweight	25.0 to 29.9
Obese	30 or above

Note: BMI = weight in kilograms divided by the square of height in meters (kg/m²).

Source: Centers for Disease Control and Prevention, "BMI-Body Mass Index," 2007.

Table 14-2 Public Attitudes on Seriousness of Obesity (in percent)

Perceived seriousness of obesity as a health problem for . . .	Very serious	Somewhat serious	Not very serious	Not at all serious
Adults				
2003	58	35	4	2
2005	68	27	4	*
Children and teenagers				
2003	61	32	4	2
2005	66	30	2	*

Note: "Don't know" responses not shown. * = less than .5 percent.

Question: How serious a health problem is obesity (among adults/in children and teenagers)? Would you say it is very serious, somewhat serious, not very serious, or not at all serious?

Sources: Stony Brook University Center for Survey Research Poll (Storrs, Conn.: Roper Center for Public Opinion Research, July 22–August 12, 2003); Stony Brook University Center for Survey Research Poll (Storrs, Conn.: Roper Center for Public Opinion Research, September 1–25, 2005).

Table 14-3 Public Attitudes on the Consequences of Being Overweight (in percent)

	A lot	A little	Not at all
An individual's weight can improve their chance for a long and healthy life[1]	83	13	1
	Very harmful	**Somewhat harmful**	**Not too/Not at all harmful**
Harmfulness of obesity to adults who are significantly overweight[2]	83	15	1
Effects of someone being moderately overweight on likelihood of . . .[3]	**More likely**	**Not much difference**	**Less likely**
Developing a chronic illness, such as diabetes or high blood pressure	73	22	3
Dying prematurely	51	39	6

Note: "Don't know" responses not shown.

Question: How much do you think a person's weight can improve a person's chances of a long and healthy life: a lot a little or not at all?

Question: In general, how harmful do you feel obesity is to adults who are significantly overweight: very harmful, somewhat harmful, not too harmful, or not at all harmful?

Question: Do you think that someone who is moderately overweight is more likely or less likely than someone who is the recommended weight to (develop a chronic illness such as diabetes or high blood pressure/die prematurely), or isn't there much difference?

Sources: [1]Pew Research Center for the People and the Press Poll (Storrs, Conn.: Roper Center for Public Opinion Research, February 8–March 7, 2006). [2]Gallup Poll (Storrs, Conn.: Roper Center for Public Opinion Research, July 12–15, 2007). [3]Harvard School of Public Health Poll (Storrs, Conn.: Roper Center for Public Opinion Research, June 23–28, 2005).

Table 14-4 Public Attitudes on the Causes of Obesity (in percent)

	One of the single most important causes	Very important cause	Somewhat important cause	Less important cause
Not getting enough physical exercise	21	65	11	3
Poor eating habits	20	65	11	4
The marketing of sweets and other high-calorie foods to children	15	50	21	13
Watching too much television	13	46	26	13
Restaurant portions are too large	8	36	31	24
Genetics, or a family history	7	43	38	11
Lack of information on good eating habits	6	39	32	23
The cost of buying healthy food	6	39	30	23
Lack of information about food content	5	32	34	28

Note: "Don't know" responses not shown.

Question: For each item I name, please tell me if you think it's one of the single most important causes of obesity in this country, very important, somewhat important, or less important than that.

Source: ABC News/*Time* Poll (Storrs, Conn.: Roper Center for Public Opinion Research, May 10–16, 2004).

Table 14-5 Personal versus External Causes of Childhood Obesity (in percent)

The biggest cause of childhood obesity	
Personal factors, such as overeating, lack of exercise, and watching too much television	64
External factors, such as exposure to junk food, lack of safe place for children to play, and limited availability of health foods in some neighborhoods	18
Both equally (vol.)	16

Note: "Something else (vol.)" and "Don't know" responses not shown. (vol.) = volunteered response.

Question: Which of the following do you think is the biggest cause of childhood obesity? Would you say personal factors, such as overeating, lack of exercise, and watching too much television, or external factors, such as exposure to junk food, lack of safe place for children to play, and limited availability of health foods in some neighborhoods?

Source: Harvard School of Public Health/Robert Wood Johnson Foundation Poll (Storrs, Conn.: Roper Center for Public Opinion Research, April 2–7, 2008).

Table 14-6 Public Perceptions about the Causes of Obesity in Adults and Children (in percent)

Primary cause of obesity in adults	Poor eating habits	Lack of physical activity	Genetics or family history
2003	48	35	4
2005	54	26	6

Primary cause of obesity in children	Poor eating habits	Lack of physical activity	Genetics or family history
2003	46	35	4
2005	51	30	3

Note: Volunteered "Combination" and "Other" responses and "Don't know" responses not shown.

Question: What do you think is the primary factor causing obesity among (adults/children)? Poor eating habits, not enough physical activity, or genetics or a strong family history?

Sources: Stony Brook University Center for Survey Research Poll (Storrs, Conn.: Roper Center for Public Opinion Research, July 22–August 12, 2003); Stony Brook University Center for Survey Research Poll (Storrs, Conn.: Roper Center for Public Opinion Research, September 1–25, 2005).

Table 14-7 Public Attitudes on Responsibility for Obesity (in percent)

	Great deal	Good amount	Just some	Hardly any
Individual Americans in their choice of diet and lack of exercise	67	20	7	4
Fast-food restaurants	43	21	19	13
Schools that allow high-calorie snacks and sweets	40	24	20	12
Manufacturers of high-calorie packaged and processed foods	36	25	22	12
Marketers and advertisers of high-calorie packaged and processed foods	35	25	24	12
Government policies and laws on food content and marketing	20	21	28	24

Note: "Don't know" responses not shown.

Question: Whatever the causes of obesity, I'd like to ask you about groups that may or may not be responsible for creating the problem. For each, please tell me if you think it bears a great deal of responsibility for the nation's obesity problem, a good amount, just some, or hardly any.

Source: ABC News/*Time* Poll (Storrs, Conn.: Roper Center for Public Opinion Research, May 10–16, 2004).

Table 14-8 Public Attitudes on Who, aside from Parents, Should Have the Main Responsibility for Teaching Children to Avoid Becoming Overweight (in percent)

Schools	55
Media	13
Food providers like restaurants	11
Health care providers	10
None other than the parents (vol.)	5
Someone else	2

Note: "Don't know" responses not shown. (vol.) = volunteered response.

Question: Aside from parents, who do you think should have the main responsibility for teaching children to avoid becoming overweight? Schools, health care providers, the media, or food providers like restaurants, or someone else?

Source: Stony Brook University Center for Survey Research Poll (Storrs, Conn.: Roper Center for Public Opinion Research, September 1–25, 2005).

Table 14-9 Public Support for Obesity Policies (in percent)

Government Action

Favor government-funded advertising campaign that promotes eating right and exercising (2004)[1]	73
Favor Medicare/Medicaid covering the cost of nutrition counseling for overweight patients (2005)[2]	64
Favor Medicare/Medicaid subsidizing the cost of fitness programs for overweight patients (2005)[2]	52
Favor government regulation of/placing limits on TV advertising for junk food and fast food aimed at children	
2004[1]	53
2005[2]	55

(Table continues)

Table 14-9 *Continued*

Favor tax on junk food	
2003[3]	26
2004[1]	40
2005[2]	41

Schools

Favor mandatory physical education in school (2005)[2]	93
Willing to pay higher taxes to cover the cost of more nutritious school lunch programs in public schools (Yes/no)	
2003[3]	49
2005[2]	59
Oppose installing vending machines in schools as a way to raise funds, because it may contribute to being overweight (2005)[2]	79

Food industry

Favor law requiring fast-food restaurants to list nutritional information (2004)[1]	70
Favor warning labels on packaged foods about the risks of being overweight (2004)[1]	66
Government should restrict the sale of unhealthy foods (2007)[4]	16
Food manufacturers should be required by law to reduce serving sizes and fat and sugar content to make their products healthier (2003)[3]	14
Parents should be able to sue soft drink and snack food companies if they believe their child is obese from eating junk food (2003)[3]	6

Note: "Don't know" responses not shown.

Question: Now we'd like to ask you some general questions about government policies. Please tell me if you would support or oppose each of the following. Do you support or oppose (government-funded advertising campaigns that promote eating right and exercising/the federal government regulating television ads for junk food and fast food that are aimed at children the way they do for cigarettes an alcohol [2004]/putting a special tax on junk food—that is things like soda, chips and candy—and using the money for programs for fight obesity [2003, 2004]/making a law requiring fast food restaurants to list nutrition information—such as calorie count—for all items on their menus [2004]/warning labels on packaged food about the health risks of being overweight, just like there are warning labels on cigarettes about the health risks of smoking [2004])?

Question: Do you think that government funded health insurance programs such as Medicare for the elderly or Medicaid for low-income people should cover the cost of nutrition counseling for overweight patients or not? (2005)

Question: Should government health insurance programs such as Medicare and Medicaid subsidize the cost of fitness programs, such as attending a gym or fitness classes, for overweight patients or not? (2005)

Question: Do you favor of oppose the government placing limits on television advertising for junk food that is aimed at children, similar to existing limits on tobacco and alcohol ads? (2005)

Question: Do you favor or oppose a new government tax on junk food in order to reduce obesity among children and adults, similar to existing government taxes on cigarettes and alcohol? (2005)

Question: Are you in favor or opposed to schools requiring children to take a physical education class throughout the school year? (2005)

Question: Would you be willing to pay higher federal taxes to cover the cost of more nutritious school lunch programs in the public schools or not? (2003, 2005)

Question: Do you think it is all right for public schools to install soft drink and snack vending machines in schools as a way to raise funds, or are you opposed to this because it may contribute to children being overweight? (2005)

Question: Here [is a question that deals] with junk food or other unhealthy foods that taste good, but have little nutritional value and may contribute to obesity. Do you think the government should restrict the sale of unhealthy food to adults, or do you think that adults in this country should be able to eat whatever they want even if the foods they eat may not be healthy? (2007)

Question: Do you think food manufacturers should be required to reduce serving sizes and fat and sugar content to make their products healthier, or is it up to individual customers to choose healthy food products? (2003)

Question: Do you think parents should be able to sue major snack food companies if they believe their children became obese from eating junk food and drinking soft drinks, or should the government pass laws to prevent these kinds of law suits? (2003)

Sources: [1]*San Jose Mercury News*/Kaiser Family Foundation, "Survey on Childhood Obesity", March 2004; [2]Stony Brook University Center for Survey Research Poll (Storrs, Conn.: Roper Center for Public Opinion Research, September 1–25, 2005); [3]Stony Brook University Center for Survey Research Poll (Storrs, Conn.: Roper Center for Public Opinion Research, July 22–August 12, 2003); [4]CNN/Opinion Research Corporation Poll (Storrs, Conn.: Roper Center for Public Opinion Research, August 6–8, 2007).

Table 14-10 Public Concerns about Personal Weight (in percent)

	Very concerned	Somewhat concerned	Not very concerned	Not at all concerned
Concern about personal weight[1]	24	36	16	25
Concern about children's weight (among parents)[1]	24	17	16	43

Note: "Don't know" responses not shown.

Question: How concerned are you about your own weight at the present time?

Question: How concerned are you about your child or children's weight? (Among parents)

Sources: Stony Brook University Center for Survey Research Poll (Storrs, Conn.: Roper Center for Public Opinion Research, September 1–25, 2005).

Table 14-11 Prevalence and Seriousness of Overweight in the Family and Community (in percent)

Someone in your household is overweight	43
and you are very concerned that this person could develop health problems in the future[1]	21
Obesity has been a cause of serious health problems in your family[2]	28
Most children in your community are[1]	
Very overweight	11
Somewhat overweight	53
About the right weight	32
Underweight	2
Don't know	2

Question: Is there anyone in your household who is overweight? (If yes) How concerned are you that this person could develop health problems in the future: very concerned, somewhat concerned, not too concerned, or not at all concerned?

Question: Has obesity ever been a cause of serious health problems in your family?

Question: Thinking about the children in your community, would you say that most are very overweight, most are a little overweight, most are the right weight, or most are underweight?

Sources: [1]Harvard School of Public Health/Robert Wood Johnson Foundation (Storrs, Conn.: Roper Center for Public Opinion Research, April 2–7, 2007). [2]Gallup Poll (Storrs, Conn.: Roper Center for Public Opinion Research, July 12–15, 2007).

Table 14-12 People's Perception of Their Own Weight (in percent)

	Very overweight	Somewhat overweight	About right	Somewhat underweight	Very underweight
Total	5	36	53	5	1
By sex					
Male	2	33	56	8	1
Female	7	40	49	3	1
By age					
18–29	2	22	67	9	0
30–49	4	39	51	5	*
50–64	7	46	42	3	1
65+	8	36	52	4	1
By household income					
Less than $25,000	6	36	48	9	1
$25,000–$49,999	4	42	49	5	*
$50,000–$74,999	5	41	49	4	0
$75,000+	5	36	56	2	0
By education					
High school grad or less	4	34	55	6	1
Some college	6	38	50	6	*
College grad+	4	39	51	5	*
By race					
White	5	38	50	6	*
Black	2	41	48	5	2
Hispanic	1	28	65	6	0

Note: "Don't know" responses not shown. * = less than .5 percent.

Question: How would you describe your own personal weight situation: very overweight, somewhat overweight, about right, somewhat underweight, or very underweight?

Source: Harvard School of Public Health Poll (Storrs, Conn.: Roper Center for Public Opinion Research, June 23–28, 2005).

Table 14-13 Public Attention toward Composition of the Food in Daily Diet (in percent)

Percent saying track closely	Fat	Number of servings of fruits and vegetables	Carbohydrates	Calories
Total	22	21	16	14
By sex				
Male	16	17	13	11
Female	27	26	18	17
By age				
18–29	14	18	12	14
30–49	22	19	16	13
50–64	26	26	19	14
65+	29	24	16	16
By household income				
Less than $25,000	24	23	17	19
$25,000–$49,999	21	20	14	13
$50,000–$74,999	21	21	13	11
$75,000+	22	25	22	17
By education				
High school grad or less	19	19	14	14
Some college	24	22	18	14
College grad+	27	27	19	15
By race				
White	22	22	15	12
Black	26	23	29	17
Hispanic	20	22	13	16

Note: "Don't know" responses not shown.

Question: Do you keep track of the (fat content/number of servings of fruits and vegetables/amount of carbohydrates/amount of calories) in your daily diet, or is that something you don't pay much attention to? (For each one the respondents keeps track of) Is that something you track closely or somewhat?

Source: Harvard School of Public Health Poll (Storrs, Conn.: Roper Center for Public Opinion Research, June 23–28, 2005).

Table 14-14 Americans' Self-Reported Amount of Exercise (in percent)

	Get as much as should	Should be getting more
Overall	34	66
By sex		
Male	39	61
Female	29	70
By age		
18–29	45	54
30–49	30	70
50–64	28	72
65+	36	64
By household income		
Less than $25,000	33	67
$25,000–$49,999	36	63
$50,000–$74,999	26	74
$75,000+	35	64
By education		
High school grad or less	34	66
Some college	35	64
College grad+	32	68
By race		
White	33	67
Black	31	69
Hispanic	37	61

Note: "Don't know" responses not shown.

Question: Do you feel that you probably get as much physical exercise as you should, or do you feel you should probably be getting more physical exercise?

Source: Harvard School of Public Health Poll (Storrs, Conn.: Roper Center for Public Opinion Research, June 23–28, 2005).

Table 14-15 Public Attitudes on Activities to Maintain a Healthy Weight (in percent)

	Extremely important	Very important	Somewhat important	Not very/not at all important
Increasing your physical activity level	52	42	5	1
Controlling the size of the portions you eat	38	44	15	3
Increasing the amount of fruits and vegetables you eat	30	49	19	2

Note: "Don't know" responses not shown.

Question: I'm going to read you a list of things that people can do to maintain a healthy weight. Please tell me how important each of the following is in maintaining a healthy weight. How about (read item)? Would you say this is extremely important, somewhat important, not very important, or not important at all?

Source: Harvard School of Public Health Poll (Storrs, Conn.: Roper Center for Public Opinion Research, June 23–28, 2005).

Table 14-16 Americans Seriously Trying to Lose Weight (self-reported, in percent)

1990	18
1996	26
1999	20
2001	25
2002	24
2003	28
2004	29
2005	27
2006	28
2007	28
2008	30

Question: At this time are you seriously trying to lose weight?

Source: Gallup Polls (Storrs, Conn.: Roper Center for Public Opinion Research, October 18–21, 1990; February 23–25, 1996; July 22–25, 1999; July 19–22, 2001; November 11–14, 2002; November 3–5, 2003; November 7–10, 2004; November 7–10, 2005; November 9–12, 2006; November 11–14, 2007; November 13–16, 2008).

Chapter 15

EMERGING INFECTIOUS DISEASES

Gillian K. SteelFisher, Robert J. Blendon, John M. Benson, and Kathleen J. Weldon

M id-twentieth century successes in the prevention and treatment of infectious diseases were impressive. The era saw the development of antibiotics, the identification of viruses, and the development of mass vaccination programs. These efforts eventually led to the elimination of polio in the United States and the eradication of smallpox throughout the world. Such triumphs created a sense that it was only a matter of time before medicine would be able to track down each infectious agent and stamp it out with parallel techniques. That has turned out not to be the case.

The current era is marked by a rise in emerging and re-emerging infectious diseases, and numerous calls for a renewed focus in this area.[1] Several complex and interrelated factors contribute to the rise, including demographic changes such as greater urban density and international travel, mass production of food products and related agricultural practices, and climate changes such as global warming. In addition, and somewhat ironically, medical successes such as the widespread availability of antibiotics contribute to the problem by creating drug-resistant bacteria. Limited public health infrastructure or upheavals due to war also impeded efforts to control infectious agents. Finally, the purposeful release of microbes, in the context of bioterrorism and biowarfare, creates an added dimension to the growth of infectious diseases that has taken on special salience in the United States since the terrorist attacks of September 11, 2001.[2]

Public opinion is especially important in the context of infectious disease control because preventing or containing the spread of infectious disease inherently requires public participation. In many cases, policies demand that everyone—not just those who are sick—become educated about an illness and take actions, whether that be covering the mouth when coughing, getting vaccinated, or stocking emergency supplies. To develop communication strategies that the public will listen to and policies that the public will adhere to, it is critical to understand public perceptions of the disease, potential policy approaches, and relevant actors. This importance is underscored by examples such as the 1994 plague outbreak in India, when the public response to the disease and related policies turned to panic unnecessarily.[3] A better understanding of public opinion may have helped avoid some of the repercussions.

This chapter takes a look at several examples of emerging infectious diseases and the American public's response to related threats and policies. Discussion here is limited to a subset of diseases that have taken the center stage in headlines and in policy circles with the United States, including mad cow disease, West Nile virus, severe acute respiratory syndrome (SARS), anthrax, and smallpox. We do this not to suggest that these are the most important diseases. Rather, we use these examples because they offer critical insights into the public's reaction because there were actual reactions. The diseases made headlines, and research firms conducted polls about public response. Chapter 10 was dedicated entirely to HIV, so HIV is not discussed here, and the outbreak in 2009 of an H1N1 flu pandemic is discussed in Chapter 16.

The chapter has five disease-specific sections. Each section starts with a brief review providing basic facts about how the illness is spread and treated, its historical context, and a summary of the major policies or special topics that dominated media and policy discussions about it. Each section then provides a review of the available public opinion data, with special focus on four critical areas: (1) public engagement, including awareness and understanding of the illness; (2) public concerns and assessments of risk; (3) the actions that members of the public took or would take in response; and (4) public views of the policies and agents that might address the illness. The chapter ends with some conclusions that cross these specific illnesses and provide a foundation for understanding public response to emerging infectious diseases more generally. Much of the public opinion data presented in this chapter are derived from polls conducted through cooperative agreements with the Centers for Disease Control and Prevention, the National Preparedness Leadership Initiative, the Association of State and Territorial Health Officials, and the National Public Health Information Coalition.

Mad Cow Disease

Bovine spongiform encephalopathy (BSE), known as mad cow disease, gained notoriety when the British government announced in March 1996 that ten young Britons had developed a devastating neurological disease that likely resulted from eating beef infected with BSE. All ten citizens had died or were dying a gruesome death that involves a progression from confusion to insanity and ultimately complete neurological dysfunction.[4] The human form of the disease was called variant Creutzfeldt-Jakob disease (vCJD), and it became a major example of a pathogen in the food supply. Examining the public response can offer critical insights into how people may respond to food-related illnesses and a mad cow disease outbreak specifically.

The United Kingdom had been aware of BSE in cows since the mid-1980s. Moreover, the disease's counterpart in sheep—scrapie—has been documented for centuries.[5] The diagnosis of vCJD in the young British citizens, however, represented the first known time that the illness had crossed the species barrier to infect humans.[6] With this step, the disease took on new public importance. The American public watched as mad cow disease was tracked from cattle in the United Kingdom to twenty European countries, as well as Canada, Israel, and Japan, and then to the United States.[7] As of March 2008, three BSE-infected cows had been found in the United States: one in Washington State (2003), one in Texas (2005), and one in Alabama (2006).[8] Researchers have determined that the risk of finding additional cows with BSE was extremely low and that the risk of human consumption of the beef and of resulting vCJD was even lower.[9] Nevertheless, each case made headlines.[10] Newspapers kept the issue in the public eye by reporting subsequent problems in the response of federal and local officials. One problem was the difficulty of tracking down all of the cows in the herds with the infected animals, which raised the question whether additional cows infected with BSE slipped under the radar of current testing.[11]

One aspect of mad cow disease that helps drive public attention is its unusual etiology, which is not well understood by scientists. Mad cow disease, vCJD, and scrapie are all believed to be caused by prions rather than by viruses or bacteria. Prions are proteins found throughout the body, but sometimes they can become pathogenic. They "infect" the body by transforming normal prions around them through an as-yet-unidentified process. The symptoms and ultimately death in the individual appear to be a function of accumulating pathogenic proteins in relevant organs, including the brain.[12] If a person or cow consumes infected organs—or muscle meat that has been contaminated by infected organs—the prions appear to be able to infect the consumer. The disease is not transmissible from human to human by air or by touch, although there may be one case of transmission by blood products.[13] The disease may take many years, even decades, to present in humans after the consumption of infected beef. Therefore, although vCJD cases are still rare—only 200 worldwide and none in the United States[14]—it is possible that more infected victims have not yet presented with symptoms.[15]

From a policy perspective, mad cow disease and vCJD face unique issues. First, because of its etiology, vaccines, antibiotics, and antivirals are not relevant for vCJD, and there is no known cure or treatment.[16] Also, because the disease is not transmissible from human to human, and only from cow to cow by the consumption of infected material in their feed, many policies focus on containment at the level of the beef and cow feed industries. Policies have been developed to prohibit the slaughter of high-risk, visibly sick cows for human consumption[17] and to change slaughtering techniques (particularly the use of stun guns) in an effort to prevent potentially infected material in the brain and spinal column from spraying onto meat that humans will eat. The Food and Drug Administration also prohibits the use of most animal parts, including brains and spinal columns of slaughtered cows, in feed for other animals.[18] And finally, after the discovery of an infected cow, the relevant beef producer may recall beef voluntarily, or do so under pressure from federal agencies, and cull other animals in the herd that may have also been exposed to BSE through the same source.[19]

Engagement

The earliest available public opinion data in the United States concerning mad cow disease come from January 2001. At this time, the media were full of stories related to mad cow disease because of developments in Europe that spread a fear of the disease to the United States.[20] France and Germany identified new cases of BSE,[21] and the European Union subsequently proposed measures to address the issue and public unrest.[22] At nearly the same time, U.K. officials admitted to a delayed and secretive initial response to mad cow disease and agreed to pay millions in compensation to families like that of the fourteen-year-old girl who died of vCJD just as the story broke—all of which heightened public concern.[23] At this point, only 40 percent of Americans said they were watching the news unfold very or fairly closely.[24] But when mad cow was identified in Canadian cattle in mid-2003, U.S. interest grew, with 54 percent of the public saying they were following the news about mad cow disease very or fairly closely.[25] When mad cow was discovered in the United States in 2004, interest jumped even higher, and 67 percent of the public was following the news very or somewhat closely.[26] As the investigation continued through 2005 and 2006, public interest declined to between 33 percent and 47 percent.[27] These figures reveal a traditional media attention cycle: attention peaks and then ebbs,[28] and interest grows as the issue moves closer to home.[29] It is also notable that engagement was higher than one might expect, given that only three diseased cows had been found in the United States and no Americans had contracted vCJD while living in the United States. These data also reveal how the public eye is drawn to dramatic events and new issues reported in the media, not necessarily to events that pose the highest risks (**Table 15–1**).[30]

Despite high levels of attention paid to the issue, the American public did not uniformly get the basic facts about mad cow disease right. Although the disease had been identified in one cow and no people in the United States at the time of the January 2004 poll, more than a quarter of the population (27 percent) believed that mad cow had been identified in people.[31] Such incorrect information may have distorted public perceptions of the risks of mad cow disease or the appropriate policies needed. Unfortunately, the polls did not ask any additional questions about other basic characteristics of the disease, such as its incubation period, contagiousness, treatment protocols, or fatality rates. This information might have clarified the public's reaction to existing policies or support for proposals.

Concern and Assessment of Risk

In 2004, after the first cow with BSE was discovered in the United States, the vast majority of the public (81 percent) said that they were not concerned that they or someone in their family would become infected. This finding appears to suggest that the American public had an accurate sense of the very low risk of contracting BSE. This conclusion is bolstered by more specific data showing that only a small percentage of the public believed they were personally at risk of contracting the illness. In 2004 only 9 percent of the public believed that they or an immediate family member was very likely or somewhat likely to become infected with mad cow disease in the following twelve months. As a benchmark, the perceived risk of catching the flu was much higher. More than two-thirds (70 percent) of the public thought they or a family member was very or somewhat likely to catch the flu.[32]

On the other hand, the disease was still perceived as significant at the national level by a substantial minority. Roughly a third of the public (34 percent) said that mad cow disease was a crisis or a major problem for the United States.[33]

Most of the public believed that the beef supply was safe. In 2004, after the first infected cow in the United States had been discovered but before a full investigation had been done, two-thirds of American adults (66 percent) thought the nation's beef supply was safe, and roughly three-quarters (74 percent) thought the beef at their local store was safe.[34] Still, these numbers indicate that somewhere between a quarter and a third of the public did not believe beef was safe. Depending on how civically engaged these people are, such a sizable minority could be quite significant for policy advocates.[35] Moreover, the actions of a minority can have an important effect on the economy.

Actions

As it turned out, a sizable minority of the public "voted" on this issue with their wallets. One in six Americans (16 percent) said that they or someone in their family had stopped ordering beef at fast-food restaurants because of reports of mad cow disease. Similarly, 14 percent said they or a family member had stopped buying beef at the grocery store (**Table 15–2**).[36]

These reported changes are suggestive of the possible financial impact that could be felt in the beef industry, in the larger food industry, and in the overall economy if there were a larger outbreak of mad cow disease or an illness with a similar profile. These results also suggest a relative willingness of the public to make straightforward changes in health behavior—at least in the short run—in the face of some emerging infectious diseases.

Views about Policies and Policymakers

Four in ten Americans (41 percent) said they had only some or very little confidence in the U.S. meat inspection system to protect people from becoming infected with mad cow disease. There was no consensus on who should be mainly responsible for preventing the spread of mad cow domestically. Nearly equal proportions thought that producers of cattle feed (33 percent), the federal government (31 percent), and the beef industry (29 percent) should be mainly responsible.[37]

West Nile Virus

West Nile virus gained American public attention in 1999, when an outbreak of the illness occurred in New York City and the surrounding areas. There were sixty-two cases of West Nile virus, and seven of the victims died.[38] Although the disease had been first isolated in 1937[39] and is believed to have been present in other parts of the world for many hundreds of years, the New York outbreak was momentous because it represented the first known cases in the Western Hemisphere.[40] West Nile remained relevant in policy circles because the virus not only presented again in the New York area but also spread across all forty-eight contiguous states. In fact, West Nile virus, a blood-borne illness transmitted largely through mosquitoes, is now considered an endemic illness in the United States.[41] It is an important example of how quickly a newly introduced disease can spread. The public's response provides insights into how people may react to new diseases that are largely transmitted through means other than person-to-person contact and specifically to future West Nile virus outbreaks.

West Nile disease is caused by an arbovirus and manifests in one of three forms.[42] In most cases (80 percent) people do not develop any discernable symptoms and may not even know they had it. In nearly all the remaining cases, the illness is self-limited with symptoms much like seasonal flu, including fever, fatigue, and loss of appetite. In very few cases, and mostly among elderly or immuno-compromised individuals, the virus infects a person's central nervous system and results in encephalitis, meningitis, or flaccid paralysis, and a relatively high fatality rate. In most outbreaks this neuroinvasive manifestation occurs in only 1 percent of cases, but in some outbreaks it has been much higher.[43] Among survivors of the neuroinvasive form, neurological problems persist for months or years. New research indicates that the long-term effect also occurs in people with the milder forms of West Nile, which suggests that the virus may be doing more damage than is apparent.[44] Currently, no vaccine for West Nile virus exists, and treatment is largely limited to supportive techniques, such as pain relief or, in the most severe cases, mechanical respiratory support.[45]

It is not known precisely how West Nile virus emerged in New York, but the typical transmission cycle goes from birds to mosquitoes to humans. An infected bird is bitten by a mosquito, which then bites and infects a human.[46] Most cases occur during the mosquito season from spring to fall, and then the numbers peter out when cold weather kills the mosquitoes. In the United States, the West Nile virus season of 2008 recorded 1,356 cases (44 deaths). In 2002 and 2003, when the disease was at its deadliest and much of the polling was done, there were 4,156 cases (284 deaths) and 9,862 cases (264 deaths), respectively.[47]

Policies focused largely on mosquito control and surveillance. Both approaches involved public interaction. The policy response came within hours of the public announcement of West Nile: helicopters and trucks spread pesticide to try to control the adult mosquito population.[48] Subsequently, other cities and areas across the United States instituted ground and air spraying campaigns. Experts were conflicted as to whether the pesticides would be effective, and whether the pesticides themselves would be more harmful to humans than the illness.[49] Public education efforts were undertaken to help reduce personal risk through protective measures, such as avoiding being outside at dawn and dusk, which are peak mosquito feeding times, wearing "covering" clothing, and wearing mosquito repellent.[50] Like the pesticide issue more broadly, the mosquito repellent recommendation became somewhat controversial as the recommended ingredient, DEET, has also been linked to neurological problems in humans.[51] For West Nile virus, teams watch bird populations as a predictor of subsequent human infection, and then public health departments track human cases through a reporting system that relies on hospitals and physicians to give information to local public health departments.[52]

Engagement

In 2002 and 2003 the majority of the public (between 61 and 79 percent) reported watching news about West Nile virus very or fairly closely.[53] The public appears to have retained some information from the media, as the majority understood that people catch this illness from mosquitoes (90 percent) and it can be transmitted through blood transfusions (72 percent). Further, only small minorities (12 percent and 11 percent) believed—incorrectly—that you could catch West Nile from being in the same room with or shaking hands with someone who has an active case. But, polls found some important points of confusion in people's understanding of transmission. Roughly half believed—incorrectly—that West Nile can be contracted by handling dead birds or drinking infected water (53 percent and 50 percent, respectively). These misunderstandings may result in inappropriate public concern and demands for unneeded policies and activities from public health departments (**Table 15–3**).[54]

Concern and Assessment of Risk

From 2002 to 2004 about one-third (32 percent to 36 percent) of Americans nationwide said they were concerned that they or someone in their families would get sick from West Nile virus in the next twelve months (or in the 2004 survey, the next three months). Only 10 percent to 16 percent said they were very concerned.[55]

Not surprisingly, concern was greater among people living in high-mosquito areas. In July 2003 nearly half (48 percent) of those living in high-mosquito areas expressed concern, compared with 17 percent of people who did not live in such areas.[56]

Actions

In high-mosquito areas, nearly four in ten (38 percent) residents reported in July 2003 that they had not taken any precautions against mosquito bites that season. Given the number of cases of West Nile in 2002 and the recurrence of the disease in humans in 2003, this finding raised an important public health concern (**Table 15–4**).

The Centers for Disease Control and Prevention (CDC) recommended using mosquito repellent containing DEET, but only 46 percent of Americans living in high-mosquito areas said they had used such a repellent, including the brands Off® and Cutter®, since the beginning of the season. Three in ten (32 percent) reported using a mosquito repellent containing citronella, and 13 percent reported using some other kind of mosquito repellent.

Fewer than half of Americans living in high-mosquito areas reported that they had taken each of four other specific recommended precautions since the beginning of the season. Four in ten said they removed standing water from spare tires, gutters, bird baths, kiddie pools, and other places where water collects (44 percent) and avoided going outdoors at the peak mosquito hours of dawn and dusk (40 percent). Three in ten (30 percent) said they wore long-sleeve shirts and other protective clothing outdoors. Twenty percent said they replaced or repaired window screens.

Much smaller numbers reported taking other precautions, such as using a "bug zapper" in their yard (11 percent) or buying mosquito netting (4 percent). Neither precaution had been specifically recommended by the CDC.

It cannot be determined from these results whether people were taking these precautions specifically to protect against getting the West Nile virus. In high-mosquito areas, separating general precautions against mosquitoes from those aimed at dealing with a specific mosquito-borne threat is difficult. Many people living in high-mosquito areas would take precautions anyway to prevent the annoyance of mosquito bites and avoid other dangers, such as encephalitis.

Again it comes as no surprise that far fewer residents of areas where there are not many mosquitoes reported taking precautions against bites (32 percent, compared with 62 percent in high-mosquito areas). No more than one in five took any of the individual precautions, including using mosquito repellents that contain DEET (19 percent).[57]

Views about Policies and Policymakers

On the sometimes controversial issue of special spraying against mosquitoes to control the spread of the West Nile virus, the study found strong support for the practice. Nationwide, large majorities of those who live in areas where spraying was done at ground level (90 percent) or from the air (77 percent) approve of these practices. Even in areas where no ground spraying was done, three-fourths (76 percent) of Americans said they would favor such spraying to prevent the spread of West Nile virus if it appeared in their area. In areas where there was no spraying from the air, support for such spraying is lower, but a majority (58 percent) would still approve of air spraying for this purpose.[58]

SARS

A near-pandemic of severe acute respiratory syndrome, or SARS, occurred in spring 2003. The first patient actually became ill in November 2002 in China's Guangdong Province, but Chinese officials did not report the outbreak to the World Health Organization (WHO) until February 2003. Subsequently, Americans watched as the disease appeared to spread quickly from person to person through thirty countries, infecting 8,096 people and killing 774 of them.[59] SARS became a visible example of how easily a true global outbreak of a new disease could start and be spread by international travelers, and it provided an excellent example of how the public might react to a true pandemic.

SARS is caused by a virus (a coronavirus more specifically), which may be a modified virus that traditionally infects civets.[60] Patients first experience a fever, often with related aches and chills, and some develop early respiratory symptoms.[61] SARS also results in gastrointestinal and urinary tract infections.[62] Typically, two to seven days after these early symptoms, patients develop a lower respiratory infection, which may include a nonproductive cough and shortness of breath. Most patients then develop pneumonia. Recommended treatment is standard care for serious pneumonia, and 10 percent to 20 percent of patients require mechanical ventilation.[63] Fatality rates are about 10 percent on average, and the severity of the disease increases with age.[64]

SARS appears to be transmitted primarily from person to person by "respiratory droplets." That is, infected people shed the virus when they sneeze or cough, and then give it to others when they touch them or share surfaces.[65] Typically one person infects only a limited group around them, but there appear to be some contributors—perhaps even specific to particular people—that create "super-infecting" situations where the virus spreads much more quickly to a large group of people.[66] In several cases, one person has spread the disease directly to more than 100 people.[67]

WHO tracked the pattern of SARS infection over time. The index case was a physician who stayed in a Hong Kong hotel and infected a number of other people who subsequently spread it to additional regions and countries. Most of the cases were in Asia, including Hong Kong, mainland China, Singapore, and Taiwan; but, a substantial number were also in Canada.[68] Only eight Americans were infected definitively with SARS, and no one died, but as many as 418 probable or suspected cases were reported over the spring and summer of 2003.[69]

The public policy response to SARS included four dimensions that had a particular relevance for the American public through extensive media coverage. The first is that public health officials across multiple countries, including the United States, used isolation and quarantine strategies to help control the spread of the disease.[70] The specific characteristics of the quarantine ranged from effective house arrest to hospital-based isolation. The second dimension was extensive media coverage of people wearing masks to protect themselves from SARS; the mask became iconic. Third, there was some discussion of providing passengers with masks to prevent contamination on planes, using airport-based quarantine facilities, and tracking down passengers once they had landed at their destination should any of the other travelers develop SARS.[71] Finally, there was significant discussion of the potential—and actual—discrimination against Asian Americans, and some universities banned international students coming from Asia.[72] Newspapers reported the public also appeared to make racially oriented decisions, as fearful consumers stayed away from Asian restaurants and Chinatowns.[73]

Engagement

News of SARS spread through most of the American public, and by April 2003 more than nine in ten Americans (93 percent) had heard of "a new form of flu in Asia, known as SARS."[74] By June about three-fourths (77 percent) of the public reported following news stories about the SARS outbreak in Asia and Canada very or fairly closely (**Table 15–5**).[75]

In May 2003, 89 percent of the public was aware that SARS is contagious, and most people could correctly identify multiple routes of transmission, including shaking hands (70 percent), being in close contact (88 percent), being on the same airplane (76 percent), and touching objects or surfaces that someone who has SARS has touched (64 percent). Only a small minority (14 percent) identified the inaccurate transmission route of eating undercooked chicken. A majority also identified blood transfusions (58 percent) and eating food that has been prepared by someone who was infected with or had been exposed to SARS (66 percent) as mechanisms of transmission.[76] Although no cases of SARS were identified through these means, the ideas are not completely off base; and WHO did issue a precaution against SARS patients donating blood.[77] Collectively, the polling data suggest that the public was generally clear that SARS passes from person to person through contact, but the specific limitations on such transmission were not clear.

A majority of the public knew that SARS was one of the diseases in which people who are exposed needed to be quarantined (84 percent) and that there was no vaccine for SARS (88 percent). Far fewer people knew that there was no effective treatment (47 percent).[78]

Concern and Assessment of Risk

Americans expressed their highest level of concern about SARS in April 2003. About one in three (32 percent) said they were concerned that they or an immediate family member would get sick from SARS in the next twelve months. One in four thought they or a family member was very or somewhat likely to contract SARS in the next twelve months. By May 2003 concern had dropped to 26 percent and the perceived likelihood of getting sick from SARS had fallen to one in six, including only 3 percent who thought getting sick from SARS was very likely.[79]

In May about one-third (35 percent) of Americans believed that SARS had made it unsafe to travel to Canada, where many cases had been reported, mainly in the Toronto area.[80] This belief likely affected American tourism to Canada.

Actions

Even though few cases of SARS had appeared in the United States, in mid-April 2003 concerns about the disease were having an impact on the American public. One in six reported avoiding people they thought might have traveled recently to Asia, and 14 percent said they were avoiding Asian restaurants or stores. Both of these actions involve an element of social stigmatization based on race and ethnicity and could have important economic effects in certain communities (**Table 15–6**).

The public took other actions in response to reports of SARS: using a disinfectant at home or at work (21 percent), avoiding public events (10 percent), carrying something to clean objects that may have been in contact with someone who has SARS (9 percent), and consulting a Web site for information about how to protect themselves from SARS (9 percent). Few Americans had talked with a doctor about health issues related to SARS or worn a face mask (3 percent). Among Americans who had traveled outside the United States in the past year (as a measure of international travelers), 17 percent said they had avoided international air travel recently because of SARS.[81]

By May 2003 fewer people were taking many of these actions. The percentage of the public who said they were avoiding people they believed had recently traveled to Asia fell to 11 percent, and the proportion who said they were avoiding Asian restaurants or stores had declined to 9 percent. Sixteen percent reported using a disinfectant at home or at work. Among those who had traveled internationally during the past year, 9 percent reported avoiding international air travel due to concerns about SARS.[82]

Views about Policies and Policymakers

Ninety-five percent of Americans said they would comply with official requests to submit to isolation in a health care facility for two or three weeks if they had SARS. Similarly, 93 percent said they would agree to be quarantined in their home for up to ten days if they were exposed to someone with SARS but did not know if they themselves had the disease.[83] Most Americans (83 percent) did not believe that President George W. Bush's executive order adding SARS to the list of diseases for which people could be quarantined threatened their personal rights or freedoms.[84]

The public also appeared to want extra cautionary measures during air travel. Nearly three-quarters of the American public (73 percent) said they would want a face mask available on a plane flying overseas if someone was coughing a lot, and nearly two-thirds (61 percent) said they would want a mask on a domestic flight.[85] Polling data that references not only SARS but contagious diseases more generally supports this point. In 2004, 94 percent of the public said they would want public health authorities to contact them if they might have been exposed to "a highly contagious disease like SARS, tuberculosis, or meningitis." In fact, roughly 80 percent even expected them to do so.[86]

Unfortunately, we have no measures of public confidence in the government and private sector entities such as airlines in developing SARS policies, or which organizations the public might hold responsible to do so. This information would be critical in developing actual policies should SARS or a similar illness present itself again.

Bioterrorism

The CDC defines bioterrorism as "the deliberate release of viruses, bacteria, or other germs (agents) used to cause illness or death in people, animals, or plants."[87] It has been present from the days of early warfare when, for example, the Greeks used animal carcasses to contaminate enemy water supplies.[88] By the twentieth century, understanding of bacteriology and virology along with other technological advances made a true science of biological warfare, and many countries, including the United States, had offensive biological weapons programs.[89] Such programs were largely secretive and rarely captured sustained media attention.[90] The events of September 11, 2001, opened up a new era in media coverage and policy discussion related to bioterrorism in the United States. In this context, it was discussed as a technologically sophisticated tool that could plausibly be used against civilians during peacetime for political purposes with widespread impact.[91] Bioterrorism was immediately a part of the media reports related to the airplane attacks.[92] In addition, it was extensively covered when the first example of a large-scale bioterrorist attack—anthrax sent through the mail—occurred on U.S. soil over the following weeks.[93] Understanding the public's response to the most frequently discussed bioterrorism agents—anthrax and smallpox—sheds light on how the public might respond to future biological attacks and how best to develop policies for such a crisis.

Anthrax

Less than a month after 9/11, the United States experienced the first of a series of attacks involving anthrax sent through the U.S. Postal Service and intended to infect members of Congress and of the press. Although the anthrax did not reach all of its apparently intended targets, twenty-two cases of anthrax were reported, mainly in four metropolitan areas: New York City, Washington, D.C., Trenton/Princeton, New Jersey, and Boca Raton, Florida.[94] As the first large-scale instance of bioterrorism on U.S. soil, it was one of the best examples of public response to such a threat.[95]

Anthrax is caused by a naturally occurring bacterium, *Bacillus anthracis,* and can take three different forms.[96] The most dangerous form is inhalation anthrax, which affects the lungs and results in cold- or flu-like symptoms, including a cough, and ultimately chest pain, shortness of breath, tiredness, and muscle aches. Inhalation anthrax can be life-threatening; in fact, five of the eleven inhalation anthrax cases in 2001 died. The other cases of anthrax in the 2001 incident were skin (cutaneous) anthrax, which is relatively benign. It starts as a sore that blisters and then becomes an ulcer with a black center. None of these symptoms is painful, and the infection responds well to treatment; more than 80 percent of victims recover even if they receive no treatment. Anthrax can also affect the gastrointestinal system, resulting in nausea, bloody diarrhea, and significant stomach pain that results in 25 percent to 50 percent mortality, but these symptoms are much less common and did not occur during the 2001 incident. Anthrax cannot be passed from one person to another; infection must be directly from the source. Treatment for anthrax includes an intense antibiotic regimen. There is a vaccine for anthrax, but it is not publicly available. It is largely reserved for the military and is controversial even in that context because of limited testing to date.[97] The CDC considers anthrax a Category A agent, which means it poses the highest level threat to national security based on its potential public health impact, the ease of its dissemination, the possibility of public panic, and the need for "special action" by public health agencies.[98]

The American public was able to watch the media as initial reports of anthrax were made public and then as each case was revealed. There was no proven link between the airplane attacks of 9/11 and the anthrax attacks. In fact, nearly seven years later, on August 6, 2008, the FBI presented a sweeping but circumstantial case that Bruce Ivins, an Army microbiologist who had killed himself a week before the announcement, was solely responsible for mailing the deadly anthrax letters.[99] But because the two attacks occurred in nearly the same time frame, and a nervous public had little information about the anthrax source, the public response to anthrax was no doubt shaped by concerns about terrorism in general. It also meant that media attention was at higher than normal levels during the crisis, which would predict greater public engagement with the issue.[100]

Much of the media attention following the anthrax attacks focused on the federal government's bioterrorism preparedness and response efforts and the investigation into the person or persons who were responsible.[101] In addition to the extensive coverage of the true attacks, the media also reported a number of anthrax hoaxes or false alarms involving benign powdery substances.[102] And finally, there were many newspaper articles citing the public's response—including precautions they were taking when opening their own household mail.[103]

Engagement

Given the historical importance of 9/11 in the United States, it is not surprising that the anthrax attacks were the most closely watched news events related to emerging infectious disease. In November–December 2001, more than eight in ten Americans said that they were following the story very (50 percent) or somewhat closely (33 percent).[104] As late as January–February 2002 nearly three-fourths (72 percent) were still following anthrax news closely (**Table 15–7**).[105]

By the end of 2001, most people understood the main elements of the facts about anthrax. Most were aware that anthrax is not contagious (75 percent), but from a public health perspective, it is alarming that 25 percent of the public got this basic fact wrong. Most people were aware that treatment is available (87 percent) and that inhalation anthrax is the most deadly form (78 percent). The majority (80 percent) were aware that fewer than ten people had died from inhalation anthrax since 9/11.[106]

Concern and Assessment of Risk

Americans' degree of concern about anthrax and their assessment of personal risk varied by the proximity of the attacks. Nationally, about one in four (24 percent) said in November–December 2001 that they were worried that they could contract anthrax from opening mail at home or at work. In two metropolitan areas where anthrax attacks occurred, the level of worry was significantly higher: 39 percent in the Trenton/Princeton area and 33 percent in metropolitan Washington. Nationally, only 9 percent thought they or an immediate family member was very or somewhat likely to contract anthrax in the next twelve months. But the proportion who felt at risk from anthrax was about twice as large in the Trenton/Princeton (21 percent) and Washington (17 percent) metropolitan areas.[107]

On the other hand, the public was concerned that more attacks would happen to someone in the United States. More than half the public (52 percent) thought it was very likely that more anthrax attacks would happen in the coming year; fully 86 percent said it would be very or somewhat likely.[108] People were split on their view as to the scope of those future attacks. Roughly half the country (45 percent) thought the anthrax situation was a few isolated cases limited to a small number of people, and the other half (50 percent) thought it was more likely the first of an ongoing series of cases that could affect large numbers of people.[109]

Actions

In November–December 2001 roughly a third (32 percent) of the public nationally said they were taking precautions with the way they handled their mail to avoid anthrax contamination. These precautions included washing hands after opening the mail (30 percent), wearing gloves while opening the mail (6 percent), and completely avoiding opening the mail (2 percent). More than half (54 percent) of Trenton/Princeton area residents said they were taking precautions with the mail (**Table 15–8**).[110]

At the height of public attention to the issue 41 percent of the country said they would be willing to take a vaccine to prevent anthrax infection.[111] The vaccine was not publicly available.

Survey data indicated increased demands on the health system nationwide, but they were not large in scale. Five percent said they or someone in their household had either talked with a doctor about health issues related to bioterrorism; 4 percent that they had gotten a prescription for or purchased antibiotics; and 3 percent that they had consulted a health professional or counselor about their anxieties.[112] Less than half of 1 percent were currently taking antibiotics as a precaution against anthrax. These figures contradict, to some degree, stories that people were flocking to doctors' offices trying to get prescriptions for Cipro (Ciprofloxacin) and other antibiotics.

Views about Policies and Policymakers

Although government approval ratings were relatively high in the wake of 9/11, the public was mistrustful of the government's response to the anthrax attacks. About half of the public felt the government was not telling people everything they needed to know about the anthrax attacks.[113] The public also may have believed that government officials had legitimate reasons to withhold information—they might not have known themselves (30 percent) or they may have been trying to prevent overreaction and panic (23 percent).[114]

More than three-fourths of the public said they were very (28 percent) or somewhat confident (52 percent) in the ability of the U.S. government to respond effectively to the health threats posed by anthrax. About two-thirds (64 percent) expressed confidence in the government to prevent additional people from being exposed to anthrax, including the 14 percent who said they were very confident.[115] Shortly after the attacks, less than a third (29 percent) felt that the local officials in their town or city were prepared for such an attack.[116]

Smallpox

Naturally occurring smallpox was eradicated from the United States in 1949 and from the world in 1977.[117] For decades, the eradication served as an example of the success of public health in addressing disease and the promise of future successes in wiping out other illnesses. With the apparent threat of smallpox gone, routine inoculation was eliminated, and the only stores of smallpox virus were in laboratories. But in the wake of 9/11 and a new focus on bioterrorism, smallpox came to represent a threat. Although it has not been released in a terrorist context, some believe that would be possible because laboratories in destabilized regions had access to the smallpox virus and might use it or sell it to terrorist organizations.[118] Ironically, because the smallpox virus was eliminated from the globe, few people are immune by virtue of surviving the disease. A new outbreak could therefore be the worst in history.[119]

Smallpox is a serious and highly contagious disease caused by the variola virus. Like anthrax, it is classified as a Category A agent by the CDC. Ninety-nine percent of cases of smallpox manifest as variola major, which includes four subtypes.[120] Historically most variola major cases were "ordinary." Far less frequently, there were some "modified" cases, which occurred in people who had been inoculated, as well as "flat" and "hemorrhagic" cases. Over all subtypes, the fatality rate is 30 percent, but flat and hemorrhagic cases nearly always end in death. The remaining 1 percent of cases were variola minor, which were much less severe with only a 1 percent fatality rate. Among those who survive smallpox, severe scarring is the norm, and blindness is a common complication.[121]

No specific treatment is available for smallpox and no known cure, but vaccination provides effective prevention. The vaccine can also mute symptoms or prevent them even if it is given after exposure; however, it must be administered before symptoms appear, which is typically seven to fourteen days after exposure. The vaccine may pose significant risks, especially for some subgroups, such as those who are immuno-compromised. The vaccine is not made with smallpox, but from a related virus that could cause fever, rash scarring, life-threatening complications (including heart problems), and even death.[122] The inoculation also causes a small scab to form, and the scab can infect others.[123]

The major federal public health policy response to the threat of smallpox was an inoculation program launched by President Bush in December 2002. It targeted the military and then frontline medical workers, who were believed to be at the greatest risk for coming into contact with smallpox.[124] Some medical workers refused to participate in the program, citing a greater risk from inoculation than from the terror threat.[125] Over time, concern grew about the known risks and newly discovered risks of heart problems. Ultimately, the inoculation program was terminated but not before there were significant negative outcomes, including seven deaths.[126] Other federal policies were also discussed to help manage public health in the event of a bioterrorist attack using smallpox, including military enforcement of quarantine (which is typically left to state powers).[127]

Engagement

Although smallpox was an important part of the bioterrorism discussion in the wake of 9/11, fewer people were tuned into news about smallpox than anthrax. Given that the anthrax attack was still unfolding at that time, this prioritization is understandable. Still, in late 2001 roughly two-thirds (65 percent) of the country were following very or somewhat closely news stories on concerns about possible future bioterrorism involving smallpox.[128] In October 2002 more than half (53 percent) were following news about the CDC's smallpox vaccination plan, a much more specific topic (**Table 15–9**).[129]

The American public had a mixed understanding of the basics of the smallpox virus. The majority (89 percent) rightly perceived that smallpox is a contagious disease. But a nearly equal percent (78 percent) believed—incorrectly—that there is treatment for smallpox to prevent someone who has come down with the disease from having serious complications or from dying.[130] This gap in understanding could reduce the public's concern about the disease and lull people into thinking that policies to prevent the spread of smallpox are not important. Moreover, if an outbreak did occur and the message got out that there was no treatment, this information could dramatically alter public perceptions of the seriousness of the disease and the measures they would need to take to keep themselves safe.

The last case of smallpox in the United States was reported in 1949, and in the world in 1977.[131] Three in ten Americans (30 percent), however, believed smallpox cases had occurred in the United States during the last five years, and 63 percent thought there had been cases somewhere else in the world in the same time frame.[132] If people are not well informed, they may not process public health messages about the risk implications of reintroducing this disease or about vaccination.

Understanding of the benefits and risks of vaccination was also limited. Less than half of the public (42 percent) realized that if a person has been exposed to smallpox but does not yet have the symptoms, getting a vaccination can provide protection. Only about one in four (27 percent) knew that someone who has physical contact with a recently vaccinated person can contract a serious infection.[133] These misperceptions may have shaped their views of vaccination programs, as well as their own personal decisions about how they want to protect themselves. In the event of an attack, much of the public does not realize that even if they are exposed to smallpox, they can take critical steps to reduce their risks and should not wait to see if pox appear before seeking medical assistance. Knowing this may make them more likely to want to get vaccinated before they face any tangible threat, or may make them delay seeking care.

Concern and Assessment of Risk

In late 2002 government reports warned of the possibility of bioterrorist attacks involving smallpox. This possibility was coupled with the potential for military action with Iraq, a country thought to have biological weapons. At that time, about half (51 percent) of the public said they were concerned that there would be a terrorist attack using smallpox in the United States during the next twelve months. After the Iraq War began in March 2003 and no biological weapons were used by the Iraqis against U.S. troops, concern about bioterrorism using smallpox declined sharply, with 28 percent expressing concern in May 2003.[134]

In late 2002 nearly two-thirds (64 percent) of the public believed that if the United States took military action against Iraq, a terrorist attack using smallpox in the homeland was very or somewhat likely.[135] Throughout the period from 9/11 until May 2003, however, no more than 12 percent of Americans thought that they or an immediate family member was very or somewhat likely to contract smallpox during the next twelve months.[136]

Actions

In late 2002, during the run-up to the Iraq War, 61 percent of the public said they would want to get a smallpox vaccination (or re-vaccination) if it were offered as a precaution against bioterrorist threats. Some people would change their mind about vaccination under certain circumstances. If there were cases of smallpox in the United States, 75 percent would choose to be vaccinated. If there were cases in their community, the proportion of Americans willing to be vaccinated increased to 88 percent (**Table 15–10**).

The actions of doctors could also influence the decision to be vaccinated. Nearly three-fourths (73 percent) of the public said they would get vaccinated if their own doctor and most other doctors were vaccinated. On the other, if their own doctor and many other doctors refused vaccination, only 21 percent of the public would want to get vaccinated.

Thirty-three percent would want to be vaccinated if they heard that "some people" had died from the smallpox vaccine, and 44 percent would want to be vaccinated if they had to stay out of work for two weeks. A small proportion (9 percent) said they would not want to be vaccinated under any of these circumstances.[137]

Two-thirds (67 percent) said they would stay in the community if cases of smallpox were reported there, and 32 percent said they would stay elsewhere until the outbreak was over. Ninety-one percent said they would stay in the community if they thought they had been exposed to the virus, but a small fraction (7 percent) would leave their community even if they thought they had been exposed.[138]

About half (52 percent) said they would go to their own doctor first for diagnosis and care if they thought they had smallpox. A sizable minority (40 percent) said they would go to a hospital emergency room.[139]

Overall, these responses suggest the need to include the clinical community in the public health policy planning and outreach. Further, they suggest the need to develop policies that will take account for a potentially contagious people moving between communities.

Views about Policies and Policymakers

The public had moderate confidence in the government's abilities to address smallpox. About two-thirds (65 percent) of Americans said they had confidence in the ability of the U.S. government to protect its citizens from terrorist attacks involving smallpox; however, this includes only 19 percent who said they had a "great deal" of confidence.[140] Two-thirds (66 percent) of the public expressed confidence in the ability of the United States to respond effectively to the health threats posed by a major outbreak of smallpox, including 27 percent who said they were very confident.[141]

More than eight in ten said they were very (43 percent) or somewhat (40 percent) confident that their own doctor could recognize the symptoms of smallpox.[142] About two-thirds believed their local emergency room was very (22 percent) or somewhat (47 percent) prepared to diagnose and treat smallpox victims.[143]

The public was asked about two of the policy issues being debated at the time, vaccination of health professionals and the vaccination of the general public. A strong majority (81 percent) favored voluntary vaccination of doctors and nurses in preparation for a bioterrorist attack. Nearly two-thirds (65 percent) were in favor of immediately offering the smallpox vaccination to the general public on a voluntary basis.[144]

Many Americans believed that they would not be able to get vaccinated quickly if cases of smallpox were detected in their community and that there would not be enough vaccine for everyone. Moreover, 72 percent believed that if it was not possible to vaccinate everyone quickly, wealthy and influential people would get the vaccine first; 43 percent believed that the distribution of the vaccine would discriminate against the elderly, and 22 percent that it would discriminate against African Americans.[145]

About three-fourths (77 percent) of Americans said that if they were diagnosed with smallpox and told they needed to be isolated in a special health facility with other smallpox patients for three to four weeks, they would agree to go. Ninety-five percent said they would agree to quarantine for two to three weeks if they were exposed but did not have symptoms.[146] More than half of the public, however, said that if they were quarantined at home for two or three weeks they would be very or somewhat worried about not being able to get food and water (57 percent) or the regular medical care and prescriptions they need (54 percent). Nearly the same number would be very or somewhat worried about not being able to see family members (50 percent) and not getting their paycheck because they would miss work (49 percent). Addressing these concerns may be important in the real-life situation of quarantine requirements.[147]

The public showed mixed support for policies that would increase state powers in the event of an infectious disease outbreak. The public largely supported policies that would require hospitals to provide care for people who think they may have smallpox (87 percent favor), for quarantining people who have smallpox (73 percent), and for destroying contaminated personal effects (69 percent). But support was much lower for policies that would affect people who have not yet been confirmed with the illness. Less than half the public supported mandatory vaccines (41 percent), and only a slim majority supported mandatory testing (51 percent) or mandatory quarantine of people suspected to have been exposed to smallpox (57 percent). Moreover, roughly a third (35 percent) believed such emergency powers would be a major threat to their personal rights and freedoms, and another third (33 percent) felt they would constitute a minor threat. Part of the reason for the lack of support may be that nearly half the public (46 percent) believes the state would abuse such powers.[148]

Conclusions and Implications for Policy

Reviewing the American public's response to these specific emerging infectious diseases—mad cow disease, West Nile virus, SARS, anthrax, and smallpox—provides a rich foundation to draw some larger conclusions about how the American public responds to biological threats, and what the responses mean for future policy and preparedness planning.

Overall, the public appears to be interested in the topic of emerging infectious diseases, with more than three-quarters of the public tuning into the news at the peak of the attention cycles for mad cow disease, West Nile virus, SARS, and anthrax. At each peak, the diseases were either just reaching the United States, or federal agencies were responding to the threat as if it were imminent by outlining preparedness strategies. This pattern of attention is consistent with the idea that the American public focuses on issues as they get closer to home.[149] Policymakers therefore can expect the public to tune into an issue only when it appears to pose a direct threat in domestic areas; public support for action is likely to wane once the threat no longer seems imminent. Sustaining support for targeted programmatic interventions, therefore, is likely to garner more public support than general infrastructural improvements in the public health system.

The American public also appears somewhat "rational"—at least in very broad terms—about the purported threats insofar as they distinguish between the overarching threat of the disease at the national level and their personal risk.[150] In the three cases where we have polling data about both aspects of risk (mad cow disease, anthrax, and smallpox), the public acknowledges that they personally have a low risk of getting the disease, but finds the threat at the national level significant. Unfortunately, the data do not reveal whether this distinction stems from a sort of altruism and concern about the people and communities most at risk from concerns about the larger financial impacts or impacts on the overall quality of life in the United States.

At the same time, a sizable minority felt they were at risk for certain diseases, even when the more factual data would suggest otherwise. More than 20 percent of the population felt they were at significant risk for contracting anthrax at the time of the mail attacks, which suggests that the public was quite fearful of this threat and felt much more closely engaged in the issue than some of the other diseases we review here.[151]

Despite their concerns, only a fraction of the public actually took steps to protect themselves from any of these diseases. Moreover, many of the steps they took were fairly easy, such as throwing away more junk mail, or steps that have immediate payoffs, such as avoiding mosquito bites. This information is consistent with a large body of literature suggesting that health behavior changes come slowly.[152] Policymakers should plan on assisting a public that is largely unprepared for an infectious disease disaster. At the same time, they need to prepare for significant economic repercussions, because even a small fraction of the public making major lifestyle changes—such as changes in food shopping habits—could have significant financial repercussions. Moreover, such behaviors may be driven by fear in a true outbreak.[153]

The public is somewhat conflicted about their views of policies and policymakers. They are fairly supportive of federal government intervention in the case of infectious diseases, with majority support for quarantine measures. That said, the public appears to be more supportive of voluntary participation than forced participation. Furthermore, data from parallel studies overseas suggest that Americans are less supportive of strict government measures than people living in other countries. A study conducted during the SARS outbreaks showed lower support among Americans for relatively intrusive measures like temperature screenings than among residents of Hong Kong, Singapore, and Taiwan.[154] And a substantial proportion of Americans do not have a lot confidence in the federal government's ability to address infectious disease outbreaks effectively. This finding is not unexpected, given studies of Americans' views of government more broadly.[155]

The public appears to have greater confidence in the health system and medicine to address outbreaks. They look to their doctors not only for clinical care but also as role models in terms of specific health practices, like vaccination. As another example, they would turn to their local emergency room in a crisis. And, if they believed the illness was very serious, they would rely on vaccines to protect them from harm, even when they are told that the vaccine itself has significant side effects and can kill people. These findings are consistent with data suggesting that the American public is enamored with science and medicine, especially as compared to their European counterparts.[156] Policymakers should, however, note that the public's views on vaccination are not absolute; rather, they depend on factors that include the perceived severity of the illness and the perceived safety of the vaccine, and their views may shift over time.

Looking historically at the beginning of the swine flu outbreak of 1976–1977, nearly three-fourths (73 percent) of the public favored a government program of mass vaccination, and a majority (54 percent) said they planned to get vaccinated (30 percent said they did not, and 16 percent were undecided).[157] But after serious side effects of the vaccine were reported, the percentage of the public who said they actually had a vaccination was only 38 percent.[158] The discussion of vaccination in Chapter 16 provides a more recent example of the limits of public support for vaccines.

Taken together, these findings suggest that policymakers would do well to develop clear, largely voluntary policies for public protection in the case of a disease outbreak. Programs must be based on hard scientific evidence and the risks clearly communicated to the public. Communication strategies should take advantage of the natural peaks and ebbs in public engagement in the issue by ensuring that clear messages are delivered when the public is paying the most attention. Moreover, success may depend on using the natural connections of the public to existing health institutions and engaging physicians and other care providers in their plans. Despite these efforts, policymakers should assume that the public will not have taken many tangible steps to prepare themselves for a crisis. Clearly, developing effective policies is not an easy task, but by taking public opinion into consideration, policymakers are likely to have more success in gaining compliance and more success in keeping the public safe.

Notes

[1] K. E. Jones, N. G. Patel, M. A. Levy, A. Storeygard, D. Balk, J. L.Gittleman, and P. Daszak, "Global Trends in Emerging Infectious Diseases," *Nature* 451 (February 21 2008): 990–993; U. Desselberger, "Emerging and Re-emerging Infectious Diseases," *Journal of Infection* 40 (January 2000): 3–15; Joshua Lederberg, Robert E. Shope, and Stanley C. Oaks Jr., eds.; Committee on Emerging Microbial Threats to Health, Institute of Medicine, *Emerging Infections: Microbial Threats to Health in the United States* (Washington, D.C.: National Academy Press, 1992).

[2] L. Scott Chavers and Sten H. Vermund, "Introduction to Emerging and Reemerging Infectious Diseases," in *Emerging Infectious Diseases: Trends and Issues,* ed. Felissa R. Lashley and Jerry D. Durham (New York: Springer Publishing, 2007), Chapter 1.

[3] V. Ramalingaswami, "Psychosocial Effects of the 1994 Plague Outbreak in Surat, India," *Military Medicine* 166 (Suppl., December 2001): 29–30.

[4] Felissa R. Lashley, "Prion Diseases: Creutzfeldt-Jakob Disease and Other Transmissible Spongiform Encephalopathies," in *Emerging Infectious Diseases,* 307.

[5] Ibid., 309.

[6] Ibid., 316.

[7] Centers for Disease Control and Prevention, "vCJD (Variant Creutzfeldt-Jacob Disease): Epidemiology of vCJD and BSE," 2005, http://www.cdc.gov/ncidod/dvrd/vcjd/epidemiology.htm.

[8] Centers for Disease Control and Prevention, "BSE (Bovine Spongiform Encephalopathy, or Mad Cow Disease)," 2009, http://www.cdc.gov/ncidod/dvrd/bse.

[9] U.S. Department of Agriculture, Animal and Plant Health Inspection Service, "An Estimate of the Prevalence of BSE in the United States," July 20, 2006, http://www.aphis.usda.gov/newsroom/hot_issues/bse/downloads/BSEprev–estFINAL_7–20–6.pdf.

[10] Shankar Vedantam, "Mad Cow Case Found in U.S. for First Time; Infected Animal Killed In Washington State," *Washington Post,* December 24, 2003, A1; Donald G. McNeil Jr., "Mad Cow Case Confirmed; U.S. Testing Will Change," *New York Times,* June 25, 2005, A7; Donald G. McNeil Jr., "Mad Cow Disease Is Confirmed in Alabama," *New York Times,* March 14, 2006, A2.

[11] Ira Dreyfuss, "Government Ends Search for More Mad Cows," Associated Press, February 10, 2004; Donald G. McNeil Jr., "Man Who Killed the Mad Cow Has Questions of His Own," *New York Times,* February 3, 2004, F2.

[12] Lashley, "Prion Diseases: Creutzfeldt-Jakob Disease and Other Transmissible Spongiform Encephalopathies," 308; Kurt Link, *Understanding New, Resurgent, and Resistant Diseases: How Man and Globalization Create and Spread Illness* (Westport, Conn.: Praeger, 2007).

[13] Centers for Disease Control and Prevention, "vCJD (Variant Creutzfeldt-Jacob Disease): Fact Sheet," 2007, http://www.cdc.gov/ncidod/dvrd/vcjd/factsheet_nvcjd.htm.

[14] These individuals presented with symptoms of vCJD while in the United States, but all had been living in another country with active cases of BSE in cattle, and that is presumed to be where they were infected.

[15] M.T. Bishop, P. Hart, L. Aitchison, H.N. Baybutt, C. Plinston, V. Thomson et al., "Predicting Susceptibility and Incubation Time of Human-to-Human Transmission of vCJD," *Lancet Neurology* 5 (May 2006): 393–398; "Outbreak of Mad Cow Disease Rattles Europe; Plague's Human Equivalent Drives Concerns Higher," *Florida Times-Union,* December 3, 2000, A24.

[16] Centers for Disease Control and Prevention, "vCJD (Variant Creutzfeldt-Jacob Disease): Fact Sheet," 2007.

[17] U.S. Department of Agriculture, Food Safety and Inspection Service, "FSIS Publishes Final Rule Prohibiting Processing of 'Downer' Cattle," July 12, 2007, http://www.fsis.usda.gov/News_&_Events/NR_071207_01/index.asp.

[18] U.S. Department of Agriculture, Food Safety and Inspection Service, "FSIS Further Strengthens Protections Against Bovine Spongiform Encephalopathy (BSE)," 2005, http://www.fsis.usda.gov/Fact_Sheets/FSIS_Further_Strengthens_Protections_Against_BSE/index.asp.

[19] U.S. Department of Agriculture, Food Safety and Inspection Service, "Washington Firm Recalls Beef Products Following Presumptive BSE Determination," Recall Release FSIS-RC-067–2003, December 23, 2003, http://www.fsis.usda.gov/Frame/FrameRedirect.asp?main=http://www.fsis.usda.gov/oa/recalls/prelease/pr067–2003.htm.

[20] Jocelyn Gecker, "Fear of Mad Cow Disease Spreads," Associated Press, November 10, 2000; Crocker Stephenson, "Europe's Pain; America's Fear; Mad Cow Disease's Shadow Lengthens as U.S. Wonders: Could It Happen Here?" *Milwaukee Journal-Sentinel,* March 25, 2001, 1A.

[21] "New Mad Cow Disease Cases in France," Associated Press, October 17, 2000; "French Officials Say Meat Is Safe; Farmers Limit Sales as Fear of Mad Cow Disease Spreads," *Washington Post,* November 10, 2000, A42; "Mad Cow Disease Hits Germany, Azores," *Milwaukee Journal-Sentinel,* November 25, 2000, 10A.

[22] "European Union Proposes Series of Measures to Control Mad Cow Disease; Ban on Animal Products in Feed, Testing of Older Cattle Are Urged," *St. Louis Post-Dispatch,* November 30, 2000, A2; Keith B. Richburg, "'Mad Cow' Disease Unites Europe in Fear; As Affliction Spreads and France Panics, EU Pushes for Continental Response," *Washington Post,* December 3, 2000, A31.

[23] "Britain Admits Cover-up, Will Pay 'Mad Cow' Disease Victims; Report Hits Delay in Notifying Public," *Florida Times-Union,* October 27, 2000, A12; "Girl, 14, Dies of Mad Cow Disease," Associated Press, October 28, 2000.

[24] Kaiser Family Foundation Poll (Storrs, Conn.: Roper Center for Public Opinion Research, January 25–29, 2001).

[25] Kaiser Family Foundation Poll (Storrs, Conn.: Roper Center for Public Opinion Research, June 5–8, 2003).

[26] Robert J. Blendon, John M. Benson, Catherine M. DesRoches, Melissa J. Herrmann, Elizabeth Raleigh, and Kathleen J. Weldon, "Mad Cow Disease," *Working Papers of the Project on the Public and Biological Security, Harvard School of Public Health* 14, February 2, 2004, http://www.hsph.harvard.edu/research/horp/files/WP14MadCow.pdf.

[27] Kaiser Family Foundation polls (Storrs, Conn.: Roper Center for Public Opinion Research, February 3–6, 2005; August 4–8, 2005; April 6–11, 2006).

[28] Anthony Downs, "Up and Down with Ecology: The Issue-Attention Cycle," *The Public Interest* 28 (Summer 1972): 38–50.

[29] Doris A. Graber, *Mass Media and American Politics,* 7th ed. (Washington, D.C.: CQ Press, 2006), Chapter 4.

[30] B. Fischhoff, "Risk Perception and Communication Unplugged: Twenty Years of Process," *Risk Analysis* 15 (April 1995): 137–145.

[31] Blendon et al., "Mad Cow Disease."

[32] Ibid.

[33] Gallup/CNN/*USA Today* Poll (Storrs, Conn.: Roper Center for Public Opinion Research, January 2–5, 2004).

[34] *Time*/CNN/Harris Interactive Poll (Storrs, Conn.: Roper Center for Public Opinion Research, December 30, 2003–January 1, 2004).

[35] Nolan McCarty, Keith T. Poole, and Howard Rosenthal, *Polarized America: The Dance of Ideology and Unequal Riches* (Cambridge, Mass.: MIT Press, 2006); Geoffrey C. Layman, Thomas M. Carsey, and Juliana Menasce Horowitz, "Party Polarization in American Politics: Characteristics, Causes, and Consequences," *Annual Review of Political Science* 9 (June 2006): 83–110.

[36] Blendon et al., "Mad Cow Disease."

[37] Ibid.

[38] Centers for Disease Control and Prevention, "West Nile Virus—Statistics, Surveillance, and Control," 2009, http://www.cdc.gov/ncidod/dvbid/westnile/surv&control.htm; D. Nash, F. Mostashari, A. Fine, J. Miller. D. O'Leary, K. Murray et al., "The Outbreak of West Nile Virus Infection in the New York City Area in 1999," *New England Journal of Medicine* 344 (June 14, 2001): 1807–14.

[39] It was isolated from a woman in the West Nile province of Uganda in Africa and thus bears the name "West Nile virus."

[40] Felissa R. Lashley, "West Nile Virus," in *Emerging Infectious Diseases*, ed. F. R. Lashley and J. D. Durham, 337; Centers for Disease Control and Prevention, "West Nile Virus—Background: Virus History and Distribution," 2004, http://www.cdc.gov/ncidod/dvbid/westnile/background .htm (accessed December 3, 2009).

[41] Lashley, "West Nile Virus," 337–338.

[42] Centers for Disease Control and Prevention, "West Nile Virus—What You Need to Know," 2006, http://www.cdc.gov/ncidod/dvbid/westnile/wnv_factsheet.htm; Lashley, "West Nile Virus," 339.

[43] Lashley, "West Nile Virus," 339–340.

[44] J. J. Sejvar, "The Long-term Outcomes of Human West Nile Virus Infection," *Clinical Infectious Diseases* 44 (June 15, 2007): 1617–24.

[45] Lashley, "West Nile Virus," 340.

[46] Centers for Disease Control and Prevention, "West Nile Virus—Vertebrate Ecology," 2009, http://www.cdc.gov/ncidod/dvbid/westnile/birds&mammals.htm.

[47] Centers for Disease Control and Prevention, "West Nile Virus—Statistics, Surveillance, and Control," 2008.

[48] Sandra Mullin, "New York City's Communication Trials by Fire, from West Nile to SARS," *Biosecurity and Bioterrorism* 1 (December 2003): 267–272.

[49] J. P. Roche, "Print Media Coverage of Risk-Risk Tradeoffs Associated with West Nile Encephalitis and Pesticide Spraying," *Journal of Urban Health* 79 (December 2002): 482–490.

[50] Centers for Disease Control and Prevention, "West Nile Virus—What You Need to Know," 2006.

[51] T. G. Osimitz and J. V. Murphy, "Neurological Effects Associated with Use of the Insect Repellent N,N-diethyl-m-toluamide (DEET)," *Journal of Toxicology: Clinical Toxicology* 35 (October 1997): 435–441.

[52] Daniel Yee, "West Nile: Finding Infected Birds Early in Season Likely Means Human Cases Later," Associated Press, March 18, 2003; Centers for Diseases Control and Prevention, "Epidemic/Epizootic West Nile Virus in the United States: Guidelines for Surveillance, Prevention and Control," 3rd revision, 2003, http://www.cdc.gov/ncidod/dvbid/westnile/ resources/wnv-guidelines-aug-2003.pdf.

[53] Kaiser Family Foundation polls (Storrs, Conn.: Roper Center for Public Opinion Research, October 10–13, 2002; October 3–5, 2003).

[54] Robert J. Blendon, John M. Benson, Catherine M. DesRoches, Melissa J. Herrmann, Elizabeth Mackie, and Kathleen J. Weldon, "West Nile Virus," *Working Papers of the Project on the Public and Biological Security, Harvard School of Public Health* 6, January 13, 2003, http:// www.hsph.harvard.edu/research/horp/files/WP6WestNile.pdf.

55 For 2002 and 2003, Robert J. Blendon, John M. Benson, Catherine M. DesRoches, Melissa J. Herrmann, and Kathleen J. Weldon, "West Nile Virus II," *Working Papers of the Project on the Public and Biological Security, Harvard School of Public Health* 12, July 31, 2003, http://www.hsph.harvard.edu/research/horp/files/WP12WestNileII.pdf; for 2004, Robert J. Blendon, John M. Benson, Catherine M. DesRoches, Melissa J. Herrmann, and Kathleen J. Weldon, "West Nile Virus III," *Working Papers of the Project on the Public and Biological Security, Harvard School of Public Health* 16, September 15, 2004, http://www.hsph.harvard.edu/research/horp/files/WP16WestNileIII.pdf.

56 Blendon et al., "West Nile Virus II." In this survey, people were defined as residents of high-mosquito areas if they said that where they live there are a lot of mosquitoes around during the summer.

57 Ibid.

58 Blendon et al., "West Nile Virus III."

59 World Health Organization, "Summary of Probable SARS Cases with Onset of Illness from 1 November 2002 to 31 July 2003," 2003, http://www.who.int/csr/sars/country/table2004_04_21/en/index.html.

60 Fang Li, "Structural Analysis of Major Species Barriers Between Humans and Palm Civets for SARS Coronavirus Infections," *Journal of Virology* 82 (July 2008): 6984–91; Y. Guan, B. J. Zheng, Y. Q. He, X. L. Liu, Z. X. Zhuang, C. L. Cheung et al., "Isolation and Characterization of Viruses Related to the SARS Coronavirus from Animals in Southern China," *Science* 302 (October 10, 2003): 276–278.

61 Centers for Disease Control and Prevention, "Severe Acute Respiratory Syndrome—Fact Sheet: Basic Information about SARS," January 13, 2004, http://www.cdc.gov/ncidod/sars/pdf/factsheet.pdf.

62 Bart L. Haagmans and Albert D. M. E. Osterhaus, "SARS: From Zoonosis to Pandemic Threat," in *Emerging Infectious Diseases,* 326.

643 Centers for Disease Control and Prevention, "Severe Acute Respiratory Syndrome—Fact Sheet: Basic Information about SARS," January 13, 2004.

64 Haagmans and Osterhaus, "SARS: From Zoonosis to Pandemic Threat," 326.

65 Centers for Disease Control and Prevention, "Severe Acute Respiratory Syndrome."

66 Haagmans and Osterhaus, "SARS: From Zoonosis to Pandemic Threat," 327.

67 M. A. J. McKenna, "Super-spreaders Fan SARS Fears; Scientists Probe Why Some Infect So Many," *Atlanta Journal-Constitution,* April 27, 2003, 1A.

68 "Update: Severe Acute Respiratory Syndrome—Toronto, Canada, 2003," *MMWR [Morbidity and Mortality Weekly Report]* 52 (June 13, 2003): 547–550, http://www.cdc.gov/mmwr/preview/mmwrhtml/mm5223a4.htm.

69 "Update: Severe Acute Respiratory Syndrome—Worldwide and United States, 2003," *MMWR [Morbidity and Mortality Weekly Report]* 52 (July 18, 2003): 664–655, http://www.cdc.gov/mmwr/preview/mmwrhtml/mm5228a4.htm.

70 DeNeen L. Brown, "Canadians Say Guard Lowered Too Quickly; Resurgence of SARS in Toronto Spurs Call for Voluntary Quarantine of 3,400," *Washington Post,* May 28, 2003, A15; Suzanne Bohan, "President Authorizes Quarantine for SARS Illness," *Alameda Times-Star* (Alameda, Calif.), April 5, 2003, Headline News.

71 William Foreman, "Fasten Your Seat Belts, Slip on Your Surgical Mask: Flying the SARS Route," Associated Press, April 18, 2003; "Georgia Reports First Case of SARS," Associated Press, April 1, 2003.

[72] Iris Chang, "Fear of SARS, Fear of Strangers," *New York Times,* May 21, 2003, A2.

[73] Jennifer Lee, Dean E. Murphy, and Yilu Zhao, "The SARS Epidemic: Asian-Americans; In U.S., Fear Is Spreading Faster than SARS," *New York Times,* April 17, 2003, A1; Bobbie Person, Francisco Sy, Kelly Holton, Barbara Govert, Arthur Liang, and the NCID/SARS Emergency Outreach Team, "Fear and Stigma: The Epidemic within the SARS Outbreak," *Emerging Infectious Disease*s 10 (February 2004): 358–363, http://www.cdc.gov/ncidod/ EID/vol10no2/03–0750.htm; Angie Chuang, "Asian Americans Fight SARS Rumors," *The Oregonian,* May 8, 2003, C03.

[74] Robert J. Blendon, John M. Benson, Catherine M. DesRoches, Melissa J. Herrmann, Elizabeth Mackie, and Kathleen J. Weldon, "Americans' Response to SARS (I)," *Working Papers of the Project on the Public and Biological Security, Harvard School of Public Health* 9, April 29, 2003, http://www.hsph.harvard.edu/research/horp/files/WP9SARSUS1.pdf.

[75] Kaiser Family Foundation Poll, June 5–8, 2003.

[76] Robert J. Blendon, John M. Benson, Catherine M. DesRoches, Melissa J. Herrmann, Elizabeth Mackie, and Kathleen J. Weldon, "SARS (II)," *Working Papers of the Project on the Public and Biological Security, Harvard School of Public Health* 10, May 21, 2003, http://www.hsph .harvard.edu/research/horp/files/WP10SARSUS2.pdf.

[77] NPR, "SARS Timeline," 2003, http://www.npr.org/news/specials/sars/timeline.html.

[78] Robert J. Blendon, John M. Benson, Catherine M. DesRoches, Elizabeth Raleigh, and Kalahn Taylor-Clark, "The Public's Response to Severe Acute Respiratory Syndrome in Toronto and the United States," *Clinical Infectious Diseases* 38 (April 1, 2004): 925–931.

[79] Blendon et al., "SARS (II)."

[80] Ibid.

[81] Ibid.

[82] Ibid.

[83] Blendon et al., "The Public's Response to Severe Acute Respiratory Syndrome."

[84] Blendon et al., "SARS (II)."

[85] Ibid.

[86] Robert J. Blendon, John M. Benson, Catherine M. DesRoches, Melissa J. Herrmann, Elizabeth Raleigh, and Kathleen J. Weldon, "Airline Contagious Diseases," *Working Papers of the Project on the Public and Biological Security, Harvard School of Public Health* 15, July 19, 2004, http:// www.hsph.harvard.edu/research/horp/files/WP15AirlineContDis.pdf.

[87] Centers for Disease Control and Prevention, "Bioterrorism Overview," 2007, http://www .bt.cdc.gov/bioterrorism/overview.asp.

[88] G. W. Christopher, T. J. Cieslak, J. A. Pavlin, and E. M. Eitzen Jr., "Biological Warfare: A Historical Perspective," *JAMA: Journal of the American Medical Association* 278 (August 6, 1997): 412–417.

[89] Nancy Khardori, "Potential Agents of Bioterrorism: Historical Perspective and Overview," in *Bioterrorism Preparedness,* ed. Nancy Khardori (Weinham, Germany: Wiley-Vach, 2006), Chapter 1.

[90] J. B. Tucker, "Historical Trends Related to Bioterrorism: An Empirical Analysis," *Emerging Infectious Diseases* 5 (July-August 1999): 498–504.

[91] Miriam Cohen, "Bioterrorism in the Context of Infectious Diseases," in *Emerging Infectious Diseases,* ed. Lashley and Durham, 416; Elizabeth Sullivan, "Expect More Attacks, U.S. Experts Warn; Biggest Nightmare of Defense Planners Now Has Come True," *Plain Dealer* (Cleveland, Ohio), September 12, 2001, A8.

[92] Helen Kennedy, Richard Sisk, Ken Bazinet, and Tim Burger, "Disaster, Then an Eerie Silence in Washington; Pentagon Target in Attack," *Daily News*, September 12, 2001, 14; "HHS Orders Medical Emergency Plan," Associated Press, September 11, 2001.

[93] Rick Weiss, "Second Anthrax Case Found in Fla.; Victim's Co-Worker Infected; FBI Launches Massive Probe as Va. Monitors a Third Man," *Washington Post*, October 9, 2001, A1; Jim Yardley and Dana Canedy, "A Nation Challenged: The Anthrax Investigation; Anxiety Grows in South Florida as Mystery of Anthrax Cases Lingers," *New York Times*, October 12, 2001, B1.

[94] Cohen, "Bioterrorism in the Context of Infectious Diseases," 427.

[95] Ibid., 416.

[96] Centers for Disease Control and Prevention, "Anthrax: What You Need to Know," 2006, http://www.bt.cdc.gov/agent/anthrax/needtoknow.asp.

[97] Centers for Disease Control and Prevention, "Anthrax—Frequently Asked Questions," 2008, http://www.cdc.gov/nczved/dfbmd/disease_listing/anthrax_gi.html; Christopher Lee, "Mandatory Anthrax Shots to Return," *Washington Post*, October 17, 2006, A3.

[98] Centers for Disease Control and Prevention, "Bioterrorism Agents/Diseases," http://www.bt.cdc.gov/agent/agentlist-category.asp#catdef.

[99] Scott Shane and Eric Lichtblau, "F.B.I. Presents Anthrax Case, Saying Scientist Acted Alone," *New York Times*, August 7, 2008, A1.

[100] Scott L. Althaus, "American News Consumption during Times of Crisis," *PS: Political Science and Politics* 35 (September 2002): 517–521.

[101] Joby Warrick and Steve Fainaru, "Bioterrorism Preparations Lacking at Lowest Levels; Despite Warnings and Funds, Local Defenses Come Up Short," *Washington Post*, October 22, 2001, A7; Eric Lipton and Kirk Johnson, "A Nation Challenged: The Anthrax Trail; Tracking Bioterror's Tangled Course," *New York Times*, December 26, 2001, A1.

[102] Tamar Lewin, "A Nation Challenged: The Hoaxes; Suspect Named in Fake Anthrax Mailings to Abortion Clinics," *New York Times*, November 30, 2001, B3; Marie McCullough, "Anthrax Hoaxes Hard to Fight; With Few Outbreaks but Many Scares, the Risks Are Too Great to Ignore," *Philadelphia Inquirer*, November 3, 2001, A1.

[103] Peter Slevin, "For a Country Already on Edge, Added Anxiety; Anthrax Scare Underscores Vulnerability," *Washington Post*, November 4, 2001, A8; Stuart Elliott, "The Media Business: Advertising; With Consumers Concerned about Unexpected Mail, Direct Marketers Will Try New Approaches," *New York Times*, October 16, 2001, C3.

[104] Kaiser Family Foundation/Harvard School of Public Health Poll (Storrs, Conn.: Roper Center for Public Opinion Research, November 29–December 2, 2001).

[105] Kaiser Family Foundation/Harvard School of Public Health Poll (Storrs, Conn.: Roper Center for Public Opinion Research, January 31–February 3, 2002).

[106] Kaiser Family Foundation/Harvard School of Public Health Poll, November 29–December 2, 2001.

[107] Robert J. Blendon, John M. Benson, Catherine M. DesRoches, William E. Pollard, Claudia Parvanta, and Melissa J. Herrmann, "The Impact of Anthrax Attacks on the American Public," *Medscape General Medicine* 4 (April 17, 2002), http://www.medscape.com/viewarticle/430197.

[108] NPR/Kaiser Family Foundation/Kennedy School of Government Poll (Storrs, Conn.: Roper Center for Public Opinion Research, October 31–November 12, 2001).

[109] ABC News/*Washington Post* Poll (Storrs, Conn.: Roper Center for Public Opinion Research, October 15, 2001).

[110] Blendon et al., "The Impact of Anthrax Attacks on the American Public."

[111] *Time*/CNN/Harris Interactive Poll (Storrs, Conn.: Roper Center for Public Opinion Research, October 12, 2001).

[112] Blendon et al., "The Impact of Anthrax Attacks on the American Public."

[113] CBS News/*New York Times* Poll (Storrs, Conn.: Roper Center for Public Opinion Research, October 25–28, 2001) (50 percent); CBS News poll (Storrs, Conn.: Roper Center for Public Opinion Research, November 13–14, 2001) (55 percent).

[114] *Newsweek*/Princeton Survey Research Associates Poll (Storrs, Conn.: Roper Center for Public Opinion Research, October 25–26, 2001).

[115] Gallup/CNN/USA Today Poll (Storrs, Conn.: Roper Center for Public Opinion Research, November 2–4, 2001).

[116] *Time*/CNN/Harris Interactive Poll, October 12, 2001.

[117] Centers for Disease Control and Prevention, "Smallpox Disease Overview," 2007, http://www.bt.cdc.gov/agent/smallpox/overview/disease-facts.asp.

[118] Link, *The Vaccine Controversy*, 45.

[119] Ibid.

[120] Centers for Disease Control and Prevention, "Smallpox Disease Overview," 2007.

[121] World Health Organization, "Smallpox," http://www.who.int/mediacentre/factsheets/smallpox/en.

[122] R. E. Eckart, S. S. Love, J. E. Atwood, M. K. Arness, D. C. Cassimatis, C. L. Campbell et al., "Incidence and Follow-up of Inflammatory Cardiac Complications after Smallpox Vaccination," *Journal of the American College of Cardiology* 44 (July 7, 2004): 201–205; Centers for Disease Control and Prevention, "Smallpox Fact Sheet—Vaccine Overview," 2007, http://www.bt.cdc.gov/agent/smallpox/vaccination/facts.asp; J. Neff, J. Modlin, G. D. Birkhead, G. Poland, R. M. Robertson, K. Sepkowitz et al., "Monitoring the Safety of a Smallpox Vaccination Program in the United States: Report of the Joint Smallpox Vaccine Safety Working Group of the Advisory Committee on Immunization Practices and the Armed Forces Epidemiological Board," *Clinical Infectious Diseases* 46 (March 15, 2008): S258–270.

[123] J. M. Neff, J. M. Lane, V. A. Fulginiti, and D. A. Henderson, "Contact Vaccinia—Transmission of Vaccinia from Smallpox Vaccination," *JAMA* 288 (October 16, 2002): 1901–5.

[124] Richard W. Stevenson and Sheryl Gay Stolberg, "Threats and Response: Vaccinations; Bush Lays Out Plan on Smallpox Shots; Military Is First," *New York Times*, December 14, 2002, A1.

[125] Jeffrey Gettleman, "Threats and Responses: Biological Defenses; Two Hospitals Refuse to Join Bush's Plan for Smallpox," *New York Times*, December 19, 2002, A19.

[126] M. K. Wynia, "Risk and Trust in Public Health: A Cautionary Tale," *American Journal of Bioethics* 6 (March/April 2006): 3–6.

[127] Mary Leonard, "Fighting Terror Legislative Moves: Posse Comitatus Act; Officials Talk of Using Military at Home, Despite Doubts," *Boston Globe*, October 31, 2001, A10; "Proposal Would Strengthen Laws for Health Emergencies," *St. Petersburg Times*, October 31, 2001, 12A.

[128] Kaiser Family Foundation/Harvard School of Public Health Poll, November 29–December 2, 2001.

[129] Kaiser Family Foundation/Harvard School of Public Health Poll, October 10–13, 2002.

[130] Robert J. Blendon, Catherine M. DesRoches, John M. Benson, Melissa J. Herrmann, Kalahn Taylor-Clark, and Kathleen J. Weldon, "The Public and the Smallpox Threat," *New England Journal of Medicine* 348 (January 30, 2003): 426–432.

[131] Centers for Disease Control and Prevention, "Smallpox Disease Overview," 2007.

[132] Blendon et al., "The Public and the Smallpox Threat."

[133] Ibid.

[134] Blendon et al., "SARS (II)."

[135] Blendon et al., "The Public and the Smallpox Threat."

[136] Blendon et al., "SARS (II)."

[137] Blendon et al., "The Public and the Smallpox Threat."

[138] Ibid.

[139] Ibid.

[140] CBS News/*New York Times* Poll, October 25–28, 2001.

[141] Gallup/CNN/*USA Today* Poll (Storrs, Conn.: Roper Center for Public Opinion Research, October 19–21, 2001).

[142] Blendon et al., "The Public and the Smallpox Threat."

[143] Robert J. Blendon, John M. Benson, Catherine M. DesRoches, Melissa J. Herrmann, Kalahn Taylor-Clark, and Kathleen J. Weldon, "Public Attitudes, Beliefs and Knowledge about Smallpox," *Working Papers of the Project on the Public and Biological Security, Harvard School of Public Health 5*, December 19, 2002, http://www.hsph.harvard.edu/research/horp/files/WP5Smallpox.pdf.

[144] Blendon et al., "The Public and the Smallpox Threat."

[145] Ibid.

[146] Ibid.

[147] Blendon et al., "Public Attitudes, Beliefs and Knowledge about Smallpox."

[148] Ibid. See also: Kalahn Taylor-Clark, Robert J. Blendon, Alan Zaslavsky, and John M. Benson, "Confidence in Crisis? Understanding Trust in Government and Public Attitudes Toward Mandatory State Health Powers," *Biosecurity and Bioterrorism* 3 (June 2005): 138–147.

[149] Graber, *Mass Media and American Politics*, Chapter 4; Shirley S. Ho, Dominique Brossard, and Dietram A. Scheufele, "The Polls—Trends: Public Reactions to Global Health Threats and Infectious Diseases," *Public Opinion Quarterly* 71 (Winter 2007): 671–692.

[150] Benjamin I. Page and Robert Y. Shapiro, *The Rational Public: Fifty Years of Trends in Americans' Policy Preferences* (Chicago: University of Chicago Press, 1992).

[151] V. T. Covello, R. G. Peters, J. G. Wojtecki, and R. C. Hyde, "Risk Communication, the West Nile Virus Epidemic, and Bioterrorism," *Journal of Urban Health* 78 (June 2001): 382–391.

[152] Karen Glanz, Frances Marcus, Barbara K. Rimer, eds., *Health Behavior and Health Education: Theory Research, and Practice*, 2nd ed. (San Francisco: Jossey-Bass, 1997).

[153] Kate MacArthur, "Avian-flu Scare Will Have Negative Effect on Poultry Biz," *Advertising Age* 76 (November 14, 2005): 4.

[154] Robert J. Blendon, Catherine M. DesRoches, Martin S. Cetron, John M. Benson, Theodore Meinhardt, and William Pollard, "Attitudes toward the Use of Quarantine in a Public Health Emergency in Four Countries," *Health Affairs* 25 (Web exclusive, January 24 2006): W15–W25.

[155] Joseph S. Nye Jr., Philip D. Zelikow, and David C. King, eds., *Why People Don't Trust Government* (Cambridge: Harvard University Press, 1997); Seymour Martin Lipset and William Schneider, *The Confidence Gap: Business, Labor and Government in the Public Mind* (New York: Free Press, 1983).

[156] Minah Kim, Robert J. Blendon, and John M. Benson, "How Interested Are Americans in New Medical Technologies? A Multicountry Comparison," *Health Affairs* 20 (September/October 2001): 194–201.

[157] Roper Report Poll (Storrs, Conn.: Roper Center for Public Opinion Research, August 28–September 4, 1976).

[158] Harris Poll (Storrs, Conn.: Roper Center for Public Opinion Research, February 1–7, 1977).

Table 15-1 Public Attitudes about Mad Cow Disease: Engagement, Concern, and Assessment of Risk, 2003–2004 (in percent)

	Very closely	Somewhat closely	Not too closely	Not at all
Following news reports about mad cow disease in the U.S.[1]	22	45	21	11

Mad cow disease in the U.S. has been found . . .[1]				
Only in cattle	66			
In both cattle and people	26			
Only people	1			

You or someone in your family becoming infected with mad cow disease in next 12 months[1]	Concerned	Not concerned
Concerned you might	18	81

	Very/somewhat likely	Not very/not at all likely
Likelihood you will	9	90

	Crisis	Major problem	Minor problem	Not a problem
How much of a problem mad cow disease is in the U.S.[2]	6	28	53	12

Safety of . . .[3]	Safe	Unsafe
The national beef supply	66	27
The beef in your local stores	74	18

Note: "Don't know" responses not shown.

Question: How closely have you been following news reports about mad cow disease in the United States? Would you say you have been following them very closely, somewhat closely, not too closely, or not at all?

Question: In the United States, to the best of your knowledge, has mad cow disease been found only in cattle, only in people, or in both cattle and people?

Question: Are you concerned that you or someone in your immediate family may become infected with mad cow disease during the next 12 months?

Question: I'm going to read you a list of things and ask you how likely it is that each of them will happen to you or someone in your immediate family during the next 12 months. How about becoming infected with mad cow disease? Do you think that is very likely to happen to you or someone in your immediate family, somewhat likely, not very likely, or not at all likely?

Question: Which of these statements do you think best describes the state of mad cow disease in the United States? . . . It is a crisis, it is a major problem for the country but is not a crisis, it is a minor problem for the country, or it is not a problem for the country at all?

Question: As you may know, last week a cow, which had been slaughtered, was discovered with mad cow disease. As a result of this discovery, do you think the nation's beef supply is safe or unsafe?

Question: Do you think the beef in your local store is safe or unsafe from mad cow disease?

Sources: [1]Blendon et al., "Mad Cow Disease," *Working Papers of the Project on the Public and Biological Security, Harvard School of Public Health* 14, February 2, 2004. [2]Gallup/CNN/*USA Today* Poll (Storrs, Conn.: Roper Center for Public Opinion Research, January 2–5, 2004). [3]*Time*/CNN/Harris Interactive Poll (Storrs, Conn.: Roper Center for Public Opinion Research, December 30, 2003–January 1, 2004).

Table 15-2 Public Attitudes about Mad Cow Disease: Actions, Policies, and Policymakers, 2004 (in percent)

In response to reports about mad cow disease in the U.S., you or someone in your family has . . .			Yes
Stopped ordering beef at fast-food restaurants			16
Stopped ordering beef in other restaurants			13
Stopped buying beef at the grocery store			14
Stopped eating hamburger or ground beef			13
Stopped eating beef altogether			7
Started buying and eating only organic or grass-fed beef			4
Done one or more of these			22

	Great deal	Good amount	Only some	Very little
Confidence in meat inspection system in the U.S. to protect Americans from mad cow disease	19	37	26	15

Who should be mainly responsible for preventing the spread of mad cow disease in the U.S.

	Yes
Producers of cattle feed	33
Federal government	31
Beef industry	29

Note: "Don't know" responses not shown.

Question: In response to reports about mad cow disease in the United States, have you or has someone in your family done any of the following? Have you (stopped ordering beef at fast-food restaurants/stopped ordering beef at other restaurants/stopped buying beef at the grocery store/stopped eating hamburger or ground beef/stopped eating beef completely/started buying and eating only organic or grass-fed beef)?

Question: How much confidence do you have in the meat inspection system in the United States to protect Americans from becoming infected by mad cow disease? A great deal of confidence, a good amount, only some, or very little?

Question: Which one of the following do you think should be mainly responsible for preventing the spread of mad cow disease in the United States? Producers of the food that cattle eat, the federal government, or the American beef industry?

Source: Blendon et al., "Mad Cow Disease," *Working Papers of the Project on the Public and Biological Security, Harvard School of Public Health* 14, February 2, 2004.

Table 15-3 Public Attitudes about West Nile Virus: Engagement, Concern, and Assessment of Risk, 2002–2004 (in percent)

	Very closely	Fairly closely	Not too closely	Not at all
Following news reports about West Nile virus[1]*				
2002	43	36	13	7
2003	26	35	21	18

	Yes	No	Don't know
Can you contract West Nile virus in the following ways (2002)[2]			
Mosquito bites	92	6	3
Blood transfusion	72	18	9
Organ transplants	56	30	14
Contact with dead birds	53	34	13
Drinking infected water	50	39	12
Being in the same room as someone who has active case of West Nile virus	12	77	11
Shaking hands with someone who has active case of West Nile virus	11	80	9

Concern about you or someone in your immediate family getting sick from West Nile virus in the next X months	Concerned
2002 (next 12 months)[2]	32
2003 (next 12 months) total[3]	32
High-mosquito–area residents	48
2004 (next 3 months)[4]	36

Note: *"Don't know" responses not shown.

Question: I'm going to read you a list of some stories covered by news organizations in the last month or so. As I read each one, tell me if you happened to follow this news story very closely, fairly closely, not too closely, or not at all closely. How closely did you follow this story? . . . The West Nile virus spreading in the United States (2002)/New cases of West Nile virus in the United States (2003).

Question: I'm going to read you a list of some ways people can get a disease. As I read each one, please tell me whether or not you think you can contract the West Nile virus that way. How about (mosquito bites/blood transfusions/organ transplants/contact with dead birds/drinking infected water/being in the same room with someone who has an active case of the West Nile virus/shaking hands with someone who has an active case of the West Nile virus). To the best of your knowledge, can you contract the West Nile virus that way, or not?

Question: Are you concerned that you or someone in your immediate family may get sick from the West Nile virus during the next 12 months, or aren't you concerned about that? (2002, 2003)

Question: Are you concerned that you or someone in your immediate family may get sick from the West Nile virus during the next 3 months, or aren't you concerned about that? (2004)

Sources: [1]Kaiser Family Foundation polls (Storrs, Conn.: Roper Center for Public Opinion Research, October 10–13, 2002; October 3–5, 2003). [2]Blendon et al., "West Nile Virus," *Working Papers of the Project on the Public and Biological Security, Harvard School of Public Health* 6, January 13, 2003. [3]Blendon et al., "West Nile Virus II," *Working Papers of the Project on the Public and Biological Security, Harvard School of Public Health* 12, July 31, 2003. [4]Blendon et al., "West Nile Virus III," *Working Papers of the Project on the Public and Biological Security, Harvard School of Public Health* 16, September 15, 2004.

Table 15-4 Public Attitudes about West Nile Virus: Actions, Policies, and Policymakers, 2003–2004 (in percent)

Since the beginning of June, things you did to avoid getting mosquito bites (responses of people living in high-mosquito areas) (2003)[1]	Took this precaution
Took any precaution	62
Used mosquito repellent containing DEET	46
Used mosquito repellent containing citronella	32
Used some other kind of mosquito repellent	13
Removed standing water from spare tires, gutters, bird baths, kiddie pools, or other places water collects	44
Avoided going outside during the peak mosquito hours of dawn and dusk	40
Wore long-sleeved shirts or other protective clothing outdoors	30
Replaced or repaired window screens	20
Used "bug zapper" in your yard	11
Bought mosquito netting	4
Special spraying against mosquitos (2004)[2]	
Approve of ground spraying to control spread of West Nile	
Among those in areas ground sprayed	90
Among those in areas not ground sprayed	76
Approve of air spraying to control spread of West Nile	
Among those in areas air sprayed	77
Among those in areas not air sprayed	58

Question: Since the beginning of June have you taken any precautions to avoid getting mosquito bites, or not?

Question: Since the beginning of June, have you used any of the following types of mosquito repellents? (Off, Cutter, or some other mosquito repellent containing DEET/Skin-So-Soft, or some other mosquito repellent containing citronella/some other kind of mosquito repellent)

Question: Since the beginning of June, have you done any of the following things to avoid getting mosquito bites? (Removed standing water from spare tires, gutters, bird baths, kiddie pools, or other places where water collects/avoided activities or areas that would bring you in contact with mosquitoes/avoided going outside during the peak mosquito hours of dawn or dusk/worn long-sleeved shirts or other protective clothing outdoors/replaced or repaired window screens/used a "bug zapper" in your yard/worn clothing that was treated with mosquito repellent before you bought it)

Question: In the area where you live, has there been any special spraying against mosquitoes to prevent the spread of the West Nile virus, or hasn't there been any special spraying? (If live in an area where there has been special spraying) Was the spraying done at ground level or from the air or both? (If live in an area where there has been special spraying at ground level) Do you approve or disapprove of this spraying done at ground level? (If live in an area where there has been special spraying from the air) Do you approve or disapprove of this spraying done from the air? (If live in an area where there has been no special spraying at ground level) What if special spraying at ground level to prevent the spread of West Nile did happen in your area? Would you approve or disapprove? (If live in an area where there has been no special spraying from the air) What if special spraying from the air to prevent the spread of West Nile did happen in your area? Would you approve or disapprove?

Sources: [1]Blendon et al., "West Nile Virus II," Working Papers of the Project on the Public and Biological Security, Harvard School of Public Health 12, July 31, 2003. [2]Blendon et al., "West Nile Virus III," Working Papers of the Project on the Public and Biological Security, Harvard School of Public Health 16, September 15, 2004.

Table 15-5 Public Attitudes about SARS: Engagement, Concern, and Assessment of Risk, 2003 (in percent)

	Very closely	Fairly closely	Not too closely	Not at all
Following news reports about outbreak of SARS in Asia and Canada[1]	42	35	13	9

		Yes	No	Don't know
Is SARS contagious[2]		89	3	8

Can you contract SARS in the following ways?[2]	Yes	No	Don't know
Being in close contact with someone who has SARS	88	7	5
Being on the same airplane as someone who has SARS	76	17	6
Shaking hands with someone who has an active case of SARS	70	23	7
Eating food prepared by someone infected with or exposed to SARS	66	24	11
Touching objects or surfaces that have been in contact with someone who has SARS	64	28	8
Blood transfusions	58	29	12
Eating undercooked chicken	14	74	12

	Yes	No	Don't know
Vaccine for SARS exists[3]	4	88	8
SARS requires quarantine[3]	84	9	7
Treatment for SARS exists[3]	36	47	17

You or someone in your immediate family getting sick from SARS in the next 12 months[2]

Concern that you might	Concerned	Not concerned
April 2003	32	68
May 2003	26	72

Likelihood you will	Very/somewhat likely	Not very/not at all likely
April 2003	25	73
May 2003	16	81

Note: Except for knowledge questions, "Don't know" responses not shown.

Question: Now I'm going to read you a list of some stories covered by news organizations in the last month or so. As I read each one, tell me if you happened to follow this news story very closely, fairly closely, not too closely, or not at all closely. How closely did you follow this story? . . . Outbreaks of severe acute respiratory syndrome, also known as SARS, in Asia and Canada.

Question: To the best of your knowledge, is SARS, the new form of flu from Asia, a disease that is contagious, meaning that it can be passed from one person to another, or is it not contagious?

Question: I'm going to read you a list of some ways people can get a disease. As I read each one, please tell me whether or not you think it is possible to contract SARS that way. How about (being in close contact with someone who has SARS/being on the same airplane with someone who has SARS/shaking hands with someone who has an active case of SARS/eating food that has been prepared by someone who was infected with or had been exposed to SARS/touching objects or surfaces that have been in contact with someone who has SARS/blood transfusions/eating undercooked chicken)? To the best of your knowledge, is it possible to contract SARS that way, or not?

Question: To the best of your knowledge, is there a vaccine against SARS, or isn't there one?

Question: Some contagious diseases require people who have been exposed to the disease to be quarantined in order to keep the disease from spreading. To the best of your knowledge, is SARS one of the diseases where people who are exposed need to be quarantined, or isn't it?

Question: To the best of your knowledge, is there an effective treatment for people who have contracted SARS, or doesn't such a treatment exist?

Question: Are you concerned that you or someone in your immediate family may get sick from SARS during the next 12 months, or aren't you concerned about that?

Question: I'm going to read you a list of things and ask you how likely it is that each of them will happen to you or someone in your immediate family during the next 12 months. How about contracting SARS, the new form of flu from Asia? Do you think that is very likely to happen to you or someone in your immediate family, somewhat likely, not very likely, or not at all likely?

Sources: [1]Kaiser Family Foundation Poll (Storrs, Conn.: Roper Center for Public Opinion Research, June 5–8, 2003). [2]Blendon et al., "SARS (II)," *Working Papers of the Project on the Public and Biological Security, Harvard School of Public Health* 10, May 21, 2003. [3]Blendon et al., "The Public's Response to Severe Acute Respiratory Syndrome in Toronto and the United States," *Clinical Infectious Diseases* 38 (April 1, 2004): 925–931.

Table 15-6 Public Attitudes about SARS: Actions, Policies, and Policymakers, 2003 (in percent)

In response to reports of SARS, you or someone in your household has . . .[1]	Percent saying yes	
	April 2003	May 2003
Used disinfectant at home or work	21	16
Avoided people who may have recently traveled to Asia	16	11
Avoided Asian restaurants or stores	14	9
Avoided public events	10	7
Carried something to clean objects that may have had contact with someone with SARS	9	6
Talked with a doctor about health issues related to SARS	5	6
Purchased a face mask	3	3
Avoided international travel (among those who traveled outside the U.S. in the past 12 months)	NA	9
Avoided travel to Canada (among those who traveled outside the U.S. in the past 12 months)	NA	5
Quarantine and Isolation	Yes	
Would agree to be isolated in health care facility for 2–3 weeks to prevent spreading the disease[2]	95	
If you were exposed to someone who had SARS and didn't know if you had the dieseases, would agree to be quarantined with families for up to 10 days[2]	93	
Quarantine for SARS does not threaten personal rights for freedoms[1]	83	

Question: In response to reports of SARS, have you or has someone in your household done any of the following? (Used a disinfectant at home or work to protect against SARS/avoided people you think may have recently visited Asia/avoided Asian restaurants or stores/avoided public events/carried something to clean any objects you think might have come into contact with someone who has SARS/talked with your doctor about health issues related to SARS/purchased a face mask/avoided international air travel, that is airline travel outside the United States [among those who have traveled outside the US in the last 12 months]/avoided travel to Canada [among those who have traveled to Canada in the last 12 months])

Question: If you had SARS and health officials told you that you needed to be isolated for two or three weeks in a health care facility to prevent spreading the disease, would you agree to go, or wouldn't you?

Question: Suppose you were exposed to someone who has SARS but you didn't know if you had the disease or not. If health officials told you that you and your family needed to be quarantined in your home for up to ten days away from other people in order to prevent spreading the disease, would you agree to do that, or wouldn't you?

Question: Recently President Bush signed an executive order adding SARS to the list of diseases for which people can be quarantined. Do you think this order threatens or does not threaten your personal rights and freedoms?

Source: [1]Blendon et al., "SARS (II)," *Working Papers of the Project on the Public and Biological Security, Harvard School of Public Health* 10, May 21, 2003. [2]Blendon et al., "The Public's Response to Severe Acute Respiratory Syndrome in Toronto and the United States," *Clinical Infectious Diseases* 38 (April 1, 2004): 925–931.

Table 15-7 Public Attitudes about Anthrax: Engagement, Concern, and Assessment of Risk, 2001 (in percent)

	Very closely	Somewhat closely	Not too/not at all closely
Following news stories about reports of anthrax cases around the country and the ongoing investigation[1]	50	33	17

	Yes	No	Don't know
Anthrax is contagious, meaning it can be passed from one person to another[1]	18	75	6
There is a treatment for those exposed to anthrax[1]	87	6	7

Worried that you could contract anthrax opening your mail at home or work[2]

National	24
Washington (D.C.) area	33
Trenton/Princeton (N.J.) area	39

Likelihood that you or someone in your household will contract anthrax in the next 12 months[2]

	Very/somewhat likely
National	9
Washington (DC) area	21
Trenton/Princeton (NJ) area	17

	Very likely	Somewhat likely	Somewhat unlikely/ not at all likely
Likelihood of more anthrax attacks in the next 12 months[3]	52	34	12

Initial reaction to cases of anthrax: think of them as . . .[4]

A few isolated cases limited to small number of people	45
First of an ongoing series that could affect large numbers of people	50

Note: Except for knowledge questions, "Don't know" responses not shown.

Question: I'm going to read you a list of some stories covered by news organizations in the last month or so. As I read each one, tell me if you happened to follow this news story very closely, fairly closely, not too closely, or not at all closely. How closely did you follow this story? . . . Reports of anthrax cases around the country and the ongoing investigation.

Question: From what you've seen or heard in the news, is anthrax a disease that is contagious, meaning that it can be passed from one person to another, or is it not contagious?

Question: Thinking about what you've heard in the news about treatments for anthrax, does a treatment exist for people who have been exposed to anthrax, or is there no treatment?

Question: As a result of recent incidents of anthrax in the mail, how worried are you that you could contract anthrax from opening your mail (at home/ at work)? Are you very worried, somewhat worried, not too worried, or not worried at all?

Question: I'm going to read you a list of things and ask you how likely it is that each of them will happen to you or someone in your immediate family during the next 12 months. How about contracting anthrax? Do you think that is very likely to happen to you or someone in your immediate family, somewhat likely, not very likely, or not at all likely?

Question: Please tell me how likely or unlikely you think it is that the following will occur in the next 12 months. . . . More anthrax attacks . . . is it very likely, somewhat likely, somewhat unlikely, or very unlikely to occur in the next 12 months?

Question: Given what you know about it, do you think of the anthrax situation as a few isolated cases limited to a small number of people, or as the first of an ongoing series of cases that could affect large numbers of people?

Sources: [1]Kaiser Family Foundation/Harvard School of Public Health Poll (Storrs, Conn.: Roper Center for Public Opinion Research, November 29–December 2, 2001). [2]Blendon et al., "The Impact of Anthrax Attacks on the American Public," *Medscape General Medicine* 4 (April 17, 2002). [3]NPR/Kaiser Family Foundation/Kennedy School of Government Poll (Storrs, Conn.: Roper Center for Public Opinion Research, October 31–November 12, 2001). [4]ABC News/*Washington Post* Poll (Storrs, Conn.: Roper Center for Public Opinion Research, October 15, 2001).

Table 15-8 Public Attitudes about Anthrax: Actions, Policies, and Policymakers, 2001 (in percent)

Currently taking precautions opening mail (wearing gloves, completely avoiding opening mail, or washing hands after opening mail)[1]			Yes
National			32
Washington (D.C.) area			37
Trenton/Princeton (N.J.) area			54

		Yes	No
Would take anthrax vaccine if available to you, even though it may produce negative side effects[2]		41	50

Government telling people everything they need to know about the anthrax attacks		Yes	No
October 2001[3]		47	50
November 2001[4]		40	55

Confidence in ability of U.S. government to . . .[5]	Very confident	Somewhat confident	Not too/not at all confident
Respond effectively to the health threats posed by anthrax	28	52	19
Prevent people from being exposed to anthrax	14	50	34

Note: "Don't know" responses not shown.

Question: Do you currently take the following precautions when opening the mail, or not? Do you (wear gloves when opening the mail/wash your hands after opening the mail)?

Question: As a result of recent incidents of anthrax in the mail, have you completely avoided opening your mail, or have you continued to open your mail?

Question: As you may know, a vaccine for anthrax exists but it may produce negative side effects. If such a vaccine were made available to you, would you take the vaccine as a precaution against a terrorist attack using anthrax or wouldn't you take such a vaccine?

Question: Do you think the government is telling people everything they need to know about the anthrax attacks, or not?

Question: How confident are you in the ability of the United States government to respond effectively to the health threats posed by a major outbreak of anthrax? Are you very confident, somewhat confident, not too confident, or not at all confident?

Question: How confident are you in the ability of the United States government to prevent additional people from being exposed to anthrax? Are you very confident, somewhat confident, not too confident, or not at all confident?

Sources: [1]Blendon et al., "The Impact of Anthrax Attacks on the American Public," *Medscape General Medicine* 4 (April 17, 2002). [2]*Time*/CNN/Harris Interactive Poll (Storrs, Conn.: Roper Center for Public Opinion Research, October 12, 2001). [3]CBS News/*New York Times* Poll (Storrs, Conn.: Roper Center for Public Opinion Research, October 25–28, 2001). [4]CBS News Poll (Storrs, Conn.: Roper Center for Public Opinion Research, November 13–14, 2001). [5]Gallup/CNN/*USA Today* Poll (Storrs, Conn.: Roper Center for Public Opinion Research, November 2–4, 2001).

Table 15-9 Public Attitudes about Smallpox: Engagement, Concern, and Assessment of Risk, 2001–2003 (in percent)

	Very closely	Fairly closely	Not too closely	Not at all closely
Following news stories about concerns with future bioterrorism involving smallpox (November–December 2001)[1]	34	31	19	14

(Table continues)

Table 15-9 *Continued*

Knowledge and beliefs[2]		Yes
Smallpox is contagious		89
If someone comes down with smallpox, there is a medical treatment that would prevent the person from dying or having other serious consequences		78
Any case of smallpox in U.S. in past 5 years		30
Any cases of smallpox anywhere else in the world in past 5 years		63
If a person has been exposed to smallpox, but doesn't have symptoms, getting a vaccination within a few days would prevent the person from coming down with the disease		42

Concern there will be a terrorist attack using smallpox in the U.S. during the next 12 months[3]	Concerned	Not concerned
October–December 2002	51	49
May 2003	28	70

Likelihood of you or someone in your immediate family contracting smallpox during next 12 months[3]	Very/somewhat likely	Not very/not at all likely
October 2001	9	88
December 2001	8	89
May 2002	8	91
October–December 2002	12	87
April 2003	12	86
May 2003	8	91

Note: "Don't know" responses not shown.

Question: I'm going to read you a list of some stories covered by news organizations in the last month or so. As I read each one, tell me if you happened to follow this news story very closely. Fairly closely, not too closely, or not at all closely. How closely did you follow this story? . . . Concerns about possible future bioterrorism involving smallpox.

Question: To the best of your knowledge, is smallpox a disease that is contagious, meaning that it can be passed from one person to another, or is it not contagious?

Question: To the best of your knowledge, if a person has been exposed to smallpox but doesn't have symptoms, would getting a vaccination within a few days prevent the person from coming down with the disease, or wouldn't a vaccination prevent it?

Question: To the best of your knowledge, have there been any cases of smallpox in the United States in the last five years or haven't there been any cases?

Question: To the best of your knowledge, have there been any cases of smallpox anywhere else in the world in the last five years or haven't there been any cases?

Question: To the best of your knowledge, if someone comes down with smallpox, is there a medical treatment that would prevent them from dying or having other serious consequences, or isn't there such a treatment?

Question: Are you concerned that there will be a terrorist attack using smallpox in the United States during the next 12 months, or aren't you concerned about that?

Question: I'm going to read you a list of things and ask you how likely it is that each of them will happen to you or someone in your immediate family during the next 12 months. How about contracting smallpox? Do you think that is very likely to happen to you or someone in your immediate family, somewhat likely, not very likely, or not at all likely?

Sources: [1]Kaiser Family Foundation/Harvard School of Public Health Poll (Storrs, Conn.: Roper Center for Public Opinion Research, November 29–December 2, 2001). [2]Blendon et al., "The Public and the Smallpox Threat," *New England Journal of Medicine* 348 (January 30, 2003): 426–432. [3]Blendon et al., "SARS (II)," *Working Papers of the Project on the Public and Biological Security, Harvard School of Public Health* 10, May 21, 2003.

Table 15-10 Public Attitudes about Smallpox: Actions, Policies, and Policymakers, 2001–2003 (in percent)

	Yes
If smallpox vaccine were made available, would get vaccinated (re-vaccinated) as a precaution against terrorist attack (with mention of serious side effects of vaccine in small number of cases)[1]	61
Would get vaccinated (re-vaccinated) if . . .[1]	
Cases were reported in the U.S.	75
Cases were reported in your community	88
Your doctor and most other doctors were getting vaccinated	73
Your doctor and many other doctors refused to get vaccinated	21
You heard some people died from the vaccine	33

(Table continues)

Table 15-10 *Continued*

Would stay in community or leave if . . .[1]	Stay	Leave
Cases of smallpox were reported in your community	67	32
Cases were reported and you thought you might have been exposed	91	7

	Very confident	Somewhat confident	Not too confident	Not at all confident
Confidence in ability of U.S. to respond effectively to the health threats posed by a major outbreak of smallpox[2]	27	39	22	10
Confident your doctor can recognize the symptoms of smallpox[1]	43	40	10	5

	Very prepared	Somewhat prepared	Not very prepared	Not at all prepared
How prepared your local hospital ER is to diagnose and treat people who have smallpox[3]	22	47	20	9

Availability of smallpox vaccinations[1]

Should be made available now on a voluntary basis to any American who wants it	65			
Should be given to the public only if there is an active outbreak in the U.S.	35			

	Would agree	Would not
If diagnosed with smallpox, would be willing to be isolated for 3–4 weeks in special health care facility with other people who have the disease[1]	77	22

Note: "Don't know" responses not shown.

Question: As you may know, a vaccine for smallpox exists, but it may produce serious side effects in a small number of cases. If such a vaccine were made available to you, would you go get (vaccinated/re-vaccinated) as a precaution against a terrorist attack using smallpox, or wouldn't you get such a vaccination?

Question: (Asked of those who said they would not get vaccinated/re-vaccinated) Here's a list of things that some people say might happen. After I read each one, please tell me if it would change your mind and make you want to be (vaccinated/re-vaccinated), or if you would still not want be (vaccinated/re-vaccinated) against smallpox. What if (cases of smallpox were reported in the United States/cases of smallpox were reported in your community/your doctor and most other doctors were getting vaccinated against smallpox)?

Question: (Asked of those who said they would get vaccinated/re-vaccinated) Here's a list of things that some people say might happen. After I read each one, please tell me if it would change your mind and make you not want to be (vaccinated/re-vaccinated), or if you would still want be (vaccinated/re-vaccinated) against smallpox. What if (your doctor and most other doctors were getting vaccinated against smallpox/your doctor and many other doctors refused to get vaccinated against smallpox because they believed the vaccine was too risky/you heard that some people who had gotten vaccinated had died from the vaccine)?

Question: If cases of smallpox were reported in your community, would you stay in your community, or would you leave and stay somewhere else until the outbreak was over? (If would leave) Suppose you thought you might have been exposed to smallpox. In that case, would you stay in your community, or would you still leave and stay somewhere else?

Question: How confident are you in the ability of the United States to respond effectively to the health threats posed by each of the following—are you very confident, somewhat confident, not too confident, or not at all confident? How about a major outbreak of smallpox?

Question: How confident are you that your doctor can recognize the symptoms of smallpox? Are you very confident, somewhat confident, not very confident, or not at all confident?

Question: How prepared do you think your local hospital emergency room is to diagnose and treat people who have smallpox? Very prepared, somewhat prepared, not very prepared, or not at all prepared?

Question: (Some/other) experts say that smallpox vaccinations should be given to the general public only if there is an actual case of smallpox in the United States. (Other/some) experts say that vaccinations should be made available now on a voluntary basis to any American who wants one. Which comes closer to your own view?

Question: If you were diagnosed with smallpox and health officials told you that you needed to be isolated for three or four weeks in a special health care facility with other people who have the disease, would you agree to go, or wouldn't you?

Sources: [1]Blendon et al., "The Public and the Smallpox Threat," *New England Journal of Medicine* 348 (January 30, 2003): 426–432. [2]Gallup/CNN/USA *Today* Poll (Storrs, Conn.: Roper Center for Public Opinion Research, October 19–21, 2001). [3]Blendon et al., "Public Attitudes, Beliefs and Knowledge about smallpox," *Working Papers of the Project on the Public and Biological Security, Harvard School of Public Health* 5, December 19, 2002.

Chapter 16

PANDEMIC INFLUENZA

Gillian K. SteelFisher, Robert J. Blendon, John M. Benson, and Kathleen J. Weldon

In the past 100 years, there have been four occurrences of a pandemic influenza, or flu. The most devastating of these was the flu of 1918–1919, which caused more than 500,000 deaths in the United States and tens of millions deaths worldwide.[1] The flu of 1957–1958 caused roughly 70,000 U.S. deaths, and the flu of 1968–1969 caused about 34,000 U.S. deaths.[2] Most recently, the H1N1 flu of 2009–2010 caused between 9,000 and 18,000 deaths in the United States.[3] Scientists expect that new deadly pandemics will continue to occur.[4] Moreover, they fear that such pandemics will look more like 1918 than 2009. To help prepare for this possibility, scientists monitor animal populations for flu viruses that could mutate to infect humans. One particularly menacing example of such a virus is the "avian flu," more technically known as a "highly pathogenic flu (H5N1)," which has a very high mortality rate among birds and has already crossed the threshold to infect 387 people, with 245 deaths among them.[5] Although the incidence of human-to-human infections of avian flu is small (most people get infected directly from a bird), further mutations could create a deadly strain that could pass easily from person to person, spreading around the globe and causing untold numbers of deaths.

If such a pandemic were to occur, two main public health strategies would likely be: (1) "community mitigation" efforts, which would literally try to keep people apart by asking them to stay at home when they are ill or by closing public and private institutions where lots of people normally gather; and (2) a mass vaccination campaign—although vaccine is unlikely to be ready at the beginning of an outbreak. Because these public health practices require public cooperation, understanding the public's responses is particularly important. In addition, scientists' or public health officials' views of these practices may not be the same as the public's views. For example, the opinions of scientists who are more knowledgeable about the benefits or risks of pharmaceutical interventions may be very different from the public's. It is therefore important to have an empirical basis for understanding the public perspective on pandemic flu.

This chapter examines the public's attitudes and behavior regarding these two major dimensions of a pandemic flu response: community mitigation efforts and vaccine. It relies on two different data sources. The first is a public opinion poll done to help public health authorities prepare for a widespread, deadly pandemic flu before a vaccine is available. A response at that time would rely on nonpharmaceutical community mitigation efforts, so the poll asks people to evaluate their likely behaviors given a hypothetical scenario. The second data source is a poll done during the 2009 H1N1 flu outbreak as a new vaccine was about to become available. Both of these polls were conducted through cooperative agreements with the Centers for Disease Control and Prevention (CDC), the National Preparedness Leadership Initiative, the Association of State and Territorial Health Officials, and the National Public Health Information Coalition.

Background: Seasonal versus Pandemic Flu

Although many people refer to any cold as "the flu," true flu (or influenza) is caused by a specific series of viruses. Flu typically presents with symptoms that include a high fever, muscle aches, and a runny nose, but complications such as pneumonia can produce significant health problems, including death.[6] These complications are typically limited to the elderly, young children, pregnant women, and those with preexisting medical conditions.[7] Influenza viruses spread from person to person through "droplets" expelled when people sneeze or cough and touch each other or the same surfaces.[8] Each year, a few strains of the influenza virus spread from person to person across the globe in a predictable pattern.[9] This kind of flu is called "seasonal" flu, and between 5 percent and 20 percent of the American public will get seasonal flu in a given year.[10] Some years the dominant flu viruses are fairly benign, and some years they do not spread among many people because a large percentage of the population has immunity to that particular virus, most likely because they had it, or a similar strain, in earlier years. Scientists try to predict which strains will be dominant in the upcoming year and develop a vaccine specifically targeted to those strains.[11]

Pandemic flu is distinct from this pattern because it is an outbreak of a new flu virus to which people have little natural immunity and for which no vaccine is available, at least initially. Such a virus spreads easily between humans and becomes a global phenomenon.[12] Certain prescription antiviral medications, such as Tamiflu® (oseltamivir) and Relenza® (zanamivir), can shorten the time a person is sick and help prevent serious flu complications, but the supply might not be sufficient to quell the pandemic if transmission rates are very high. Moreover, in a pandemic flu outbreak, there might not be enough time to develop a vaccine before the illness reaches a large percentage of the population.

Community Mitigation Measures in a Severe Pandemic

In February 2007 the CDC issued the *Community Strategy for Pandemic Influenza Mitigation* (known as "Community Mitigation Guidance"), which describes the measures that would be used to reduce transmission of a pandemic flu virus. These community mitigation interventions include: (1) isolation and treatment with influenza antiviral medications of all persons with confirmed or probable pandemic influenza; (2) voluntary home quarantine of and provision of antiviral medications as prophylaxis to members of households with individuals with confirmed or probable influenza (if sufficient quantities of effective medications exist and a feasible means of distributing them is in place); (3) dismissal of students from schools and closure of child-care facilities along with preventing the recongregation of children and teenagers in community settings; and (4) social distancing of adults in the community and workplace, which may include cancellation of large public gatherings and alteration of workplace environments and schedules to the extent possible to decrease social density.[13]

Researchers differ over the potential effectiveness of such community mitigation measures. Evidence to determine the best strategies for protecting people during a pandemic is very limited. Several studies based on findings from mathematical models and historical analyses suggest that early implementation of multiple measures such as social distancing, school closures, and isolation of sick individuals may be effective in reducing the transmission of the virus.[14] Other researchers cite uncertainty[15] or believe such measures may not be effective.[16] In particular, the use of quarantine—or the isolation of people thought to have been infected with a disease but not yet showing symptoms—may be less effective for pandemic flu than for diseases like smallpox and SARS.[17] Smallpox and SARS have relatively long incubation periods of fourteen days and ten days, respectively, so time is available to quarantine people before they become ill and can infect others. By contrast, flu has a short incubation period of one to four days with an average of two days.[18] Identifying cases and quarantining people who may have been exposed before they expose others is much more difficult in that time frame.

The next section looks at pandemic influenza as a case study of an emerging infectious disease for which no strain-specific vaccination or sufficient antiviral medicines are available at the outset. It is based on a nationwide poll conducted in 2008 to gauge the public's possible reaction to the use of social distancing and other nonpharmaceutical interventions during a severe pandemic.[19] Predicting public reactions to a crisis with which people have had little experience is obviously difficult to do. This poll, however, described a hypothetical scenario to elicit some of the potential responses of people to these situations, and therefore it sheds light on the response that people anticipate they would have.

Familiarity with Pandemic Flu

To determine whether people understood what public health officials mean when they talk about pandemic influenza, the survey asked how familiar respondents were with the term *pandemic flu* and found that it was unfamiliar to a majority of Americans. About one-third (34 percent) said they knew what the term meant; 29 percent reported that they had heard of the term, but did not know what it meant, and 36 percent had never heard of it.[20]

Setting Up a Scenario

Because many people were unfamiliar with pandemic influenza, the survey presented a hypothetical scenario:

> Now I want to ask you some questions about a possible outbreak in the U.S. of pandemic flu, a new type of flu that spreads rapidly among humans and causes severe illness. Currently

there have not been any cases of pandemic flu in the U.S. However, imagine that there was a severe outbreak in the U.S. and possibly in your community and a lot of people were getting sick from the flu and the flu was spreading rapidly from person to person.

This scenario was intentionally designed to describe a severe situation without being overly alarming. Respondents were then asked how they would respond to and be affected by the circumstances that would arise from such an outbreak.

A note of caution is in order in interpreting the results. Even when only a small proportion of the population may be affected by a problem or be unable to cooperate with public health authorities, this proportion can translate into millions of people who may have difficulty.

Home

During a severe pandemic, it is likely that public health authorities will recommend that all but the sickest persons remain at home rather than go to a hospital if they are ill. In the survey people were asked about their response to a variety of recommendations that public health officials might make. More than nine in ten (92 percent) said they would stay at home and away from other people for seven to ten days if they had pandemic flu. In addition, 85 percent said they and all members of their household would stay at home for that period if another member of their household was sick (**Table 16–1**).[21]

More than eight in ten (84 percent) said they would be able to take care of sick household members at home for seven to ten days, if public health officials recommended it. About three-fourths (76 percent), however, said they would be worried that if they stayed at home with a household member who was sick from pandemic flu, they themselves would get sick.

Nearly three-fourths (74 percent) said they would have someone to take care of them at home if they became sick with pandemic flu and had to remain at home for seven to ten days. About one in four (24 percent) said they would not have someone to take care of them. People living in one-adult households were far more likely (42 percent to 19 percent) than people from households with more than one adult to say they would not have anyone to take care of them. About one-third of adults who were in fair or poor health (39 percent), disabled (36 percent), or from low-income households (32 percent) said they would not have anyone to take care of them.

A substantial proportion of the public believed that they or a household member would be likely to experience various problems if they stayed at home for seven to ten days and avoided contact with anyone outside their household. More than four in ten thought it very or somewhat likely that they or a household member might lose pay and have money problems (49 percent) or be unable to get the health care or prescription drugs they needed (43 percent).

School Closings

One of the major interventions for potentially reducing transmission of the influenza virus during a pandemic would be to dismiss students from schools and close child-care facilities. Depending upon the severity of the pandemic, the duration of school dismissal could range from a few weeks to up to three months.

After hearing a brief description of an outbreak scenario in which schools and child-care facilities were closed, adults who had major responsibility in their household for children under age five in day care or ages five to seventeen in school were asked a series of questions. If schools and day care were closed for one month, 93 percent of adults who had major responsibility for children in day care or school and had at least one employed adult in the household thought they would be able to arrange care so that at least one employed adult in the household could go to work. Almost as many (86 percent) thought they would be able to do so for three months (**Table 16–2**).[22]

Of those who said they could arrange care for one month so that at least one adult would be able to work, nearly nine in ten said they or another family member would mainly take care of the children if schools and day-care facilities were closed. About six in ten (61 percent) said that at least one employed person would have to stay home from work. Among adults with major responsibility for school-age children, about three-fourths (74 percent) thought that if schools were closed for three months and public health officials recommended it, they would be able to keep their children and teenagers from taking public transportation, going to public events, and gathering outside home while schools were closed.

About three in ten adults (29 percent) who have major responsibility for children in day care or school reported that a child in their household received free breakfast or lunch at day care or school. Asked specifically in the context of an outbreak of pandemic influenza, 38 percent of those whose children got free meals at school (10 percent of the total who have responsibility for children in this age group) said that if these facilities were closed for three months, the lack of free meals would be a problem.

Work

Employed people were asked about the problems they might face being out of work for various lengths of time. The longer people were out of work, the greater the number who thought they would face financial problems. Most employed people (74 percent) believed they could miss seven to ten days of work without having serious financial problems, and one in four (25 percent) said they would face such problems. About six in ten (59 percent) thought they would have serious financial problems if they stayed home for one month. More than three-fourths (79 percent) believed they would have such problems if they stayed home from work for three months (**Table 16–3**).[23]

About three in ten employed people (28 percent) said that if they had to stay home for one month because of a serious outbreak of pandemic flu, they would be able to work from home for that long. Seventeen percent said they would be able to work from home for three months.

Employed people were also asked about their current employers' plans and policies for dealing with an outbreak of pandemic flu. Few working people (19 percent) were aware of any plan at their workplace to respond to a serious outbreak of pandemic flu.

A majority (55 percent) of employed adults said they would stay home from work if public officials said they should, and 39 percent said they would go to work if their employers told them to report to their jobs. One in four employed adults (25 percent) were worried that, in the event of a serious outbreak of pandemic flu in their community, their employers would make them go to work even if they were sick.

Nearly half (46 percent) of employed people believed that their workplace would stay open during a serious outbreak of pandemic flu and public health officials recommended that some businesses in their community should shut down. Forty-eight percent thought their workplace would shut down.

Only about one-third (34 percent) of employed people thought that if they stayed home from work, they would still get paid; 42 percent thought they would not get paid, and 24 percent did not know. Lower-income respondents (from households earning less than $25,000) were significantly less likely (16 percent to 45 percent) than higher-income respondents (from households earning $50,000 or more) to believe they would still get paid.

Willingness to Cooperate with Other Public Health Recommendations

When given a scenario about a potential outbreak of pandemic influenza, the initial response of more than eight in ten respondents was to say that they would cooperate if public health officials recommended that for one month they curtail various activities of their daily lives. Nine in ten said they would stay in town during a serious outbreak if public health officials recommended it (**Table 16–4**).[24]

Potential Problems Responding to Public Health Recommendations, by Household Income, Race/Ethnicity, and Health Status

The survey results indicate that community mitigation measures could cause particular problems for people from lower-income families and for racial and ethnic minorities. On a number of measures, lower-income Americans (households with an annual income under $25,000) were more likely than higher-income Americans (households with an annual income of $50,000 or more) to believe they would experience problems responding to public health recommendations. Similarly, on many of these measures a higher proportion of African Americans and Hispanic Americans than whites believed they would experience problems. The same held true for people who described their own health status as fair or poor (**Table 16–5**).[25]

More than half of adults from low-income households (58 percent), Hispanics (70 percent), African Americans (54 percent), and people in fair or poor health (55 percent) said that if they were asked to stay home for seven to ten days and avoid contact with people outside their household, it was likely that they or a household member would lose pay and have financial problems. A majority of low-income adults (57 percent), Hispanics (61 percent), and people in fair or poor health (59 percent) also thought it was likely that they or a household member would be unable to get the health care or prescription drugs they needed. More than half of low-income adults (54 percent) and about four in ten Hispanics (45 percent) and people in fair or poor health (38 percent) believed they would have serious financial problems if they had to stay home from work for seven to ten days.

People in fair or poor health (18 percent), disabled persons (18 percent), and chronically ill adults (15 percent) were significantly more likely than others to say they would be unable to take care of a sick household member for seven to ten days at home. Also, these groups were less likely to have someone who could care for them at home if they were sick (**Table 16–6**).[26]

Case Study Conclusions

The poll results suggest that if community mitigation measures are instituted for a severe influenza pandemic, most respondents would comply with these recommendations, but would be challenged to do so if their income or job were severely compromised.

The findings from this poll provide important insights about what the public might do if a pandemic occurred in the near future; however, no one can be certain how the public would actually react. These results need to be interpreted with caution in advance of a severe pandemic that could cause prolonged disruption of daily life and widespread illness or death in a community. The poll results suggest that adherence rates may be high during the early stages of a pandemic, but the results may not be as predictive of how well the public would comply over the course of several months. The predictive ability of polls like this one will be better in areas where people have a greater amount of personal experience, such as workplace issues and income.

The willingness to adhere to community mitigation measures may also be influenced by the severity of the illness people observe in the community during a pandemic, relative to the need for income and the level of community and individual/family disruption. In addition, public response is likely to be affected by the perceived effectiveness of government and voluntary agencies in dealing with this crisis situation.

The 2009 H1N1 Flu Pandemic and Vaccine

In March 2009 a new strain of influenza emerged in Mexico with the makings of a pandemic: the population had little natural immunity to the virus; it spread easily from person to person; and it appeared to have a high mortality rate. This new flu was called "novel influenza A (H1N1)," but was referred to popularly and in the media at that time as "swine flu" because it seemed to have arisen from contact between humans and pigs. H1N1 appeared in the United States in April and spread to every U.S. region within weeks.[27] By June H1N1 had spread to seventy-four countries and was given the World Health Organization's highest level pandemic rating of phase 6.[28] An effort to develop an H1N1 vaccine began almost immediately, but it would not be ready until the fall.[29] Mortality rates were not as high in the intervening summer months as they had initially appeared, but scientists were concerned that the rate would increase when the traditional flu season began in the fall or that the virus could mutate to become more deadly as the outbreak unfolded.[30]

A poll conducted in September 2009—at the beginning of the flu season and before the vaccine was available—provides data about how the public responds to vaccine in the face of an unknown, but real, threat rather than a hypothetical scenario. We present the findings here.[31] In interpreting them, it is important to know that evidence about the disease suggested that it targeted not only the groups that usually are more likely to suffer from seasonal flu complications but also children and young adults at greater rates than expected. Moreover, the CDC's Advisory Committee on Immunization Practices recommended that certain groups be prioritized for the vaccine because the supply would not be sufficient to reach everyone at first.[32] The priority groups were pregnant women, people who live with or care for infants younger than six months old, health care and emergency medical personnel, anyone ages six months through twenty-four years, and adults ages twenty-five to sixty-four with certain chronic medical conditions or weakened immune systems. As more vaccine became available, the recommendations said that healthy adults twenty-five to sixty-four and those sixty-five and older should be vaccinated.[33]

Public Concern about H1N1

In September 2009 about three-fourths of U.S. adults (76 percent) believed that in the coming fall and winter, widespread cases of H1N1 were likely, "with people getting very sick." Fewer were concerned that they would personally be affected. Only about half of adults (52 percent) were concerned that they or their family members would get sick with H1N1 in the next twelve months. These data make clear that it is important to assess both public concern about a disease in general and concern about a disease as it affects people personally.[34]

Public Views of Vaccine Safety

Only one-third (33 percent) of the public thought the H1N1 vaccine was "very safe" generally for most people to take. About half (55 percent) thought it was "somewhat safe," and 9 percent believed it was "not very" or "not at all" safe. By comparison, 57 percent considered the seasonal flu vaccine to be very safe.[35]

Public Intent to Get the H1N1 Vaccine

In this context, the public had mixed feelings about getting a vaccine that was recommended by public health officials. Just over half (53 percent) of adults said they personally would get the vaccine; about four in ten (41 percent) said they would not; and 6 percent were undecided. Three-fourths of those who reported that they intended to get the vaccine said they were "absolutely certain" that they would. This result means that overall, only 40 percent of Americans said they were absolutely certain they would get the vaccine, leaving a majority (60 percent) saying they were not absolutely certain they would do so.

Seven in ten parents of children under age eighteen (70 percent) said they intended to get the vaccine for one or more of their children; 21 percent did not intend to get the vaccine for any of their children; and 7 percent were uncertain. About three-fourths (73 percent) of parents who intended to get their children vaccinated said they were absolutely certain they would, meaning that 51 percent of all parents said they were absolutely certain to get the vaccine and nearly half (49 percent) were not.[36]

Reasons for Vaccine Hesitation

The main reasons that people were not absolutely certain of getting the vaccine were their beliefs about the severity of the illness for themselves. When asked directly about the reasons for not getting the vaccine (or not being certain about getting it), two of the top reasons given related to this issue: 28 percent of adults who were not absolutely certain to get the vaccine said they did not think they were at risk of getting a serious case of the illness, and 26 percent said they thought they could get medication to treat H1N1 if they did get sick—implying that the illness was not a very serious concern for them personally. Among parents, limited concern about the illness also played a role in their vaccine decision: 27 percent said a major reason for their decision was their belief that their child was not at risk for a serious case of the illness. Decisions about vaccination changed if people were sure that serious cases were in close proximity to them. Sixty percent of adults who initially said they did not intend to get the vaccine for themselves, and parents who initially said they did not intend to get the vaccine for their children, also said that they would change their mind if "there were people in [their] community who were sick or dying from Influenza A—H1N1."

Concerns about the safety of the vaccine affected adults' hesitation about getting the vaccine, and were an even stronger influence for parents. Roughly one-fifth of adults who were not absolutely certain to get the vaccine said a "major" reason was concern about getting H1N1 (21 percent) or another serious illness (20 percent) from the vaccine. Thirty percent of adults who were not absolutely certain they would get the vaccine for themselves said that a major reason was their concern about other side effects. Among parents who were not absolutely certain that they would get the H1N1 vaccine for their children, the three top major reasons for their decisions were: (1) they were concerned that their children could get other illnesses from the vaccine (33 percent); (2) they did not trust public health officials to provide correct information about the safety of the vaccine (31 percent); and (3) they were concerned about the side effects of the vaccine (38 percent).[37]

Conclusions about Public Support for Vaccines from H1N1 Case Study

Data from this poll suggest that the public weighs two factors when making a decision about whether to get a flu vaccine for themselves or for their children: the seriousness of the illness and any concern they might have about the safety of the vaccine. In the event of a future outbreak of pandemic flu, the vaccination rate will depend on public perceptions of these issues. Moreover, trust in public health officials to provide them with accurate information will be important to their decision making. Despite evidence that the American public relies on medicine and scientific technology to address disease (see Chapter 15), it is clear that there are limits to public support for vaccines: if people have concerns about the safety of the vaccine or disbelief about the severity of the illness, it is likely that a sizable share of the public will not get vaccinated in a future pandemic flu outbreak.

Public Opinion Concerning Pandemic Flu: What to Expect in a True Pandemic

In the simplest terms, the findings from these two case studies suggest that decisions to comply with public health measures, both nonpharmaceutical and vaccine-related, during a pandemic flu outbreak depend on the public's perception of their personal risk of the illness, as well as the barriers to instituting proposed public health interventions—whether such barriers are concerns about keeping a job or concerns about the clinical risks of a vaccine. One can expect resistance to public health interventions when the public disagrees about the severity of the illness or the proposed interventions are burdensome. There may also be differences in public response if disease prevalence itself is not uniform; people in the epicenter of outbreak will be more compliant, but those farther away may do little to protect themselves before the disease gets closer. One implication is that people are unlikely to adopt protective measures well in advance of a pandemic flu, but compliance may be higher with interventions that are effective even when started later in the pandemic cycle if the disease threat continues. Further, if interventions are particularly burdensome for some parts of the population, adoption will not be uniform, unless the illness threat is very severe. Therefore, certain subgroups in the population may be especially vulnerable to the disease because it will be difficult for them to comply with recommended interventions. If so, their opinions about the outbreak and how well it was handled by public health authorities may be different from the larger population. In the long run, these different experiences may contribute to variations seen in public opinion not only about pandemic flu response, but also about public health emergency response more broadly.

Notes

[1] National Institute of Allergy and Infectious Diseases, "Flu (Influenza): Timeline of Human Flu Pandemics," http://www3.niaid.nih.gov/topics/Flu/Research/Pandemic/TimelineHumanPandemics.htm; World Health Organization, "Ten Concerns of Avian Influenza Becomes a Pandemic," October 14, 2005, http://www.who.int/csr/disease/influenza/pandemic10things/en.

[2] Ibid.

[3] Centers for Disease Control and Prevention, "CDC Estimates of 2009 H1N1 Influenza Cases, Hospitalizations and Death in the United States, April 2009–March 13, 2010," April 19, 2010, http://www.cdc.gov/h1n1flu/estimates/April_March_13.htm.

[4] Madeleine Drexler, *Secret Agents: The Menace of Emerging Infections* (Washington, D.C.: Joseph Henry Press, 2002), 190; M. A. Hamburg, S. A. Hearne, J. Levi, K. Elliott, L. M. Segal, and M. J. Earls, "A Killer Flu? Planning for the Devastating Effects of the Inevitable Pandemic," in *Emerging Infectious Diseases and the Threat to Occupational Health in the U.S. and Canada*, ed. William Charney (Boca Raton, Fla.: CRC Press/Taylor and Francis Group, 2006), Chapter 9. It is also notable that there is some skepticism of this prediction. See, for example: Merrill Goozner, "Spreading Fear Like a Virus," *Washington Post*, November 23, 2005, C9.

[5] Centers for Disease Control and Prevention, "Avian Influenza A Virus Infections of Humans," http://www.cdc.gov/flu/avian/gen-info/avian-flu-humans.htm.

[6] Centers for Disease Control and Prevention, "People at High Risk of Developing Flu-Related Complications," http://www.cdc.gov/h1n1flu/highrisk.htm.

[7] Centers for Disease Control and Prevention, "Seasonal Influenza: The Disease," http://www.cdc.gov/flu/about/disease/index.htm.

[8] Ibid.

[9] C.A. Russell, T. C. Jones, I. G. Barr, N. J. Cox, R. J. Garten, V. Gregory, et al., "The Global Circulation of Seasonal Influenza A (H3N2) Viruses," *Science* 320 (April 18, 2008): 340–346; J. J. Cannell, R. Vieth, J. C. Umhau, M. F. Holick, W. B. Grant, S. Madronich et al., "Epidemic Influenza and Vitamin D," *Epidemiology and Infection* 134 (December 2006): 1129–40.

[10] Centers for Disease Control and Prevention, "Influenza: The Disease."

[11] Kurt Link, *The Vaccine Controversy: The History, Use, and Safety of Vaccinations* (Westport, Conn.: Praeger, 2005), 99. The group responsible for selecting strains reflected in the vaccine

in a given year is the Global Influenza Network. More information available at: World Health Organization, "WHO Global Influenza Surveillance Network," http://www.who.int/csr/disease/influenza/surveillance/en.

[12] Centers for Disease Control and Prevention, Flu.gov, "About the Flu," http://www.pandemicflu.gov/general/whatis.html.

[13] Centers for Disease Control and Prevention, "Community Strategy for Pandemic Influenza Mitigation," February 2007, http://pandemicflu.gov/professional/community/commitigation.html.

[14] Richard J. Hatchett, Carter E. Mecher, and Marc Lipsitch, "Public Health Interventions and Epidemic Intensity during the 1918 Influenza Pandemic," *Proceedings of the National Academy of Sciences of the United States of America* 104 (e-publication; April 6, 2007): 7582–7; Martin C. J. Bootsma and Neil M. Ferguson, "The Effect of Public Health Measures on the 1918 Influenza Pandemic in U.S. Cities," *Proceedings of the National Academy of Sciences of the United States of America* 104 (e-publication; April 6, 2007): 7588–93; Howard Markel, Harvey B. Lipman, J. Alexander Navarro, Alexandra Sloan, Joseph R. Michalsen, Alexandra Minna Stern, and Martin S. Cetron, "Nonpharmaceutical Interventions Implemented by US Cities during the 1918–1919 Influenza Pandemic," *JAMA: Journal of the American Medical Association* 298 (August 8, 2007): 644–654; N. M. Ferguson, D. A. Cummings, C. Fraser, J. C. Cajka, P. C. Cooley, and D. S. Burke, "Strategies for Mitigating an Influenza Pandemic," *Nature* 442 (e-publication; April 26, 2006): 448–452; Robert J. Glass, Laura M. Glass, Walter E. Beyeler, and H. Jason Min, "Targeted Social Distancing Design for Pandemic Influenza," *Emerging Infectious Diseases* 12 (November 2006), http://www.cdc.gov/ncidod/EID/vol12no11/06–0255.htm.

[15] Institute of Medicine; Committee on Modeling Community Containment for Pandemic Influenza, *Modeling Community Containment for Pandemic Influenza. A Letter Report* (Washington, D.C.: National Academies Press, 2006).

[16] Thomas V. Inglesby, Jennifer B. Nuzzo, Tara O'Toole, and D. A. Henderson, "Disease Mitigation Measures in the Control of Pandemic Influenza," *Biosecurity and Bioterrorism* 4 (December 2006): 366–375; Eric Toner, "Do Public Health and Infection Control Measures Prevent the Spread of Flu?" *Biosecurity and Bioterrorism* 4 (March 2006): 84–86.

[17] Globalsecurity.org, "Flu Pandemic Mitigation—Quarantine and Isolation," 2009, http://www.globalsecurity.org/security/ops/hsc-scen-3_flu-pandemic-quarantine.htm; Centers for Disease Control and Prevention, "Community Strategy for Pandemic Influenza Mitigation."

[18] Centers for Disease Control and Prevention, "Interim Guidance on Infection Control Measures for 2009 H1N1 Influenza in Healthcare Settings, Including Protection of Healthcare Personnel," May 3, 2010, http://www.cdc.gov/h1n1flu/guidelines_infection_control.htm.

[19] Harvard School of Public Health Poll (Storrs, Conn.: Roper Center for Public Opinion Research, May 6–June 19, 2008). For the findings from a similar survey conducted in 2006, see Robert J. Blendon, Lisa M. Koonin, John M. Benson, Martin S. Cetron, William E. Pollard, Elizabeth W. Mitchell, Kathleen J. Weldon, and Melissa J. Herrmann, "Public Response to Community Mitigation Measures for Pandemic Influenza," *Emerging Infectious Diseases* 14 (May 2008): 778–786.

[20] Harvard School of Public Health Poll (Storrs, Conn.: Roper Center for Public Opinion Research, May 6–June 19, 2008).

[21] Ibid.

[22] Ibid.

[23] Ibid.

[24] Ibid.

[25] Ibid.

[26] Ibid.

[27] National Institute of Allergy and Infectious Diseases, "Flu (Influenza): Timeline of Human Flu Pandemics."

[28] Margaret Chan, "World Now at the Start of 2009 Influenza Pandemic, June 11, 2009, http://www.who.int/mediacentre/news/statements/2009/h1n1_pandemic_phase6_20090611/en/index.html.

[29] Rob Stein, "Preparing for Swine Flu's Return: New Wave Expected after Virus Flourished in Southern Hemisphere," *Washington Post,* August 10, 2009, http://www.washingtonpost.com/wp-dyn/content/article/2009/08/09/AR2009080902447.html; Julie Steenhuysen, "As Swine Flu Wanes, U.S. Prepares for Second Wave," Reuters, June 4, 2009, http://www.reuters.com/article/healthNews/idUSN0423008520090605.

[30] World Health Organization, "Pandemic (H1N1) 2009—Update 96," April 16, 2010, http://www.who.int/csr/don/2010_04_16/en/index.html; Guillermo Dominquez-Cherit, Stephen E. Lapinsky, Alejandro E. Macias, Ruxandra Pinto, Lourdes Espinosa-Perez, Alethse de la Torre, et al., "Critically Ill Patients with 2009 Influenza A (H1N1) in Mexico," *JAMA* 302 (November 2, 2009): 1880–7; World Health Organization, "Ten Concerns if Avian Influenza Becomes a Pandemic."

[31] Harvard School of Public Health, "Public Views of the H1N1 Vaccine: Topline Results," September 2009, http://www.hsph.harvard.edu/news/press-releases/files/H1N1_Vaccine_Topline_10.1.09.doc.

[32] Centers for Disease Control and Prevention, "2009 H1N1 Vaccination Recommendations," http://www.cdc.gov/h1n1flu/vaccination/acip.htm.

[33] Centers for Disease Control and Prevention, "2009 H1N1 Influenza Vaccine: What You Need to Know," http://www.cdc.gov/vaccines/pubs/vis/downloads/vis-inact-h1n1.pdf.

[34] Harvard School of Public Health, "Public Views of the H1N1 Vaccine."

[35] Ibid.

[36] Ibid.

[37] Ibid.

Table 16-1 How Americans Think They Would Respond to a Serious Outbreak of Pandemic Flu: Home (in percent)

	Yes	No	Not applicable/ Don't know
Would stay at home for 7 to 10 days if public health officials recommended because you had flu	92	5	2
You and all members of household would stay at home for 7 to 10 days if public health officials recommended because a member of household had flu	85	11	4
If public health officials recommended, would be able to take care of sick household member for 7 to 10 days at home	84	10	6
If stayed at home with sick household member, would be worried about getting sick yourself	76	22	2
Have someone who could care for you at home if you were sick	74	24	2

(Table continues)

Table 16-1 *Continued*

Likelihood of having these problems if you had to stay home 7 to 10 days	Likely	Not likely	Not applicable/ Don't know
You or a member of your household might lose pay and have money problems	49	50	1
You or a member of your household might have a hard time being stuck at home for so long	49	50	1
You or a member of your household might be unable to get the health care or prescription drugs that you need	43	55	2
You might not be able to get baby formula, diapers, or other important things for a baby in your household (among those with major responsibility for children aged 0–2)	42	58	–
You might not be able to get care for a disabled person in your household (among those in household with a disabled person)	38	45	17
You might not be able to get care for an older person in your household (among those in household with person aged 65+)	37	46	17
You might have difficulty taking care of the (child/children) under age 5 in your household (among those with major responsibility for children under age 5)	33	66	1
You or a member of your household might lose your job or business as a result of having to stay home	28	72	1

Question: Public health officials think many people will get sick if there is a severe outbreak of pandemic flu. Those less severely sick would need to be taken care of at home rather than at hospitals. Only the sickest people would be hospitalized. I'm going to ask you some questions about two situations: if you yourself were sick, or if you were taking care of someone in your household who was sick from pandemic flu. Suppose you had pandemic flu and health officials recommended that you stay at home, away from other people for 7 to 10 days. Is this something you would do, or not?

Question: What if another member of your household was sick from pandemic flu and health officials recommended that you and all members of your household should stay at home, away from other people for 7 to 10 days? Is this something you and other members of your household would do voluntarily, or not?

Question: If public health officials said you should be prepared to take care of members of your household at home for 7 to 10 days if they become sick, would you be able to do that, or not?

Question: If you stayed at home with a household member who was sick from pandemic flu, how worried would you be that you would get sick from the disease yourself? Would you be very worried, somewhat worried, not too worried, or not at all worried?

Question: If you were sick with pandemic flu and you had to remain at home for 7 to 10 days, is there someone who could care for you at home, or not?

Question: Here is a list of problems people might have while staying at home in the event of an outbreak of pandemic flu. If you were asked to stay at home for 7 to 10 days and avoid contact with anyone outside your household, how likely do you think it is that each of the following would happen to you or a member of your household? How about (you or a member of your household might lose pay and have money problems/you or a member of your household might have a hard time being stuck at home for so long/you might not be able to get baby formula, diapers, or other important things for a baby in your household [among those who have major responsibility for children aged 0 to 2 years old]/you or a member of your household might be unable to get the health care or prescription drugs that you need/you might not be able to get care for a disabled person in your household [among households with disabled person]/you might not be able to get care for an older person in your household [among those in households with person aged 65+]/you might have difficulty taking care of the (child/children) under age 5 in your household [among those who have major responsibility for children under 5 years old]/you or a member of your household might lose your job or business as a result of having to stay home)? Do you think that is very likely, somewhat likely, not too likely, or not at all likely?

Source: Harvard School of Public Health Poll (Storrs, Conn.: Roper Center for Public Opinion Research, May 6–June 19, 2008).

Table 16-2 How Americans Think They Would Respond to a Serious Outbreak of Pandemic Flu: School Closings (in percent)

	Yes	No	Don't know
If schools/day care closed for one month, could arrange care so that at least one employed adult in household could go to work[1]	93	4	3
If schools/day care closed for three months, could arrange care so that at least one employed adult in household could go to work[1]	86	9	5
At least one employed person would have to stay home from work[1]	61	37	2
Child in household gets free breakfast or lunch at school or day care[2]	29	71	–
If school/day care closed for three months, would be problem that children could not get free meals[2]	10	89	1

Notes: [1]Among respondents who have major responsibility for children under 5 in day care or age 5–17 in the household and have at least one working adult in the household. [2]Among respondents who have major responsibility for children under 5 in day care or age 5–17 in the household.

Question: In order to keep pandemic flu from spreading and to protect the safety of children, some communities may close schools and day-care facilities for some period of time. The length of school and day-care closures would probably be tied to how serious the pandemic flu outbreak is. For instance, if there was a severe epidemic, schools and day care might be closed for a long period of time. If schools and day-care facilities were closed for one month to protect children because of a serious outbreak of the disease, would you be able to arrange care for the children so that at least one adult in your family could go to work, or not?

Question: What if schools and day care were closed for three months because there was a severe outbreak of pandemic flu in your community? Would you be able to arrange care for the children who live in your household so that at least one adult in your family could go to work, or not?

Question: If schools and day care were closed for one month, how many of the employed people in your household if any do you think would have to stay home from work?

Question: Do any of the children in your household get free breakfast or lunch at school or child care? (If yes) If schools and child care were closed for three months, how much of a problem would it be that these children could not get these free meals at school or child care? Would it be a major problem, a minor problem, or not a problem?

Source: Harvard School of Public Health Poll (Storrs, Conn.: Roper Center for Public Opinion Research, May 6–June 19, 2008).

Table 16-3 How Americans Think They Would Respond to a Serious Outbreak of Pandemic Flu: Work (in percent)

	Yes	No	Don't know
Among employed respondents			
Would be a serious financial problem if had to stay home for work for 7 to 10 days	25	74	1
Would be a serious financial problem if had to stay home for work for one month	59	41	1
Would be a serious financial problem if had to stay home for work for three months	79	21	1
If had to stay home for one month, would be able to work from home for that long	28	71	1
If had to stay home for three months, would be able to work from home for that long	17	81	2

(Table continues)

Table 16-3 *Continued*

Workplace has plan for outbreak of pandemic flu	19	63	18
Would stay home if public health official said you should, even if employer told you to come to work	55	39	6
Worried employer would make you go to work if sick during outbreak	25	74	1
Workplace would shut down if public health officials recommended business in your community do so	46	48	6
If had to stay home from work, would still get paid	34	42	24

Question: If cases of pandemic flu remained in your community for some time, public health officials might recommend that people stay home from work so they do not catch or spread the disease. How long do you think you could stay home from work before it became a serious financial problem? Would it become a serious financial problem if you stayed out of work for 7–10 days? (If no) How about one month? Would that become a serious financial problem? (If no) How about three months? Would that become a serious financial problem? (among employed respondents)

Question: If you had to stay home for one month because of a serious outbreak of pandemic flu, would you be able to work from home for that long, or not? (If yes) Would you be able to work from home for three months or not? (among employed respondents)

Question: Has your workplace developed a plan to respond to a possible outbreak of pandemic flu? (among employed respondents)

Question: If public health officials said you should stay home from work, but your employer told you to come to work, would you stay at home or go to work? (among employed respondents)

Question: If there were a severe outbreak of pandemic flu in your community, how worried are you that your employer would make you go to work even if you were sick? Are you very worried, somewhat worried, not too worried, or not at all worried? (among employed respondents)

Question: If the pandemic flu was very serious and public health officials recommended that some businesses in your community should shut down, do you think your workplace would shut down, or would it stay open? (among employed respondents)

Question: If there were a severe outbreak of pandemic flu in your community and you had to stay away from work, would you still get paid or not, or don't you know? (among employed respondents)

Source: Harvard School of Public Health Poll (Storrs, Conn.: Roper Center for Public Opinion Research, May 6–June 19, 2008).

Table 16-4 How Americans Think They Would Respond to a Serious Outbreak of Pandemic Flu: Other Recommendations (in percent)

Would follow recommendation if public health officials said for one month you should . . .	Yes	No
Avoid air travel	93	5
Avoid public events like movies, sporting events, or concerts	92	6
Avoid going to malls and department stores	91	8
Cancel doctor or hospital appointments that are not critical at the time	88	10
Limit your use of public transportation, buses and trains	87	5
Reduce contact with people outside your own household as much as possible	86	13
Postpone family or personal events such as parties, weddings, or funerals	81	16
Avoid going to church or religious services	81	17

	Likely	Not likely
Would stay in town or city during serious outbreak if public health officials recommended you do so	90	9

Note: "Don't know" responses not shown.

Question: I'm going to read you a list of steps that public health officials might advise. This would be to prevent the spread of severe flu and help protect you and your family from catching it. As I read each one, please tell me if you would follow such a recommendation, or not. What if they said that for one month you should (Avoid air travel/Avoid crowded public events like movies, sporting events, or concerts/Avoid going to malls and department stores/Cancel doctor or hospital appointments that are not critical at the time/Limit your use of public transportation, buses, and trains/Reduce contact with people outside your own household as much as possible/Postpone family or personal events such as parties, weddings, or funerals/Avoid going to church or religious services)? Do you think you would do that, or not?

Question: Suppose there was a serious outbreak of pandemic flu in your town or city and health officials recommended that you and members of your household stay in your town or city. How likely is it that you would stay in your town or city—very likely, somewhat likely, not too likely, or not at all likely?

Source: Harvard School of Public Health Poll (Storrs, Conn.: Roper Center for Public Opinion Research, May 6–June 19, 2008).

Table 16-5 Potential Problems Responding to Public Health Recommendations, by Household Incomes, Race/Ethnicity, and Health Status (in percent)

	Total	Household income			Race/Ethnicity			Health status	
		<$25K	$25–49.9K	$50K+	Hispanic	Black (Non-Hispanic)	White (Non-Hispanic)	Fair/Poor	Excellent/very good/good
If asked to stay home 7 to 10 days, likely that:									
You or a member of your household might lose pay and have money problems	49	58	57	40	70	54	44	55	48
You or a member of your household might be unable to get the health care or prescription drugs that you need	43	57	48	33	61	48	38	59	40
You or a member of your household might lose your job or business as a result of having to stay home	28	39	31	20	57	32	21	39	26
Employed respondents									
Would be a serious financial problem if had to stay home for work for 7 to 10 days	25	54	37	15	45	24	22	38	23
Would be a serious financial problem if had to stay home for work for one month	59	82	77	43	75	61	55	69	56
Would be a serious financial problem if had to stay home for work for three months	79	93	90	69	90	85	75	86	76

Question: Here is a list of problems people might have while staying at home in the event of an outbreak of pandemic flu. If you were asked to stay at home for 7 to 10 days and avoid contact with anyone outside your household, how likely do you think it is that each of the following would happen to you or a member of your household? How about (You or a member of your household might lose pay and have money problems/You or a member of your household might be unable to get the health care or prescription drugs that you need/You or a member of your household might lose your job or business as a result of having to stay home)? Do you think that is very likely, somewhat likely, not too likely, or not at all likely?

Question: If cases of pandemic flu remained in your community for some time, public health officials might recommend that people stay home from work so they do not catch or spread the disease. How long do you think you could stay home from work before it became a serious financial problem? Would it become a serious financial problem if you stayed out of work for 7–10 days? (If could stay out of work or are unsure for 7 to 10 days without it becoming a financial problem) How about one month? Would that become a serious financial problem? (If could stay out of work or are unsure for 1 month without it becoming a financial) How about three months? Would that become a serious financial problem?

Source: Harvard School of Public Health Poll (Storrs, Conn.: Roper Center for Public Opinion Research, May 6–June 19, 2008).

Table 16-6 Potential Problems with Care at Home, by Health Status, Disability, and Chronic Illness (in percent)

	Total	Health status		Disabled		Chronic illness	
		Fair/poor	Excellent/very good/good	Yes	No	Yes	No
If public health officials recommended, would not be able to take care of sick household member for 7 to 10 days at home	10	18	9	18	8	15	9
Do not have someone who could care for you at home if you were sick	24	39	21	36	21	31	22

Question: If public health officials said you should be prepared to take care of members of your household at home for 7 to 10 days if they become sick, would you be able to do that, or not?

Question: If you were sick with pandemic flu and you had to remain at home for 7 to 10 days, is there someone who could care for you at home, or not?

Source: Harvard School of Public Health Poll (Storrs, Conn.: Roper Center for Public Opinion Research, May 6–June 19, 2008).

Chapter 17

AMERICANS' VIEWS ABOUT RACIAL AND ETHNIC HEALTH CARE DISPARITIES

Mollyann Brodie, John M. Connolly, and Claudia Deane

Introduction

Members of racial and ethnic minority groups are at a disadvantage when it comes to health and health care in America. Although important differences exist across different groups, in general people of color are less likely to be in good health or to have good health outcomes, less likely to have health insurance, and less likely to receive good quality care.

Differences in health status—the most important bottom line measure—have been vexingly persistent over time. With the exception of Asian Americans, racial and ethnic minority population groups are more likely to report being in poor health overall, and more likely to report suffering specific health problems, including diabetes or obesity.[1] Differences in health status translate into shorter lives: infant mortality rates, as well as overall mortality ratios among different age groups, are higher among African Americans and Native Americans than among other groups.[2] The infant mortality rate for children born to college-educated African American women is more than twice that for white women with the same level of education. The number of infant deaths per 1,000 live births among mothers over age twenty who are college graduates is 11.5 for African Americans, compared to 4.2 for whites.[3] The life expectancy for African American men is lower than the life expectancy for white men in comparable income brackets.[4] Other examples of the problem are distressingly easy to find. The death rate from diabetes for black children is more than double that of white children (2.46 deaths per 1 million vs. 0.91 deaths per 1 million for white children).[5] African American children are hospitalized for asthma at a rate four to five times that of white children (527 per 100,000 vs. 144 per 100,000).[6]

The authors thank Marsha Lillie-Blanton, formerly of the Kaiser Family Foundation, and Cara James of the Kaiser Family Foundation for their input in the writing of this chapter.

The HIV/AIDS death rate for African Americans is more than seven times that of whites,[7] and the death rate from all types of cancer is 25 percent higher for African Americans than it is for whites.[8]

One of the fault lines underpinning these different outcomes is unequal access to high-quality health insurance, the kind of insurance that makes it possible to afford the services of good doctors and hospitals and the right kind of medications. Members of racial and ethnic minority groups are less likely than whites to have private health insurance and more likely than whites to have health insurance that places strict limits on the types of services patients may receive.[9] Among non-elderly whites, three in four (76 percent) report having private health insurance; 12 percent say they have Medicaid or another public health insurance; and 12 percent report being uninsured. In contrast, just over half (52 percent) of non-elderly African Americans say they have private insurance; more than a quarter (27 percent) report using a government health plan; and about a fifth (21 percent) report being uninsured. Even fewer non-elderly Hispanics report having private health insurance, and more say they are uninsured. About four in ten non-elderly Hispanics (42 percent) report having private insurance; a quarter (24 percent) say they are using a government program; and one in three (34 percent) say they do not have any health insurance.[10] Speaking even more broadly, racial and ethnic minorities have more limited access to care than whites. Adult Hispanics and African Americans are less likely than whites to have seen a doctor over the course of a year, even after controlling for possible differences in their health.[11] Hispanics report not getting care for an illness or injury as soon as they wanted at twice the rate of non-Hispanic whites.[12] Black patients have been found to be less likely than white patients to have access to board-certified physicians or high-quality subspecialists.[13] Added to all these differences are variations in the sources of care, with members of racial and ethnic minority groups less likely to receive continuous treatment from private practice doctors and more likely to rely on emergency room care.[14]

Even those people of color who do have health insurance and equivalent access to health care may suffer different treatment within the health care system, and it is these inequities that have received intense attention from a number of private and government bodies in recent years. In 2002 the Institute of Medicine (IOM) released a comprehensive report, *Unequal Treatment: Confronting Racial and Ethnic Disparities in Health Care*.[15] The report defines a health care disparity as a difference "in the quality of care received by racial and ethnic minorities and non-minorities who have equal access to care." Even with this strict definition—holding constant factors such as access to a doctor and type of health insurance—the IOM found that marked racial and ethnic disparities in health care are both pervasive and persistent. The causes of these differences are complex and nuanced. The IOM grouped these causes roughly into three categories: how the organizational structure of health care systems might impact people of color differently; the often unnoticed biases and behaviors of health care providers; and the behavior of patients themselves.[16]

The 2008 National Healthcare Disparities Report, issued by the Agency for Healthcare Research and Quality, documented disparities across all dimensions of health care quality, including safety and effectiveness. The report also found disparities in the various types of care—including preventive care, treatment of acute conditions, and management of chronic disease—and across many care settings, from primary care to hospitals to nursing homes and even to dental offices.[17] These differences are particularly disturbing in light of the growing body of research demonstrating that disparities in quality of care are associated with higher rates of mortality among members of racial and ethnic minority groups.[18] Moreover, the current racial disparities in health care, particularly when it comes to quality, are not getting any better.[19]

The existing income differences between whites and racial and ethnic minority groups certainly contribute to exacerbating racial disparities in health care, but even when income levels are held constant, differences in health, access to care, and quality persist.[20]

Beneath these big-picture trends are the individual, real-life problems and day-to-day worries faced by people of color, experiences that are reflected in any number of survey results. Surveys have found that African Americans and Latinos more frequently report having problems in the health care system and are more likely to be worried about things going wrong with their own medical care or health insurance coverage.[21] Insured African Americans are more than twice as likely as insured whites to say they are very worried about losing or not being able to afford their coverage going forward, and three times as likely to be very worried about their benefits being cut back.[22] More than half (54 percent) of Latinos say they are not confident they have enough money or health insurance to cover a major illness, compared to about a third (36 percent) of whites.[23]

This chapter examines the views of the American public concerning the existence and pervasiveness of these racial and ethnic disparities in health care. It also focuses more closely on the views of African Americans and Latinos. It then assesses opinions about proposed policy solutions to these problems.

Americans' Perceptions of Racial and Ethnic Disparities in Health, Access to Care, and Quality of Care

Despite the stark and persistent disparities in many measures of health status, access to care, and quality of care among different racial and ethnic groups, public awareness of these differences remains limited. In nearly all cases, and likely because of their different personal experiences as laid out above, members of minority groups are more aware of the existing groupwide disparities than are the white population, whose views as the majority of the population drive the overall numbers.

Two commonly used metrics of health status are life expectancy and infant mortality. On these topics in 2006 roughly a third of the public believed that the average African American was worse off than the average white person. The rest of the public incorrectly believed either that the two groups were equally well off, that African Americans were better off, or said they did not know enough to venture a response.[24] A plurality of the public (40 percent) believed that the Latino population is currently roughly equivalent to the white population in infant mortality, and this is actually correct (**Table 17–1 and Table 17–2**).[25]

On having health insurance, roughly four in ten Americans in 2006 believed that African Americans (38 percent) and Latinos (41 percent) were worse off than whites. The majority either did not know or misperceived the situation.[26]

Americans are also largely unaware that members of racial and ethnic minority groups are less likely to get the health care they need. In 2005 half the public said there was not much difference in the ability of the average African American to get needed health care compared to the average white person, and 45 percent held the same view about the average Latino. Smaller shares more accurately said that it was harder for members of these groups to get health care, with 35 percent having this opinion about African Americans and 37 percent saying so about Latinos.[27] And despite documented disparities in quality of care, majorities of adults in 2006 said they thought African Americans and Latinos received either the same or better quality care than whites.[28]

Although the medical and research communities have increased their focus on these differences, public awareness of disparities has been stagnant in recent years, and actually shows signs of decrease. Between 1999 and 2006 the proportion of the public perceiving African Americans to be just as well off as whites on common measures of health remained relatively steady, and the shares saying they were worse off went down somewhat. The share saying they thought the average African American was worse off than the average white person in terms of infant mortality fell from 44 percent to 33 percent in this period.[29] In fact, the gap in infant mortality did not change over this time period.[30]

Differing Perceptions by Race and Ethnicity

Not surprisingly, awareness of health and health care disparities varies widely across racial and ethnic groups, with whites least likely to be aware of inequities. In 2006 a majority of African Americans (65 percent) correctly responded that the average member of their racial group was worse off than the average white person in terms of health insurance status. Much smaller shares of whites (36 percent) and Latinos (34 percent) held that view. A majority of African Americans (55 percent) believed that most African Americans received lower quality health care than whites, but considerably smaller shares of whites (24 percent) and Latinos (33 percent) had this opinion.

Latinos were somewhat more mixed in their assessments of the challenges facing their own ethnic group. About half (48 percent) believed their group received poorer quality of care than whites, but four in ten correctly recognized that the average Latino was worse off when it came to having health insurance.[31]

Just as the lack of public awareness of disparities has persisted as a trend in public opinion, differences between the views of members of various racial and ethnic minority groups have proved to be an enduring trait of opinion as well.[32]

It would be beneficial to report the views of racial and ethnic groups that make up smaller shares of the American public, such as Asian Americans or Native Americans, and to be able to look at Latinos by their original country of origin, as Cubans, Puerto Ricans, Mexicans, and other groups may face different experiences and challenges. But here survey research runs into a challenge. The average national survey includes respondents from all racial and ethnic groups in proportion to their share of the population. This means that a standard survey of 1,000 respondents would normally include at least 100 African Americans and 100 Latinos because each group represents upwards of 10 percent of the adult American population. These subsamples are large enough to report the opinions of each group separately. But because Asian Americans and other racial groups are significantly smaller shares of the U.S. population, there are not usually enough respondents in these categories to report their opinions separately. Studies are certainly done of these populations, but they are more costly to conduct and many fewer are available.[33]

Racial and Ethnic Discrimination in Health Care

Although most Americans are unaware of many aspects of the disparate treatment racial and ethnic minorities experience in the health care system, most believe that racism is a problem generally in the country and in the health care system. In 2003, 87 percent said they thought racism was a problem facing the country, including 42 percent who saw it as a major problem. More specifically, nearly two in three Americans (64 percent) believed that racism was a problem in health care, although only 20 percent saw it as a major problem (**Table 17–3**).[34]

That said, the public ranks race and ethnicity relatively low on their list of factors they think determine whether an individual receives "high-quality health care." In 2004, 46 percent said that race and ethnicity were important in this respect, and half said these characteristics were either not too important (12 percent) or not at all important (38 percent). In comparison, significantly larger shares of Americans said that access to health insurance (81 percent), employment status (68 percent), income (67 percent), age (60 percent), and living in an urban or rural area (56 percent) were important in determining one's quality of care (**Table 17–4**).[35]

In keeping with public opinion on other questions related to health disparities, the views of Latinos and African Americans on racism and ethnic discrimination in health care differ from those of whites. In 2003 Latinos (31 percent) and African Americans (41 percent) were twice as likely as whites (16 percent) to say that racism is a major problem in health care.[36] In 2005, 53 percent of Americans overall and 48 percent of whites believed that "some people, because of their race or ethnicity, had serious problems getting quality health care in the United States." Significantly larger shares of Latinos (69 percent) and African Americans (67 percent) held this opinion (**Table 17–5**).[37]

These differing perceptions are likely rooted in the personal experiences of members of racial and ethnic minority groups. Twenty-three percent of African Americans and 21 percent of Latinos reported in 2005 that sometime in the past five years they had received poor quality medical treatment because of their race or ethnic background. Roughly the same proportion of Latinos (21 percent) reported receiving poor treatment because of their accent or English language skills (**Table 17–6**).[38] Expanding beyond the individual to members of their circle of family and friends, more than a third of African Americans and Latinos say that they themselves, a family member, or a friend has been treated unfairly when getting medical care because of their racial or ethnic background. This number is more than twice as many in each group as among the white population.[39]

The prevalence of these experiences reverberates among people of color, translating experiences among a subset of individuals into a more widespread worry that carries even to those who have not themselves experienced discrimination in the medical sector. Majorities of African Americans (65 percent) and Latinos (58 percent) say they are very or somewhat concerned that they or a family member may face discrimination when seeking medical care in the future.[40] These broad-based concerns may also stem from the discrimination that members of racial and ethnic minority groups experience in other common situations—such as 50 percent of black men reporting they have been unfairly stopped by the police—and extrapolate those experiences to the medical field.[41]

Possible Policy Solutions and the Role of Government

On the whole, the majority of Americans believe the government has at least some responsibility to ensure greater racial and ethnic equality in health care. In 2001, when respondents were asked whether it was the federal government's responsibility to make sure that minorities have equality with whites in health care services, even if it meant they had to pay more in taxes, 62 percent of the public said it was a government responsibility (**Table 17–7**).[42] When asked in 2003 to choose from a wider list of actors in the health care system whom they thought should be primarily responsible for ensuring equal treatment, responses were more evenly divided. A small plurality (32 percent) chose the government, while others chose doctors (25 percent), individual patients (19 percent), or health insurance companies (13 percent).[43] And when given the option in 1999 of saying this responsibility belonged to both the government and the medical community, more than half chose that response (**Table 17–8**).[44] These responses suggest that many Americans not only identify the government and health care providers as responsible for greater equity in health care, but also feel it is a responsibility that should be shared.

In keeping with other racial differences of opinion on the government's role in public policy, white Americans are significantly less likely than African Americans and Latinos to feel that it is the government's responsibility to intervene in racial and ethnic inequities in medical care, although a narrow majority do accept this premise. African Americans were nearly unanimous (90 percent) in favor of government involvement, but whites were more closely divided, with 55 percent saying it was a government responsibility and 41 percent disagreeing.[45] On the question asking about a more extended list of actors, whites were divided, with between two and three in ten saying the major responsibility should be with government (28 percent), the medical community (27 percent), and patients (21 percent); larger pluralities of African Americans (47 percent) and Latinos (41 percent) named the government.[46]

Although majorities across racial and ethnic groups feel the government ought to do more to eliminate disparities, support for action often wanes, as it does with most issues, when higher taxes are attached. In 2005 support fell appreciably from a majority (65 percent) saying they thought the government should do more in this area to 39 percent if increased taxes were a consequence of these efforts (**Table 17–9**). Support also fell among African Americans and Latinos on this question, but it remained a majority (57 percent and 61 percent, respectively). Whites went from a majority in favor (57 percent) to a majority opposed (57 percent).[47]

Conclusion

The existence of racial disparities in health status, access to health insurance and care, and quality of care has been extensively documented in both the medical and popular press. Nevertheless, many Americans, particularly whites, remain unaware of the existence of these problems. That disparities seem to stem from a complicated mix of factors makes the situation that much more opaque for many lay observers. It also makes solutions harder to crystallize for the public.

The vexing question of race in America is no less thorny when it comes to health care than it is on employment or education, with many members of racial and ethnic minority groups reporting the existence of problems that many whites either do not see or do not believe. The issue, as is also true more broadly, pits Americans' entrenched belief in equal treatment against their complicated views on whether minorities continue to face barriers that the majority population does not. And although the public is open to having the government act to remedy inequalities in health care, there is no agreement as to what share of the responsibility rests with government compared to the medical community or patients themselves. The willingness to use public tax dollars to fund efforts at change is also limited.

Although public awareness of the problems remains low, awareness among policy and political decision makers seems to be on the rise. Government has reacted: in 2000 the National Center on Minority Health and Health Disparities was created as a part of the National Institutes of Health.[48] And members of Congress continue to introduce legislation aimed at alleviating racial disparities in health.[49] At the industry level, nine major health insurers have joined to form the National Health Plan Collaborative, a group that attempts to test possible solutions for unequal treatment in health service delivery.[50] And the National Business Group on Health has joined with the U.S. Department of Health and Human Services' Office of Minority Health to launch an initiative aimed at reducing disparities.[51] Finally, health care providers are also paying attention: both the American Medical Association and the National Medical Association have commissions on the topic. Still, the disparities persist, and, as racial and ethnic minorities continue to grow as a percentage of the U.S. population, the problems become that much more extensive.

To the extent that change requires public support, the data suggest the first step would be to raise awareness of the existence and pervasiveness of racial disparities, especially those—such as the gaps in life expectancy and infant mortality—that are long-standing, well-documented, and most easily understood by the public. Some of this awareness may come from numbers alone: as racial and ethnic minorities become a larger share of the population, greater numbers of white Americans may be exposed through personal interactions or media reports to the problem of disparate treatment in the health care system. Experts in the field are quick to acknowledge that solutions to these problems are neither obvious nor easy because of the numerous factors that cause disparities. As the data in this chapter suggest, the path forward might be made smoother by mobilizing support around solutions that involve shared responsibility across the government, the private sector, and individuals.

Notes

[1] Kaiser Family Foundation, "Key Facts: Race, Ethnicity & Medical Care," January 2007, http://www.kff.org/minorityhealth/6069.cfm.

[2] Centers for Disease Control and Prevention, "Life Expectancy at Birth, at 65 Years of Age, and at 75 Years of Age, by Race and Sex," 2004, http://www.cdc.gov/nchs/data/hus/hus06.pdf#027; Arialdi M. Miniño, Melonia P. Heron, and Betty L. Smith, "Deaths: Preliminary Data for 2004," *National Vital Statistics Reports* 54 (June 28, 2006), http://www.cdc.gov/nchs/data/nvsr/nvsr54/nvsr54_19.pdf.

[3] Kaiser Family Foundation, "Infant Mortality Rates for Mothers Age 20+, by Race/Ethnicity and Education, 2001–2003," May 2008, http://facts.kff.org/chart.aspx?ch=372.

[4] Kaiser Family Foundation, "Life Expectancy at Age 25 for U.S. Black and White Men with Similar Income Levels," May 2008, http://facts.kff.org/chart.aspx?ch=498.

[5] Kaiser Family Foundation, "Diabetes Death Rates for Black Children More Than Double That of Whites, Report Finds," November 16, 2007, http://dailyreports.kff.org/Daily-Reports/2007/November/16/dr00048924.aspx.

[6] Kaiser Family Foundation, "Eliminating Racial/Ethnic Disparities in Health Care: What Are the Options?" October 2008, http://www.kff.org/minorityhealth/h08_7830.cfm.

[7] Office of Minority Health and Health Disparities, Centers for Disease Control and Prevention, "About Minority Health," 2007, http://www.cdc.gov/omhd/AMH/AMH.htm.

[8] National Cancer Institute, National Institutes of Health, "Fact Sheet: Cancer Health Disparities," March 2008, http://www.cancer.gov/cancertopics/factsheet/cancer-health-disparities/disparities.

[9] Institute of Medicine, "What Healthcare Consumers Need to Know about Racial and Ethnic Disparities in Healthcare," March 2002, http://www.iom.edu/Object.File/Master/4/176/PatientversionFINAL.pdf.

[10] Kaiser Family Foundation, "Health Insurance Status, by Race/Ethnicity: Total Nonelderly Population, 2007," December 2008, http://facts.kff.org/chart.aspx?ch=365.

[11] Morehouse Medical Treatment and Effectiveness Center, "Racial and Ethnic Differences in Access to Medical Care: A Synthesis of the Literature," October 1999, http://www.kff.org/minorityhealth/upload/A-Synthesis-of-the-Literature-Racial-Ethnic-Differences-in-Access-to-Medical-Care-Report.pdf.

[12] Kaiser Family Foundation, "Three Largest Disparities in Quality of Care for Hispanics in the U.S., 2005," December 2006, http://facts.kff.org/chart.aspx?ch=227.

[13] Peter B. Bach, Hoangmai H. Pham, Deborah Schrag, Ramsey C. Tate, and J. Lee Hargraves, "Primary Care Physicians Who Treat Blacks and Whites," *New England Journal of Medicine* 351 (August 5, 2004): 575–584, http://content.nejm.org/cgi/content/full/351/6/575.

[14] M. P. Doescher, B. G. Saver, K. Fiscella, and P. Franks, "Racial/Ethnic Inequities in Continuity and Site of Care: Location, Location, Location," *Health Services Research* 36 (December 2001): 78–89.

[15] Brian D. Smedley, Adrienne Y. Stith, and Alan R. Nelson, Editors, Committee on Understanding and Eliminating Racial and Ethnic Disparities in Health Care, Board of Health Sciences Policy, Institute of Medicine, *Unequal Treatment: Confronting Racial and Ethnic Disparities in Health Care* (Washington, D.C.: National Academy Press, 2002).

[16] Institute of Medicine, "What Healthcare Consumers Need to Know about Racial and Ethnic Disparities in Healthcare," March 2002.

[17] Agency for Healthcare Research and Quality, "Key Themes and Highlights from the National Healthcare Disparities Report," 2008, http://www.ahrq.gov/qual/nhdr08/Key.htm.

[18] P. B. Bach, L. D. Cramer, J. L. Warren, and C. B. Begg, "Racial Differences in the Treatment of Early-Stage Lung Cancer," *New England Journal of Medicine* 341 (October 14, 1999): 1198–205; E. D. Peterson, L. K. Shaw, E. R. DeLong, D. B. Pryor, R. M. Califf, and D. B. Mark, "Racial Variation in the Use of Coronary-Revascularization Procedures: Are the Differences Real? Do They Matter?" *New England Journal of Medicine* 336 (February 13, 1997): 480–486.

[19] Agency for Healthcare Research and Quality, "Key Themes and Highlights from the National Healthcare Disparities Report," 2008.

[20] Smedley et al., *Unequal Treatment,* 79.

[21] Kaiser Family Foundation, "Race, Ethnicity and Medical Care: A Survey of Public Perceptions and Experiences," October 1999, http://www.kff.org/minorityhealth/loader .cfm?url=/commonspot/security/getfile.cfm&PageID=13294; Harvard School of Public Health/Robert Wood Johnson Foundation, "Americans' Views of Disparities in Health Care," December 2005, http://www.rwjf.org/files/research/Disparities_Survey_Report .pdf; Kalahn Taylor-Clark, Robert J. Blendon, and John M. Benson, "African Americans' Views on Health Policy: Implications for the 2004 Elections," *Health Affairs,* Web Exclusive, December 3, 2003, http://content.healthaffairs.org/cgi/reprint/hlthaff.w3.576v1; Pew Hispanic Center/Kaiser Family Foundation, "2002 National Survey of Latinos," December 2002, http://www.kff.org/kaiserpolls/upload/2002-National-Survey-of-Latinos-Toplines-Survey.pdf; Economic Policy Institute, "Health Care Insecurity Greatest among Hispanics," Economic Snapshots, February 20, 2008, http://www.epi.org/content.cfm/ webfeatures_snapshots_20080220.

[22] Taylor-Clark, Blendon, and Benson, "African Americans' Views on Health Policy," *Health Affairs,* 2003.

[23] *USA Today*/Kaiser Family Foundation/Harvard School of Public Health Poll (Storrs, Conn.: Roper Center for Public Opinion Research, April 25–June 9, 2005).

[24] Kaiser Family Foundation Poll (Storrs, Conn.: Roper Center for Public Opinion Research, April 6–11, 2006).

[25] Because the question of whether Latinos' life expectancy differs from that of whites is the subject of some debate among academics, we do not assess the public's views on this topic here. See, for example, David P. Smith and Benjamin S. Bradshaw, "Rethinking the Hispanic Paradox: Death Rates and Life Expectancy for US Non-Hispanic White and Hispanic Populations," *American Journal of Public Health* 96 (September 2006): 1686–92.

[26] Kaiser Family Foundation Poll, April 6–11, 2006.

[27] Harvard School of Public Health/Robert Wood Johnson Foundation, "Americans' Views of Disparities in Health Care," December 2005.

[28] Kaiser Family Foundation Poll, April 6–11, 2006.

[29] Kaiser Family Foundation, "Race, Ethnicity and Medical Care: A Survey of Public Perceptions and Experiences," October 1999; Kaiser Family Foundation Poll, April 6–11, 2006.

[30] National Center for Health Statistics, Centers for Disease Control and Prevention, *Health, United States, 2006,* Table 19, http://www.cdc.gov/nchs/data/hus/hus06.pdf.

[31] Kaiser Family Foundation Poll, April 6–11, 2006.

[32] Ibid.; Kaiser Family Foundation, "Race, Ethnicity and Medical Care: A Survey of Public Perceptions and Experiences," October 1999.

[33] Two recent articles based on surveys with large enough samples of these smaller-incidence racial/ethnic groups to analyze reported these groups' experiences indicative of disparities in the health care system. But neither of the articles reported the groups' views *about* the existence or prevalence of disparities in the health care system in general or policies to reduce disparities. See Robert J. Blendon, Tami Buhr, Elaine F. Cassidy, Debra J. Perez, Kelly A. Hunt, Channtal Fleischfresser, John M. Benson, and Melissa J. Herrmann, "Disparities in Health: Perspectives of a Multi-Ethnic, Multi-Racial America," *Health Affairs* 26 (September/October 2007): 1437–47;

Robert J. Blendon, Tami Buhr, Elaine F. Cassidy, Debra J. Perez, Tara Sussman, John M. Benson, and Melissa J. Herrmann, "Disparities in Physician Care: Experiences and Perceptions of a Multi-Ethnic America," *Health Affairs* 27 (March/April 2008): 507–517.

[34] Aetna/National Conference for Community and Justice/Princeton Survey Research Associates, "Racial and Ethnic Disparities in Healthcare: A Public Opinion Update," 2003, http://www.nccjstl.org/downloads/AetnaNCCJ2003survey.pdf.

[35] Research!America/American Public Health Association/Harris Interactive Poll (Storrs, Conn.: Roper Center for Public Opinion Research, October 1–10, 2004).

[36] Aetna/National Conference for Community and Justice/Princeton Survey Research Associates, "Racial and Ethnic Disparities in Healthcare," 2003.

[37] Harvard School of Public Health/Robert Wood Johnson Foundation, "Americans' Views of Disparities in Health Care," December 2005.

[38] Ibid.

[39] Kaiser Family Foundation, "Race, Ethnicity and Medical Care: A Survey of Public Perceptions and Experiences," October 1999.

[40] Ibid.

[41] *Washington Post*/Kaiser Family Foundation/Harvard University, "Race and Ethnicity in 2001: Attitudes, Perceptions, and Experiences," August 2001.

[42] Ibid.

[43] Aetna/National Conference for Community and Justice/Princeton Survey Research Associate, "Racial and Ethnic Disparities in Healthcare," 2003.

[44] Kaiser Family Foundation, "Race, Ethnicity and Medical Care: A Survey of Public Perceptions and Experiences," October 1999.

[45] *Washington Post*/Kaiser Family Foundation/Harvard University, "Race and Ethnicity in 2001: Attitudes, Perceptions, and Experiences," August 2001.

[46] Aetna/National Conference for Community and Justice/Princeton Survey Research Associate, "Racial and Ethnic Disparities in Healthcare," 2003.

[47] Harvard School of Public Health/Robert Wood Johnson Foundation, "Americans' Views of Disparities in Health Care," December 2005.

[48] National Center for Minority Health and Health Disparities, http://ncmhd.nih.gov.

[49] Kaiser Family Foundation, "Key Health Disparities-Focused Legislation Introduced in the 110th Congress," December 2007, http://www.kff.org/minorityhealth/upload/7724.pdf.

[50] National Health Plan Collaborative, "Phase One Summary Report," November 2006, http://www.rwjf.org/files/publications/other/NHPCSummaryReport2006.pdf.

[51] National Business Group on Health, "National Business Group on Health and HHS Office of Minority Health Launch Initiative to Reduce Racial and Ethnic Health Disparities," February 11, 2008, http://www.businessgrouphealth.org/pressrelease.cfm?ID=101.

Table 17-1 Americans' Perceptions of Health and Health Care Disparities between Whites and African Americans, by Race/Ethnicity, 1999 and 2006 (in percent)

	1999	2006			
			Responses of . . .		
	Total adults	Total adults	Whites*	African Americans*	Latinos
Infant Mortality					
The average African American is					
Worse off	44	33	33	46	33
Just as well off	39	43	44	32	43
Better off	7	8	6	13	8
Don't know	9	17	17	9	16
Life Expectancy					
The average African American is					
Worse off	42	36	37	50	31
Just as well off	42	40	42	29	40
Better off	7	8	6	13	12
Don't know	9	16	16	9	17
Having health insurance					
The average African American is					
Worse off	44	38	36	65	34
Just as well off	46	39	42	15	40
Better off	3	9	8	12	13
Don't know	6	14	15	8	13
Quality of Care					
Most African Americans receive					
Lower quality	29	28	24	55	33
Same quality	60	57	62	36	49
Higher quality	1	3	2	3	9
Don't know	10	12	12	6	9

Note: * = excluding Latinos.

Question: (For the next few questions I would like you to think about African Americans in our country today/Thinking about African Americans in our country today . . .) Do you think the average African American is better off, worse off, or just as well off as the average white person (in terms of/when it comes to each of the following)? (Infant mortality—that is, a baby's chance of surviving after birth/Life expectancy—that is, how long someone can expect to live/[having/being covered by] health insurance)?

Question: When going to a doctor or health clinic for health care services, do you think most African Americans receive the same quality of health care as whites, higher quality of care, or lower quality of health care as most whites?

Sources: Kaiser Family Foundation, "Race, Ethnicity and Medical Care: A Survey of Public Perceptions and Experiences," October 1999; Kaiser Family Foundation Poll (Storrs, Conn.: Roper Center for Public Opinion Research, April 6–11, 2006).

Table 17-2 Americans' Perceptions of Health and Health Care Disparities between Whites and Latinos by Race/Ethnicity, 1999 and 2006 (in percent)

	1999	2006			
	Total adults	Total adults	Whites*	African Americans*	Latinos
Infant Mortality					
The average Latino is					
Worse off	37	29	31	30	25
Just as well off	44	40	39	33	47
Better off	4	10	8	16	14
Don't know	15	21	21	22	13
Life Expectancy					
The average Latino is					
Worse off	35	30	30	36	32
Just as well off	45	40	43	33	34
Better off	4	9	8	13	16
Don't know	15	21	20	18	18
Having health insurance					
The average Latino is					
Worse off	50	41	41	39	41
Just as well off	37	27	28	17	36
Better off	4	14	13	26	9
Don't know	9	18	18	18	14
Quality of Care					
Most Latinos receive					
Lower quality	35	32	26	58	48
Same quality	52	50	55	29	38
Higher quality	3	5	4	7	5
Don't know	10	14	14	6	8

Note: * = excluding Latinos.

Question: (Now thinking about Latinos in our country today . . .) Do you think the average Latino is better off, worse off, or just as well off as the average white person (in terms of/when it comes to each of the following)? (Infant mortality—that is, a baby's chance of surviving after birth/Life expectancy—that is, how long someone can expect to live/[having/being covered by] health insurance)?

Question: When going to a doctor or health clinic for health care services, do you think most Latinos receive the same quality of health care as whites, higher quality of care, or lower quality of health care as most whites?

Sources: Kaiser Family Foundation, "Race, Ethnicity and Medical Care: A Survey of Public Perceptions and Experiences," October 1999; Kaiser Family Foundation Poll (Storrs, Conn.: Roper Center for Public Opinion Research, April 6–11, 2006).

Table 17-3 Americans' Perceptions of Racism in Health Care, by Race/Ethnicity (in percent)

	Responses of . . .		
	Whites*	African Americans*	Latinos
Racism in health care is . . .			
Major problem	16	41	31
Minor problem	46	40	43
Not a problem at all	30	16	23

Note: * = excluding Latinos. "Don't know" responses not shown.

Question: As I mention some different areas of our society, please tell me if you think racism—that is, people being treated worse than others because of their race or ethnicity—is a major problem, a minor problem, or not a problem at all in this area of society.) Is racism a major problem, a minor problem, or not a problem at all in . . . health care?

Source: Aetna/National Conference for Community and Justice/Princeton Survey Research Associates, "Racial and Ethnic Disparities in Healthcare," 2003.

Table 17-4 Americans' Views on the Importance of Various Factors in Determining if Someone Receives High Quality Health Care (in percent)

	Very important	Somewhat important	Not too important	Not at all important
Access to health insurance	65	16	4	16
Employment status	46	22	8	21
Income	44	23	9	22
Age	37	23	10	27
Living in an urban or rural area	33	23	11	30
Race or ethnicity	29	17	12	38
Gender	24	16	15	42

Note: "Don't know" responses not shown.

Question: The quality of health care varies among populations in the United States. How important do you think each of the following is in determining if someone receives high-quality health care? Is (access to health insurance/employment status/ income/age/whether you live in a rural vs. urban area/ race or ethnicity/gender) very important, somewhat important, not too important or not at all important in determining if someone receives high-quality health care?

Source: Research!America/American Public Health Association/Harris Interactive Poll (Storrs, Conn.: Roper Center for Public Opinion Research, October 1–10, 2004).

Table 17-5 Americans' Perceptions of Whether Some People Have Serious Problems Getting Quality Health Care Because of Race/Ethnicity, by Race/Ethnicity (in percent)

	Responses of . . .			
	Total adults	Whites*	African Americans*	Latinos
Have serious problems	53	48	67	69
Don't have serious problems	34	38	27	23
Don't know	12	13	6	8

Note: * = excluding Latinos.

Question: Do you think some people in this country, because of their race or ethnicity, have serious problems getting quality health care, or don't you think they have serious problems?

Source: Harvard School of Public Health/Robert Wood Johnson Foundation, "Americans' Views of Disparities in Health Care," December 2005.

Table 17-6 Reported Incidence of Getting Poor Quality Medical Care Because of Discrimination, by Race/Ethnicity

	Responses of . . .		
Percent reporting that they received poor quality medical treatment or care because of . . .	Whites*	African Americans*	Latinos
Your race or ethnic background	1	23	21
Your accent or how well you speak English	2	5	21

Note: * = excluding Latinos.

Question: During the past five years, have you ever felt that you got poor quality medical treatment or care because of your race or ethnic background?

Question: During the past five years, have you ever felt that you got poor quality medical treatment or care because of your accent or how well you speak English?

Source: Harvard School of Public Health/Robert Wood Johnson Foundation, "Americans' Views of Disparities in Health Care," December 2005.

Table 17-7 Americans' Attitudes about the Responsibility of the Federal Government to Make Sure Members of Minority Groups Have Health Care Services Equal to Whites, by Race/Ethnicity (in percent)

	Responses of . . .			
	Total adults	Whites*	African Americans*	Latinos
Responsibility of the federal government	62	55	90	78
Not the responsibility of the federal government	34	41	8	19
Don't know	3	4	2	2

Note: * = excluding Latinos.

Question: Do you believe it is the responsibility of the federal government to make sure minorities have equality with whites in each of the following areas, even if it means you will have to pay more in taxes? . . . Health services equal to whites.

Source: Washington Post/Kaiser Family Foundation/Harvard University, "Race and Ethnicity in 2001: Attitudes, Perceptions, and Experiences," August 2001.

Table 17-8 Americans' Views about Responsibility for Ensuring that Patients Get the Same Quality of Health Care Regardless of Race/Ethnic Background, by Race/Ethnicity (in percent)

Who should be primarily responsible?	Responses of . . .			
	Total adults	Whites*	African Americans*	Latinos
When respondents were offered several choices[1]				
The government	32	28	47	41
Doctors	25	27	20	20
Patients themselves	19	21	11	11
Health insurance companies	13	14	11	16
Medical schools	2	1	1	5
Medical researchers	1	1	2	2
When respondents were given a choice between two/both/neither[2]				
The medical community	20	23	7	14
The government	13	11	23	20
Both	55	53	64	59
Neither	10	11	5	5

Notes: * = excluding Latinos. "Don't know" responses not shown.

Question: In your opinion, who should be primarily responsible for ensuring that patients get the same quality of health care to meet their needs regardless of their race and ethnic background . . . the government, doctors, patients themselves, health insurance companies, medical schools, or medical researchers?

Question: In your opinion, who should be primarily responsible for ensuring that patients get the same quality health care to meet their needs regardless of their race and ethnic background? The government, the medical community, both, or neither?

Sources: [1]Aetna/National Conference for Community and Justice/Princeton Survey Research Associates Poll (Storrs, Conn.: Roper Center for Public Opinion Research, January 2–16, 2003); [2]Kaiser Family Foundation, "Race, Ethnicity and Medical Care: A Survey of Public Perceptions and Experiences," October 1999.

Table 17-9 Americans' Willingness to Pay More in Taxes to Have the Federal Government Ensure Equality for Members of Minority Groups in Access to Quality Health Care, by Race/Ethnicity (in percent)

	Responses of . . .			
	Total adults	Whites*	African Americans*	Latinos
Federal government should do more than it does now (net)	65	57	91	84
. . . and willing to pay more in taxes	39	33	57	61
. . . but not willing to pay more in taxes	22	21	31	17
. . . don't know if willing to pay more in taxes	4	3	3	6
Federal government should not do more	29	36	6	11
Don't know if government should do more	5	6	2	5

Note: * = excluding Latinos.

Question: Do you think the federal government should do more than it does now to ensure that racial and ethnic minorities have the same chance to get good quality health care as whites have, or not? (If yes) Would you be willing or unwilling to pay more in taxes to ensure that racial and ethnic minorities have the same chance to get good quality health care as whites have?

Source: Harvard School of Public Health/Robert Wood Johnson Foundation, "Americans' Views of Disparities in Health Care," December 2005.

Chapter 18

THE VIEWS OF AFRICAN AMERICANS AND HISPANICS ON HEALTH POLICY

Kalahn Taylor-Clark and John M. Benson

This chapter focuses on the health care experiences and attitudes of the two largest racial and ethnic minority groups in the United States: African Americans and Hispanics.[1] The experiences and views of other racial and ethnic minorities are obviously important, but because those groups make up somewhat smaller proportions of the adult U.S. population, most polls do not interview enough of them to allow for reliable statistical analyses. In addition, important differences exist among various subpopulations of African Americans and Hispanics, but few surveys allow for reliable analyses of differences in the views of Mexican or Cuban Americans, to name just two.[2]

Although the U.S. health care system is arguably the most advanced in the world in terms of resources and technologies, several segments of the American public, including the poor and racial and ethnic minorities, suffer disproportionately from poorer health status, care, and outcomes compared to their wealthier and white counterparts.[3] Research has documented persistent and pervasive inequalities in health care treatment among racial and ethnic minority populations in the United States, even after controlling for other sociodemographic characteristics, such as age, income, and insurance status.[4] Several studies show that health care disparities are associated with poorer health outcomes for African Americans and Hispanics.[5]

African Americans and Hispanics report fair or poor health status significantly more often than do whites.[6] African Americans have substantially higher age-adjusted death rates than whites and Hispanics.[7] Life expectancy at birth is five years less for African Americans than for whites.[8] In addition, infant mortality is twice as high for African Americans as it is for whites and Hispanics (Table 18–1).[9]

Among the non-elderly (less than 65 years old), African Americans and Hispanics are more likely than whites to be uninsured or covered by public insurance, such as Medicaid. Non-elderly blacks (18 percent) and Hispanics (35 percent) are significantly more likely than non-elderly whites (13 percent) to be uninsured. Non-elderly African Americans (26 percent) and Hispanics (23 percent) are more likely than non-elderly whites (10 percent) to get coverage from Medicaid.[10] African Americans are also overrepresented among those under age sixty-five receiving disability benefits through Medicare.[11] More than two-thirds (69 percent) of non-elderly whites receive health insurance coverage from their employer (69 percent), compared to about half (49 percent) of non-elderly blacks and about four in ten non-elderly Hispanics (38 percent).[12]

Although unemployment among racial and ethnic minorities is implicated as a cause of disparities in health insurance coverage, the data show large differences in coverage even among employed Americans. Hispanic workers (40 percent) are nearly three times as likely as white workers (14 percent), and almost twice as likely as black workers (23 percent), to be uninsured, and black workers are more likely than white workers to be uninsured.[13]

The personal experiences of African Americans and Hispanics in accessing high-quality health care are important in understanding their views on the U.S. health care system. African Americans and Hispanics perceive greater challenges in accessing high-quality care for themselves and their own families than do whites. African Americans (32 percent) and Hispanics (29 percent) are more likely than whites (18 percent) to believe that, if they were sick, they would not have access to the best medical care in their community.[14] African Americans are significantly more likely than whites to believe that not enough high-quality doctors practice in their community, and along with Hispanics are more likely than whites to believe their community does not have enough high-quality hospitals (**Table 18–2**).[15]

African Americans and Hispanics are more likely than whites to rate the medical services they received in the past twelve months, including the care they received from their regular health care provider, as fair or poor.[16] They are also more likely to report getting poor medical treatment in the past five years based on their racial or ethnic background or an inability to pay for care. Hispanics, in particular, are more likely than African Americans or whites to say that they have received poor medical treatment because of language barriers.[17]

Research by the Agency for Healthcare Quality and Research indicates worsening disparities in the receipt of timely health care for Hispanics and blacks. The agency's report also documents worsening disparities (compared with whites) in listening, explaining, respect, and visit length of health care providers for adult Hispanic patients.[18]

In assessing the health care attitudes of African Americans and Hispanics, it is important to keep in mind the history of racial and ethnic relations in the United States in general and in health care in particular. Abuses of medical ethics, such as the Tuskegee syphilis study, are likely to have a negative impact on the views of African Americans about the health care system. In that study, southern African American men, who did not know they were receiving placebo treatment for syphilis, were tracked by the federal government to study the effects of untreated disease.[19]

Health Care as a Voting Issue

Health care is more likely to be an important voting issue for African Americans than for whites. In all but one of the six presidential elections from 1988 through 2008, African Americans were more likely than whites to cite health care as one of the most important issues in their voting decision.[20] In the four presidential elections (1996 through 2008) where polling measured the attitudes of Hispanic voters, they were about equally likely as whites to say that health care was one of the most important issues in their vote.[21] On nearly every specific health policy measure, African Americans were significantly more likely than whites to report that such issues were very important in determining for whom they would vote in the 2004 presidential election.[22]

Views of the U.S. Health Care System

African American registered voters are more likely than white registered voters (31 percent to 23 percent) to say that the U.S. health care system has so much wrong that it needs to be completely overhauled, and they are less likely (17 percent to 30 percent) to say that the system works pretty well and needs minor or no change.[23] Among the general public, a majority of all three groups rates the nation's system for providing medical care as fair or poor, but African Americans (76 percent) are significantly more likely than whites (69 percent) and Hispanics (57 percent) to give fair or poor ratings.[24] Majorities of all three groups believe that the federal government spends too little on health care, with African Americans the most likely to hold this view (**Table 18–3**).[25]

Health Care Priorities

Overall, the public believes that health care costs and the problem of the uninsured are the two highest health care priorities for government action, with a somewhat smaller number citing the quality of health care. Among registered voters interviewed prior to the 2008 election, "making health care and health insurance more affordable" was the top issue that Hispanics and whites most wanted to see the next president address, and "expanding health insurance coverage for the uninsured" was second. These two priorities were about equal for African American registered voters, who were about twice as likely as whites (35 percent to 18 percent) to cite covering the uninsured as the top issue (**Table 18–4**).[26]

When the public was asked after the 2008 election what the most important goal should be for any health care reform plan, the priorities were the same: costs, covering the uninsured, and quality. Once again, health care costs were the top priority for Hispanics and whites, and costs and the uninsured were about equal as a priority among African Americans, who were significantly more likely than whites to consider covering the uninsured as the top priority.[27]

Views on Health Care Policy

This section examines important differences between African Americans, Hispanics, and whites on a variety of health policy issues. These issues include covering more of the uninsured, government regulation of various aspects of health care, Medicaid and Medicare, diseases and conditions that threaten the health of the American public, and health care disparities.

Covering the Uninsured

In the period before the enactment in 2010 of health care reform legislation, overwhelming majorities of all three racial/ethnic groups favored the government doing more to provide health insurance for more Americans.[28] They disagreed, however, on the how much they wanted the government to do and how to do it. About three-fourths (73 percent) of African Americans preferred a major effort to provide health insurance for nearly all uninsured people, which would involve a substantial increase in spending. About half of Hispanics (49 percent) and 43 percent of whites favored this option. Half of Hispanics (50 percent) and 54 percent of whites favored a limited effort or keeping things as they are now. Nearly two-thirds (64 percent) of African Americans, compared with a minority of Hispanics (39 percent) and whites (46 percent), expressed willingness to pay more in insurance premiums or taxes to increase the number who have health insurance (**Table 18–5**).[29]

In 2009, more than three-fourths of African Americans (78 percent) and Hispanics (79 percent), compared with about half (47 percent) of whites, favored a national health insurance plan, financed by tax money, that would pay for most forms of health care. Respondents were also asked about a law that would require everyone to have health insurance that they buy themselves or get through an employer, similar to the law that requires people who drive cars to have auto insurance. People who cannot afford to buy health insurance would get help from the government to pay the premiums. Again about three-fourths of African Americans (78 percent) and Hispanics (70 percent) favored such a law, compared with about half of whites (53 percent).[30]

Government Regulation

African Americans (62 percent) are more likely than Hispanics (48 percent) and whites (50 percent) to believe that more regulation of health care costs is needed, and they are more likely than Hispanics (59 percent to 47 percent) to believe the same is true for prescription drug costs.[31] On prescription drug safety, African Americans (64 percent) are far more likely than whites (43 percent) and especially Hispanics (25 percent) to think government regulation is necessary.[32] The three racial/ethnic groups do not differ significantly in their views about the federal government imposing limits on health insurance company profits, with about two-thirds in favor (**Table 18–6**).[33]

Safety Net: Medicaid and Medicare

Large majorities of all three racial/ethnic groups believe that Medicaid and Medicare are very important programs in general.[34] About two-thirds of African Americans (68 percent) and Hispanics (65 percent) say that Medicare is very important to them and their families, but only about half (49 percent) of whites think of Medicare that way (**Table 18–7**).[35]

African Americans (57 percent) are more likely than Hispanics (39 percent) and whites (41 percent) to believe spending on Medicare should be increased. The majority of the latter two groups think that spending on Medicare should be kept about the same. African Americans are almost twice as likely as whites (54 percent to 29 percent) to believe that Medicaid spending should be increased.[36]

Diseases and Health Conditions that Pose Greatest Threats

When the public was asked in 2009 what they thought were the two diseases or health conditions that posed the greatest threat to the American people, three diseases topped the list: cancer, heart disease, and HIV/AIDS. But the three racial/ethnic groups differed in their responses.

Cancer ranked first in the minds of Hispanics (56 percent) and whites (60 percent). A larger proportion of African Americans cited HIV/AIDS (54 percent) than cancer (46 percent) as a top threat. Blacks were more than three times as likely as whites (17 percent) to name HIV/AIDS as one of the top two threats (**Table 18–8**).[37]

These findings should come as no surprise, given that in 2006 the rate of new AIDS cases among adults and adolescents (age 13 and over) was nine times higher for African Americans than the rate for whites. The rate for Hispanics was three times higher than the rate for whites. The share of AIDS diagnoses accounted for by African Americans rose from 25 percent in 1985 to 49 percent in 2006.[38] The HIV/AIDS death rate for African Americans is more than seven times that of whites.[39]

African Americans and whites were more likely than Hispanics to list heart disease. African Americans and Hispanics were more likely than whites to cite diabetes as a top threat.[40] In fact, Hispanics are almost twice as likely as whites to die from diabetes.[41]

Nearly three in ten Hispanics (29 percent) saw influenza as a top threat, compared with 11 percent of African Americans and 16 percent of whites.[42] The higher number for Hispanics may result from the timing of the poll. It was conducted shortly after an outbreak in the United States and elsewhere of H1N1 flu (popularly called "swine flu" at the time), which was first noticed in Mexico and was the source of considerable concern among the U.S. Hispanic community.[43]

In most areas of public health, African Americans are more supportive than whites of increased federal spending. About two-thirds (68 percent) of African Americans, compared with less than half of Hispanics (42 percent) and whites (48 percent), believe that the federal government is spending too little on HIV/AIDS domestically.[44] Large majorities of African Americans and Hispanics, compared with 45 percent of whites, believe the federal government should spend more on preventing the spread of infectious diseases like H1N1 flu and providing vaccines to prevent illnesses like yearly flu, measles, and mumps. Majorities of all three groups believe the federal government should spend more to prevent chronic illnesses, such as heart disease, cancer, and arthritis, with African Americans being especially likely to support more spending.[45]

Health Care Disparities

African Americans and Hispanics are more likely than whites to believe that minorities (not just their own) receive worse access to care when they are sick, and that they get worse quality of care once they are hospitalized and when they see doctors in their own community. About six in ten African Americans (61 percent) and about half of Hispanics (48 percent) believe that when people of their own race or ethnicity are sick, it is harder for them than for whites to get the health care they need. By contrast, only about three in ten whites believe that African Americans (27 percent) and Hispanics (31 percent) have a harder time than whites getting care when they are sick (**Table 18–9**).[46]

Overwhelming majorities of African Americans (91 percent) and Hispanics (84 percent), compared with 57 percent of whites, believe that the federal government should do more to ensure that racial and ethnic minorities have the same chance as whites to get good quality health care.[47] About six in ten African Americans (61 percent) and about half of Hispanics (52 percent), compared with only 32 percent of whites, believe that as part of a health reform plan the federal government should spend more to improve the health of minority populations.[48]

Conclusion

The reported experiences of black, Hispanic, and white Americans in the U.S. health care system differ significantly. Although large majorities of all three groups are satisfied with the medical care they have received recently, especially from their regular doctor or other health care provider, African Americans and Hispanics are more likely than whites to rate care negatively. They are also more likely to report having received poor medical care in the past five years because of their racial or ethnic background, their inability to pay for care, and, for Hispanics, the language barriers.

Because African Americans and Hispanics have lower median household incomes than whites (**Table 18–1**),[49] the problems and experiences associated with lower income often cannot be disentangled from the negative experiences reported by those two groups. Studies have shown, however, that health care treatment inequalities among racial and ethnic minorities remain even after controlling for income, and that lower-income blacks consistently report more health and social problems than do lower-income whites.[50]

The views of black, Hispanic, and white Americans diverge on several major health policy issues. African Americans are more critical of the U.S. health care system than are their Hispanic or white counterparts and more likely to believe the federal government spends too little on health care.

African Americans are significantly more likely than whites to think that covering the uninsured should be the top health care priority. They are far more likely than Hispanics and whites to favor a major effort to cover most of the uninsured, even if it involves a substantial increase in spending, and they are more willing to pay higher taxes or premiums to achieve this goal. African Americans and Hispanics are more likely than whites to support a national health insurance plan and require individuals to have health insurance, with subsidies for those who cannot afford to buy insurance.

African Americans are generally supportive of greater government regulation of health care costs, prescription drug costs and safety, and health insurance company profits, sometimes significantly more so than Hispanics or whites. African Americans and Hispanics are significantly more likely than whites to say that the Medicaid program is very important in general, and they are more likely than whites to believe Medicaid spending should be increased. They are also more likely than whites to say that the Medicare program is very important to their own family.

As to the diseases or health conditions that threaten Americans, the three groups have somewhat different views. Hispanics and whites see cancer as the top threat, but African Americans express particular concern about HIV/AIDS. Large majorities African Americans support increased government spending in a number of public health areas, whereas whites are often evenly divided in the support for more spending.

Even with extensive documentation of health care disparities, more than two-thirds of whites do not believe that racial/ethnic minorities get worse care. African Americans and Hispanics are more supportive than whites of efforts to reduce health care inequalities.

Notes

[1] The terms *African American* and *black* are used interchangeably in this chapter. There is some disagreement over the use of the terms *Hispanic* and *Latino*. The U.S. Census employs both terms. This chapter uses Hispanic because that is the term more commonly used in the demographic questions of public opinion polls nationally. *White, black,* and *African American* are terms that refer to race; *Hispanic* refers to an ethnicity, whereby individuals may be of any race. In the U.S. Census and in most public opinion polls, Hispanic/Latino ethnicity is asked separately from race. In this chapter, except where noted, white refers to non-Hispanic white, and black or African American refers to non-Hispanic black or African American.

[2] Two polls provide important information about disparities among racial and ethnic subpopulations, but they have few public policy measures. See Robert J. Blendon, Tami Buhr, Elaine F. Cassidy, Debra J. Perez, Kelly A. Hunt, Channtal Fleischfresser, John M. Benson, and Melissa J. Herrmann, "Disparities in Health: Perspectives of a Multi-Ethnic, Multi-Racial America," *Health Affairs* 26 (September/October 2007): 1437–47; Robert J. Blendon, Tami Buhr, Elaine F. Cassidy, Debra J. Perez, Tara Sussman, John M. Benson, and Melissa J. Herrmann, "Disparities in Physician Care: Experiences and Perceptions of a Multi-Ethnic America," *Health Affairs* 27 (March/April 2008): 507–517.

[3] David R. Williams and Toni D. Rucker, "Understanding and Addressing Racial Disparities in Health Care," *Health Care Financing Review* 21 (Summer 2000): 75–90.

[4] Brian D. Smedley, Adrienne Y. Stith, and Alan R. Nelson, Editors, Committee on Understanding and Eliminating Racial and Ethnic Disparities in Health Care, Board of Health Sciences Policy, Institute of Medicine, *Unequal Treatment: Confronting Racial and Ethnic Disparities in Health Care* (Washington, D.C.: National Academy Press, 2002).

[5] Ibid.; A. M. Epstein, J. Z. Ayanian, J. H. Keogh, S. J. Noonan, N. Armistead, P. D. Cleary, J. S. Weissman, J. A. David-Kasdan, D. Carlson, J. Fuller, D. Marsh, and R. M. Conti, "Racial Disparities in Access to Renal Transplantation: Clinically Appropriate or Due to Underuse or Overuse?" *New England Journal of Medicine* 343 (November 23, 2000): 1537–44; P. B. Bach, L. D. Cramer, J. L. Warren, and C. B. Begg, "Racial Differences in the Treatment of Early-Stage Lung Cancer," *New England Journal of Medicine* 341 (October 14, 1999): 1198–1205.

[6] National Center for Health Statistics, *Health, United States, 2008,* http://www.cdc.gov/nchs/data/hus/hus08.pdf, Table 60.

[7] National Center for Health Statistics, *Health, United States, 2008,* Table 27.

[8] National Center for Health Statistics, *Health, United States, 2008,* Table 26. These figures are for total whites and blacks, rather than non-Hispanic whites and blacks. The question of whether Latinos' life expectancy differs from that of whites is the subject of some debate among academics. See David P. Smith and Benjamin S. Bradshaw, "Rethinking the Hispanic Paradox: Death Rates and Life Expectancy for US Non-Hispanic White and Hispanic Populations," *American Journal of Public Health* 96 (September 2006): 1686–92.

[9] National Center for Health Statistics, *Health, United States, 2008,* Table 22.

[10] National Center for Health Statistics, *Health, United States, 2008,* Tables 139–140.

[11] Kaiser Family Foundation, "Key Facts: Race, Ethnicity and Medical Care," January 2007, http://www.kff.org/minorityhealth/upload/6069-02.pdf.

[12] National Center for Health Statistics, *Health, United States, 2008,* Table 138.

[13] Kaiser Family Foundation, "Key Facts: Race, Ethnicity and Medical Care," January 2007, 18.

[14] Harvard School of Public Health/Robert Wood Johnson Foundation Poll (Storrs, Conn.: Roper Center for Public Opinion Research, July 5–September 18, 2006). Throughout the chapter, the groups' responses to polling questions were compared by testing differences between proportions using Fisher's Exact Test. When responses between groups are said to differ, the differences are statistically significant at the $p \leq .05$ level.

[15] Harvard School of Public Health/Robert Wood Johnson Foundation Poll (Storrs, Conn.: Roper Center for Public Opinion Research, March 26–30, 2008).

[16] Harvard School of Public Health/Robert Wood Johnson Foundation Poll (Storrs, Conn.: Roper Center for Public Opinion Research, May 17–August 10, 2007).

[17] Harvard School of Public Health/Robert Wood Johnson Foundation Poll, July 5–September 18, 2006.

[18] Agency for Healthcare Research and Quality, "National Healthcare Disparities Report, 2005," http://www.ahrq.gov/qual/nhdr05/nhdr05.htm, Table 2.3a.

[19] Tuskegee University, "Research Ethics: The Tuskegee Syphilis Study," http://www.tuskegee.edu/Global/Story.asp?s=1207598; James H. Jones, *Bad Blood: The Tuskegee Syphilis Experiment* (New York: Free Press, 1981).

[20] The only exception was 1996, when equal proportions of blacks and whites cited health care as one of the most important issues in their vote. Robert J. Blendon, Drew E. Altman, John M. Benson, Mollyann Brodie, Tami Buhr, Claudia Deane, and Sasha Buscho, "Voters and Health Care Reform in the 2008 Presidential Election," *New England Journal of Medicine* 359 (November 6, 2008): 2050–61.

[21] Ibid.

[22] Kalahn Taylor-Clark, Robert J. Blendon, and John M. Benson, "African Americans' Views on Health Policy: Implications for the 2004 Elections," *Health Affairs* W3 (July-December 2003 Supplement): 576–585. The survey on which these conclusions were based did not have enough Hispanic respondents for reliable analysis.

[23] Kaiser Family Foundation/Harvard School of Public Health Poll (Storrs, Conn.: Roper Center for Public Opinion Research, September 10–21, 2008).

[24] Harvard School of Public Health/Robert Wood Johnson Foundation Poll (Storrs, Conn.: Roper Center for Public Opinion Research, June 17–21, 2009).

[25] Kaiser Family Foundation/Harvard School of Public Health Poll (Storrs, Conn.: Roper Center for Public Opinion Research, November 9–19, 2006).

[26] Kaiser Family Foundation/Harvard School of Public Health Poll, September 10–21, 2008.

[27] Kaiser Family Foundation/Harvard School of Public Health Poll (Storrs, Conn.: Roper Center for Public Opinion Research, December 4–14, 2008).

[28] Kaiser Family Foundation/Harvard School of Public Health Poll, November 9–19, 2006.

[29] Kaiser Family Foundation/Harvard School of Public Health Poll, December 4–14, 2008.

[30] Harvard School of Public Health/Robert Wood Johnson Foundation Poll, June 17–21, 2009.

[31] Kaiser Family Foundation/Harvard School of Public Health Poll, December 4–14, 2008.

[32] *USA Today*/Kaiser Family Foundation/Harvard School of Public Health Poll (Storrs, Conn.: Roper Center for Public Opinion Research, January 3–23, 2008).

[33] Kaiser Family Foundation/Harvard School of Public Health Poll, December 4–14, 2008.

[34] Kaiser Family Foundation Poll (Storrs, Conn.: Roper Center for Public Opinion Research, April 1–May 1, 2005).

[35] Kaiser Family Foundation Poll (Storrs, Conn.: Roper Center for Public Opinion Research, May 2–8, 2009).

[36] Kaiser Family Foundation/Harvard School of Public Health Poll, December 4–14, 2008.

[37] Harvard School of Public Health/Robert Wood Johnson Foundation Poll (Storrs, Conn.: Roper Center for Public Opinion Research, June 24–28, 2009).

[38] Kaiser Family Foundation, "Black Americans and HIV/AIDS," HIV/AIDS Policy Fact Sheet, October 2008, http://www.kff.org/hivaids/upload/6089–061.pdf; Kaiser Family Foundation, "Latinos and HIV/AIDS," HIV/AIDS Policy Fact Sheet, October 2008, http://www.kff.org/hivaids/upload/6007–061.pdf.

[39] Office of Minority Health and Health Disparities, Centers for Disease Control and Prevention, "About Minority Health," 2007, http://www.cdc.gov/omhd/AMH/AMH.htm.

[40] Harvard School of Public Health/Robert Wood Johnson Foundation Poll, June 24–28, 2009.

[41] Office of Minority Health and Health Disparities, Centers for Disease Control and Prevention, "About Minority Health," 2007.

[42] Harvard School of Public Health/Robert Wood Johnson Foundation Poll, June 24–28, 2009.

[43] "Outbreak of Swine-Origin Influenza A (H1N1) Virus Infection—Mexico, March-April 2009," *MMWR: Morbidity and Mortality Weekly Review* 58 (April 30, 2009): 1–3, http://www.cdc.gov/mmwr/preview/mmwrhtml/mm58d0430a2.htm.

[44] Kaiser Family Foundation, "2009 Survey of Americans on HIV/AIDS: Summary of Findings on the Domestic Epidemic," April 2009, http://www.kff.org/kaiserpolls/upload/7889.pdf.

[45] Harvard School of Public Health/Robert Wood Johnson Foundation Poll (Storrs, Conn.: Roper Center for Public Opinion Research, September 10–14, 2009).

[46] Harvard School of Public Health/Robert Wood Johnson Foundation Poll (Storrs, Conn.: Roper Center for Public Opinion Research, September 14–18, 2005).

[47] Ibid. See James M. Avery, "Racial Differences in Public Opinion," in *Polling America: An Encyclopedia of Public Opinion*, ed. Samuel J. Best and Benjamin Radcliff, (Westport, Conn.: Greenwood Press, 2005), 634–641, for a discussion of public opinion on "racial" policies and "implicitly racial" policies.

[48] Harvard School of Public Health/Robert Wood Johnson Foundation Poll, September 10–14, 2009.

[49] U.S. Census Bureau, *Income, Poverty, and Health Insurance Coverage in the United States: 2007*, August 2008, http://www.census.gov/prod/2008pubs/p60–235.pdf.

[50] Smedley et al., *Unequal Treatment: Confronting Racial and Ethnic Disparities in Health Care* (Washington, D.C.: National Academy Press, 2002); Robert J. Blendon, Ann C. Scheck, Karen Donelan, Craig A. Hill, Mark Smith, Dennis Beatrice, and Drew Altman, "How White and African Americans View Their Health and Social Problems," *JAMA: Journal of the American Medical Association* 273 (January 25, 1995): 341–346.

Table 18-1 Health Indicators and Health Insurance, by Race/Ethnicity

	Black (non-Hispanic)	Hispanic	White (non-Hispanic)
Fair or poor health (self-assessed), percent (2006)[1]	14	13	8
Life expectancy at birth, in years (2005)[1]	73*	—	78*
Infant mortality, per 1,000 live births (2003–2005)[1]	14	6	6
Health insurance from employer (<65 years old), percent (2006)[1]	49	38	69
Health insurance from Medicaid (<65 years old), percent (2006)[1]	26	23	10
Uninsured (<65 years old), percent (2006)[1]	18	35	13
Uninsured among workers (age 18–64 years old), percent (2005)[2]	23	40	14
Racial/ethnic composition of . . .			
U.S. population, percent (2005)[2]	12	14	67
AIDS diagnoses, percent (2006)[3]	49	19	30
Age 65+ Medicare recipients, percent (2003)[2]	8	7	81
Age <65 Medicare recipients (disabled), percent (2003)[2]	19	10	66
Household income, median (2007)[4]	$33,916	$38,679	$54,920

Note: *Total blacks and whites, rather than non-Hispanic blacks and whites.

Sources: [1]National Center for Health Statistics, *Health, United States, 2008.* [2]Kaiser Family Foundation, "Key Facts: Race, Ethnicity and Medical Care," January 2007. [3]Kaiser Family Foundation, "Latinos and HIV/AIDS," HIV/AIDS Policy Fact Sheet, October 2008. [4]U.S. Census Bureau, *Income, Poverty, and Health Insurance Coverage in the United States: 2007.*

Table 18-2 Personal Experience with the Health Care System, by Race/Ethnicity (in percent)

	Black (non-Hispanic)	Hispanic	White (non-Hispanic)
If sick, think you would not have access to best medical care in community[1]	32	29	18
Believe there are not enough high quality doctors in community[2]	41	27	31
Believe there are not enough high quality hospitals in community[2]	40	40	28
Rate medical/health services you used in past 12 months as fair or poor (among those who made one or more visits to doctor or other health care provider in past year)[3]	27	28	14
Rate quality of medical care you received from your regular doctor/health care provider in last 12 months as fair or poor (among those who have regular doctor/provider)[3]	16	19	9
Got poor quality medical treatment/care in past five years because . . .[1]			
Not able to pay	33	21	16
Your racial/ethnic background	26	16	4
Something in your medical history	15	10	9
Your accent/how well you speak English	9	20	3

Question: If you were sick, do you think you would have access to the best medical care in your community, or not?

Question: In your community, do you believe there are enough high quality doctors, or not?

Question: In your community, do you believe there are enough high quality hospitals, or not?

Question: (Asked of those who made one or more visits to doctor or other health care provider in past year) Overall, how would you rate the medical and health services that you have used in the past 12 months? Was the medical care excellent, good, fair, or poor?

Question: (Asked of those who have regular doctor/provider) Overall, how would you rate the quality of medical care that you have received from your regular doctor or health care provider in the past 12 months? Was the medical care excellent, good, fair, or poor?

Question: During the past five years, have you ever felt that you got poor quality medical treatment or care because (you were not able to pay for care/of your racial or ethnic background/of something in your medical history/of your accent or how well you speak English)?

Sources: [1]Harvard School of Public Health/Robert Wood Johnson Foundation Poll (Storrs, Conn.: Roper Center for Public Opinion Research, July 5–September 18, 2006). [2]Harvard School of Public Health/Robert Wood Johnson Foundation Poll (Storrs, Conn.: Roper Center for Public Opinion Research, March 26–30, 2008). [3]Harvard School of Public Health/Robert Wood Johnson Foundation Poll (Storrs, Conn.: Roper Center for Public Opinion Research, May 17–August 10, 2007).

Table 18-3 Views of the Health Care System, by Race/Ethnicity (in percent)

	Black (non-Hispanic)	Hispanic	White (non-Hispanic)
Views of health care system (registered voters)[1]			
So much wrong that it needs to be completely overhauled	31	27	23
Some good things, but major changes needed	51	45	46
Works pretty well, but minor changed needed	16	24	28
Works well, does not need to be changed	1	4	2

(Table continues)

Table 18-3 *Continued*

Rate nation's system for providing medical care as fair or poor[2]	76	57	69
Believe federal government spends too little on health care[3]	88	66	64

Question: Which one of the following comes closest to your view about the health care system in America today? . . . There is so much wrong with our health care system that it needs to be completely overhauled. There are some good things about our health care system, but major changes are needed. The health care system works pretty well, but minor changes are needed. The health care system works well and does not need to be changed.

Question: How would you rate the nation's system for providing medical care to Americans? Would you say excellent, good, fair, or poor?

Question: Do you think the federal government spends too much, too little, or the right amount on health care?

Sources: [1]Kaiser Family Foundation/Harvard School of Public Health Poll (Storrs, Conn.: Roper Center for Public Opinion Research, September 10–21, 2008). [2]Harvard School of Public Health/Robert Wood Johnson Foundation Poll (Storrs, Conn.: Roper Center for Public Opinion Research, June 17–21, 2009). [3]Kaiser Family Foundation/Harvard School of Public Health Poll (Storrs, Conn.: Roper Center for Public Opinion Research, November 9–19, 2006).

Table 18-4 Americans' Health Care Priorities, by Race/Ethnicity (in percent)

	Black (non-Hispanic)	Hispanic	White (non-Hispanic)
Health care issue you would most like to see the next president take action on (registered voters)[1]			
Making health care and health insurance more affordable	40	40	47
Expanding health insurance coverage for the uninsured	35	29	18
Improving the quality of care and reducing medical errors	9	14	11
Reducing spending on government health programs like Medicare and Medicaid	3	6	8
Improving Medicare and the Medicare prescription drug program	9	11	12
None (vol.)	1	0	1
Most important goal of health reform plan (total adults)[2]			
Making health care and health insurance more affordable	41	49	37
Finding a way to provide health insurance coverage to most Americans	38	29	28
Reforming the existing health care system to provide higher quality, more cost-effective care	13	12	19
None are very important	2	7	13

Note: Volunteered responses of "other," "combination," and "don't know" are not shown. (vol.) = volunteered response.

Question: Thinking specifically about health care, which one of the following health care issues would you most like to see the next president take action on? . . . Making health care and health insurance more affordable, expanding health insurance coverage for the uninsured, improving the quality of care and reducing medical errors, reducing spending on government health programs like Medicare and Medicaid, improving Medicare and the Medicare prescription drug program.

Question: If the new president and Congress decide to take on health care reform, how important is each of the following as a goal of any health care reform plan? What about . . . (making health care and health insurance more affordable/finding a way to provide health insurance coverage to most Americans/ reforming the existing health care system to provide higher quality, more cost-effective care)? Is this very important, somewhat important, not too important, or not at all important as a goal of health care reform? (If "very important" to more than one item, ask) Of the things you said are very important, which of these do you think should be the most important goal of any health care reform plan? . . . Making health care and health insurance more affordable, finding a way to provide health insurance coverage to most Americans, reforming the existing health care system to provide higher quality, more cost-effective care.

Sources: [1]Kaiser Family Foundation/Harvard School of Public Health Poll (Storrs, Conn.: Roper Center for Public Opinion Research, September 10–21, 2008). [2]Kaiser Family Foundation/Harvard School of Public Health Poll (Storrs, Conn.: Roper Center for Public Opinion Research, December 4–14, 2008).

Table 18-5 Views about Covering the Uninsured, by Race/Ethnicity (in percent)

	Black (non-Hispanic)	Hispanic	White (non-Hispanic)
Health care reform proposal you would like to see[1]			
Major effort to provide health insurance for nearly all uninsured, substantial increase in spending	73	49	43
Limited effort to cover only some groups of uninsured, but less new spending	11	21	29
Keep things as they are	14	29	25
Willing to pay more in insurance premiums or taxes to increase number who have health insurance[1]	64	39	46
Favor national health insurance financed by tax money, paying for most forms of health care[2]	78	79	47
Favor individual health insurance mandate with people who cannot afford to buy insurance getting help from government to pay premiums[2]	78	70	53

Question: Which one of the following three things would you like to see in a health care reform proposal from the new president and Congress? Would you want them to propose . . . option 1: a new health plan that would make a major effort to provide health insurance for nearly all uninsured Americans and would involve a substantial increase in spending; option 2: a new health plan that is more limited and would cover only some groups of uninsured Americans, but would involve less new spending; or option 3: keeping things basically as they are?

Question: Would you be willing to pay more—either in higher health insurance premiums or higher taxes—in order to increase the number of Americans who have health insurance, or not?

Question: Do you favor or oppose national health insurance, which would be financed by tax money, paying for most forms of health care?

Question: Do you favor or oppose having a law that requires everyone to have health insurance that they buy themselves or get through an employer. This would be similar to the law that requires people who drive cars to have auto insurance. People who cannot afford to buy health insurance would get help from the government to pay their health insurance premiums.

Sources: [1]Kaiser Family Foundation/Harvard School of Public Health Poll (Storrs, Conn.: Roper Center for Public Opinion Research, December 4–14, 2008). [2]Harvard School of Public Health/Robert Wood Johnson Foundation Poll (Storrs, Conn.: Roper Center for Public Opinion Research, June 17–21, 2009).

Table 18-6 Views about Government Regulation, by Race/Ethnicity (in percent)

	Black (non-Hispanic)	Hispanic	White (non-Hispanic)
Not enough government regulation of health care costs[1]	62	48	50
Not enough government regulation of prescription drug costs[1]	59	47	52
Not enough government regulation of prescription drug safety[2]	64	25	43
Favor federal government imposing limits on health insurance company profits[1]	62	67	63

Question: Overall, do you think there is too much, not enough, or about the right amount of government regulation of health care costs?

Question: Overall, do you think there is too much, not enough, or about the right amount of government regulation of the price of prescription drugs?

Question: I'd like your opinion of current government regulation of prescription drugs in some different areas. How about . . . making sure prescription drugs are safe for people to use? Is there too much regulation in this area, not as much as there should be, or about the right amount of regulation?

Question: Do you favor or oppose the federal government imposing limits on the profits of health insurance companies?

Source: [1]Kaiser Family Foundation/Harvard School of Public Health Poll (Storrs, Conn.: Roper Center for Public Opinion Research, December 4–14, 2008). [2]*USA Today*/Kaiser Family Foundation/Harvard School of Public Health Poll (Storrs, Conn.: Roper Center for Public Opinion Research, January 3–23, 2008).

Table 18-7 Views about Medicaid and Medicare, by Race/Ethnicity (in percent)

	Black (non-Hispanic)	Hispanic	White (non-Hispanic)
Medicaid is a very important program[1]	90	85	70
Medicare is a very important program[1]	93	90	82
Medicare program is very important to you/ your family[2]	68	65	49
Want to see spending in Medicaid . . .[3]			
Increased	54	44	29
Kept about the same	38	43	59
Decreased	7	13	11
Want to see spending on Medicare . . .[3]			
Increased	57	39	41
Kept about the same	39	51	53
Decreased	3	10	5

Note: "Don't know" responses not shown.

Question: I'm going to read you a list of federal government programs and for each one, please tell me how important you think this program is. What about (Medicaid/Medicare)? Is this very important, somewhat important, not very important, or not at all important?

Question: How important, if at all, is the Medicare program to you and your family?

Question: As you know, the federal government has a substantial budget deficit and there are many competing spending priorities facing the next president and Congress. Thinking about the federal budget, do you want to see the next president and Congress increase spending on (Medicaid, the program that provides health insurance and long-term care to low-income families and people with disabilities/Medicare, the program that provides health insurance primarily to people age 65 and older), decrease spending, or keep it about the same?

Sources: [1]Kaiser Family Foundation Poll (Storrs, Conn.: Roper Center for Public Opinion Research, April 1–May 1, 2005). [2]Kaiser Family Foundation Poll (Storrs, Conn.: Roper Center for Public Opinion Research, May 2–8, 2009). [3]Kaiser Family Foundation/Harvard School of Public Health Poll (Storrs, Conn.: Roper Center for Public Opinion Research, December 4–14, 2008).

Table 18-8 Views about Health Threats, by Race/Ethnicity (in percent)

	Black (non-Hispanic)	Hispanic	White (non-Hispanic)
Diseases or health conditions you think pose the greatest threats to the American public*[1]			
Cancer	46	56	60
Heart disease	23	7	33
HIV/AIDS	54	39	17
Influenza (all types)	11	29	16
Diabetes	17	21	10
Obesity	7	9	9
Federal government spends too little on HIV/AIDS in U.S.[2]	68	42	48
Federal government should spend more on . . .[3]			
Preventing chronic illnesses, such as heart disease, cancer, and arthritis	89	61	57

(Table continues)

Table 18-8 *Continued*

Preventing the spread of infectious diseases, such as H1N1 flu	80	72	45
Providing vaccines to prevent illnesses like the yearly flu, measles, and mumps	69	73	45

Note: *Respondents could mention up to two diseases/conditions. Top six responses for total population shown.

Question: What two diseases or health conditions do you think pose the greatest threats to the American public? (open-ended)

Question: Thinking about the HIV/AIDS epidemic in the United States specifically, in general, do you think the federal government spends too much money on HIV/AIDS, too little money on HIV/AIDS, or about the right amount?

Question: I'm going to read you a list of some different public health programs that are being discussed as part of a new health reform bill. For each one, please tell me if you think the federal government should spend more, spend less, or spend about the same as it does now. How about (preventing chronic illnesses, such as heart disease, cancer, and arthritis/preventing the spread of infectious diseases, such as H1N1 or swine flu/providing vaccines to prevent illnesses like the yearly flu, measles, and mumps)? Should the federal government spend more, less, or about the same as it does now?

Sources: [1]Harvard School of Public Health/Robert Wood Johnson Foundation Poll (Storrs, Conn.: Roper Center for Public Opinion Research, June 24–28, 2009). [2]Kaiser Family Foundation, "2009 Survey of Americans on HIV/AIDS: Summary of Findings on the Domestic Epidemic," April 2009. [3]Harvard School of Public Health/Robert Wood Johnson Foundation Poll (Storrs, Conn.: Roper Center for Public Opinion Research, September 10–14, 2009).

Table 18-9 Views about Health Care Disparities, by Race/Ethnicity (in percent)

	Black (non-Hispanic)	Hispanic	White (non-Hispanic)
When African Americans get sick, it is harder for them than for whites to get the health care they need[1]	61	53	27
When African Americans are hospitalized, they get worse quality care than whites do[1]	47	35	14
When African Americans see doctors in their own communities, they get worse quality health care than whites do[1]	39	19	13
When Latinos get sick, it is harder for them than whites to get the health care they need[1]	57	48	31
When Latinos are hospitalized, they get worse quality care than whites do[1]	43	45	15
When Latinos see doctors in their own communities, they get worse quality health care than whites do[1]	37	31	13
Federal government should do more to ensure that racial and ethnic minorities have the same chance as whites have to get good quality health care[1]	91	84	57
Federal government should spend more to improve the health of minority populations[2]	61	52	32

Question: When (African Americans/Latinos or Hispanic Americans) are sick, do you think it is easier or harder for them to get the health care they need than it is for white Americans, or don't you think there is much difference?

Question: When (African Americans/Latinos or Hispanic Americans) are hospitalized, do you think they get the same quality of health care as white Americans get, or not? (If not the same) Do (African Americans/Latinos or Hispanic Americans) get better or worse quality health care than whites when they are hospitalized?

Question: When (African Americans/Latinos or Hispanic Americans) see doctors in their local community, do you think they get the same quality of medical treatment or care as white Americans get, or not? (If not the same) Do (African Americans/Latinos or Hispanic Americans) get better or worse medical treatment or care than whites when they see doctors?

Question: Do you think the federal government should do more than it does now to ensure that racial and ethnic minorities have the same chance to get good quality health care as whites have, or not?

Question: I'm going to read you a list of some different public health programs that are being discussed as part of a new health reform bill. For each one, please tell me if you think the federal government should spend more, spend less, or spend about the same as it does now. How about improving the health of minority populations? Should the federal government spend more, less, or about the same as it does now?

Sources: [1]Harvard School of Public Health/Robert Wood Johnson Foundation Poll (Storrs, Conn.: Roper Center for Public Opinion Research, September 14–18, 2005). [2]Harvard School of Public Health/Robert Wood Johnson Foundation Poll (Storrs, Conn.: Roper Center for Public Opinion Research, September 10–14, 2009).

WOMEN'S PERSPECTIVES ON HEALTH CARE POLICY

Gillian K. SteelFisher, Tara Sussman Oakman, and John M. Benson

Introduction

The roles that women and men play in everyday American life have evolved dramatically in recent decades, and now women and men take on many of the same major life tasks such as paid work and child care.[1] That said, important differences still exist between women's and men's typical behaviors, particularly in the sphere of health. As patients, women have special health care needs, including care related to childbearing. Women face higher incidences of certain illnesses such as arthritis, which are not typically thought of as "women's issues."[2] Women are more likely than men to rely on public health care programs, including Medicaid and Medicare,[3] which may impact not only their financial relationship with health care providers but also the kind of care they receive. Women are more likely than men to be families' primary decision maker for health care services and health insurance and to be informal caregivers for their children and parents.[4] For these reasons, women are central players in the health sphere and may have experiences, needs, and opinions different from men.

Women's opinions in the health care policy sphere are crucial not only because of their participation in health care, but also because of their participation in elections. In recent years women have been more likely than men to vote, and they make up a larger number of voters.[5] Understanding women's opinions in health care policy is therefore necessary to understand the major components of American public opinion overall, as well as how public opinion influences policymakers and shapes health care policy.

Despite the clear case for studying women's opinions in health care policy, the idea that women's opinions about policy of any sort may be different from men's in important ways and are worthy of independent study is relatively new. In fact, before the 1980 presidential election, very little was written about women's political opinions or behaviors at all. Women were considered either to be apolitical or to have opinions that mirrored men's; therefore, few political scientists explored women's political opinions.[6] But in 1980 a well-publicized "gender gap" in voting emerged, with more women than men voting for the Democratic candidate, incumbent president Jimmy Carter, than for the Republican candidate, former governor Ronald Reagan, who won the election. It was later shown that the gender gap in 1980 was largely due to a change in voting behaviors by men rather than women, with more men voting Republican, and that such sex differences in voting were nothing new.[7] Nevertheless, the identification of a substantial difference between the sexes in this pivotal election year meant that scholars and the media began to consider more seriously women's voting behaviors and the political opinions behind their choices.

Most of the literature about the gender gap focuses on differences in voting related to candidates, and little focuses on differences in opinions related to policy—with almost none on health care policy specifically. Moreover, much of the literature utilizes data from the 1970s and 1980s, and few updates about gender differences in policy in general have been published. Nevertheless, some consensus is seen in the relatively few articles about women's and men's policy-related opinions.

First, although some differences exist between men's and women's opinions, differences are not found on every question, and even consistent differences are not large. Somewhat surprisingly, surveys find little difference between women's and men's views on "women's issues" such as abortion.[8]

Second, the largest and most consistent differences in women's and men's opinions are found in the policy spheres related to the military and violence. Women are more dovish than men and pay less attention to military issues. Surveys find moderate differences between women and men in what are frequently called "compassion issues," which usually involve income distribution and government intervention to support people with low incomes and other groups. These issues include welfare and education and sometimes health care policy. In general, women are more supportive of compassion policies than men,[9] perhaps because they are more likely to care about vulnerable people who need such programs, as some theorists suggest,[10] or perhaps because women themselves are more likely to be poor or to participate in such programs,[11] or because they see the programs as necessary social or economic institutions.[12] Women may also be more comfortable with government intervention in general; women are, for example, more supportive than men of government regulation of industry in areas such as environmental policy.[13]

Finally, surveys reveal modest differences between women and men on what are referred to as "traditional values," or "family values"; on how to deal with matters that some see as "socially deviant," such as pornography and illicit drug use; and on maintaining "conservative" behaviors, such as prayer in school and limits on sex education.[14] On such issues, women are slightly more conservative than men, opting to uphold the "traditional" behavior and to condemn the "socially deviant" behavior. Research also suggests that women were more likely to be willing to constrain civil rights of groups perceived to pose a threat to "traditional" American values, including communists, socialists, and atheists.[15] The data, however, suggest heterosexual women are more supportive than heterosexual men of certain gay rights.[16]

This chapter explores possible differences between the opinions of women and men on health care policy by focusing on four main topics: (1) the experiences of women and men with the health care system and the problems and worries they have about health care; (2) the interest women and men have in health care issues and the salience of health care as a voting issue; (3) the views of women and men about the nation's health care system and the need for health care reform; and (4) views of women and men on major health care policy issues, including many issues discussed in this book.

In the tables, differences in response between women and men that are statistically significant are indicated with an asterisk. In the text, the opinions or experiences of women and men are said to differ only if that difference is statistically significant. It is important to note that past analyses in this field have suggested that women tend to answer knowledge-related questions with "don't know" more frequently than men, and this may be compounded in areas like policy where some suggest women have less knowledge.[17] We did not find large differences between the sexes where data about the "don't know" responses were available, and so we did not include such data in this chapter.

Finally, before we begin this review, we acknowledge a legitimate complaint—that in studying women's opinions and the reasons women are different from men, it can appear that the male opinion is accepted as the norm. To be clear, the explicit assumption of this chapter is that views of neither sex (or any other way people are grouped for that matter) should be seen as the norm. That said, women may hold a different place in the health care sphere from men, and this chapter acknowledges the possibility of health-specific reasons as well as broader sociological or political reasons for differences in women's and men's opinions.[18] The chapter does not explore differences between subgroups of women, but readers should also keep in mind that women do not constitute a monolithic group that is different only from men. Instead, women are a multifaceted segment of the population with many differences of opinion among themselves that on some subjects may be more varied than the differences between women and men.

Experience with the Health Care System

In general, women have more contact with the health care system than men do. Women are more likely than men (87 percent to 74 percent) to have made at least one visit to a doctor or other health care provider in the past year. They are also more likely than men (83 percent to 73 percent) to report having a regular doctor or health care provider.[19] Women are significantly more likely (62 percent to 46 percent) to say they currently take a prescription drug.[20] Even in areas that may not be directly related to their own health care, women are more likely to have contact with the health care or public health system. Thirty-seven percent of women, compared with 29 percent of men, report ever having had contact with their state health department (**Table 19–1**).[21]

Financial Problems and Worries Related to Health Care

Women are more likely than men to report problems paying medical bills and to be worried about a variety of potential problems involving health insurance and future health care costs. Nearly three in ten women (29 percent), compared with 19 percent of men, report problems paying medical bills during the past twelve months (**Table 19–2**).[22]

Women are more likely than men (38 percent to 31 percent) to report that they are very worried about not being able to afford needed health care services.[23] Among those who have health insurance, women are more likely than men (14 percent to 8 percent) to say they are very worried about losing their health insurance coverage during the next six months.[24] Looking ahead with no time period specified, women are also more likely than men to say they are very worried that they will not be able to pay medical costs when they are elderly (44 percent to 36 percent), pay medical costs in the event of a serious illness or accident (41 percent to 32 percent), afford prescription drugs they need (34 percent to 28 percent), and afford nursing home care (39 percent to 32 percent).[25]

In addition, more women than men report having cut back on treatment or prescriptions for reasons directly related to high health care costs. Thirty-two percent of women, but only 22 percent of men, say that they have skipped a recommended treatment or health care test; 22 percent of women and 14 percent of men report skipping doses or cutting pills in half, presumably to make them last longer; and 37 percent of women and 28 percent of men say that they have put off or postponed needed medical care.[26]

Women, on average, use more health care services than men do and therefore have more opportunities to experience problems paying for care, which may explain some of these differences.[27] Women are also more likely to have lower incomes than men, putting them at greater risk for financial trouble in the health care system.[28]

Interest in Health Care Issues

Women are more likely than men to say they closely follow news stories about a variety of health care issues. An analysis of how closely Americans reported following 218 health news stories between 1996 and 2002 showed that 68 stories (31 percent) were followed more closely by women, while only 9 stories (4 percent) were followed more closely by men. Women were particularly more attentive to news stories about diseases—especially cancer and flu—and about prescription drugs.[29]

In 2004 a larger proportion of women than men said that they were closely following news stories about the withdrawal of the drug Vioxx (66 percent to 54 percent) and about an FDA study on the link between antidepressants and the risk of suicide in children (60 percent to 44 percent).[30] In 2008 more than 70 percent of women, compared with 55 percent of men, said they closely followed news stories about food and health safety issues.[31] As the debate over health care reform started to heat up in August and September 2009, about two-thirds of women (66 percent), compared with less than half of men (47 percent), said they were closely following the discussions in Washington.[32]

What these results tell us is that health care–related issues are generally more salient for women than for men, probably because women have greater exposure to the U.S. health care system as more frequent users of health care services as patients and caregivers and because they are more likely to be lower income and to rely more heavily on public programs or to feel more financially vulnerable.

In general, surveys find little difference between women and men in the level of knowledge about health-related issues. Women are more likely than men to give correct answers when it comes to disease-related questions.[33] Men are more likely than women to give correct answers to questions about some health care policy facts, as well as political and policy issues that are not directly related to health care, but do impact health conditions and/or policy, such as economic policy, the federal budget, gun control, and Social Security.[34]

Health Care as a Voting Issue

In every presidential election from 1988 through 2008, with the exception of 1992, women were more likely than men to be "health care voters"; that is, they were more likely than men to say that health care was the most important issue or one of the two most important issues in deciding their vote.[35] In a survey of registered voters shortly before 2008 presidential election, 38 percent of women, compared with 26 percent of men, said that health care would be one of the two most important issues in their voting decision (**Table 19–3**).[36]

Asked shortly before the 2004 election how important thirteen health care and related issues would be in deciding their vote for president, a higher proportion of women than men described eleven of them as "extremely important." These issues included the cost of health care and health insurance (cited as extremely important by 38 percent of women, compared with 26 percent of men), the number of Americans without health insurance (36 percent to 26 percent), the cost of prescription drugs (36 percent to 26 percent), prescription drugs for seniors (35 percent to 24 percent), Medicare (32 percent to 21 percent), problems with health care quality (29 percent to 16 percent), abortion (27 percent to 18 percent), gun control (26 percent to 18 percent), racial disparities in health care (24 percent to 12 percent), medical malpractice (22 percent to 12 percent), and aid to developing countries to prevent and treat HIV/AIDS (16 percent to 12 percent). The only two issues on which women were not statistically more likely than men to say were extremely important were bioterrorism and stem cell research.[37]

Views of the Health Care System

Although majorities of women and men give negative ratings to the nation's health care system and believe the health care system is either in a state of crisis or has major problems, women are more likely than men to hold these negative views. About three-fourths of women rate the nation's system for providing medical care as fair or poor (73 percent) and believe the system is in crisis or has major problems (76 percent) (**Table 19–4**).[38]

Americans are mixed in their impressions of how the U.S. health care system compares with those in countries such as Canada, France, and Great Britain. With the exception of quality of care, surveys find few differences between men and women on this front. Fifty-two percent of both sexes say the United States is worse than other countries at making sure everyone can get affordable health care, and 56 percent of both groups say the United States is worse at controlling health care costs. The public is much more upbeat about how the U.S. system compares to other countries in the waiting times either to see specialists or be admitted to a hospital. A majority agrees that the U.S. system is better, and only 16 percent of men and women say the U.S. system is worse. Men are more likely than women (61 percent to 50 percent) to believe that patients in the United States receive a better quality of care than patients in the other countries.[39]

Women are more likely than men to see health care reform as an important priority for government action. Asked shortly after the 2008 election how important they thought each of nine issues should be as priorities for the new president and Congress, nearly half of women (48 percent), compared with 39 percent of men, said that reforming health care should be one of the top priorities. In the same poll, two-thirds (67 percent) of women said that given the serious economic problems facing the country, it was more important than ever to take on health care reform now. About half (54 percent) of men expressed that opinion, but 44 percent said the United States cannot afford to take on health care reform right now. Only three in ten women shared that view (**Table 19–5**).[40]

Health Care Policy Issues

This section examines the views of women and men on particular health care policy issues, including the uninsured, government regulation of health care, health care quality, Medicare and Medicaid, and health care spending. The emphasis in the tables is more on the differences than the similarities, but generally speaking, the differences of opinion between the sexes are modest.

The Uninsured

Finding ways to increase the number of Americans who have health insurance was an important issue in the 2008 presidential election and in the debate over the health care reform law that was enacted in 2010. In 2008 a large majority of the public believed that the high number of Americans who do not have health insurance was a very serious problem. Women were especially likely to hold this view: 80 percent of women, compared with 67 percent of men.[41] Women were more likely than men (53 percent to 42 percent) to want to see a health care reform proposal that would make a major effort to provide health insurance to nearly all Americans, even though such a proposal would entail substantial new spending. About one-fourth of both women and men wanted to see a more limited effort that would cover some groups of uninsured and involve less new spending than a more comprehensive effort would. Men were more likely (28 percent to 21 percent) than women to want to keep things basically as they were (**Table 19–6**).[42]

A plurality (42 percent) of women believed that the responsibility of expanding coverage should lie with the federal government. Men were about equally divided between seeing individuals and the federal government as having that responsibility.[43]

In 2008 women were more supportive than men of several approaches to coverage for the uninsured, especially those that involve an expansion of state and federal programs. About four in five women favored expanding Medicare to cover uninsured people ages fifty-five through sixty-four (81 percent) and expanding state government programs for low-income people (78 percent). Support among men for both ideas was about ten percentage points lower (**Table 19–7**).[44]

Women were also supportive of instituting additional requirements on employers and individuals as ways to expand insurance coverage. Seventy-eight percent of women favored requiring employers to offer health insurance to their workers or contribute to a government fund that will pay to cover the uninsured. Women's enthusiasm for this idea may be explained in part by the fact that women are more likely than men to be in jobs that do not offer health benefits, such as part-time positions or service occupations.[45] Men also supported this requirement, but to a lesser extent (64 percent). In addition, 72 percent of women, compared with 62 percent of men, favored requiring individuals to have health insurance, either from their employer or from another source, with tax credits or other aid to help lower- and middle-income people pay for it. Women, like men, were also highly supportive of policy proposals to offer tax breaks or other incentives to businesses to provide health insurance to their employees.[46]

One of the major stumbling blocks that policymakers faced in ensuring health coverage for all Americans was how to pay for it. Although women were more likely than men to consider the problem of the uninsured to be very serious and were more favorable than men toward many of the different approaches to correct this problem, they were not more likely than men to say that they would be willing to pay either higher health insurance premiums or higher taxes to achieve it. Only 48 percent of women and 49 percent of men indicated that they would be willing to pay more to increase the number of Americans who have insurance.[47]

Children receive special attention from federal and state governments through the State Children's Health Insurance Program (SCHIP), now known as CHIP. This program was created through the 1997 Balanced Budget Act and provides federal funding to states to extend insurance coverage to more children than would qualify under Medicaid. During the debate over SCHIP reauthorization in 2007, the general public supported an increase in funding for the program to expand coverage. Women were especially supportive. Nearly three-quarters (73 percent) of women favored spending an additional $35 billion over the next five years to maintain coverage for children already in the program and to expand coverage to an additional 3.8 million uninsured children.[48]

On covering the uninsured and uninsured children, surveys reveal some differences between women's and men's opinions, but these differences do not persist across the board and do not signify wide gulfs between the sexes.

Government Regulation of Costs, Drug Safety, and Profits

About half of the public believes the government does not do enough to regulate health care and prescription drug costs. Women are slightly more likely than men (54 percent to 47 percent) to believe this about health care costs, and about half of both women and men believe this is true about prescription drug prices (**Table 19–8**).[49]

More women than men appear to be concerned about the safety of prescription drugs. About half (49 percent) of women, compared with 38 percent of men, believe the government should regulate more to ensure the safety of prescription drugs. A plurality (49 percent) of men believes the amount of drug safety regulation is about right.[50]

A majority of the public favors the federal government imposing limits on the profits of health insurance companies. Women are significantly more likely than men (68 percent to 56 percent) to hold this view.[51]

Health Care Quality

Consistent with the patterns noted so far are some modest differences between women and men in their perceptions of health care quality in the United States. Although Americans in general are dissatisfied with the quality of care, women are somewhat more likely than men (59 percent to 52 percent) to report being dissatisfied (**Table 19–9**).[52]

Americans are, however, more upbeat about the quality of their own care than about the quality of health care in the nation as a whole. Large majorities of both women and men rate the quality of care they received the last time they visited a doctor as excellent or good, and women are more likely than men (50 percent to 40 percent) to say the quality was excellent.[53]

The incidence of medical errors is a subset of the health care quality debate that has received considerable national attention. Americans attribute medical errors to a wide range of system-related problems: overwork, stress and fatigue, health professionals not working together as a team, poor training of health professionals, doctors not having enough time with patients, and a lack of computerized medical records. Women are more likely than men to consider many of these issues "very important." These views are also popular among men, but to a lesser extent, suggesting that men and women may not disagree on the root causes of medical errors, but that the issue may be more salient for women than for men.[54]

Women are more likely than men to see several potential solutions to the problem of medical errors as being "very effective." Eighty-two percent of women and 75 percent of men said giving doctors more time to spend with patients would be very effective; 79 percent of women and 65 percent of men said the same about better training of health professionals; and 78 percent of women and 65 percent of men said that requiring hospitals to develop systems to avoid medical errors would be very effective.

On looking for information about quality of care, women are more likely than men to report that they would engage in information-seeking behaviors, including asking family, friends, and co-workers (71 percent of women, compared with 58 percent of men); asking their doctor, nurse, or other health professional (69 percent to 60 percent); contacting their health plan (39 percent to 32 percent); and contacting a state agency (18 percent to 13 percent).[55] This pattern may best be explained by women being more likely to be responsible for their families' health care services and insurance-related decisions.

Medicare and Medicaid

Two of the most important features of the U.S. health care system are the public insurance programs for elderly and low-income individuals—Medicare and Medicaid, respectively—and here the views of women and men are generally comparable. Large majorities of both women and men believe that Medicare is a very important program.[56] In addition, women and men have similar views about the appropriate level of federal spending on Medicare and Medicaid (**Table 19–10**).[57]

With regard to the Medicare prescription drug benefit, enacted in 2003, men and women had similar opinions when asked about it in the early stages of implementation in April 2006. At that time, a plurality of both women and men felt unfavorably toward the program.[58]

One area with wide differences between women and men is their concern for the future of Medicare. Sixty percent of women on Medicare are very concerned that they will not continue to receive the current level of benefits they now receive; only 38 percent of men feel this way. Among people who are not yet eligible for Medicare, 62 percent of women are very concerned that the benefits seniors enjoy now will not be available to them when they retire, compared with 53 percent of men.[59] These differences may be explained by the fact that women tend to rely on Medicare benefits more than men do and rely on them longer time because their life expectancies are slightly higher. Life expectancy at birth is eighty-one years for women and seventy-six years for men.[60]

On reforming Medicare so that it is sustainable for the foreseeable future, women and men tend to agree on most of the potential options. The most popular solutions among both groups are allowing the federal government to use its buying power to negotiate with drug companies to get lower drug prices, reducing payments to doctors and hospitals, requiring higher-income seniors to pay more for Medicare, increasing the payroll taxes workers and employers pay to help fund Medicare, and reducing Medicare payments to HMOs and other private insurers.

Women are less likely than men (29 percent to 39 percent) to favor raising the Medicare eligibility age from sixty-five to sixty-seven for future retirees. Women are also less likely than men to support turning Medicare into a program that serves only low-income seniors instead of all seniors (20 percent to 31 percent), cutting back the Medicare drug benefit (18 percent to 29 percent), and requiring all seniors to pay a larger share of Medicare costs out of their own pocket (7 percent to 16 percent).[61] It should be noted that a majority of both women and men oppose each of these measures.

Health Care Spending

A majority of women and men believe the federal government is spending too little on health care, and women are significantly more likely than men (71 percent to 60 percent) to hold this view.[62] A majority of both sexes believe that spending to prevent the spread of disease and improve health should be kept about the same, but women are more likely than men (39 percent to 28 percent) to believe that such spending should be increased (**Table 19–11**).[63]

Conclusions

Some general conclusions emerge from the polling data presented in this chapter. First, they confirm that for a number of reasons discussed in the introduction, women have more contact with the health care system than men do. They also are more likely to experience financial problems with the health care system and to worry about future problems involving health insurance and health care costs.

Women generally pay more attention to news stories about health care issues, particularly those involving diseases and prescription drugs. In addition, health care issues have consistently been more important to women than to men in deciding how to vote in presidential elections. Women generally have a slightly lower opinion than men of the nation's health care system, although they are no more likely than men to be critical of their own medical care.

But on most health care policy issues, the views of women and men do not differ greatly. Women are more likely than men to believe that federal spending on health care should be increased, but the differences are not big. They are also slightly more supportive of government regulation of health care, with the largest difference being on the safety of prescription drugs.

Although more women than men rely on Medicare and Medicaid, the sexes do not differ very much in their overall views of these government programs. On some proposed Medicare changes that are unpopular overall, such as reducing future benefits, increasing out-of-pocket costs for recipients, and raising the retirement age, women are even less supportive than men. And, women are far more worried than men that the Medicare benefits seniors now enjoy will not be there in the future.

Where women do differ from men is on the problem of the uninsured. During the period before the enactment in 2010 of a major health care reform law, women were more likely than men to see the number of uninsured Americans as a very serious problem, and they were more likely than men to want a major effort to fix the problem. Women were more likely than men to support a variety of proposals to increase the number of Americans who have health insurance, but were no more likely than men to be willing to pay more in higher premiums or taxes to achieve this goal.

In summary, women's and men's policy views differ on some important issues, but for the most part the differences are relatively small, especially when compared with the often wide differences seen between whites and African Americans and between whites and Hispanic Americans. This pattern of modest differences is roughly consistent with polling data in other policy areas, as described in the introduction. In addition, we see that in health care policy, as in other areas, women are more likely to be supportive of government reform and regulation, and slightly more protective of not tampering with existing government efforts, including Medicare and Medicaid. Perhaps the most important conclusions from the data presented in this chapter are that health care issues are significantly more salient to women than to men and that women are more likely than men to vote based on these issues. Therefore, even though their policy prescriptions may not be very different from those of men, women are more likely to want to hear candidates discuss their positions on health care and to see government take action on these issues.

Notes

[1] Mark Aguair and Erik Hurst, "Measuring Trends in Leisure: The Allocation of Time over Five Decades," *Quarterly Journal of Economics* 122 (August 2007): 969–1006.

[2] Kaiser Family Foundation, "Women and Health Care: A National Profile," July 2005, http://www.kff.org/womenshealth/7336.cfm.

[3] Ibid.

[4] Ibid.

[5] Susan Carroll, "Women Voters and the Gender Gap," American Political Science Association, 2009, http://www.apsanet.org/content_5270.cfm; Center for American Women and Politics, Eagleton Institute of Politics, Rutgers, "Gender Differences in Voter Turnout," 2008, http://www.cawp.rutgers.edu/fast_facts/voters/documents/genderdiff.pdf.

[6] Kristi Andersen, "Working Women and Political Participation, 1952–1972," *American Journal of Political Science* 19 (July 1975): 439–453; Kent L. Tedin, David W. Brady, Mary E. Buxton, Barbara M. Goran, and Judy L. Thompson, "Social Background and Political Differences between Pro- and Anti-ERA Activists," *American Politics Quarterly* 5 (July 1977): 395–408.

[7] Daniel Wirls, "Reinterpreting the Gender Gap," *Public Opinion Quarterly* 50 (Fall 1986): 316–330; Barbara Norrander, "The Evolution of the Gender Gap," *Public Opinion Quarterly* 63 (Winter 1999): 566–576.

[8] Robert S. Erikson and Kent L. Tedin, *American Public Opinion: Its Origins, Content, and Impact,* updated 7th ed. (New York: Pearson/Longman, 2007), 222–225.

[9] Ibid.; Robert Y. Shapiro and Harpreet Mahajan, "Gender Differences in Policy Preferences: A Summary of Trends from the 1960s to the 1980s," *Public Opinion Quarterly* 50 (Spring 1986): 42–61.

[10] Carol Gilligan, *In a Different Voice: Psychological Theories and Women's Development* (Cambridge: Harvard University Press, 1982); Sara Ruddick, *Maternal Thinking: Toward a Politics of Peace* (London: The Women's Press, 1990).

[11] U.S. Census Bureau, Current Population Survey, Annual Social and Economic (ASEC) Supplement, "POV01: Age and Sex of All People, Family Members and Unrelated Individuals Iterated by Income-to-Poverty Ratio and Race: 2008," http://www.census.gov/hhes/www/cpstables/032009/pov/new01_100_01.htm; Carmen DeNavas-Wait, Bernadette D. Proctor, and Jessica C. Smith, U.S. Census Bureau, Current Population Reports, P60–236, *Income, Poverty and Health Insurance Coverage in the United States, 2008,* Table 1, http://www.census.gov/hhes/www/income/income.html; U.S. Department of Health and Human Services, Health Resources and Services Administration, *Women's Health USA 2004,* I. Population Characteristics, http://mchb.hrsa.gov/whusa04/pages/ch1.htm; Steven P. Erie and Martin Rein, "Women and the Welfare State: Potential for a New Progressive Alliance?" in *The Politics of the Gender Gap: Social Construction of Political Influence,* vol. 2, ed. Carol M. Mueller (Newbury Park: Sage Publications, 1988), 173–191.

[12] Ethel Klein, *Gender Politics: From Consciousness to Mass Politics* (Cambridge: Harvard University Press, 1984).

[13] Shapiro and Mahajan, "Gender Differences in Policy Preferences."

[14] Ibid.

[15] Ibid.; Ewa A. Golebiowksa, "Gender Gap in Political Tolerance," *Political Behavior* 21 (March 1999): 43–66.

[16] Gregory M. Herek, "Gender Gaps in Public Opinion about Lesbians and Gay Men," *Public Opinion Quarterly* 66 (Spring 2002): 40–66.

[17] Michael X. Delli Carpini and Scott Keeter, *What Americans Know About Politics and Why It Matters* (New Haven: Yale University Press, 1996).

[18] Because of space limitations, this chapter cannot fully explore the array of theories put forth to explain differences between women's and men's opinions, although this literature would likely enrich the study of public opinion in health care policy.

[19] Kaiser Family Foundation, "Women and Health Care," July 2005.

[20] *USA Today*/Kaiser Family Foundation/Harvard School of Public Health Poll (Storrs, Conn.: Roper Center for Public Opinion Research, January 3–23, 2008).

[21] Harvard School of Public Health/Robert Wood Johnson Foundation Poll (Storrs, Conn.: Roper Center for Public Opinion Research, June 24–28, 2009).

[22] Harvard School of Public Health/Robert Wood Johnson Foundation Poll (Storrs, Conn.: Roper Center for Public Opinion Research, June 17–21, 2009).

[23] Kaiser Family Foundation Poll (Storrs, Conn.: Roper Center for Public Opinion Research, April 2–8, 2009).

[24] Harvard School of Public Health/Robert Wood Johnson Foundation Poll, June 17–21, 2009.

[25] *USA Today*/Kaiser Family Foundation/Harvard School of Public Health Poll (Storrs, Conn.: Roper Center for Public Opinion Research, April 25–June 9, 2005).

[26] Ibid.

[27] Sheila D. Rustgi, Michelle M. Doty, and Sara R. Commins, "Women at Risk: Why Many Women Are Forgoing Needed Health Care," Commonwealth Fund Issue Brief, May 2009, http://www.commonwealthfund.org/~/media/Files/Publications/Issue%20Brief/2009/May/Women%20at%20Risk/PDF_1262_Rustgi_women_at_risk_issue_brief_Final.pdf.

[28] U.S. Census Bureau, Current Population Survey, Annual Social and Economic (ASEC) Supplement, "POV01: Age and Sex of All People, Family Members and Unrelated Individuals Iterated by Income-to-Poverty Ratio and Race: 2008"; DeNavas-Wait, Proctor, and Smith, *Income, Poverty and Health Insurance Coverage*, Table 1.

[29] Mollyann Brodie, Elizabeth C. Hamel, Drew E. Altman, Robert J. Blendon, and John M. Benson, "Health News and the American Public, 1996–2002," *Journal of Health Politics, Policy and Law* 28 (October 2003): 927–950.

[30] Kaiser Family Foundation/Harvard School of Public Health Poll (Storrs, Conn.: Roper Center for Public Opinion Research, October 14–17, 2004).

[31] Harvard School of Public Health Poll (Storrs, Conn.: Roper Center for Public Opinion Research, May 12–June 1, 2008).

[32] NPR/Kaiser Family Foundation/Harvard School of Public Health Poll (Storrs, Conn.: Roper Center for Public Opinion Research, August 27–September 13, 2009).

[33] Brodie et al., "Health News and the American Public, 1996–2002."

[34] Ibid.; Delli Carpini and Keeter, *What Americans Know About Politics and Why It Matters.*

[35] Robert J. Blendon, Drew E. Altman, John M. Benson, Mollyann Brodie, Tami Buhr, Claudia Deane, and Sasha Buscho, "Voters and Health Reform in the 2008 Presidential Election," *New England Journal of Medicine* 359 (November 6, 2008): 2050–61.

[36] Kaiser Family Foundation/Harvard School of Public Health Poll (Storrs, Conn.: Roper Center for Public Opinion Research, September 10–21, 2008).

[37] Kaiser Family Foundation/Harvard School of Public Health Poll, October 14–17, 2004.

[38] Harvard School of Public Health/Robert Wood Johnson Foundation Poll, June 17–21, 2009.

[39] Harvard School of Public Health/Harris Interactive Poll (Storrs, Conn.: Roper Center for Public Opinion Research, March 5–8, 2008).

[40] Kaiser Family Foundation/Harvard School of Public Health Poll (Storrs, Conn.: Roper Center for Public Opinion Research, December 4–14, 2008).

[41] NPR/Kaiser Family Foundation/Harvard School of Public Health Poll (Storrs, Conn.: Roper Center for Public Opinion Research, February 14–24, 2008),

[42] Kaiser Family Foundation/Harvard School of Public Health Poll, December 4–14, 2008.

[43] Kaiser Family Foundation/Harvard School of Public Health Poll, September 10–21, 2008.

[44] Kaiser Family Foundation/Harvard School of Public Health Poll, December 4–14, 2008.

[45] U.S. Department of Labor, "Quick Stats on Women Workers, 2008," http://www.dol.gov/wb/stats/main.htm.

[46] Kaiser Family Foundation/Harvard School of Public Health Poll, December 4–14, 2008.

[47] Ibid.

[48] NPR/Kaiser Family Foundation/Harvard School of Public Health Poll (Storrs, Conn.: Roper Center for Public Opinion Research, October 8–13, 2007).

[49] Kaiser Family Foundation/Harvard School of Public Health Poll, December 4–14, 2008.

[50] *USA Today*/Kaiser Family Foundation/Harvard School of Public Health Poll, January 3–23, 2008.

[51] Kaiser Family Foundation/Harvard School of Public Health Poll, December 4–14, 2008.

[52] Kaiser Family Foundation/Agency for Healthcare Research and Quality/Harvard School of Public Health Poll (Storrs, Conn.: Roper Center for Public Opinion Research, July 7–September 5, 2004).

[53] Harvard School of Public Health/Robert Wood Johnson Foundation Poll (Storrs, Conn.: Roper Center for Public Opinion Research, March 26–30, 2008).

[54] Kaiser Family Foundation/Agency for Healthcare Research and Quality/Harvard School of Public Health Poll, July 7–September 5, 2004.

[55] Ibid.

[56] Kaiser Family Foundation Poll (Storrs, Conn.: Roper Center for Public Opinion Research, April 1–May 1, 2005).

[57] Kaiser Family Foundation/Harvard School of Public Health Poll, December 4–14, 2008.

[58] Kaiser Family Foundation Poll (Storrs, Conn.: Roper Center for Public Opinion Research, April 6–11, 2006).

[59] Kaiser Family Foundation/Harvard School of Public Health Poll (Storrs, Conn.: Roper Center for Public Opinion Research, April 25–June 1, 2003).

[60] National Center for Health Statistics, *Health, United States, 2008,* Table 26, http://www.cdc.gov/nchs/data/hus/hus08.pdf.

[61] Kaiser Family Foundation/Harvard School of Public Health Poll, December 4–14, 2008.

[62] Kaiser Family Foundation/Harvard School of Public Health Poll (Storrs, Conn.: Roper Center for Public Opinion Research, November 9–29, 2006).

[63] Kaiser Family Foundation/Harvard School of Public Health Poll, December 4–14, 2008.

Table 19-1 Contact with the Health Care System, by Sex (in percent)

	Women	Men
At least one visit to health care provider in past year[1]	87*	74
Have a regular health care provider[1]	83*	73
Reported use of prescription drugs, current[2]	62*	46
Had contact with state health department, ever[3]	37*	29

Note: *Statistically significant difference between women's and men's responses.

Question: In the past 12 months, have you seen a doctor or health care provider?

Question: Do you have a regular doctor or health care provider you usually see?

Question: Do you currently take any prescription medicine or not?

Question: Have you ever had any contact with your state's health department, or not?

Sources: [1]Kaiser Family Foundation, "Women and Health Care: A National Profile," July 2005. [2]*USA Today*/Kaiser Family Foundation/Harvard School of Public Health Poll (Storrs, Conn.: Roper Center for Public Opinion Research, January 3–23, 2008). [3]Harvard School of Public Health/Robert Wood Johnson Foundation Poll (Storrs, Conn.: Roper Center for Public Opinion Research, June 24–28, 2009).

Table 19-2 Financial Problems and Worries Related to Health Care, by Sex (in percent)

	Women	Men
Had problem paying medical bills, past 12 months[1]	29*	19
Very worried about not being to afford the health care services you think you need, no time period specified[2]	38*	31
Very worried about losing health insurance, next 6 months (among adults who have health insurance)[1]	14*	8
Worries about health care, no time period specified (percent very worried)[3]		
Won't be able to pay medical costs when elderly	44*	36
Won't be able to pay medical costs in event of serious illness or accident	41*	32
Won't be able to afford prescription drugs you need	34*	28
Won't be able to afford nursing home care	39*	32

Note: *Statistically significant difference between women's and men's responses.

Question: In the past 12 months, have you had problems paying medical bills, or not?

Question: How worried are you about not being able to afford the health care services you think you need? Are you very worried, somewhat worried, not too worried, or not at all worried?

Question: (Asked of adults who have health insurance) Thinking about the next six months, how worried are you that you will lose your health insurance coverage? Are you very worried, somewhat worried, not too worried, or not at all worried?

Question: How worried are you that (you won't be able to pay medical costs when you are elderly/you won't be able to pay medical costs in the event of a serious illness or accident/you won't be able to afford the prescription drugs you need/you won't be able to afford nursing home and home care services)? Are you very worried, somewhat worried, not too worried, not at all worried?

Sources: [1]Harvard School of Public Health/Robert Wood Johnson Foundation Poll (Storrs, Conn.: Roper Center for Public Opinion Research, June 17–21, 2009). [2]Kaiser Family Foundation Poll (Storrs, Conn.: Roper Center for Public Opinion Research, April 2–8, 2009). [3]*USA Today*/Kaiser Family Foundation/Harvard School of Public Health Poll (Storrs, Conn.: Roper Center for Public Opinion Research, April 25–June 9, 2005).

Table 19-3 Health Care as a Voting Issue, by Sex (in percent)

	Women	Men
One of two most important issues in deciding your vote for president (2008, registered voters)[1]		
Economy	66	69
Energy, including gas prices	30	37*
Health care	38*	26
War in Iraq	31	27
Terrorism	20	17
Illegal immigration	11	11
Health care issues extremely important in deciding your vote for president (2004)[2]		
Cost of health care and health insurance	38*	26
Number of Americans without health insurance	36*	26
Cost of prescription drugs	36*	26
Prescription drug benefits for seniors	35*	24
Medicare	32*	21
Bioterrorism	28	25
Problems with health care quality	29*	16
Abortion	27*	18
Gun control	26*	18
Racial disparities in health care	24*	12
Medical malpractice	22*	12
Stem cell research	19	14
Aid to developing countries to prevent and treat HIV/AIDS	16*	12

Note: *Statistically significant difference between women's and men's responses.

Question: Thinking ahead to the November 2008 election, which of the following issues will be most important to you when you decide how to vote for president? And which of these issues will be the second most important to you when you decide how to vote for president? The economy; energy, including gas prices; health care; the war in Iraq; terrorism; illegal immigration.

Question: I'm going to read you a list of specific health care issues. For each one, please tell me how important it will be in your vote for president this year. Will it be extremely important in deciding your vote, very important, somewhat important, or not important? (The cost of health care and health insurance/The number of Americans without health insurance/The cost of prescription drugs/Prescription drug benefits for seniors/Medicare/Bioterrorism/Problems with health care quality/Abortion/Gun control/Racial disparities in health care/Medical malpractice/Stem cell research/Aid to developing countries to prevent and treat HIV/AIDS).

Sources: [1]Kaiser Family Foundation/Harvard School of Public Health Poll (Storrs, Conn.: Roper Center for Public Opinion Research, September 10–21, 2008). [2]Kaiser Family Foundation/Harvard School of Public Health Poll (Storrs, Conn.: Roper Center for Public Opinion Research, October 14–17, 2004).

Table 19-4 Views of the U.S. Health Care System, by Sex (in percent)

	Women	Men
Rating the nation's system for providing medical care[1]		
Excellent/good	25	32*
Fair/poor	73*	66
Don't know	2	2
U.S. health care system[1]		
Is in a state of crisis/Has major problems	76*	64
Has minor/no problems	23	34*
Don't know	1	2

(Table continues)

Table 19-4 *Continued*

U.S. health care system compared with Canada, France,
and Great Britain when it comes to . . .[2]

Quality of care patients receive		
U.S. system is better	50	61*
U.S. system is worse	17	14
Same (vol.)	9	7
Don't know	23	18
Making sure everyone can get affordable health care[2]		
U.S. system is better	24	29
U.S. system is worse	52	52
Same (vol.)	5	3
Don't know	18	16

Note: *Statistically significant difference between women's and men's responses. (vol.) = volunteered response.

Question: How would you rate the nation's system for providing medical care to Americans? Would you say excellent, good, fair, or poor?

Question: Which of these statements do you think best describes the U.S. health care system today—it is in a state of crisis, it has major problems, it has minor problems, or it does not have any problems?

Question: Thinking about the countries I have just mentioned [Canada, France, and Great Britain], would you say that, in general, the United States has a better health care system or a worse health care system than these countries when it comes to (the quality of care patients receive/making sure everyone can get affordable health care)?

Sources: [1]Harvard School of Public Health/Robert Wood Johnson Foundation Poll (Storrs, Conn.: Roper Center for Public Opinion Research, June 17–21, 2009). [2]Harvard School of Public Health/Harris Interactive Poll (Storrs, Conn.: Roper Center for Public Opinion Research, March 5–8, 2008).

Table 19-5 Importance of Health Care Reform, by Sex (in percent)

	Women	Men
Priorities for the new president and Congress		
(percent saying each should be one of their top priorities)		
Improving the country's economic situation	74	71
Fighting terrorism	50	46
Reforming health care	48*	39
Reducing the federal budget deficit	39	39
Providing more support to improve public schools	38	36
Working to create more clean energy sources	39	34
Dealing with Iraq	36	35
Dealing with Afghanistan	32	29
Improving America's image in the world	26	25
Given the serious economic problems facing the country . . .		
It is more important than ever to take on health care reform now	67*	54
We cannot afford to take on health care reform right now	30	44*
Don't know	3	2

Note: *Statistically significant difference between women's and men's responses.

Question: I'm going to read you a list of some different things the new president and Congress might try to act on next year. As I read each one, tell me if you think it should be one of their top priorities, very important but not a top priority, somewhat important, or not that important. What about (improving the country's economic situation/fighting terrorism/reforming health care/reducing the federal budget deficit/providing more support to improve public schools/working to create more clean energy sources/dealing with Iraq/dealing with Afghanistan/improving America's image in the world)? Should this be one of their top priorities, very important but not a top priority, somewhat important, or not that important?

Question: Which comes closer to describing your own views? Given the serious economic problems facing the country, we cannot afford to take on health care reform right now, or it is more important than ever to take on health care reform now.

Source: Kaiser Family Foundation/Harvard School of Public Health Poll (Storrs, Conn.: Roper Center for Public Opinion Research, December 4–14, 2008).

Table 19-6 Views about the Uninsured, by Sex (in percent)

	Women	Men
Seriousness of number of Americans who do not have health insurance[1]		
Very serious	80*	67
Somewhat serious	15	23*
Not too serious	4	8
Not at all serious	1	3
Would like to see in a health care reform proposal[2]		
Major effort to provide health insurance to nearly all uninsured, would involve substantial spending increase	53*	42
More limited effort, would cover only some groups of uninsured, would involve less new spending	24	27
Keep things basically as they are	21	28*
Don't know	2	3
Who should have most responsibility for helping ensure Americans receive health insurance coverage? (registered voters)[3]		
Federal government	42*	34
Individuals themselves	28	35*
Employers and businesses	25	26
All of them (vol.)	2	2
Don't know	3	3

Note: *Statistically significant difference between women's and men's responses. (vol.) = volunteered response.

Question: An issue that has received attention in the news lately is the number of Americans who do not have health insurance. How serious do you think this problem is? Very serious, somewhat serious, not too serious, or not at all serious?

Question: Which one of the following three things would you like to see in a health care reform proposal from the new president and Congress? Would you want them to propose a new health plan that would make a major effort to provide health insurance for nearly all uninsured Americans and would involve a substantial increase in spending; a new health plan that is more limited and would cover only some groups of uninsured Americans, but would involve less new spending; or keeping things basically as they are?

Question: Which one of the following do you think should have the most responsibility for helping ensure that Americans receive health insurance coverage? The federal government, employers and businesses, or individuals themselves?

Sources: [1]NPR/Kaiser Family Foundation/Harvard School of Public Health Poll (Storrs, Conn.: Roper Center for Public Opinion Research, February 14–24, 2008). [2]Kaiser Family Foundation/Harvard School of Public Health Poll (Storrs, Conn.: Roper Center for Public Opinion Research, December 4–14, 2008). [3]Kaiser Family Foundation/Harvard School of Public Health Poll (Storrs, Conn.: Roper Center for Public Opinion Research, September 10–21, 2008).

Table 19-7 Views about Ways to Increase the Number of Americans Covered by Health Insurance, by Sex

	Percent favor	
	Women	Men
Offering tax breaks or other incentives to businesses that provide health insurance for their employees	85	85
Helping those who are unemployed to afford health insurance coverage	89*	74
Requiring all parents to have health insurance for their children, either from their employer or from another source, with financial help for those who can't afford it	86*	72
Expanding Medicare to cover people between the ages of 55 and 64 who do not have health insurance	81*	70
Expanding state government programs for low-income people, such as Medicaid or the State Children's Health Insurance Program	78*	68
Requiring employers to offer health insurance to their workers or pay money into a government fund that will pay to cover those without insurance	78*	64
Requiring all Americans to have health insurance, either from their employer or from another source, with financial help for those who can't afford it	72*	62
Offering tax credits to help people buy private health insurance	68	61
Having a national health plan in which all Americans would get their insurance from a single government plan	47	44
Giving people fixed amounts of money to buy health insurance on their own instead of getting it at work	30	29

Note: *Statistically significant difference between women's and men's responses.

Question: I'm going to read you some different ways to increase the number of Americans covered by health insurance. As I read each one, please tell me whether you would favor it or oppose it. (INSERT EACH OPTION). Do you favor or oppose this?

Source: Kaiser Family Foundation/Harvard School of Public Health Poll (Storrs, Conn.: Roper Center for Public Opinion Research, December 4–14, 2008).

Table 19-8 Views about Health Care Costs and Government Regulation, by Sex (in percent)

	Women	Men
Government regulation of health care costs[1]		
Not enough regulation	54*	47
About right	18	23
Too much regulation	23	27
Don't know	5	3

(Table continues)

Table 19-8 *Continued*

	Women	Men
Government regulation of prescription drug prices[1]		
Not enough regulation	52	52
About right	21	21
Too much regulation	22	23
Don't know	5	4
Government making sure prescription drugs are safe[2]		
Not enough regulation	49*	38
About right	44	49
Too much regulation	5	11*
Don't know	2	2
Federal government imposing limits on profits of health insurance companies[1]		
Favor	68*	56
Oppose	28	43*
Don't know	3	1

Note: *Statistically significant difference between women's and men's responses.

Question: Overall, do you think there is too much, not enough, or about the right amount of government regulation of health care costs?

Question: Overall, do you think there is too much, not enough, or about the right amount of government regulation of the price of prescription drugs?

Question: I'd like your opinion of current government regulation of prescription drugs in some different areas. How about making sure prescription drugs are safe for people to use? Is there too much regulation in this area, not as much as there should be, or about the right amount of regulation?

Question: Do you favor or oppose the federal government imposing limits on the profits of health insurance companies?

Sources: [1]Kaiser Family Foundation/Harvard School of Public Health Poll (Storrs, Conn.: Roper Center for Public Opinion Research, December 4–14, 2008). [2]*USA Today*/Kaiser Family Foundation/Harvard School of Public Health Poll (Storrs, Conn.: Roper Center for Public Opinion Research, January 3–23, 2008).

Table 19-9 Views about Quality of Health Care, by Sex (in percent)

	Women	Men
Satisfaction with the quality of care in this country[1]		
Satisfied	39	45*
Dissatisfied	59*	52
Rating of quality of care you received the last time you visited a doctor[2]		
Excellent	50*	40
Good	35	40
Fair	12	14
Poor	2	4
Don't know	0	2

Note: *Statistically significant difference between women's and men's responses.

Question: Thinking about the country as a whole, are you generally satisfied or dissatisfied with the quality of health care in this country?

Question: Thinking specifically about care from a doctor, how would you rate the quality of care that you received the last time you visited a doctor: excellent, good, fair, or poor?

Sources: [1]Kaiser Family Foundation/Agency for Healthcare Research and Quality/Harvard School of Public Health Poll (Storrs, Conn.: Roper Center for Public Opinion Research, July 7–September 5, 2004). [2]Harvard School of Public Health/Robert Wood Johnson Foundation Poll (Storrs, Conn.: Roper Center for Public Opinion Research, March 26–30, 2008).

Table 19-10 Views about Medicare and Medicaid, by Sex (in percent)

	Women	Men
Importance of Medicare program[1]		
Very important	86	80
Somewhat important	12	15
Not very/Not at all important	0	3
Don't know	2	2
Federal spending on Medicare[2]		
Increase	44	41
Keep about the same	51	50
Decrease	3	8*
Don't know	1	1
Federal spending on Medicaid[2]		
Increase	38	30
Keep about the same	50	58
Decrease	11	11
Don't know	1	1
Concern that you will not continue to receive the level of Medicare benefits you now receive (among those on Medicare)[3]		
Very concerned	60*	38
Somewhat concerned	25	25
Not very concerned	8	16*
Not at all concerned	7	17*
Concern that benefits seniors have today will not be available to you when you retire (among those not on Medicare)[3]		
Very concerned	62*	53
Somewhat concerned	25	28
Not very concerned	8	8
Not at all concerned	7	10

Note: *Statistically significant difference between women's and men's responses.

Question: I'm going to read you a list of federal government programs and for each one, please tell me how important you think this program is. Is it very important, somewhat important, not very important, or not at all important? What about . . . Medicare?

Question: As you know, the federal government has a substantial budget deficit and there are many competing spending priorities facing the next president and Congress. Thinking about the federal budget, do you want to see the next president and Congress increase spending on (Medicare, the program that provides health insurance primarily to people age 65 and older/Medicaid, the program that provides health insurance and long-term care to low-income families and people with disabilities), decrease spending, or keep it about the same?

Question: (Asked of those on Medicare) How concerned are you that, in the future, you will not continue to receive the current level of Medicare benefits you now receive? Would you say you are very concerned, somewhat concerned, not too concerned, or not at all concerned?

Question: (Asked of those not on Medicare) How concerned are you that the Medicare benefits seniors have today will not be available for you when you retire? Would you say you are very concerned, somewhat concerned, not too concerned, or not at all concerned?

Sources: [1]Kaiser Family Foundation Poll (Storrs, Conn.: Roper Center for Public Opinion Research, April 1–May 1, 2005). [2]Kaiser Family Foundation/Harvard School of Public Health Poll (Storrs, Conn.: Roper Center for Public Opinion Research, December 4–14, 2008). [3]Kaiser Family Foundation/Harvard School of Public Health Poll (Storrs, Conn.: Roper Center for Public Opinion Research, April 25–June 1, 2003).

Table 19-11 Views about Health Care Spending, by Sex (in percent)

	Women	Men
Federal government spending on health care[1]		
Too little	72*	61
Right amount	14	16
Too much	7	15*
Don't know	7	8
Federal spending on programs to prevent the spread **of disease and improve health[2]**		
Increase	39*	28
Keep about the same	53	57
Decrease	6	13*
Don't know	2	2

Note: *Statistically significant difference between women's and men's responses.

Question: Do you think the federal government spends too much, too little, or the right amount on health care?

Question: As you know, the federal government has a substantial budget deficit and there are many competing spending priorities facing the next president and Congress. Thinking about the federal budget, do you want to see the next president and Congress increase spending on . . . public health programs to prevent the spread of disease and improve health, decrease spending, or keep it about the same?

Sources: [1]Kaiser Family Foundation/Harvard School of Public Health Poll (Storrs, Conn.: Roper Center for Public Opinion Research, November 9–29, 2006). [2]Kaiser Family Foundation/Harvard School of Public Health Poll (Storrs, Conn.: Roper Center for Public Opinion Research, December 4–14, 2008).

Chapter 20

ELECTIONS, PARTISAN VIEWS, AND HEALTH POLICY

Robert J. Blendon and John M. Benson

Differences between Democrats and Republicans in their views about health policy issues are a central factor in understanding the debates that occur over health care in the United States. Proposals for health reform are usually organized around the views put forth by the two political parties and their leaders. Elected leaders must first win the nomination of their own party and subsequently rely on loyalists' support in the general election, so their policy positions often reflect the general preferences of their party adherents.[1] In an area such as health care, with its concrete human problems that almost everyone experiences, we might expect to find little variation in views between the partisans of the two parties. But as this chapter shows, that expectation is not correct.

Research by a number of writers has found that the political parties (including their elected officials, activists, and those in the general public who identify with the party) are divided on many major policy issues. Many of these writers believe the polarization on issues has intensified in recent times.[2]

Scholars trying to explain the rise in polarization point to a number of factors. The first is the impact of the party realignment of southern whites starting in the late 1960s. White southern Democrats left their party en masse and re-identified themselves as Republicans. Because many southern Democrats saw themselves as conservative (including on religious issues), their move changed the distribution of opinions within both parties, making the Republicans more conservative and the Democrats more liberal. Also identified as important factors leading to polarization are certain social and political trends: wider income disparities between adherents of each party; the re-segregation in housing by place, income, and ethnicity; the impact of the growth in the number of immigrants on the composition of the two parties; and redistricting efforts that have led to congressional districts in which constituents' views have become more homogenous.[3]

The Partisan Divide

We examine this partisan divide as it may effect health policy along five dimensions: (1) attitudes about how much the government should do to solve big problems, (2) attitudes toward the state of the U.S. health care system, (3) people's views about their own health care, (4) attitudes about health reform, and (5) attitudes about what are considered controversial health/social policy issues. In addition, we discuss the consequences of political party polarization for health policy's role in presidential elections and presidential initiatives.

Attitudes about the Role of Government

Since World War II, many advocates for major health reform have argued that government must be the driver in changing the nature and functioning of the U.S. health care system. The underlying value expressed by this belief is that government should do more to solve major problems, including health care. Fifty-eight percent of Democrats favor government doing more about larger problems, but only 28 percent of Republicans share that view. The majority of Republicans (64 percent) believe government is already trying to do too many things, and they are not in favor of government doing even more in the future (Table 20–1).[4]

A related question is whether the public would rather have a smaller government that provides fewer services or a bigger government that provides more services. Any debate about government's future participation in health care starts out with a wide difference on this underlying value: 68 percent of Republicans prefer smaller government; 60 percent of Democrats prefer a bigger government providing more services.[5]

Attitudes about the State of the U.S. Health Care System

When it comes to the state of the U.S. health care system, the parties are divided on a wide range of measures. Democrats are more critical of the health care system than Republicans. Three-fourths (76 percent) of Democrats rate the health system as fair or poor, compared with 56 percent of Republicans.[6] About half (52 percent) of Democrats think the health care systems of other countries are better than the U.S. system; only 19 percent of Republicans express this view.[7] More than three-fourths (78 percent) of Democrats are dissatisfied with the quality of health care in this country, compared with 40 percent of Republicans. The majority of both parties' constituents agree in being dissatisfied with the cost of health care and in seeing as a serious problem that many Americans do not have health insurance. But Democrats are more likely than Republicans (89 percent to 66 percent) to be dissatisfied about health care costs. On the number of uninsured people, 94 percent of Democrats believe it is a *very* serious problem, compared to 55 percent of Republicans.[8]

Democrats are significantly more likely than Republicans to see serious problems with the health care system. More than three-fourths (79 percent) of Democrats believe that the health care system is in crisis or has major problems, compared with 56 percent of Republicans.[9] Nearly half (46 percent) of Democrats believe the current health care system has so many flaws that it needs to be completely rebuilt, a view shared by only 28 percent of Republicans. On the other side of the equation, 22 percent of Republicans, compared with only 7 percent of Democrats, see the U.S. system working pretty well.[10]

Views about Their Own Health Care

The differences in actual life experiences with health care do not mirror the polarized views between the political parties. Large majorities of individuals in both parties give relatively high ratings for the medical care they received in the last year. Asked whether they had experienced problems in the past year paying their medical bills or not being able to obtain the health care they or a family member needed, most people in both parties reported that they had not. But for the substantial minority who did have these problems, the data show they are more likely to be Democrats than Republicans (**Table 20–2**).[11]

People who did not report having a recent health care problem may still worry about their situation getting worse in the future, and such concerns may shape individuals' views about health policy issues on opinion surveys. Democrats are more likely than Republicans to say they are very worried about the future of their own health care situation. Among the insured, Democrats are more likely than Republicans (42 percent to 24 percent) to be very worried about losing their health insurance. Democrats are also more likely to be very worried that the quality of health care services they receive might get worse (41 percent to 20 percent) in the future. Democrats and Republicans are, however, about equally likely to be very worried about having to pay more in the future for their health care and health insurance.[12]

Attitudes about Health Reform

The widest differences between the parties can be seen when examining health policy preferences for the country. A number of questions measure the public's broad views of the government's role in health care. Others focus on some specific policy issues that have been a subject of debate in recent years.

Asked whose responsibility it was to ensure that people have health insurance, the plurality of Republicans (45 percent, compared with only 13 percent of Democrats) selected individuals as the locus of responsibility. In contrast, the plurality of Democrats (39 percent, compared with only 13 percent of Republicans) said that government should be mainly responsible (**Table 20–3**).[13]

Democrats and Republicans also have very different views on whether the government would do a better or worse job than private health insurance at providing medical coverage and holding down health care costs. Six out of ten Republicans believe the government would do a worse job than private insurance companies, and a plurality (41 percent) of Democrats think the government would do a better job. Nearly six in ten (56 percent) Democrats think the government would do a better job than private insurance companies at holding down health care costs, and a plurality (48 percent) of Republicans believe the government would do a worse job.[14]

When respondents are asked whether the government should guarantee health insurance coverage for all Americans, a large majority of Democrats agree (79 percent). Only 41 percent of Republicans have this view.[15]

An even wider division between the parties appears when the public is asked if they favor or oppose a national health insurance plan, which would be financed by tax money and would pay for most forms of health care. Three-fourths (75 percent) of Democrats support this policy proposal, compared with just over one-fourth (27 percent) of Republicans.[16]

Similar divisions occur when discussing "socialized medicine," a term that has had controversial connotations for decades. Seven in ten Democrats think socialized medicine would be better than the current health care system, while an equal proportion of Republicans believed it would be worse.[17]

Another policy proposal aimed at covering more of the uninsured would require by law that everyone have health insurance, similar to requirements that people who drive cars have auto insurance. Those who cannot afford to buy health insurance would get government assistance to pay the premiums. This policy proposal is sometimes called an "individual mandate." Two-thirds (66 percent) of Democrats support such a proposal, and Republicans are evenly divided (48 percent in favor, 48 percent opposed).[18]

The partisan divide is also apparent when the question is willingness to pay higher taxes so that all Americans have health insurance they cannot lose. About three-fourths (74 percent) of Democrats say they are willing to pay higher taxes for this purpose, compared to 46 percent of Republicans.[19]

Taken together, public opinion data show a wide gap between Republicans and Democrats in their views about the future direction of U.S. health policy. Only a small part of this polarization of attitudes is likely to be attributable to differing health care experiences, but the differences between the two parties are substantial when it comes to worries about their health care and insurance in the future.

Attitudes about Health-related Social Issues

The picture of polarization in health-related attitudes would not be complete without noting the wide divisions on abortion and stem cell research.[20] Fifty-five percent of Republicans believe abortion should be illegal in all or most cases. Sixty-three percent of Democrats believe abortion should be legal in all or most cases, and 32 percent believe abortion should be illegal in all or most cases.[21] A similar pattern is apparent when the topic is embryonic stem cell research: the majority of Republicans (52 percent) opposes such research, and the majority of Democrats favors it (71 percent).[22] At play in these partisan differences are the varying perceptions Republicans and Democrats have about the influence religion should have in politics and public life. The plurality of Republicans would like to see religion have greater influence, and the plurality of Democrats prefers religion having less influence.[23] As shown in **Table 20–4**, the more religion-oriented party (Republicans) favors more limits on abortion and stem cell research, and the less religion-oriented party (Democrats) favors less.

Health Care and Elections

One of the ways the partisan gap in opinion shapes the outcome of health policy debates in the United States is through its impact on elections, particularly presidential elections. Prior research has shown that no single issue determines the outcome of a national election; rather, factors such as a candidate's character, experience, or leadership qualities also influence voters' decisions. But the issues perceived to be important to voters in their choices among presidential candidates do help to set the public policy agenda for the next president and Congress.[24] In health care, elections have sometimes provided the impetus for subsequent health reform efforts. Health care has been one of the top six issues in every presidential campaign since 1988. It has ranked higher than many other national problems that are often discussed by political leaders and the media (**Table 20–5**).[25]

The priority given to health care as a voting issue for Republicans and Democrats reflects the level of concern each group has about the need to change the U.S. health care system and what they think government should or should not do. Election results reflect the substantial partisan differences in the priority given to health care as a voting issue, the health issues that are deemed important, and the policy solutions seen as most desirable.

The media and polling organizations have been conducting national presidential election-day exit polls of voters since the 1960s. Many of the earlier surveys did not use a list of issues to determine which were most important to voters in their choice of a candidate, and when they did, health care was not on the list. The first election exit poll that included the health care issue was in 1988, and it came in response to the emphasis Governor Michael Dukakis of Massachusetts placed on it in his campaign as the Democratic nominee for president. Since then health care has been included as a potential voting issue in at least one of the national exit polls in the six subsequent presidential elections and a number of individual polling surveys.

Health care as a voting issue has ranked higher among Democratic voters than Republican voters in each of the last six elections (**Table 20–5**).[26] Democratic voters also report being concerned about a wider range of health care problems when they consider their vote choice. Two weeks before the 2004 presidential election, registered voters were given a list of specific health and health care issues and asked how important each of them would be in their vote for president. Democratic registered voters were more likely than Republican registered voters to say that ten of the thirteen issues on the list were extremely important to their vote. These issues included the cost of health care and insurance, the cost of prescription drugs, the number of uninsured, a prescription drug benefit for seniors, Medicare, problems with health care quality, gun control, racial disparities in health care, stem cell research, and aid to developing countries to prevent and treat HIV/AIDS. The only issue called extremely important by a higher proportion of Republican than Democratic registered voters was abortion. Republican and Democratic registered voters did not differ significantly on the importance of bioterrorism or malpractice (**Table 20–6**).[27]

In the 2008 election cycle, Republicans and Democrats had different priorities for which health care issues they wanted their presidential candidates to address if elected. Democrats were more likely to see the uninsured as the top issue for presidential candidates to talk about, and Republicans candidates saw the cost of health care and insurance as their highest priority. As for their candidates' health care proposals, the majority (65 percent) of Democrats wanted to see a major effort to provide health insurance for all or nearly all of the uninsured, a view shared by only 26 percent of Republicans. The majority of Republicans favored either a more limited plan that would cover only some of the uninsured but involve less new spending than an effort to cover nearly all of the uninsured (35 percent) or keeping things as they are (28 percent). Given two choices about what the main goal of efforts to improve the health care system should be, seven in ten Democrats said making sure everyone is covered. About six in ten Republicans (61 percent) said these efforts should focus first on making health insurance more available and affordable in the private marketplace, even if everyone did not get covered (**Table 20–7**).[28]

The deep partisan divide in elections carries over into major health care debates after the election is over. The best example of this is the 1992 presidential election, in which the health care issue was important and a major national health reform proposal was put forth by President Bill Clinton in the early part of his first term.

The Clinton Plan as a Case Study

The idea that national health reform might become an important voting issue in the 1992 presidential election emerged from the results of a special election for U.S. senator in Pennsylvania in November 1991. In that race, voter interest in reform of the American health care system was central to the come-from-behind victory of Democratic senator Harris Wofford, who had been appointed to the seat in May, over Republican candidate Richard Thornburgh. A postelection poll of Pennsylvania voters showed that 50 percent identified "national health insurance" as one of the two issues that mattered the most in deciding how to vote; 21 percent said the issue was "the single most important factor" in their voting decision.[29] The results of that race suggested that health care had arrived as a major political issue, one that could decide the outcome of an election. Wofford had demonstrated that talking about health care was an effective way to reach people about their economic fears and insecurities.

National political candidates were quick to learn. Not long after the Wofford victory, President George H. W. Bush outlined a health reform plan that would offer low- and moderate-income uninsured Americans an income tax refund to help purchase private health insurance. To control costs, financial incentives would encourage enrolling in less costly plans such as HMOs or other managed care plans. During the 1992 presidential campaign, Democratic nominee Bill Clinton proposed a plan in which businesses would be required to purchase private health insurance for their employees. Those who were unemployed or worked part-time would receive private insurance paid for by a government-funded program. To control costs, government would set a limit on health care spending overall.

The continued media attention to health care as a national problem helped make it a prominent issue in 1992. Analysis of an election-night telephone survey and the national election day exit poll shows that health care was an important concern to voters and was a factor in Clinton's victory over Bush (Republican) and independent candidate Ross Perot. Each survey asked voters to identify the two issues most important in deciding on their choice for president. Among the nine issues offered on a checklist in the national exit poll, health care tied for second, behind economy/jobs and tied with the deficit as an issue. In both 1992 election surveys, health care outranked traditionally important voting issues such as abortion, crime, taxes, and foreign policy.[30]

These findings contrast sharply with those from the 1988 presidential race between Bush and Dukakis, when a national exit poll found that health care ranked fifth in importance to voters.[31] Health care ranked lower even though Dukakis had made it a central issue of his campaign. Part of the rationale for his presidential candidacy was his leadership in enacting a universal health care bill in Massachusetts while he was governor.

The importance of health care as an issue in the 1992 election pointed to a continuation of the debate. The results suggested that President-elect Clinton had a general mandate for health reform that would expand coverage and contain costs. He did not, however, have a mandate for a particular plan, and he faced the formidable challenge of building consensus on a specific health reform program.

In a series of polls conducted during the campaign, voters consistently expressed the belief that Governor Clinton would do a better job than President Bush or Ross Perot in responding to the problem of providing affordable health care to all Americans. In the final survey in the series, 52 percent named Clinton; 18 percent said Bush; and 16 percent said Perot.[32]

Voter support for Clinton's health care reform plan during the campaign, however, was not as strong as the perception that he would do a better job than the other candidates. In an election night survey self-described voters were given short descriptions (without mentioning the candidates' names) of the three candidates' proposals. These voters split about evenly between Bush's health care plan (33 percent), Clinton's plan (28 percent), and a single-payer national health care plan (32 percent).[33] Because of the lack of voter agreement about a specific national plan, creating consensus for one particular plan presented a difficult challenge for the new president (Table 20–8).

In spring 1993 President Clinton created a task force of experts, chaired by his wife, Hillary Rodham Clinton, to construct a health care reform plan to be submitted to Congress. The president presented the outline of the plan in September. Many of the specific policy details that later became controversial were not presented in the September speech. Over the subsequent eight months, as these details emerged, the plan became more controversial and raised doubts among many Americans. Ultimately, Congress did not pass the Clinton plan.

Partisan divisions were apparent from the beginning. More than eight in ten Democrats (83 percent) supported Clinton's original outline of the national health plan proposal, but support among Republicans was only 35 percent. By April 1994 support among Democrats had fallen to 58 percent and to 25 percent among Republicans (Table 20–9).[34] The parties' polarization continued. Although the two parties may agree that the U.S. health care system has serious problems, they do not come close to agreeing about what, if anything, government should do to solve these problems.

Health Care in the 2008 Presidential Election

During the 2008 presidential campaign, the two major party candidates outlined health care reform proposals. Senator John McCain, the Republican candidate, proposed eliminating the current tax exclusion for employer-sponsored health coverage and using the new revenue to pay for a refundable tax credit that would encourage individuals and families to purchase health insurance in the marketplace. He also proposed increasing competition in the insurance market by allowing insurance to be sold across state lines.

Senator Barack Obama, the Democratic candidate, proposed a plan that would require that all children have health insurance and would require employers to have health insurance plans for their employees or contribute to the cost of helping people buy insurance from a new "national health insurance exchange." The exchange would include a range of private insurance plans in addition to a public option.[35]

Partisan divisions were once again at work in the 2008 election and can be seen by contrasting the health care views of registered voters who said they intended to vote for McCain or for Obama. The analysis that follows focuses on the issues that were raised by the two presidential candidates during the campaign.

Health Care as a Priority Issue

In the 2008 national election day exit poll, voters were asked to choose from a list of options the most important issue affecting their vote. Those who said they voted for Obama ranked health care a distant second after the economy, and those who said they voted for McCain ranked health care fifth. The majority of Obama voters (68 percent) indicated that the candidates' positions on the issues were more important to their voting decision than the candidates' leadership and personal qualities (30 percent); McCain voters said the candidates' leadership and personal qualities (49 percent) were equally important as their stands on the issues (48 percent) (**Table 20–10**).[36]

Health Care Priorities for the Next President

Asked in a preelection poll to choose from a list of five problem areas their top health care priority for the new administration, registered voters overall, McCain voters, and Obama voters ranked affordability of health care as the top priority. Second among registered voters overall was expanding health insurance coverage for the uninsured. Obama voters were significantly more likely than McCain voters (33 percent to 10 percent) to name the issue of the uninsured as most important.[37]

The Need for Health System Reform

More than two-thirds of registered voters said either that the current health care system had so much wrong with it that it need to be overhauled (24 percent) or needed major changes (46 percent). Obama voters were more likely than McCain voters to say that the health care system needed to be overhauled (28 percent to 16 percent) and less likely to see the system as needing minor or no changes (16 percent to 43 percent).[38]

Health Care Coverage

A fundamental difference in views was revealed when registered voters were asked who they thought should have the most responsibility for helping ensure that Americans receive health insurance coverage. The majority of Obama voters (54 percent, compared with only 20 percent of McCain voters) thought the federal government should be most responsible. McCain voters were significantly more likely than Obama voters (47 percent to 18 percent) to say that the responsibility lies with the individual. Asked to choose among three approaches to increase health insurance coverage, registered voters were equally divided between support for a large, nearly universal plan and more limited approaches. Obama voters were more than twice as likely as McCain voters to favor a large national health plan (65 percent to 26 percent), and the majority of McCain voters selected the two more limited coverage expansion options, including nearly one-third (31 percent) saying we should leave things the way they are.[39]

Health Care Costs

Broad differences between Obama and McCain voters were also visible on slowing the rise in health care costs. Obama voters were significantly more likely than McCain voters (73 percent to 41 percent) to believe the president and Congress could do "a lot" about the cost.

About two-thirds of registered voters thought the federal government should be more involved than it is at present in trying to control health care costs. Obama voters were significantly more likely than McCain voters (85 percent to 46 percent) to hold this view. But most registered voters did not believe that the federal government should be the *central* player in slowing the growth of health care costs. When given five possible choices as to who should have the most responsibility for dealing with costs, pluralities of Obama voters (36 percent) and McCain voters (31 percent) said health insurance companies. The proportion that believed the federal government should have the most responsibility was twice as high among Obama voters as among McCain voters (30 percent to 15 percent).

Given four options for what the 2008 winner's top priority should be on reducing health care costs, registered voters overall, as well as both candidates' supporters, chose as their top priority the more personal option: reducing the amount people pay for their health care and insurance. Only a minority selected as the top priority reducing the nation's overall health care spending or government's health spending. On this question, McCain and Obama voters had similar priorities.

Elements of Health Reform

Registered voters were also asked about seven elements of health reform that the two presidential candidates discussed (**Table 20–11**). To assess what the voters strongly supported, we focus on those elements a majority of respondents viewed "very" favorably and found only one: requiring health insurance companies to cover anyone who applies, even those with a prior illness. Of McCain voters, no majority viewed any of the seven elements very favorably, while the majority of Obama voters viewed four reform elements very favorably, suggesting support for a much broader agenda.

Asked how important it was that health care reform proposals did not raise taxes, a majority (57 percent) of registered voters said it was the most important or a very important consideration. McCain voters were significantly more likely than Obama voters (70 percent to 45 percent) to express this concern about health reform not leading to higher taxes.[40]

Health Care Spending

Registered voters were asked to consider the substantial federal deficit and priorities other than health facing the next administration and then to identify what they would like the next president to propose in each of six areas of federal government health spending: Medicare, Medicaid, biomedical research, programs to prevent disease and improve health, medical care for veterans, and programs to protect against bioterrorism. The majority thought that federal spending on medical care for veterans (72 percent) and programs to prevent disease and improve health (53 percent) should be increased. No more than 12 percent of registered voters thought that federal spending in any of the six areas should be decreased (**Table 20–10**).

The only area where the majority of McCain voters thought federal spending should be increased was medical care for veterans, a view shared by Obama voters. McCain voters were more likely than Obama voters to favor increased spending on programs to protect against bioterrorism. Obama voters were more likely than McCain voters to say that federal health spending should be increased in the other four areas: programs to prevent disease and improve health, Medicare, biomedical research, and Medicaid.[41]

Abortion

Obama and McCain voters differed sharply in their views about abortion policy. More than two-thirds (72 percent) of Obama voters believed that abortion should be legal in all or most cases, compared with 35 percent of McCain voters. A majority (60 percent) of McCain voters thought abortion should be illegal in all or most cases, compared with only 24 percent of Obama voters.[42]

Expectations for Change

Not only did the two candidates' voters differ on many policy views, but also they had different expectations about the importance of the outcome of the election for major change in health care. In a preelection poll of registered voters, the majority of Obama voters (59 percent) expressed the belief that the outcome of the election would make a great deal of difference for health care. Only a minority of McCain voters shared this view (40 percent).[43]

What do these results suggest about the future of health reform? They point to how partisan views shape the way many Americans see health policy issues and the way their views affect future reform debate. In the 2008 election, a large majority of voters favored major changes in the U.S. health care system, but supporters of the two major candidates and political parties differed greatly on the policy direction and magnitude of such change. In contrast to Obama's backers, McCain's supporters placed a lower priority on a major reform of health care and favored less participation by the federal government in increasing coverage for the uninsured. They also advocated a smaller role for government regulation of health care costs and more emphasis on the private sector, as well as more restrained federal health spending.

McCain's supporters believed that free market competition and greater responsibility by individuals should be central in addressing the nation's health care problems. Obama's supporters saw the need for increased government action and the federal government as a more central actor in the reform of the system.

These broad partisan differences in visions about the future of health reform in the United States made it very difficult to achieve the enactment of comprehensive legislation. The results of the 2008 election, when the Democrats gained control of the presidency and both houses of Congress, provided a "window of opportunity" for the Democratic Party's health care vision to be enacted in 2010. This opening might not have lasted past the next election. The important take-away message is that one reason the U.S. health system has been so difficult to change is the huge gulf that exists between the two parties' perspectives on the nature of that reform.

Notes

[1] Geoffrey C. Layman, Thomas M. Carsey, and Juliana Menasce Horowitz, "Party Polarization in American Politics: Characteristics, Causes, and Consequences," *Annual Review of Political Science* 9 (June 2006): 83–110.

[2] Ibid.; Nolan McCarty, Keith T. Poole, and Howard Rosenthal, *Polarized America: The Dance of Ideology and Unequal Riches* (Cambridge, Mass.: MIT Press, 2006), 71–138; Ronald Brownstein, *The Second Civil War: How Extreme Partisanship Has Paralyzed Washington and Polarized America* (New York: Penguin Press, 2007), 137–262; Alan I. Abramowitz and Kyle L. Saunders, "Ideological Realignments in the U.S. Electorate," *Journal of Politics* 60 (August 1998): 634–652; Paul DiMaggio, John Evans, and Bethany Bryson, "Have Americans' Social Attitudes Become More Polarized?" *American Journal of Sociology* 102 (November 1996): 690–755; Edward G. Carmines and Geoffrey C. Layman, "Issue Evolution in Postwar American Politics: Old Certainties and Fresh Tensions," in Byron E. Shafer, ed., *Present Discontents: American Politics in the Very Late Twentieth Century* (Chatham, N.J.: Chatham House, 1997), 89–134; Gary C. Jacobson, "Party Polarization in National Politics: The Electoral Connection," in Jon R. Bond and Richard Fleisher, eds., *Polarized Politics: Congress and the President in a Partisan Era* (Washington, D.C.: CQ Press, 2000), 9–30; Geoffrey C. Layman and Thomas M. Carsey, "Party Polarization and Party Structuring of Policy Attitudes: A Comparison of Three NES Panel Studies," *Political Behavior* 24 (September 2002): 199–236; Richard Fleisher and Jon R. Bond, "Evidence of Increasing Polarization among Ordinary Citizens," in Jeffrey E. Cohen, Richard Fleisher, and Paul Kantor, eds., *American Political Parties: Decline or Resurgence?* (Washington D.C.: CQ Press, 2001), 55–77; Jeffrey M. Stonecash, Mark D. Brewer, and Mack D. Mariani, *Diverging Parties: Social Change, Realignment, and Party Polarization* (Boulder, Colo.: Westview, 2003); Bond and Fleisher, *Polarized Politics;* Barry C. Burden, "The Polarizing Effects of Congressional Primaries," in Peter F. Galderisi, Marni Ezra, and Michael Lyons, eds., *Congressional Primaries and the Politics of Representation* (Lanham, Md.: Rowman and Littlefield, 2001), 95–115; John H. Aldrich and David W. Rohde, "The Logic of Conditional Party Government: Revisiting the Electoral Connection," in Lawrence C. Dodd and Bruce I. Oppenheimer, eds., *Congress Reconsidered,* 7th ed., (Washington, D.C.: CQ Press, 2001), 269–292.

[3] McCarty, Poole, and Rosenthal, *Polarized America,* 2006; Brownstein, *The Second Civil War,* 2007; Abramowitz and Saunders, "Ideological Realignments in the U.S. Electorate," 1998; Jacobson, "Party Polarization in National Politics," 2000; Stonecash, Brewer, and Mariani, *Diverging Parties,* 2003; Aldrich and Rohde, "The Logic of Conditional Party Government," 2001.

[4] *Washington Post*/Kaiser Family Foundation/Harvard University, "Survey of Political Independents," July 2007, http://www.kff.org/kaiserpolls/upload/7665.pdf.

[5] Pew Research Center for the People & the Press, "Trends in Political Values and Core Attitudes: 1987–2007," March 22, 2007, http://people-press.org/reports/pdf/312.pdf.

[6] Harvard School of Public Health/Robert Wood Johnson Foundation Poll (Storrs, Conn.: Roper Center for Public Opinion Research, June 17–21, 2009).

[7] Harvard School of Public Health/Harris Interactive Poll, "Most Republicans Think the U.S. Health Care System is the Best in the World; Democrats Disagree," March 20, 2008, http://www.hsph.harvard.edu/news/press-releases/2008-releases/republicans-democrats-disagree-us-health-care-system.html.

[8] CBS News Poll, "Health Care and the Democratic Presidential Campaign," September 17, 2007, http://www.cbsnews.com/htdocs/pdf/Sep07b-HRC-HEALTH.pdf.

[9] Harvard School of Public Health/Robert Wood Johnson Foundation Poll, June 17–21, 2009.

[10] CBS News/*New York Times* Poll, "The President, Congress and 2008 Campaign," July 19, 2007, http://www.cbsnews.com/htdocs/pdf/071907_bush.pdf.

[11] Harvard School of Public Health/Robert Wood Johnson Foundation Poll, June 17–21, 2009.

[12] Kaiser Family Foundation Poll, "Kaiser Health Tracking Poll: Election 2008," June 2007, http://www.kff.org/kaiserpolls/upload/7656.pdf.

[13] *Los Angeles Times*/Bloomberg Poll, "Public Pessimistic on the Economy: Most Pick Democrats over Republicans on Health Care Reform," October 24, 2007, http://www.latimes.com/media/acrobat/2007–10/33450977.pdf.

[14] CBS News/*New York Times* Poll, "U.S. Health Care Politics," March 1, 2007, http://www.cbsnews.com/htdocs/CBSNews_polls/health_care.pdf.

[15] Ibid.

[16] Harvard School of Public Health/Robert Wood Johnson Foundation Poll, June 17–21, 2009.

[17] Harvard School of Public Health/Harris Interactive Poll, "Poll Finds Americans Split by Political Party over Whether Socialized Medicine Better or Worse than Current System," February 14, 2008, http://www.hsph.harvard.edu/news/press-releases/2008-releases/poll-americans-split-by-political-party-over-socialized-medicine.html. "Socialized medicine" is discussed at greater length in Chapter 3.

[18] Harvard School of Public Health/Robert Wood Johnson Foundation Poll, June 17–21, 2009. Such a proposal is part of the health care law in Massachusetts, which has achieved nearly universal health insurance coverage. For an extensive discussion of the Massachusetts law, see Chapter 6.

[19] CBS News/*New York Times* Poll, "U.S. Health Care Politics," March 1, 2007.

[20] A number of authors have described the polarization in these areas. John C. Green, James L. Guth, Corwin E. Smidt, and Lyman A. Kellstedt, *Religion and the Culture Wars* (Lanham, Md.: Rowman and Littlefield, 1996); Donald Green, Bradley Palmquist, and Eric Schickler, *Partisan Hearts and Minds* (New Haven, Conn.: Yale University Press, 2002); Andrew Kohut, John C. Green, Scott Keeter, and Robert C. Toth, *The Diminishing Divide: Religion's Changing Role in American Politics* (Washington, D.C.: Brookings Institution, 2000); Geoffrey C. Layman, *The Great Divide: Religious and Cultural Conflicts in American Party Politics* (New York: Columbia University Press, 2001).

[21] *Washington Post*/Kaiser Family Foundation/Harvard University, "Survey of Political Independents," July 2007. See Chapters 11 and 12 for further discussion of public attitudes about abortion and stem cell research.

[22] Virginia Commonwealth University Life Sciences/Center for Public Policy, "VCU Life Sciences Survey 2008," http://www.vcu.edu/lifesci/images2/survey2008.pdf.

[23] *Washington Post*/Kaiser Family Foundation/Harvard University, "Survey of Political Independents," July 2007.

[24] Richard G. Niemi and Herbert F. Weisberg, "What Determines the Vote?" in Richard G. Niemi and Herbert F. Weisberg, eds., *Classics in Voting Behavior* (Washington, D.C.: CQ Press, 1993), 93–106; Gregory B. Markus and Philip E. Converse, "A Dynamic Simultaneous Equation Model of Electoral Choice," in *Classics in Voting Behavior,* 140–159; Morris P. Fiorina, *Retrospective Voting in American National Elections* (New Haven, Conn.: Yale University Press, 1981).

[25] ABC News National Election Day Exit Poll (Storrs, Conn.: Roper Center for Public Opinion Research, November 8, 1988); Voter Research and Surveys National Election Day Exit Poll (Storrs, Conn.: Roper Center for Public Opinion Research, November 3, 1992); *Los Angeles Times* National Election Day Exit Poll (Storrs, Conn.: Roper Center for Public Opinion Research, November 5, 1996); *Los Angeles Times* National Election Day Exit Poll (Storrs, Conn.: Roper Center for Public Opinion Research, November 7, 2000); National Election Pool/Edison Media Research/Mitofsky International National Election Day Exit Poll (Storrs, Conn.: Roper Center for Public Opinion Research, November 2, 2004); Robert J. Blendon, Drew E. Altman, John M. Benson, Mollyann Brodie, Tami Buhr, Claudia Deane, and Sasha Buscho, "Voters and Health Care Reform in the 2008 Presidential Election," *New England Journal of Medicine* 359 (November 6, 2008): 2050–61.

[26] Ibid.

[27] Robert J. Blendon, Mollyann Brodie, Drew E. Altman, John M. Benson, and Elizabeth C. Hamel, "Voters and Health Care in the 2004 Election," *Health Affairs* 24 (Web exclusive, March 1, 2005): 86–96.

[28] Kaiser Family Foundation, "Kaiser Health Tracking Poll: Election 2008," April 2008, http://www.kff.org/kaiserpolls/upload/7771.pdf; Kaiser Family Foundation, "Kaiser Health Tracking Poll: Election 2008," March 2008, http://www.kff.org/kaiserpolls/upload/7751.pdf.

[29] Robert J. Blendon, Drew E. Altman, John M. Benson, Humphrey Taylor, Matt James, and Mark Smith, "Health Care Reform and the 1992 Election," *The Polling Report* 8 (December 14, 1992): 1, 6–7.

[30] Ibid.

[31] Robert J. Blendon and Karen Donelan, "The 1988 Election: How Important Was Health?" *Health Affairs* 8 (Fall 1989): 6–15.

[32] Blendon et al, "Health Care Reform and the 1992 Election," 1992.

[33] Ibid.

[34] Robert J. Blendon, Mollyann Brodie, and John Benson, "What Happened to Americans' Support for the Clinton Health Plan?" *Health Affairs* 14 (Summer 1995): 7–23.

[35] Kaiser Family Foundation, "2008 Presidential Candidate Health Care Proposals: Side-by-Side Summary," http://www.health08.org/sidebyside_results.cfm?c=5&c=16.

[36] Jackie Calmes and Megan Thee, "Voter Poll Finds Obama Built a Broad Coalition," *New York Times,* November 5, 2008, P9, citing data from the 2008 National Election Pool/Edison Media Research/Mitofsky International National Election Day Exit Poll.

[37] Blendon et al., "Voters and Health Care Reform in the 2008 Presidential Election," 2008.

[38] Ibid.

[39] Ibid.

[40] Ibid.

[41] Ibid.

[42] Ibid.

[43] Harvard School of Public Health/Harris Interactive Poll, "On Key Policy Areas, Majority of Voters Say Presidential Election Outcome Will Make a Great Deal of Difference," October 28, 2008, http://www.hsph.harvard.edu/news/press-releases/2008-releases/key-policy-areas-majority-voters-say-presidential-election-outcome-make-great-deal-of-difference.html.

Table 20-1 Republicans' and Democrats' Views on the Role of Government and the State of the U.S. Health Care System (in percent)

	Total	Republican	Democrat
Role of government[1]			
Washington is trying to do too many things	48	64	35
Government should do more	45	28	58
Would rather have a smaller government providing fewer services or a bigger government providing more services[2]			
Smaller government	45	68	28
Bigger government	43	26	60
Depends (vol.)	4	2	3
Rating of nation's system for providing medical care to Americans[3]			
Excellent/good	28	42	21
Fair/poor	69	56	76
Best health care system[4]			
The U.S.	45	68	32
Other countries	39	19	52
Don't know/No answer	15	13	16
Quality of health care in this country[5]			
Satisfied	32	58	20
Dissatisfied	66	40	78
Cost of health care in this country[5]			
Satisfied	16	32	10
Dissatisfied	81	66	89

(Table continues)

Table 20-1 *Continued*

Problem that many Americans do not have health insurance[5]			
Very serious	76	55	94
Somewhat serious	16	28	6
Not too serious	5	11	0
Not at all serious	3	6	0
The state of health care system[3]			
In crisis	18	6	22
Has major problems	52	50	57
Has minor problems	24	38	17
Has no problems	4	3	2
Health care system[6]			
Works pretty well	11	22	7
Some good things, needs fundamental changes	50	49	47
So much wrong, need to completely rebuild	38	28	46

Note: "Don't know" responses not shown. (vol.) = volunteered responses.

Question: Some people think the government in Washington is trying to do too many things that should be left to individuals and private businesses. Others disagree and think the government should do more to solve our country's biggest problems. Which of these two views is closer to your own?

Question: If you had to choose, would you rather have a smaller government providing fewer services or a bigger government providing more services?

Question: How would you rate the nation's system for providing medical care to Americans: excellent, good, fair, or poor?

Question: Some people say that the United States has the best health care system in the world. Others say that the health care systems of some other countries are better than the United States. How about you? Do you think that, in general, the United States has the best health care system or are there other countries with better health care systems?

Question: Thinking about the country as a whole, are you generally satisfied or dissatisfied with the quality of health care in this country?

Question: Thinking about the country as a whole, are you generally satisfied or dissatisfied with the cost of health care in this country?

Question: How serious a problem is it for the United States that many Americans do not have health insurance—very serious, somewhat serious, not too serious, or not at all serious?

Question: Which of these statements do you think best describes the U.S. health care system today—it is in a state of crisis, it has major problems, it has minor problems, or it does not have any problems?

Question: Which of the following three statements comes closest to expressing your overall view of the health care system in the United States? . . . On the whole, the healthcare system works pretty well and only minor changes are necessary to make it work better. There are some good things in our health care system, but fundamental changes are needed. Our healthcare system has so much wrong with it that we need to completely rebuild it.

Sources: [1]*Washington Post*/Kaiser Family Foundation/Harvard University, "Survey of Political Independents," July 2007. [2]Pew Research Center for the People and the Press, "Trends in Political Values and Core Attitudes: 1987–2007," March 22, 2007. [3]Harvard School of Public Health/Robert Wood Johnson Foundation Poll (Storrs, Conn.: Roper Center for Public Opinion Research, June 17–21, 2009). [4]Harvard School of Public Health/Harris Interactive Poll, "Most Republicans Think the U.S. Health Care System is the Best in the World; Democrats Disagree," March 20, 2008. [5]CBS News Poll, "Health Care and the Democratic Presidential Campaign," September 17, 2007. [6]CBS News/*New York Times* Poll, "The President, Congress and 2008 Campaign," July 19, 2007.

Table 20-2 Republicans' and Democrats' Views on Their Own Health Care (in percent)

	Total	Republican	Democrat
Rating of their own medical care (among those receiving care in the last year)[1]			
Excellent/good	82	91	78
Fair/poor	18	9	22
Problem paying medical bills in last year[1]			
Yes	24	15	23
No	76	85	77
Needed medical care but did not receive it in last year[1]			
Yes	18	13	19
No	82	86	81
Worried about losing your health insurance coverage (among those who have health insurance)[2]			
Very worried	34	24	42
Somewhat worried	20	19	17
Not too worried	20	24	21
Not at all worried	25	32	20
Worried about the quality of health care services you receive getting worse[2]			
Very worried	32	20	41
Somewhat worried	28	32	27
Not too worried	19	22	17
Not at all worried	20	25	15
Worried about having to pay more for your health care or health insurance[2]			
Very worried	41	34	37
Somewhat worried	34	32	38
Not too worried	14	17	13
Not at all worried	11	16	11

Note: "Don't know" responses not shown.

Question: (Asked of those who had received medical care during the past 12 months) Overall, how would you rate that medical care: excellent, good, fair, or poor?

Question: In the past 12 months, have you had problems paying medical bills, or not?

Question: Was there a time over the past 12 months when you or another family member living in your household needed medical care, but did not get it?

Question: I'm going to read you a list of things that some people worry about and others do not. I'd like you to tell me how worried you are about each of the following things. How worried are you about (losing your health insurance coverage/the quality of health care services you receive getting worse/having to pay more for your health care or health insurance)? Are you very worried, somewhat worried, not too worried, or not at all worried?

Sources: [1]Harvard School of Public Health/Robert Wood Johnson Foundation Poll (Storrs, Conn.: Roper Center for Public Opinion Research, June 17–21, 2009). [2]Kaiser Family Foundation, "Kaiser Health Tracking Poll: Election 2008," June 2007.

Table 20-3 Republicans' and Democrats' Views on Health Reform (in percent)

	Total	Republican	Democrat
Whose responsibility is it to ensure that people have health insurance?[1]			
Individual persons	24	45	13
Government	29	13	39
Employers	23	19	19
Shared (vol.)	19	18	20
Government compared with private insurance in providing medical coverage[2]			
Government better	30	21	41
Government worse	44	60	36
Same (vol.)	3	2	3
Don't know	23	17	20
Government compared with private insurance in holding down health care costs[2]			
Better	47	42	56
Worse	37	48	29
Same (vol.)	2	2	3
Don't know	14	8	12
Role of federal government[2]			
Should guarantee health insurance for all Americans	64	41	79
Not responsibility of federal government	27	51	13
National health insurance financed by tax money[3]			
Favor	55	27	75
Oppose	38	68	18
Socialized medicine[4]			
Better than current system	45	17	70
Worse than current system	39	70	16
About the same (vol.)	4	4	2
Don't know	12	9	12
Require by law all Americans to have health insurance (individual mandate). Those who can't afford to buy it receive help from govt.[3]			
Favor	58	48	66
Oppose	38	48	31

(Table continues)

Table 20-3 *Continued*

Pay higher taxes for all Americans to have health insurance[2]			
Willing	60	46	74
Not willing	34	49	22

Note: "Don't know" responses not shown, except where the percentage for any of the groups of respondents is 10 percent or more. (vol.) = volunteered responses.

Question: Which of the following statements comes closest to your view? "It is the government's responsibility to ensure that its citizens have health insurance." "It is the employer's responsibility to ensure that their employees have health insurance." "It is the responsibility of the individuals to secure their own health insurance without the help of the government or their employer."

Question: Do you think the government would do a better or worse job than private insurance companies in providing medical coverage?

Question: Do you think the government would do a better or worse job than private insurance companies in holding down health care costs?

Question: Do you think the federal government should guarantee health insurance for all Americans, or isn't this the responsibility of the federal government?

Question: Do you favor or oppose national health insurance, which would be financed by tax money, paying for most forms of health care?

Question: (Asked of those who said they knew at all what the term "socialized medicine" meant) So far as you understand the phrase, do you think that if we had socialized medicine in this country that the health care system would be better or worse than what we have now?

Question: Do you favor or oppose having a law that requires everyone to have health insurance that they buy themselves or get through an employer. This would be similar to the law that requires people who drive cars to have auto insurance. People who cannot afford to buy health insurance would get help from the government to pay their health insurance premiums.

Question: Would you be willing or not willing to pay higher taxes so that all Americans have health insurance they can't lose, no matter what?

Sources: [1]*Los Angeles Times*/Bloomberg Poll, "Public Pessimistic on the Economy: Most Pick Democrats over Republicans on Health Care Reform," October 24, 2007. [2]*CBS News*/*New York Times* Poll, "U.S. Health Care Politics," March 1, 2007. [3]Harvard School of Public Health/Robert Wood Johnson Foundation Poll (Storrs, Conn.: Roper Center for Public Opinion Research, June 17–21, 2009). [4]Harvard School of Public Health/Harris Interactive Poll, "Poll Finds Americans Split by Political Party over Whether Socialized Medicine Better or Worse than Current System," February 14, 2008.

Table 20-4 Republicans' and Democrats' Views on Health-related Social Policy Issues (in percent)

	Total	Republican	Democrat
Abortion[1]			
Should be legal in all/most cases	56	42	63
Should be illegal in all/most cases	40	55	32
Medical research that uses stem cells from human embryos[2]			
Favor	57	40	71
Oppose	36	52	23
Preferred influence of religion in politics and public life[1]			
Greater influence	29	42	26
About the same influence	36	41	32
Less influence	34	17	40

Note: "Don't know" responses not shown.

Question: Do you think abortion should be legal in all cases, legal in most cases, illegal in most cases, or illegal in all cases?

Question: On the whole, how much do you favor or oppose medical research that uses stem cells from human embryos? Do you strongly favor, somewhat favor, somewhat oppose, or strongly oppose this?

Question: Would you rather see religion have greater influence in politics and public life than it does now, less influence, or about the same influence as it does now?

Sources: [1]*Washington Post*/Kaiser Family Foundation/Harvard University, "Survey of Political Independents," July 2007. [2]Virginia Commonwealth University Life Sciences/Center for Public Policy, "VCU Life Sciences Survey 2008."

Table 20-5 Voters' Ranking of Health Care as an Important Issue in Their Presidential Vote, by Party Identification, 1988–2008 (in percent)

Rank	Issue (percentage of respondents)		
	Total voters	Republican voters	Democratic voters
1988			
1	Economy/Jobs (22)	National defense (27)	Economy/Jobs (23)
2	National defense (16)	Economy/Jobs (22)	Problems of the poor (21)
3	Problems of the poor (12)	Taxes (15)	**Health care/Medicare/ Prescription drugs (15)**
4	Taxes (11)	Foreign affairs/Policy (9)	Federal budget deficit (10)
5	**Health care/Medicare/ Prescription drugs (10)**	Federal budget deficit (6)	Taxes (8)
6	Federal budget deficit (8)	Crime/Drugs (4) **Health care/Medicare/ Prescription drugs (4)**	National defense (7)
1992			
1	Economy/Jobs (42)	Economy/Jobs (37)	Economy/Jobs (48)
2	**Health care/Medicare/ Prescription drugs (20)**	Family/Moral/ Ethical values (21)	**Health care/Medicare/ Prescription drugs (27)**
3	Federal budget deficit (20)	Federal budget deficit (21)	Federal budget deficit (19)
4	Family/Moral/Ethical values (15)	Taxes (20)	Education (17)
5	Taxes (14)	Foreign affairs/ Policy (15)	Family/Moral/ Ethical values (10)
6	Education (13)	Abortion (15)	Taxes (10)
1996			
1	Family/Moral/Ethical values (39)	Family/Moral/Ethical values (63)	Economy/Jobs (47)
2	Economy/Jobs (35)	Taxes (25)	Education (35)
3	Education (24)	Economy/Jobs (23)	Family/Moral/Ethical values (20)
4	Taxes (15)	Federal budget deficit (14)	**Health care/Medicare/ Prescription drugs (18)**
5	Federal budget deficit (12)	Abortion (12)	Federal budget deficit (9)
6	**Health care/Medicare/ Prescription drugs (12)**	Education (12)	Environment (8)
2000			
1	Family/Moral/Ethical values (35)	Family/Moral/Ethical Values (54)	Economy/Jobs (33)
2	Education (25)	Taxes (26)	Education (30)
3	Economy/Jobs (25)	Education (19)	Social Security (26)
4	Social Security (20)	Social Security (17)	**Health care/Medicare/ Prescription drugs (22)**

(Table continues)

Table 20-5 *Continued*

5	**Health care/Medicare/Prescription drugs (16)**	Economy/Jobs (17)	Family/Moral/Ethical values (19)
6	Taxes (16)	Abortion (17)	Environment (12) Abortion (12)

2004

1	Family/Moral/Ethical values (22)	Family/Moral/Ethical values (35)	Economy/Jobs (33)
2	Economy/Jobs (20)	Terrorism (31)	Iraq (19)
3	Terrorism (19)	Iraq (9)	**Health care/Medicare/Prescription drugs (13)**
4	Iraq (15)	Economy/Jobs (8)	Family/Moral/Ethical values (10)
5	**Health care/Medicare/Prescription drugs (8)**	Taxes (6)	Terrorism (8)
6	Taxes (5)	**Health care/Medicare/Prescription drugs (4)**	Education (6)

	Total registered voters	Republican registered voters	Democratic registered voters

2008

1	Economy/Jobs (48)	Economy/Jobs (41)	Economy/Jobs (55)
2	Energy/gas prices (13)	Energy/gas prices (15)	**Health care (15)**
3	**Health care (12)**	Terrorism (15)	War in Iraq (13)
4	War in Iraq (11)	War in Iraq (9)	Energy/gas prices (9)
5	Terrorism (8)	**Health care (9)**	Terrorism (2)
6	Illegal immigration (4)	Illegal immigration (7)	Illegal immigration (2)

Note: The top six responses are shown for each presidential election year. The data from 1988–2004 come from national election day exit polls, self-administered by voters as they left the voting booth; the 2008 data come from a preelection day poll conducted by telephone. When two or more issues were closely related, they were combined into one category on this table to make the data more comparable over time. In 1992, 2004, and 2008 respondents could give only a single response. In the other years, respondents could give up to two responses.

Question: Please put a check mark next to the one issue where you most liked the stand of the presidential candidate you voted for: taxes, health care, national defense, the federal budget deficit, problems of the poor, foreign affairs, the national economy, crime, creating jobs. (1988)

Question: Which one or two issues mattered most in deciding how you voted (for president)? Health care, federal budget deficit, abortion, education, economy/jobs, environment, taxes, foreign policy, family values? (1992)

Question: Which issues, if any, were most important in deciding how you would vote for president today? Moral and ethical values, education, jobs/the economy, the environment, taxes, abortion, health care, poverty, federal budget deficit, crime/drugs, foreign affairs, or none of the above? (1996)

Question: Which issues, if any, were most important in deciding how you would vote for president today? Moral and ethical values, education, jobs/the economy, the environment, taxes, abortion, health care, Social Security, budget surplus, Medicare/prescription drugs, foreign affairs, or none of the above? (2000)

Question: Which one issue mattered most in deciding how you voted for president? Taxes, education, Iraq, terrorism, economy/jobs, moral values, health care? (2004)

Question: Thinking ahead to the November 2008 presidential election, which of the following issues will be most important to you when deciding how to vote for president? The economy, the war in Iraq, health care, illegal immigration, terrorism, energy, including gas prices? (2008)

Sources: ABC News National Election Day Exit Poll (Storrs, Conn.: Roper Center for Public Opinion Research, November 8, 1988); Voter Research and Surveys National Election Day Exit Poll (Storrs, Conn.: Roper Center for Public Opinion Research, November 3, 1992); *Los Angeles Times* National Election Day Exit Poll (Storrs, Conn.: Roper Center for Public Opinion Research, November 5, 1996); *Los Angeles Times* National Election Day Exit Poll (Storrs, Conn.: Roper Center for Public Opinion Research, November 7, 2000); National Election Poll/Edison Media Research/Mitofsky International National Election Day Exit Poll (Storrs, Conn.: Roper Center for Public Opinion Research, November 2, 2004); Robert J. Blendon, Drew E. Altman, John M. Benson, Mollyann Brodie, Tami Buhr, Claudia Deane, and Sasha Buscho, "Voters and Health Care Reform in the 2008 Presidential Election," *New England Journal of Medicine* 359 (November 6, 2008): 2050–61.

Table 20-6 Importance of Health Care in Voters' Preferences in the 2004 Presidential Election, by Party Identification

Percent saying extremely important

	Total registered voters	Republican registered voters	Democratic registered voters
The cost of health care and health insurance	31	20	39
The number of Americans without health insurance	31	17	43
The cost of prescription drugs	30	17	38
Prescription drug benefits for seniors	29	16	39
Bioterrorism	27	28	26
Medicare	26	14	35
Problems with health care quality	23	14	30
Abortion	23	30	18
Gun control	22	18	27
Racial disparities in health care	19	9	27
Medical malpractice	18	20	17
Stem cell research	17	15	22
Aid to developing countries to prevent and treat HIV/AIDS	13	7	19

Question: I'm going to read you a list of specific health care issues. For each one, please tell me how important it will be in your vote for president this year. (First/How about) (Read each item) Will it be extremely important in deciding your vote, very important, somewhat important, or not important?

Source: Robert J. Blendon, Mollyann Brodie, Drew E. Altman, John M. Benson, and Elizabeth C. Hamel, "Voters and Health Care in the 2004 Election," *Health Affairs* 24 (Web exclusive, March 1, 2005): 86–96.

Table 20-7 What Registered Voters Wanted to Hear from the 2008 Presidential Candidates about Health Care, by Party Identification (in percent)

	Total registered voters	Republican registered voters	Democratic registered voters
Health care issue you would most like to hear presidential candidates talk about[1]			
Reducing the costs of health care and health insurance	41	43	35
Expanding health insurance coverage for uninsured	30	19	45
Improving quality of care and reducing medical errors	15	16	12
Reducing spending on government health programs like Medicare and Medicaid	9	16	5

(Table continues)

Table 20-7 *Continued*

What you would like to see in presidential candidates' health care proposals[2]			
New health plan that would make a major effort to provide health insurance for all or nearly all of uninsured, but would involve substantial increase in spending	47	26	65
A new health plan that is more limited and would only cover some of the uninsured. But would involve less new spending	28	35	24
Keeping things basically as they are	15	28	6
Preferred approach to improving health care system[1]			
The main goal of these efforts should be to make sure that everyone is covered by health insurance	54	35	70
These efforts should focus first on making health insurance more available and affordable in the private marketplace, even if everyone doesn't get covered	42	61	26

Note: "Don't know" responses not shown.

Question: Now thinking specifically about health care, which one of the following health care issues would you most like to hear the presidential candidates talk about? Reducing the costs of health care and health insurance, expanding health insurance coverage for the uninsured, improving the quality of care and reducing medical errors, or reducing spending on government health programs like Medicare and Medicaid?

Question: Which one of the following three things would you like to see in a health care reform proposal from a presidential candidate? Would you want your candidate to propose . . . a new health plan that would make a major effort to provide health insurance for all or nearly all of the uninsured but would involve a substantial increase in spending, or a new health plan that is more limited and would cover only some of the uninsured but would involve less new spending, or keeping things basically as they are?

Question: The presidential candidates have proposed different approaches to improving the health care system in the United States. Which of the following comes closest to your view? The main goal of these efforts should be to make sure that everyone is covered by health insurance (or) These efforts should focus first on making health insurance more available and affordable in the private marketplace, even if everyone doesn't get covered.

Sources: [1]Kaiser Family Foundation, "Kaiser Health Tracking Poll: Election 2008," April 2008. [2]Kaiser Family Foundation, "Kaiser Health Tracking Poll: Election 2008," March 2008.

Table 20-8 Public Support for Various Health Care Reform Plans Put Forth by Presidential and Other Candidates in the 1992 Election (in percent)

Employer mandate (Clinton)	28
Tax credits (Bush)	33
Single-payer	32
Leaving things as are (vol.)	2

Note: "Don't know" responses not shown. (vol.) = volunteered responses.

Question: Which of the following proposals for health care reform would you favor? (1) A plan in which businesses are required to purchase private health insurance for their employees. Those who are unemployed or work part-time would receive private insurance paid for by a government-funded program. To control costs, government would set a limit on health care spending overall; (2) A plan which would offer low- and moderate-income uninsured Americans an income tax refund to help purchase private health insurance. To control costs, financial incentives would encourage enrolling in less costly plans such as HMOs or managed care plans; (3) A national plan financed by taxpayers in which all Americans would receive their insurance from a single government plan. To control costs, government would set the fees charged by doctors and hospitals.

Source: Robert J. Blendon, Drew E. Altman, John M. Benson, Humphrey Taylor, Matt James, and Mark Smith, "Health Care Reform and the 1992 Election," *The Polling Report* 8 (December 14, 1992): 1, 6–7.

Table 20-9 Public Approval of the Clinton Health Care Reform Plan, by Party Identification, 1993 and 1994

	Percent approving	
	September 1993	April 1994
Total	59	43
Republicans	35	25
Democrats	83	58

Question: From what you have heard or read, do you favor or oppose the Clinton administration's health care reform proposals? (1993)

Question: From everything you have heard or read about the plan so far, do you favor or oppose President Clinton's plan to reform health care? (1994)

Source: Robert J. Blendon, Mollyann Brodie, and John Benson, "What Happened to American's Support for the Clinton Health Plan?" *Health Affairs* 14(Summer 1995): 7–23.

Table 20-10 Registered Voters' Attitudes about Health Care and Health Care Policy, by 2008 Presidential Voting Intention (in percent)

	Total Registered Voters	McCain Voters	Obama Voters
Most important issue in deciding whom to vote for[1]			
Economy	63	60	65
War in Iraq	10	8	11
Health care	9	5	13
Terrorism	9	17	2
Energy policy	7	7	7
Most important in deciding whom to vote for[1]			
Candidates' positions on issues	59	48	68
Candidates' leadership and personal qualities	40	49	30
Health care priorities for next president[2]			
Making health care/insurance more affordable	45	44	46
Expanding health insurance coverage for uninsured	22	10	33
Improving Medicare/Rx drug program	11	14	9
Improving the quality of care and reducing medical errors	11	15	8
Reducing spending on government health programs like Medicare and Medicaid	7	13	2
View of health care system[2]			
So much wrong with our health care system that it needs to be completely overhauled	24	16	28
Some good things about our health system, but major changes are needed	46	40	55
Works pretty well, but minor changes are needed	26	39	15
Works well and does not need to be changed	3	4	1

(Table continues)

Table 20-10 *Continued*

Who should have the most responsibility for helping to ensure Americans receive health insurance coverage[2]			
The federal government	38	20	54
Individuals themselves	31	47	18
Employers and businesses	25	30	23
Preferred health insurance coverage[2]			
Make major effort to provide health insurance to all/would involve substantial increase in spending	47	26	65
Work to provide health insurance for some of the uninsured/would inolve less new spending	30	36	26
Keep things basically as they are	17	31	5
How much can president and Congress do about health care costs[2]			
A lot	58	41	73
A little	25	34	19
Mostly beyond their control	15	22	7
Federal government involvement in trying to control health care costs[2]			
Should be more directly involved	66	46	85
Should be less directly involved	15	27	5
Stay about the same	16	23	9
Who should have the most responsibility for slowing the rise in health care costs[2]			
Health insurance companies	33	31	36
Doctors and hospitals	24	27	20
The federal government	23	15	30
Individuals themselves	11	16	6
Employers and businesses	4	5	4
Priorities to address rising health costs[2]			
Reducing the amount people pay for their health care and insurance	50	44	57
Reducing what the nation as a whole spends on health care	22	24	21
Reducing the amount employers pay to provide health insurance to their workers	10	11	9
Reducing future spending on government health insurance programs like Medicare and Medicaid	9	12	6

(Table continues)

Table 20-10 *Continued*

Federal spending on health care (percent wants spending increase)[2]			
Medical care for veterans	72	70	73
Programs to prevent disease and improve health	53	39	67
Medicare	41	31	49
Programs to protect against bioterrorism	38	41	35
Biomedical research	34	24	45
Medicaid	33	22	42
Abortion policy preference[2]			
Legal in all/most cases	54	35	72
Illegal in all/most cases	41	60	24

Note: "Don't know" responses not shown.

Question: Which one issue mattered most in deciding how to vote for president? Energy policy, war in Iraq, economy, terrorism, health care.

Question: Which was more important in your vote for president today? Candidates' positions on the issues or candidates' leadership/personal qualities.

Question: Now thinking specifically about health care, which one of the following health care issues would you most like to see the next president take action on? Making health care and health insurance more affordable, expanding health insurance coverage for the uninsured, improving the quality of care and reducing medical errors, reducing spending on government health programs like Medicare and Medicaid, and improving Medicare and the Medicare prescription drug program?

Question: Which one of the following comes closest to your view about the health care system in America today? There is so much wrong with our health care system that it needs to be completely overhauled; there are some good things about our health care system, but major changes are needed; the health care system works pretty well, but minor changes are needed; or the health care system works well and does not need to be changed?

Question: Which one of the following do you think should have the most responsibility for helping ensure that Americans receive health insurance coverage? The federal government, employers and businesses, or individuals themselves?

Question: When it comes to health insurance coverage, which of the following would you like the next president to propose: A new health plan that would make a major effort to provide health insurance for all or nearly all of the uninsured BUT would involve a substantial increase in spending; a new health plan that is more limited and would cover only some of the uninsured BUT would involve less new spending; or keeping things basically as they are?

Question: Do you think that the cost of health care is something the president and Congress can do a lot about, do a little about, or is that mostly beyond their control?

Question: Do you think the federal government should become more directly involved in trying to control health care costs, less directly involved, or should their involvement stay about the same?

Question: Which one of the following do you think should have the most responsibility for slowing the rise in health care costs? The federal government, employers and businesses, health insurance companies, doctors and hospitals, or individuals themselves?

Question: Which of the following should be the next president's top priority when it comes to addressing rising health care costs? Reducing the amount people pay for their health care and health insurance, reducing what the nation as a whole spends on health care, reducing future spending on government health insurance programs like Medicare and Medicaid, or reducing the amount employers pay to provide health insurance to their workers?

Question: As you know, the federal government has a substantial budget deficit and there are many competing spending priorities facing the next president. Thinking about the federal budget, do you want to see the next president increase spending on (Medicare, Medicaid, biomedical research, programs to prevent disease and improve health, medical care for veterans, programs to protect against bioterrorism), decrease spending, or keep it about the same?

Question: Do you think abortion should be legal in all cases, legal in most cases, illegal in most cases, or illegal in all cases?

Source: [1]Jackie Calmes and Megan Thee, "Voter Poll Finds Obama Built a Broad Coalition," *New York Times,* November 5, 2008, 9. [2]Robert J. Blendon, Drew E. Altman, John M. Benson, Mollyann Brodie, Tami Buhr, Claudia Deane, and Sasha Buscho, "Voters and Health Care Reform in the 2008 Presidential Election," *New England Journal of Medicine* 359 (November 6, 2008): 2050–61.

Table 20-11 Registered Voters' Attitudes about Elements of Health Reform, by 2008 Presidential Voting Intention (in percent)

	Total registered voters	McCain voters	Obama voters
Percent very favorable about these elements of health reform			
Requiring health insurance companies to cover anyone who applies, even if they have a prior illness	56	46	64
Changing the tax system so that everyone who buys health insurance would get the same tax break whether they get coverage at work or on their own	48	49	48
Requiring parents whose children are not currently covered to buy health insurance for their children, with financial assistance from the government for those who can't afford it	42	29	54
Expanding high risk insurance pools to cover people who have an illness that makes it hard to buy insurance in the regular market	45	36	57
Financial assistance from the government to help low and middle-income people purchase insurance	44	28	57
Using tax incentives to encourage more people to sign up for health savings accounts	34	38	31
Requiring employers to either offer health insurance to their workers or pay money into a government pool that provides coverage for those who aren't covered	39	26	50
Importance to you that health care proposal not raise taxes			
Most important consideration	17	23	12
Very important consideration	40	47	33
Somewhat important	35	26	42
Not important at all	8	3	13

Note: "Don't know" responses not shown.

Question: Following are some elements that are being discussed as the presidential candidates debate over health care. For each, please tell me if you find this element favorable or unfavorable. How about (Requiring health insurance companies to cover anyone who applies, even if they have a prior illness/Changing the tax system so that everyone who buys health insurance would get the same tax break whether they get coverage at work or on their own/Expanding high risk insurance pools to cover people who have an illness that makes it hard to buy insurance in the regular market/Financial assistance from the government to help low and middle-income people purchase insurance/Requiring parents whose children are not currently covered to buy health insurance for their children, with financial help from the government for those who can't afford it/Requiring employers to either offer health insurance to their workers or pay money into a government pool that provides coverage for those who aren't covered/Using tax incentives to encourage more people to sign up for health savings accounts)? Do you find this favorable or unfavorable? Is that somewhat or very (favorable/unfavorable)?

Question: When considering health care proposals, how important is it to you that the proposal NOT raise taxes: Is that the most important consideration for you, a very important consideration for you, somewhat important, or not important at all?

Source: Robert J. Blendon, Drew E. Altman, John M. Benson, Mollyann Brodie, Tami Buhr, Claudia Deane, and Sasha Buscho, "Voters and Health Care Reform in the 2008 Presidential Election," *New England Journal of Medicine* 359 (November 6, 2008): 2050–61.

Chapter 21

PUBLIC OPINION ON HEALTH CARE REFORM THROUGH THE PRISM OF OBAMA'S 2009–2010 REFORM EFFORT

Claudia Deane, Mollyann Brodie, Robert J. Blendon, John M. Benson, and Drew E. Altman

In March 2010, after more than a year of intense discussions and negotiations, President Barack Obama signed the Patient Protection and Affordability Act into law, the first major comprehensive health reform legislation to pass the Congress in many decades. The debate over the legislation—which passed the House and the Senate on a party line vote, with most Democrats in favor and all Republicans opposed—touched on most aspects of public opinion discussed in this volume. As the historic reform process passes from the legislative battle to the massive effort required for implementation, advocates and detractors are beginning a new campaign to win the hearts and minds of the American people on health reform. Given the continuing relevance of the current effort at reform, it is helpful to conclude by looking at public opinion on health care policy through the prism of this ultimately successful attempt to overhaul the system and revisiting major themes along the way.

Health Care Reform Hits the Big Time

As illustrated in Chapter 3, in recent years health care reform was repeatedly included on the list of problems the public would like the nation's leaders to tackle.[1] But health care has been one of *several* tough issues on the public's priority list, along with consistent post-9/11 concerns about combating terrorism and fighting wars in Afghanistan and Iraq, and ever-present concerns about the worsening economic situation.

Two developments helped move health care reform up on the legislators' to-do lists in 2009. First was the 2008 presidential primaries, unusually competitive in that both major parties were holding open races; that is, no incumbent president or vice president was vying for either party's nomination. The top Democratic contenders, Senators Barack Obama, Hillary Rodham Clinton, and John Edwards, relentlessly stressed the shortcomings of the current health care system—both in terms of national fiscal health and in terms of the ways in which it failed individuals—and it became a reliable focus of their ongoing public debates. Each proposed fairly substantial increases in coverage, with the differences among their plans being fairly minor, described by one candidate as "in the weeds."[2] Health care reform was less of an issue in the Republican primaries, although to the extent it became a factor, the proposed changes—such as increased tax credits for buying health insurance—were targeted at moving the country closer to an individual market for health coverage rather than expanding the employer-based system, the Democrats' preference.

Public opinion both led and followed party leaders throughout the primary. The Democratic rank and file were more likely to say the health care system needed serious fixes, more likely to put health care reform at the top of their priority list, and more likely to say they hoped their nominee would put forward a "major effort" to expand coverage.[3] This interest likely led Democratic nominees to push the plans they did, and their pushing in turn likely spurred public support all the more. On the Republican side, voters put a relatively higher priority on other issues, such as antiterrorism, taxes, and immigration; health care did not become a major feature of the contest.[4] To the extent it was featured, it was efforts to move the system toward a more market-based approach rather than coverage-related issues that were in the foreground. As a result of the prominence of health care in the Democratic contest, however, it became an issue in the general election, with the Democratic primary base energized around the ideas put forward by their eventual nominee and eager to hold him to some of these promises.

Then came the second major factor spurring health care reform to the top of Washington's to-do list: an economic downturn the likes of which many younger Americans had never experienced. In late 2008 the National Bureau of Economic Research confirmed what many Americans already felt in their pocketbooks: the country was in a recession. By the time President Obama took office in January 2009, many were drawing parallels to the Great Depression, and there was talk of the world's financial system grinding to a halt. Banks and automakers came close to failing and were bailed out by the federal government. Gas prices soared and settled back down in repeating cycles. Congress passed stimulus bills to boost the economy and keep unemployment checks coming.

The economic crisis interacted with the health care policy agenda in conflicting ways. It offered a vital competing priority to health care reform but made such reform more important. In terms of issue competition, the first Kaiser Health Tracking Poll of 2009, fielded in February, found the economy by far the top issue on the public's agenda, named by seven in ten (71 percent) as a top priority. In comparison, health care was tied with fighting terrorism for third place on the agenda, named by four in ten (39 percent).[5]

But at the same time, as people found their incomes tightening, and others lost their health care coverage altogether, the rising cost of health care made it impossible for some who needed medical treatment to get it and threatened to bankrupt others, heightening the need for reform. As seen in Chapter 4, in 2009 roughly half of the American public consistently reported that they or someone in their immediate household had put off some kind of health care over the past year—from routine dental care to treatment for more serious issues—because they could not afford it. Others obtained the care they needed but then ran into real problems paying for it. More than one in four said that they or someone in their family had experienced serious problems paying for medical care over the past year.[6] Worries ran ahead of real experiences to plague even those with employer-sponsored coverage, many of whom reported concerns about their rising insurance premiums, skyrocketing out-of-pocket costs, and whether they would be able to get and afford coverage should they become unemployed.[7]

Health care, in other words, became a true pocketbook issue for Americans, part and parcel of the very real economic complaints that the new administration was trying to address and therefore tied into any efforts to address the country's financial woes. Throughout 2009 the Kaiser Family Foundation's monthly tracking survey found that the majority of Americans—between five and six in ten—agreed that "given the serious economic conditions facing the country, it is more important than ever to take on health care reform," while roughly four in ten said that given these economic challenges the country could not afford to address health care now.[8]

As was true in the primaries, however, persistent, significant differences between self-identified Republicans and Democrats became apparent on this question, with a large majority of Democrats pressing for short-term action on health care and a majority of Republicans expressing a desire to wait or not tackle the issue at all. As is often the case, political independents tilted the balance, with more in favor of tackling the issue in the short term.

Legislative Action and Initial Public Reaction

The public was only one actor in the complex policymaking process, and the public put the economy rather than health care at the top of its legislative agenda. Public opinion alone was not going to drive congressional committees to begin marking up health care bills.

But the newly installed Obama administration made clear it wanted to make health care reform a priority. In March the White House held a widely publicized meeting, the Forum on Health Care Reform, which included major industry stakeholders. The president also made clear that he had learned from the stumbles of the Clinton era and was going to let Congress take the lead in drafting the actual legislative proposals. And Congress—now controlled by Democrats, who for years had been frustrated with their inability to successfully tackle health care reform—did take the lead.

By the end of July, the Senate Committee on Health, Education, Labor, and Pensions (HELP) and the three House committees of jurisdiction had passed versions of health care reform. The Senate Finance Committee completed the roundup in October, but not before a rocky August recess, during which some members of Congress were shouted down by protestors expressing worries about a government takeover of health care and fears about supposed "death panels" that were going to determine which senior citizens were costing too much, and a September rally in support of health care reform pegged to Obama's address to a joint session of Congress.[9]

As the debate over health care reform became more public and more intense, and as actual legislative proposals began to appear, an important strand of public opinion featured in this book became more apparent: people's general satisfaction with their existing health coverage and their fear of what change could mean for them. As seen in Chapter 3, most Americans currently have health care coverage, and more than eight in ten are satisfied with the quality of that care (89 percent), rating it "excellent" or "good" (81 percent).[10] As noted in Chapter 4, important nuances attach to this finding: Americans are much less satisfied with the *cost* of their coverage than with its quality, and they are much more likely to be dissatisfied with both cost and quality when they evaluate the country's health care more broadly.[11] But this said, as the debate over reform intensified, the high level of satisfaction was increasingly cited by opponents as a reason the public might fear change.

With personal concerns and personal satisfactions in some ways at odds, survey researchers focused their attention on what many experts argue is the most meaningful measure of public opinion on policy change: what Americans thought the legislation, once passed, would mean for them personally.[12] More than opinion on the details of proposals or views on how they would impact the country generally, this question seems to have driven public reaction to the Clinton reforms in 1994. Survey researchers attempted to measure this sentiment by asking Americans a classic survey item about whether they thought they and their family would be better off, worse off, or about the same if the president and Congress passed health care reform. The same question was asked about the fate of the country.

Results of these questions were unusually divergent across survey organizations as the debate heated up, but several consistent patterns eventually emerged. First, in no survey did a majority of Americans say they thought they would be better off if health care reform passed. Neither, however, did a consistent majority say they thought they would be worse off. Instead, opinion was mixed and somewhat variable, with a good-sized minority saying they did not think they would be impacted either way. In the broadest brush: in every survey the group concerned about being harmed or not impacted by the legislation was larger than the group that thought it would be helped.[13] Second, as one would guess based on the public's more negative view about health care nationally compared to their own health care, a consistently larger share of the public thought health reform would be good for the nation than thought it would be good for them.[14] Third, as the debate continued, the primary movement in these questions was a decrease in the percentage of Americans who thought health care reform would not impact their own situation and a corresponding increase in the percentage who thought it would leave them worse off.[15] And finally, views of impact were dramatically different among Democrats compared to Republicans, with Democrats significantly more likely to anticipate their own situation being improved by the passage of health reform (**Tables 21–1 and 21–2**).[16]

As noted, some puzzling inconsistencies in the data on personal effects also showed up. In particular, significantly more range than usual was seen across surveys in the size of the group anticipating they would be better off. The Kaiser tracking survey consistently found the most positive results, with somewhat more Americans reporting they would be better off than worse off. The Fox News survey conducted by Opinion Dynamics consistently found the least positive results, with a majority reporting they would be worse off. These variations were likely caused by a combination of differences in descriptions of reform proposals, in mentions of President Obama and Congress, and in the positions of items in the questionnaire. These technical aspects of survey research can have a particularly significant impact on polls fielded in the middle of a heated public debate, when public opinion is likely to be inherently unstable.

Serving Many Masters

One of the challenges facing legislators in crafting health reform proposals, and then in selling them to an interested but somewhat nervous public, was that this round of reform was attempting to meet so many different goals. Given that the Democratic Party was in control of the White House and both branches of Congress, it is perhaps no surprise that reform was first and foremost targeted at providing more of the uninsured with health care coverage. As seen in Chapter 5, most Americans—and nearly all Democrats—agree with this goal, even if many are unwilling to make personal sacrifices to see it happen.[17]

But reform was also trying to do other things, the most difficult of which was to tackle the costs of health care, a major preoccupation of the public, which does not fully understand the roots of the rapid increases in the price of care. The effort to control costs spanned the personal to the national, with legislators attempting to ensure that Americans could continue to afford care and that the country could continue to afford to pay its Medicare bills (to, in a phrase that became omnipresent during the debate, "bend the cost curve").

But there was more. Various policymakers were also interested in making delivery systems reforms of the kind discussed in Chapter 9, not only for increased efficiency and safety, but also as a way to control costs. Survey data suggested that although Americans might appreciate the results of these reforms, few average voters—not being policy experts—were demanding such changes. In fact, as the debate progressed, discussion of topics such as comparative effectiveness research allowed some opponents to raise the specter of the dreaded "rationing." Some of these reforms, such as greater emphasis on electronic medical records, passed as part of the stimulus bill early in 2009 and were not an important part of the health care reform debate that unfolded in the late summer and fall.

Wellness reforms were also woven into the debate, including suggestions that those who maintained healthier lifestyles should reap rewards in the form of lower insurance premiums, and these ideas found their way into the Senate HELP proposal. Most Americans were sympathetic to the idea of higher premiums for smokers, but less sympathetic if they would be applied to overweight people,[18] a problem afflicting a much larger percentage of the public (see Chapter 14).

Finally, of greater interest to the public than either wellness or delivery reforms, policymakers also began talking about making insurance market reforms; in particular, requiring insurance companies to accept individuals with preexisting conditions. With nearly six in ten Americans reporting that they or someone in their family likely would qualify as having an existing illness of some sort, this proposal was met with overwhelming public approval from the earliest days of the debate, and it remained one of the few aspects of the legislation backed by majorities of self-identified Republicans, Democrats, and independents.[19] For policymakers, it was also one critical step—along with an individual mandate—toward making universal coverage affordable.

From Goals to Bills

In general, it is significantly easier to get public agreement on goals than it is to find agreement on specific ways of reaching those goals. Yes, health care should be cheaper, and yes, everyone who needs health care should get it, but how do we get from here to there?

From early on in the polling on health care reform, surveys found that a variety of methods of providing coverage—from expanding existing programs such as Medicaid to providing tax credits to imposing an employer mandate—received majority support (**Table 21–3**). Yet when people were pressed to rank their top choice as a means of expansion, opinion fractured into nearly equal-sized minorities across the spectrum of options.[20]

When legislators approached health care reform in 2009, they took advantage of this division of preference by combining approaches somewhat in the way Massachusetts did in 2006 (see Chapter 6). The bills that were considered in the House and Senate included some expansions of existing government programs such as Medicaid, some effort to provide individuals with government subsidies to purchase health insurance in the open market, and some efforts to reform the marketplace. The bills avoided a complete remake of the existing employer-based system, again congruent with a public that does not seem interested in rebuilding the system from the ground up. This approach frustrated the vocal and committed group of single-payer advocates on the left as well as the pure market advocates of the right.

Among the most controversial aspects of this more moderate, mixed approach was the introduction of a so-called public plan, a government-administered insurance option that would be made available, depending on the bill, to some of the people searching for health insurance and would compete with private insurance companies. Over the course of 2009 much ink was spilled and many voices were raised over this proposal, which to some liberals seemed an indispensable part of health care reform and to some conservatives an unwanted step toward a fully government-run health care system. The public, meanwhile consistently gave the public option majority support.[21] Until, that is, they were provided with arguments against it.

Messaging and Malleability

When the 2009 debate over health care reform began, most Americans were not aware of the possible tradeoffs—real or alleged—involved in achieving the goals so many embraced. And it is at this point in any policy debate that the public campaign becomes critically important: opponents emphasize the costs of change, proponents stress the benefits.[22]

As is evident throughout this book, and as legions of marketers and public relations experts already know, messaging matters. Public opinion on health care is not exempt from the rules that govern public opinion more generally in how negative, as well as positive, messages can change people's minds.

From the start of the 2009 debate, the similarities with the 1993–1994 reform effort were clear in terms of which messages had the power to make people feel warmer toward a particular reform and which would send them running for the hills. Among the messages the public found most strongly positive were requiring insurance companies to cover preexisting conditions, not increasing the federal budget deficit, and improving the country for future generations. Three things the public really did not want to see in a health care reform plan were limitations on their choice of doctors; more power for the federal government they already saw as too large and growing; and anything perceived as harming Medicare.

In 2009 surveys found majority support for a variety of ways of expanding coverage. At the same time, however, surveys also suggested that faced with some combination of negative messages in the form of arguments, supporters could, in the blink of an eye, be turned into wary opponents. In other words, support for specific approaches was soft, moveable. An October survey found that 66 percent of the public was in favor of imposing a requirement that every American carry health insurance, a finding that had been fairly robust throughout the fall. But when supporters of the individual mandate were told that this might mean some people would be required to buy health insurance that they found too expensive or did not want, support fell to 21 percent. Support for the public option, which was at 57 percent initially in the same survey, fell to 32 percent when supporters were given a commonly voiced argument suggesting that this would give the federal government an unfair advantage in the insurance market.[23] Surveys also found that opposition to various proposals was somewhat malleable, but changes in support levels were less dramatic because opponents were usually fewer in number and somewhat more difficult to move off their position.

One situation that differentiated the Obama-era effort from the Clintons' was that, unlike in 1993–1994, many of the major stakeholder groups, such as business and the insurance industry, began with an interest in reform and a seat at the table. Although many developed qualms during the process, they mainly spent the first half of the year making nice. In other words, the messages were still potent: they just were not deployed as early or with as much vehemence. Second, mindful of how negative ads helped to scuttle the Clinton health care bill, pro-reform groups such as labor unions came out of the gate with their own on-air positive messaging, and for most of the year more people reported seeing positive ads than negative ones. This balance shifted in the fall as legislation began to make strides in the House and Senate and business began to heavily outspend reform supporters.[24] By November 2009 just under half of Americans said they had seen a health care reform ad in the course of the past week: 37 percent of that group saw only ads opposed; 29 percent saw ads in favor; and 31 percent saw both kinds.[25] Over the course of the fifteen years since the Clinton effort failed, the media landscape had changed drastically, with the growth of online news sources and opinion blogs providing an outlet both for ads and immediate rebuttals to them.

The Divisive Question of the Proper Role for Government

One question that reflects a real flashpoint and a dividing line in public opinion concerns the role of government in policy and in people's day-to-day lives. And it was the differing opinions of the proper role of government in health care, as embodied in the discussion of a public plan, that to some extent took over—and some would say distracted from—the health care reform debate in 2009.

Overall, polls consistently made it clear that a government-run system, or single-payer system, was the least popular option with the public, although consistently favored by a sizable minority. One survey found that by almost a two-to-one margin, Americans thought it would be "a bad thing" (58 percent) rather than a good thing (32 percent) if the government ran the health care system.[26] The question of the public plan got entangled in this larger ideological debate, even though in reality the proposals were about whether the government should create and administer a health insurance plan that would compete with private plans in exchanges or nonprofit cooperatives that would be created as an option for new customers who received government insurance subsidies. Some of these proposed public plans were weaker—only kicking in via a trigger mechanism if not enough people were getting affordable plans, or having to negotiate their prices with providers rather than pay Medicare rates. Others were more robust. All divided Republicans from Democrats on Capitol Hill, and most even divided conservative Democrats from their more liberal and moderate fellow party members.

The same pattern held true for the public, again in some sort of symbiotic relationship with their leaders. Surveys have repeatedly confirmed the conventional wisdom about the basic ideological layout of the two parties' membership. Republicans are, in general, more likely to distrust federal government involvement in most areas of policy, which makes rank-and-file members of the GOP less likely from the start to be interested in any government-led reform of the health care system. This tendency was exacerbated in 2009, however, because the Democratic Party was in control of both houses of Congress as well as the White House. As noted in Chapter 2, partisans are more likely to trust government when their own party controls the institutions of government. Add to a basic distrust of government a basic distrust of the particular party leading the government and it is easy to understand why surveys throughout 2009 found self-identified Republicans—representing roughly three in ten Americans—markedly less supportive of nearly every aspect of health care reform, beginning with whether the economically challenged country should be tackling it at all and extending to opposition to the public plan and most other specific proposals on the table. These partisan divisions seemed to attach themselves to the public plan option in particular and played out on Capitol Hill in the form of strident debates.

Even more generally, however, researchers found that the top reason provided by opponents was concern about increased government involvement in health care.[27] And in October 2009 twice as many said that the then-current proposals entailed too much government involvement as said they entailed too little (42 percent compared to 21 percent).[28]

Seniors, Medicare, and Health Care Reform

Perhaps no demographic group is watched more closely in politics than senior citizens, who make up a large portion of the voting public in presidential elections and an even larger proportion of the voters who turn out for primaries and off-year contests. Seniors—all of whom are eligible for health care coverage through the federal Medicare program—hold an unusual place in health care reform debates, not only immune from many of the ramifications of change but also in many ways less likely to personally benefit from any additional access to coverage.

Medicare came into play in the 2009 debate in at least two important ways: as an impetus for reform, in that its costs, as discussed in Chapter 7, are rising at a rate that is difficult to sustain, as well as being the source of potential health care savings that could cancel out new spending and keep the various plans deficit neutral. As we also saw in Chapter 7, however, Medicare is a widely popular program. Little support exists for changing it and less for making anything seen as a cutback in benefits.

As the debate played out, this protectiveness over Medicare became entangled in confusion as to whether and how the possible reductions in benefits—mainly targeted at a layer of additional benefits, such as coverage for hearing aids and eyeglasses, being offered to those enrolled in some Medicare Advantage plans—would affect the average senior. Seniors—the only age group to go solidly for Republican candidate John McCain in the 2008 general election[29]—responded by souring on the plan at a much more rapid rate than younger Americans. From February to October of 2009, the proportion of seniors who said they expected they would be worse off under health care reform rose by twenty-nine percentage points, compared to a fourteen-percentage-point jump among adults under age sixty-five.[30] By October, then, those under age sixty-five were more likely to think health care reform would leave them better off than worse off by a margin of 44 percent to 25 percent, and seniors were more likely to think their own situation would suffer if reform took place (36 percent said they would be worse off compared to 27 percent who thought they would benefit).[31]

Footing the Bill

Of all the difficult tasks involved in something as complicated as reforming the vast network of providers, insurers, manufacturers, employers, and patients that make up the U.S. health care system, none is more difficult than determining how to pay for it. Dealing with costs here really meant at least two things for legislators: first, and perhaps most obviously, it meant finding the funds needed to pay for any new changes they wanted to make, such as providing federal subsidies to the lower-income uninsured. But second, and perhaps even more important, it meant finding ways to rein in the amount the country is set to spend on health care in upcoming years, completely aside from any of the proposed coverage expansions in the various bills.

From the perspective of public opinion, the financing mechanisms were of primary interest, particularly those costs that were expected to fall on the shoulders of the average taxpayer. Throughout 2009 policy experts and legislators offered a variety of proposals to control costs and find revenues. Some proposals, such as efforts to cut waste in the system, were relatively uncontroversial. But most, particularly the many proposals that would increase taxes on some or all of the population, were the opposite.

As discussed in Chapter 5, surveys fielded over the past two decades repeatedly have found the public nearly evenly divided in their willingness to personally pay more—either in higher premiums or higher taxes—to extend health insurance to more Americans. This widespread unwillingness to pay more was exacerbated by the fact that in mid-2009, six in ten Americans believed that "if policymakers made the right changes, they could reform the health care system without spending more money to do it."[32]

Surveys found that few of the specific funding mechanisms proposed in 2009 received clear and consistent majority support. In general, support was highest for proposals that were targeted at the fewest number of people. Most Americans said they would back taxes on alcoholic beverages (67 percent), cigarettes (63 percent), and the very wealthy (63 percent). Taxing employer-sponsored health care benefits was broadly unpopular (27 percent in favor).[33] The public was more closely divided on taxing the health care benefits of those employees receiving the most generous coverage from their employers (45 percent in favor, 50 percent opposed).[34] The idea of directly taxing insurance companies who offer the "gold standard" policies received narrow majority (55 percent) support.[35] Reining in future provider payment increases in Medicare was divisive among the public at large (45 percent in favor, 45 percent opposed), and opposed by a majority of seniors.[36]

Overall, then, finding popular ways to finance the bill was one of the biggest challenges facing legislators in 2009 and 2010. This challenge was exacerbated by the economic and political reality that passing a bill and *not* paying for it was not an option during a difficult recession and a time of heightened awareness of federal budget deficits.

The Public's Yea or Nay: Public Divided on Plan up through and after Final Votes

In the weeks immediately before passage of health care reform, the multitudes of public surveys seemed to agree on one main finding: in none of them did a significant majority of Americans say they favored the legislation that was about to pass.[37] Instead, opinion ranged from an even split between opponents and proponents to a narrow majority tilting against passage. As observers had come to expect, final opinion reflected the sort of vast partisan divide discussed in Chapter 20, with Democrats overwhelmingly in favor of passage, Republicans fairly unified in their opposition, and independents more divided.[38] Views as to whether the legislation would be of personal benefit also remained quite mixed, with roughly one-third expecting to benefit, but just as many expecting to suffer harm, and another third not expecting any impact.[39] This lukewarm reaction to the final legislation was a dramatic contrast to the continuing majorities who said they were in favor of tackling health care reform (58 percent),[40] the majorities who approved of any number of specific changes included in the bill,[41] and the majority that worried that they themselves could someday be without coverage if the government did not create a system covering everyone (56 percent).[42] This public opinion pattern is similar to that seen during the debate over the Clinton health plan in 1994.[43] In 2010, however, the political dynamics were much different and led to a different result.

It is worth noting, as seen in Chapter 7, that another recent major change to the health care system—the expansion of the Medicare program to include a prescription drug benefit—was also viewed unfavorably by a majority of Americans on passage, as was the decision to expand the program using private insurance plans as a vehicle. Yet it passed both houses of Congress, was signed by President George W. Bush, and once the new benefits were implemented, became a popular new program. On the other hand, the 1988 Medicare Catastrophic Coverage Act was popular at the time it was enacted only to be repealed a year later in response to the angry reaction of seniors upon implementation.

What's Next?

It would require a working crystal ball to divine how public opinion on health reform may develop now that the law has passed and the interpretation and implementation phase is beginning. As a starting point, it is important to understand that despite the massive media attention focused on the political debate over reform,[44] and that most Americans reported following these discussions,[45] a vast amount of confusion remained about the final law even after its passage. A survey fielded weeks after enactment found that 56 percent of Americans did not feel they had enough information about the reform law to understand how it might impact them personally, and 55 percent felt confused about it.[46]

Two forces will shape opinion going forward. The first, and most important, is the unfolding of the implementation process, as reforms, subsidies, mandates, and marketplaces are put into place over the next several years. To the extent that these changes touch people's lives, they will most directly affect Americans' judgments about health reform, not only those Americans who are directly affected, but also the even-larger circle of people who have a friend or family member who is affected.[47] The second will be the media coverage of reform, including coverage of the ongoing implementation, how it is working or not working, and how the issue plays in the political arena over time.

A Final Word about the Limitations of Polls

The national discussion over major, historic health care reform provides an ideal opportunity to leave readers with a clear-eyed view of what surveys concerning health care policy can and cannot add to the debate. The chapters compiled here are intended to stand on their own as a testament to how surveys of the public illuminate problems and needs, tell policymakers which of their programs are working and which are not, give leaders a rough roadmap to follow in creating policies that will be well received, set constraints around acceptable and unacceptable alternatives, and highlight areas where more public education is needed.

The conclusion of this final chapter uses the example of health care reform to add some cautionary words about what surveys cannot do. Surveys represent the will of the public. In a democracy, what the public wants is an important consideration. But average Americans are not, and should not be expected to be, policy experts. People can tell you which proposals sound good to them, but they cannot evaluate which particular proposals actually have a chance of working in this complex health care network we have created. One cannot rely on surveys to discover the best way to bend the nation's health care cost curve, for example. Surveys are perhaps better used to find out where the public wants policymakers to go rather than to map out a way to get there.

At some point, leaders may need to override some specific aspects of majority will to get to where the public wants them to go. One example is that the public has expressed a desire for government-subsidized coverage provided to more low-income, uninsured Americans *and* for any health care reform bill to be deficit neutral. For both of these things to happen, the reform must be paid for either with cuts or with new revenues, but neither option has popular support. Overcoming this disconnect will require leadership.

Public opinion is not always educated opinion. Most Americans, for example, do not know that most of the uninsured live in households where at least one person has a job. If they knew that many of their fellow citizens were working full time and were still not insured, they might be more sympathetic to spending federal resources to expand coverage or feel more vulnerable themselves. But many do not know, despite extensive (and sometimes expensive) public education campaigns aimed at informing them and the efforts of several presidents making full use of their bully pulpit.

On a related note, public opinion might be more focused on the short term than the long term in ways that reflect the media attention cycle and are not helpful for policymakers. For example, the sense of public urgency associated with the domestic AIDS crisis hit a new low just when the Centers for Disease Control and Prevention upwardly revised their estimate of new infections.[48] Basing action on public interest in this issue, then, would likely leave the country in a dangerous position in the longer term.

Public opinion surveys represent a snapshot of public views *at that moment*. They can measure whether the public supports a legislative policy as Americans understand it while it is in the planning stages, which is a different beast from gaining public support for a legislative policy once it is actually being implemented and its realities are being experienced on a day-to-day basis.

One classic example is the passage of the Medicare prescription drug bill, as outlined in Chapter 7.[49] The public moved from: (1) majority support of the expansion, to (2) a position of real wariness as the legislation began to be implemented, to (3) expressing a good deal of satisfaction once the benefits had fully kicked in. It is very possible that the public's reaction to the *hypothetical* individual mandate—one proposed change that would have a very real, tangible impact on those without insurance coverage—although expressed quite genuinely could be different from their reaction to the actual mandate, which begins in 2014.

Public opinion is also very volatile in periods when people are undergoing a steep learning curve and are exposed to multiple competing messages. In this environment, differences in methodology across various polls might lead to quite variable results, a situation that might not occur in calmer times or on subjects with which the public was long familiar. Some topics in the health reform legislation are just too complicated for polls to address adequately or responsibly in the space of a necessarily abbreviated survey item. Those taking polls should be keenly aware that when fielding questions on the public option or on taxing particularly generous employer-provided policies, they may be reaching the limits of what polling can tackle, with the items inevitably falling short of the nuance inherent in the policy proposals. Moreover, some topics are too complicated even for the most detailed and policy-oriented survey researchers to attempt to write into a questionnaire: the appropriate levels of premium subsidies to provide to various income groups, as measured by where they fall on the federal poverty scale; the preference for regional cooperatives versus a national exchange; the best way to create a temporary high-risk pool to cover those who have been denied coverage; the best way to restructure payments to Medicare Advantage plans.

Polls of the general public do not always reflect the will of that committed group of Americans who show up at the voting booth regularly, including in lower-turnout, congressional off-year elections. Republicans are somewhat more likely to turn out than Democrats, the insured more likely to vote than the uninsured, and senior citizens more likely than younger Americans. In each case, then, their opinions might be considered to hold somewhat more weight in our political system. Because these voters are more likely to get the attention of policymakers, surveys of the general public are not always the best barometers of the political pressures being experienced by individual members of Congress.

Not all polls are created equal. Survey research is a field in the midst of dramatic change, a byproduct of the communications revolution affecting Americans' daily lives. Standards are shifting, but are not infinitely elastic, and care must still be taken to pay attention to the methodology of a public opinion poll along with its findings.[50]

In the end, the public's long-term bottom line on health care reform will be determined by whether most people think what they *get* is worth what they *pay*. But in the policy-making process, who will get what and how much is not always clear, and even the best poll cannot figure out and then explain to each American what the personal tradeoffs will be. The best leaders, policymakers, and students of policy will use surveys to understand the public's experiences, fears, and interests along with their policy preferences and use these findings as one element in their plans for the nation's policy future.

Notes

[1] Robert J. Blendon and John M. Benson, "The American Public and the Next Phase of the Health Care Reform Debate," *New England Journal of Medicine* 361 (November 19, 2009): e48, pages 1–4, http://content.nejm.org/cgi/reprint/361/21/e48.pdf.

[2] John Edwards, describing differences with the health care plan of Hillary Rodham Clinton. See excerpt at "Democratic Candidates Discuss Health Care Proposals in Forums," PBS NewsHour, December 25, 2007, http://www.pbs.org/newshour/bb/politics/july-dec07/healthcare_12–25.html.

[3] Robert J. Blendon, Drew E. Altman, Claudia Deane, John M. Benson, Mollyann Brodie, and Tami Buhr, "Health Care in the 2008 Presidential Primaries," *New England Journal of Medicine* 358 (January 24, 2008): 414–422, http://content.nejm.org/cgi/reprint/358/4/414.pdf.

[4] Ibid.

[5] Kaiser Family Foundation, "Kaiser Health Tracking Poll: February 2009," http://www.kff.org/kaiserpolls/upload/7867.pdf.

[6] Kaiser Family Foundation, "Kaiser Health Tracking Poll: November 2009," http://www.kff.org/kaiserpolls/upload/8018.pdf.

7 See, for example, Kaiser Family Foundation, "Data Note: Americans' Satisfaction with Insurance Coverage," September 2009, http://www.kff.org/kaiserpolls/upload/7979.pdf.

8 Kaiser Family Foundation, "Kaiser Health Tracking Poll: November 2009."

9 See, for example, Ian Urbina, "Beyond the Beltway, Health Debate Turns Hostile," *New York Times*, August 8, 2009, http://www.nytimes.com/2009/08/08/us/politics/08townhall.html?_r=1; "Barney Frank Confronts Woman at Townhall Comparing Obama to Hitler," http://www.youtube.com/watch?v=nYlZiWK2Iy8.

10 ABC News/Kaiser Family Foundation/*USA Today*, "Health Care in America 2006 Survey," October 2006, http://www.kff.org/kaiserpolls/upload/7573.pdf; Gallup Poll (Storrs, Conn.: Roper Center for Public Opinion Research, November 5–8, 2009).

11 ABC News/Kaiser Family Foundation/*USA Today*, "Health Care in America 2006 Survey."

12 Blendon and Benson, "The American Public and the Next Phase of the Health Care Reform Debate."

13 CBS New/*New York Times* Poll, http://documents.nytimes.com/new-york-times-cbs-news-poll-the-war-in-afghanistan#p=9; CBS News, "The Politics of Health Care Reform," http://www.cbsnews.com/htdocs/pdf/poll_health_care_032210.pdf?tag=contentMain;contentBody; NBC News/*Wall Street Journal* Poll, October 22–25, 2009, http://online.wsj.com/public/resources/documents/wsjnbc-10272009.pdf; Kaiser Family Foundation, "Kaiser Health Tracking Poll: March 2010," http://www.kff.org/kaiserpolls/upload/8058-T.pdf.

14 Kaiser Family Foundation, "Kaiser Health Tracking Poll: March 2010."

15 Trend data in NBC News/*Wall Street Journal* Poll, October 22–25, 2009, and in Kaiser Family Foundation, "Kaiser Health Tracking Poll: March 2010."

16 CBS News, "The Politics of Health Care Reform."

17 CBS News/*New York Times* Poll, "U.S. Health Care Politics," March 1, 2007, http://www.cbsnews.com/htdocs/CBSNews_polls/health_care.pdf.

18 ABC News/Kaiser Family Foundation/*USA Today*, "Health Care in America 2006 Survey."

19 Kaiser Family Foundation, "Kaiser Health Tracking Poll," September 2009, http://www.kff.org/kaiserpolls/upload/7990.pdf.

20 Ibid.

21 Sarah Dutton, "Support for Public Options Remains Strong, Polls Show," cbsnews.com, October 20, 2009, http://www.cbsnews.com/blogs/2009/10/20/politics/politicalhotsheet/entry5401123.shtml.

22 Anthony Downs, "Up and Down with Ecology: The 'Issue-Attention Cycle,'" *The Public Interest* 28 (Summer 1972): 38–50.

23 Kaiser Family Foundation, "Kaiser Health Tracking Poll: October 2009," http://www.kff.org/kaiserpolls/upload/7998.pdf.

24 Alan Fram, "Business Foes of Health Care Revamp Ramp up Effort," *USA Today*, November 17, 2009, http://www.usatoday.com/money/topstories/2009–11–17–2639414209_x.htm.

25 Kaiser Family Foundation, "Kaiser Health Tracking Poll: November 2009."

26 Quinnipiac University, "U.S. Voters Back Public Insurance 2–1, But Won't Use It, Quinnipiac University National Poll Finds," July 1, 2009, http://www.quinnipiac.edu/x1284.xml?ReleaseID=1344&What=&strArea=;&strTime=3.

[27] Frank Newport, Jeffrey M. Jones, and Lydia Saad, "Americans on Healthcare Reform: Five Key Realities," October 30, 2009, http://www.gallup.com/poll/123989/Americans-Healthcare-Reform-Five-Key-Realities.aspx?version=print.

[28] ABC News/*Washington Post* Poll, October 15–18, 2009, http://www.washingtonpost.com/wp-srv/politics/polls/postpoll_101909.html.

[29] Edison Media Research/Mitofsky International/National Election Pool, National Election Day Exit Poll 2008, abcnews.com, http://abcnews.go.com/PollingUnit/ExitPolls.

[30] Kaiser Family Foundation Poll (Storrs, Conn.: Roper Center for Public Opinion Research, February 3–12, 2009); Kaiser Family Foundation, "Kaiser Health Tracking Poll: October 2009."

[31] Kaiser Family Foundation, "Kaiser Health Tracking Poll: October 2009 Chartpack" http://www.kff.org/kaiserpolls/upload/7999.pdf.

[32] Kaiser Family Foundation, "Kaiser Health Tracking Poll: June 2009," http://www.kff.org/kaiserpolls/upload/7923.pdf.

[33] Quinnipiac University Poll (Storrs, Conn.: Roper Center for Public Opinion Research, July 27–August 3, 2009).

[34] Kaiser Family Foundation, "Kaiser Health Tracking Poll: August 2009," http://www.kff.org/kaiserpolls/upload/7964.pdf.

[35] Kaiser Family Foundation, "Kaiser Health Tracking Poll: October 2009."

[36] Kaiser Family Foundation, "Kaiser Health Tracking Poll: November 2009 Chartpack," http://www.kff.org/kaiserpolls/upload/8019.pdf.

[37] Robert J. Blendon and John M. Benson, "Public Opinion at the Time of the Vote on Health Care Reform," *New England Journal of Medicine* 362 (April 22, 2010): e55, pages 1–6, http://healthcarereform.nejm.org/?p=3284&query=home.

[38] CBS News, "The Politics of Health Care Reform"; Blendon and Benson, "Public Opinion at the Time of the Vote on Health Care Reform."

[39] Blendon and Benson, "Public Opinion at the Time of the Vote on Health Care Reform."

[40] Kaiser Family Foundation, "Kaiser Health Tracking Poll: November 2009."

[41] Kaiser Family Foundation, "Kaiser Health Tracking Poll," September 2009; Blendon and Benson, "Public Opinion at the Time of the Vote on Health Care Reform."

[42] CBS News/*New York Times* Poll (Storrs, Conn.: Roper Center for Public Opinion Research, September 19–23, 2009).

[43] Blendon and Benson, "The American Public and the Next Phase of the Health Care Reform Debate."

[44] Pew Research Center, Project for Excellence in Journalism, "The Big Three—Health Care, War, and the Economy—Dominate Again," October 26–November 1, 2009, http://www.journalism.org/index_report/pej_news_coverage_index_october_26november_1_2009.

[45] Pew Research Center for the People and the Press, News Interest Index, "Public Closely Tracking Health Care Debate," December 16, 2009, http://people-press.org/reports/pdf/571.pdf.

[46] Kaiser Family Foundation, "Kaiser Health Tracking Poll: April 2010," http://www.kff.org/kaiserpolls/upload/8067-T.pdf.

[47] Mollyann Brodie, Drew Altman, Claudia Deane, Sasha Buscho, and Elizabeth Hamel, "Liking the Pieces, Not the Package: Contradictions in Public Opinion during Health Reform," *Health Affairs* 29 (June 2010): 1125–30.

[48] Drew Altman, "America Has Gone Quiet on HIV/AIDS," April 2, 2009, http://www.kff.org/hivaids/040209_altman.cfm.

[49] See Mark Blumenthal, "If Reform Passes, What Then?" *National Journal,* October 5, 2009, http://www.nationaljournal.com/njonline/no_20091005_8338.php.

[50] One good place to go for questions about survey methodology is the Web site of the American Association for Public Opinion Research, or AAPOR, http://www.aapor.org//AM/Template.cfm?Section=Home.

Table 21-1 Perceived Future Impact of the 2009–2010 Health Care Reform Plans (in percent)

Effect of health care reforms under consideration on you personally	Help	Not much effect	Hurt	Don't know
2009				
August[1]	18	46	31	5
September[1]	23	44	26	7
October[1]	18	45	31	6
November[1]	19	41	34	6
December[1]	16	42	34	8
2010				
March total[2]	20	38	35	7
Republicans	8	21	67	4
Independents	13	42	37	8
Democrats	35	43	13	9

Effect of Obama's health care plan on quality of your own health care[3]	Get better	Stay about the same	Get worse	Do Not have an opinion/ Not sure
2009				
April	22	29	24	25
July	21	29	39	11
August	24	27	40	9
September	19	34	36	11
October	21	27	40	12

Question: From what you've heard or read, do you think the (health care reforms under consideration in Congress/current health care reform bill) will mostly help you personally, will mostly hurt you personally, or don't you think they will have much of an effect on you personally?

Question: From what you have heard about Barack Obama's health care plan, do you believe it will result in the quality of your health care getting better, worse, or staying about the same as now? If you do not have an opinion, please just say so.

Sources: [1]CBS News/*New York Times* trend data, August–December 2009. [2]CBS News, "The Politics of Health Care," March 18–21, 2010. [3]NBC News/*Wall Street Journal* trend data, April–October 2009.

Table 21-2 Perceived Future Impact on Family and the Country of Passing Health Care Reform (in percent)

	Better off	Wouldn't make a difference	Worse off
Effect on you and your family			
2009			
February	38	43	11
April	43	36	14
June	39	36	16
July	39	32	21
August	36	27	31
September	42	28	23
October	41	28	27
November	42	27	24
December	35	32	27
2010			
January	32	29	33
February	34	26	32
March	35	28	32
Effect on the country as a whole			
2009			
February	59	19	12
April	56	21	15
June	57	19	16
July	51	16	23
August	45	14	34
September	53	14	26
October	53	12	28
November	54	11	27
December	45	17	31
2010			
January	42	12	37
February	45	12	34
March	45	14	34

Note: Volunteered responses "It depends" and "Don't know" not shown.

Question: Do you think you and your family would be better off or worse off if the president and Congress passed health care reform, or don't you think it would make much difference?

Question: Do you think the country as a whole would be better off or worse off if the president and Congress passed health care reform, or don't you think it would make much difference?

Source: Trend data in Kaiser Family Foundation, "Kaiser Health Tracking Poll: March 2010."

Table 21-3 Public Support for Different Ways to Increase the Number of Americans with Health Insurance (in percent)

Percent in favor	
Expanding state government programs for low-income people, such as Medicaid and the State Children's Health Insurance Program	82
Expanding Medicare to cover people between the ages of 55 and 64 who do not have health insurance	74
Requiring all Americans to have health insurance, either from their employer or from another source, with financial help for those who can't afford it	68
Requiring employers to offer health insurance to their workers or pay money into a government fund that will pay to cover those without insurance	67
Offering tax credits to help people buy private health insurance	67
Having a national health plan—or single-payer plan—in which all Americans would get their insurance from a single government plan	40

Question: Now I'm going to read you some different ways to increase the number of Americans covered by health insurance. As I read each one, please tell me whether you would favor it or oppose it.

Source: Kaiser Family Foundation, "Kaiser Health Tracking Poll," September 2009.

INDEX

Tables are indicated by t following the page number.